LEGENDS OF THE AFRICAN FRONTIER

LEGENDS OF THE AFRICAN FRONTIER

BY

DAVID CHANDLER

SAFARI PRESS

Chandler, David

Second edition

Safari Press

2008, Long Beach, California

ISBN 1-57157-285-6

Library of Congress Catalog Card Number: 2006927696

10 9 8 7 6 5 4 3 2 1

Printed in USA

Readers wishing to receive the Safari Press catalog, featuring many fine books on big-game hunting, wingshooting, and sporting firearms, should write to Safari Press Inc., P.O. Box 3095, Long Beach, CA 90803, USA. Tel: (714) 894-9080 or visit our Web site at www.safaripress.com.

This book is dedicated to my mother,

Audrey Donovan Mahoney

TABLE OF CONTENTS

FOREWORD vii
INTRODUCTION viii
CHAPTER 1 A 1
CHAPTER 2 B 16
CHAPTER 3 C 59
CHAPTER 4 D 91
CHAPTER 5 E 115
CHAPTER 6 F 123
CHAPTER 7 G 135
CHAPTER 8 H 153
CHAPTER 9 I 180
CHAPTER 10 J 182
CHAPTER 11 K 203
CHAPTER 12 L 213
CHAPTER 13 MAC/MC 231
CHAPTER 14 M 238
CHAPTER 15 N 261
CHAPTER 16 O 269
CHAPTER 17 P 272
CHAPTER 18 Q 295
CHAPTER 19 R 296
CHAPTER 20 S 312
CHAPTER 21 T 348
CHAPTER 22 U 366
CHAPTER 23 V 368
CHAPTER 24 W 376
CHAPTER 25 Y 391
CHAPTER 26 Z 392
GLOSSARY 394
BIBLIOGRAPHY 404

FOREWORD

I once read Negley Farson describe an introduction or foreword to a book as the monkey that walks ahead of a circus parade when it comes to town. In the olden days a circus would set up its tents somewhere on the outskirts of town and then run a parade through the main street to let the whole town preview the circus acts that would be showing the following weekend. The monkey would act as a precursor of bigger things to come, and it would be followed by lions, elephants, and tigers. Admittedly my writing a foreword for this book, *Legends of the African Frontier,* is very much like that monkey, a precursor of a more important attraction.

I have read this manuscript from A through Z, literally. And, quite frankly, I am immensely impressed by how much work Dave Chandler put into this endeavor. Somebody from marketing at Safari Press came up with the fact that the author had to have spent twelve years compiling this book. My only comment was that I am surprised it did not take him 120 ycars! I havc a collcction of some 1,400 titles on big-game hunting in Asia and Africa, so I consider myself somewhat of a study on Africana books, but I have to admit that I have read only a couple hundred of these books completely. In order for Dave Chandler to have come up with over 1,200 biographical sketches on Africa's early hunters and explorers, he must have read well over 1,500 books on the subject matter, and possibly even 2,000. He tells me that most of these books came from his own collection, but he also got quite a few from the rare book section of public libraries. I am not sure that I have read 1,500 books in my lifetime, let alone 1,500 books on one subject matter . . . and all that in an estimated time span of twelve years! This was certainly a labor of love.

The antiquarian (African) big-game, hunting-book world is a small one. I know of several self-proclaimed experts in this field, but while most of these bibliophiles have vast knowledge of the writings of the time period covered by this manuscript, I dare say none of them have read as many books nor done as much research as the author has in the preparation of this work for publication. If you are a history buff or if you are interested in looking up a name you've come across in your readings but had no idea who that person was, this is the book for you. Chandler's exhaustive guide is like a Who's Who of African big-game hunting. It will not only entertain; it will also educate.

This is not a book that you can read from cover to cover in a matter of a few days. It is a work that you will refer to again and again as you seek to bring into focus all those fascinating characters who walked on the Dark Continent so many years ago—characters who have now largely faded away into the mists of time. Of course, most know the names of Walter Bell, Frederick Selous, and James Sutherland, for these men were truly famous. But there were so many more people who came with a rifle to Africa for one reason or another and who left their mark. For instancc, did you know that Sclous considered George Wood to have "probably shot more elephants than any Englishman living"? These people are also featured in these pages.

As always, a work like this is hard to start but even harder to finish. Who should you include and who will you leave out? Chandler told me that at one point he had about 1,800 biographical sketches prepared for this manuscript. However, as it matured, he realized that he had to cut it off somewhere or it would never end. So he decided to concentrate on a specific time period and on those who had made their way through the continent with a sporting gun. Here, presented in a few hundred pages, are no less than 150 years of fascinating history of a time long since past but, thanks to David Chandler's careful research, by no means forgotten.

Ludo Wurfbain, Publisher
Safari Press
December 2006

INTRODUCTION

This is a book about African hunters, more specifically those early European settlers and sportsmen who hunted in Africa. The book covers a time period approximately from 1800 to 1945, with a few exceptions outside those dates. The term "hunter' is defined loosely, by necessity, for just about all the explorers, missionaries, prospectors, and colonists on the so-called Dark Continent survived at least in part on the fruits of the chase. A few people are profiled just to illustrate a particular point about life in Old Africa, but I've focused to a large extent on those who made their living "off their guns": the ivory hunters, the hide hunters, and the many others who made their livelihood with a rifle.

The opportunities to do so, for possibly the last time in history, were legion. Throughout most of this time period, elephant ivory went for about £1 per pound of weight, at a time when £500 was a very respectable annual income. Hippo and buffalo meat was sold in markets all over Africa, and the hides of buffalo, hippo, rhino, and even giraffe fetched good prices. The explorer Dracopoli reported that an ounce of tail feathers from the humble marabou stork was worth about £12 in 1913, and the famous Karamojo Bell made enough money hunting elephant to buy an estate in Scotland and to keep him and his wife in style until his death at age seventy-one. Generations of colonial families in Kenya, Rhodesia, and South Africa found the exploitation of wildlife to be their main source of income.

There are a few tricks to getting the most from this book. I have presumed a certain familiarity with African history and sport on the part of the reader. As a reminder, the initials "BSAC" stand for the British South African Company, the huge corporation dominated by Cecil Rhodes that opened up Rhodesia to European settlement. "PH" is "professional hunter." Other initials are more esoteric: "EARB" stands for *East African Red Book,* an invaluable almanac published in 1930 by a Nairobi newspaper, and "RW" stands in for "Rowland Ward," the ubiquitous big-game record book that was an essential part of a hunter's kit during the time period in question. References to "RW99" or "Rowland Ward 1927" are to the 1899 and 1927 editions of that work, which I cite frequently in order to give the reader the flavor of a particular hunter's activities. There is more information about EARB and RW in the text and in the glossary.

Biographies are listed alphabetically by the last name, and, in the case of British double names, by the last element (see below). The full formal name (John Lethbridge) is in the heading, while the more common name (Jackie Lethbridge) is mentioned first in the text of the entry. Popular nicknames ("Karamojo" Bell) are included in the heading.

The political map has changed entirely from colonial days, and the reader will do well to remember that British East Africa included Kenya and Uganda; that Tanganyika was a German colony from the 1880s until 1919 when it became a British mandate until the 1960s; and that Zimbabwe and Zambia were once Southern and Northern Rhodesia, respectively. Northern Rhodesia was itself divided into Northeastern Rhodesia and Northwestern Rhodesia from 1896 through 1911. In the southern part of the continent, Namibia was once the German colony of South-West Africa, and like Tanganyika, was similarly taken over by the British after World War I; it was later administered by the South Africans. Bechuanaland is now Botswana.

I feel compelled to mention a few things to avoid unwarranted criticism. This is a book about European hunters; no slight is intended by the limited space allotted to native Africans. Some of the major tribal leaders are included to provide historical context, but to do the subject justice would require an entirely new book.

The biographies are as accurate as possible, considering the spotty nature of the source materials. Every effort has been made to cross-check every fact, but when the pipes are dirty you can't expect the water to be clear. African sporting and hunting literature is erratic and has never been placed on a solid academic basis, with many of the best-known stories available in multiple versions. I have tried to elicit the kernels of truth behind each person's life, but there are undoubtedly numerous errors and omissions. These are entirely my responsibility, and I can only remind the reader in my defense that to research a book of this scope completely is a project that would take many lifetimes. Alas, I have but one.

I leave it to other writers of greater resources and skill to expound on what I have begun.

One final note. Let me state right up front that I am not an expert: I'm a fan and a lifelong reader of the old African hunting literature, starting back when you could still buy the books for less than the price of a Vegas vacation. If a hunter-writer is what you want, check out Tony Sanchez-Ariño. He's the real thing, a bona fide African hunter of vast experience who has considerable literary skills to boot. But you don't have to have hitchhikers buried in the yard to write a book about serial killers, and you don't have to be a veteran of Gettysburg to write about the Civil War. The bookstores are full of books about the Mafia by people who never whacked an enemy or broke a welcher's leg. What I do possess is a deep, lifetime obsession with the literature and a modest talent for research.

This project was a monster, and it evolved into something far beyond the capabilities of one man—this one man, anyway. Thanks are due to Jann Kerr and David Hartley of Hartley Safaris, who provided information that was helpful in the article concerning that grand old patriarch, Henry Hartley. Also to Izak and Willem Barnard, the progeny of Bvekenya, whose generosity was overwhelming. Diane Hardwick Shannon went to great lengths to provide me with information on her great-uncle Alfred Arkell-Hardwick. Thanks also to Pat Shipman; James Mellon; curator Malcolm Harman of the Powell-Cotton Museum at Quex Park; George Gloss and the staff at Boston's Brattle Books; Dr. Edward Miner of the University of Iowa; and Leszek Kosek for information on individual entries.

Special thanks to Ann Littlewood, Scott Miller, Michelle McColgan, Denise Miller, and Jennie Wolf. I am eternally indebted to Rich Fitzpatrick of the Bookrack in Braintree, Massachusetts, for his help in finding manuscripts about Old Africa; Judy Gorman; Diane Flaherty Martin; Linda Peterson; Diana Mitchell Carbone; Michael, Meg, and Hannah Littlewood; Christine O'Neill; Jean Hogarty; Mary Hogarty; Beth and Casey Benoit; Frank Gallagher of Boston and Guadalcanal; Clayton Chandler; Audrey Mahoney; Diane, Ian, and Brendan Maguire of Plymouth Massachusetts; Deirdra Mahoney; Dr. Harmony Allison; Colleen LaBelle; Sheila Timilty; Cheri Cavanaugh. Ludo Wurfbain and the staff and editors at Safari Press have been simply incredible. As always, what is good in this project comes from them; the errors are mine, and that there weren't more mistakes is a tribute to them all.

RAISON D'ÊTRE

The American writer Negley Farson said it best in his introduction to W. D. M. Bell's 1949 classic, *Karamojo Safari.* Speaking of the early big-game hunters of Africa, Farson wrote, "The life of every one of them is an epic, could they but tell it." Every man and woman listed in this book deserves a full-length biography, but only a few have received one. This work is a small attempt to keep their names alive and, I hope, to act as a starting point for researchers with greater resources, time, and skill.

DISCOVERIES

For the sake of clarity and ease of use, "discovery" is used in the traditional Western sense. If I say Livingstone discovered a lake, I mean he was the first European that we definitely know of who visited that body of water and wrote about it. Obviously, the local Africans discovered all the significant and insignificant parts of Africa long before the Europeans got there. I make no attempt to attach special glory to the white man's travels, but, equally obviously, it is the careers of the various European and American hunters/explorers and what they were known for during their lives that is the primary focus of this book.

SPELLING AND WORD USAGE

African locales, tribal names, personal names, and other features have always been a source of wonder and frustration for Western lexicographers and writers. In order to maintain consistency throughout this book, I have taken a very simple approach: Although the same name was often spelled differently in different sources, I have taken the most used spelling for that entry and used it consistently throughout the book. I make no claim whatsoever for accuracy, and when in doubt I have tried to err on the side of ease of comprehension. Any other approach would have suffered from innumerable drawbacks, not the least of which is my total inadequacy in the linguistic field. One example (among many) that I am sure will infuriate at least some people is my preference of the word Masai for that noble, arrogant warrior people, in opposition to what I'm told is the preferred Maasai or other variations. Any way you spell it, the word literally refers to the speakers of the Ma or Maa language. I have gone with Masai, as that is the spelling found in almost all of the sources before 1945.

Another example is my choice of the word Matabele over the preferred Ndebele. My only excuse is that all of the contemporary sources used the former term. And then, of course, there is the name of the great warrior-king who broke away from Shaka and fathered Lobengula—out of the dozens of possible spellings I have tried to stick with Mzilikazi. I just like the way that one looks.

Biographies are listed alphabetically by the last name, and, in the case of British double names, by the last element (Roualeyn Gordon CUMMING), except where hyphenated (Robert BADEN-Powell). The full formal name (John Lethbridge) is in the heading, while the more common name (Jackie Lethbridge) is mentioned first in the text of the entry. Popular nicknames ("Karamojo" Bell) are included in the heading.

RACISM

I want to draw attention to the fact that the colonial and precolonial eras witnessed racial attitudes that are rightfully held in abhorrence today. It is impossible to write the history of those eras without quoting some inexcusable language and attitudes, but it is not the purpose of a historian to sugarcoat his subject. The past is what it was, and no purpose is served by attempting to leave out the unpleasant bits. I have tried to accommodate modern sensibilities by rejecting the most offensive terms, and have adopted modern usage where able. For instance, the series of conflicts now called the Frontier Wars were for generations known as the "Kaffir" Wars, and as that word has extremely negative connotations I have gladly adopted the modern usage. But the line is a fuzzy one, and I am not politically savvy enough to avoid offending everyone. I have tried to get out of this trap by the admittedly cowardly expedient of using the terminology favored by the source. Thus the Kavirondo and the Hottentots remain so in the text, although they are now known by preferred names in modern works. I apologize for the inevitable offense, but history itself is often offensive. I ask the reader to understand that any transgressions on my part are the result of ignorance, not insensitivity or racism.

Even the most "enlightened" Europeans (by which I mean "Westerners" or "Europeans and Americans" throughout the book) believed in a hierarchy of human variation, situated at the top of which was always their own particular heritage. The frightful treatment of Ota Benga by the supposedly learned William Hornaday is appalling to modern sensibilities. No less despicable is the role that Bill Buckley forced his employee Juma to perform. There were degrees of racism, to be sure: The hearts of men like Major Barttelot and William Finaughty were stained by an unabashed hatred and fear of other cultures and people, but even relatively innocuous souls such as Mary Kingsley, Harry Johnston, James Stevenson-Hamilton, and Denis Lyell were imbued with feelings of racial and cultural superiority. Only a few—Karamojo Bell leaps to mind—were able to view the exotic African with neither prejudice nor condescension. Nearly all the men and women profiled in this book formed strong personal friendships with individual Africans, and some (like Harry Johnston) visibly matured in their awareness of human universality, but the situation as a whole did not change much during the period covered in this book.

CONTENT

A lot of thought and anxiety went into what to put into this book and what to leave out. The original draft was more than twice as long and obviously had to be pared, but that was easier said than done. The initial concept called for a reference book that would help historians and readers of out-of-print safari books identify names and events that would crop up in their reading. In its simplest form, then, the book only included pure hunters. Unfortunately, that distinction was impossible to keep. It's easy enough to include Bror Blixen and exclude Bishop Tucker of Uganda, but once the simple choices are made the line between hunter and nonhunter becomes blurred.

Two main factors obscure the line. First, hunting was the number one sport of the British upper class during the time period included in this book. If you were a British officer or official stationed in Africa, you were expected to hunt. Thus, hunting became socially important to an extent that's hard for a modern reader to understand. Gerald Portal, for instance, was a military officer on a political mission, but his diary devotes more space to the local game than it does to the political situation he was sent to investigate. Second, for nearly every European in Africa during the early years, shooting wild animals was a major—in many cases *the* major—source of food. District commissioners, explorers, Victorian lady travelers, butterfly collectors, traders—they all hunted regularly, and the most book-bound missionary had more big-game hunting experience than many of today's top-ranking members of Safari Club International. Of necessity, then, the book grew to include those whose occupations and vocations required a rifle as part of their essential equipment. The one exception is military men who were in Africa solely to campaign against a human enemy. This is not a military history and the wars have been left out, except for enough exposition to put everything into context.

Accordingly, in these pages you will find a plethora of explorers, engineers, surveyors, doctors, tourists, and other folks not generally thought of as hunters. I've included anybody who made a living off his or her guns, as well as those whose names commonly appear in the literature of Africa from that time period. I have, however, made a few exceptions. I have included people whose stories were simply too interesting to leave out, and I have added someone occasionally just to illustrate a particular facet of life in colonial Africa.

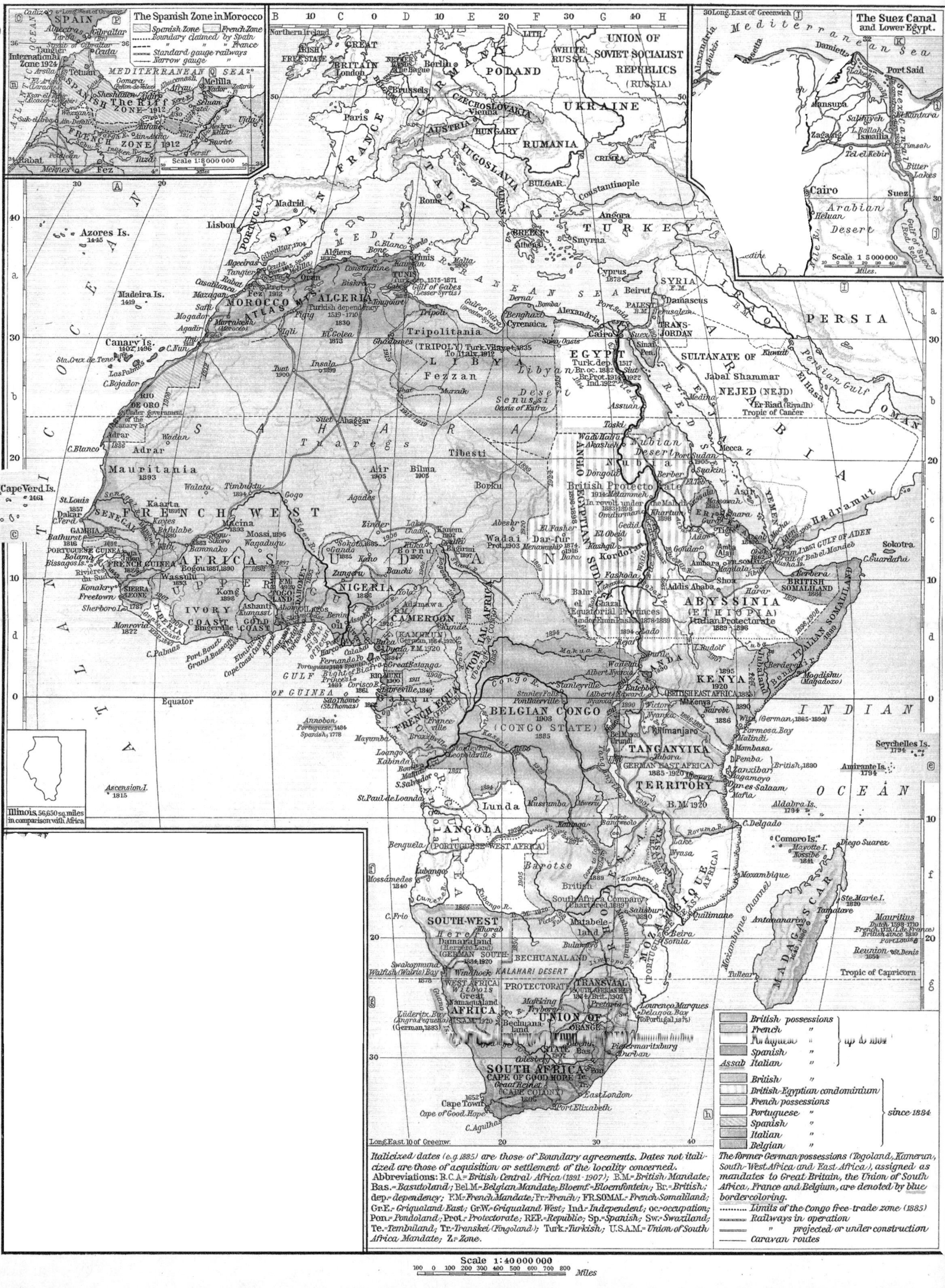

The Spanish Zone in Morocco
Spanish Zone
French Zone
Boundary claimed by Spain
" " " France
Standard gauge railways
Narrow gauge
SPAIN
Gibraltar
Tangier
International Zone 1924
MEDITERRANEAN SEA
Tetuan
Ceuta
Melilla
The Riff
SPANISH ZONE 1912
FRENCH ZONE 1912
Rabat
Fez
Meknes
Scale 1:8 000 000
The Suez Canal and Lower Egypt.
Mediterranean Sea
Alexandria
Rosetta
Damietta
Port Said
Mansura
Ismailia
Zagazig
Tel el Kebir
Cairo
Suez
Bitter Lakes
Arabian Desert
Scale 1:5 000 000
Northern Ireland
IRISH FREE STATE
GREAT BRITAIN
London
Paris
Berlin
POLAND
UNION OF SOVIET SOCIALIST REPUBLICS (RUSSIA)
WHITE RUSSIA
UKRAINE
CZECHOSLOVAKIA
AUSTRIA
HUNGARY
RUMANIA
YUGOSLAVIA
ITALY
FRANCE
SPAIN
PORTUGAL
Madrid
Lisbon
Rome
BULGAR.
Constantinople
TURKEY
Angora
GREECE
Athens
Smyrna
Cyprus 1878
SYRIA F.M.
Beirut
Damascus
PALEST. B.M.
Jerusalem
TRANS-JORDAN
PERSIA
ARABIA
SULTANATE OF NEJED (NEJD)
Mecca
YEMEN
Hadramut
OMAN
Persian Gulf
Tropic of Cancer
Azores Is.
Madeira Is.
Canary Is.
Cape Verd Is.
ATLANTIC OCEAN
MEDITERRANEAN SEA
MOROCCO
ALGERIA
TUNIS
Tripolitania
LIBYA
Fezzan
Cyrenaica
EGYPT
Libyan Desert
RIO DE ORO
Adrar
Mauritania 1893
SAHARA
Tuaregs
Tibesti
FRENCH WEST AFRICA
SENEGAL
GAMBIA
PORTUGUESE GUINEA
FRENCH GUINEA
SIERRA LEONE
LIBERIA
IVORY COAST
GOLD COAST
TOGO LAND
DAHOMEY
NIGERIA
CAMEROON (KAMERUN)
SUDAN
Wadai
Dar-fur
ANGLO-EGYPTIAN SUDAN
British Protectorate
Nubian Desert
ABYSSINIA (ETHIOPIA)
Italian Protectorate 1889-1896
ERITREA
FR. SOMAL.
BRITISH SOMALILAND
ITALIAN SOMALILAND
GULF OF ADEN
Sokotra
KENYA 1920
UGANDA
BRITISH EAST AFRICA 1885
Equator
GULF OF GUINEA
FRENCH EQUATORIAL AFRICA
BELGIAN CONGO 1908 (CONGO STATE) 1885
TANGANYIKA TERRITORY
GERMAN EAST AFRICA 1885-1920
INDIAN OCEAN
Seychelles Is.
Zanzibar
ANGOLA (PORTUGUESE WEST AFRICA)
Lunda
Barotse
British South Africa Company (Chartered) 1889
RHODESIA
NYASALAND
MOZAMBIQUE (PORTUGUESE EAST AFRICA)
MADAGASCAR
Comoro Is.
Mauritius
Reunion
Tropic of Capricorn
SOUTH-WEST AFRICA
Damaraland
(GERMAN SOUTH WEST AFRICA) 1884-1920
KALAHARI DESERT
BECHUANALAND PROTECTORATE
TRANSVAAL
UNION OF SOUTH AFRICA
ORANGE
NATAL
CAPE OF GOOD HOPE (CAPE COLONY)
Cape Town
Cape of Good Hope
Durban
Port Elizabeth
East London
Ascension I.
Illinois, 56,650 sq. miles in comparison with Africa
British possessions
French "
Portuguese "
Spanish "
Assab Italian "
up to 1884
British "
British-Egyptian condominium
French possessions
Portuguese "
Spanish "
Italian "
Belgian "
since 1884
The former German possessions (Togoland, Kamerun, South-West Africa and East Africa), assigned as mandates to Great Britain, the Union of South Africa, France and Belgium, are denoted by blue bordercoloring.
Limits of the Congo free-trade zone (1885)
Railways in operation
" projected or under construction
Caravan routes
Italicized dates (e.g. 1885) are those of Boundary agreements. Dates not italicized are those of acquisition or settlement of the locality concerned.
Abbreviations: B.C.A.=British Central Africa (1891-1907); B.M.=British Mandate; Bas.=Basutoland; Bel.M.=Belgian Mandate; Bloemf.=Bloemfontein; Br.=British; dep.=dependency; F.M.=French Mandate; Fr.=French; FR.SOMAL.=French Somaliland; Gr.E.=Griqualand East; Gr.W.=Griqualand West; Ind.=Independent; oc.=occupation; Pon.=Pondoland; Prot.=Protectorate; REP.=Republic; Sp.=Spanish; Sw.=Swaziland; Te.=Tembuland; Tr.=Transkei (Fingoland); Turk.=Turkish; U.S.A.M.=Union of South Africa Mandate; Z.=Zone.
Long. East 10 of Greenw.
Scale 1:40 000 000
Miles

A

Abbott, William Louis (1860–1936). Dr. Abbott, a wealthy Philadelphian, quit medicine at an early age in favor of natural history. In the late 1880s he traveled to East Africa, where he spent several years exploring and collecting specimens, mainly around the Kilimanjaro region and in Masailand. With his generous nature and outstanding financial resources, Abbott was in a position to help others, and indeed was of great assistance to both the Teleki/von Hoehnel and Chandler safaris. Later he went on numerous expeditions to remote corners of the world, making zoological, botanical, and anthropological collections for the Smithsonian.

Abruzzi, Duke of (1873–1933). Also called Prince Luigi Amadeo of Savoy, the duke of Abruzzi was a scion of the Italian royal house and a respected explorer and sportsman. In 1896 he climbed the second highest mountain in Alaska, Mount Saint Elias, and in 1899 explored to within two hundred miles of the North Pole. In 1906 he organized an expedition to explore the Ruwenzori Mountains. His team included crack veteran mountaineers, scientific experts, porters, and askaris.

The duke's safari, a very well organized and equipped affair, set out from Mombasa on the Uganda railway to Lake Victoria, then via steamer to Entebbe. From there on it was all on foot, through the jungles and swamps of Uganda to Fort Portal. At that place the colonial government, concerned lest something fatally stab, sting, or eat an Italian prince on British soil, added so many soldiers to the safari that the entire body now exceeded four hundred men. The mountains were now only fifty miles away, but such was the nature of the terrain and the mass of the expedition that it took weeks to reach their base. Finally the duke established his main camp at an altitude of nine thousand feet. The duke and the elite mountaineering crew of his safari pushed on while the various scientific experts remained to collect geological, botanical, and zoological specimens.

The final assault on Ruwenzori's summit was made by the duke and three expert Swiss climbers, professional guides in their own land. The climb was hazardous and almost disastrous, a thick fog setting in as they negotiated the twin peaks that constituted the mountain's highest point. Ultimately, Abruzzi's expedition was a complete success, on both a mountaineering and a scientific level. The duke left twin flags on the peaks, those of Italy and Great Britain, and named them after those nations' reigning queens, Margherita and Alexandra. He didn't live to see those two countries go to war in 1940.

Ackroyd, R. Dr. Ackroyd was the curator of the Kensington Museum in London in the 1920s. He frequently went on safari to collect specimens, often hiring J. A. Hunter as his professional hunter. Ackroyd had entries in the 1928 Rowland Ward record book for BUSHBUCK, LELWEL HARTEBEEST, DORCAS GAZELLE, BUFFALO, DEFASSA WATERBUCK, AND LORD DERBY ELAND.

Adamson, George (1906–1989). Before his name became associated with "Elsa the Lioness" and the book *Born Free,* George Adamson was known as a tough, hard-drinking game warden of the Northern Frontier District, Kenya's toughest province. Born in Etawah, India, in 1906, George was one of two sons (his brother Terence was born in 1907). His mother was a member of an old India family whose own mother had lived through the Great Mutiny of 1857. His father was an indigo planter. The two married in 1900.

At age eighteen George went to Capetown while the rest of the family moved to a small coffee plantation at Limuvo near Nairobi. As a young man Adamson cast around for an occupation. One early attempt was running a transport business, the Nairobi-Arusha Mail Service. This business failed comically when he agreed to deliver a large shipment of matches, and they caught fire and destroyed his truck. Adamson also tried his hand at building roads, growing coffee and sisal, and trading in beeswax and natural resins. In the mid-1920s he ran a short-lived goat business with partners Hugh Grant and Roger Courtney, both of whom went on to have interesting careers in their own right.

Throughout it all George developed his hunting skills, sometimes for food and sometimes for profit. When funds were low, he and Terence would scrape up £25 for an elephant license and go looking for big ivory. Generally they would triple or quadruple their investment. George developed his bush skills further with a job in locust control, using poison and fire to destroy the voracious insects, and by doing some gold prospecting. In 1934 Adamson and his mining partner, a friend named Neil Baxendale, took an adventurous safari in the Lake Rudolf area. Shortly afterward George became a professional hunter for a safari firm called Gethin and Hewlett.

He quickly made a name for himself in the hunting business. The outdoor life appealed to him, and, being a tough, rugged young man, he had an aptitude for it. By July of 1938 he had been offered and accepted a post as a temporary assistant game warden for the Kenya Game Department. The salary was £8 per week.

Adamson's first post was at Isiolo in the Northern Frontier Province, and his jurisdiction covered an area larger than Great Britain. The Kenya Game Department was woefully understaffed in 1938, consisting of less than a dozen full game wardens and their various temporary assistants, all of them white. Adamson commanded a small force of about thirty African game rangers. His transportation, in the early days, consisted of camels and donkeys and whatever motor vehicle he could patch together or borrow on his own salary.

Adamson had found his place in the world. He developed a reputation for bushcraft and toughness that was second to none. He killed several man-eating lion. At one point the animals almost turned the tables on him. The Samburu tribe had lost nine people to man-eaters in a year. Adamson went up to "sort things out." The day before he arrived, a young boy had been eaten by three lion that had chased him around a pasture. Adamson camped and prepared to track the killer pride.

That night a lioness tried to break through his zareba and attack his men. Adamson shot her. One down. Two hours later another lioness attacked. Adamson shot and missed, the lioness escaping into the night. Adamson went back to sleep and in the morning was shaken to find paw prints just inches from his head—one of the man-eaters had managed to sneak in but for some reason hadn't killed him.

Following the lion's spoor in the morning, they came to a patch of scrub. Adamson went in with a ranger on either side of him. A lioness sprang onto one of the rangers, and the other ranger shot and killed her. Two down. A fresh flesh wound showed that this was the second lioness from the night before, the one that Adamson thought he had missed.

They continued to follow the spoor for ten hours under the scorching tropical sun. Finally the exasperated lion turned and charged. Three down and game over.

A short time after this incident, again in Samburu territory, Adamson was mauled by a lioness when his bolt-action rifle jammed. The wound turned septic, and he spent several days in the bush in excruciating pain while the Samburu fetched assistance. Other duties were less physically painful but emotionally draining; for example, Adamson found a camel that had been stuck up to the neck in the mud of the dried-up Lorian swamp for more than a month, and mercifully put the insane animal out of its misery.

When the African part of World War II broke out in 1939, Adamson found himself right on the front line, smack on the border between British Kenya and Italian Somaliland. He became a military intelligence officer, an almost traditional posting for big-game hunters, and conducted operations against the Italians in Somaliland. For a time he served as an irregular partisan under his old friend Hugh Grant. He engaged in a bit of skirmishing, but his biggest contribution was controlling native spies who reported on enemy troop strengths. There were some communication difficulties—for example, the local Somalis, who for the most part opposed the Italian occupation, often couldn't tell the difference between, say, a milk truck and an armored car. But mostly Adamson's operations went smoothly.

Indeed, he found that war was not all hell. For one three-month period Adamson lived at a tiny desert outpost called Afmadu, where he shared his quarters with a beautiful Somali woman named Fatima. According to biographer Adrian House (1993), for years afterward the mention of her name would produce a "twinkle in George's eyes."

In 1942, after Italian Somaliland had fallen to the English forces, Adamson was able to return to his game department job. He met his future wife, Joy Gessner, at a party at the home of District Commissioner Willie Hale (later Kenya's chief game warden). At the time, Joy, a talented but neurotic German girl originally from Silesia, was married to a Swiss botanist named Peter Bally. The couple had been having trouble and had decided to call it quits. When her divorce came through a year later, Joy, four years younger than George, became Mrs. Adamson. She possessed considerable talent as an artist and was commissioned to do official portraits of native tribesmen and plants and animals.

George's career in the game department continued during the troubled years of the Mau Mau in the early 1950s, when he was put in charge of a small unit of irregular riflemen, in addition to his regular duties. Known as Adamson Force, this unit was very successful at evicting terrorists in the arid wastes near Isiolo. There were frequent shootouts, in all of which Adamson Force come out on top. George personally shot and killed at least twenty terrorists during these skirmishes, and captured many more. His unit was credited with preventing the various terrorist groups from frequently crossing over the border to Somalia, as had been their habit when hotly pursued.

His relationship with Joy became increasingly troubled, despite attempts at reconciliation, such as a 1953 safari through the Sahara and Europe, and a camping trip to South Island in Lake Turkana. On the island the Adamsons found a campsite and other artifacts

Terence Adamson (left) and George Adamson in the 1920s.

that had belonged to two men named Martin and Dyson, members of the 1934 Vivian Fuchs expedition to the lake who had disappeared without a trace. Adamson theorized that the men had torn the bottom of their canvas boat while trying to reach safety on the mainland and had been eaten by crocodiles. Others have speculated that their light craft was tipped over by hippo, which were ubiquitous in the area at the time.

The trips, while interesting, did nothing to ease the strain on the marriage. In retrospect the Adamsons were obviously incompatible. Joy was a neurotic Bohemian while George was a quiet man who liked to drink alone. However, he was deeply in love with his wife and they never divorced, despite numerous infidelities on Joy's side and her blatant financial exploitation. For example, for many years George paid all her taxes from his paltry income, which was considered "shared," while any money she made (and the money coming in for the Elsa Foundation was considerable) was hers and hers alone.

Joy was an odd woman. Although undoubtedly gifted intellectually, she seems to have been ruled entirely by her emotions of the moment. She saw no hypocrisy in wearing a leopard fur coat (a picture of her in it has been published) or a colobus monkey cape while campaigning vigorously, even violently, for the sentimentification of wildlife. George and Joy were separated and estranged their last ten or fifteen years, living apart in a sort of armed truce. It seemed he had always liked her more than she liked him, anyway.

In the mid-1950s the Adamsons embarked on their famous crusade to rehabilitate "tame" lions into the wild. Quite an industry was founded on this premise, including books written by Joy (such as *Born Free, Living Free,* and various sequels), movies, a television show, and the Elsa Foundation. George wrote a memoir of his career in the game department titled *Bwana Game* (1968), as well as a later autobiography, *My Pride and Joy* (1987). The two books cover pretty much the same territory, though the latter has good pictures and brings George and Joy's story up until just before George's death.

In actuality, the lion-rehab program was more of a propaganda device than a zoological accomplishment. The stunning success of *Born Free* contributed immensely to the sentimentification of wildlife politics, but the fact remained that lion are lion, not people or even overgrown kittens. The scorecard undoubtedly favored the animals. Of the seventeen lion released by the Adamsons, George put one down, poachers or herdsmen killed four, and four were killed by other animals (mainly other lion), leaving eight survivors—about twice the expected natural survival rate. On the other hand, quite a few of the "rehabilitated" lion were too habituated to humans to be considered safe. One lioness peripherally associated with the Adamsons killed an African man near the Ura River as early as 1960. Adamson shot another, a big male called Boy, after it had killed a Meru employee named Stanley on 6 June 1971. Two years earlier Boy had bitten the young son of Game Warden Peter Jenkins, fortunately not fatally. Another lion mauled George's brother Terence. Rumors of other incidents, many admittedly spurious, repeatedly made the rounds of the Kenya Game and Parks departments. The authorities made several attempts to curtail the program or to at least move it to more remote areas, but the Adamsons' strong personalities and the force of public opinion acted as a powerful brake on these efforts.

On 3 January 1980, Joy Adamson was killed at her camp while taking a solitary stroll in the bush. George had long warned her against this habit. Early reports indicated that a lion was a culprit. The medical examiner, however, ruled that a sword was the murder weapon, and in due time one of her Kenyan staff was convicted of murder. There is still some controversy over these findings.

George's last years were spent in a constant battle against both poachers and the game department administration, which not unreasonably kept trying to move the lion project into more and more isolated districts in an effort to stop the big cats from killing people. Exiled to a remote camp at Kora, George grieved over the loss of Joy to the end of his days and never lost his toughness and bravery. His own life ended in 1989 when he rushed to the rescue of one of his men who was beset by African *shiftas* (bandits or poachers). They were waiting for him and riddled the cab of his Land Rover with AK-47 slugs, killing him and two assistants.

Adamson, Terence (1907–1986). Terence was George Adamson's brother and an honorary game warden of Kenya. Terence did some work with elephant and buffalo control in the 1940s, and in the 1950s worked for locust and game control at Isiolo, Garissa, and Voi. Locust control involved poisoning the insects in the flightless "hopper" stage of their life cycle, using an arsenic compound mixed with bran. The poison was specially designed to be fatal to locusts but too diluted to cause much harm to larger creatures. When African farmers balked at the application of the compound, claiming that their goats would die from eating the stuff, Terence would eat a mouthful in front of their eyes to calm their fears.

In the early 1980s Terence was bitten in the face by one of the Adamsons' tame lion, a male called Shade, leaving him with a permanent scar. The quintessential story about Terence, a quiet, thoughtful man, concerns the cheap suit he was given upon his release from the military in 1945. Owning no other formal clothes, Terence buried the suit in an airtight can on his property, digging it up years later when he made his only overseas trip. When he returned home he put the suit back in the can and reburied it.

Afrika, Jonathan. This Bechuana hunter traveled extensively with Thomas Morris and Carl Anderson. In 1884 he was seriously mauled by a lioness and recovered on the banks of the Zambezi River. Afrika had been forbidden to hunt by the Bechuana King Khama, but ignored the ban. Some of Khama's men ambushed him in the late 1880s and speared him to death.

Afrikander, Jonker (1785–1861). Afrikander was the patriarch of the so-called Orlam Afrikanders, a clan of mixed ancestry that held sway over a section of South-West Africa in the nineteenth century. One of the clan's chief opponents was explorer and naturalist Carl J. Andersson, who led what amounted to a private army against them. Jonker, the strongest leader of the group, died in 1861. The remaining Orlam Afrikanders were defeated by Andersson's men at a decisive battle on 15 June 1863 and effectively dispossessed.

Aga Khan, The (1877–1957). A religious leader and dedicated sportsman, the Aga Khan (given name Aga Sultan Sir Mohammed Shah) was the forty-eighth of his line, the leader of the Ismaili sect of the Shi'a Muslims. He was considered the spiritual leader of some eleven or twelve million people. Born in Karachi, he succeeded his father in 1885 and began active administration of the Imamate in 1893. He was a strong, active man who helped his people maintain a sense of community even though they were scattered all over India, Burma, the Middle East, and Arabia.

The Aga Khan earned the gratitude of the Allies during World War I when he unflinchingly supported their cause, even though Islamic Turkey was in the enemy camp. He was also influential in keeping India interested in the war. He used his strong position to urge leniency toward Turkey after the Armistice.

From 1924 to 1928 the Aga Khan took a sort of leave from his official duties and devoted himself, in his words, "almost exclusively to my personal and private life." In the 1930s he was again involved in Indian affairs and was a popular figure at the League of Nations. Although he supported the Munich agreement, he was a staunch ally of the West against Hitler and the Nazis in 1939–1940. At the fall of France, however, he took refuge in Switzerland, where he remained, suffering from ill health, until the German defeat in 1944.

By war's end he had lost much of his relevance and influence in India, where Jinnah had taken over the leadership of the Shi'a community, and in the West, where his inactivity during the war was held against him despite his poor health. For the remaining years of his life he was a decidedly minor figure on the world stage.

The Aga Khan had two great sporting interests. One was horse racing and breeding—his horses had an outstanding record in major British races from 1922–1954. The second was big-game hunting. He made numerous African safaris and gathered an impressive set of trophies. The Aga Khan's 1946 safari with Leslie Tarlton and Andy Andersson was noted for its state-of-the-art communications system and a seventy-five-hundred-foot airstrip built to accommodate the Khan's fleet of private aircraft. On a later safari the Aga Khan was guided by the flamboyant, tragic Mark Howard-Williams. A surprising number of the memoirs of professional hunters from that era mention the Aga Khan and his various expeditions. The 1928 edition of Rowland Ward credits him with owning an African elephant tusk weighing 162 pounds and another of 124 pounds.

Akeley, Carl Ethan (1864–1926). Born on a Vermont farm on 19 May 1864, less than a year after the Battle of Gettysburg, Carl Akeley grew up spreading fertilizer and picking apples all week and hunting in the Green Mountains on Saturdays. He learned fowling, tracking, shooting, and the handling of hounds from a local sportsman named Os Mitchell, all skills that proved handy in Carl's adult occupation. It was during other hunting trips to the Adirondacks with Mitchell and Carl's father, Webster Akeley, that the young boy saw his first mounted animals, deer and bear and moose on the walls of hunting lodges.

Rural taxidermy in the 1870s was a sorry art. There still exist in New England roadside bars and old farms that display moose heads or even "Eastern panthers" that resemble nothing more than a sack stuffed with old socks. To the modern eye these specimens look like the work of amateurs or schoolboys, but they represent the typical professional taxidermy product of that time. It was as if no one realized how lifelike a mounted animal could appear, so no one bothered striving for that effect.

Even as a twelve-year-old, Akeley recognized that these stuffed specimens were poor reflections of what the animal looked like in life. In 1876 he made his first attempt at taxidermy himself, on a neighbor's canary. With no training or other outside influence, he produced a mount superior to what was hanging in those New York hunting lodges.

About 1878 Akeley made a trip to Rochester, New York, where he saw his first good mounts, some specimens prepared by an English painter named David Bruce. Akeley was so impressed that he asked Bruce to become his teacher. The painter instead referred him to a Rochester company called Ward's Natural Science Establishment. Prof. Henry A. Ward, an acerbic little man, agreed to take Akeley on as an apprentice for wages of $3.50 per week.

The Ward company was composed of fifteen separate buildings loaded with specimens in various degrees of preparation, chemical baths, unlabeled boxes, and bustling apprentices. The company had two main sources of revenue. Museums would pay Ward to prepare specimens for exhibit, and various consortiums and individuals would pay to have their specimens mounted for resale.

Though grateful for the learning experience, Akeley was appalled by the mass-production philosophy of the Ward company. Professor Ward had made taxidermy a successful business, but in doing so he had forsaken the scientific, educational, and even the artistic aspects of the skill. The taxidermists were treated like unskilled labor, working eleven hours six days a week with no holidays or sick time. Most of them held their tongues because they realized they were getting specialized training available nowhere else. Daily, the company received large tubs full of the disarticulated bones of exotic animals. Merely in the routine performance of their duties, the apprentices learned zoology, anatomy, and other areas of natural history. Akeley, however, was young and enthusiastic, full of big ideas, and incapable of keeping his mouth shut. He soon found himself fired.

With at least the basics of the trade under his belt, Akeley had no trouble getting another taxidermy job, this one in Brooklyn. John Wallace, like Ward, made a business of preparing skins and trophy heads for resale. Also like

Ward, Wallace was grouchy and hard to get along with, and cut every corner he could in the preparation of his mounts. Even after Wallace had agreed to a substantial wage increase, Akeley got back in touch with Ward and the two agreed to give it another go.

Soon Akeley, with the help of another progressive young taxidermist named William Wheeler, convinced Professor Ward that the secret to greater commercial success lay not in mass-production but in creating a superior product—craftsmanship over quantity, as it was called. One early opportunity came in 1885 when Jumbo, the great African elephant of the Barnum and London Combined Circus, was killed by a train in Saint Thomas, Ontario. Ward got the call to try to preserve the huge beast. Barnum personally negotiated the details with Professor Ward, and Akeley and another worker named Critchley were left to do the actual work. They were given five months to complete the unprecedented task.

A core part of Akeley's emerging method was to take great care with the central mannequin around which the hide would be stretched. Jumbo's new skeleton was made from steamed basswood and oak, with thousands of nails holding the skin tight. One of Akeley's techniques was to mold the skin flush with the mannequin, as opposed earlier taxidermists' practice of putting a layer of stuffing in between. Akeley and Critchley took great care in assembling the mount, but the schedule did not permit proper drying of the hide and it shrank and shifted constantly on the massive frame. Still, it looked great. When the final product was wheeled out of its Rochester workshop en route to the train that would take it to Barnum, the observers (estimated at nearly half the population of Rochester) were amazed at its lifelike appearance. Despite the rush, Jumbo was a success.

Carl Akeley (left) and George Eastman in Tanganyika.

Other successes followed swiftly. For his next production, Akeley created a mount with an Indian motif showing an elephant battling a tiger. Reviewers loved the natural display. But although the new relationship with Professor Ward was working out well, Akeley wanted to be his own boss. Accordingly, in November 1886 he moved to Wisconsin, where his erstwhile coworker William Wheeler had become a curator at the Milwaukee Public Museum. Akeley's new post was as the museum's part-time taxidermist. He would work four hours a day and study toward his college degree. He was just twenty-two years old.

The young taxidermist set out to prove his theory that quality lifelike specimens mounted flush over a mannequin would draw crowds. His first professional displays were a reindeer group and an orangutan group. He also perfected his technique by studying anatomy and modeling with clay, so as to prepare better the mannequins. His best work at this time, however, was a breakthrough exhibit showing the most mundane of animals—a family of muskrats—at home in their natural habitat. Akeley built a cross-section of the muskrat lodge and associated trails, and draped the scene with the trees and foliage that belonged in any North American swamp. The result was the first museum group anywhere to show mammals in their full natural habitat. It was an outstanding critical success.

Milwaukee was where Akeley truly learned his craft. By 1890 he was a full-time employee of the museum and had abandoned pursuit of his college degree (in 1940 his wife, Mary Jobe Akeley, wrote, "He became convinced that college would have been the death of his dreams"). In that year, however, Wheeler resigned to take a post at Clark University. Akeley resigned as well, partly because he missed Wheeler's friendship and patronage and partly because the museum's directors kept adding mundane housekeeping tasks to his job description, like sweeping the floor and taking out the trash. He set up his own shop on Grand Avenue in Milwaukee, doing work for local sportsmen and museums. Another big opportunity presented itself with the 1892 World Columbian Exposition in Chicago. Akeley prepared a horse mount (a difficult animal to make lifelike) that was the taxidermy hit of the exposition.

By the time he entered his thirties Akeley had achieved national recognition. He now set out to make his name internationally. He met Dr. Daniel Elliot, curator of zoology at Chicago's prestigious Field Museum. Elliott was outfitting a collecting expedition to East Africa, and Akeley agreed to sign on as the expedition taxidermist. The team spent nearly six months in 1896 hunting in Somalia, collecting wild ass, greater kudu, oryx, spotted hyena, striped hyena, cheetah, hartebeest, and dibatag.

It was during this expedition that Akeley had his famous experience with a leopard. Pursuing the wounded animal through a donga (dried streambed), Akeley was charged at short range. As he brought his rifle up he realized he had not reloaded after firing the shot that had wounded the beast. The leopard sprang upon him, simultaneously trying to bite his throat open while her hind claws ripped at him in an attempt at disembowelment. Akeley threw himself atop the cat and tried to crush her with his knee, meanwhile letting the leopard chew his arm up in order to keep the teeth occupied (this, incidentally, is the strategy recommended by professionals). After what seemed an eternity he heard a snap and the leopard's struggles weakened—he had broken a rib. By continually applying the same pressure he finally managed to kill the animal. He staggered back to camp, where his wounds were doused with permanganate of potash. ("During this process I nearly regretted that the leopard had not won," he said later, as quoted by his wife in 1940.)

This event made Akeley the Victorian equivalent of a sporting superstar. To kill a leopard with your bare hands was quite a feat. But to kill a leopard with your bare hands and then mount the skin in a superb trophy was the stuff of legend. By the time Akeley's wounds had healed, his name was known throughout the hunting and natural-history world. He was immediately appointed the Field Museum's director of taxidermy. Over the next twelve years he completed fifteen large groupings showing African mammals in their natural surroundings. Many of these groups later resided in his legacy, the Akeley Memorial African Hall. Akeley trained and mentored other aspiring taxidermists including James L. Clark, Louis Jonas, Robert H. Rockwell, Raymond B. Potter, and Albert E. Butler.

Also during this time frame Akeley pioneered two new taxidermy techniques. The first was the use of the lighter, more flexible papier-mâché for his mannequins instead of the traditional wood, plaster, and metal. The other groundbreaking idea was to use colored beeswax to simulate the vegetation for his habitat displays. Both of these techniques soon became standards in the trade.

Akeley started making periodic trips overseas to collect animals and supervise their preparation in the field. In 1906 he went on an extended hunting trip with elephant hunter R. J. Cuninghame to the Aberdares and then to Mount Kilimanjaro. This was really Akeley's initiation to the finer points of African big-game hunting, in particular the habits and hunting of elephant. In 1909 he joined up with the historic Roosevelt safari in Kenya and Uganda, skinning elephant shot by both Theodore and Kermit Roosevelt. While they continued to the Nile valley, Akeley left to explore Mount Elgon, where he experimented with close-up wildlife photography on rhino and other dangerous game.

His experiences there led him to design and build a portable motion-picture camera suitable for making nature films. The Akeley camera made its debut in Man-o'-War's Kentucky Derby run and was later chosen for military use in World War I. As Akeley had planned, the camera was particularly useful for rugged outdoor work, accompanying important scientific expeditions to the Arctic, the Amazon, Lapland, Siberia, the Himalayas, and Guiana, among other places.

It was at this time (1910) that Akeley had another run-in with an angry wild animal. While filming elephant at an altitude of nine thousand feet on Mount Kenya, he was surprised by a big bull that burst from brush at the side of the trail. As he swung up his rifle, the safety switch stuck in the "on" position, rendering it useless. When the elephant tried to skewer him, Akeley somehow slipped in between the two tusks, which sank into the ground on either side of him. Though this move prevented impalement, it did not stop Akeley from being badly crushed by the bull's massive forehead as it tried to drive him into the earth. The elephant did not grind him entirely into the dirt; Akeley always thought that the tusks had hit a stone or something in the ground that prevented it. Unlike many elephant that attack humans, this one did not stay around to make sure of the outcome. After some grinding and pushing, the big bull moved off, back into the leafy bush.

At first Akeley's Kikuyu and Swahili retainers refused to help him—it went against their tribal training to touch a dead person. Instead they built a campfire and stood around discussing the matter. It eventually became apparent to them that the white man might live, and they carried him back to camp. His initial treatment consisted of hot beef soup extract, quinine, and a bottle of brandy—presumably all the restoratives on hand.

Akeley was found to have a punctured lung and several broken ribs. The flesh of his face fell down over his eyes, and his nose was broken. During his recovery in a Nairobi hospital he compared notes with three other elephant hunters, Alan Black, George Outram, and Horatio Hutchinson, all of whom were laid up with moderate-to-severe injuries caused by their intended quarry.

World War I saw Akeley, now over fifty years old, turning down a commission as a major to work as a "dollar-a-day" volunteer scientist. Not only did Akeley provide his specialized camera to the United States armed forces, he also designed an effective bulletproof mirror for huge military searchlights as well as making improvements on primitive tanks. The war brought him out of Chicago to an office in New York. He was just preparing to go overseas when the Armistice was declared. Among the taxidermy work he managed to squeeze in during the war years was a splendid okapi mount finished in 1917 for the American Museum of Natural History.

For a few years in the late 1910s Akeley shared an apartment with explorers Vilhjalmur Stefansson (Arctic) and Herbert Spinden (Central and South America). This unusual living arrangement was brought about by the war—all three men were in New York on military business. They split a suite of rooms near the American Museum, and in a boys'-fantasy "open house," other explorers, archaeologists, and international big-game hunters frequently dropped by to consult, plan, and brag. This lasted until about 1920, when Akeley moved his living quarters into the Explorer's Club. Akeley's book *In Brightest Africa* was patterned after one by Stefansson, *The Friendly Arctic,* and reversing the stereotypical view was the central theme in each. Stefansson was a long-term friend not only of Akeley but also of Mary Jobe Akeley; in fact, it was the Arctic explorer who had first introduced the future husband and wife.

The year 1921 saw Akeley embarking on his famous "gorilla expedition." He had seen a gorilla mount at Professor Ward's workshop way back in 1882 and had always wanted an opportunity to model one correctly. He had been planning to collect some specimens in 1910, but the elephant incident ruined his plans. He set out again in August 1921, financed mostly by $10,000 of his own money and accompanied by four adult friends and a five-year-old child, the daughter of two of the friends. They headed for the Lake Kivu district to collect mountain gorilla.

Akeley made two discoveries of a personal nature on this trip, his fourth expedition to Africa. First, he discovered that what he had read about the gorilla was wrong. It was not a bloodthirsty, treacherous animal eager to attack any human being in its reach. Rather the gorilla was an intelligent, docile, often even gentle creature. His other personal discovery was that Kivu and its surrounding mountains were the most beautiful country he had ever seen. He promptly decided to commission a painting of the glorious panorama for a backdrop to his gorilla group. He may have expressed the thought that he might someday be buried there. This was not a premonition; at the time he was fifty-seven years old, in good health, and of a strong constitution, and privately expressed in letters the opinion that he had a good twenty working years left in him.

Akeley's gorilla group was probably the culmination of his career. He collected five specimens, a family group of four animals and a massive bull called the "Giant of Karisimbi." The mounting was so effective that when professional hunter T. Alexander Barns first saw the Giant he exclaimed, "Well, thank God! At last a gorilla has been mounted that looks like a gorilla."

Despite his optimistic estimate of his remaining working life, the sands of time were running out on Carl Akeley. Ironically, his life ended on the threshold of the fulfillment of his greatest dream. He had long planned and dreamed about building a great African Hall, designed so that realistic mounts would create the impression of a pristine African savanna prior to the depredations of man. The stumbling block had always been money. In the mid-1920s Akeley finally managed to round up the requisite financing by recruiting millionaire George Eastman (of Kodak camera fame) as a backer. Eastman was an avid sportsman who was also backing Martin and Osa Johnson during those years. He agreed to finance a 1926 African expedition (to be Akeley's fifth) that would collect the animals necessary to finish the African Hall.

The Akeley-Eastman-Pomeroy Expedition (Daniel Pomeroy was another investor) set sail for Africa in January 1926. Members included Akeley, his second wife Mary Jobe Akeley, taxidermist Robert Rockwell, artist Arthur Jansson, and artist William Leigh. The American

Museum's Richard Raddatz went as a taxidermist's helper, auto mechanic, and general handyman. The artists were along mainly to paint the magnificent scene that Akeley desired as a backdrop for the gorilla group, as well as other backdrops. After stopping in Europe, the team entered Africa via Mombasa. They quickly collected specimens of lion, buffalo, klipspringer, and a great bull giraffe before moving into Rwanda and the Lake Kivu area. Eastman joined the expedition but spent much of his time away from the others on private shooting safaris. This was entirely appropriate—he was leaving the collecting work to the professionals while he indulged in his own sport.

It quickly became apparent, however, that this expedition faced a challenge that none of the previous ones had seen. Carl Akeley's health was breaking down. Time after time he had to stop and rest at various nursing homes and missions. After a few days he would feel better and the team would move along. A week or two more in the bush, however, and Akeley would collapse again and be carried into the nearest refuge. As word got around that his health was failing and that this would probably be his last African trip, a stream of important visitors began visiting the safari camp. These included white hunters like Leslie and Alan Tarlton, Blayney Percival, and Mrs. Philip Percival. Akeley was quickly fading. Ironically, after two of Africa's major beasts, the leopard and the elephant, had tried and failed to take his life, Carl Akeley was being brought down by lowly African microbes.

He died on 17 November 1926 and was buried on the saddle between two of the mountains overlooking Lake Kivu—amid the same spectacular scene that had so impressed him five years earlier. He never lived to see it, but the Akeley African Hall of the American Museum was dedicated on 19 May 1936, the seventy-second anniversary of his birth. The entrance way was framed by statues of African warriors (by sculptor Malvina Hoffman) and two perfectly matched elephant tusks weighing 167 and 169 pounds, respectively. The exhibit contained eight huge double groups and twenty single groups, all of them testaments to the high standards that Akeley had created for taxidermy. The doors opened

Carl and Mary Akeley with a group of Lumbwa warriors.

to the public on New Year's Day 1938. The hall was a huge success.

Akeley, Delia Julia (1875–1970). Delia, Carl Akeley's first wife, accompanied him on his early African expeditions, including the 1910 trip on which he was nearly killed by an elephant. Delia was cut in the Jane Goodall–Dian Fossey mold and devoted herself wholeheartedly to studying vervet monkeys. So single-minded was her obsession that she neglected other aspects of her life, and many of her friends credited the monkeys (especially one particular pet called J. T. that Delia brought back to New York) with breaking up her marriage. At any rate, her husband started to go on expeditions with another woman, which was sufficient monkey business for the divorce court. In 1924 Delia, without her ex-husband, returned to Africa, sponsored by the Brooklyn Museum of Arts and Sciences. During this expedition it is thought that she may have been the first white woman to transverse Africa from east to west. She was the author of *Jungle Portraits* (1930).

Both Delia Akeley and Carl's second wife, Mary Jobe Akeley, were fascinating, adventurous women—and they couldn't stand each other. In all of Carl Akeley's later works, and in all of Mary Jobe Akeley's works, Delia is never even mentioned.

Akeley, Mary L. Jobe (1878–1966). The second wife of Carl Akeley was a respected explorer (of Canada's northwestern wilderness areas) in her own right. She was introduced to Akeley by their mutual friend, the arctic explorer Vilhjalmur Stefansson. Mary accompanied Carl Akeley on his last expedition and was by his side as he died on 17 November 1926. Mary Jobe went on to write several books, including *Carl Akeley's Africa; Adventures in the African Jungle; Lions, Gorillas, and Their Neighbors,* and *Restless Jungle.* Her 1940 book, *The Wilderness Lives Again,* is a biography of her husband with an emphasis on his taxidermy. She died in Mystic, Connecticut, having outlived her husband by forty years.

Albassini, Joao "Jowawa" (1813–1888). In the first half of the nineteenth century, this legendary Portuguese hunter and trader (whose name is also spelled Albasini) was reputed to be the first white man in the lowveld of the eastern Transvaal. The son of a sea captain, Albassini set up a trading post at Delagoa Bay at the age of eighteen in 1831. Beginning in 1838, he began to hunt broadly in the interior with the Boer hunter Carel Trichardt. Around 1840 he built a brick house on the Sabi River near what is now called the Hippo Pool in Kruger National Park, about fifteen miles from Pretorius Kop. From this headquarters he traded with the local tribespeople and sent out four hundred hired African hunters to bring in ivory and hides and, occasionally, slaves. He periodically shipped the tusks to Delagoa Bay for sale. Albassini's operations were so efficient that the warden and naturalist James Stevenson-Hamilton (1924) considered his ivory and hide hunters responsible for the extinction of elephant and white rhino in the region.

Such was his authority that Albassini was considered a high-ranking chief among the Shangaan people, and had indunas (chiefs or kings) who reported to him. Albassini helped protect the local inhabitants from their raiding Swazi neighbors. In 1858 he was appointed Portugal's vice consul in the area and, a year or two later, became a native commissioner for the Transvaal government.

Albassini married a Boer girl, Gertina van Rensberg, around the year 1850. He then built a large farm in what is now Kruger National Park, with an irrigation ditch nearly two miles long leading to the Sabi River. Game Ranger Harry Wolhuter and C. A. Yates found the ruins of the famous brick house many years later. Yates took a photograph of the ruins, which were overgrown with shrubs and brush.

Alexander, Boyd (1873–1910). Boyd Alexander was born as one of a pair of twins (his brother was named Robert) in Kent, England on 16 January 1873. Boyd was educated at Radley College and in 1893 joined the British army as an enlisted man assigned to the 7th battalion of the Rifle Brigade. It is unclear whether he quit the army or was allowed several extended leaves, but he visited the Cape Verde Islands in 1897 and a year later went to the Zambezi and Kafue Rivers in Rhodesia. He was intensely interested in ornithology and made some valuable contributions to that field.

In 1899 Alexander was a member of the Gold Coast Constabulary and a year later was engaged in the relief of Kumasi during the Asante campaign. He then received a commission in the Rifle Brigade, but continued to take his extended leaves (if that's what they were), collecting birds in West Africa in 1902. On 31 March 1904 he began a lengthy expedition into northern Nigeria, accompanied by his younger brother Capt. Claud Alexander, Capt. G. B. Gosling, P. A. Talbot, and a taxidermist and servant named Jose Lopes, who had been with Boyd Alexander since 1897.

The safari proceeded at a leisurely pace, stopping periodically for Alexander to collect birds and for Gosling, an ardent hunter, to go after big game (a giraffe he shot on this trip made it into the Rowland Ward records). Claud Alexander and Talbot charted the hitherto little-known Murchison Mountains, and despite sickness and the usual trouble with the locals, things seemed to be going well. Around the beginning of October, however, Claud Alexander came down with a particularly virulent fever, and on 13 November he died at the village of Maifoni.

Boyd Alexander buried his brother and then led the rest of the expedition to Lake Chad, where they spent several months exploring that remote district. Their observations later resulted in the first accurate British maps of the area. Talbot left the safari in early 1905, and the rest of the group set off down the Bamingi River toward the Shari on 26 May. They mapped the Shari and a section of the Bangui River and then started up the Welle, where Gosling died from blackwater fever at the village of Niangara.

Thus only Boyd Alexander and the reliable Jose Lopes were left out of the original staff. Alexander kept going, however, and visited the Lado Enclave, the Yei River, and the Bahr el Jebel. By July of 1906 he was back on the Welle and five months later reached the Nile and started home. For his tremendous accomplishments on this safari Captain Alexander was awarded the Gold Medal of the Geographical Society of Antwerp and the Founder's Medal of the Royal Geographical Society in 1908.

After a prolonged stay in England, Alexander and Lopes returned to West Africa in late 1908. They visited the coastal islands and Mount Cameroon in 1909, and then once again headed inland toward Lake Chad. The situation had deteriorated in the intervening years, and Boyd Alexander was murdered by tribesmen at Nyeri, seventy miles north of Abeshr in Wadai, on 2 April 1910. Jose Lopes, who escaped the ambush, buried his body next to that of his brother. Boyd Alexander was the author of *From the Niger to the Nile* (1907). His girlfriend, Olive Macleod, traveled to West Africa to try to uncover the mystery of his death.

Alexander, Sir James Edward (1803–1885). General Alexander was a British soldier and explorer whose military career included campaigns in India, Burma, South Africa, and the Crimea. As an explorer, he made an extended trip through the Karoo north into central Africa in 1836–1837. He was the author of *Travels Through Russia and the Crimea* (1830) and *Expedition of Discovery into the Interior of Africa* (1838), among other works.

Allen, "Yank." An American hunter of the 1920s, from Texas, Allen was hired by a cattle rancher in Southern Rhodesia to control the native lion. During his tenure he shot more than two hundred of them, using a .577 black-powder Express double rifle. Allen once tripped while being charged by a wounded lion, an unenviable situation. In trying to catch himself, he jammed his rifle on the ground and broke the stock off. Somehow he managed to get enough leverage to swing the rifle down on the lion's head and kill it. Yank Allen was apparently not a man to fool with.

Allen, Frank Maurice "Bunny" (1906–2002). Born on 17 April 1906, Bunny Allen came to Kenya in 1927 from England aboard the steamship *Ussukuma*. He was of Gypsy descent and had some reputation as an amateur boxer and sparring partner. His first safari was in 1928 under the tutelage of Bror Blixen. A year later he assisted Denys Finch Hatton in guiding the Prince of Wales.

Allen worked a lot with Nanyuki professional hunter Raymond Hook, who taught him many of the ins and outs of the business. He also impressed Archie Ritchie, who contracted him to do control work. He quickly became a successful professional and was hired to work on many of the safari films being shot in Kenya, from *King Solomon's Mines* and *Mogambo* in the 1950s to *Out of Africa* in 1985.

For *Mogambo* Allen not only organized a staff of twenty professional hunters and over a thousand Samburu warriors, he also appeared on-screen as Clark Gable's stunt double. Allen, a suave, charming sort, was rumored to have been romantically involved with Gable's co-stars Grace Kelly and Ava Gardner.

Allen carried around a scar across the bridge of his nose, the gift of a Voi leopard early in his career. Bunny Allen lived to a very old age, retiring to the island of Lamu on the Indian Ocean, where he died at the age of ninety-five on 14 January 2002.

His two sons followed him in the field. David Allen was a Kenya game warden stationed at Nanyuki. Anton Allen became a professional hunter in Tanganyika and proudly bore the marks of his trade, twice being badly hurt by a buffalo and once by a leopard.

Amabile. An Italian explorer operating along the White Nile, Amabile was sent to prison by Petherick for slave trading in the 1850s.

Andersson, Gordon Henry "Andy" (1878–1946). The story goes that Maj. G. H. "Andy" Andersson (late of Paget's Horse and 18th Royal Hussars) met Jim Sutherland aboard a ship and was so interested in the elephant hunter's tales that he resigned his commission to hunt full time. His first safari took place in Somaliland in 1904, and it wasn't a rousing success—he was mauled by a lion. He got better at it, though, good enough to become a founding member of EAPHA (see glossary) in 1934.

In 1910 Andersson hunted elephant in Uganda on a special government control permit, and later did elephant control work in Tanganyika. He accompanied the duke and duchess of York during their 1924 expedition—the first of the really "royal" safaris—and hunted with the Prince of Wales during the prince's two East African trips. Despite a severe and permanent limp from an early leg wound, he was considered one of the premier professional hunters in Kenya in the 1920s and 1930s.

Andersson, Karell Johann (1827–1867). This Swedish hunter was also known as Carl John Andersson, Charles John Andersson, and similar variations. He was an early explorer of the Kalahari, Namibia, and Botswana areas, following the usual pattern in which the search for new hunting experiences led to geographic discoveries. In 1850 he went with Francis Galton from Walfisch Bay to Ovamboland, continuing on alone to Lake Ngami in 1853–1854. In 1856 he worked as a mines inspector at Swakop. Then, in 1859–1860, Andersson hunted up around the Okavango Delta area. With his wife he lived by the Damara River, lording it over the indigenous people. For some time he ran a flourishing ivory trading business in Otyimbingue. In 1866 he set out on his last journey, to the Kunene River, but this venture ended in a fatal sickness.

Like most of the early hunters, Andersson has been criticized for his excesses. He once shot sixty rhino in a period of a few months. Men like Andersson and Gordon Cumming seem to have been just overwhelmed at the number of shooting opportunities. It wasn't entirely one-sided—Andersson was nearly killed by a black rhino one day. He was the author of several books, including *Lake Ngami* (1855) and *The Okavango River* (1861).

In 1867 Andersson was buried by his friend Axel Eriksson along the trail near the Kunene River after his death from peritonitis. For many years his gravesite was lost, but it was rediscovered in the 1940s by Native Commissioner Cocky Hahn.

Andersson's last letter to his wife still survives: "Oh, beloved wife! We shall never meet in this life, but surely in the next. I had thought to turn this journey to good account for my poor family; it is to be hoped it will bring you something to your home. Poor wife! I can see you overwhelmed with grief when this reaches you and you understand that my bones are bleaching in this distant wilderness. I feel ill-prepared to pass out of this world, but I trust in God's mercy and His immeasurable love . . . I am too weak to write much."

Andersson's wife, Sarah Jane Aitchison (1832–1917), was left with no support after his death and opened a haberdashery in South-West Africa.

Angebauer, Karl (1882–1952). A German hunter who lived in South-West Africa in the first two decades of the twentieth century, Angebauer fled Namibia in the exodus of German citizens after the Great War, and later wrote several books about his hunting adventures.

Ansorge, W. J. (1850–1913). Ansorge was a veteran of six trips into the interior of Africa, visiting Uganda, the Zambezi Valley, and the Shire River region. He was a hunter and a prolific insect collector, and the author of *Under the African Sun* (1899).

Antinori, Orazio (1811–1882). This Italian explorer and zoologist explored the upper Nile and into Abyssinia. In 1876 he led an important scientific expedition into the land of the Shoa, in southeast Abyssinia, where he died.

Archer, Sir Geoffrey Francis (1882–1964). A nephew of Sir Frederick Jackson, Archer was the first district officer at Marsabit in 1909. The foundation of the house later built by Martin and Osa Johnson was made from stones used by Archer in constructing Marsabit's first building. A year later, Archer supervised the government takeover of the Boma Trading Company's assets in the Northern Frontier District. In 1920 Archer led the campaign against the Mad Mullah in Somaliland, and from 1922–1924 he was governor and commander-in-chief in Uganda. He was a member of the Kenya administration from 1902–1912 and the founder of Archer's Post. A big man, he was an avid amateur ornithologist. ROWLAND WARD 1928: NILE LECHWE, WHITE RHINO, IMPALA, SITATUNGA, ELEPHANT, MOUNTAIN BUSHBUCK (NYALA), SOMALI (SWAYNE) HARTEBEEST.

Arkell-Hardwick, Alfred (1878–1912). See Hardwick, Alfred Arkell.

Arnot, Frederick Stanley (1858–1914). Arnot was a British missionary of the denomination called the Plymouth Brethren. He was invited to Barotseland by

George Westbeech in 1882 and stayed at the Barotse capital of Lealui for eighteen months. There he opened a small mission school for royal and noble children, and advised the Barotse king, Lubosi, to ally himself with Khama rather than Lobengula. Arnot became just the sixth European known to cross the African continent, traveling from Durban to Benguela in 1881–1884. In 1884 he moved to Katanga, where he continued his missionary endeavors for thirty years. Many years passed before he made even a single convert.

Arnot was the author of *Bihe and Garenganze: A Record of Four Years Work and Journeying in Central Africa* (1893), a collection of letters written between missionaries at the two locations in the title.

Ashley, Wilfred William (1867–1938). William Ashley, Baron Mount Temple, inherited the estate of Broadlands through his grandmother, Lady Palmerston. Ashley had a long career in public service, toiling as a justice of the peace, alderman of the county of Hampshire, member of Parliament, member of the House of Lords from 1932, and a battalion commander during the Great War. He was an extensive traveler and frequently went on safari to Africa, where he earned several rankings in the record book. One of his two daughters, Edwina, married Lord Louis Mountbatten of Burma. ROWLAND 1928: KONGONI, LESSER KUDU.

Athlone, Earl of (1874–1957). Born Alexander Augustus Frederick William Alfred George Cambridge at Kensington Palace on 14 April 1874, Athlone was the son of Princess Mary Adelaide and the Duke of Teck, and the brother of the future Queen Mary of Great Britain. Originally known as Prince Alexander of Teck, he (and the rest of the British royal family) abandoned his Germanic name in 1917 and took the surname Cambridge and the title earl of Athlone.

Athlone joined the 7th Hussars as a second lieutenant in 1894 and fought in the Matabele rebellion in 1896–1897, being mentioned in dispatches. In the Boer War he served in the Inniskilling Dragoons, again being mentioned and receiving the DSO (see glossary). Several of his comrades wrote of him as a tough but cheerful officer who did not attempt to take advantage of his exalted rank.

After marrying Queen Victoria's granddaughter, Princess Alice, in 1904, the earl continued to serve in the army. He was appointed governor general of Canada in 1914 but cancelled the appointment when the war broke out in August so he could serve with his regiment (by now the 2nd Life Guards) as a lieutenant colonel. During the war he served mainly on staff appointments with allied headquarters and with the Belgian army, and was twice mentioned in dispatches and much decorated.

Athlone retired from the army when the war ended and for the rest of his life worked mainly in politics and in education reform. He served as governor general of South Africa in 1923–1931, longer than the standard five-year term. His later years were marred by the death of his son in a French car accident in 1928.

Athlone was a respected sportsmen and often took time out from his duties to go hunting. His trophy room at Kensington Palace was filled with magnificent mounted specimens and paintings by African artists who had been commissioned by Princess Alice. In 1940–1945 the earl finally got his long-postponed term as governor general of Canada. He died where he had been born, at Kensington Palace, on 16 January 1957. ROWLAND WARD 1928: ELEPHANT (SOUTH-WEST AFRICA).

Atkinson, A. Eustace (1869–xxxx). When Lord Delamere's mother, worried about her son's health, wanted him to bring a physician along on his 1895 African hunting trip, Dr. Atkinson was selected by the taxidermists at Rowland Ward to be the hunting companion. Atkinson was twenty-six years old, handsome, and charming, but with a hard streak underneath the affable exterior. The pair hunted in India and Norway before arriving in East Africa in 1896. In December of that year they finally left the Somalian jumping-off place of Berbera with a safari of two hundred camels and one hundred rifles. In March 1897 Delamere waited on the Juba River while Atkinson traveled to Zanzibar with a bank draft of £1,000 to replenish supplies. Apparently while in Zanzibar, Atkinson first fully realized the value of ivory, a passion for which would forever change the young doctor's life.

By early summer of 1897 Delamere and Atkinson were reunited and hunting near Marsabit Mountain, where Atkinson killed twenty-one elephant in twenty-one days. After Marsabit they hunted elephant along Lake Rudolf. By the time they returned to civilization Atkinson had an ivory profit of £1,000 and Delamere £14,000, an enormous sum in the days when a district commissioner was paid an annual salary of £400. On their way out of the backcountry they met with Dr. Johann Kolb, the German naturalist who was gored to death by a rhino just days later.

Obsessed with the profit potential of ivory, Atkinson settled permanently in Kenya, where he not only hunted elephant himself but also hired both white hunters and

Africans to hunt for him. Atkinson traded for ivory in a big way as well, and it was this latter activity that almost got him hanged, a fate that he richly deserved.

In July of 1902 he met near Lake Rudolf with some Rendille tribesmen who had some tusks for sale. Atkinson was accompanied by two white employees named Smith and Vincent. The Rendille were holding out for what Atkinson felt was an exorbitant price. Throughout the discussion the doctor sat on a keg that he told the Africans contained their payment in Austrian Maria Theresa dollars, the universal currency of the district. Dissatisfied with the way things were going, Atkinson surreptitiously lit a fuse attached to the keg and walked away. The keg was filled with gunpowder.

The resulting explosion tore apart the Rendille tribesmen, killing or maiming almost all of them. An explosion of that magnitude causes a concussion blast that can lacerate human lungs due to the sudden change in air pressure. It was then a simple matter for the three Europeans and their two hundred porters to steal the Rendille's ivory and make for the coast. Atkinson made a critical mistake, however, by failing to pay his porters the wages due them. Inevitably, some of the porters talked and soon Atkinson, Smith, and Vincent found themselves arrested and charged with murder. About the only thing that could be said in their defense was that some of the Rendille chiefs had made some ugly threats during the trade talks. Nonetheless, it could hardly be said that Atkinson and friends acted in self-defense, for they could easily have packed up their caravan and moved away.

In Kenya in 1902, however, it proved impossible to hang a white man for killing a black man. The talkative porters were bullied and threatened into silence, and in the end only three witnesses, all of them secondhand and including elephant hunter Arthur Neumann, testified for the prosecution. For his testimony Neumann especially incurred the wrath of his fellow Europeans in the colony, at least some of who thought that he'd perjured himself. To the chagrin of Governor Sir Charles Eliot, a deal was worked out with the prosecution whereby Smith and Vincent were deported from the colony and Dr. Atkinson quietly retired to his potato farm for a year.

Whether Atkinson was frightened by his near miss with the hangman or had some flash of remorse is unknown, but he quit the ivory business and devoted the rest of his long life to farming and running a lumber business. Atkinson became one of Kenya's wealthiest old settlers and lived out his life at a fine ranch at Karura. His unpleasant side still surfaced from time to time. In 1903 he was one of the leaders in the fight to prevent Jewish settlement on the Uasin Gishu plateau, and he seems to have been motivated purely by anti-Semitism. It was widely believed that he was the lover of Lady Florence Delamere before her death in 1914.

Austin, Herbert Henry (1868–1937). Born in Burma, Austin served in the British army in India and with the Uganda Railway Survey. In 1897 he signed on as second-in-command of Maj. James MacDonald's Juba Expedition to the Upper Nile. Ostensibly a scientific endeavor, the expedition's real purpose was to contain the French force under Marchand that was precipitating a crisis between Britain and France. In August 1898 MacDonald split his force into two wings, and one wing, under Austin, was sent to the Omo Delta on Lake Rudolf. Austin acquitted himself well, and his small force of five hundred men successfully circumnavigated Lake Rudolf and produced the first good maps of the area. He also signed thirteen separate treaties with various African entities along the lake, an act of much political importance during the mad "Scramble for Africa."

In 1900 Austin was chosen to head one of two survey teams, the Abyssinian Frontier Expedition, sent to Ethiopia to help gather knowledge about frontier conditions. It was also considered important that an official British force be sent through the area to bolster Britain's legal claims. The British government wanted the purpose of the expedition to be a secret, so Austin was instructed to emphasize its hunting and sporting aspects to the inhabitants of the district and to the world press. This was a common ploy that never fooled anybody.

The company of sixty-two men and 157 pack animals left Khartoum in December 1900 and headed south. The camels were driven by thirty-two men from the Jehadia tribe, and the twenty soldiers were Sudanese. There were four servants, and the three other men were Major Austin and his two British officers (Maj. Richard Bright and Maj. John Garner). The party made good time, and Austin's experienced engineering eye produced a remarkable survey. On 4 April 1901 they reached Mount Nakua, overlooking Lake Rudolf. This was the end of the surveying part of the expedition, and all that really remained was to successfully bring the men out to the coast. All had gone well, and Austin and his men were superbly confident. But at this moment portents of disaster began to creep in.

First, a promised relief column loaded with food failed to appear at the rendezvous. Austin's men were growing short on rations, a cause for concern. Second, the local inhabitants, generally considered friendly, became reclusive and refused to barter food with the Englishmen. Austin had no way of knowing that recent raids from Ethiopia had left the tribal people so panicked and distressed that they were in no position and had no inclination to help any strangers. Austin had hoped to buy food in the Omo Delta region, but this was now out of the question because the local Africans refused to sell what little they had. Austin declined to attack the villages and seize food, and with less than two weeks of rations remaining, the decision was made to change the plan and exit the Lake Rudolf district to the south and head for Uganda.

This meant traversing the territory inhabited by the Turkana people. Unknown to Austin, the Turkana had also suffered badly at the hands of the Ethiopian raiders and were at a fever pitch. On 5 May 1901 two Sudanese soldiers and Austin's Mohammedan cook were ambushed and speared to death by Murle tribesmen. That night the Murle launched two frenzied attacks upon Austin's camp, to be beaten back only by disciplined rifle fire.

Escaping from the Murle, the expedition moved farther into Turkana territory, where Austin promptly became so ill that they had to camp in the same place for a few days. The daily ration was reduced to a quarter-pound of meat and grain per man, and the camels were slaughtered and eaten. On 19 May three of the Jehadia camel drivers died from starvation and a fourth was killed by the Turkana, who had surrounded the camp. Shortly thereafter Austin ordered some of the remaining donkeys to be killed for food.

By the second of June, sixteen of the Jehadia were dead as well as three of the Sudanese. Only a few donkeys were left to carry the most essential supplies, and Austin and the other English officers had to constantly guard the animals. One of the younger Jehadia, named Abdul, was continually caught trying to pilfer food from the general stores. Warnings and floggings did no good. Frustrated, Austin finally had the youth shot by a firing squad.

The expedition eventually struggled out of Turkana territory on 14 June, which at least reduced the threat of ambush. Men continued to die of starvation and other causes (one of the Sudanese soldiers died after eating poisoned berries), and by 1 July only seventeen Africans out of the combined force of fifty-nine were still alive. The British medical officer with the expedition, Dr. John Garner, pointed out that most of those who starved to death were Jehadia, who had begun the ordeal less well nourished. None of the Europeans, who were presumably healthier to begin with, died. Austin, however, came down with scurvy toward the end of the expedition and temporarily went blind.

The remnants of the Abyssinian Frontier Expedition reached the British post at Lake Baringo at the end of July 1901. Thirty of thirty-two Jehadia had died, as well as nine of twenty Sudanese and three of the four servants. Austin would have been dead in a day or two if they hadn't reached Baringo. The expedition could only be considered an unmitigated disaster.

Somehow, Austin's career survived the fiasco. He was made a companion of the Order of Saint Michael and Saint George and given further commands in India and the Near East. He retired in 1920 as a general, and died in 1937. A prolific writer, he was the author of *Among Swamps and Giants in Equatorial Africa* (1902), *Some Rambles of a Sapper* (1928), and *With MacDonald in Uganda* (1903).

Aylmer, G. Percy V. Aylmer was a British sportsman who accompanied Frank James, W. D. James, and Ethelbert Lort Phillips on safari into the deep hinterlands of Somalia in 1881–1882 and again in 1884, reaching as far as the Shebele River. ROWLAND WARD 1899: SCOTTISH RED DEER, ABYSSINIAN BUFFALO.

Ayre, Aubrey Fitzpatrick "Pat" (1886–1975). Pat Ayre of Nanyuki was a professional hunter whose clients included the duke and duchess of York (1924) and George Eastman (1926). Affiliated with the Newland & Tarlton and the Safariland firms, Ayre in 1934 was one of the charter members of EAPHA (see glossary). The hunter/writer W. Robert Foran considered Ayre one of the best three professional hunters ever to work in Kenya (1958).

Ayre, W. H. (xxxx–1941). A member of EAPHA (see glossary) from 1938, W. H. Ayre was killed in action in Abyssinia in 1941.

B

Baden-Powell, Sir Robert Stephenson Smith (1857–1941). Born in London on 27 February 1857 as the son of an Oxford geometry professor, Baden-Powell led the kind of daring life suitable for the founder of the Boy Scouts. He did so well on his 1876 army entrance examination that he was allowed to skip the British military academy at Sandhurst and was commissioned directly as an officer of the 13th Hussars, then stationed in India. A light horseman, he specialized in scouting and skirmishing and in the early 1880s wrote several books on light-cavalry tactics. In 1888 he served against the Zulus in South Africa, and in 1891 he was posted as an intelligence officer for the Mediterranean, where he oversaw a network of Victorian spies.

After serving in the Asante War of 1895–1896, during which he played a key role in designing the war's successful British strategy, Baden-Powell went to Rhodesia, where he helped to subdue the Matabele and Shona rebellions. As a staff officer under General Carrington in 1896 he performed well, proving himself relentless in the defense of British imperialism. In September of that year a patrol led by Baden-Powell captured the Matabele priest Uwini, and the future founder of the Boy Scouts ordered the rebel leader to be shot after an informal court-martial.

In 1897 Baden-Powell was promoted to commander of the 5th Dragoon Guards. The outbreak of the Boer War fortuitously found him in Mafeking, South Africa, which was soon under siege by the Boers. Baden-Powell performed magnificently, and when the siege was lifted by a relief column in May of 1900 he was rewarded by being placed in command of the newly established South African Constabulary. He returned to Britain in 1901 and was soon promoted to the prestigious position of inspector general of the cavalry. In 1908 he was placed in command of the Northumbrian Division and retired from the army in 1910 as a lieutenant general.

His true passion in later life was the organization called the Boy Scouts. Baden-Powell had authored an 1899 book titled *Aids to Scouting,* designed as a supplement to his light cavalry texts. Upon returning to England from the Boer War, he found that the book had acquired a huge following among young boys. This piqued his interest. A model Victorian soldier and imperialist, he was very interested in promoting the martial virtues that Britain would need to run her overseas Empire. He edited *Aids to Scouting* to appeal to a young, civilian audience, and the book was reprinted as *Scouting for Boys* (1908). The Boy Scouts were founded in 1907, followed in 1909 by the Girl Guides and later by the Wolf Cubs, Sea Scouts, and Rover Scouts. The concept was hugely successful, teaching young boys and girls the arts of hunting, scouting, and husbandry while fostering a love for the outdoors. International chapters were soon opening up at a frantic pace: The notorious Nazi Hitler Jugend (Youth) began as the German Boy Scouts, and the ubiquitous Hitler Youth dagger was simply the Scout knife with a different emblem (many modern fake Hitler Youth knives are made by putting the Nazi diamond on an existing Boy Scout original). Baden-Powell was proclaimed chief scout of the world in the same year that saw the first international Scout "Jamboree" (a word he coined), a huge festival that attracted scouts of many nations. It was held annually until interrupted by the tensions just before World War II.

General Sir Robert Baden-Powell in his elderly years.

In 1929 Baden-Powell was made Baron Baden-Powell of Gilwell and received many honors for his variety of distinguished service. He married Olave Saint Clair in 1912; she was acclaimed as Chief Girl Guide in 1918. During the last years of his life the couple lived in Nyeri, Kenya, near the famous Treetops Hotel, at which they were frequent visitors. The founder and owner of Treetops, Eric Sherbrooke Walker, had served Baden-Powell as far back as 1908 as scout commissioner and private secretary. Walker permitted his old boss to build a small cottage on the grounds of the Outspan Hotel, another hostel owned by Walker. The cottage was named Paxtoo after B-P's former home in Bentley, England, which was called Pax.

Baden-Powell loved Africa and happily lived out his life at Paxtoo. In his younger days he had been an enthusiastic hunter, and especially enjoyed stalking wild boar in India, but he never hunted an elephant, awed as he was by that animal's immensity and intelligence. During the last decades of his life he traded his gun for a movie camera and filmed many scenes of animal life. He died on 8 January 1941 at the age of eighty-two. He was the author of numerous books, including *Cavalry Instruction, My Adventures as a Spy, The Downfall of Prempeh, Paddle Your Own Canoe,* and *Birds and Beasts in Africa.*

Bagge, Stephen Salisbury (1859–xxxx). Widely considered one of the more talented British provincial commissioners of his day, Bagge lived in Uganda for fifteen years before taking a post in the Kenya administration in 1902. Before that, he had been a rancher in Texas. Bagge was a sub-commissioner (1902–1907) and then provincial commissioner at Naivasha (1907–1910). ROWLAND WARD 1928: BUFFALO.

Bailey, Sir Abe (1864–1940). Bailey was born at Cradock in Cape Colony, the only son of a general storekeeper from Yorkshire. Educated in England, Bailey returned to South Africa in 1881 and worked at his father's store for five years before moving to the goldfields at Barberton in the Transvaal. He brought along £100 in capital funds, which he promptly lost. Then, borrowing £10 from a friend, Bailey took out a broker's license and began working on the stock exchange. In 1887 he moved his operations to the Rand and within a few years began working in real estate. His business dealings were so successful that he wound up as the chairman of fourteen companies that were amalgamated into the Abe Bailey and London and Rhodesian Mining Group.

Bailey's interests were varied—he loved hunting, racing, and hosting elaborate large dinners to which the cream of London society was invited (Harry Johnston, Rudyard Kipling, etc.). He was made KCMG (see glossary) in 1911 and a baronet in 1919. He married Caroline Mary Paddon in 1894 (she died in 1902) and Mary Westenra, the daughter of Lord Rossmore, in 1911. He had three sons and four daughters. Bailey was an original member of the Transvaal Game Protection Association. His former farm and hunting ranch in South Africa is now the Abe Bailey Nature Reserve.

In the 1930s a newspaper reporter uncovered a man named George Honeyball, an old wheelwright who years before was one of the first to discover the great gold reefs of the Rand. Honeyball never made any money from his discovery, and when writer Negley Farson found him he was living in abject poverty in Johannesburg. Bailey sent him a gift of £100, the largest amount of money that Honeyball had ever had in his life. ROWLAND WARD 1928: HARTEBEEST, SPRINGBOK, BONGO (NO. 1, 39½ INCHES, KENYA), GEMSBOK (NO. 1, 48 INCHES, BECHUANALAND), LORD DERBY ELAND.

Bailey became ill in the late 1930s and had both legs amputated, one in July 1937 and the other nine months later. He passed away on 10 August 1940, leaving 25 percent of his estate (and his art collection) to the Abe Bailey Trust for the advancement of the South African people. He also left £100,000 for research at the Royal Institute of International Affairs.

Bailey's second wife, Lady Mary Bailey (1890–1960), had a distinguished career of her own. After earning her pilot's license in 1927, she became the first woman to fly across the Irish Sea and (with Mrs. Geoffrey de Havilland) set a woman's light-aircraft altitude record of 17,280 feet in 1927. She won the coveted Britannia Trophy in 1930 for her successful flight from London to Cape Town and back.

Bailey, Henry. Bailey went to the Belgian Congo in 1884 and remained there for four years, exploring, prospecting, and hunting big game. Under the pen name Bula N'Zau ("Elephant Crusher," supposedly his African nickname) he wrote a book, published in 1894 as *Travel and Adventure in the Congo Free State, and Its Big Game Shooting.* The book concentrates on hunting, mainly elephant but also buffalo, hippo, leopard, antelope, and a solitary gorilla (for which last the *Scottish Geographical Magazine* criticized him—conservationist sympathies were not entirely absent in the late nineteenth century). Bailey wove in the usual odd natural-history anecdotes such as poisonous snakes being killed by tobacco juice and geese roosting in trees, as well as one of the more horrific stories about *siafu* ants.

Baillie, John. Baillie came to South Africa in 1820 as part of a great wave of some five thousand settlers. He spent much of the next decade hunting and trading in the interior. Accompanied by John Rex, the grandson of King George III, he explored the Buffalo River and founded the town of East London at its mouth.

Baillie's later life was hard. He was financially ruined in one of the endless frontier wars (also losing a son, Lt. Charles Baillie) and served eighteen months in jail with another son for killing a man in a fight. He tried several times to establish either a farm or a trading station, but failed each time. He finally drowned while attempting to rescue some men who were stranded on a grounded ship.

Bain, Andrew Geddes (1797–1864). Bain and John Burnet Biddulph were a pair of English traders from Graaff-Reinet who traveled through much of South Africa in the 1820s. With another man named Benjamin Kift, they went on a trading trip in 1826 up through Kuruman and into the domain of a native king named Sebegho, collecting ivory and skins as they went. Sebegho persuaded them to help in an intertribal battle, which they did. When they returned to Graaff-Reinet eight months after leaving, they had achieved no great financial success but had penetrated farther north than any other European explorers of the time.

Kift became a noted professional hunter. Biddulph continued to run his store at Graaff-Reinet, helping to equip William Cornwallis Harris a few years later. Bain led an additional company north in 1834, following the Dr. Andrew Smith Expedition. The Smith group was no ordinary get-rich-quick assemblage of traders but rather an official expedition of discovery sponsored by the Cape of Good Hope Association for Exploring Central Africa. Bain intended to follow Smith as far as the Orange River and then go off on his own. He had commissions from American naturalists to collect animal specimens and also intended to make a profit by hunting for ivory and rhino and giraffe hide.

For some reason, after splitting from Smith, Bain's company was attacked by Matabele warriors under the control of Mzilikazi. William Cornwallis Harris reported that some Griquas riding with Bain had stolen some of Mzilikazi's cattle, and the attack was in retaliation for that deed. Other sources ascribe no such reasonable motive. At any rate, Bain and four others fought their way to safety after killing several of their assailants and losing all of their goods, and straggled back to civilization more dead than alive.

Baines, Thomas (1822–1875). Born at King's-Lynn, Norfolk, England, Baines arrived in Cape Colony in 1842. He accompanied the British army as a civilian artist in the Frontier War of 1848–1851, and explored northwestern Australia with Augustus Gregory in 1855–1856. He was the official artist and commissary of the Livingstone Zambezi Expedition in 1858, and in 1861–1862 traveled with Chapman to Victoria Falls, where he made very precise drawings of the falls. During these trips he "spent much time hunting elephants, rhinoceri, lions, hartebeests, ostriches, quaggas, and buffaloes" (Buel, 1889). He also went on to participate in several safaris led by Henry Hartley.

Baines was fired from the Livingstone expedition because of allegations of theft made by Charles Livingstone. Those accusations were later shown to be unfounded. The real source of trouble seems to have been that Charles Livingstone, brother of the expedition's leader, felt that Baines should take orders from him and would constantly demand that the artist perform menial tasks. Baines finally exploded and protested that he was the expedition's artist and commissary, not Charles's personal servant. From then on his termination was inevitable. The Livingstones kept his paintings, and such was their vindictiveness that Baines's name was largely eliminated from Livingstone's official Narrative of the expedition.

Baines went on the professional lecture tour in England in 1864–1868. During 1869–1871 he conducted another African expedition, this one to find gold fields in Mashonaland. A respected artist, Baines wrote *Explorations in Southwestern Africa* (1864) and *The Gold Regions of Southeastern Africa* (1877). He also wrote an article, "How I Shot My First Elephant," that was published in the *Eclectic Magazine of Foreign Literature Science and Art* in 1868.

Baird, John Lawrence (1874–1941). Baird was a member of the Archibald Butter–Philip Maud Abyssinian Boundary Survey Expedition of 1902–1903. On 22 May 1903 he was badly injured by a lion he had been hunting, saved only by quick and courageous action by his Somali gunbearers. Baird later became governor general of Australia.

Baker, Julian A. (xxxx–1922). Nephew of Sir Samuel Baker, Julian was a commander in the Royal Navy and captain of the HMS *Foam*. While cruising off the west coast of Africa, Baker went ashore to hunt for red buffalo. A reliable native armed with a second rifle accompanied him. They spotted a bull buffalo at a range of one hundred yards. Baker fired and hit the animal, which plunged into a small bush and apparently went down. Baker ran forward, but just as he approached, the buffalo roared to its feet. His rifle misfired, and in short order he was over the bull's head, impaled through the thigh. By gripping one horn, Baker, who must have been in great shape, managed to pull the other horn from his thigh. The buffalo tried to gore him again, but the resourceful officer kept one hand on the horn and tried twisting the bull's nose with the other. With great presence of mind and bravery, the native assistant threw away his rifle, apparently believing he was too close to use it, and began stabbing the buffalo with his long hunting knife.

The buffalo finally collapsed from loss of blood. Julian Baker was incapacitated for over three months, but survived to become a rear admiral of the Royal Navy. Samuel Baker kept the bull's head as a trophy.

Baker, Sir Samuel White (1821–1893). Sam Baker was born in Enfield, England on 8 June 1821, a member of a successful family with a long history of lucrative overseas business ventures. After a spell spent running a sugar estate on Mauritius, Baker in 1847 moved to Ceylon, where he founded a sanatorium and a township and enjoyed the island's big-game hunting opportunities. He wrote about his early shooting adventures in his first books, *The Rifle and the Hound in Ceylon* (1854) and *Eight Years Wandering in Ceylon* (1855). His first wife, Henrietta, died in 1855 after bearing seven children, three of whom died as infants. Baker lost much of his zest for hunting at this time in his life. After a brief stint with the Turkish railway service, in 1859 Baker went on a European tour with the Maharajah Duleep Singh, a playboy Sikh prince who was the deposed ruler of the Punjab and sort of Queen Victoria's pet.

The story of how Baker met his second wife has been shrouded in mystery. Most accounts merely describe her as a young Hungarian woman, but writer Pat Shipman, who had access to Baker family papers, claimed in 2004 that Florence Szasz (c. 1845–1916) was a slave in Wallachia when Baker saw her at an auction. He bid for, but lost out on, the beautiful blonde teenager (the year of her birth has also been disputed, but Shipman reported that she was startlingly young). No matter—Baker bribed a guard, absconded with the girl, and escaped back into Christian Europe just ahead of the retainers of the winning bidder, the pasha of Viddin.

Whether it started as true love or an extreme midlife crisis (thirty-eight-year-old man rescues fifteen-year-old girl) can't be judged, but despite the unorthodox beginning, Sam and Florence Baker became one of history's great couples. Eager to participate in the quest for the Nile's source, Sam went to North Africa and led a caravan into Abyssinia, where he and his wife and men spent the summer and fall of 1861. By June of 1862 his hastily formed expedition had reached Khartoum, with the gifted Florence sharing every hardship and triumph. Among other, more ephemeral qualities, she possessed the extremely practical skill of speaking Arabic, which was to prove essential many times in the years ahead.

Throughout 1862 the pair explored the upper reaches of the White Nile. They were the first to provide relief for Speke and Grant upon their exit from the jungles around Lake Victoria, giving them much-needed supplies and support. In 1863 the Bakers discovered Lake Albert and

Sir Samuel Baker in the 1860s.

Murchison Falls, and were stranded for much of 1864 in Bunyoro. They suffered every conceivable hardship, from starvation to sunstroke to malaria to blackwater fever to mendacious natives and dangerous slave traders. Finally, in 1865 they pulled out to Gondokoro and from there made it back to civilization.

As a young man Baker was obsessed with hunting; his love of sport was the driving force behind all the major decisions of his early life, up until the death of Henrietta and, later, the fateful day that he met his future second wife. From that point on he was more devoted to Florence and to achieving success and glory for Britain as an explorer and anti-slavery crusader. Like many sportsmen who had almost unlimited hunting opportunities while young (he admitted to killing "some hundreds" of elephant, not to mention lesser species), in his later, more reflective years Baker grew rather remorseful over his youthful bloodletting. Though it was a gradual lessening of interest, not a sudden stop, and he never entirely gave up hunting, by 1881 the formerly reckless Victorian hunter was surprising his American guide by taking just one bison and being content to merely glass the rest of the herd.

The Bakers' return to England in 1865 (when he received the Gold Medal of the Royal Geographical Society) was marred only by the reluctance of the British upper class, including the queen, to accept Florence as Baker's wife and a "lady." Lurid imaginations painted her as a debauchee of the harem rather than a frightened, virginal girl of amazing resourcefulness. Happily, though, in the long run her innate decency and strong character convinced all of her worth and she wound up being one of the more esteemed women of the era.

Almost everyone who met Samuel and Florence Baker in Africa before they were famous was deeply skeptical that the pair was married. It was just naturally assumed that Baker was traveling with his beautiful and very much younger mistress (he was in his forties, she was a teenager). It is interesting to note that neither Speke nor Grant mentioned Mrs. Baker when they wrote about the end of their expedition in Gondokoro—while they did mention other European women, including Mrs Petherick, the Baroness van Capellan, and Alexine Tinne. Author Frederick Bradnum showed surprising naiveté in his 1969 work *The Long Walks* when he suggested that Baker must have hidden Florence from their sight. The obvious truth was that Speke and Grant assumed the lovely Hungarian girl was merely Baker's mistress and were observing the gentleman's code of silence, the Victorian version of the motto "What happens in Vegas stays in Vegas."

Sam Baker (known as "Baker of the Nile") was knighted in 1866, and sent back to Egypt in 1869. There he took the post of governor general of Equatoria province, charged with the destruction of the slave trade. Here, too, Florence shared his hardships. The campaign against the slavers was of mixed success, largely because corruption was too pervasive to get any real support from the Egyptian government and courts. Baker's term in office expired in 1873, and the couple returned to Britain, claiming success.

Baker's personality was an odd one. He was a bit of a loner, albeit deeply attached to each of his wives, especially Florence. He lacked the British "public school" spirit and was not one to socialize, except in the hunting field. As an administrator he was a pragmatic man and quick to resort to force. His "pull-no-punches" approach both intimidated and provoked the people of Equatoria province. Most modern writers tend to blame Baker for the combative mood that often greeted later Europeans visiting the natives of the Sudan. Be that as it may, he generally got things done, and he no doubt performed as well as anyone could under difficult circumstances.

Samuel Baker continued writing during his African years and after his retirement. His later books included *The Albert Nyanza* (1863), *The Nile Tributaries of Abyssinia* (1867), *Ismailia* (1874), *Cyprus as I Saw It* (1879), and his classic *Wild Beasts and Their Ways* (1890). The last named is a rollicking memoir of hunting stories and adventures spanning more than forty years, one of the best hunting (and natural-history) books of that era. He was also a contributor to *Big Game Shooting* 1894, part of the Badminton Library of Sport and Pastimes. One of the great Victorian figures, he died on 30 December 1893. His wife, the former slave girl, died Lady Florence Baker in 1916.

Baker, Valentine (1825–1887). The brother of Samuel Baker, Valentine was the distinguished colonel of the 10th Hussars and a founder of the elite Marlborough Club. To the Victorian public he was known as "Baker of the Tenth" as opposed to "Baker of the Nile." He lost both his commission and his club membership in 1875 as a result of a bizarre scandal. On 17 June Baker (who must have been drunk) accosted a young woman, Kate Dickinson, in a railway car traveling from Aldershot to London. By all accounts Miss Dickinson was a reserved and respectable young lady. Baker tried to kiss her and slid his hand under her dress. Dickinson broke away and somehow, in her flight, ended up clinging to the outside of the railroad carriage with the colonel holding onto her. Baker wound up being convicted of two counts of assault but was acquitted of attempted rape—which was somewhat surprising, since it was widely known that he had approached the girl with his trousers unbuttoned. Queen Victoria was not amused; rather, she was horrified, and Baker was thrown out of both the army and his club.

Influential friends got Baker (who had considerable military, if not amatory, talents) a post as commander of the Turkish army, and he began his rehabilitation by trouncing the Russians in 1877. The Marlborough Club thereupon reinstated his membership. Apparently it was who you slaughtered that counted, not who you tried to rape. He was in line to take the prestigious position of commanding general of the Egyptian army, but Victoria blocked the appointment. He had to settle for commander of the Egyptian police, at least until the man who did get the army appointment, Hicks Pasha, was killed with most of his men in Kordofan in 1883. The next year Baker was defeated by the Mahdi's army at Tokar, losing twenty-five hundred men out of a total of thirty-five hundred, but it was recognized that the rout was not his fault—apparently, the troops he had been given were of execrable quality. In 1887 Queen Victoria finally agreed to his reinstatement, but Baker died before he got the news. He was buried with full military honors.

Baldwin, William Charles (1827–1903). Born the son of an English clergyman on 3 March 1827, William Baldwin tried his hand at farming and as a clerk in Liverpool before emigrating at the age of twenty-four. On his first trip into the African countryside, he was one of thirteen men who went out to hunt elephant and hippo near Saint Lucia Bay. A few months later only six were still alive—the rest had fallen to the virulent tropical diseases that were so deadly before the introduction of modern medicines.

From 1852–1860 he hunted and traded in the hinterlands of South Africa, detailing his experiences in the classic *African Hunting and Adventure* (1863). Baldwin was only the second confirmed European to see the famous Victoria Falls of the Zambezi, and it has been estimated that he covered a total of twelve thousand to fifteen thousand miles during his African travels. He returned to England in 1861 and never went back to Africa.

Between the profits he made hunting in Africa and the proceeds of *African Hunting,* Baldwin was able to live a sportsman's existence for the rest of his life, hunting and fishing in Britain and Canada. He stayed healthy and was still riding in arduous steeplechases at the age of seventy. Baldwin died on 17 November 1903. *African Hunting,* incidentally, is one of the most readable and enjoyable of the early safari books, and scarcely dated even after one hundred fifty years.

Banks, Frederick Grant (1875–1954). Known to everyone as "Deaf" Banks due to a severe hearing problem, he was an old-time hunter who worked the Lado Enclave starting in 1904. When others wondered how he could risk hunting elephant, given his disability, Banks replied that the lack of sound enabled him to concentrate better. After the Lado Enclave was incorporated into British Africa, Banks went straight and became an elephant control officer and Uganda game ranger, based at Fort Portal. Throughout his career he relied upon a .577 Nitro Express double rifle for heavy game.

Banks was one of that breed of adventuresome hunters who always seemed to be landing in a scrape. On different occasions during his career he was tossed by a buffalo, trampled by an elephant, and badly injured when his own rifle exploded. His hut was once struck by lightning and burned down with the loss of all his possessions. One of his best-known exploits was when he shot one elephant on a steep incline and it fell and carried two more with it off a cliff—the famous "three elephant with one shot" story. This took place in the Toro district of Uganda. Banks served as an infantryman in Uganda during World War I, occasionally going out on commando raids led by Capt. Tracy Philips and Capt. R. J. D. "Samaki" Salmon.

During his poaching days in the Lado Enclave, Banks launched a scheme to capture a baby white rhino and sell it to a European or American zoo for a large profit. This was not impossible: An Austrian named Fleischer had pulled it off, and Ewart Grogan of "Cape to Cairo" fame had recently accepted a commission from the American Museum of Natural History for two of the creatures. The usual method was to shoot the cow and wrestle the calf into submission. The first part of Banks's plan went admirably, but he had trouble with the second when the young rhino proved much stronger than it looked. He tried to wrap his arms around the calf's neck and throw it to the ground, but the rhino butted him sharply. Banks wound up on the creature's back, riding it like a mechanical bull as the frantic beast tried to buck him off. He finally fell from the saddle, badly bruised, and decided to stick to elephant hunting. He was happy to hear later that Grogan's efforts had failed in precisely the same way.

Banks retired from the Uganda Game Department in 1941. Estimates of the total number of elephant he killed, both while poaching and doing control work, range from 1,050 to 3,000. He died peacefully in London on 31 May 1954.

Bvekenya Barnard, circa 1920.

Barnard, Stephanus Cecil Rutgert "Bvekenya" (1886–1962). Born outside of Knysna in Cape Colony on 19 September 1886, Stephanus Barnard was a celebrated elephant hunter in Rhodesia, Mozambique, and the northern Transvaal from about 1910 through the 1920s. In the early 1890s his father moved the family from Knysna to a new farm in the western part of the Transvaal. After a promising start, the family was virtually ruined by the rinderpest epidemic of 1896, which killed all their livestock. They scraped along for three years until the outbreak of the Boer War, when Barnard's father was conscripted into the Boer army and then captured by the British.

Young Stephanus became the head of the household of five children (four older boys had already left home, most to fight alongside their father), a responsibility that was heightened when his mother died in 1902. Stephanus supported the family by taking on odd jobs and teamster work. After his father returned, the younger Barnard decided to find his own way in the world and on 3 April 1906, the nineteen-year-old left to wander southern Africa in search of his destiny.

A brief period as a vagabond in the Transvaal and the Orange Free State ended when Barnard enlisted in the South African Constabulary. The first three years of the enlistment were considered a probationary period, at the end of which either party could decide to part with the other. Barnard, who neither smoked nor drank, saved his money and when the time came to make his choice opted to leave the police and try his hand at professional hunting. In early 1910 he purchased a wagon, camp gear, ten donkeys, a mule, and a pair of rifles, including a .303 bolt-action service model. He then went north into the wilderness to see if he could make his fortune at the ivory game.

Barnard centered his activities around a place called Crook's Corner, in the Transvaal just across the Limpopo River from Southern Rhodesia. The Corner was the location of a small trading station and the center of a tiny community of hunters, misfits, and shifty characters who made a living by recruiting African laborers for the distant mines. It was close to the borders of three countries (Southern Rhodesia, the Union of South Africa, and Portuguese East Africa), and, therefore, a convenient place for ivory dealing and other activities that might cause a man to flirt with the wrong side of the law. Should the police come, it was a relatively easy matter to slip across the appropriate boundary. A convenient beacon marked the point where the three borders met.

Barnard had his problems at first, including narrowly escaping being impaled in a native elephant trap, as well as being jumped in his camp one night by a band of Shangaan ruffians who tried to murder him and steal his kit. Barnard escaped the robbers but lost all of his possessions, including his rifles. He did manage to gouge out one of his attacker's eyes before fleeing. Returning briefly to civilization to fetch clothes and a new weapon (a short-barreled 9.5mm Mannlicher-Schoenauer), Barnard went back to the bush around Crook's Corner and began his elephant-hunting career.

His first elephant had tusks of 51 and 49 pounds; not huge, but a good start. The second was a belligerent bull that had killed at least three Shangaans; its tusks weighed in at 75 pounds per side. Barnard shot a third bull with 60-pound tusks shortly afterward. With ivory selling for about £1 for every 3 pounds of weight, Barnard's first week or so in the business earned him more than £120, an amount of money that was a great deal higher than what he would have made if he had stayed in the police. Harry Wolhuter, a game ranger in the Sabi Game Reserve not far south of Crook's Corner, was then making about £30 per month by working on the right side of the law.

Barnard, now called "Bvekenya" ("the man who swaggers"), soon became a legend in the area around the three international borders. He continually slipped into Portuguese territory time and again to hunt and to avenge himself on the Shangaans who had robbed him a few years before. When he caught up with the culprits, he beat them with a *sjambok* and burnt their homes. The Portuguese responded by swearing out warrants for his arrest and eventually sentenced him in absentia to twenty-five years imprisonment. Bvekenya scoffed at the sentence; they would have to catch him first. Of more concern were the various warrants issued for his arrest in Southern Rhodesia and the Transvaal. He spent most of his time in British territory and was somewhat dismayed at being considered a criminal by his own people. Being wanted by the authorities in three countries cancelled some of the advantages of Crook's Corner, for there no longer was a friendly border to run to. Bvekenya built a semipermanent camp in the area and took to digging up the famous border beacon and placing it in convenient spots to redefine the border, depending upon which nation's police force seemed more intent on capturing him.

Bvekenya built another new camp along the Chefu River called Mazimbe, a place where he could rest, store tusks and supplies, and manufacture whips and *sjamboks*, a very profitable sideline of his ivory business. He hunted elephant, of course, but also giraffe, buffalo, sable, and hippo for their hides. Bvekenya came to know the area between the Limpopo and Great Sabi Rivers better than any other man, at times ranging eastward to within a few miles of the Indian Ocean coast. He tried his hand at sheep herding (without success) and labor recruiting for the mines of South Africa. He also raised tame eland, both for the meat and the milk.

Dividing his time between the Chefu camp (which was in Portuguese territory) and the one near Crook's Corner (in South Africa), Bvekenya was at the latter camp one day in 1918 when he was finally arrested by two Rhodesian police troopers. He pointed out that they were on the wrong side of the border, but they didn't seem to care, and kidnapped him at gunpoint. After a forced march to Fort Victoria, Bvekenya was convicted of illegally shooting a hippo—all the other charges were dismissed due to lack of evidence or were considered too old. He was fined £5 and released. On his way back to Crook's Corner Bvekenya shot seven elephants to even the score.

Poaching in those days was a much less reprehensible affair than it is now, for the men involved (including Bvekenya) generally followed sporting traditions and pursued their quarry under fair-chase conditions. Wildlife was a lot more abundant and the poachers saw no harm in evading what were sometimes frankly cryptic game regulations. This seeming contradiction of faithfully adhering to the sportsman's code while breaking the hunting laws now seems almost quaint, especially after decades of indiscriminate high-tech poaching with air searches, automatic weapons, 4-wheel drive vehicles, and radio communications. Although they wouldn't come right out and say it, the colonial game officers recognized the distinction themselves: A man who poached ivory would often eventually be hired as a game ranger while a man who used "unsportsmanlike" techniques would never be considered.

In 1919 Bvekenya bought a farm at Soutpansberg (near the current camp of Punda Maria in Kruger National Park) and tried to go straight, but civilized life bored him. After four years he returned to his old haunts, armed this time with a .465 Holland & Holland double. He also tried a .425 Magnum Express but didn't like the weapon. The .465 H&H produced tremendous results, and he considered it the finest rifle he ever used. Unlike Bell and other fans of the brain shot, Bvekenya usually went for the side shot at the heart and lungs. He always had plenty of time to track wounded elephants through the bush if necessary.

Bvekenya spent five years in the field during this last phase of his poaching career. By the late 1920s, however, the days of the great elephant poachers were fading out. Bvekenya could still make an exceptional profit—in 1928 he shot forty-five bulls—but civilization and law enforcement were encroaching on his hunting grounds. He had beaten the odds for longer than he had any right to expect, and in 1929, shortly after a close call with a pair of deadly green mambas, he started thinking about calling it quits.

No story about Bvekenya would be complete without mention of Zhulamiti (or Dhulamithi), a legendary elephant with tusks "taller than the trees." Bvekenya always said that his meeting with this behemoth was what made him give up hunting. After a fleeting first sighting west of the Great Sabi River, Bvekenya stalked the animal, which had tusks estimated at 200 pounds per side, for years. He finally got his chance to shoot the magnificent tusker near Gonarezhou in November 1929, but at the last moment he refused to pull the trigger and hung up his elephant rifle instead. He packed up his kit and went back to the farm.

Bvekenya's sportsmanship and skill were so much admired that when he finally went straight he was given a job in the game department. He married a woman named Maria Badenhorst, and they had four sons and a daughter. His third son, Izak Barnard, went on to become one of the founders of the Botswana safari industry and as of 2005 both Izak and Bvekenya's grandson, Willem Barnard, were still active in the business.

For decades after Bvekenya's retirement, the question remained "What ever happened to Dhulamithi?" Despite a legend that the massive bull lived until the 1960s, when it was reported shot by a South African general named Verster, the best evidence indicates that the grand elephant was killed around late 1931 and that its tusks, weighing in at 160 and 161 pounds, were exported to London by an ivory dealer in Lourenço Marques named Balmer. The final disposition of the tusks is unknown.

Barnes, James Hugh. A Kenya professional hunter with a penchant for early photographic safaris, Barnes's clients included photographers Marius Maxwell and Cherry Kearton. The 1930 *East African Red Book Resident Directory* for Kenya Colony lists Barnes at Post Office Box 862, Nairobi.

Barnes, Thomas Alexander (1881–1930). T. Alexander Barnes owned a three-thousand-acre cattle ranch near Fort Jameson, North-East Rhodesia, in 1903, adjacent to a ranch owned by hunter Denis Lyell. He often hung out with Lyell and fellow hunter Martin Ryan. Barnes did a lot of collecting work for various museums, getting as much as £150 for an elephant skin (not including the tusks). As early as 1906, he was also guiding hunters professionally—"gents" from England.

A tough man, Barnes once was bitten in the leg by a nine-foot crocodile while crossing a stream; he blew the reptile's head off, rubbed some salt on the wound to disinfect it, then walked many miles to the hospital at Fort Jameson for treatment. He and Lyell later estimated the crocodile's length from the tooth marks on his leg. Barnes was respected for his stamina and his ability to walk hundreds of miles on the trail of an elephant if need be.

In 1921–1922 Barnes went on several gorilla hunts in the Kivu district of Rwanda and the Belgian Congo, including one for the British Museum. In 1924 Barnes was hired to guide two Americans, Alfred Collins of Philadelphia and Edmund Heller of Chicago's Field Museum, on an expedition to the Kivu district with the goal of obtaining two gorilla specimens. Barnes grew tired of the chase and abandoned the expedition, which continued (successfully) without him. Despite this experience, Barnes began campaigning hard for the Belgian government to add one or two gorillas to the hunting license, and even began advertising "Alexander Barnes Adventure Tours" with gorilla hunts as a prime inducement.

The author of *Wonderland of the Eastern Congo, Across the Great Crater-Land to the Congo,* and *An African Eldorado,* Barnes was killed in Chicago on 4 March 1930, when he stepped in front of a train while trying to avoid a speeding car. Generally speaking, his books are well illustrated with Barnes's own photographs, but are somewhat stiffly written.

Barnshaw, A. L. Barnshaw was an agent for the British Central Africa Company at the station of Gwazas on the Upper Shire River, Nyasaland, 1903. He later became an elephant hunter.

In April 1907 Barnshaw wrote to his friend Denis Lyell, describing that season's elephant hunting. He had killed twelve bulls, and they carried tusks of the following sizes: 80 and 74 pounds, 67 and 45, 54 and 54, 40 and 38, 70 and 48½, 32 and 31, and several 15-pounders. These might be considered representative for southern and central Africa, where the ivory just didn't reach the size it did in more northern countries.

Six weeks later Barnshaw sent another letter to Lyell that described his hunting adventures in the interim period. He had killed three more elephant, all with tusks weighing between 52 and 30 pounds, but had failed to get eight larger bulls. He had wounded one of the larger animals, but it escaped after a long chase. It was soon tracked down and killed by the intrepid elephant hunter Mickey Norton and was found to have tusks weighing 86 and 84 pounds.

Barth, Heinrich (1821–1865). Barth was a native of Hamburg who traveled through Algeria, Tunisia, Syria, Greece, and Turkey before 1848. In 1849 he started out from Tripoli with Richardson and Overweg and spent the next five years (1849–1855) roaming the Sahara and West Africa. Richardson and Overweg both died before the expedition was over, but Barth finished the journey, which is considered the first really sound scientific survey of central and West Africa. He is credited with discovering the upper reaches of the Benue River for the West in 1851. He later wrote numerous works on his extensive journeys, and died at home in Berlin at the age of forty-four.

Barttelot, Edmund Musgrave (1860–1888). The tropical hardships and responsibility of command seemed to unhinge Barttelot; he became unreasonable and paranoid, claiming that Stanley was trying to murder him and checking his provisions for poison. He treated the African porters and askaris poorly and even began to turn on the European officers working under him.

An accident that occurred while he was hunting probably didn't help Barttelot's state of mind. Just a few days after settling in, he and a medical officer named Bonny went hunting for antelope. Barttelot was inexperienced with African game and might have been overanxious—a day or two earlier he and James Jameson had narrowly escaped being injured by a large rhino they had been trying to shoot. At any rate Barttelot wounded a buffalo and carelessly approached the fallen beast with a knife in his hand and trailing his rifle. The wounded buffalo surged to its feet and, with its dying strength, gored Barttelot in the thigh and knocked him unconscious. Bonny was able to revive the major and get him back to camp, but the shock may have contributed to Barttelot's increasingly erratic behavior.

Whatever the cause, Barttelot soon revealed himself as one of the worst characters ever to explore old Africa, and that's saying a lot. He was an unabashed racist—to the point that it stood out even in that racist environment (Stanley had to admonish him about how he spoke to the porters). His behavior toward the soldiers and bearers of the column was execrable: He shot one man for stealing some goat meat, kicked a teenaged servant to death, and murdered several other men. Barttelot would stand there watching the men with a wide, toothy smile on his face, daring them to balk him. On the march he would poke stragglers and cripples with a spiked stick to make them move faster.

He didn't treat his European comrades much better. Four days after dispatching Herbert Ward on a pointless fifteen-hundred-mile trip to Saint Paul de Loanda (to send an equally pointless telegram to London), Barttelot sent a runner after Ward with an insulting letter that essentially warned the junior officer not to steal any company funds en route. To his credit, Ward sent back a terse message that he would "demand explanation and satisfaction" upon his return, and dutifully carried out his meaningless mission.

Finally, on the morning of 19 July 1888, Barttelot made the mistake of threatening a Manyara woman for singing while she worked. The deranged major was standing over the woman with his loaded revolver when her husband, a man named Sanga, shot and killed him with a single bullet through his heart. Sanga was executed by a firing squad less than a month later, on the orders of a Belgian court-martial that was presided over by the provincial governor, Tippu Tib, and included the Belgian officers Baert, Haneuse, and Bodson. Baert later wrote that Sanga, who came from a culture in which the penalty for homicide was usually a fine, "shrieked and swooned" when he learned that he was going to be shot.

After Barttelot's death, his brother published a book defending the dead officer and blaming the entire Rear Column fiasco on Stanley. Neither the public nor history was fooled.

Bates, George Latimer (1863–1940). Bates was a turn-of-the-century American sportsman and hunter who collected numerous zoological specimens from the Cameroons. One of his most prominent trophies was the first giant forest hog shot in that area.

Bates, Henry. Hunter in Namibia, 1875–1878.

Battell, Andrew (1565–1614). Battell was an English sailor from Essex who sometime around the year 1515 was shipwrecked off the coast of Brazil. He was rescued by Portuguese seamen who, fearful he would reveal geographical secrets, kept him on board as sort of a combination mascot and hostage for several years as they sailed back and forth between Brazil and Angola. Eventually he was set ashore in the Congo watershed. After making his way home following nearly twenty years of captivity and strange travel, he created a mild sensation with his memoirs. Few thinking Englishmen seriously believed his far-fetched tales of the Pygmies and great apes (chimpanzees) that he had seen in his travels.

Baumann, Oscar (1864–1899). Dr. Baumann was a German explorer who conducted surveys around Kilimanjaro and the Pangani River in 1890. He later roamed through the Congo and Rwanda, discovering Lake Kivu.

Baumann was commissioned in 1891 by the German Anti-Slavery Society and the German East African Railway Company to survey possible rail routes in northern Tanganyika. He made it a point to avoid all the known tracks and thereby made a significant exploration of the area to the southeast of Lake Victoria. Baumann was an advocate of a joint Anglo–German East African railway, an idea that came to naught.

Baumann was the author of *Durch Massailand Zur Nilquelle: Reisen und Forschungen der Massai—Expedition des Deutschen Antisklavereikomite in den Jahren, 1891–1893* (*Travels Through Masailand to the Source of the Nile: Travels and Discoveries of the Masai Expedition of the German Anti-Slavery Committee*), published in Berlin in 1894.

Bauszus, Hans (1871–xxxx). Bauszus was a German hunter and settler in South-West Africa, and an officer of the colonial Schutztruppe (Defense Force) before World War I. After the war he returned to Germany and rose to become a high-ranking officer of the Nazi SS (number 131 on the 1942 seniority list; Heinrich Himmler was number 1), being promoted to SS Brigadefuehrer in 1937. His decorations included the Iron Cross First Class and the Wound Badge.

Bear, Fred (1902–1988). Bear was a well-known American bowmaker and bowhunting enthusiast who made several safaris to Africa in an attempt to prove the feasibility of the sport. Bowhunting had been banned in most African countries as unsportsmanlike. Bear showed that in the hands of a well-trained archer it was not only sporting but also within the best traditions of fair chase. The key words in that sentence, however, are "well trained." Not every archer is a Fred Bear. When lesser archers used the weapon on African game, the animals often escaped, wounded but alive, to suffer in the bush, and often the professional hunters would have to finish them off. This was not only unpopular with the professionals (who wants to track a buffalo in the bush with an arrow sticking in it?) but also often led to friction with the client.

Beard, R. L. He was an American hunter and adventurer who traveled through both northern and southern Nigeria during 1903–1906.

Beaton, Ken (1912–1954). A rising star with the newly established Kenya Parks Department in 1945, Beaton was responsible for the original survey and administrative design of Tsavo National Park. It was Beaton who recommended that the huge park, chosen for its arid uselessness rather than any wildlife or scenic virtues, be divided into two sections. Tsavo West contained the most visually impressive terrain, and its 3,000 square miles were assigned to wardens Tabs Taberer and Peter Jenkins, while David Sheldrick and Bill Woodley developed and guarded the 5,000 square miles of Tsavo East.

Beaton moved westward to become the first director and chief warden of Uganda Parks in the early 1950s. As such, he was responsible for picking the sites of the first two national parks of Uganda, wisely choosing Murchison Falls and what came to be known as Queen Elizabeth National Park. An interesting description of the factors going into his decision and the birthing pains of the parks can be found in Colin Willock's *The Enormous Zoo.*

While he was still in Kenya, Beaton kept a quasi-official log of events at Nairobi National Park. The log was published weekly in the *East African Standard* and was quite popular. Beaton died from illness at a young age. He was the author of *A Warden's Diary* (1949).

Beaumont. Born in Paris, Monsieur Beaumont was working as a mechanic for a German firm in the years right after World War I when he was sent to assemble machinery in Bangui, French Equatorial Africa. When that job was finished, he took to elephant hunting with his new friend

Ken Beaton of the Uganda National Parks.

Nollet. He spent the next twenty-five or thirty years doing just that, killing about five hundred elephant overall.

Beck, Henry Houghton. This English writer and hunter, who first visited Africa in 1880, replaced Harry Johnston during the second half of Lord Mayo's Angola hunting trip in 1882. He hunted in Angola, the Belgian Congo, and, on his way home, Portuguese Guinea. After the Mayo expedition Beck was sent on a reporting trip to Mount Kilimanjaro. The rest of his career consisted of extended trips that combined hunting, journalism, and book research.

His African travels were extensive. In 1886–1888 he visited the Cameroons and Nigeria, and in 1889 he surveyed the southern section of Lake Rukwa with a Dr. Cross. During 1889–1895 he made numerous trips to British Central Africa and in 1897 returned to Tunis and North Africa. He was the author of *History of South Africa and the Boer-British War* (1901), as well as *Famous Battles, The Greco-Turkish War, Cuba's Fight for Freedom and the War with Spain,* and similar works.

Beit, Alfred (1853–1906). This South African mining magnate, originally from Hamburg, came to South Africa in 1875 as representative for the Lippert Company of merchants. A hard-working man with a gift for finance, he became rich in the Transvaal and Rhodesia as an officer of BSAC (see glossary) (director 1889–1897, but resigned due to his involvement in the Jameson raid) and later DeBeers.

Beit enjoyed hunting and was mentioned in numerous memoirs. A small, likable man, he and Percy Fitzpatrick accompanied Lord Randolph Churchill on the Transvaal leg of Churchill's 1891–1892 safari to Mashonaland. ROWLAND WARD 1928: BLACK RHINO.

Alfred Beit.

Bell, Sir Henry Hesketh (1864–1952). Born in the West Indies, Bell served in the colonial administrations of several Caribbean islands before becoming high commissioner of Uganda in 1905. His tenure in Uganda was notable for the inroads that were made against the sleeping sickness and the origin of the cotton industry. Bell served as governor of Northern Nigeria from 1910–1911, and Mauritius from 1916–1924, when he was forced to retire. He lived the rest of his life in France and the Bahamas before dying on a trip to London.

Bell spent much of his Uganda term out in the field hunting and engaging in natural-history studies. Quite a few photographs show him playing with a captive python, for instance, or surrounded by his huge assortment of hunting trophies, including an impressive pair of elephant tusks that must have topped the scales at one hundred pounds each.

Bell, Walter Dalrymple Maitland "Karamojo" (1880–1951). Walter "Karamojo" Bell is known for two things. First, he was the foremost proponent of using a small-caliber rifle on elephant. His marksmanship was such that he could place a .223 bullet in the precise spot necessary to bring down an infuriated seven-ton bull. Second, along with Arthur Neumann and Jim Sutherland, Bell was an elephant hunter par excellence. His adventures and exploits, not to mention his considerable profits, inspired generations of young hunters to take to the African bush. Even today his books are exciting accounts of a world gone by.

Bell was born near Edinburgh in 1880. An orphan by the age of six (his father was a prosperous timber merchant), he was an avid reader of American buffalo-hunting tales and the works of the pioneer elephant hunters,

Sir Hesketh Bell and his game bag, Uganda, 1908.

particularly his fellow Scotsman Gordon Cumming. At a very early age he tried to pawn some family heirlooms to finance a hunting expedition to America's bison country. Since Bell was only about seven years old, the pawnbroker's suspicions were raised and the plan was quickly thwarted. For a while the problem child was apprenticed by his guardians to a sailing firm, and by the time he was fourteen Bell had visited New Zealand and Tasmania, not to mention being sent to a boarding school in Germany. His overriding ambition, however, was always to hunt in Africa.

He finally got his chance at the age of seventeen, in 1897. Armed with a single-shot .303 rifle, Bell arrived in British East Africa and took a job as a guard on a mule train that brought supplies to men working on the Uganda Railway. Wanting more firepower, he traded the .303 for a black-powder .450 that fired hollow copper-point bullets. The rifle performed well on antelope for the pot, but almost got him killed when he finally confronted his first dangerous game. He wounded a lion and barely escaped the ensuing charge. Only after much prolonged shooting did the king of beasts fall, and Bell discovered that the problem lay in the copper-point bullets. They had simply smacked the lion and then disintegrated, causing nowhere near the damage they should have.

This close call marked the beginning of Bell's almost obsessive interest in bullets and ballistics. He soon acquired another rifle. While he was still working with the railway transport outfit, he first met John Boyes, the notorious "King of the Kikuyu," who was engaged in similar work.

Bell's first stay in Africa turned out to be a brief one. Wracked with malaria, he decided to recover his health and perhaps make his fortune by joining the Klondike Gold Rush that had all of Alaska aflame in 1898. Stopping in England en route, he picked up a .360 single-shot Fraser rifle. After arriving in the Yukon, Bell entered into a hunting scheme with a man he knew only as "Bill." Bill and Bell spent an entire Klondike winter deep in the woods hunting moose and other game with the intention of becoming rich selling the food to starving prospectors. Food storage was no problem—the moose carcasses were simply stacked frozen in the snow. They had some trouble with wolves but soon amassed a huge stockpile of moose meat. Bill loaded up their dogsled with the meat and Bell's Fraser rifle (and the pair's only ax) and took off to Dawson, where he would sell the meat and then come back to pick up Bell and the next shipment. The two stood to make a healthy profit, although the young Bell was a bit daunted at having to stay alone in the wilderness with just a revolver, no ax, and a big pile of moose meat that the wolves were trying to raid.

Bill made several trips into Dawson, selling the meat for $1.75 per pound and banking the money. By winter's end the pair had built up a substantial bank account. Given his orphan's background, Bell could hardly be called new to the ways of the world, but he still had a deep faith and trust in human nature. That trust was soon to be betrayed.

Bill never returned from the final trip, disappearing with the rifle, the revolver, and all their money. By the time Bell realized that he had worked and suffered all winter only to be duped and robbed by his partner, his only recourse was to stagger into Dawson and ask if anyone knew where Bill was. There were thousands of Bills in the Yukon that year—if that was the man's real name. Without a last name and more information, Bell's pursuit was hopeless.

Showing the resourcefulness that marked his entire career, the penniless Bell hit upon a scheme to get him out of the frozen north. The Boer War had just begun, so he enlisted in the Canadian army as a cavalry trooper. This got him back to Africa, where he was promptly captured by the Boers. After escaping, Bell became attached to regimental headquarters as a scout. As he put it in *Bell of Africa,* "What we did was draw double rations and rustle Boer ponies wherever we could find them." It sure beat freezing in the Yukon.

Alas, the war ended, and young Bell traveled north to Uganda, where he fell in with a man named Ormsby who had once teamed with the gunrunner Charlie Stoles, whose execution by the Belgians had caused an international scandal. Ormsby took Bell on the boy's first elephant hunt, in the Unyoro section of Uganda. It was here that Bell formed his first opinions on the techniques of elephant hunting, and mastered the brain shot. At this time he was using a .303 rifle.

In 1902 Bell decided to hunt in the area north of Uganda known as Karamoja. This was a remote region inhabited by primitive and warlike tribes, but was said to be chockfull of big elephant. Bell traveled to the town of Mumias near Mount Elgon to prepare for his epic safari, the fulfillment of a lifelong dream. He was twenty-two years old.

At Mumias Bell gathered together his outfit. His caravan was fairly well armed. In addition to his own rifles, he had eight askaris armed with Snider rifles. It was sort of a ragtag expedition, partly because all the regular porters were out on other safaris at the time. Bell had to slap together such men as he could get. He was learning the inscrutable ways and incongruities of Africa. He recalled in *Bell of Africa* that "As usual, all the small loads seemed to be jauntily and lightly perched on the massive heads and necks of the biggest porters, while the big loads looked doubly big in comparison to the spindly shanks which appeared below them."

On the seventh day out they reached the Turkwell River; beyond lay the unexplored Karamoja. The first two Karamojans Bell met—haughty spearmen who sauntered into camp one afternoon—laughed at his puny rifles when he said he was there to shoot elephant. They had seen Swahili and Arab hunters fire muskets at the massive pachyderms with little effect. They simply had no conception of the power of a modern rifle.

The word for elephant in Karamojan, according to Bell, is *atome!* That exclamation rang through the camp the next morning. Bell ran ahead to catch up with the small herd of elephant that the scouts had spotted. His rifle cracked twice, and by the time the haughty spearmen came up, two great elephant lay dead. Suitably impressed, the local inhabitants soon came streaming from their villages to gather a share of the meat. It was the beginning of a fruitful association between Bell and the Karamojans. Wherever he went in Africa, Bell had a knack for striking just the right demeanor when meeting new populations for the first time. When he needed to be firm, he was—or threatening or conciliatory, as the situation required. Those Europeans

Hesketh Bell and a python on the steps of Government House, Entebbe.

who did not master such skills in the early days often came to unpleasant ends.

This first Karamoja safari was a profitable venture, but on a somewhat small scale. He never really got past the border areas of Karamoja. After various small side trips, Bell decided to return to Mumias, loaded down with as much ivory as he could transport. Rather than calling it quits or, like many pioneers, spending the profits on drink and women, Bell reinvested everything into a new, larger, grander safari. He would make elephant hunting a business.

And so he did. Bell hunted in Karamoja and the surrounding districts (northwest of Lake Rudolf) for five years, from 1902 to 1907, in what could be considered five separate safaris but was really one massive campaign against the elephant. He shot hundreds of them during this time, with an average tusk weight of fifty-three pounds, which was amazing considering that about 10 percent of the animals had broken or single tusks.

Bell was typical of his generation of elephant hunters in that he was driven by a combination of greed and desire for adventure. But he was atypical in his monumental success. During his career he shot 1,011 elephant, virtually all bulls. Bell brought back from just one of his expeditions 14,000 pounds of ivory, worth £8,400, at a time when the annual salary of a British provincial commissioner was £500. All told, during his hunting years Bell made enough money to live in comfort in Scotland the second half of his life.

His success was due to his character, marksmanship, daring, and, above all, his organizational skills. He was fortunate in that he appeared on the African stage at the opportune time for an elephant hunter—the one time in history when a daring sportsman could legally make a fortune hunting elephant. Prior to the late 1890s, the primitive weapons available were too weak and unreliable to kill big-game animals on such a scale. Bell belonged to the first generation of hunters who had access to magazine rifles, efficient smokeless powder, and modern ammunition. Conversely, he also belonged to the last generation before hunters were restricted by bag limits and licenses. This combination of unprecedented lethality and weak hunting laws is what gave Bell and a few others the chance to literally make a fortune by spending a few seasons in the bush.

Furthermore, he approached elephant hunting as a craft, not just as a business (businessmen sent others out to do their hunting). Bell worked as a craftsman, doing the work himself but covering every angle so as to maximize his chances of success and his profits. A Bell safari was an independent operation, all centered around and dependent upon his effective marksmanship. He shot elephant for their ivory, of course, but he also shot antelopes to feed his men, buffalo and rhino to make their shoes and sandals, and giraffe for their skin, which he would trade to villagers for millet and other foodstuffs. The local natives placed a premium on giraffe hide and used it to make sandals and shields. Every operation was designed to minimize costs and ensure that the ivory obtained on the trip would cover the costs and permit a tidy profit.

Bell was notorious for advocating the use of a small-bore rifle on African big game, especially the elephant. When he started hunting for ivory in the early 1900s, most men used monstrously large elephant guns. Bell preferred using anything from a .318 down to a .256, and of course had tremendous success. But then he was one of the top three or four marksmen ever to hunt Africa, depending on who you ask. It was perfectly feasible for Karamojo Bell to make a perfect brain shot every time, day in and day out, but many young Englishmen found themselves flattened or worse when they tried to emulate the feat. Few hunters could shoot well enough to get away with such a light rifle.

In 1908 Bell moved his operations farther north, to that part of the Sudan near the Gelo River, and to western Abyssinia. He continued his great success, averaging fifty-six pounds per tusk. But his time in the district was cut short by the opening of the Lado Enclave upon King Leopold's death. Professional hunters from all over Africa flocked to the tiny province west of the Nile and north of Lake Albert, where for six months there was no effective legal authority and the elephant had never been hunted. It was an elephant hunter's paradise.

Bell was at his peak. For nine months he tore through the Lado, shooting 210 elephants, almost one a day. He shared the Lado with such legendary hunters as Robert Foran, Mickey Norton, William Buckley, John Boyes, Quentin Grogan, Bill Judd, and scores of others. His average tusk weight was down (twenty-seven pounds), but this was due to both the competition and the smaller elephant found in this district.

After the Lado, Bell hunted ivory in Liberia, but that excursion turned out to be his first real disappointment. The elephant were small and the conditions unbelievably tough. From there he went to the Ubangi River in French Equatorial Africa in 1912. His exploits there were broken up by the outbreak of war in 1914.

Like many of the great hunters, Bell performed distinguished service during the war. He joined the Royal Flying Corps. According to *Bell of Africa,* the RFC was so short of men that the only qualification needed was the ability to ride a bicycle. After getting his pilot's wings, he was told he was headed for France but at the last minute was shipped to a South African squadron fighting in East Africa. Here he flew a type of two-seater biplane called the BE.2.C., horrid contraptions that were mainly remarkable for the frequency with which the Red Baron could shoot them down. A gifted flyer, Bell remained a true hunter in his heart, writing in his memoirs, "The amount of game you could see from the air was disappointing."

After flying in East Africa, Bell was transferred to the Balkans, where a desultory campaign was being carried out against the Turks and Germans. Bell was actually credited with shooting down a German plane with one shot, although he always said it was an accident. Still, at war's end Bell could legitimately claim status as at least a minor war hero. He even did some time floating in the Mediterranean when his troop ship was torpedoed by a U-boat. His chief lament about this last episode was that the Germans sank his favorite rifle.

With war's end, Bell's hunting days were far from over. The early 1920s saw him hunting in the Ivory Coast and along the Niger River. For a time he stalked elephant in the traditionally French district around Fort Lamy and Chad. Later he guided two rich Americans, publisher Malcolm Forbes and a man named Gerrit, on an extended motorized hunting trip through Chad and Sudan.

In 1932 Bell left Africa for good and settled down quietly in Scotland with his wife. They had a charming little estate in Ross-shire called Corriemoillie, and Bell settled down to tamer pursuits. He had tried his hand at writing in the early 1920s and was rather surprised to have his work published in the periodical *Country Life.* These early stories were published in book form as *The Wanderings of an Elephant Hunter.*

Later, in his retirement, he wrote *Karamojo Safari,* as fascinating a book as has ever been written. It is a detailed account of an early 1900s elephant hunt. If not for this book, much of our knowledge of the minutia of these affairs would be irretrievably lost. The scale of the book allows the reader to get a feel for and insight into the rhythm of a great ivory safari. These expeditions lasted months, if not years. Like war, they could be said to consist of long periods of drudgery punctuated by moments of sheer terror. Bell also had some success as an artist, selling at least one painting on exhibit in Scotland. His drawings, of course, were used to illustrate his books and magazine articles.

W. D. M. Bell.

Bell was one of the very few British hunters to write frankly about sex. Consider this comparison between Western women and the women of Ubangi Shari, given in *Bell of Africa:* "Compare the service of the two. One with her head full of her 'rights' kicks you around like a piece of dirt, refuses you this, refuses you that. The other—oh, well! Perhaps I had better not! No! Not even a peep at paradise."

Bell wrote candidly about the sex lives of his African porters and interpreters and the tribal people he met. Unusually for a white observer of that era, he handled the subject with frankness and good humor and without a hint of mockery or disdain. For instance, in *Karamojo Safari* he tells how he asked his Karamojan friend, Pyjale, why a certain group of women looked so pale and tired. Bell thought they must be ill. "Pyjale said that their men had returned the day before from a week's foray in no-man's land and that the girls had been put through it during the night. Think of that!" In the same book, Bell recounted how one of his servants, an African called Swede, was taking a ribbing from the other porters after his recent marriage. Apparently Swede had paid a high bride price, consistent with that paid for a virgin. "When his obdurate wife had finally surrendered," Bell wrote, "he had encountered the wide highway where he had expected the narrow path." Such observations by Bell give us an exceedingly rare glimpse into the vital and energized lives of his men. Though other early hunters painted only two categories of safari staff—either silent and dutiful or stubborn and mutinous—Bell's African friends come alive on the page.

From 1932 to 1939 Bell indulged in another favorite pastime, boating. His steel-hulled racing boat *Trenchemer* (named after the flagship of Richard the Lion Hearted) was a tremendous success and provided him and his wife with countless hours of enjoyment until it was impounded for war use in 1939.

During World War II, Bell was active in the Home Guard. He also hunted rabbits, grouse, and other small creatures in the hills near his estate. When the war ended he again enjoyed cruising on *Trenchemer,* but a mild heart attack in July 1948 forced him to slow down, and failing health caused him to give up sailing and sell the boat in 1950. A final heart attack a year later killed him.

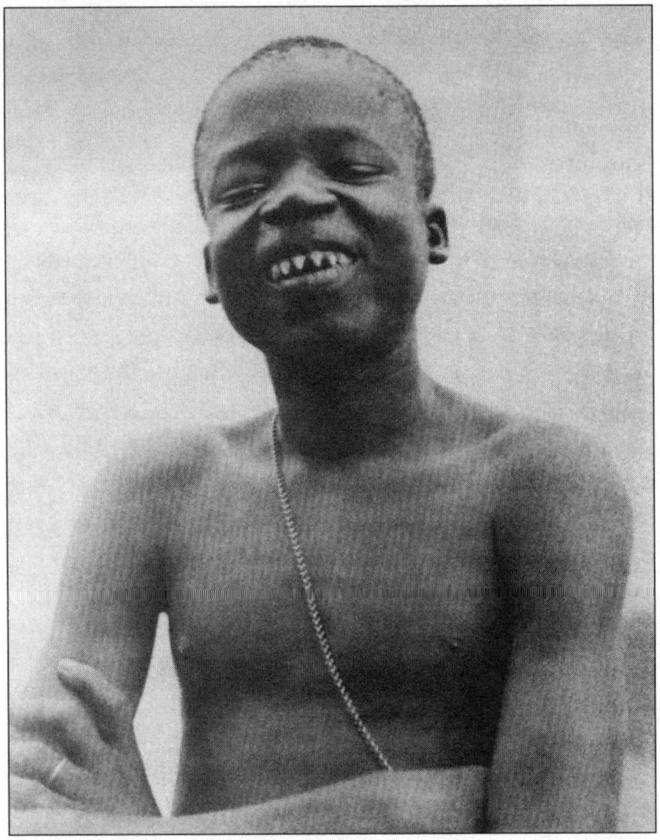
Ota Benga, the "Pygmy in the zoo," displays his filed teeth.

Shortly after Bell's death the writer Robert Ruark managed to buy two of the legendary hunter's rifles from the firm of Westley Richards, where they were on consignment from Bell's widow. Ruark purchased a Jeffery .450-400 Nitro Express double rifle and Bell's famous .275 Rigby Mauser. Ruark had them engraved on the buttstock "Mark Robert Selby from Uncle Bob Ruark" and presented them to his godson, the two-year-old son of professional hunter Harry Selby. According to an article by professional hunter Joe Coogan in the November 2004 edition of *American Rifleman,* the Bell Rigby has remained in the Selby family ever since. From time to time it has been brought out for purposes old Karamojo Bell most certainly would have approved of—among them a 1973 Botswana hunt on which Mark Selby's young sister Gail took her first elephant.

Benga, Ota (c. 1883–1916). Ota was a Batwa Pygmy born in the Congo forest in roughly 1883. He was your typical aboriginal hunter, wise in the ways of the bush and somewhat naïve in the ways of the world. In 1904 he was captured by an enemy tribe and his wife and child were slaughtered and eventually sold to Samuel Verner, a "special agent" of the St. Louis World's Fair. Verner was in the Congo recruiting, by hook or by crook, a band of twelve Pygmies to appear at the Fair. Ota Benga soon formed a close bond with Verner and became essentially the supervisor of the troupe. The forest people danced and put on shows similar to those performed by Native Americans in the old Wild West shows. Ota Benga even met and was befriended by Geronimo, the legendary Apache chief.

When the Fair was over the troupe performed in New Orleans, and seemed to immensely enjoy Mardi Gras. Then most of the men were returned to Africa. Ota for some reason wanted to stay in America. A story was later bandied about that Ota was marked for a cannibal feast if he remained in Africa. This was nonsense, a pure fabrication by people who could not conceive that an African—and a Pygmy at that—could have any goals or desires beyond purely physical needs and fears. The truth of the matter seems to be that Ota wanted to learn to read and pick up other aspects of the white man's culture. At any rate, Ota accompanied Verner when the other Batwa were brought back to the Congo, and then returned with the "special agent" to New York.

Like millions of other aspiring hopefuls, Ota Benga was treated harshly in the Big Apple. William Hornaday, director of the Bronx Zoo, who was generally considered a progressive thinker, had Ota displayed in a cage alongside an orangutan. The black community erupted in furious protest. Hornaday defended his action by claiming not only that the cage was simply a matter of convenience but also that Ota liked the accommodation. Throughout the summer of 1906 the controversy raged on and on, ending with Hornaday virtually begging Verner to take Ota off his hands. The zoo owed Verner money for a captive chimpanzee, however, and until he was paid off, Verner was in no hurry to solve Hornaday's problem. For his part, Ota Benga was not appalled or distressed at his treatment. Rather, he seems to have had a sense of showmanship and would engage in mock battles with the zoo staff to try to stir up excitement around his cage. Still, a cage is a cage, and everybody involved was generally relieved when Ota was finally moved to an orphanage in the fall of 1906. He was about twenty-three years old.

The rest of his story is a sad one. The orphanage was tough, and so was the job Ota had in a Virginia tobacco field afterward. His greatest enjoyment at the orphanage seems to have been the game of baseball. The hunter from the Congo forest took to the ball field like a black Ty Cobb, or like his fellow orphan down in Baltimore, George Herman Ruth. Ota's enthusiastic base running delighted onlookers, and for the rest of his life he could not pass a baseball game without stopping to watch. His work in the tobacco fields brought no such joy, but at least the countryside around Lynchburg, Virginia, brought plenty of hunting and fishing opportunities. Years later old black men in Lynchburg could still recall being taught to fish by the strange man from Africa.

Ota changed his name to Otto Bingo and finally learned to read. He never totally took on Western ways, however, and was known to sleep in the woods and barter for rides on the streetcar with a dead rabbit or some eggs. He wasn't alone, having many black friends and some white ones, including a deep but platonic friendship with a married woman named Anne Spencer. Not alone—but lonely. After moving to Virginia, he never again heard from Verner. Sometimes at night Ota would disappear deep into the woods and sing songs from his childhood.

Toward the end, as depression took hold, he broke off the caps that had been placed over his teeth, which in boyhood had been filed into sharp points. Finally, one day in 1916, Otto Bingo stole a revolver, built a bonfire, stripped himself, and danced around it. When neighborhood children came to watch, he uncharacteristically snarled at them to leave (he had always been a good-natured man).

When his song was over, Ota Benga shot himself in the heart. Far away in New York, William Hornaday, upon hearing of Benga's suicide, commented, with an abysmal lack of understanding, that Benga "felt that he would rather die than work for a living."

Bennett, William (xxxx–1911). Billy Bennett ran the steamer *Kenia* on the route between Butiaba on Lake Albert and the Nile River port of Nimule in the early 1900s. This government launch carried mail, officials, and troops as well as passengers and poachers to and from the Lado Enclave. Bennett was nicknamed the "Admiral of the Nile Flotilla" by no less a personage than Winston Churchill. Unlike many nicknames in written history, this one seems to have been in widespread use at the time. Wistfully observing the huge profits being made from ivory, Bennett would often leave his ship and start hunting elephant.

At first he would deviate only slightly from his government route and hunt ivory for just a day or two. He was remarkably unsuccessful, and the side trips only got him into trouble. Once, the district commissioner demanded to know the reason for a delay of several days in bringing the mail to Nimule. Bennett could hardly admit he was trying to poach ivory, even on the Belgian side of the river, so he made up a story about a swarm of safari ants taking over the ship. Nobody believed him, but he was given credit for imagination and the DC let the matter drop. It's not like they were ever going to find any illegal ivory on Billy Bennett's ship.

Bennett decided that the problem was his busy work schedule. There simply wasn't enough time to both run a steamer and make money from ivory. So he decided to quit the shipping business and devote himself full time to elephant hunting. He should have stuck with sailing. Bennett was a well-liked, amiable man and eager to please. He played the accordion and was considered sort of everybody's mascot. But he was not at all ready to successfully lead an expedition through savage, virtually uncharted territory.

On his first lengthy safari into the Lado Enclave he got exactly one tusk in three months. That one was given to him by a friendly chief who apparently felt sorry for him. His second foray ended in disaster when the local Africans took him captive, robbed him of his guns and a considerable stockpile of ivory, and left him naked on the banks of the

Nile. They captured him by a ruse, pretending to be ignorant of modern rifles until he obligingly showed them how to unload his entire magazine. Then they took him prisoner and killed all fourteen of his porters. These Africans were reputed to be cannibals. Bennett got suspicious when his captors started feeding him well and insisted he take a bath every day. Fortunately, an armed party of European hunters entered the district and Bennett was released.

Bennett's friends among the elephant hunters chipped in to replenish his outfit—John Boyes, for example, gave him a .450 rifle. They also tried to school him in the finer arts of the game—Bob Foran, for one, went shooting elephant with him. It didn't help. On his third trip by himself Bennett was robbed again, escaping with his life only by hiding in a swamp. Apparently a "glass-is-half-full" type of guy, he was preparing for a fourth trip in 1911 when he died of blackwater fever.

Bere, Rennie Montague (1907–1991). Rennie Bere was a game ranger in Uganda from the 1930s on, rising to become director of Uganda Parks in the 1950s.

Berg, Bengt (1885–1967). A Swedish zoologist and wildlife artist and photographer, Berg went on several safaris with Bror Blixen as his professional. A Berg-owned Kuhnert oil painting of an elephant is reproduced in Blixen's *The Africa Letters*.

Berg wrote more than twenty-five books, mainly on the birds of Africa, Asia, and Scandinavia. An avid ornithologist, he is credited with introducing the Canadian goose into Sweden.

Beringe, Friedrich Robert von (1865–1940). The man who "discovered" the mountain gorilla (in the same sense that Sir Harry Johnston discovered the okapi) has been largely neglected by history. What little has been written about him is vague and inaccurate. The crowning insult is that virtually nobody even gets his name right.

Friedrich Robert von Beringe was born to a Prussian military family in 1865. His surname is often misspelled as "Beringer," and his Christian name of Robert is almost always given as "Oscar" or "Oskar." He held a commission in the elite 1st Hussar Regiment—the "Death's Head Hussars"—from 1894–1906. In 1898 he led a successful punitive expedition against the fractious Watumbi people of Tanganyika. He was rewarded by being made a captain and given command of the German outpost at Usambara on the northern tip of Lake Tanganyika, now Bujumbura, the capital of Burundi.

In 1902 von Beringe commanded another expedition, this one made up of a Dr. Engeland, Sergeant Erhardt, and about twenty askaris. His purposes were to impress the local African leaders to the north of Usambara with German power and, if possible, get their signatures on some treaties granting trade and political concessions to the Reich. It was on this mission that he made his historic discovery. On 17 October 1902 von Beringe and Engeland shot two large apes at an altitude of ninety-three hundred feet on the slopes of Mount Sabinio in the Virunga range. After much struggle they managed to get one of the two-hundred-pound carcasses back to camp, where they could examine it thoroughly. The animal turned out to be the first known specimen of the mountain gorilla.

The skin and skeleton of the ape were shipped back to Germany, where they were examined and the results were publicized by Prof. Paul Matschie (1861–1926). Matschie was notorious for being a "splitter"—an anatomist who proclaims different species on the basis of even tiny morphological differences (the opposite being "lumper"). He had apparently "identified" several new species of ape before this one, but his identifications were not recognized by his fellow scientists. With von Beringe's animal, however, he got it right—modern authorities consider the mountain gorilla as belonging to a distinctly different subspecies than the lowland gorilla. In fact, more recent controversies swirl over whether the Eastern lowland gorilla should be considered a species separate from the Western variety, and whether a certain type found in Uganda might be considered a fourth race. The eternal struggle between lumpers and splitters rivals that between good and evil.

All this was beyond the scope of von Beringe's interest. To him all that mattered was that he had shot a distinctly different ape and uncovered the existence of at least some sort of gorilla in a region where that animal was previously unknown. Even more important to him were his military duties. The 1902 treaty mission bore him no lasting fruits professionally, but a year later he was given command of a much larger force.

The 1903 punitive expedition commanded by von Beringe consisted of eight Europeans, 115 askaris, two machine guns, and some three hundred local spearmen. The campaign was necessitated by a rebellion led by a courageous young African leader named Muezi Kasabo, who gave the Germans a pretty good chase for their money. After a series of skirmishes, however, Kasabo was finally run to earth and surrendered to his enemies.

Shortly after that expedition von Beringe returned to Germany, where he served with the 11th Dragoons and the Lithuanian Dragoons of the Prussian army. Promoted to major in 1908, he retired in 1913 due to ill health caused by diabetes. He lived most of the rest of his life as a semi-invalid in Dresden, and died in 1940. He has been described by those who knew him as a quiet, thoughtful man.

Besser, Hans. A German naturalist and hunter, Besser claimed to have shot a twenty-five-foot crocodile on the Mbaka River. He was the author of *Natur und Jagdstudien in Deutsch Ostafrika (Nature and Hunting Studies in German East Africa),* published in 1917.

Bester, Paul. Bester was the first ranger hired by Major Stevenson-Hamilton to patrol the Sabi Game Reserve in 1902. Harry Wolhuter was the second. Wolhuter had a long and famous career as a ranger; Bester didn't.

Bezedenhout. Bezedenhout was a Dutch hunter and ivory poacher working in the Congo in the 1920s and 1930s. He was said to be the first to photograph a wild okapi in its natural surroundings. John Hunter wrote of a safari he conducted in the 1930s along with Bezedenhout and British Museum director Dr. R. Ackroyd.

Bia, Lucien (1852–1892). Bia, a captain, led a large expedition (commissioned by King Leopold) to Katanga in 1891. His European officers included Francqui, Derscheid, and Cornet. The main focus of Bia's trip seems to have been to survey the mineral and mining potential of the area. He found plenty of copper but no gold and little else.

The expedition was wracked with illness and famine, losing 253 men out of an original force of 598. On 15 April 1892 Bia and Francqui, the only officer still on his feet, took 128 of the healthiest men and set out for Lake Mweru. Bia's health collapsed and he had to be carried in a *machila* (a hammock swung on a long pole). They struggled on to Chitambo's town, where Livingstone had died. Bia had been commissioned by the London Royal Geographical Society to affix a plaque to a tree there. This done, they turned west to head home. After a march of some 280 miles, Bia died of bilious fever on 30 August 1892.

Francqui continued on, and one of the expedition's major accomplishments, the discovery of the Lualaba source, is rightly credited to him. The survivors of the expedition joined with Delcommune at Gongo Lutete in early 1893.

Binger, Louis-Gustave (1856–1937). Louis-Gustave Binger was a French explorer who arrived in West Africa on military service in the 1880s. He was noted for his expedition to the country called Kong (now the northern part of the Ivory Coast) in 1887–1889. Starting from Bamako on the Niger River in the spring of 1887, Captain Binger attempted to march straight to Kong but was embroiled in a local war between two African kings, Samory and Tieba. At one point he was held against his will for some weeks by Samory. Finally getting on his way, he was deserted by his guides. At this time a rumor of his death reached France.

After recovering among some friendly Africans called the Senefu, Binger resumed his trip. He brought preprinted treaty forms along with him and signed treaties with numerous small potentates en route to Kong, which he finally reached on 20 February 1888, a year to the day since he had left Bordeaux. Binger was thus credited with connecting the French colonies in Senegambia with the settlements on the Guinea Coast to form an unbroken chain of French territory.

His second West African expedition, which ended in 1892, covered about twelve hundred miles, three hundred of which had never before been traversed by Europeans. He was accompanied by Dr. Crozat, Lieutenant Braulot, and Marcel Monnier. The purpose of this expedition was to survey the border between the French Ivory Coast and the British Gold Coast. He became governor of Ivory Coast in 1893, and was an under-secretary of the French Colonial Office in the 1900s.

Binger was the author of *Du Niger au Golfe de Guinee.* He was awarded the Founder's Medal by the Royal Geographical Society in 1899.

Bingle, Frederick. Hunter in Namibia in the 1870s.

Binks, Herbert K. (1880–1971). Herbert "Pop" Binks arrived in Rhodesia from England in 1900. Trained as a pharmacist, he soon moved on to Nairobi. Originally he worked as a farmer but soon established himself as a big-game photographer and photo developer. He was Kenya's first professional photographer and did a considerable amount of elephant hunting. Binks was the author of *African Rainbow* (1959).

Bird. A man named Bird was the manager of the African Lakes Company store at Tete in the early 1900s. In 1906 he was transferred to Feira, upriver from Tete on the Zambezi.

On the way to his new station he was hunting for the pot when he wounded a small antelope, which ran off down a hippo path. Bird quickly followed and, running carelessly, tripped over a rope that was the trigger of an African hippo trap. A giant spear fell out of a tree and hit him in the neck, killing him instantly.

Bish. An ivory hunter and poacher of the first third of the twentieth century, Bish once put twelve bullets into a bull elephant that was trying to climb up an anthill after him, before finally killing it. He collected the second largest set of tusks then known, at 195 and 197 pounds. Something of a character, he was once jailed in the Belgian Congo for refusing to cough up some smuggled gold. His only request in jail was that the police keep watch on his prized bicycle. Eventually the Belgian authorities reluctantly released the recalcitrant Bish, who peddled away on his bike without revealing the hiding place of the gold. It was, of course, built into the frame of the bicycle.

Black, Alan Lindsey (1881–1963). Born in London to a wealthy family, Alan Black went to East Africa at an early age and started hunting around 1900. A quiet man, he often went off into the bush for extended safaris by himself. He made enough money for his needs by filling meat contracts for the railroad and local markets. He quickly made a reputation for hunting skill and reliability, and when Newland and Tarlton started their safari company in 1904, Black was one of the first hunters they enlisted.

Skilled with both rifle and bow, Black was injured in an early elephant hunt with R. J. Cuninghame. The two were charged by a pair of elephant. Cuninghame dropped one, but the other threw Black into the air and stepped on him before being shot. Black was fortunate to escape with just a broken arm and a few broken ribs.

In 1911 Black went along as the professional hunter on the wealthy American Paul Rainey's experiment in hunting lion with dogs. Rainey imported a pack of bear and puma hounds from the American West and set them out to track African lion. This is a dangerous sport: American mountain lions climb trees when at bay, but the African variety try to kill you. There were several close calls, particularly when an angry lion was dropped only yards from American photographer John Hemment. Overall the experiment was a guarded success, but not something the Kenyan participants were anxious to repeat. The use of dogs to hunt lion was later prohibited.

Three years later Rainey had another bright idea—to film a lion charging right at the camera. This was clearly a potentially lethal plan, and Black refused. Professional hunter Fritz Schindelar later accepted Rainey's proposal, a decision that cost him his life.

During World War I Black served in the 25th battalion of the Royal Fusiliers, the so-called "Legion of Frontiersmen." Commanded by Jim Driscoll, the unit's ranks included other prominent hunters such as Fred Selous, Cherry Kearton, George Outram, and Martin Ryan. The battalion performed distinguished service during the arduous East African campaign.

Black continued his hunting career after the war. When Newland & Tarlton folded up in 1919, he joined the Safariland firm. Black was one of the white hunters on the famous "Royal" safaris of the Prince of Wales in the 1920s, and guided Lord Egerton on his first African hunting trip in 1938. He outlived much of his generation, having seen Kenya grow from a struggling infant colony to an independent African state, and died in 1963.

Black, Derek. This legendary hunter of southern Africa wandered Bechuanaland, Angola, and Namibia in the 1870s–1890s.

Blaine, Gilbert (1874–1955). A British sportsman and respected naturalist, Gilbert Blaine was the hunter who shot the first recorded giant sable in 1919. Blaine, who was born in Bath, England, in 1874, was a soldier and the holder of the Military Cross. Retiring as a lieutenant colonel, he was a prolific magazine writer, and a contributor to the *Big Game Shooting in Africa* volume of the Lonsdale Library (1932).

Blaine went on a number of long safaris with H. C. Maydon, including to the Red Sea region and to Ethiopia, where they collected mountain nyala and walia ibex. He was also very interested in falconry. Blaine died in retirement in Scotland on 12 August 1955. ROWLAND WARD 1928: ANGOLAN SPRINGBOK, ANGOLAN GEMSBOK, LORD DERBY ELAND, PATTERSON ELAND, BONGO, LECHWE (#2), GERENUK, SITATUNGA, SOEMMERRING GAZELLE, PELZELN GAZELLE, GRANT GAZELLE, DORCAS GAZELLE, ERITREAN GAZELLE, SPRINGBOK, WHITE ORYX, BLACK DUIKER, HIROLA, BUFFALO, ELEPHANT.

Blancou, Lucien. Blancou was a French game ranger in the 1830s and 1840s, rising to the post of chief game warden for French Equatorial Africa in the 1850s.

Bland Sutton, Sir John (1865–1936). Bland Sutton was a respected surgeon and close friend of Rudyard Kipling;

in fact, he performed surgery on Kipling in 1922. He was the author of *Men and Creatures in Uganda, and Man and Beast in Eastern Ethiopia* (1911).

Blixen-Finecke, Baron Bror von (1886–1946). Better known as Bror Blixen, he is best known to the general public because of one of the women he married. His first of three marriages was in 1914 to Karen Dinesen, who used the pen name Isak Dinesen, author of *Out of Africa,* which was made into a popular movie.

Blixen, a Swedish aristocrat (his twin brother Hans died in an airplane crash in 1917), came to East Africa in 1913 but didn't gravitate to professional hunting until after World War I. Always strapped for cash, he was a tough, persistent hunter who soon attracted many celebrity clients, including the wealthy polo player Winston Guest, the German artist Kuhnert, and the Prince of Wales. He acquired a reputation for hard living as well as hard hunting but, fortunately for him, was one of those lucky souls whose innate personal charm outweighed his drinking, romantic peccadilloes, and financial irresponsibility.

Blixen's autobiography, *African Hunter* (1938), was ghostwritten and is a mediocre collection of largely secondhand anecdotes. His *Africa Letters,* edited by Romulus Kleen, is much better. When you read the letters you have to wonder why Blixen felt he needed a ghostwriter in the first place, but he undoubtedly just lacked confidence in his literary ability. In modern parlance he was street-smart but uneducated—Karen once said that he wasn't sure whether the Crusades had happened before or after the French Revolution.

Blixen-Finecke, Baroness Karen von (1885–1962). The author of *Out of Africa* (under the pen name Isak Dinesen), Karen Blixen (universally called Tania or Tanne) became a cult figure on the level of Ayn Rand and Mary Shelley, although in recent years Beryl Markham has threatened her position as leading lady of colonial Kenya's Golden Age. A resident in Africa only from 1914–1931 (she had a farm there), Blixen knew and was involved with most of the leading figures of her day. Her strength of character and resolve have become admired symbols. Her published letters and the detailed reminiscences of other people have revealed all-too-human frailties and flaws, but these have not tarnished her image. Tania stands as an example of many abstractions, from female equality to self-sufficiency to noblesse oblige. That she failed in her goal to keep her farm solvent is but a comment on some greater lesson of life.

Literary analyses and biographies abound. For this book's purposes, what kind of a hunter was Karen Blixen? When she first came to Kenya in 1914, she'd had some slight experience with field sports in her native Europe and readily took to the rugged adventure of African hunting. Tania frequently went on safari with her husband, Bror Blixen, and later with her lover, Denys Finch Hatton. She possessed a great pool of physical courage. When lion attacked her ox team in the bush, she set upon them with a whip and drove them away. She excelled at riding and soon at shooting ("I was a fairly good shot with a rifle, but I cannot photograph," she wrote in 1960), and was frequently seen riding the hills of her Ngong farm with a rifle strapped to her saddle and her pack of dogs loping behind.

Before long she lost her taste for killing plains game, except when necessary to feed the hundreds of Kikuyu squatters who lived on her land. But she never lost her taste for the sights and sounds of the hunt. Late in her rich and varied life, when asked what moment she would choose to relive if she could do so, she replied, "To go on safari once more with Bror."

Her decision not to hunt antelopes and other grazers, except in cases of need, did not extend to lions. In her last and best African book, *Shadows on the Grass* (1960), Blixen wrote, "Lion-hunting was irresistible to me; I shot my last lion a short time before I left Africa." She once sent a prime lion skin to the Danish King, Christian X. It was presented to him by one of Blixen's relatives and apparently was well received.

Tania had a jealous streak, and it is tempting to think that in shooting a lion she was really taking on her rival

White hunter Bror Blixen.

Markham, a tall, lithe blonde that more than one man compared to a predatory feline. But it is unfair to indulge in such cheap psychoanalysis, and anyway, Karen Blixen undoubtedly hunted lion for the same reasons the men of her day did so.

Blower, John. Blower was a Tanganyika game warden who patrolled the Serengeti before it became a national park. He later became chief game warden of Uganda.

Blunt, David Enderby (1891–1971). Born on 10 September 1891, David Blunt joined the Royal Navy in 1904 as a midshipman, and was promoted to sub-lieutenant on 15 May 1912. It was a common practice in Edwardian days for prospective naval officers to serve an apprenticeship as a boy midshipman before rising to more responsible duties. Blunt was chosen to be one of the earliest officers of the elite submarine service, and served in that branch until eye problems forced his reassignment to training duties. By the end of WWI he held the rank of commander. Blunt retired from the navy for health reasons in 1919 and moved to Africa.

Over the next six years Blunt held a variety of positions, including managing the Senna sugar estate in Portuguese East Africa, the Roshaugh sisal plantation in Tanganyika, and his own 250-acre cotton farm. In the spring of 1925 he was hired as a temporary cultivation protector (control officer) in the Elephant Control Scheme section of the Game Preservation Department of Tanganyika. He used a .416 Rigby rifle for most of his elephant work. As a control officer, Blunt operated mainly in Tanganyika's Lindi province, in the far south of the colony. In his first season at Lindi, he shot ninety elephant. In 1926 he was loaned on detached duty to the veterinary department to catch buffalo calves in the Rufiji River valley. The veterinary authorities were trying to crossbreed Cape buffalo with domestic Indian buffalo, hopefully thereby getting a beast of burden that was immune to the effects of the tsetse fly. The program was not a success.

After taking some sick leave in 1928, Blunt was sent to Lake Rukwa to make a survey of the region's game population and to carry out a local campaign of elephant control. That autumn he was moved to Tanga province where, it was alleged, a particular herd of elephants had developed the unfriendly habit of attacking motor vehicles. He operated out of Arusha for a while and then was returned to his duties in Lindi province. In 1931 he was let go when all of the "temporary" officials were laid off due to financial cutbacks.

After his layoff, he wrote an excellent book on elephant natural history and the problems of control work. It was titled, appropriately, *Elephant*, and was published in 1933 with an introduction by Lord Lonsdale. It's an outstanding work that has never been surpassed. John Taylor (1948) called *Elephant* "one of the very few books on big game and big game hunting I have ever read in which I cannot pick a hole or two," and Denis Lyell (1935) predicted "this book of Commander Blunt's should become a standard work on the subject."

Despite being laid off, Blunt never really lost his yen for the outdoor life, except when the necessities of wartime intervened. During the Second World War Blunt was assigned as commander of merchant ship defenses in Calcutta harbor. He turned down the offer of an assignment in Britain because he could no longer tolerate the cold northern climate.

After WWII, he was occasionally employed at his old task of training submarine crews (this time in Kenya), but his main activities still involved hunting and fishing. Blunt was a member of EAPHA from 1952. As an honorary Kenya game warden (which means it was a part-time, paid position), Blunt was called upon in 1955 to shoot out some troublesome buffalo in the bush at Nyali, near Mombasa. His contract called for piecework; he was paid fifty shillings per buffalo killed. He was getting rather old for such strenuous work, and after narrowly escaping serious injury from an enraged bull, Blunt called it a career. Eric Rundgren finished the job of wiping out the Nyali herd—twenty-eight buffalo in all—at, incidentally, double the fee Blunt had been paid.

Blunt married Winifred Bent in 1938 and had two children, a daughter, Sarah, and a son, Nicky, who became a respected professional hunter. In the last decades of his life Commander Blunt conducted some photographic safaris and also operated a big-game fishing business in Kenya waters. He died in 1971, fondly remembered as one of the steadiest and most reliable professionals of his time. *Elephant* was reprinted in 1985 and still holds pride of place on any Africana bookshelf.

There's an interesting bibliographical story about *Elephant*. The book was originally published almost simultaneously in New York and in London, with most of the London copies being shipped to East Africa for sale. Postal regulations required that articles being shipped within the British Empire had to sprayed with insecticide to prevent the spread of disease, and books were no exception. The insecticide left a residue, and for that reason many of the London-printed first-edition copies of *Elephant* are stained on the cover.

Bodelschwingh, Friedrich von (1831–1910). This aristocratic German landowner and farmer took Holy Orders and founded a nationwide system of charitable homes and hospices. He was the leading figure behind the German missionary movement in Africa.

Boislamber, Claude Hettier de. A leading French big-game hunter during the first half of the twentieth century, De Boislamber used a .375 Holland and Holland and was noted for being able to get off two shots as quickly as other men could fire a double rifle.

Bombay (Sidi Mubarak) (c. 1825–1885). A native of the Yao tribe, Sidi Mubarak was captured by slavers at an early age and taken to India. Bombay (he preferred this nickname, reflecting his adopted city) returned to Africa as a freedman and enlisted in the army of the sultan of Zanzibar in the early 1850s. In 1857 he was one of six Zanzibari soldiers assigned to help escort Burton and Speke on their explorations of the central lakes. He never returned to his military duties. Bombay went on to have a unique career in African exploring. Between 1857 and 1876 he was a member of the Burton and Speke, Speke and Grant, Stanley's trek to find Livingstone, and Verney Cameron expeditions. Few men of any race trekked across as much previously unknown territory as Bombay did.

A short, powerful, moody man with his teeth filed into points, Bombay was an invaluable asset to have on staff. He was hardworking, resourceful, adept at managing porters, and had a feel for languages. Burton lauded him as a tough, responsible aide who "worked like a horse" and called him "a gem." Only Stanley, of all the men Bombay served under, had a problem with him, but Stanley was an almost impossible man to work for—or with, for that matter. Stanley went out of his way to insult and even beat Bombay, acts that cost Stanley much respect among the porters. Bombay's wages for the Stanley expedition amounted to $80 a year, plus a muzzleloading rifle, a cheap pistol, a knife, and a hatchet.

After guiding Verney Cameron's safari in 1874–1875, Bombay was preparing to set out on yet another expedition—this one into Uganda for the Church Missionary society in August 1876—when, just prior to departure, he was notified that the Royal Geographical Society had awarded him a lifelong pension in recognition of his contributions to African exploration. Obviously Henry Rawlinson, then president of the society, appreciated Bombay's efforts, even if Stanley didn't. Sidi Mubarak Bombay promptly retired to Zanzibar and lived out his life a happy and comfortable man.

Bonchamps, Marquis Christian de. Bonchamps was a French aristocrat and noted big-game hunter who was a member of the Grant Stairs expedition to Katanga in 1891. In 1897 Bonchamps (along with Gabriel de Bonvalot) led an expedition heading west from Addis Ababa toward the Nile. This was supposedly a scientific survey, but its real goal was to support Marchand's grab at Fashoda. Expedition members included an entomologist, a mining engineer, and a landscape painter named Maurice Potter. The Bonchamps-Bonvalot expedition was the second attempt to supplement Marchand; the first, sent out from Addis Ababa on 27 August under the command of a Captain Clochette, had disintegrated after the death of its leader.

Bonvalot had trouble getting along with the French ambassador to Ethiopia, Leonce Lagarde, and found himself getting nowhere with Menelik, the Ethiopian emperor, as well. Frustrated, he quit and went back to Paris. This left Bonchamps in sole command. Unlike his partner, Bonchamps was a cheery, optimistic soul who felt he had every chance of succeeding. He met personally with Menelik before leaving and managed to get that monarch's lukewarm support. Menelik agreed to provide guides and letters of introduction to Ethiopian officials Bonchamps might meet on the way. Bonchamps finally left Addis Ababa to officially begin his expedition, carrying secret orders to claim the western bank of the Nile for France and the eastern bank for Menelik. In an effort to avoid the local Mahdist warriors, Bonchamps led his men along a rugged route through a series of swamps. Almost all the camels bought for the expedition died. Menelik's letters of introduction proved positively harmful; they were worded in such a way that the Ethiopian officials realized the emperor did not wish them to provide any real assistance to the French. Beset by fever, hunger, and floods, the Bonchamps expedition struggled to within one hundred miles of Fashoda but, at the end of December 1897, was forced to retreat back to Addis Ababa.

Ironically, for an expedition conceived as a politic maneuver disguised as a scientific venture, the Bonchamps expedition turned out to be a political failure but a definite scientific success. The route chosen to avoid the Mahdists was previously unmapped; Bonchamp's men made detailed surveys that added greatly to the known geography of the region. Also, due largely to Bonchamp's penchant for hunting, the expedition produced a large number of valuable natural-history specimens.

Bond, Brian W. A member of the Kenya administration from 1920–1940, Major Bond was a lusty Irish WW1 veteran who was first district officer and then district commissioner at Kitui, Ukamba province. He was known as "BB" and had won a Military Cross during the war. ROWLAND WARD 1928: KONGONI, PATTERSON ELAND.

Booysen Brothers. Two brothers with this name hunted with John Burger in the Belgian Congo. Around 1920 Burger and one of the brothers went elephant hunting in the Lualaba area. Every day the two would split up in the morning and return to base camp at night. One day Booysen came back to base in the early afternoon and spotted a baby elephant, alone, on the edge of the camp. Insanely, Booysen, an experienced hunter, tried to capture the calf alive.

When Burger returned to camp some hours later, all that remained of Mr. Booysen was, in Burger's words, "a pulp of mangled flesh" (1957). The mother elephant had of course been in the vicinity and promptly rescued her calf.

Not long after that, the other Booysen brother, obviously not the superstitious sort, was also hunting the Lualaba country with Burger. This time the two camped a few miles apart. This Booysen, a crack shot, wounded a lion one day and was mauled trying to follow it up in thick bush. Burger notes that this second scion of the Booysen brood survived but lost an arm and a leg, and lived out his days a permanent cripple.

Borelli, Jules (1852–1941). Borelli was a French explorer who conducted extensive safaris through Ethiopia, particularly the area north of Lake Rudolf. Leaving from Egypt in September 1885, he discovered the Omo River and made a significant survey of the Sobat region. Borelli was held up by the Emperor, Menelik, in the city of Antoto for almost a year and a half. When he finally was allowed to proceed, he headed for Lake Rudolf, which he called Lake Schambara. The delay allowed Teleki and von Hoehnel to reach the lake about three months before him. Borelli never actually got to the lake, and turned back, discouraged and sick with malaria, in the summer of 1888.

He wrote a book about his journeys, *Ethiopia Meridionale: Journal de Mon Voyage aux Pays Amhara, Oromo et Sidama, Septembre 1885 à Novembre 1888* (Paris, 1890) and published a map. Von Hoehnel, who later met Borelli in Egypt, advised him that his map was inaccurate; in fact, according to the map, Borelli had walked right through Lake Turkana without seeing it. A few years later the Italian explorer Bottego set out on his safari, stubbornly relying on Borelli's map, and was heading in the wrong direction when the Ethiopians stopped his progress.

Botha, Jacobus (c. 1690–c. 1792). The prototypical Boer elephant hunter, Botha was the patriarch of a family that included twelve sons. He pioneered the Boer technique of moving his entire family via wagon to a campsite, setting up a home there, and hunting the vicinity on horseback. Elephant being plentiful on the Cape back then, Botha twice shot twenty-two of the animals in a single day. He would often make lesser kills of ten or twelve. He retired to a farm in Swellendam a very rich man.

Botha, Pieter (1846–1933). He was a Boer elephant hunter who accompanied Jan van Zyl on a notorious 1879 hunt in Angola, where the hunters slaughtered 104 elephant that were mired in a swamp. The incident caused a great deal of public outrage.

Bottego, Vittorio (1860–1897). An Italian cavalry officer, Captain Bottego was chosen for the elite Special Africa Corps in 1887. He spent his time on garrison and patrol duties as well as collecting natural-history specimens for the Parma Museum. His first mission of exploration was into the Danakil in 1891. In 1892–1893 he explored Jubaland, accompanied part of the way by the erratic Captain Matteo Grixoni, who deserted after threatening to shoot Bottego. In late 1895 Bottego embarked on an extensive and well-prepared expedition into Somaliland and Ethiopia, a trip probably meant to augment the planned Italian military occupation of the latter country. Bottego reached Lake Rudolf in the summer of 1896, unaware of the catastrophic Italian defeat at Adowa on 1 March.

Harassed by Ethiopian irregulars, Bottego and his force of about two hundred men wintered on the shores of the lake. Still ignorant of Adowa and the subsequent renunciation of Italian claims to Abyssinia, Bottego worked hard at his original brief to explore and expand Italian influence. He alternately skirmished and parlayed with the local Ethiopian authorities, which must have been perplexed by his attitude. Finally the Ethiopians tired of the game and launched a dawn attack on his camp. By this time Bottego's force was down to about ninety men. Outnumbered at least ten to one, it was overrun in short order. Bottego (shot in the head) and most of his men were killed, and the others were captured and led off to Addis Ababa. The carefully collected specimens and geographical measurements were destroyed.

Bournan. According to Charles Williams (1859), Bournan was a resident of Cape Colony and an "athletic and powerful man" who was attacked and knocked down by a leopard. After a vicious struggle, he managed to get atop the leopard and kill it with his knife. "It was long before his previous strength was restored."

Bowker-Douglas, Russell. A Kenya hunter of the early 1900s, Bowker was involved in the 1907 "rickshaw floggings" with Ewart Grogan (see entry on Grogan for details). At the start of war in 1914 he formed a volunteer unit called Bowker's Horse, one of the members of which was the Swedish aristocrat Bror Blixen. Bowker-Douglas later hunted extensively in Tanganyika and formed the Tanganyika Tours and Safaris company in Arusha. He also owned the Lake Manyara Hotel for many years.

Bowring, Richard. A Kenya professional hunter from 1911–1936. The 1930 *East African Red Book* gave his address as Post Office Box 794, Nairobi.

Boyce, William Dickson (1858–1929). A Chicago newspaper magnate and hot-air-balloon enthusiast, W. D. Boyce led the 1909 Balloonograph Expedition to Kenya. The idea was to photograph wildlife from the air. The expedition consisted of Boyce, two photographers, and several journalists. Boyce tried to hire the band of the King's African Rifles to play at the expedition's ceremonious departure for the Rift Valley, but was refused because in a newspaper article he had once referred to Nairobi as a "military backwash."

The results of the expedition were less than spectacular, largely because Boyce hadn't foreseen the effect Kenya's thin air would have on the gas. Accordingly, it was almost impossible for the balloon to gain altitude. When they finally did get the thing aloft, the animals were spooked by the strange aerial object floating low in the sky and made great efforts to hide and crouch down whenever it neared. Boyce and his photographers got very few pictures worth printing.

It got so bad that the head writer made up a bunch of spectacular adventures while sitting in the lobby of the Norfolk Hotel drinking gin, and sent that letter off as his story. Boyce's newspapers didn't print the letter, but rival publishers got word of the affair and had a field day exposing the fraudulent report. Boyce got his revenge by firing the reporter and turning him in to the Kenya Game Department for shooting animals without a license, citing the writer's fictitious report as his evidence.

Boyce played a key role in the early days of the Boy Scouts of America. Various stories have him seeing the British Scouts in action in Kenya, and being assisted by a helpful Scout when lost in a London fog. He is known to have met with Robert Baden-Powell, founder of the original British Scouts, and obtained the official Boy Scouts of America charter from the U.S. Congress in 1916. During the American Scouts' uncertain founding days, he supported the organization with a generous donation of $1,000 per month. He passed away in 1929, stricken with grief after his only son died from an embolism.

Boyes, John (1874–1951). Born 24 May 1874 in Hull, Yorkshire, John Boyes was educated largely in Germany and spoke with a slight Teutonic accent all his life. A restless soul, he ran away to sea as a youngster. As early as 1888 he was working on fishing trawlers and tramp steamers. His travels brought him to Brazil, where he was stricken with yellow fever. Boyes was quarantined in a vermin-infested hospital where the staff routinely euthanized the most serious cases. He was saved by his shipmates, who overpowered the hospital orderlies and brought him back aboard ship.

After recovering, Boyes spent several years sailing on merchant ships in the Atlantic and Indian Oceans, and spent some time trading in the backwaters of West Africa for the Royal Niger Company. This first taste of the Dark Continent got Africa—and malaria—into his blood. Boyes also joined the Royal Naval Reserve about this time, for at this point in his life he still had dreams of a career in the Royal Navy. In the mid-1890s, however, he finally had to give up his life at sea due to failing eyesight, apparently caused by his sickness in Brazil. The poor vision meant that he could never qualify for a master's license, which in turn meant he would always have to serve as a common sailor. So he turned his back on Neptune and looked to Africa to make his fortune.

Boyes landed in South Africa in 1896 and enlisted in the Matabeleland Mounted Police and the Africander Corps during the Matabele Rebellion later that year. He was one of the soldiers who captured the rebel leader Uwini (Boyes called him Umwini), who was shot per order of Robert Baden-Powell in September 1896. When the revolt ended, Boyes opened and managed the Colonial Fruit and Produce Store in Bulawayo. Though

John Boyes, "King of the Wakikuyu" and one-time owner of Mount Kenya.

he was a qualified success as a grocer, an old man named Elstop (who had hunted with Selous) convinced him that adventure—and greater profit—lay in East Africa. So the young man sold out his grocery business and worked his passage to Mombasa, arriving there in 1898 after narrowly avoiding shipwreck or worse on the short trip from Zanzibar.

Boyes went into the interior with a trader named Gibbons. They soon split up. At first things did not look good for Boyes, virtually the sole white man in the district. But by a series of daring and clever escapades, Boyes managed to first ingratiate himself to, and later intimidate, the Kikuyu. Before too long he was playing one branch of the Kikuyu against the others, and soon found himself the paramount political figure among the clans. He was not averse to using force to solidify his position, at one point braining a dissident sub-chief with a knobkerrie (short wooden club). One rebellious clan, the Chinga, was put down with great ferocity.

Boyes looked at his ascendancy as a commercial venture rather than a political one, and used his influence to convince the Kikuyu to trade with the British. He did a good turn for both the Kikuyu and his own countrymen by organizing large caravans to carry grain to the isolated British garrisons in central Kenya, where it was sold for a lucrative profit. He later (1911) said that the "most striking incidents of my life at this time" occurred during these caravans—on two separate occasions elephant burst out of the brush and killed a porter on the trail.

Of course, there were problems being the self-styled "King of the Kikuyu." It was a turbulent and dangerous time in the Kikuyu homeland. The tribe, which later developed a reputation for education and intelligence, at that time was better known for its intransigence and ferocity. His old partner Gibbons angered a distant Kikuyu clan and was attacked by them; most of Gibbons's porters and a European named Findlay were speared to death in the massacre. In addition, the British authorities did not take kindly to Boyes's empire building, as they saw it, and eventually dispatched officers to arrest him. Boyes saved them trouble by going along quietly. His procession to Nairobi was impressive, if not ludicrous: Two hundred of his loyal men, all armed, accompanied the ten terrified Sudanese soldiers detailed to escort him, while Boyes himself rode on a mule. The askari sergeant in charge of the file containing the complaint and evidence against Boyes handed it over to the "criminal" for safekeeping. He was charged with dacoity (an Indian crime analogous to banditry), of impersonating a government, and of flying the British flag without authorization. The charges were ridiculous and soon dismissed.

Boyes's precise status among the Kikuyu is hard to determine at this late date. He himself made great truck by proclaiming to one and all that he had been recognized as the "king" of the tribe; some Europeans, however, ridiculed his claim and reported that many of his so-called "subjects" considered him a preposterous nut, or at least just an eccentric trader. Whatever his exact position in the tribe, there seems to be little doubt that for a short time at least he wielded a great deal of influence on Kikuyu affairs.

After his "reign" ended so abruptly, Boyes was involved in a variety of adventures, including hunting ivory in the Lado Enclave, running mules from Abyssinia to Kenya, and managing a variety of transport businesses. His sheep-trading enterprise greatly alleviated the shortage of food for early Kenya settlers. In the summer of 1901 Boyes served as the chief of scouts attached to the Kalyera

Punitive Expedition, serving under Capt. St. A. Wake. The Kalyera, rowdy relatives of Boyes's old Kikuyu friends, had been raiding caravans and spearing Swahili traders. They were subdued only after Boyes personally shot and killed one of their leading warriors, a vigorous young subchief named Kasusa. After an interval of cattle trading in German East Africa, Boyes tried his hand at land speculation around Nairobi, and began to make some influential friends. In 1904 Boyes went along on safari to the Uasin Gishu plateau with American millionaire W. N. McMillan, Charlie Bulpett, and Maj. G. Ringer, founder of the Norfolk Hotel.

Boyes wasn't the first elephant hunter to go to the legendary Lado Enclave—that distinction probably belongs to Bill Buckley. Boyes followed along in what might be called the second wave, a rash of ivory hunters who arrived in the area in 1907–1908. Boyes actually passed Russell Bowker-Douglas and the Brittlebank brothers on the road to Lado. This was before the death of King Leopold, the event that would start the clock ticking on the handing-over of the territory from Belgian to British control, under the terms of a 1905 treaty. But once the treaty had been signed and the provisions were widely known, the Belgians lost interest in building up an area that they were soon going to lose. The British government wasn't interested in the place yet either, so the hunters and poachers, operating largely from Koba on the British side of the Nile, had a field day for a few years.

The British representative at Koba, a son of Hannington, the murdered Bishop of Uganda, kept order in the town itself but actively encouraged the hunters' extra-territorial activities. A bar called the Harbour Lights was the center of the social scene in Koba. There the outdoorsmen would gather for a drink, a card game, and a bath, plus a chance to brag, tell stories, and get up to speed on everyone else's adventures. It was a great place to be young and a hunter, and John Boyes was in the thick of it.

Boyes lasted several years in the Lado, occasionally going over to the Congo or the Sudan in pursuit of the elephant herds. He was associated with most of the great names of the era—Bell, Pickering, Knowles, McQueen, Craven—but hunted much of the time with a mysterious Scandinavian who went by the name of Selland. On their first expedition into the Enclave, Boyes and Selland each came out with twelve hundred pounds of ivory. Subsequent trips brought out similar amounts. Selland died of blackwater fever while Boyes was away on a trip to England.

Boyes lived most of the second part of his life on a thousand-acre farm near Nairobi. He remained a colorful figure in Kenya until his death in 1951. He was the author of two books, *John Boyes: King of the Wakikuyu* (1912) and *The Company of Adventurers* (1928), the latter mainly about his days in the Lado.

The year of Boyes's birth illustrates one problem of nailing down information about the old hunters. Several sources list it as 1873, including the introduction to the 1998 reprint edition of *The Company of Adventurers,* which apparently lifted it from J. A. Hunter and Daniel Mannix's *Tales of the African Frontier.* I've seen another source with a birth date of 1871. The United States Library of Congress gives the correct date of 1874, and that is also the date Boyes himself used in *King of the Wakikuyu.*

Bozas, Vicomte Robert du Bourg de (1871–1902). De Bozas was a French aristocrat who led a crack French scientific expedition to Lake Rudolf in 1901–1902. It was a tough safari—two of his men were killed by Murle tribesmen, and de Bozas felt it necessary to conduct a punitive raid on a Murle village.

The de Bozas expedition was composed of a variety of French scientists, and was not without issue. For instance, they were the first to recognize the Rift Valley's unique access to fossils. The original plan was to restock supplies on the Nile and then proceed to the Congo basin. De Bozas caught tetanus, however, and died on the fringes of the Congo on Christmas Eve 1902. The remaining expedition members threw in the towel and went home.

Bradshaw, Benjamin Frederick. Bradshaw was an employee of George Westbeech but struck out on his own in early 1877. For the next few years he made his living by hunting and collecting museum specimens in the Zambezi Valley. Bradshaw visited Victoria Falls with Fred Selous in October 1877.

Brander Dunbar, James, and Archibald Dunbar Brander. This gets confusing. James Brander Dunbar (1875–1969) and Archibald Dunbar Brander (1877–1953) were brothers. Your eyes aren't playing tricks on you; they couldn't get the names straight themselves. Their grandmother, a Lady Mary Dunbar, stood to inherit a considerable estate if she adopted the name Brander. Accordingly, her son and his sons, James and Archibald, received both names. The two boys were baptized James Dunbar Brander and Archibald Dunbar Brander. As with

Arthur Conan Doyle or Roualeyn Gordon Cumming, the surname had two parts. All well and good, but James felt that his Dunbar heritage was more prestigious and also that he had some chance of inheriting another estate on that side of the family, so when he reached maturity he began styling himself James Brander Dunbar. Archie kept it the other way.

Jim served in the Boer War as an officer of the King's African Rifles. After the war he was stationed in Nyasaland with fellow officers Stigand and Mostyn. Short but very strongly built, he had a notable 1903 billiard-room wrestling match with Stigand that ended only when their struggle threatened to throw the pool table off-kilter. Subsequently he was a district commissioner in Zululand. Through it all he was an avid hunter. By the time he returned to Scotland he had collected more than sixty species of African big game. Jim enjoyed espousing a controversial theory that African animals had a poor sense of smell and that wind direction played no role in successful hunting. He served in the Cameron Highlanders during the 1914 war and spent the remainder of his long life (he died the year Neil Armstrong walked on the moon) managing the family estate at Pitgaveny on Loch Spynie, hunting birds and deer.

Brother Archibald, considered the better marksman of the two, spent most of his working life with the Indian Forestry Service. This, of course, gave him ample opportunity to hunt and fish, as well as write. In 1923 Archie published *Wild Animals in Central India*, considered a classic of its type. He was awarded a sporting medal in 1937 by Germany's master of the hunt, a fellow named Hermann Goering. Archie died in 1953.

Brazza, Pierre Savorgnan de (1852–1905). Pierre Savorgnan de Brazza, although a French hero, was actually an Italian count born in Rome. In 1875 he went on a three-year African trading venture to the Ogowe River in West Africa with a Dr. Ballay, in the course of which he explored the entire Ogowe basin and discovered the Alima and Likouala Rivers. The French government commissioned him in 1879 to undertake a political mission in the same region. He signed dozens of treaties with local chiefs, bringing them and their people under French "protection," and established a station at Franceville on the Upper Ogowe. He also founded Brazzaville and explored the Niari River region. In the course of this safari he met the British explorer Stanley. Unlike Stanley, who went exploring for the sake of fame and fortune, Brazza was motivated by patriotism and a sense of adventure. This first expedition, at least, actually cost him money. The French government advanced him 26,000 francs, but he had to kick in 16,000 francs of his own before it ended.

In 1880 Brazza returned to Africa and made yet another survey of the Ogowe, as well as exploring likely locations for settlement along the coast. In 1883 he was appointed governor of the French Congo, the capital city of which bore his name, and spent the next decade consolidating French control over the area. In 1891 he led an expedition up the Sangha River, opening up a trade route toward Lake Chad.

Brazza was an exceptionally able man, and one of the few who could live up to the stereotypical image of an African explorer. At a famous meeting at a lecture in Paris, Henry Stanley, the guest of honor, spoke first and attacked Brazza, mocking him viciously and calling him "a barefoot tramp." Brazza then quietly asked to say a few words. The crowd expected retaliation, but instead the Italian praised his rival, commending him for his courageous deeds and calling for international cooperation in the exploration of the Dark Continent. The audience was left with no illusions as to which explorer was the greater man.

As governor of the French Congo, Brazza attempted to run the colony in a progressive manner. His administration was honest and fair, in stark contrast to his neighbors in the Belgian Congo. Money was lacking, however, and Brazza was unable to build much infrastructure or otherwise put the colony on a solid footing. He made an impassioned plea for development funds, especially money to build a railroad (in vain—the railway from the Atlantic Ocean to Brazzaville was not completed until 1934), but in 1898 the French government chose to recall him.

He was replaced by a corrupt governor named Emil Gentil. France thereupon resorted to the cost-saving device developed and used successfully by Great Britain—giving private companies concessions on huge tracts of land and depending on them to develop it. Conditions in the Congo, however, drove the concession companies to the same brutal methods employed by the Free State, and soon after Brazza's recall the French Congo could rightly be called a "Heart of Darkness" in its own right.

The scandals of the Free State soon boiled over into the French Congo, and the public clamored for the situation to be corrected and corrupt officials brought to justice. The government responded by sending the colony's founder, Brazza, back to the Congo to investigate the situation. Brazza was particularly disturbed by allegations that two French officers, Toque and Gaud, had systemically massacred hundreds of innocent Congolese, including many women and children.

Brazza's return to Africa in 1905 was an eye-opener. He was shocked by the brutality of the administration. The corruption and cruelty went far beyond Toque and Gaud, extending up to the directors of the concession companies and Governor Gentil. He began to compose a scathing report that would expose the concession system and force reforms.

In the summer of 1905 Brazza, still investigating in Africa, was stricken with a serious attack of dysentery. Plans had already been made for the veteran explorer to return to Paris, but his condition necessitated that the ship bringing him to France stop at Dakar so that he could receive medical treatment. He died in Dakar on 14 September 1905. The damning report was sealed by the French government and the concession system continued, even though the sadistic methods had proved a failure. By 1906, out of forty concession companies, twenty-one had lost money and nine had folded completely.

Bright, Richard George Tyndall. Major Bright was a British officer on the staff of Col. J. R. L. MacDonald when the latter was dispatched to forestall the Frenchman Marchand's drive on the Nile in 1895. In 1899–1900 Bright accompanied Herbert Austin on an expedition that successfully mapped the Sobat River basin. After a trip back to England to publish the maps, Bright again joined Austin on the latter's disastrous 1901 Lake Turkana expedition. Bright took over effective command of the expedition after Austin became sick and lost his sight, probably as a result of scurvy. ROWLAND WARD 1928: LELWEL HARTEBEEST.

Brittlebank, William. A graduate of both Eton and the Klondike Gold Rush, Brittlebank was one of the "gentleman poachers" of the Lado Enclave. His older brother accompanied him on most of his travels, but William was the acknowledged leader in their affairs. He was a successful elephant hunter, despite having to wear special metal boots due to ankle injuries he had sustained in Alaska.

Brittlebank prospected for many years in Australia, Siberia, Baluchistan, Rhodesia, and the Klondike before coming to Kenya. An 1873 book he wrote on a famine in Persia is still considered a classic. He arrived in East Africa early enough to open the first account in the Mombasa branch of the National Bank of India (legally and fiscally, East Africa was considered an extension of India during the early colonial days). He took a job conducting transport for the Uganda railway and for a time supervised Walter "Karamojo" Bell when the elephant hunter was temporarily working for the railroad.

Brittlebank worked as a geologist and prospector for F. R. Burnham's East African Syndicate for a short time until he was captured by the Abyssinians. Upon his release from captivity he went to the Kilo gold fields in the Belgian Congo. Later he was joined once again by his brother and started hunting elephant in the Lado Enclave.

While hunting around Lake Albert, he discovered oil (he had previously been the discoverer of the Persian oil deposits). Exploitation of the oil field was delayed while he tried to get the appropriate permits and financing. He was finally granted the first permit for oil exploration ever issued in Uganda, in 1913, but he never actually got around to telling anybody precisely where his deposit was located. Brittlebank planned to return to the area after World War I to exploit his find, but died while on a prospecting trip to the Kenya coast. His brother died soon after. As of 2005 at least three oil companies were still searching for Brittlebank's lost oil deposit, concentrating mainly on the likeliest area, the so-called Albertine Rift.

Brocklehurst, H. C. A British game warden in the Sudan, Brocklehurst was also the author of *Game Animals of the Sudan* (1931). ROWLAND WARD 1928: WHITE RHINO (MONGALLA), ELEPHANT, BONGO, LORD DERBY ELAND, SITATUNGA.

Bronson, Edgar Beecher (1856–1917). This American cattleman and sportsman was a friend of Owen Letcher, and the two traveled together to Mombasa in 1908. Bronson later shot an elephant in Kenya's Kavirondo Hills that stood 11 feet, 4 inches tall at the shoulder and had just one tusk that weighed 84 pounds. The bull was ranked third in the 1928 edition of Rowland Ward's record book. In 1910 he hunted in the Sotik country with John Alfred Jordan. He was the author of *In Closed Territory* and several books about the American West.

Brooks, William. Brooks hunted South-West Africa with William Chapman and died around 1875.

Broughton, Sir John Henry "Jock" Delves (1883–1942). Broughton was a British baronet who had been schooled at Eton. Although he missed combat service in World War One due to a vague illness, he was also an officer in the Irish Guards from 1902–1919. Rudyard Kipling's son was a fellow officer in the same regiment; young Kipling was killed in the trenches as were many, if not most, of the Guard's 1914 officer corps. Broughton, described by one admirer as possibly "the best-looking officer in the Irish Guards" (Fox, 1982) sat out the war in Britain, tending to administrative duties.

Discharged finally for medical reasons, he went to Kenya in the 1920s first to hunt but ended up buying several coffee plantations. He frequently went on safari with professional John Hunter. Despite arthritis and a hobbled right hand from a 1915 auto accident, Broughton (pronounced "Brawton") was an avid hunter and a decent shot; he stalked and killed a total of twenty elephants between 1920 and his own death twenty-two years later.

In January 1941 when the earl of Erroll was found shot to death outside of Nairobi, suspicion fell on Broughton. Erroll had been having an affair with Broughton's wife, the 27-year old Diana Caldwell Broughton. The affair was quite open and brazen, and Diana (who had married the much older Broughton just months before) was apparently posed to take advantage of a bizarre prenuptial agreement wherein Broughton would support her financially if she left him for a younger man.

The case against Broughton was built primarily on ballistic evidence, which proved insufficient. Broughton was acquitted in a spectacular trial but committed suicide soon afterward, injecting himself with an overdose of barbiturates. Broughton's suicide may not have been connected with the Erroll murder because he also faced an indictment over some missing trust-fund money. The Erroll affair was the subject of the 1982 book *White Mischief* by James Fox.

Browne, Sir Granville St. John Orde (1883–1947). A graduate of the Royal Military Academy and a major in the Royal Artillery, Orde Browne arrived in East Africa in 1909. During the First World War, he was mentioned in dispatches four times, a highly desirable recognition of courage equivalent to a decoration. He was a district commissioner in Kenya in 1909, a provincial commissioner in Tanganyika Territory in the 1920s, and British resident in the Cameroons 1929–1932. He was also a Fellow in the Royal Geographical Society, the Royal Zoological Society, the American Geographical Society, and l'Institut d'Anthropologie Suisse. Orde-Browne was the author of *The Vanishing Tribes of Kenya* (1925). ROWLAND WARD 1928: BLACK RHINO, BUFFALO (54 INCHES), GIANT FOREST HOG (#1).

Brown, William Harvey (1862–1913). Brown, an American scientist, was a member of the United States Eclipse Expedition, sent in 1889 to observe a solar eclipse at Cape Town. Once in South Africa, Brown requested and received permission from the Expedition to travel into the interior to collect specimens for the Smithsonian Institution. He signed a six-month contract with Cecil Rhodes and Frank Johnson's "Pioneer Column," and thus became part of the spearhead that occupied Mashonaland in 1890. The official photographer of the Eclipse Expedition, one C. A. Orr of Chicago, also joined the Pioneers.

Brown then took his bonus and, like most of his fellow Pioneers, began prospecting and hunting in the Rhodesian countryside. All this while he was still employed by the Smithsonian, and until at least 1894 he periodically sent natural-history and cultural specimens back to the States. Among the settlers he was known as "Yankee" Brown, for his American origin, as well as "Curio" Brown, due to his constant collection of "curiosities" for the museum. Adrian Darter, in his 1914 *The Pioneers of Mashonaland,* recalled how he and Yankee Brown had collected a cheetah family while on the march. Brown fought in the Matabele War in 1893 and in the rebellion two years later. Much of his later life is obscure, but he died in Salisbury, Southern Rhodesia, in 1913.

In 1892 Brown went on a hunting trip to the wooded hills northwest of Salisbury, teaming up with brothers Arthur and Herbert Eyre. While the Eyres were chiefly interested in tracking down a bull white rhino they had spotted on a previous trip (in 1895 Arthur Eyre finally caught up with the animal, said to be the last white rhino in Southern Rhodesia), Brown was chiefly interested in fulfilling his obligations to the Smithsonian. A previous shipment of specimens had gone missing en route to Kimberley, and Brown was doubtlessly under some pressure to produce. During six weeks in the field he shot and preserved a total of forty-nine large mammals, including six buffalo, two zebra, eleven eland, three waterbuck, three roan antelope, two sable, six reedbuck, five wild dogs, three warthogs, and one each of black rhino, tsessebe, kudu, bushbuck, oribi, bushpig, baboon, and lioness.

Brown belonged to the Gordon Cumming school of hunting and quite literally seems to have tried to put a bullet into every living creature he came across in the field. His account of a buffalo hunt in Mashonaland in 1893 is particularly revealing, for he continually stalked and charged the herd, indiscriminately firing at every animal he saw. He was one of the last hunters to describe taking on a mindless glee in his war on nature—by the turn of the century nearly all big-game hunting books contained at least a token passage decrying the activities of "game butchers," even when their bags were exorbitant and wasteful by modern standards. Brown had the time-honored excuse of being a collector for a distinguished museum and thus could claim to be furthering science and education with his excesses. But his Victorian bloodlust still shows through, such as when he remarks in his book that he continued to pursue the herd "as buffalo heads were in demand in Salisbury."

Nevertheless, *On the South African Frontier (*1899) is a great book. The 430-page tome has not received the attention it deserves, although it was reprinted in 1970 as part of the excellent Africana series put out by Negro Universities Press. Brown included chapters on the Pioneer Column, the Matabele Wars, big-game hunting, gold mining, and many other aspects of early Rhodesian history, creating an essential and entertaining reference for students of the period.

One of Brown's minor anecdotes is simply too good not to pass along. In late 1893 he decided to spend a few months raising hogs and cattle for market. As a Pioneer he was entitled to a free "farm right" and had established his about six miles outside Salisbury. He bought several pigs in Salisbury for starter stock and loaded them onto his wagon for a trip to his farm several miles away. Just before setting out he was stopped by a friend, the hunter Stuart Meikle, who warned him (apparently with a straight face) that he must not let the pigs see the wheels of the wagon as it turned around. Such a sight, Meikle warned, always proved fatal to swine in South Africa. Unfortunately, Brown did not note his response to this unusual advice, but he seems to have considered the warning some sort of odd joke. A lot of weird characters roamed Rhodesia in those days, and Brown chalked Meikle up as just one more harmless nut.

All went well for the first five miles of the trip, but as Brown maneuvered the wagon across a stream near his destination, he happened to glance behind and see that all the pigs were in a position to watch the rear wheels rotate. Further examination revealed the hogs to be gasping for air and on the brink of collapse, and though Brown quickly stopped the wagon and cooled them with water, all the animals died. To top it off, all of Brown's African workers deserted him that same night, and the American was left to wonder if it was all just an eerie coincidence, a bizarre natural law, or something even spookier.

Brownell, Clarence Melville. Brownell was a young American doctor who traveled to Khartoum in 1860 for the commendable purpose of exploring unknown Africa. He apparently had no particular agenda in mind, just a vague plan to walk from one end of the continent to the other, similar to Ewart Grogan's "Cape-to-Cairo" walk. Brownell was not as lucky or as skillful as Grogan—he died from fever before he even got out of the Sudan.

Broyon, Philippe. This Swiss trader was an influential figure—and one of the first European visitors—at Mpwapwa in Tanganyika in the 1870s.

Bruce, Sir David (1855–1931). Originally from Melbourne, Australia, Bruce joined the British Army Medical Service in 1883 after graduating from Edinburgh University medical college. He was especially interested in the new science of bacteriology. Within two years he had identified the microbe that caused the fatal disease called Malta fever, and twenty years later he identified the transmission vector of Malta fever, which is passed in goat's milk. In 1894 he was sent to Zululand, where he discovered that nagana and other livestock diseases were caused by the trypanosome *Trypanosoma brucei.* The next big step in his amazing career came in 1903, when he went to Uganda and identified the tsetse fly as the proximate cause of sleeping sickness. He returned to Uganda in 1908 to continue his research, and went to Nyasaland in 1911.

Bruce was knighted, was made commandant of the Royal Army Medical College in Millbank during World War I, and became president of the British Association in 1924. For health reasons he spent most of his declining years at Madeira. Throughout his career he worked closely with his wife, Mary Elizabeth Steele Bruce, a distinguished medical researcher in her own right (she was honored for her work in fighting trench fever and tetanus). Mary Elizabeth Bruce died in London on 23 November 1931; Dr. Sir David Bruce died during her funeral four days later. They had no children.

Despite the value of his medical work, Bruce left behind a mixed reputation. Several hunters who sought jobs providing meat for his sleeping-sickness commission quit after he sought to pay them a ridiculously low amount for their work. And Dr. J. B. Daley, a junior member of the commission in 1910–1911, recorded in his diary that Bruce suffered from insecurities and compensated by acting in a domineering and even tyrannical manner. He was very hard on the European members of the team and worse on the African staff, often having the latter flogged for minor infractions.

Bruce, James (1730–1794). Bruce was a British explorer who discovered the source of the Blue Nile, the shorter of the Nile's two branches. Arriving in Cairo in 1768, he went down the eastern side of the Red Sea, crossed over to Massawa, and found the Blue Nile source at Geesh Springs and Lake Tana. In 1773 he traveled west to Khartoum and north to Cairo, where he committed the faux pas of announcing his discoveries to the French authorities rather than waiting until he reached English territory. This political mistake caused his discoveries to be distinctly underreported in Britain, and he got nowhere near the personal acclaim and recognition accorded later explorers of the White Nile. This injustice has been amply corrected by history—Bruce has become one of the best-known and most written-about African adventurers of his day.

Bryden, Henry Anderson (1854–1937). A British sportsman and journalist, Bryden hunted all over South Africa and was considered an expert on the subject. He was the author of *Gun and Camera in Southern Africa* (1893), a typical Victorian hunting travelogue with chapters on native habits, giraffe, eland hunting, et cetera. He did place a somewhat unusual emphasis on birdlife and fishing, which makes this work more interesting than some. Bryden assisted Rowland Ward with the early editions of *Records of Big Game.*

Bryden was one of the first writers to warn the public about the overhunting of African wildlife. In 1895 he reported that African hunters in the employ of European traders had killed some three hundred giraffe near Lake Ngami over the course of just a few months. The hides were eventually sold to traders at a profit of some £5 apiece. The resulting outcry helped get the giraffe added to the lists of royal game in several of the British colonies. Ironically, Bryden himself had a listing in the 1928 edition of Rowland Ward's record book for giraffe, as well as for springbok and Somali (Swayne) hartebeest.

Bruyn, Pieter de. De Bruyn was a Boer elephant hunter of the early eighteenth century. Except for some hypothetical shipwrecked sailors, he was probably the first white man to see the interior of South-West Africa.

Bucheri (xxxx–1908). This Italian hunter and trader was attacked and killed by the Lugwara tribe between Wadelai and Dufile on the Nile in 1908. Apparently Bucheri, a mean sort, was given to molesting African women. According to Tony Sanchez-Ariño (1995), he also cheated the tribesmen out of money that had been promised for provisions. A party of avenging warriors raided Bucheri's camp in the Lado Enclave and chased him through the forest. As he was struggling across a jungle stream, one of the warriors shot him with an old muzzleloader. They carried him back to their village, injured but alive, and selectively cut pieces off him until he died.

Either Bucheri or an Austrian hunter, Fleischer, was among the first to capture a baby white rhino for exhibit in European zoos. Most sources attribute the feat to the Austrian, but at least one (Boyes, 1927) alludes to Bucheri. Noted hunter Robert Foran claimed to have been told about the calf directly by Fleischer himself. Boyes reported that Bucheri (who he does not mention by name, but the association is fairly clear) was killed in a dispute over the purchase of milk for the rhino. In the same paragraph Boyes mentioned another unnamed hunter, a "German," who was killed by an elephant around the same time in the Congo. This brief statement corresponds with what is known about Fleischer's death. Given Boyes's reputation for inaccuracy, it is more likely that Fleischer was the man in question in the rhino incident and that Boyes, writing twenty years after the fact, was simply confused about which of the two men owned the rhino calf. On the other hand, Boyes was in the area at the time of both deaths and apparently knew Fleischer pretty well.

Buchta, Riccardo (1845–1894). Also see Richard Buchta. An Austrian-Italian (born in Radlof, Galicia) explorer in the Sudan, Buchta was both the first professional-quality photographer to make a study of the Upper Nile and a superior artist with pencil and brush. His photographs of the people and places of that region in 1878–1882 are of great historical interest.

His first published book was *Der Sudan und der Mahdi* (1884), followed by *Der Sudan Unter Aegyptischer Herrschaft* (1888). His most spectacular accomplishment, however, was a very expensive volume entitled *Album of the Human Types of the Upper Nile.* Quiet by nature, Buchta was frequently overlooked in his home city of Vienna as others less accomplished promoted themselves and their projects to Buchta's disadvantage. He was finally starting to get some recognition, including a high decoration personally awarded by the Emperor Franz Josef, when he died 27 July 1894, of an apoplectic stroke.

Buck, Frank (1888–1950). Buck was an entertainer, animal dealer, author of *Bring 'Em Back Alive* (1930), and star of numerous short films about animal collecting. In the introduction to his memoirs Buck estimated that he had delivered 39 elephants, 60 tigers, 48 leopards, 52 orangutans, 20 hyenas, 40 bears, 31 gibbons, 5,000 monkeys, 40 kangaroos, 90 pythons longer than 20 feet, 15 crocodiles, and more than 100,000 birds to American destinations, as well as handling rarities like ratels, anoas, and a babirussa. Many more animals were killed undergoing capture and during transit.

His films included *Bring 'Em Back Alive* (1932), *Fang and Claw* (1936), *Jungle Menace* (1937), *Jacare, Killer of the Amazon* (1942), and *Africa Screams* (1950). The animal fights in his films were staged, a secret the studio tried desperately to keep from the public. He got some negative publicity in 1936 when professional hunter Donald Ker unthinkingly told a newspaper reporter that Buck had never been in Africa and that all his stunts were staged in a camp in India. Buck took it good-naturedly. He was, after all, in show business.

Buckley, William (1873–1948). Born in London in 1873, Buckley immigrated to South Africa during one of the gold rushes of the early 1890s. Too young for the 1890 Mashonaland campaign, he signed up for the Mashonaland Border Police at the start of the 1893 rebellion. He saw hard service and would have been one of the dead at Maj. Allan Wilson's "last stand," but his place was taken by another that day, Buckley being down with fever.

After his Matabele service (he also served in the Matabele war of 1896), Buckley tried his hand at trading and prospecting (even returning to England in 1896 to raise capital for a mining company), but by 1902 he had drifted north to Kenya and become an elephant hunter. He was one of those driven entirely by the huge profit a man could make from ivory in those days. He hunted in the Karamoja region of Uganda and in 1904 teamed up with Pete Pearson, another well-known elephant hunter, and began stalking the huge pachyderms all over Uganda. Buckley also hunted elephant in the Congo, Tanganyika, and the French colonies of West Africa (he was fluent in French).

Buckley was the first prominent European ivory hunter to work the Lado Enclave, making his initial safari there in 1903. He had been promised an unrestricted elephant-hunting license from the Congo Free State, but as the weeks went by and the license didn't arrive, he grew impatient and began operating without it. Any objections from the local Belgian authorities were quickly dispelled with a few well-placed bribes. The main rush to the Lado didn't take place until five or six years later, after the death of King Leopold of Belgium.

In contrast to men like Karamojo Bell, Buckley was an ardent admirer of large-caliber rifles, the bigger the better. While hunting in the enclave, he grew dissatisfied with his .450 Express rifle and ordered a custom .600 rifle from London. According to John Boyes (1927), who liked and admired Buckley, "While awaiting its arrival he was fond of talking about the big slaughter of elephant he would put up when it came." Finally a large box was delivered, postmarked from England. Buckley eagerly tore the crate open, only to find a consignment of Bibles printed in an African language. It seems that a Uganda bishop named Buckley had ordered the books, and the shipments had somehow got mixed. What the missionary did with the heavy rifle has not been recorded.

Buckley's biggest elephant, a huge bull sporting tusks of 145 and 137 pounds, was shot, according to his 1930 book *Big Game Hunting in Central Africa,* near "the village of M'Boga, about fifteen miles inland of the Nile." That's all Buckley wrote about the location of that hunt. Professional hunter and author Tony Sanchez-Ariño wrote in his excellent 1995 book *The Last of the Few* that the event took place in the Lado Enclave in 1905. Detailed period maps don't show a place called M'Boga in the Lado Enclave or by the Nile, but there was a M'Boga not too far away, about fifteen miles inland from the Semliki River just southwest of Lake Albert, in British territory in the Ruwenzori foothills. Buckley was known to hunt that area as well. The exact area remains a mystery. Sanchez-Ariño gathered much of his information by word-of-mouth from veteran hunters, and there may be a little haziness in the recollection of a hunt that took place a century ago.

Buckley served in the East African campaign in World War I. Like Sutherland and many other hunters, he was an intelligence officer. After the war he resumed hunting in Uganda. When old age started closing in, he retired to a modest home near Mombasa, where he died in 1948. Before his death, he was honored by the country of Rhodesia and the city of Bulawayo as one of the last surviving pioneers from the wars of the 1890s.

Buckley's an odd one. His book came out in 1930, and like everything else he did, it seems to have been motivated purely by the desire for financial gain. You can tell that he looked around at his elephant-hunting buddies who had written books, said "Hey, I can do that too," and put pen to paper in the hope of making a quick buck. He comes across as a tough, no-nonsense character, and his treatment of the local Africans was somewhat crude, even by that era's standards. Buckley wrote a passage about a "game" he would play with

Count Alexander Xavieryevich Bulatovich, circa 1899.

a servant named Juma that is so degrading it rivals anything Finaughty may have done. Juma had foolishly made the statement that he was Buckley's dog, probably just a cultural device among his people designed to show respect, but from then on Buckley would make Juma bark and beg like a real dog to get fed his scraps of meat. Buckley used to entertain his guests with this act. But you get the sense that Buckley wasn't all bad, a damn good man to have on your side and a tough but honest bloke you could do business with. Boyes wrote that Buckley was popular among his fellow hunters and an excellent guy to have around a campfire, with an inexhaustible supply of stories and tall tales. This doesn't really come across in Buckley's book.

Bulatovich, Alexander Xavieryevich (1870–1919). Captain Bulatovich was a Russian Imperial Guard officer of great promise who was born to a high-ranking noble family in Orel. In 1896 he was detailed to the Ethiopian army as part of a medical detachment sent to treat Ethiopian wounded after the battle of Adowa. Bulatovich was an extremely intelligent, well-read man who took the trouble to learn to speak Amharic and Ge'ez, Ethiopia's two major languages, in the short period of time after he was ordered to go there. In contrast, a good proportion of British officers served their entire careers in India without ever learning the native tongues.

Ethiopian Emperor Menelik was tremendously impressed with the young Russian nobleman and requested that he accompany several Ethiopian expeditions in the winter and spring of 1896–1897. These expeditions took the form of short military excursions into the countryside, during which some scientific work was done (meteorological readings, natural-history collecting, map surveying). Bulatovich got permission from his Russian superiors to go on these treks and performed his duties in a competent if somewhat flashy fashion. He returned to Russia in May 1897.

Bulatovich was sent back to Ethiopia six months later as part of the official Russian delegation. The Russian government obviously hoped to take advantage of the young man's budding relationship with the Emperor. Menelik asked Bulatovich to accompany the army of Wolda Giorgis, which was being sent to secure the Lake Rudolf region for Ethiopia. Once again permission was obtained, and Bulatovich signed on as a sort of executive-scientific officer.

The Giorgis expedition is mainly remembered for the brutal foraging required to feed 30,000 men—entire villages were massacred and the countryside was denuded of cattle. Both Giorgis and Bulatovich tried to temper the carnage, but there was no other way to feed the huge host, and the undisciplined warriors simply could not be restrained from shooting and raping the tribal people who lived in the district. Bulatovich was particularly appalled by the destruction of an entire community that had built lush farms in the Oyma River valley.

The main mission of Giorgis's army was to secure Ethiopian control of the region. To this end, Bulatovich designed a chain of small forts along the Omo and Kori Rivers to facilitate Ethiopian administration. The only European force operating in the area at the time was a small British contingent under Herbert Austin, and they quickly withdrew when faced with five thousand Ethiopian soldiers at the northern tip of Lake Rudolf.

Bulatovich left Giorgis in May of 1898 and returned to Russia, where he lectured on Ethiopia before the Russian Geographical Society on 25 January 1899. He published a report and a map of the regions he had traveled. He brought with him back to Russia a three-year-old boy who had been castrated and whose Omo delta village had been ransacked by Giorgis's troops. Bulatovich named the boy Vaska and enrolled him in a school in Saint Petersburg. The boy did well at first, but as he grew older he was increasingly harassed by other students because of his physical deformity—eunuchs develop distinctive physical qualities, and these were not lost on the other boys. The harassment reached the point that Bulatovich returned Vaska to Ethiopia in 1906, and his fate thereafter is unknown.

Bulatovich made a survey of the Blue Nile for Menelik in 1899 but was then transferred to Port Arthur, where he fought in the Russo-Japanese War. After the war he quit the army and became a monk known as Father Anthony and lived in a Greek monastery at Mount Athos for several years. He suffered from chronic ill health, the result of the inevitable African microbes. He volunteered to work for the Red Cross during WW1, and after Russia's surrender to the Germans he applied to enter a monastery near Petrograd. His application was not immediately accepted, because some of his beliefs were thought to be heretical. While his application was under review he lived in a tiny woodland hovel, where he was murdered by bandits on 5 December 1919.

Bulpett, Charles W. L. (1851–1939). Universally known in his later years as "Uncle Charles," Bulpett was a wealthy Victorian adventurer and bon vivant who lived well into the twentieth century. As a young man he swam across the Hellespont, the strait that separates Europe from Asia, and was an early explorer of the upper reaches of the White Nile. In later life he was an influential figure in the new Kenya colony, living as a permanent house guest of Sir William Northrup MacMillan at Chiromo. As president of the Muthaiga Club, Bulpett was a popular part of "White Highlands" society, a close friend of Lord Delamere, Denys Finch Hatton, Karen Blixen, and others of that circle. The title of his 1907 memoir—*A Picnic Party in Wildest Africa*—reflects the man's personality. So was his favorite motto, which was adopted in spirit by most upper-class Kenyans of the time. It went like this, as quoted by Karen Blixen: "The person who can take delight in a sweet tune without wanting to learn it, in a beautiful woman without wanting to possess her, or in a magnificent head of game without wanting to shoot it, has not got a human heart."

Bulpett went on safari to the Athi Plains, the Uasin Gishu plateau, and the Kavirondo district with John Boyes, William Northrup McMillan, and Maj. G. Ringer in 1904. The expedition is the subject of a chapter of Boyes's book *The Company of Adventurers* (1928). Bulpett edited and wrote the introduction to Boyes's 1911 work, *King of the Wakikuyu*. ROWLAND WARD 1928: SOMALI (SWAYNE) HARTEBEEST, ELEPHANT.

Burbridge, Ben. Burbridge was a prominent American hunter of the 1920s who made four lengthy trips to Africa. He had a bit of a reputation as a gorilla expert, and was the subject of some criticism as he shot and captured at least nine of them between 1922 and 1925. He also hunted extensively in East Africa. Burbridge was the author of *Gorilla: Tracking and Capturing the Ape-Man of Africa* (1928), and directed and starred in the five-reel motion picture *The Gorilla Hunt* (1926). Some critics believe the film to have been a source and inspiration for the classic *King Kong*.

Burchell, William J. (1781–1863). In 1808 Burchell was a botanist for the East India Company, and engaged to be married. He was on the island of Saint Helena (not yet Napoleon's place of exile) to join his fiancée, but was jilted when she fell in love with the captain of the ship that was bringing her there. Heartbroken, Burchell quit his post and moved to Cape Colony to start a new life.

The rich plant life of Africa fascinated him, and he soon decided to dedicate himself to its study. In June 1811 Burchell set out for the interior with a few wagons and some Hottentot attendants. For the next four years he roamed as far north as Bechuanaland, covering over 4,500 miles, collecting more than 40,000 plant specimens, and making some 500 drawings. He taught himself numerous skills, such as hunting, taxidermy, and even surgery, once amputating three mutilated fingers from the hand of a Hottentot named Gert whose muzzleloader had exploded. Burchell recorded eating twenty-three species of antelope, as well as other animals such as zebra, rhino, and hippo; he rated eland the best (better than beef) and put zebra at the bottom.

Burchell discovered for science several new animals such as the quagga and the white rhinoceros. He seems to have had some ambition to find and kill a unicorn, and even wrote his mother that he expected to be paid at least £7,500 for a unicorn hide. This early example of putting the cart before the horse is a neat indicator of the type of motivation shared by many of the first British explorers in Africa, a combination of greed and zest for adventure that made these men move mountains. Burchell had remarkably little trouble during his journeys in the hinterland (a previous expedition, led by two intrepid explorers named Donovan and Cowan, had disappeared without a trace in 1808), except for some tense moments when a local chief named Mothibe threateningly demanded weapons. Like Joseph Thomson in East Africa years later, Burchell relied upon tact and passivity, an approach that sometimes worked and sometimes didn't. The closest he came to violence was when he used the threat of a pistol to keep his own men in line.

It's somewhat ironic that if Burchell had never been jilted by his bride-to-be, the great tragedy of his life, he would no doubt be long forgotten. As it was, he acquired a considerable measure of fame, wrote a book *(Travels in the Interior of Southern Africa),* lectured at Oxford, and undertook another five-year expedition in the Amazon rain forest. It somehow wasn't enough, and years later, sick and depressed, he committed suicide. He never married.

Burckhardt, John Louis (1794–1817). Born in Switzerland, Burckhardt defected to England in 1806 to avoid conscription by the French army. Two years later he propositioned London's African Association for their sponsorship of an expedition to North Africa. Burckhardt, the diligent type, prepared for his mission by studying Arabic in Syria for more than two years before finally traveling to Fezzan by way of Cairo and the Nile.

In 1812 he visited Dongola on the upper Nile and later went to Berbera and Suakin. He was one of many of a long tradition of European explorers who sought to disguise themselves as Muslims when transiting Arab territories, and was more successful than most, doubtless due to his assiduous preparation. After returning to Egypt in 1815 to tour the Sinai, Burckhardt decided to try to discover the source of the Niger. He died at Cairo on 15 April 1817 while waiting for the arrival of a caravan that had agreed to conduct him to Fezzan, his proposed starting point. The African Association printed his observations of travel in Nubia, Syria, and Arabia in 1819, 1822, and 1829 respectively.

Burger, John F. One man whose name has become inextricably linked with hunting the African buffalo was John Burger. Born around 1896 in the arid region of South Africa known as the Great Karoo, Burger's father owned a farm with a flock of about five thousand sheep. A combination of disasters—drought, a massive herd of springbok that trampled to death hundreds of lambs and fouled the wells, and then a lethal hailstorm—reduced the flock to less than two thousand animals. As a small boy Burger had a variety of distinctively African experiences. During the Boer War, he and his entire family were once arrested by a Boer patrol.

Another incident was far more serious. The young Burger (whose relations with black Africans during his life were generally good) was involved in a street fight during which he brained a Hottentot boy with a rock. Thinking he had killed his opponent, Burger ran away and hid in the bush overnight. The next day he returned to face the music, fortunately finding that the other boy had survived.

The incident should not be considered evidence that Burger was more racist than other white youths of his time. Teenage violence certainly is not a new development in human history; street fights and rock fights have been common among young men in all eras and places. What matters to a young man is the group his peers belong to, be it defined racially or culturally. In my own high school the athletic kids were always fighting the "stoner" kids, and both groups despised the band kids. The fact that the street fights in Burger's day developed along racial lines is just a product of that time and place, nothing more.

When his father died in 1905, the young Burger and his family moved to the Orange Free State and from there to Rhodesia. En route to the new home the Burgers passed through Bechuanaland, where Burger witnessed a man-eating lion leap from ambush and snatch away an unfortunate African. That same night Burger met the legendary Bechuana king, Khama. Burger went along on a hunt with the great Selous at age twelve, an episode he would remember his entire life.

Growing up in Bulawayo, Burger matured into a strong and steady youth. It was a tough society, and he had to develop skills as a fighter. He learned boxing and was taught the exotic martial art jujitsu by an English champion named Stephens, who went by the name Ozaka. He worked as a printer's apprentice. Both printing and boxing were to serve him well in later life.

When World War I broke out, Burger joined the British army and served in the East African campaign. Invalided from the service in 1917 due to illness, Burger returned to Bulawayo and resumed work as a printer. He also began to promote boxing matches.

Around 1919 Burger moved to the Belgian Congo, where he spent the next fifteen years pursuing a variety of careers. First he signed up as a "copper sampler," work that today would be done by a geologist. He roamed the Congo countryside with a large retinue, collecting likely rocks and testing the ores for copper content. At this time Burger began his first large-scale hunting activity, driven by the safari's need to live off the local game animals. Burger learned the fine points of shooting antelope and buffalo, and also indulged himself in some elephant hunting. He was successful both as a hunter and as a sampler, but neither vocation paid enough to meet his commitments, so he was always on the lookout for other moneymaking opportunities.

One of his successful ventures was as a boxer, like fellow hunter Jim Sutherland. Burger fought professionally in the Congo for about five years, from 1919–1924, and was considered the region's unofficial champion. In his last match he went some fifteen rounds to a split-decision, only to find that the promoters had absconded with the £600 purse, which he and his opponent were supposed to share. The opponent, a Swiss man who had just lost his job for participating in the fight (boxing was still widely considered immoral by proper society), committed suicide in his despair over the theft.

Burger's most profitable activity in the Congo was as a manager for a caterer, filling meat contracts for mining concerns and other large businesses. As a supervisor, his greatest assets were his physical strength and fighting ability. The catering business brought out the tougher elements of Congo societies, mostly hardened, alcoholic thugs from Europe who were willing to risk tropical disease and death for what they thought was an easy outdoor job. The previous manager of the catering company had been badly beaten by one of the employees and was laid up in the hospital with a number of broken ribs and other bones.

Burger quickly asserted himself with his fists and turned the company into an efficient operation. Businesses with large demands for food supplies flocked to his door, and Burger was continually promoted and given lucrative bonuses. He began to speculate in various other enterprises, making money hand-over-fist in printing, importing, and other activities.

In 1929 Burger, rolling in dough, established a motion-picture theater business, setting up cinemas in Elisabethville and Jadotville and beginning construction in other Congo towns. The films—the first "talkies"—would be shipped in from Europe. Burger stood to make a fortune, but then the Depression began and the price of copper—the chief raw material of the Congo—fell cataclysmically. Burger was wiped out and, like millions of other men at the time, had to search about for a new profession.

In the early 1930s Burger, now broke, heard of a gold strike at Lupa in Tanganyika. Lacking the funds to go there himself, he wangled a commission as a journalist for the Belgian *Essor* newspaper chain. While reporting news of the gold rush to the home offices in the Congo and Brussels, Burger tried his hand at prospecting as well. Once again, he proved to be successful at this new endeavor, inventing several devices that made the actual mining simpler and more efficient. He wasn't fond of the actual work of mining, so he set himself up as a middleman, buying gold from the miners and reselling it in Tanganyika's port cities. This proved very profitable, and by 1939 he not only owned and managed his own gold mine in Tanganyika's southern highlands, he was also employed as a manager and accountant for a major mining company and occasionally took work for locust control in the Rift Valley.

The job of a locust control officer was to find a swarm, continually report its size (in square miles) and direction, and follow it until the insects spawned. When the flightless "hoppers" emerged, the officer would clear openings in their path, dig trenches in the openings, and fill them with a mixture of bran and Gamaxene, a deadly poison. The poisonous mix was of relatively low lethality—Terence Adamson, on locust control in Kenya in the 1940s, used to assuage the fears of doubtful farmers by eating a handful of the stuff. The hoppers, however, would gorge themselves on the mix and die in droves. Sometimes fire was used as a weapon as well. It was a very effective program.

So far as hunting went, this period was the most prolific of Burger's life. It was here that he acquired his reputation for shooting buffalo. The area's great herds of buffalo represented the cheapest and most available meat to feed the workers at the various mines that he managed. During the course of his life he shot more than a thousand of the animals. With that reputation came numerous requests from the game department and local Africans to help get rid of dangerous old buffalo bulls that had taken up residence in populated areas. During World War II he was classified as a "priority war worker" and tasked with the responsibility to provide food for two thousand African villagers. He diversified yet again, buying a small tobacco farm and distilling quality moonshine on a small scale. He still worked with locust control and regularly submitted newspaper articles to various news services.

In 1947 Burger finally retired from hunting and his other businesses and devoted himself full time to writing. Moving back to South Africa for his retirement, he turned out several fine books in the next decade or so, including the classic of buffalo hunting, *Horned Death,* which solidified his reputation as history's premier buffalo hunter. Although other men killed more of the beasts, to this day

Maj. Frederick Russell Burnham.

it is Burger's name that first comes up when the subject is discussed. His other books included *African Adventures* (1957), *African Jungle Memories* (1958), *African Campfire Nights* (1959), and *My Forty Years in Africa* (1960).

Burgess (xxxx–1860). A Scotsman named Burgess went hunting in Bechuanaland in the late 1850s, accompanied by two friends named Henry Reader and Sir James Lamont. In June of 1860 the trio met up with missionary John Mackenzie and his party along the Mareetsane River, where they camped together for a night or two and held a religious service. A short time later Burgess was killed in his own wagon when he accidentally dropped a lit pipe into a barrel of gunpowder.

Burkitt, Roland Wilks. Dr. Roland Burkitt arrived in Kenya in 1911 and set up his practice in Nairobi. Trained as a surgeon, he became Nairobi's first private medical practitioner and took on all manner of cases. Burkitt was a forceful, vivacious man with an odd mix of modern and ancient medical theories—many people dreaded seeking his help. He was an advocate of the old-fashioned practice of bleeding, for example, and his cures often included parts of venomous snakes. He developed a unique cure for malaria that involved pouring cold water over the shivering, naked patient until the blood parasites presumably froze to death. This technique was hard on the patient but often surprisingly successful, and it was felt that most of those who died under this regimen were no doubt goners anyway. The method was later successfully applied to horses and mules suffering from nagana. After he bought a Rigby car in 1919, he began treating patients by driving them around naked so that the cold could work its beneficial effects.

Burkitt also displayed a talent for more modern medicine. In one celebrated case, farmer Stanley Polhill was dragged into the machinery of a mechanical harvester-combine, which ripped his torso completely open and tore one lung away. After a horrible thirty-mile trip to the hospital, Polhill's remaining lung collapsed and the man was fading fast. Dr. Burkitt quickly constructed a breathing machine from football and bicycle pumps and had African hospital staff members, working in two-hour shifts, pump air around the clock. Polhill was in the hospital for over a year but survived his horrendous injuries.

Burnham, Frederick Russell (1861–1947). Major Burnham was an American adventurer from the western frontier who went to Africa and served in the Matabele wars and the Boer War. As a young man scouting and fighting the Apaches and cattle rustlers, Burnham flirted with being on the wrong side of the law. For many years he was involved in one of the bloody and interminable Arizona range wars of the Old West of Doc Holliday and Wyatt Earp.

Lured to Africa by the prospect of unlimited hunting and adventure, Burnham figured prominently as a scout in the first Matabele war. He worked closely with Selous, Maurice Gifford, and other legendary figures on reconnaissance, patrol, and courier duties. Frequently operating at night in enemy territory, Burnham was one of the last scouts to be detached from Maj. Allan Wilson's doomed strike force the very night of Wilson's Last Stand. After the war Burnham tried his hand at prospecting and also led a lucrative hippo-hunting expedition into the Congo in 1895.

During the Matabele Uprising of 1896, Burnham, now the "Chief of Scouts," played an even larger role than in the previous campaign by assassinating—there is no other word—a Matabele religious leader known as the M'Limo at the entrance of a holy cavern near Mwange. The widely publicized exploit greatly boosted morale in the European ranks but was actually a tragic mistake: The man killed by Burnham and an accomplice, a district officer named Armstrong, was a leader of the sole remaining pro-British faction among the Matabele. The murder nearly pushed the few remaining loyal Matabeles onto the rebel side. Nevertheless the assassination cheered the beleaguered Britons, and Burnham was still bragging about it in his memoirs thirty years later.

Having lost a four-year-old daughter in the rebellion, Burnham and his wife then traveled to the Klondike at the start of the Alaska Gold Rush. There Burnham was one of the few to actually find gold and get it back to a bank. He did distinguished service in the Boer War (again as "Chief of Scouts") and was decorated with the DSO (see glossary). Later he was a prominent businessman with varied interests, including a mining company named the East Africa Syndicate, and spent a considerable amount of time big-game hunting in East Africa.

During World War I Burnham, by then largely living on a ranch in California, was commissioned by the United States government to try to find deposits of the strategically valuable metals tungsten and manganese. Virtually all of the North American continent south of the Arctic Circle had at one time or another been visited by old-time prospectors in the nineteenth century, but tungsten and manganese had held little value back then and they had been interested only in gold and silver. The two other metals became vitally important in modern technology, and Burnham spent the war years taking old prospecting friends—most of whom he hadn't seen in thirty years—back out into the Rocky Mountains, the Sierra Madre, and the western Badlands to rediscover old deposits that had once been of only scientific interest. Relying mostly on the traditional miners' tools including mules, picks, and shovels, Burnham and his grizzled companions found only modest amounts of tungsten and manganese, though their finds were of vital strategic importance.

His autobiography, "elicited and arranged" by Mary Nixon Everett, came out in 1928. This riveting adventure story is one of the better examples of its genre, clearly benefiting from the professional touch-up. Burnham comes across as an extremely competent, somewhat hard man, but not a sociopath like Finaughty or Meinertzhagen. Despite his killing of the wrong man in the Matabele rebellion, Burnham was a valuable addition to British colonial forces in Africa and a personification of Winston Churchill's fondest hope, the union of the best of both Britain and America in one man. Much of the early success of Baden-Powell's Boy Scouts organizations in both countries can be attributed to the popularity of Burnham's military scouting techniques.

In the American West, Burnham had learned an old duck hunter's trick: With a heavy rifle he would fire directly beneath a swimming duck. The vibration would kill the duck without a wound, similar to "barking" a squirrel. While scouting for Major Forbes in the 1893 Matabele campaign, Burnham presented the major with a duck that had been killed in this manner. Forbes refused to believe it, saying Burnham must have obtained the duck through "some Yankee trick." In his book Burnham never actually comes right out and says it, but you get the feeling he believed Forbes was a complete idiot.

Burnham was the author of *Scouting on Two Continents* (1928) and the subject of Peter van Wyk's *Burnham: King of Scouts* (2003).

Burrough, H. S. Captain Burrough once shot an elephant in Uganda whose tusks had a combined weight of 340 pounds, making it one of the largest ever.

Burrows, Guy. Burrows was the author of *Land of the Pygmies,* in which he claimed that mountain gorillas lived near Stanley Falls. Harry Johnston thought the photo reproduced in Burrows's book might actually be of a specimen taken in the Virunga Mountains by the German hunter Beringe.

Burton, Sir Richard Francis (1821–1890). The author of forty-three books and one hundred articles, and the translator of thirty other books, Sir Richard Burton was the ultimate Victorian explorer. A true Renaissance man, he combined success at warfare, geology, poetry, languages, natural sciences, ethnology, and, of course, hunting—all under one hat.

Burton's father was Col. Netterville Burton of the 36th Regiment of Foot. Colonel Burton liked to travel, and young Richard spent his formative years moving from place to place on the European mainland. He returned to England in 1840 to attend Oxford but was dismissed as an undergraduate for a breach of discipline. He managed to get a commission in the army of the East India Company and went to Bombay in late 1842, being posted as regimental interpreter (he spoke Arabic, Persian, and Hindustani fluently). Burton served in the Sind campaign of 1843.

In 1853 Burton first achieved distinction by entering Mecca in disguise—a forbidden and dangerous adventure for a non-Muslim. He wasn't the first Westerner to do so but provided the best description of those who made the attempt. In 1855 he embarked on a Nile expedition with three other British officers, one of them John Speke. Their camp was attacked by bandits near Berbera in Somalia. One officer was killed and Burton took a horrendous spear wound in the face, causing the expedition to be curtailed. Ever after he sported a spectacular scar, often hidden by whiskers. After a short break to fight the Crimean War, Burton and Speke returned to Africa. Anxious to discover the source of the Nile, the two soldiers went to Zanzibar and headed inland from there.

On this 1857 expedition to find the great African "inland sea," the two soldiers discovered Lake Tanganyika but not its outflow. Burton fell ill with a serious case of malaria and was left at Tabora while Speke, almost blind from fever himself, went on to discover Lake Victoria. Speke, a strange, selfish, single-minded man, returned to civilization without Burton and proclaimed Lake Victoria the source of the Nile. This began a bitter feud between the two erstwhile friends that ended only with Speke's sudden and mysterious death in 1864. For many years Burton vehemently denounced the idea that the Victoria Nyanza could be the source of the great river, preferring instead Lake Tanganyika, which is actually part of the Congo watershed.

Burton made many more travels in Africa, Arabia, and South America and held diplomatic posts at Fernando Po (1861), Brazil (1864), Syria (1868–1872), and Trieste (1872–1890). His relations with the Foreign Office were always somewhat strained, for he was very outspoken, and his writings included frank anthropological material and even erotic translations like *Arabian Nights*. Burton liked to be controversial and the center of attention, and these qualities, coupled with his enthusiastic sampling of native sexual mores wherever he went, hampered his career in the repressive (if hypocritical) Victorian society. It was even rumored that an early effort of Burton's in the field of military intelligence, a report on the homosexual brothels that might be tempting Her Majesty's troops in India, was the result of firsthand experience.

A tremendously prolific writer, Burton was the author of many works, among them *Personal Narrative of a Pilgrimage to El Medinah and Meccah* (1855), *Lake Regions of Central Africa* (1860), *A Mission to the King of Dahomey* (1864), *Explorations of the Highlands of Brazil* (1868), and *Gold Mines of Midian* (1878). Burton was knighted in 1886 in recognition of his many services. He died in Trieste on 20 October 1890, leaving behind his wife, Isabel Arundell Burton (1831–1896), who had shared many of his triumphs and controversies. For personal reasons Isabel burned forty years of Sir Richard's notes and journals upon his death.

Butler, A. L. Butler was the superintendent of the Sudan Game Department in the early 1910s and a contributor to *Big Game Shooting in Africa* (1932), part of the Lonsdale Library. He is mentioned in Pease's *Book of the Lion* (1913). ROWLAND WARD 1928: NILE LECHWE, SITATUNGA.

Butter, Archibald Edward (1874–1928). Butter was a wealthy Scotsman who went along as an extra hunter on the 1899–1900 Harrison-Whitehouse expedition to the Lake Turkana region. On this trip Butter, armed with a Mauser magazine rifle, shot a legendary albino topi that had first been described by the explorer Wellby a year before, donating the unique trophy to the British Museum. He did some elephant hunting as well: The 1928 edition of Rowland Ward has the "late A. E. Butter" owning a pair of elephant tusks from Lake Rudolf that totaled 268 pounds of ivory. During this period of his life Butter made frequent short hunting trips into the countryside of Ethiopia and Somaliland.

In 1902 Butter was back in Ethiopia, commissioned by British agent John Lane Harrington to conduct a border survey. He was accompanied by his friend John Baird, Captain Philip Maud of the Royal Engineers, a doctor named Wakeman, and an Italian named Count Giuseppe Colli di Felizzano, who was brought along at the behest of the Foreign Office. Other members of the team included Mohamed Hassan, who had been safari headman on the Wellby expedition of some years previous, Shazad Mir of the 11th Bengal Lancers, and eighty-odd African soldiers and porters.

For six months they explored the border zone, preparing meticulous notes and charts far superior to the inaccurate maps done by the Harrison-Whitehouse Expedition. It wasn't all work: Like most Victorian officials, the men of the Butter expedition took plenty of time out to hunt. The Europeans on the team hunted and shot some twenty rhino, and Butter himself took nineteen of the thirty-nine lion killed. On 22 May 1903, the inevitable accident occurred when John Baird was badly hurt by a charging lion. One of his Somali gunbearers grabbed the lion's tail and distracted the beast long enough for another gunbearer to shoot it.

When the final report was presented to parliament in November 1904, the team had divided opinions. The disagreement arose over the difference between what might be called the "geographical" frontier versus the "military" frontier. Butter recommended a border that split the Galla tribes from other races and followed what might be topographically considered the logical line. Maud, on the other hand, proposed a boundary that was militarily and strategically much stronger in Britain's favor. The government selected Butter's recommendation, soon known in Africa as the "Red Line."

Butter's day in Africa was over at that point. Still a young man, he retired to farm and raise thoroughbred dogs. He died young in 1928. In addition to the trophies cited above, Butter also had rankings in the 1928 Rowland Ward record book for lesser kudu.

Buxton, Clarence Edward Victor (1892–1967). The son of a baronet, Buxton was a member of the Kenya administration during 1919–1938. He was district commissioner at Kajiado in the 1920s and 1930s, and at Narok in 1935. In that capacity he often helped obtain provisions and porters for numerous safaris, including those of the Prince of Wales and those of Martin and Osa Johnson. As a hunter, Buxton was a "small-rifle" aficionado, using the .256 for almost all game. As a DC he apparently preferred the .303 service rifle—at least, that is what he used when he and seven askaris shot into an unruly mob of about a hundred Masai warriors on 25 June 1935. Two were killed and two wounded. An inquest ruled that it was justifiable homicide, and there was some talk of prosecuting the Masai for rioting, but it fizzled out.

Like many of Kenya's early administrators, Buxton was somewhat eccentric—in fact, many of his colleagues considered him quite mad. He was a proponent of a plan to get the Masai interested in sports instead of warfare. To this end he issued them cricket bats and polo sticks, built a soccer stadium, and encouraged the warriors to use their donkeys as polo ponies. The scheme was not entirely successful.

Dashing and bold despite his eccentricities, Buxton was considered an up-and-coming politico, possibly even a future governor. Then, suddenly, his career in Kenya ended when he left his wife and four children to take up with the beautiful young wife of a junior government analyst. Named as respondent in the analyst's suit for divorce, Buxton denied the charge that he had committed adultery with the young lady in Nairobi Game Park.

"In the game park?" he snorted. "Preposterous! Too many ticks." His superiors were scandalized, as much by the lying as by the adultery.

Buxton was accordingly exiled to a minor diplomatic post in Palestine, a move considered a punishment just shy of dismissal. Two years later, now married to his erstwhile mistress, he resigned his position and retired to his East African farm at Limuru.

Buxton, Edward North (1840–1924). Buxton, an early pioneer in the field of wildlife photography, was an inspiration for Schilling, Kearton, and Maxwell. Telephoto lenses were not yet in use, so most of Buxton's close-ups were of animals that had been shot by him or another hunter. The author of *Two African Trips* (1902), Buxton assisted Frederick Selous in the planning of former President Roosevelt's 1909 safari. ROWLAND WARD 1928: ATLAS GAZELLE, SITATUNGA, KONGONI.

Buys, Coenraad de (1761–1821). Last name also spelled *De Buuys.* Born in 1761, Coenraad de Buys was a Boer frontiersman who forged a place in South African history akin to that of his American counterparts Daniel Boone and Davy Crockett. He was the first white man to settle in the Transvaal, a stalwart Boer leader, and even the stepfather of the Xhosa chieftain Ngquika (c.1775–1829), also known as Gaika. De Buys took Ngqika's mother as a common law wife in the late 1790s and thereafter exerted a tremendous amount of influence on Xhosa affairs. He was responsible for at least some of the animosity between the Xhosa and the British, having convinced Ngquika that the English were the European equivalent of the Bushmen, who were considered by the Xhosa to be a subservient and treacherous race.

Stories and legends with De Buys as a central figure have somewhat clouded the historical picture of the man. For our purposes it is sufficient to point out that he spent much of his life causing trouble for the English, stirring up not only the Xhosa but also the various mixed-race clans, like the Bastaards and the Griquas, that populated southern Africa. His dislike of all things Anglican was the one constant of his life, which extended not only to soldiers and settlers but to missionaries as well. He hampered the designs and progress of the British missions at every opportunity.

At various times De Buys was a hunter, a trader, a Boer burgher, and the acknowledged leader of several African villages. By the end of his life he had largely renounced his European heritage and gone completely "native," even to the extent of using a bow and arrow for hunting and warfare. A lusty sort, he took numerous African and mixed-blooded women as wives and concubines—he never married a European woman—and by the 1810s was living largely on the move as the lord of a wandering band of Griquas, natives, escaped slaves, and deserters from the British and Portuguese armies and navies. They fought and hunted and robbed as they moved from place to place, preying particularly on the Sotho. The English eventually posted a reward for his capture and at the same time offered him a pardon if he would merely come in and give them the benefit of his unparalleled geographic knowledge. De Buys spurned the overture.

His end befitted a legend. In August 1821 he was leading his band along the far reaches of the Limpopo River when one of his favorite wives took sick and died. Suddenly tired, De Buys bade farewell to his family and his followers and slipped away from camp during the night. Nobody ever saw him again, and it is unknown how and when he died. Legends of his death and his possible fate were bandied about campfires for years. His numerous progeny formed their own branch of the South African people, the Buysvolk, and spread out through the bush: William Cornwallis Harris reported two of De Buys' sons living among friendly natives near Delagoa Bay in 1836. Several thousand Buysvolk live to this day in the northern Transvaal and other parts of southern Africa.

C

Caldwell, Keith F. T. An ex-officer with the rank of captain, Caldwell became an assistant game warden in Kenya in 1922 and senior assistant game warden in 1925. He helped organize the Uganda Game Department in 1925. He had to resign sometime around 1932 due to ill health, but he kept his hand in and was a trustee of Uganda, Kenya, and Tanganyika parks through the 1950s. He is thought to be the first man to drive from Nairobi to Paris via Sudan, Darfur, French Equatorial Africa, Gibraltar, and Spain.

Cameron, Verney Lovett (1844–1894). Born near Weymouth, England, in 1844, Cameron, a preacher's son, joined the Royal Navy in 1857. He served in the Mediterranean, the West Indies, and the Red Sea and served with distinction in the 1868 Abyssinian campaign.

In 1873 Cameron led the second Royal Geographical Society expedition to search for Livingstone. Robert Moffatt, Livingstone's nephew and the missionary Moffatt's grandson, went with Cameron but died of malaria soon after entering Africa. When the party reached Tabora on the way to Lake Tanganyika in September of 1873, Lieutenant Cameron received word that Livingstone was dead. He had the explorer's body (recovered at Unyanyemba) and possessions escorted to Zanzibar by Lieutenant Murphy and Dr. Dillon, and continued on throughout 1874–1875, exploring Lake Tanganyika and the Congo and Zambezi watersheds. Cameron recovered some of Livingstone's papers and one of his maps at the village of Ujiji. He was the first European explorer to cross equatorial Africa from east to west, arriving at Benguela in November 1875. His many side excursions on this adventure helped considerably to fill in the map of Africa.

Cameron was widely applauded upon his return to England, receiving the Gold Medal from both the Paris and London Geographical Societies. He was promoted to commander, Royal Navy, made a C.B.,* and given an honorary doctorate from Oxford.

With a reputation like that, Cameron couldn't just sit at home, so in 1878 he made a trip through Turkey and Persia, publishing *Our Future Highway* upon his return. In 1882 he and Sir Richard Burton (a close friend) went to the interior of Guinea to prospect for gold, but not enough of the precious metal was found to justify the expenses of mining it. Always an enthusiastic hunter, Cameron collected numerous natural-history specimens in Guinea. He spent the rest of his life involved in a number of commercial development schemes. On 26 March 1894 he was returning from a hunt at Leighton Buzzard when he was thrown from his horse and killed.

Cameron was the author of *Across Africa* (1877), an influential book that told of great riches to be made by exploiting the continent's resources. He also wrote *The Cruise of the Black Prince Privateer* and *The Adventures of Herbert Massey in Eastern Africa,* and translated *Steam Tactics.*

**Commander of the Bath*

Campbell, Alexander Duncombe (1872–1899). Campbell was a young man from Cape Colony who joined the 1890 Pioneer Company that spearheaded the occupation of Mashonaland. He was very interested in beekeeping and hoped to establish a honey business on the farm that was part of his Pioneer payment. This farm was built about twenty miles east of Salisbury.

William Harvey Brown told a story about the Africans who worked on Campbell's farm. Like many laborers, they were prone to drinking to excess, and after tasting one particularly good batch of local beer they spent the better part of a month drinking and carousing. During the party they lost track of the phases of the moon, so when they finally sobered up they knew it was a new moon but didn't know which one. According to Brown, they spent the next three months profoundly discussing the matter and trying to reach a consensus on what month it was. Work on the farm came to a standstill as the entire staff debated this interesting chronological problem.

Campbell is listed in Adrian Darter's 1914 book as having been murdered near Salisbury in 1896, presumably during the Matabele Rebellion, but the same book lists his death as taking place in 1899. In Brown's 1899 book Campbell is indicated in the index as still being alive, so I have gone with the later date.

Campbell, John (1766–xxxx). Campbell had an illustrious career as a missionary and explorer in Bechuanaland, the Transvaal, and Namaqualand. He arrived in South Africa in 1806 and is credited with discovering the source of the Limpopo River in 1820. He returned to England in 1821 and never went back to Africa. His two-volume memoir, *Travels in South Africa* (1815 and 1822), is loaded with detailed historical, zoological, botanical, geographical, and anthropological information, and helped inspire the young David Livingstone.

Canonne, Etienne (1902–1976). Etienne Canonne can perhaps best be summarized by his nickname, Pas de Molesse, which loosely translates as "speed it up" or "get the lead out." At the age of eighteen, inspired by tales by Theodore Lefebvre and other great French hunters, Canonne left his village in northern France, bought a rifle, and moved to French Equatorial Africa. He had no intention of doing anything but hunt big game.

He started his career by hunting elephant on a large scale, as well as rhino. For a time in the late 1920s rhino horn was fetching a very high price, and everyone with a rifle was taking potshots at the beasts whenever possible. In 1927 over eight hundred rhino horns were shipped from Fort Archambault alone, and the rhino population in French Africa never recovered. Canonne himself is known to have killed at least three hundred fifty of the animals during this period. Obviously, the French government was slower to impose restrictions and bag limits than were the other colonial powers.

When they finally started doing so, Canonne switched to meat hunting, making a good living killing thousands of hippo along the Auk River and shipping their dried meat to Fort Archambault, where it was purchased to feed native railway crews. Each hippo supplied about two hundred pounds of dried meat, and Canonne was paid up to a franc per pound. Another hunter, named Tiran, had the same business going on the Shari River.

In the late 1930s, when France finally started getting serious with game laws, Pas de Molesse became a safari guide in the Kenya mold. His center of operations grew to be called Fort Canonne. He was quite successful in this role, specializing in Lord Derby eland, and built a number of permanent hunting camps connected by well-maintained tracks. This allowed him to move clients from area to area quickly in pursuit of big game.

When World War II broke out, Canonne immediately enlisted, serving in Abyssinia and with the Free French at Bir Hakeim. Postwar, disillusioned by the spread of civilization in Africa, he settled in Europe. Every year or so Canonne would make a trip to Ubangi or Chad to talk up old friends and shoot an elephant or two. He was perhaps the best of the noted French hunters.

Capellan, Baroness Adriana van (xxxx–1863). Van Capellan and her sister, Harriet Tinne, were wealthy Dutch aristocrats who traveled to Khartoum in 1861 with the vague idea of rescuing the Speke and Grant expedition coming out of the interior. They were accompanied by Harriet's daughter, Alexine Tinne, a Dr. Steudner, an Italian named Contarini, and two Dutch maids. The ladies made a fine impression on Samuel and Florence Baker but were ill-served by their own people—their agent, a French official named Georges Thibault, arranged for them to be grossly overcharged for all their supplies and conveyances. For instance, the Baroness paid £1,000 to rent a steamer similar to the one that Baker paid £40 to own outright. It is to be presumed that Thibault profited greatly from this and similar transactions.

It is sad to relate that despite their courage and cheerful innocence, the van Capellans met a tragic fate. Leaving their expensive steamer to explore the Bahr al Ghazal, they caught fever and almost all the party died, including the Baroness, the charming Harriet Tinne, the maidservants, and the two European men. Only Alexine, the youngest, survived. She was to meet her destiny years later, killed by Tuareg tribesmen in the Sahara.

Capello, Hermenegildo Augusto de Brito (1839–xxxx). A Portuguese naval officer and explorer, Capello traveled with Ivens and Serpa Pinto to Angola in 1877. When Serpa Pinto went on to the Transvaal, Capello explored much of Angola. In 1884–1885 he and Ivens crossed Africa from Portuguese West Africa to Portuguese East Africa, exploring along the way the Zambezi, Lualaba, and Congo watersheds. Capello was the author of several books, including *From Benguela to Yacca* (1881).

Cardoso, Candido (1805–1880). A Portuguese adventurer and explorer, Cardoso was born in the Mozambique town of Tete. By the late 1830s he had become an important trader and an influential politician. In both capacities (and as President of the Mines Commission from 1857) Cardoso met with important colonial figures such as Livingstone and Kirk. One of the final intrigues of his long life was an unsuccessful 1872 attempt to bring the tribes of the Shire highlands under Portuguese rule.

Carpenter, Geoffrey Douglas Hale (1882–1953). A member of the Royal Zoological Society, Carpenter first came to East Africa in 1910 as a member of the Royal Society's Sleeping Sickness Commission, a post he held until 1913.

He spent the four Commission years studying wildlife on Lake Victoria. One of his tasks was to assess whether crocodiles played any part in the sleeping-sickness cycle. To this end he would tether small crocs and see if the tsetse flies were attracted to them or ignored them (tsetse are notoriously attracted to certain colors and combinations). He once watched as forty tsetse flies bit a captive crocodile in a seventy-minute period, concentrating on the eyelids, back legs, and neck. The results of this and other experiments proved that the flies actually preferred the blood of crocodiles and monitor lizards to that of people.

Another result of Carpenter's observations was the discovery that crocodiles have unusual distribution patterns in waters they inhabit. In Carpenter's study area, Lake Victoria, the saurians were very scarce on the Sese Islands but exceedingly numerous on Tavu Island. There may well be subtle differences in salinity, acidity, temperature, or some other factor that account for this unequal distribution. In Lake Rudolf, for instance, the crocs are overwhelmingly found on the eastern shore (about 75 percent of them on the northeast shore) as opposed to the west.

When war broke out, Carpenter served as a captain in the East African campaign for the duration. By 1930 he was the specialist-in-charge of sleeping sickness for Uganda. He was the author of *A Naturalist on Lake Victoria* (1920) and *A Naturalist in East Africa.*

Carpenter, Robert Ruliph Morgan (1877–1949). Ruli Carpenter was an American businessman (chairman of the board of the DuPont company) from Wilmington, Delaware, who, inspired by Carl Akeley, went to Africa in 1936 to bring back specimens of Cape buffalo for a taxidermy group. His professional hunter was the young Donald Ker. His intended quarry nearly killed him, but in the end Carpenter prevailed and the Philadelphia Academy of Science soon boasted a buffalo habitat group.

Carr, Norman (1912–1997). Another legendary figure whose career is largely beyond the time frame of this volume, Carr started out as an elephant hunter and graduated to a position with elephant control in Northern Rhodesia in 1939. In this capacity he killed several thousand elephant before turning his talents to the creation of Kafue National Park in 1957. He retired from government in 1961 and developed the hunting and tourism business in Zambia's Luangwa Valley.

Carr is credited with popularizing the modern style of conducting Rhodesian hunting safaris on foot and, later, ecotourism. He was an extremely influential and popular figure in Northern Rhodesia—more than eight thousand people attended his funeral in April 1997, including the former president of Zambia, Kenneth Kaunda.

Casati, Gaetano (1838–1902). Major Casati was an Italian explorer of the Egyptian Sudan and second in command to Emin Pasha. He was sent to Africa in 1879 by the Italian Society for Commercial Exploration, under whose auspices he explored the Bahr el Ghazal, the territories of the Nyam-Nyam, and the Monbutto. In 1883 he joined with Emin Pasha and Wilhelm Junker. In 1886 Emin sent him on a diplomatic trip to the Bunyoro king Kabarega. The two men disliked each other on sight, and Kabarega kept the Italian captive for the next three years. Some accounts say Casati was tortured during his captivity; others paint it as a sort of house arrest. At any rate he was released in 1889.

Casati was one of the earliest explorers in the Well-Ubangi River system, but by the time he returned to civilization to publish his findings, they had long been trumped by other travelers.

Most of Casati's journals and papers were lost during his captivity by Kabarega, but he managed to reconstruct events from memory and in 1891 published a two-volume set, *Zehn Jahre in Aequatoria und Die Rueckkehr Mit Emin Pasha (Ten Years in Equatoria and the Return of Emin Pasha)* in Berlin, and *Dieci Anni in Equatoria* in Italy.

Casement, Roger David (1864–1916). Born in Dublin, Casement traveled widely in Africa in his early years. In 1890 he was supervising railway construction in the Congo (where he sometimes lived with the novelist Joseph Conrad) and getting his first look at the Free State administration. In 1892 Casement became consul at Lourenço Marques, then in 1898 transferred to Luanda and subsequently to the Congo. His 1903 report on the use of slave labor in the rubber industry caused a sensation and was a major factor in the dissolution of the Free State and the Belgian annexation of the Congo in 1908.

In 1906 Casement was transferred to Brazil and became consul general in Rio de Janeiro in 1909. Once again he exposed maltreatment of the local people by European overseers—his 1912 report on the practices of the Peruvian Amazon Company was as important as his Congo work, if less remembered today. He was knighted for his services in 1911.

In 1913 Casement helped found the Irish National Volunteers, a republican group, and a year later, at the outbreak of the Great War, he began treasonous communication with Imperial Germany, hoping to use the war to gain Irish independence. He traveled to Germany in late 1914 and toured the German POW camps trying to enlist Irish soldiers in an Irish Brigade for the German army. He found few followers.

Casement returned to Ireland in 1916 on a U-boat that was carrying weapons to the Irish insurgents. There he hoped to persuade the Nationalists to postpone the planned rebellion, largely because he mistrusted German promises that they would send an expeditionary force to assist. The rebellion went off, regardless, on Easter Sunday 1916, and failed. Casement was arrested by the British on 24 April 1916, stripped of his knighthood, and hanged on August 3. Among his private diaries and papers were found numerous proofs of his homosexual activities, especially in Africa, and the British used this fact to further blacken Casement's name.

Cavendish, Henry Sheppard Hart (1876–1948). A British aristocrat, Cavendish first visited Africa on a hunting trip to South Africa in 1895. After reading of Donaldson Smith's Lake Rudolf expedition in his morning newspaper, Cavendish fixed on that location for his next hunt. He also decided to add to British prestige by being the first European to explore the western shore of the lake. Accompanied by a friend, Lt. H. Andrew, Cavendish began following Smith's old track in September of 1896. At one point they met up with the Elliot expedition, on which a young taxidermist named Carl Akeley was soon to meet his famous leopard.

After reaching the Daua River in December 1896, Cavendish and Andrew settled down to some serious elephant hunting, averaging a kill a day. They later claimed to have got along well with the local Boran tribesmen, but reports from Lord Delamere and the British explorer Henry Austin contradict this statement and accused Cavendish (who had a large and well-armed entourage) of robbing and brutalizing the natives. After wearing out their welcome, the party moved on to Lake Stephanie, where Cavendish narrowly escaped being killed by a wounded elephant. The bull spent twenty minutes over his body, trying to crush him with its knees, but Cavendish managed to scramble up near the animal's chin and avoided the full force of the blows. His gunbearers thought him dead, but he actually escaped with just some bad bruises.

Returning to Lake Rudolf, the party shot more elephant and had a number of skirmishes with the local Turkana. Again Austin reported later that Cavendish was the aggressor and greed the motive.

On their trip back to the coast, Cavendish and his friends stopped at Lake Baringo in July 1897. Here Lieutenant Andrew was badly hurt by a rhino. They returned to the coast via the Uganda Railway, which was under construction at the time. By January 1898 Cavendish was accepting the accolades of the Royal Geographical Society. Widely admired as an explorer and considerably richer for his efforts, he became Baron Waterpark in 1932.

Cervera. Under the auspices of the Madrid Geographical Society, a Captain Cervera led an expedition into the Sahara, setting out on 16 June 1886 from Rio de Oro. His object was to explore the Hadrar region, rumored to be lush and well watered. A little more than a month later, on July 24, Cervera and his men staggered out of the desert, half dead from hunger and thirst and continually harassed by the local tribes. The rumors were false.

Chadwick, W. S. An English big-game hunter of the 1920s, he wrote *Man-Killers and Marauders* (1929).

Chaille-Long, Charles (1842–1917). Born in Maryland of French descent (his last name was pronounced with a long "o"), Captain Chaille-Long fought for the Union during the American Civil War, seeing action at Gettysburg. After the war he was recruited by Thaddeus Mott for the Khedive of Egypt. In 1869 Chaille-Long was commissioned a lieutenant colonel in the Egyptian army (his top rank in the Union army was captain). One of his first assignments was to build fortifications along the Suez Canal. Another assignment was as a French instructor at the newly established Egyptian military academy. Chaille-Long was something of a fop, known for his garish uniforms and aristocratic affectations.

Under the Beau Brummel exterior, however, he was tough as nails and well equipped mentally and physically for African exploration. By 1874 he was chief-of-staff to Charles Gordon of Khartoum, and that same year was sent on a lengthy geographic expedition through central Africa. From Gondokoro he led his safari into Uganda, unwisely setting out during the rainy season. It took fifty-eight days to reach the Kabaka's capital near Kampala. The Kabaka, Mutesa, received Chaille-Long peacefully and apparently signed a treaty of alliance with the former Union captain. Chaille-Long presented Mutesa with an electric battery that enthralled the royal court, and managed to procure the loan of forty canoes to be used to cross Lake Victoria.

Mutesa warned him it would take at least a month to cross the lake, but Chaille-Long didn't believe him. The American landed on an island relatively close to the near mainland and mistook it for the far shore.

Accordingly, he was the brunt of much ridicule when he later published his "finding" that Lake Victoria was only about ten miles wide.

The trip back to Gondokoro was eventful and nearly fatal. First the expedition suffered badly from malnutrition, and second they were almost wiped out when attacked by Bunyoro tribesmen near Lake Kioga on 17 August 1874. Chaille-Long and two of his officers were armed with rifles and managed to keep the hostile warriors at a distance, but one group got in close and nearly speared the commander before being shot down. At nightfall the Africans shied away, but it had been a very near thing.

It took another two months before the expedition, suffering from hunger and a variety of tropical diseases, managed to stagger back into Gondokoro. But after a brief recovery period Chaille-Long was back in the saddle. In 1875 he led a new expedition into the Nyam-Nyam country, successfully adding to Egyptian influence and being promoted to full colonel in the process. Subsequently he served in Jubaland.

There was a major upheaval in the Egyptian government in the mid-1870s, and the Khedive was forced to abdicate. Most of the fifty or so American Civil War veterans who had served in Egypt were let go at this time. Chaille-Long was one of the few who were asked to remain, but he decided he'd had enough of Africa. He resigned his Egyptian rank in 1877 and returned to the States. In 1887 he was appointed United States consul general in Korea, capping a rather unique career for a nineteenth-century Maryland boy. He was the author of *Central Africa: Naked Truth About Naked People* (1876) and *Three Prophets: Chinese Gordon, the Mahdi and Arabi Pasha* (1884).

In J. L. Cloudsley-Thompson's *Animal Twilight* he quotes Chaille-Long's journal entry of 17 May 1874 (when Long was with Gordon) as recording that a native a day was falling victim to crocodiles along his stretch of the Nile. Cloudsley-Thompson, an otherwise excellent naturalist who for some reason believed that crocodiles aren't dangerous, dismissed Long's observation as an exaggeration, citing no evidence whatsoever except his own opinion. Eyewitness testimony is notoriously unreliable, but since Chaille-Long was there in 1874 and Cloudsley-Thompson wasn't, I'd like to hear at least some evidence for why Chaille-Long should be discredited. This aspect of *Animal Twilight* (an overall good book, by the way) is a great example of how folks are going to believe what they want to believe, Cambridge education or not. Cloudsley-Thompson felt that crocodiles aren't dangerous, so Chaille-Long must be exaggerating, period. That was that.

Chaillu, Paul Belloni du (1835–1907). The son of a wealthy French trader with business connections in Africa, du Chaillu did some boyhood explorations around his father's store in French West Africa in 1851. After moving to America in 1855, he went on a scientific expedition for the Philadelphia Academy of Natural Sciences from 1855–1859, exploring the flora and fauna of the Congo basin. Du Chaillu was the first Westerner to write about the gorilla and the Pygmies. His reports were considered so fantastic that many thought them a hoax.

Du Chaillu returned to Africa in 1863–1865. His total contribution to Western science was impressive—in pursuit of specimens, he shot more than one thousand mammals and two thousand birds. He also suffered from at least fifty different episodes of malarial fever. Later expeditions took du Chaillu to Lapland and the Arctic Ocean. He died in Saint Petersburg, Russia, in 1907.

Among his other accomplishments, du Chaillu discovered the bongo in Gabon. He was the author of *Explorations and Adventures in Equatorial Africa* (1861), *A Journey to Ashangoland* (1867), *My Apingi Kingdom* (1870), *The Country of the Dwarfs,* (1872), *Adventures in the Great Forest of Equatorial Africa and the Country of the Dwarfs* (1890), and other works not connected with Africa.

Chanler, William Astor (1867–1934). A wealthy orphan, William Astor Chanler was a prominent New York sportsman and big-game hunter and the son of a United States Congressman. A founder of the Boone and Crockett Club, Chanler first hunted Africa in May 1889 at the tender age of twenty-two. That summer he led a 118-man (he was a precise record keeper) safari from south of Kilimanjaro through the lands of the Masai to a point north of Mount Kenya. His friend George Galvin came along for company. On this expedition, Chanler was one of the first Western hunters to witness healthy elephant trying to assist a wounded one. He didn't wind things up until October, heading back to the coast with an impressive assortment of trophies. As far as weaponry goes, Chanler carried a .577 B.P. Express, an 8-bore rifle, and a .450—he believed in being well armed.

This first expedition, basically a hunting trip, was marred by trouble with the African porters. Chanler was young, easy-going, highly educated, and refined, so it was easy to misjudge him, to miss his innate toughness and determination. He was also inexperienced in the ways of the world and made the mistake of paying the men a large advance on salary. Whatever the reason, the porters were mutinous and several deserted. Chanler asserted himself and restored discipline by having some of the more insubordinate men severely flogged. This may seem shocking to modern readers, but it is important to remember that an 1890 safari was essentially a military operation. Expeditions that started out as benign scientific forays often came under attack and were occasionally wiped out. Everyone understood the need for discipline on the march, and corporal punishment was well within the bounds of what was considered acceptable. Sometimes even stronger measures were called for, as will be seen.

After touring Europe and making a trip back home, Chanler and Galvin returned to East Africa. In September 1892 Chanler led another expedition, this one intended to explore Mount Kenya and Lake Rudolf. He was accompanied by George Galvin and Ludwig von Hoehnel, late of the Baron Teleki expedition. The British consul general in Zanzibar, Sir Gerald Portal, had promised his support, but Gen. Lloyd Mathews, nominally Portal's subordinate, did everything he could to disrupt the affair. It is thought that Mathews did not wish to see a rich American succeed in what he felt was England's bailiwick.

William Astor Chanler.

Right at the outset Chanler made another mistake involving the porters. In a hurry to get moving, he hired the first bunch of men he could get his hands on, basically the flotsam and jetsam of Zanzibar and Mombasa. Von Hoehnel was appalled—with his greater experience he had arranged to hire a large group of porters from a reliable Tanganyika community. What was done was done, however, and von Hoehnel reluctantly conceded the issue. Chanler, after all, was footing the bill. Months later Von Hoehnel had the dubious satisfaction of hearing Chanler admit he had made a mistake.

The safari left the port town of Lamu on 18 September 1892. The plan was to follow the Tana River northwest toward Mount Kenya and Lake Rudolf. The party was about sixty-three men strong and consisted of Chanler, von Hoehnel, Galvin, a few Somali camel men, the porters, and twelve Sudanese askaris armed with bolt-action magazine rifles. There was trouble with deserters right from the start, and the entire trip saw a constant reshuffling of staff, with deserting and fired porters being replaced by new men. The size of the crew varied considerably, at times reaching nearly a hundred men. However, these personnel problems caused delays that were rather pleasantly used as good excuses for hunting.

In December 1892 Chanler and von Hoehnel discovered Chanler Falls on the Uaso Nyiro River, and soon after properly mapped Mount Kenya for the first time. Like most explorers of his day, Chanler collected thousands of specimens of small animals and insects, which were later donated to the Smithsonian Institution. The company then headed for what was marked on the map as Lake Lorian and were the first Westerners to discover that the lake was really a big swamp. The air around the swamp was alive with mosquitoes and pestilence, and most if not all of the men came down with malaria and other fevers at this point. The local inhabitants, warriors of the Meru people, also began to harass them, and three porters were speared to death in the next several weeks. If nothing else, the unseen yet constant presence of the lurking warriors cut down the desertion rate.

Once clear of the swamps, however, the porters seemed to decide that they'd had enough. Twenty of them deserted during the next phase of the march. There is suspicion that General Mathews had suborned some of the men, in particular the headman, Hamidi. At any rate, it seems that at this time Chanler attempted to restore discipline by having one of the more recalcitrant deserters shot by a firing squad.

This rash act didn't help matters much. The entire safari was falling apart. On 24 August 1893 von Hoehnel was badly gored by a rhino and had to be carried, almost unconscious, in a litter some 280 miles to the base camp at Daitcho. The march was continually disrupted by other rhino charges; von Hoehnel wrote later that they actually counted some twenty-five such incidents. The animals seem to have been in some sort of mating-season frenzy—at least one other man, a porter, was tossed and killed by a rhino. The other porters (those Chanler hadn't shot) were surly and unhappy, and it was obviously time to call the whole affair off.

Amazingly, Chanler disagreed. Beneath his rich-kid exterior he was hard as nails. He sent Hamidi back to the coast to recruit more porters, nursed von Hoehnel back to health, and prepared to set out again. By December 1893 Chanler was ready to set out, with eighty new porters picked by Hamidi. Once again, however, the nefarious hand of General Mathews played its part. The new porters deserted en masse with much of Chanler's cash and equipment. The safari, like it or not, was at an end.

The aftermath in Mombasa and Zanzibar was marked by bitter anticlimax. The deserters were not punished by the authorities, further evidence of Mathews's complicity in their malfeasance. Chanler was not charged in any way with the firing-squad incident. It was conceded that as the leader of a safari in the field actually undergoing attack by hostile warriors, he was within his rights to run his expedition along military lines. Most of the knowledgeable onlookers who knew the details of the affair sided with Chanler. Mathews's refusal to prosecute the deserters was unprecedented.

Chanler wrote a book about his African expeditions titled *Through Jungle and Desert: Travels in Eastern Africa* (1896). His written version of the porter's death describes it as the result of an accident, not a firing squad. This must have been a ploy to boost sales, or possibly an attempt to avoid tarnishing his political future back in the States, since Chanler freely admitted to the authorities that he'd had the man shot.

After leaving Africa Chanler went to Asia and crossed the continent on a bicycle with his friend James Creelman. This feat earned the two men the Gold Medal of the Traveler's Club of New York. He also served in the Spanish-American War alongside his friends Frederick Remington and journalist Richard Harding Davis. In later life Chanler wrote two novels, both under pseudonyms: *A Man's Game* (1921) by John Brent and *The Sacrifice* (1925) by Robert Hart. He served a term as a United States Congressman (like his father) from 1899–1901 and seems to have run some sort of private spying service in Paris before World War I. In 1910 he fought as an officer in the Turkish army against the Italians at Tripoli.

Chanler was a quixotic man of many contrasts. His toughness and hardness have been noted; he was also thoughtful, generous, and loyal. The shooting of the Swahili deserter was a bit out of character, given that Chanler was known as a level-headed fellow—indeed, Richard Harding Davis called him "the most sensible individual I have yet met." It should also be taken in perspective: Other hunters did the same thing, including Henry Stanley, who during the course of his African explorations sentenced five men to death, two of whom were eventually hanged (the others were released).

Chanler stood by his friends, keeping the less fortunate of them from hitting rock bottom. George Galvin, for instance, never lacked for a job his entire life. Many years after his African adventures were over, with his own health failing (he had a leg amputated after an accident in 1914), Chanler learned that the value of von Hoehnel's Austrian naval pension had been wiped out by ruinous inflation after World War I. In 1929 Chanler sent von Hoehnel a one-time gift of 10,000 French francs (about $40 in 1930s American money—it bought a lot more back then) and two years later began sending regular monthly checks of 1,000 francs each. Chanler arranged matters so that the payments continued even after his own death in 1934.

Chanler's nephew, Col. William C. Chanler, was the influential deputy chief of the United States War Department's Civil Affairs Division during World War II and played a significant part in the prosecution of Nazi war criminals at Nürnberg.

Chapin, James P. (1889–1964). Chapin was an American naturalist associated with Herbert Lang and the American Museum of Natural History. The Belgian government granted Lang the use of facilities from 1909–1915 to use as a base for collecting birds and mammals from the Congo basin. Chapin, a Columbia undergraduate, signed on as Lang's assistant. One of the items he collected proved to be a feather of the Congo peacock, a bird hitherto unknown to Western science.

Chapin didn't realize the significance of his discovery until the 1930s. The feather sat unidentified for years before Chapin came across an identical feather in a European museum and realized that the specimens had been misidentified. Investigation revealed that the European specimen had been donated by a Congo commercial firm in 1914. Chapin recognized that this bird represented at least a new species (it was actually a new genus) and, using the donation records as a geographic guide, took his shotgun to the Ituri in 1937 and collected seven or eight specimens of the newly described Congo peacock *(Afropavo congensis).* This was the first new genus of bird discovered in over forty years and created a sensation in scientific circles.

Chapman, Abel (1851–1929). A rich British sportsman, Chapman was a highly respected hunter, artist, and ornithologist. He was a close friend of Selous and Millais, and late in life corresponded frequently with Dennis Lyell. Chapman was a sportsman of the "wealthy trophy hunter" type. He was likely to pass up an easy shot at a buck with less-than-record horns and return to camp to muse about the day's bad luck over iced champagne. Although the 1928 Rowland Ward book lists him as bagging high-ranking examples of elephant, black rhino, American bison, Cape buffalo, roan antelope, European elk, and Spanish red deer, among others, Chapman is best remembered for his prowess at studying and shooting birds. *His Bird Life of the Borders* and *Art of Wildfowling* are classics of the genre.

In the late 1890s Chapman went on a hunting trip north of the Sabi River in the Transvaal. He was struck by the area's topography and wildlife potential, and in 1900 wrote up a draft proposal for the extension of the Sabi Game Reserve. The detailed proposal included a discussion of the necessary funding and staff. Many of his ideas were eventually carried out by the Reserve administration and the Transvaal government.

Abel Chapman and rhino in Kenya, 1906.

Denis Lyell's *African Adventures* reprints a number of letters to Lyell from Chapman on topics ranging from mutual acquaintances like Stigand to grouse to salmon fishing to biltong to a pet theory of Chapman's called "colour protection." In addition to his books, Chapman was a prolific magazine writer and enjoyed few things more than tossing out a controversial "bomb" and watching other hunters go purple arguing over it. Despite his penchant for controversy, he was generally well liked, being regarded as an affable old uncle who liked to hunt. His other books included *On Safari* (1908), *Savage Sudan* (1921), and *Retrospect* (1928). *Savage Sudan,* Chapman's account of his safari in that country, is an excellent look at hunting in the old days in a region that has been neglected in comparison to the many writings about Somaliland and Kenya.

Chapman, Edward. South African hunter and member of the Chapman-Wood-Francis hunting syndicate, Chapman owned a store at his hometown of Kuruman, which he would leave frequently to hunt elephant. From 1860 he made annual trading trips into Matabeland. In 1864 he met the twenty-one-year-old William Finaughty and hired him to join that year's trip. At the conclusion of this venture Finaughty worked in Chapman's Kuruman store for a while. The two made another commercial junket into Matabeland in 1865. Finaughty stayed in the interior while Chapman continued his pattern of full-time trading and part-time hunting. Like the others of his syndicate, Chapman's preferred method of elephant hunting was to pursue the beasts on horseback, and once the elephant retreated into the tsetse areas, his hunting days were over.

Chapman, James (1831–1872). James Chapman was described by Finaughty in *The Recollections of an Elephant Hunter* as "the famous interior man" and by Harry Johnston in *The Story of My Life* as "the great midnineteenth century explorer." He is known to have traveled with the celebrated Canadian elephant hunter Fred Green, and in 1860 brought a huge wooden camera to Walvis Bay, where he took the first known photographs of South-West Africa and its inhabitants. He was the third European to see Victoria Falls. He might have been the second, but on his first attempt his African guides were afraid to approach the source of the thundering noise any closer than a few miles.

There was still some trepidation on his next, successful attempt, as he wrote in his *Travels*: "We approached the brink with trembling, and, carefully parting the bushes with our hands, looked at once on the first grand view."

A hunter first and foremost, his description of the vast multitude of game found around Victoria Falls—"spoors of elephant, rhinoceros, buffalo, and hippopotami, besides other animals, all over the very brink of the precipice"—was yet another enticement to young Victorian sportsmen to get themselves out to Africa.

Chapman had several long expeditions into the interior, including a hunting trip to Lake Ngami with Sam Edwards in 1856, another expedition to the same area with the Posselt brothers in 1859–1860, and to Hereroland in the early 1860s. During the last-named journey, he declined an invitation to join up with Carl Andersson and wage war against the Orlam Afrikaners and other alleged cattle thieves, and returned to Cape Town.

In the late 1860s Chapman held a variety of government positions in Cape Colony, including a customs post and several stints of supervising convicted criminals. He briefly returned to elephant hunting in South-West Africa in 1870 and had some initial success but quit after a few close calls with wounded tuskers. His son, James Chapman, was a noted explorer in Angola.

Cheesman, Robert E. Major Cheesman was British consul in northwestern Ethiopia in 1925–1934. He had previously served in India, Iraq, and Saudi Arabia. An avid hunter and explorer, he was the author of *Lake Tana and the Blue Nile* (1936). Critically acclaimed, the book was a second version, written from memory, but upon returning to London Cheesman discovered that a thief had stolen the original completed manuscript from his car. The advertisement of a reward brought no relief, and Cheesman had to reconstruct the entire book.

Cherry, William Stamps. Cherry was an American mechanic from Chicago who spent several years elephant hunting in the Congo around the turn of the twentieth century. He first went to Africa as the engineer of a Congo steamer that carried supplies in support of the French expedition under Marchand to Fashoda in 1897. Cherry signed on with the steamship company solely from a desire to earn his passage into the heart of big-game country. He spent the next few years hunting elephants with mixed results. He was a complete neophyte and went after huge animals with a ridiculously small rifle.

After almost getting killed on his very first attempt, Cherry switched to a proper elephant gun but got a bad concussion when he fired both barrels at once. He finally got the hang of it and had fair success for a couple of years before quitting for good about 1905. African cultural artifacts donated by Cherry are in the possession of the Field Museum of Chicago, and have been displayed in New York and Los Angeles.

Christy, Cuthbert (1863–1932). A doctor and naturalist, Christy served on the 1902 Uganda sleeping-sickness expedition, the 1903 Liverpool School of Tropical Medicine expedition to the Congo, and was involved in the African elephant domestication attempts at Api. Christy held government posts in the Congo and the Sudan, and during World War I he served in East Africa and Mesopotamia. He had the unique distinction of twice being savagely attacked by wounded giant forest hogs.

He was the author of *Big Game and Pygmies* (1924), which white hunter R. J. Cuninghame called in a private letter "the best reading I have known for many years" (Lyell, 1935). Considered an expert on the forest buffalo, *Syncerus caffer nanus,* Dr. Christy met his end in the Ituri forest, gored to death by a buffalo.

Churchill, Lord Randolph (1849–1895). Winston's father, Lord Randolph Churchill, went on a well-publicized safari to Mashonaland in 1891, guided by an intrepid huntsman named Hans Lee. On the Transvaal section of the safari Churchill was accompanied by a famous businessman, Alfred Beit, and Percy Fitzpatrick, then a Barberton journalist but later the prosperous author of *Jock and the Bushveld.* Churchill brought an ornate wheelchair as a gift to the Matabele king, Lobengula, who had become stout and troubled by gout over the years.

Other, less useful, items slowed the safari down. Churchill, who apparently had come prepared for any contingency, finally relented and held a public auction of his more frivolous goods at Fort Salisbury, Rhodesia. He made a profit of 300 percent on personal luxuries like cologne, and even made a killing on some trade beads he had bought in South Africa.

Churchill's journal of the expedition was serialized in an English newspaper, the *Daily Graphic.* Once a rising parliamentary star, his career in politics was cut short by syphilis. He was the author of *Men, Mines, and Animals in South Africa* (1892).

Churchill, Winston Leonard Spencer (1874–1965). Few people nowadays realize that Churchill was famous long before the rise of Hitler and World War II, in fact even before World War I and Gallipoli. He was always flamboyant and outspoken, and these attributes, combined with his writings, brought him a significant degree of celebrity early in the century. In a 1909 *McClure's Magazine* article, for example, concerning the upcoming safari of President Roosevelt, author T. R. MacMechen wrote, "Winston Churchill, who was in British East Africa last spring, rode on the pilot of the engine to observe the game. Churchill saw six lions from the train." Note that MacMechen didn't feel it necessary to tell the reader just who Churchill was, even in an American magazine. Among his many other books, Churchill was the author of *My African Journey* (1908).

Churchill served as under-secretary in the Colonial Office from 1906–1911, during which term he toured East Africa and the Sudan. While he respected Baron Lugard who was actively engaged in expanding British interests, Churchill was anxious to curb increasing British commitments in Africa. After Lugard led one bloody punitive trip in 1906 that left two thousand West Africans dead, Churchill wrote to his superior, Lord Elgin, suggesting the Empire withdraw from much of Nigeria. He scoffed at the idea of a "white man's burden": "I see no reason," he wrote, "why savage tribes should not be allowed to eat each other without restraint." Elgin ignored the suggestion. ROWLAND WARD 1928: WHITE-BEARDED WILDEBEEST (NO. 2), ROAN ANTELOPE.

Cigar. A Hottentot and former jockey from Grahamstown, Cigar got his first experience at elephant hunting with Bill Finaughty. It didn't go well. Cigar was nervous around elephant at this stage of his career, and when he got a chance to shoot one he just froze. Finaughty took him off elephant duty and had him hunt rhino. At this he was more successful, killing one with an abnormally thin 46½-inch horn. If the Rowland Ward record book had been published at the time, this trophy would have been well up in the listings.

Cigar later went on to fame hunting with Fred Selous and other "big-name" sportsmen. Selous described him (1883) as a "slight built, active Hottentot possessed of wonderful powers of endurance, and a very good game shot, though a bad marksman at a target. These qualities, added to lots of pluck, made him a most successful elephant hunter." Clearly Cigar had overcome his earlier jitters at confronting the big pachyderms. On one hunt with Selous, he brought down four elephant single-handed, and he is generally considered to have taught Selous the finer points of the sport. Edward Tabler, who wrote the foreword and notes to the 1973 reprint of Finaughty's memoirs, suggested that it may have been hunting on horseback that bothered Cigar. Once he switched to stalking the animals on foot, he became a legend at the game.

Clapperton, Hugh (1788–1827). He was a British explorer who discovered Lake Chad in 1822. Three years later he went on an expedition to Nigeria and died there in 1827.

Clark, James L. (1883–1969). Clark, a graduate of the Rhode Island School of Design, of all places, joined the staff of New York's American Museum of Natural History in 1902. The museum director, Herman C. Bumpus, was interested in the idea of improving taxidermy by the use of sculpting techniques. Early experiments in this regard had failed because nobody on the museum staff was a competent sculptor, so Bumpus solicited the young Clark who was a talented artist.

Clark's first assignment was an American elk. He spent a week at the Bronx Zoo watching the animal and learning its musculature and how it moved. The result was satisfactory. Over the next seven years, Clark was sent on a number of collecting trips to Canada and the American West where he learned the rudiments of big-game hunting and how to properly prepare an animal mount in the field.

Clark got an opportunity to go to East Africa in late 1908 to work as an assistant to the photographer A. Radclyffe Dugmore. Clark's job was to hold a rifle to protect the photographer while he shot pictures of dangerous game. After Dugmore was finished and returned to the States, Clark played the same role for motion-picture photographer Cherry Kearton. This experience taught Clark how to manage an African safari as well as an expedition to collect specimens. It can be said that by 1910 his education was essentially complete.

Clark renewed his connection with the natural history museum and soon began leading his own expeditions into the Dark Continent. He collected buffalo, giraffe, elephant, lion, and rhino, as well as a large assortment of smaller mammals. He also went to Asia where he collected ibex and Marco Polo sheep. During an expedition to the Gobi Desert in 1926, he was captured by Mongolian soldiers (along with writer William Morden) and tortured before

James L. Clark and a bull elephant, Kenya, 1909.

being released; both Clark and Morden later wrote about the episode.

Deeply influenced by Carl Akeley, Clark took over Akeley's "African Hall" exhibit after Akeley's death in 1926. He also constructed an "Asiatic Gallery" along the same lines. Clark's artistry as a sculptor combined with Akeley's tried-and-tested taxidermy techniques produced uniquely lifelike mounts. He was a successful photographer as well, and his several books are enhanced by fine photographic images. Clark was early recognized as one of the great figures in natural history and remained active in the field well into his eighties.

Considering himself first and foremost an artist, Clark was no mean big-game hunter; he personally collected a magnificent lion exhibit in 1928 and often went on safari by himself with only three gunbearers and some water carriers for company. On other trips he was accompanied by professional hunters such as George Hurst. He had the usual assortment of hunting adventures, including being treed by a herd of elephants that were out for blood. On another occasion he was stalking an elephant herd from one side while, unknown to him, professional hunter George Outram and two Russian clients were hunting the same herd from the opposite direction.

Clark's book *Trails of Hunted Animals* (1929) is an excellent representative of the "museum-collector" genre, a bit more comprehensive than most because Clark's activities were not confined to Africa. Alongside the chapters on stalking elephant and rhino, Clark included descriptions of North American and Asian conditions and game. There is a dividing line between natural history/Africana books of the nineteenth and early twentieth centuries, and that split occurred sometime about 1920 or 1930. Around that point authors became much more focused. Your older writers tended to wander, to cram in as much as they could about their travels, whether it was on point or not; sometime in the first half of the last century that changed and writers started becoming more serious and their books much narrower in scope. Perhaps it has something to do with the influx of the "serious scientists" into the field in the 1940s and 1950s. At any rate, part of Clark's charm is that he successfully straddled both worlds. A sharp observer with an artist's eye, he freely roamed through his subject matter, discussing sculpture, African society, safari planning, and elephant hunting with equal competence, yet his scientific methods were those of the twentieth and not the previous century.

In addition to *Trails of the Hunted,* Clark was the author of the classic *Great Arc of the Wild Sheep* (1964), *Good*

F.N. Clarke with a rogue elephant shot near the Lado Enclave.

Hunting (1966), and *In the Steps of the Great American Museum Collector Carl Ethan Akeley* (1968).

Clarke, F. N. Clarke came to Africa in 1904, prospecting for gold around Lake Albert with a partner named MacAlister. MacAlister died of blackwater fever, and Clarke bought a 10.75mm Mauser and switched to elephant hunting. He went up to the Lado Enclave and was very successful hunting with the likes of Billy Pickering and Bob Foran. He did a lot of ivory poaching in the Enclave but quit some months after his close friend Pickering got his head ripped off by an elephant (some sources say it was Clarke who found Pickering's head). Clarke's understanding was that Pickering had just frozen when charged by an elephant, and that's what led to his death.

The same thing happened to Clarke on the Semliki River a few months later. He had a clear shot at a big bull just six yards away but couldn't pull the trigger. He knew then that his nerves were shot and it was time to quit the racket.

Clarke became an assistant game warden back in Kenya in 1919, rising to the position of Acting Warden for the entire country in 1932. He retired to his farm at Nakuru, about a hundred miles northeast of Nairobi. He was still farming there in the 1950s.

Clarkson, Matthew. Clarkson was a friend of Selous who hunted with him, H. C. Collison, and George Wood in Mashonaland in 1877 and 1878. He was no slouch as a hunter: One day he and Wood bagged eight bull elephant, and another day he and Selous took five more. In March of 1879 Clarkson was leaving Klerksdorp with Collison and another hunter named French, heading for a rendezvous with Selous, when a thunderstorm brewed up. Clarkson was sitting in his wagon talking with Collison when he was struck in the head by a bolt of lightning and died instantly. Collison was knocked unconscious but recovered.

Clochette, Michel (xxxx–1897). Captain Clochette was a French explorer sent from Abyssinia toward the Nile in August of 1897, during the Fashoda crisis. Like the later Bonchamps expedition, Clochette's safari was a political move disguised as an expedition of discovery. He was given a budget of 100,000 francs (Bonchamps received only 55,000) and was assured of the Ethiopian Emperor Menelik's support. That support proved ephemeral—Clochette and his men wandered through the uncharted wastes of western Abyssinia until he was kicked in the stomach by his horse, which ruptured his liver, and he died a slow and painful death. The expedition fizzled out.

Clutterbuck, Charles Baldwin (1871–1957). Clutterbuck, the father of Beryl Markham, attended public school at Reston and was commissioned a lieutenant in the King's Own Scottish Borderers in 1890. He served in Burma in 1891 but spent the major part of his military career back in England, hunting and attending to the various other duties (largely social) of a Victorian officer.

Compelled to resign in 1897, probably because of debt (the official notice said it was for being absent without leave), Clutterbuck married Clara Alexander and fathered two children before relocating to Kenya in the early 1900s. He tended horses for Lord Delamere and settled at Njoro. There his wife Clara promptly deserted him. In her defense, she was unable to make the psychological transition from life in the staid English countryside to being a pioneer wife on the African frontier. She ran off with an army officer, taking her son with her, and didn't see her daughter Beryl for many years. Clara married the officer, Harry Alexander, in 1914; he was killed on the Western Front four years later.

Charles Clutterbuck built a large farm and played the traditional role of the British colonist, overseeing various agricultural projects and supervising the hundreds of African workers who lived on his land. He was an occasional elephant hunter and is known to have visited the Lado Enclave with the Craven brothers. One day in early 1906 Clutterbuck went elephant hunting on the Mau Plateau. He wounded an old bull that got away. The next day Clutterbuck followed up the trail and found that the bull had died in a small stream where it had sat down to try to quench its thirst. The huge creature's body acted as a dam and diverted the water into a new underground channel, which it followed for more than a mile before resurfacing.

An expert trainer of racehorses, Clutterbuck moved to Peru in the 1920s and for years was a successful horse trainer in South Africa. He was often out of contact with his famous daughter Beryl, but there was no permanent breach between them. When he died in 1957, still working with horses, he left most of his estate to his second wife, but his "best horse" was bequeathed to Beryl. Unfortunately, health regulations prohibited transporting horses from South Africa to Kenya, so she was never able to claim her legacy.

Codrington, Robert Edward (1867–1908). A graduate of Marlborough College, Codrington became a sergeant in the Bechuanaland Police in 1889. He saw combat in the Matabele War and then joined the Foreign Office, being assigned first to Nyasaland. In July 1898 he became deputy administrator of North-East Rhodesia (a British South African Company post) and was administrator from 1900 to 1907. In April 1907 he became administrator of North-West Rhodesia, a post he held until his death eighteen months later. A stern man, he left his mark on the Rhodesias by establishing an honest and efficient civil service, hiring young, well-educated men straight from England, and eschewing local patronage.

Coetsee, Jacobus. A farmer from Piketberg in South Africa, Coetsee was the premier Boer elephant hunter of his day. In 1775, accompanied by ten African retainers, he claimed to be the first European to explore up to the Gariep River. In reality, another Boer ivory hunter, Pieter De Bruyn, had beat him by a few decades. At any rate, Coetsee guided another expedition under his friend Hendrik Hop to the same vicinity in 1760.

Coetser, J. J. He was appointed game ranger of the Sabi Reserve in 1919 and assigned to the reserve's extreme north. He called the new station he built Punda Maria. The nice explanation was that he confused the Swahili term for zebra, which is *punda miliya*—that is, "donkey stripes." Those less charitable pointed out that a literal translation was "donkey Maria," which just happened to be the name of his wife, who left him in short order. He later destroyed his career by trying to ingratiate himself with a prominent (and unusually honest) politician by offering to let him hunt in the otherwise off-limits reserve.

Coillard, Francois (1834–1904). An influential French missionary of the Paris Missionary Society, Coillard arrived in Cape Colony in 1857 and Basutoland in 1858. His twenty years in Basutoland gave him a great deal of influence among the Africans of the region. In 1877 he tried to open a new mission among the Matabele but was rebuffed by Lobengula. Coillard and his associates, including his wife Christina (nee Mackintosh, married 1861 and died 1891), moved on to set up with Lobengula's enemy, Khama. In 1884, assisted by the trader George Westbeech, Coillard established a mission and mission school in Barotseland. With the exception of two years spent in France putting together his classic book *On the Threshold of Central Africa* (1898), Coillard stayed in Barotseland from 1886 until his death in 1904.

Cole, Galbraith Lowry Egerton and Reginald Berkeley Cole. Berkeley Cole (1882–1925) and his brother Galbraith (1881–1929) were younger sons of the earl of Enniskillen. Their half-sister Florence was the first wife of Lord Delamere. Galbraith went out to East Africa in 1903 and Berkeley followed three years later. Galbraith, an expert on sheep, set up a thirty-thousand-acre ranch northwest of Nairobi at Elmentaita while his brother established his own cattle ranch at Londiani and a farm at Mount Kenya. Both men had health issues, Galbraith severe arthritis and Berkeley a weak heart. This did not prevent them from vigorously pursuing busy lives of farming, hunting, and public service.

Berkeley fought in the Boer War in 1900 and later was western Kenya's elected member of the Legislative Council for five years, where he actively promoted better education and railway development. He never married—his doctors suggested it would somehow tax his heart—but he did keep a faithful and much-loved Somali mistress. He was the founder of the Muthaiga Club, which he started after becoming disgusted with the pretensions of the British government officials at the Nairobi Club.

When war broke out in 1914 Berkeley formed an irregular unit of eight hundred Somali riflemen known as "Cole's Scouts" that performed invaluable reconnaissance and skirmishing duties. Photographs of the Scouts show their ponies painted with stripes so as to resemble zebra. For a while Berkeley's close friend Denys Finch Hatton worked with the outfit. The Scouts, great fighters but averse to military discipline, were eventually disbanded, and both Berkeley and Finch Hatton joined the staff of the regular British army establishment in East Africa.

Galbraith and Berkeley Cole.

In November 1918 the Masai erupted in revolt, largely because of perverse British wartime policies. The final straw had come when Imperial officers tried to forcibly conscript two hundred fifty Masai warriors into the regular armed forces. The Masai blooded their spears on several Indian farm owners, and the entire province braced for battle. Berkeley was instrumental in persuading the colonial authorities to drop the demand for conscription and thus helped restore peace.

After the war Berkeley continued with his agricultural and social activities (he was close to Karen Blixen, author of *Out of Africa*, and Elspeth Huxley described him as having "fine looks, supple conversation, gray eyes, and a gay Irish wit"), but his health was failing fast. He was frequently ordered to bed for extended periods. On 21 April 1925 he died at his farm on the slopes of Mount Kenya, his passing much regretted.

His brother Galbraith arrived in Kenya in 1903. He was the first European man (after their discoverer) to see Thomson's Falls. When Berkeley joined him, Galbraith established a huge sheep ranch at Elmentaita called Keekopey.

In 1911 Galbraith was deported from British East Africa in an unusual legal move. He had caught three Masai warriors rustling sheep on his ranch. When one of them tried to run away, Galbraith, who had suffered serious losses to sheep thieves, shot and killed him. He was tried for murder and acquitted on the spurious grounds of "justifiable homicide." The British government, unwilling to place the value of a sheep higher than that of a man, ordered him deported for "inciting racial enmity," a little-used provision of the Indian Penal Code (Indian law applied in British East Africa).

The situation was particularly sensitive because a similar acquittal of a white man who had killed a black man had just taken place in Rhodesia, and the civilized world was beginning to wonder about British colonial justice. The authorities gave Cole an out—if he stated he was not aiming to kill the poacher but merely trying to stop him, the deportation order would be cancelled. Galbraith refused. He had warned the Masai that he would kill them if they stole his stock, and he had meant it. He had shot to kill. It was not for nothing that his African name was Debr Lao, or "one-tongue" (as in one who speaks only the truth). His honest if impolitic answer sealed his fate.

Cole was deported in 1911. For a short time he lived in German East Africa, but by the outbreak of war he was back in British territory illegally, under the alias of "Egerton." The deportation order was lifted in October 1914, and he returned to his ranch at Keekopey.

His arthritis kept him off active service during World War I. In 1918 he married Lady Eleanor "Nell" Balfour, a niece of the former prime minister. Karen Blixen described her in a 12 August 1918 letter as "an extremely nice, sweet girl." They had some happy years together, but Galbraith's deteriorating health foreshadowed his doom. He took to crutches, but with indomitable spirit he even followed up a wounded lion and killed it in the bush while balancing on his "sticks." By October 1929 daily life had become unbearable. In her last act of love Nell loaded his revolver and then went out for a walk. Galbraith Lowry Egerton Cole, lion hunter, had to ask his Somali servant to brace his arm steady so that he could pull the trigger and end his own life at age forty-eight.

Cole, Vernon. District commissioner at Voi in 1931. Denys Finch Hatton spent the night before his fatal plane crash (14 May 1931) visiting with Cole and his wife Hilda. Other guests included John A. Hunter. In the morning, Finch Hatton packed his cockpit with citrus fruit from Hilda's garden and flew off. Hunter and Cole recovered several charred oranges from the wreckage of the plane.

Colenbrander, Johann (1856–1918). Colenbrander was one of the many outstanding scouts and hunters who hailed from Natal. At one time he was as famous as his contemporary, Frederick Selous, but he is largely forgotten today. His parents emigrated from Holland in 1849, and Johann was born seven years later. He grew up on a remote farm and played with the local Zulu kids, learning their language as well as English and Dutch.

Colenbrander fought in the Anglo-Zulu War of 1879 and earned himself the epithet "White Whirlwind" for his energy and bravery in action. At war's end he stayed in the area and became friendly with Zibhebhu, the leader of the Mandlakazi Zulus, one of the factions struggling to regain what little internal power remained in the conquered kingdom. When civil war broke out in 1883, Colenbrander was one of five white advisers assisting Zibhebhu in his campaign against Cetshwayo and his uSuthu faction. The uSuthu were smashed, seemingly decisively, at the Battle of oNdini on 21 July 1883. Colenbrander played a part in the battle and especially in the pursuit of the retreating uSuthu, most of whose leaders were slaughtered in the massacre that followed the battle. "Being all fat and big-bellied," he wrote, "they had no chance of escape."

The surviving uSuthu attempted to save themselves by making a deal with the devil—they applied to their traditional enemies, the Boers, for help. The uSuthu and their new allies launched an offensive under the command of Cetshwayo's son Dinuzulu and began to regain their lost ground. The four other white advisers promptly deserted Zibhebhu, but Colenbrander remained loyal to the cause. In an attempt to even the scales, he went to Natal, where he advertised in local newspapers for mercenaries to join the Mandlakazi side. The ads promised "satisfactory remuneration," but the response was small. He had recruited only a few "filibusters" (he claimed twenty, but other sources said half that number) before the Natal authorities shut him down. The last thing they wanted to see was Europeans embroiled on both sides of a Zulu civil war. Colenbrander's return to Zululand was blocked by uSuthu scouts, and before he could slip past them the war ended with a decisive uSuthu victory at Tshaneni on 5 June 1884. The Boers took the best farmland in the Zulu kingdom as a reward for their participation.

Colenbrander moved next to Matabeleland and served as the agent for the British South African Company at Bulawayo in the early 1890s. He also worked as one of Lobengula's interpreters and fostered a fairly close relationship with the Matabele king. During the crisis of 1893 Colenbrander was one of the few Europeans at Bulawayo who believed (or claimed to believe) that Lobengula wanted war with the British. Others in a position to know, like the trader James Dawson and the missionaries John S. Moffatt and C. D. Helm, felt that Lobengula wanted peace. Colenbrander played a double game: His dire telegrams to Cecil Rhodes, the head of the BSAC (see glossary), played a major part in the chartered company's decision to invade. He also passed on reports of German agents operating in Matabeleland, as a further spur to Rhodes and the BSAC.

Moffatt and others considered that Colenbrander deliberately misrepresented the facts in order to give the chartered company an excuse to topple the Matabele nation. In a letter to his wife in October 1893, Moffatt wrote that Colenbrander "squirmed about and was evidently very uncomfortable" when the missionary confronted him with the evidence of his duplicity. According to Moffatt, Colenbrander claimed that Rhodes had ordered him to report everything he heard, whether he believed it or not. This was disingenuous to say the least, for it appears clear that Colenbrander had strongly advocated British intervention. To be fair, Matabele internal politics were complex, and even if Lobengula himself did want peace (which seems likely), it was a peace on Lobengula's terms, and besides, it was by no means certain that even that legendary despot could restrain his young warriors from raiding British territories. At the end of the sharp but short war, Colenbrander was rewarded by the BSAC with a farm near Bulawayo.

In the 1896 Matabele and Mashona rebellion Colenbrander organized a hundred fifty South Africans into an irregular unit called the "Cape Boys" and participated in the fighting around Bulawayo. He later served as a British colonel during the Boer War, commanding an independent column and a light cavalry battalion called Kitchener's Flying Scouts.

In the early 1900s Colenbrander, who seems to have had no talent for money, was involved in a series of unsuccessful business ventures. One gets the impression of a man barely keeping his head above water. One of his more successful affairs was a contract to dispose of surplus horses and mules for the British army after the war ended. He sold many of these animals in the Transvaal, including a number to Major Stevenson-Hamilton and the nascent staff of the Sabi Game Reserve. Colenbrander was married three times, to Mollie Mullens (1883), Yvonne Nunn, and Kathleen Gloster (1911), and had at least three children.

Colenbrander met an unusual death for an African adventurer, perishing during the making of a motion picture, of all things. In 1918 he was hired to help recruit laborers for the movie *The Symbol of Sacrifice,* produced by I. W. Schlesinger. Colenbrander played the part of Lord Chelmsford in the film, and also did what would today be called stunt work. This latter role proved his undoing. He died senselessly, drowning on film while swimming across the Klip River. The South African writer Tom V. Bulpin wrote a somewhat fictionalized version of his life, *The White Whirlwind* (1961).

Collins, Alfred. Collins, an American naturalist, led a 1924 expedition (along with Heller of the Field Museum) to collect two gorillas in the region west of Lake Kivu. Alexander Barns was brought along as professional hunter. Barns gave up after a while, but the two Americans persevered and got their gorillas.

Colvile, Gilbert de Previle (1888–1966). The only son of Gen. Sir Henry Colvile (1852–1907), Gilbert graduated from Sandhurst Military College and was preparing to accept his commission when he accidentally shot off several of his own toes while hunting rabbits. The injury disqualified him from military service, and he immigrated to East Africa soon after his father's death in 1907. He quickly "went native," living in a shack and wearing improperly tanned skins for clothing. His mother, the widow Lady Colvile, built a hotel near Gilgil that she ran until her death in 1930.

Gilbert Colvile was an odd man, small, miserly, eccentric, and misanthropic. He was more at ease with the Masai than with his own people, and indeed became a great one for lion hunting, shooting more than two hundred fifty in his career. He was something of a pyromaniac, and on at least two occasions he set fire to small islands that belonged to a neighbor, who was using them as a bird sanctuary.

He may have been hostile and violent, but he was not stupid. His first ranch, Ndabibi, consisted of forty thousand acres north of Lake Naivasha. Colvile was a shrewd businessman and one of those people who knew where every dollar he ever made had gone. Eventually he owned five ranches with a total area of more than a quarter-million acres. The largest holding was one hundred sixty thousand acres at Lariak. More than twenty thousand head of cattle grazed his lands, and in his time he was possibly the richest man in Kenya.

In the early 1940s, however, after the murder of a man named Joss Errol, Colvile struck up a friendship with the widow of the suspected murderer, Diana Broughton (nee Caldwell). A more mismatched pair could hardly be imagined. Diana Broughton was a renowned socialite given to luxury and hedonism, Colvile a slovenly old grouch. The two shocked Kenya, however, by marrying and staying married, apparently happily, for twelve years. Diana smoothed some of Gilbert's rougher edges while he taught her to ride and hunt. The couple had one son, who died in infancy. They also adopted a daughter.

Eventually, however, they drifted apart and divorced. Diana married Tom Delamere, and Gilbert Colvile retired to Oserian, the mansion he had built for her, often living quite happily in a shabby hut on the estate's grounds. He was a lonely man in his old age—his closest friends (other than the Masai) were his ex-wife and her new husband. He suffered a stroke in 1966 and died shortly thereafter. ROWLAND WARD 1928: LECHWE (NORTH-WEST RHODESIA), BUFFALO.

Colvile, Sir Henry (1852–1907). Henry Colvile (also erroneously spelled Colville) was born in Kirkby Mallory, Leicestershire, on 10 July 1852. He came from a distinguished family: His father, Col. Charles Robert Colvile, was a member of Parliament in 1841–1849 and again in 1865–1868, while his mother, Katharine Russell, was the daughter of a Royal Navy captain and the twenty-third Baroness de Clifford. The family was also related to the duke of Bedford. Young Henry Colvile was commissioned as a lieutenant in the Grenadier Guards in 1870 and by 1884 was a captain in the intelligence section in Sudan. He fought in the battles of Tel-el-Kebir and Tamai in 1884 and was twice mentioned in dispatches.

Later that same year he was placed in charge of a unit that was to specifically rescue Charles Gordon from Khartoum. Unfortunately, the entire army reached the capital days after Gordon's death. Colvile was knighted (CB) on 25 August 1885 as a reward for his service, and was promoted to colonel a year later. During his career he was mentioned in dispatches numerous times and acquired a reputation as one of the British army's best intelligence officers.

Colvile was assistant commissioner of Uganda from 1893 to 1895. In Uganda he led the campaign against the African king Kabarega, an old enemy of the Buganda Kabaka, Mwanga. He wrote a book about the campaign called *The Land of the Nile Springs* (1895), and was made KCMG (see glossary) in 1895, as well as being promoted to major general three years later.

Colvile was placed in charge of the 9th Division during the Boer War but was relieved of his command after an unfortunate series of events. A column under General Broadwood was ambushed and destroyed by the Boers at Sanna's Post on 30–31 March 1900, and

Colvile arrived too late to rescue them. Lord Roberts blamed Colvile for the disaster, claiming the intelligence officer reacted lethargically to the news of the ambush. Two months later Colvile was in a similar situation and, incredibly, reacted the same way. He had been ordered by Lord Roberts to take the town of Heilbron and was carrying out his orders when he received an urgent appeal from a Colonel Spragge, who was surrounded with his men at Lindley. Colvile stuck to his orders and ignored the appeal, a decision that spelled doom for his military reputation. Lord Roberts sacked him, and Colvile was sent to command a brigade at Gibraltar.

Unfortunately for Colvile, his nemesis Lord Roberts became commander-in-chief of the British army in November 1900. One of his first acts in that capacity was to ship Colvile home in disgrace. In January 1901 Colvile was placed on the retired list. He responded to the charges with a self-justifying book, *The Work of the Ninth Division* (1901).

Sir Henry went home to Bagshot in Surrey. On 24 November 1907 he was riding a motorized bicycle when he drove headfirst into an automobile and died within minutes. His other books included *The Accursed Land* (1884), an account of a cartographic survey of Jordan, and *The History of the Soudan Campaign* (1889). His son, Gilbert Colville, became one of the richest men in East Africa.

During the early 1890s, the reign of the British-supported Kabaka in Uganda, Mwanga, was threatened by his rival, Kabarega. Col. Sir Henry Colville led the chief British force involved, a well-disciplined battalion of some four hundred Sudanese. While Colville and his men were pursuing Kabarega's army, the rebel king tried two powerful charms to stop the British advance. Kabarega's spiritual advisers assured him these would work. The first charm was to impale a man. When that failed to hinder Colville, the second charm was resorted to. This one involved burying a ram alive, with only its head showing, in the center of the path the British were expected to take. This charm also failed to work as desired.

Comber, Thomas James (xxxx–1887). Comber was a British missionary and explorer in the Congo and Cameroon in the 1870s–1880s. After service in the Cameroons, he was sent to the Congo with George Grenfell in 1878, first on a short trip and then, in June 1878, on an extended expedition to the interior. They reached the Tungwa territory but were turned back by the chief of the Tungwa, one Bwaka-Matu. Comber returned to London, giving a lecture on the subject before the Royal Geographical Society early in 1879.

Comber returned to West Africa later in 1879, accompanied by his wife, who unfortunately died in short order. After a brief period of mourning, Comber set out to find a new route from the town of San Salvador overland to Stanley Pool, through the Makuta district south of the Congo. The problem, as it had been before, was the Tungwa tribe. Three times Comber and his companions, John S. Hartland and H. E. Crudgington, set out to establish the new trail but were turned back each time. On the fourth try, in the fall of 1880, Comber and Hartland and the one porter who hadn't already deserted were attacked by villagers in one of Bwaka-Matu's towns and struck with sticks and stones. As the missionaries retreated, Comber was shot in the middle of the back. The bullet apparently went straight through his body without striking his lungs or any vital organs. Comber managed to struggle to his feet, and the three men ran for miles, finally escaping their pursuers. Other villagers harassed them with rocks and threatened them with knives, but they covered eighty miles in three days and reached safety in San Salvador. Once there, Comber almost immediately achieved further distinction by becoming the first recorded Congo missionary to come down with blackwater fever.

Despite these hardships, Comber continued attempting the southern route to Stanley Pool. He was nothing if not persistent, and made a staggering thirteen attempts over the next several years. Meanwhile, in 1881 Crudgington and another man by the name of Bentley walked some five hundred miles in forty-three days, reaching Stanley Pool and back again by going north of the Congo. Bentley's achievement prompted the group's friends in London to ship out a collapsible steel boat named the *Plymouth*, which Comber and the others assembled on the upstream side of the Congo cataracts. They used the *Plymouth* to establish the first upstream British mission station at Wathen, across from the French post at Manyanga.

Comber continued his Congo explorations and his missionary work for the next six years. He paid a great price for his devotion to the cause, succumbing to fever in 1887.

Conan Doyle, Sir Arthur (1859–1930). The creator of Sherlock Holmes was much interested in African affairs, particularly in South Africa. During the Boer War he worked as senior physician in a British field hospital and was knighted in 1902 for his service to the Crown. Conan Doyle wrote two books on that conflict, *The Great Boer War* (1900) and *The War in South Africa: Its Cause and Conduct* (1902).

After losing his son in World War I, Conan Doyle found solace in spiritualism. He became a firm believer in the biological existence of fairies and was a great supporter of the poorly faked Cottingsley fairy photographs. Indeed, the fact that such a distinguished and intellectually inclined public figure endorsed the photos was largely responsible for giving the hoax what credibility it had. In the 1920s Conan Doyle visited southern Africa to lecture on fairies and went on safari to Rhodesia to search for them. He was unsuccessful. He did not view fairies as psychic or supernatural beings but rather as actual zoological entities that were somehow obscured from normal viewing. Two of his books on the subject were *The Coming of the Fairies* (1921) and *Our African Winter* (1929). In these works he adopted the traditional stance of the paranormally inclined, a concept that has since been amplified by many UFO-ologists and cryptozoologists—that is, scoffing at those who disagreed with him as being "close-minded." There is a fine line between being open-minded and having a hole in your head.

Connaught, Duke of (1850–1942). Born Prince Arthur William Patrick Albert, the third son and seventh child of Queen Victoria, he was the godson of the duke of Wellington and was born on the duke's eighty-first birthday. Prince Arthur had his problems as a child, including a severe case of smallpox in 1867, but he graduated the Royal Military Academy at Woolwich in 1868 and was commissioned as a lieutenant in the Royal Engineers. In 1870 he saw action as an officer of the Rifle Brigade against the Irish Fenian rebels in Canada and showed signs of great courage. In 1873, by then a captain, he visited his sister in her Grand Duchy of Hesse-Darmstadt, where he immensely enjoyed hunting wild boars with a spear. Originally a somewhat reckless partygoer, he was cured of that during a trip to Rome in 1874—the late nights of drinking and womanizing sated his curiosity. Then he began to look for more responsible ways of enjoying life.

In particular Prince Arthur began working tirelessly on his military duties, and in 1876 his hard work was rewarded with the command of his old unit, the first battalion of the Rifle Brigade. Three years later he fell in love with and married Princess Louise Margaret Alexandra Victoria Agnes, the third daughter of the so-called "Red Prince," Prince Frederick Charles Nicholas of Prussia. In an age of arranged royal marriages, the emotional love affair was unique. Queen Victoria at first had reservations about her son's new bride, but an initial visit from the vivacious and intelligent Princess Louise soon won her over. The couple remained happily married until the Princess's death in 1917.

Prince Arthur, who became the duke of Connaught and Strathearn and the earl of Sussex in 1874, was serious about the army and refused to take undue advantage of his high birth to further his career. In the late 1870s he was offered the opportunity to skip a rank and go straight from lieutenant colonel to brigadier, but he refused, stating that he had risen properly through the commissioned ranks so far and did not want to miss out on the experience of being a colonel. This dedication would be noteworthy in any age, and was particularly so in class-conscious Victorian Britain.

The duke served in the 1882 Egyptian campaign (mentioned in dispatches three times) and later went on an extended hunting trip up the Nile. In the early 1880s he was assigned to India and became, as lieutenant general, commander of the Bombay district in 1886. He held this post for four years, and both he and the duchess took a deep and enduring interest in Indian affairs, even learning to speak the local language, something all too few British officers did during the Raj. His overriding ambition was to become either commander-in-chief of India or commander-in-chief of the army, but for political reasons the various prime ministers of his time felt unable to recommend the appointment. His entry in the *Dictionary of National Biography* describes the duke as being "extremely vexed" over this turn of events. Based on his military record, it appears that he should have been capable of the job, but the British government around the turn of the last century was sensitive to charges of nepotism, and there was no lack of qualified candidates (such as Lord Roberts and Kitchener) who could perform the duties of a commander-in-chief without causing a political firestorm. It does seem a discouraging way of rewarding a hard-working and by all accounts conscientious officer.

The duke idled away at lesser posts such as commander of the Portsmouth district and of the school at Aldershot. In 1899 Connaught was in line to become duke of Saxe-Coburg-Gotha, the reigning prince having died early that year. After some hesitation, he (and his son Arthur) renounced his rights to the duchy and it descended to Charles Edward, the duke of Albany. Three years later Connaught was promoted to field marshal and, shortly afterward, became inspector general of the army.

The duke and duchess of Connaught went on a celebrated East African safari in 1910. Their entourage gives an indication of how royalty hunted in style: It included two professional hunters including Philip

Percival, a lady-in-waiting, an equerry (officer in charge of horses), two headmen, eight Somali gunbearers, fourteen askaris, four cooks, a baker, five Kikuyu teamsters for the mules, and a variety of other African staff. This trip and a subsequent one to South Africa the following year were made in connection with his official duties as inspector general.

The year 1911 saw Connaught begin a term as governor general of Canada, one of the most prestigious posts in the Empire. He governed with much pomp and circumstance, and the fact that a son of the great queen held the post certainly helped foster Canadian interest in the war against Germany. He ran into some constitutional trouble, however, for it was decidedly difficult for an experienced and dedicated professional soldier to keep from sticking his nose into Canadian military affairs, where legally it did not belong. This understandable tendency led to a bitter feud with the Canadian minister of Militia, Sir Sam Hughes. The minister was, admittedly, a tough man to get along with and an eccentric veteran of the Boer War.

In 1916 Connaught's term ended, and he found himself in a sort of semiretirement. His wife had passed away in 1917, so the duke toured the Mediterranean area immediately after the war and went hunting up the Nile once again. In 1921 he visited India and later that year suffered another personal tragedy when his eldest daughter, the crown princess of Sweden, died suddenly.

After 1928 he seldom went abroad, restricting himself largely to entertaining guests at his homes in England and southern France. He was extremely proud of his military service and reveled most in the honor of having been made an honorary junior officer of the elite French Chasseurs Alpins. Connaught was active in Freemasonry and became grand master of the United Lodge in 1901. His son and heir Arthur died in 1938, and with the death of his daughter Margaret in 1921 and the marriage of his other daughter Victoria to a lower station in the peerage, the duchy and the Earldom of Sussex went to his grandson, the earl of Macduff, upon Connaught's death in 1942. Thus both peerages went extinct. ROWLAND WARD 1928 (THE DUKE): BUFFALO.

Conrad, Joseph (1857–1924). This Polish novelist (a naturalized British citizen as of 1886) authored such works as *Heart of Darkness, Lord Jim, Typhoon,* and *The Mirror of the Sea.* During the 1880s Conrad served in the British merchant marine (rated as third mate 1880, first mate 1883, master 1886).

In 1890 Conrad visited Africa as an employee of the Societe Anonyme Belge pour le Commerce du Haut-Congo, sailing upriver to the Belgian station at Matadi, where he stayed for fifteen days, rooming with Roger Casement, a manager of the Congo railway construction company. Casement later was a major opponent of the Free State administration and was hanged by the British for treason in 1916 after an attempt to align Ireland with Germany in World War I. Conrad then went on a grueling overland march through the jungle past Stanley Falls, where he was to take command of an inland steamer. Finding his ship disabled, he transferred to the SS *Roi des Belges* as mate and spent two months steaming from Stanley Falls to Kinshasa.

Conrad's Congo experience lasted less than a year, but it had lasting effects. His health was ruined: He suffered from dysentery, fever, and gout and permanently lost much of his innate physical strength. Something inside him changed too, and 1890 marks a threshold between Conrad the reflexive sailor and Conrad the thinking writer. The two stories he wrote based on the Congo, *An Outpost of Progress* and *Heart of Darkness,* are dark and riddled with irony and moral poverty.

Conrad spent the rest of his life in England and was rewarded with a government pension in 1905. At the outset of World War I he was trapped with his family on holiday in Poland and barely escaped back to the West, assisted by the American ambassador to Austria-Hungary, Frederic Penfield. Conrad was offered a knighthood in 1924 but declined the honor. He died suddenly from heart failure on 3 August 1924 and was buried at Canterbury.

Conus, Adrien. Of mixed French and Russian descent, Conus first came to French Equatorial Africa in the 1920s as an engineer. Quickly taking to his rifles, he established himself as a premier elephant and rhino hunter as well as a successful gold prospector. He was one of those hunters who, like Taylor and Lyell, could aptly be called a "gun nut." When France tightened up its game laws in the late 1930s, Conus ostensibly went into the transport business, but rumors persisted that he was still involved in ivory poaching.

With the coming of Hitler's war and the fall of France, Conus joined the Free French and played a role in keeping the Ubangi-Shari in the Allied camp. He served in the North African campaign, fighting at Bir Hakeim and other battles. In 1943, as a major, he was transferred to intelligence work in England, from where he conducted several missions in occupied Europe. Legend has it that he was once actually up in front of a German firing squad before he could escape. In

1945, with the Allied forces moving up to the Rhine, Conus volunteered for a dangerous rescue mission behind Nazi lines. Not only did he return with the freed prisoners, he also came across a German nobleman's hunting lodge and "liberated" the man's expensive sporting rifles. He later served briefly in Indochina during the Vietnam-French war.

Back in Africa, Conus was appointed game warden of French Equatorial Africa. This surprised some who recalled his past as a poacher, but the French were merely copying the British practice that had worked successfully so many times. Rushby, Ionides, Adamson, and others had all technically "poached" ivory before taking jobs with the game department. In those days poaching of that kind was not considered morally reprehensible, as it would be later. It was like cheating on your taxes—so long as the poacher was white and refrained from unsportsmanlike methods of killing his prey.

Conus found, however, that his health was no longer up to active life in the bush. He spent a considerable amount of time in a hospital in France, trying to recover from the ravages of various chronic tropical diseases. Knowing he was dying, he went on one last safari to Bangui. Accompanied by his longtime tracker and friend, Zoum M'Bala (Sango for "elephant man"), Conus found the trail of a bull and followed it. His fever raging and his heart failing, he caught up with the tusker near a swamp. His heart beat its last as he squeezed the trigger of the big Express rifle. Fulfilling the ambition of many a great huntsman, Col. Adrien Conus died in the actual act of shooting one last elephant.

Cook, Sir Albert (1870–1950). Dr. Albert Cook (he obtained his M.D. in 1901) arrived in East Africa in 1897, accompanied by fifteen other missionaries, three of whom were women (one of them, a Katharine Timpson, he would marry four years later). The party landed at Mombasa and walked to Uganda, virtually every member developing malaria and other tropical ailments on the march. By February 1897 they had reached the Kabaka Mwanga's capital at Mengo, near Kampala, and established their mission. At first Cook was ordered by the mission leader to concentrate on saving souls and not lives, and so he had little opportunity to practice medicine for almost the first year. Only when Uganda erupted in a virtual religious civil war in late 1897 were his restrictions removed and Cook allowed to tend to the wounded and sick.

Cook built a mud infirmary with a floor made of cow dung—it was found that the dung suppressed chiggers. The doctor was immediately busy dressing wounds and working with the various tropical ailments such as malaria, blackwater fever, elephantiasis, dysentery, and snakebite. According to the chapter on Cook in *Tales of the African Frontier* by Daniel Mannix and John Hunter, a typical day for Cook in the early days involved seeing one hundred thirty patients and performing five surgeries. Soon he was faced with even more serious problems in the form of epidemics of smallpox and sleeping sickness. He was able to curtail the smallpox epidemic with the help of a new vaccine, but the sleeping sickness ravaged the countryside. Cook asked village chiefs to send him a stick whenever someone died of the disease, and he soon had a pile of over forty thousand such sticks. Sir Harry Johnston estimated that in the first few years of the 1900s the total African dead in Uganda from sleeping sickness totaled 240,000.

Despite the burden of his daily workload, Cook made two significant medical discoveries in Uganda. The first was his identification of a particular bacteria and tick as the source of a certain tick fever. The second was the identification of a certain parasitical worm as the cause of a particular blood disease that was ravaging the native population.

Dr. Cook, now aided by his wife Katharine and sometimes his brother, Dr. J. H. Cook, carried on his work in Uganda for decades despite overwork, hard conditions, and misfortunes such as a fire that destroyed the infirmary and most of his instruments. He was knighted in 1932, and attended the coronation of George VI on one of their few trips back home. His record in several conflicts (from the Nubian Mutiny to the World War) brought him two British orders, a Belgian order, three war medals, numerous clasps, and three Mentions-in-Dispatches.

Lady Cook died in 1938 and Dr. Sir Albert Cook followed her in 1950. He was the author of several medical texts.

Cooke, Edward A. Cooke was a colorful Australian who promoted the so-called "first ever" Cape-to-Cairo walk in 1928. The feat had already been accomplished by Ewart Grogan, but no matter. Cooke, who described himself as an Australian air force officer to the newspapers, was not one to let a simple fact stand in the way of a good headline. Amidst much fanfare he began his hike in late 1928 accompanied by R. A. Monson, a journalist who had answered a newspaper advertisement. The pair had gone about 1,000 miles before Cooke was revealed as a liar and a fraud (among other things, if he had ever served at all in the RAAF it was as a private, not as an officer) and forced to quit the expedition in disgrace. Monson went on without him.

Cooke then changed his name to Edward Roberts, "a renowned motorcyclist," and started off on a Cape-to-Cairo bike ride. Once again he received favorable press coverage. He got as far as Bulawayo before he was recognized and arrested for traveling on a phony passport.

Coolidge, Harold Jefferson (1904–1985). Dr. Coolidge was a curator of Harvard's Museum of Comparative Zoology and a member of the 1927 Harvard-African expedition under Dr. R. P. Strong. The safari was guided by professional hunter Marcus Daly. Dr. Coolidge collected mountain gorilla specimens and later wrote the 1929 paper "Revision of the Genus Gorilla," which differentiated between the two subspecies, mountain gorilla and lowland gorilla. Coolidge later was one of the organizers of the 1959 George Schaller gorilla-study expedition to Albert National Park. ROWLAND WARD 1928: ELEPHANT (105 AND 103 POUNDS, ITURI FOREST).

Cooper, Richard A. F. Dick Cooper, a wealthy Englishman, was a close friend and frequent safari partner of Bror Blixen. The two would go on hunts that would last months at a time. In 1927 Cooper bought a parcel of land near Lake Manyara in Tanganyika, and built a coffee plantation that he named Singu Estates. Blixen, who was always in dire financial straits, was hired on as manager for the sum of £800 per year. It was while Blixen was living at Singu Estates in 1928 that the Prince of Wales voiced his famous admonishment, "I say, Blixen, you really oughtn't to let your wife live in a tumbledown place like this."

On safari in the mid-1930s, Cooper had a romantic tryst with Ernest Hemingway's paramour, Jane Kendall Mason, the glamorous blonde heiress who was the inspiration for "Margot" in the story *The Short Happy Life of Francis Macomber.* Cooper was both a man of action and a high-society bon vivant. In the 1914–1918 War he had earned the Military Cross and the French croix de guerre, and claimed to have shot down three German planes with his double-barreled hunting rifle.

According to Romulus Kleen (*Bror Blixen: The Africa Letters,* 1988), Cooper had inherited profitable oilfields in Wyoming and had to stay there six months out of the year as a condition of the inheritance. He would therefore split his time between Wyoming and Africa. He drowned while duck hunting at Lake Manyara in the early 1950s.

Cooper had listings in the 1928 Rowland Ward Book for buffalo, bongo, and white rhino, the last a bull with a 35¼-inch horn shot on the French Congo border.

Cooper-Chadwick, John (1864–xxxx). Born in Ireland, Cooper-Chadwick rejected an apprenticeship as an office clerk and fled to Africa, signing on as a trooper with Charles Warren's Bechuanaland Expedition in 1885. When that corps disbanded, he enlisted in the Bechuanaland Border Police, and later tried his hand at prospecting throughout the Zambezi Valley. He spent the late 1880s hunting and trading in Matabeleland.

In May 1891, Cooper-Chadwick was hunting game birds for his supper when he had a horrific accident. While carelessly leaning on his double-barreled shotgun, it discharged. (He later speculated that one of his dogs brushed against it.) The shot tore through both his hands, which had to be amputated. The wound never healed properly and required many additional surgeries in subsequent years.

Despite his handicap, upon his return home Cooper-Chadwick entertained his father by writing stories of his life in the bush, using a pen strapped to the stump of his wrist. In 1894 these notes were enlarged and published as *Three Years with Lobengula.* Cooper-Chadwick lived a long life and served as a lecturer to the troops on World War II.

Coquelin. A young Frenchman by this name arrived in Ubangi-Shari in 1908 and began making a name for himself as an elephant hunter. Using a .450 single Express, he killed 107 elephant over the next two years. In 1910 he went after number 108, but something went awry and young Coquelin was impaled on the animal's tusk. Though eviscerated, he managed somehow to get back to camp, but died of his injuries nine days later.

Corbett, Edward James "Jim" (1875–1955). Lt. Col. Jim Corbett is a legendary figure in big-game circles, and is so respected that generations of African hunters have worked his name into their books even though all of his most famous exploits took place in India. Neither a trophy seeker nor a professional hunter, Corbett specialized in going after the most dangerous game imaginable—man-eating big cats. His best-selling books detail how he ended the careers of various tigers and leopards that between them killed thousands of human beings. A major Indian national park was named after him, and his name is still a legend in the Kumaon hills that he hunted over a century ago.

In his last years Corbett moved to Africa, settling at Nyeri in Kenya. He was frequently seen at Treetops Lodge, where, according to Alastair Scobie (1954), he entertained guests by "calling up" leopards using nothing more than his voice. Temple-Perkins recalled in his 1955 memoir

Kingdom of the Elephant how he guided Corbett and the retired chief game warden of Malaysia, Peter Powell, on a photographic safari at Katwe on Lake Edward. Corbett was stiffened by arthritis and a recent accident but didn't flinch while filming a group of seven bull elephant in a nearby stampede. Corbett must be considered one of the greatest woodsmen of his or any other age. He was the author of *Man-Eaters of Kumaon* (1946), *The Man-Eating Leopard of Rudraprayag* (1948), *My India* (1952), *Jungle Lore* (1953), and *The Temple Tiger* (1955).

Corbett, N. E. F. District commissioner at Eldoret in Kenya, he helped arrange a Nandi lion hunt for former President Roosevelt in 1909. Four years later he was one of the first British officials to report seeing what might have been the legendary "Nandi bear"—it was a beast "slightly bigger than a hyena" with thick reddish fur. "The annoying thing," he wrote to C. W. Hobley, "was that I had been past exactly the same place half an hour before with my gun after a duck, and when I returned I had nothing but a fishing rod. I saw it about 12:30 midday—almost the same time that Mr. Kennet saw one at another place." Heuvelmann (1958) speculated that Corbett, who did not have good eyesight, saw either a Cape hunting dog or a hyena. It is somewhat difficult to believe, however, that a district commissioner of 1913, with all the opportunities to observe wildlife that he would have had, would make a mistake like that. Being nearsighted myself, I can damn well tell whether I can see something or not, and I'm not likely to mistake a familiar animal for an unknown one. One has to give Corbett the same benefit of the doubt.

Cormon, Edouard. During most of the early and middle twentieth century, Monsieur Cormon lived in a house in Ubangi-Shari near the Belgian border. This was quite convenient as Cormon was wont to slip over that border and bag an occasional—or occasional dozen or two—elephant.

A polished, well-read man, Cormon also had numerous "guns in the bush" at all times. This was the French term for providing African hunters with rifles and ammunition; they could keep and sell the meat of any elephant that they shot provided they turned over the ivory. The law in French Equatorial Africa (of which Ubangi-Shari was a part) permitted European residents to have a total of six guns in the bush at any given time.

In his early days Cormon was a fervent socialist but wound up a prosperous businessman, selling ivory and native pepper. He is generally considered to have shot about five hundred elephant. His favorite weapon was a .416 Rigby.

Cornell, C. A. An administrative officer in Kenya from 1921 to about 1954, "Daddy" Cornell was the district commissioner at Isiolo in the 1920s and then later at Lamu. Elspeth Huxley described him (1985) as "reserved in manner, perhaps shy, a misogynist by reputation and a disgruntled man."

While DC at Isiolo, Cornell conducted a vicious feud with Trafford, the neighboring DC at Thomson's Falls. The two actually got in a fistfight at a meeting, angry over a boundary dispute. Cornell also had trouble with Gilbert Colvile, one of the richest ranchers in Kenya. Colvile was campaigning hard in the 1930s to establish that Theodore Powys had been murdered by the Samburu. Cornell apparently believed the official version, that Powys was killed by a lion. He managed to shanghai one of Colvile's star witnesses, a Samburu warrior named Lekada, to Isiolo, where he had the man severely beaten. For punishment, Cornell was sent to Moyale, where he spent several years before being transferred to Lamu.

After the harsh conditions at Isiolo and Moyale, Cornell seemed to regard Lamu (which for a spell in the 1960s was a hippie beach resort) as a part-time job. District Commissioner Chenevix Trench, in his excellent book *Men Who Ruled Kenya* (1993), wrote that Cornell had four rubber stamps made up for use on his paperwork at Lamu. The stamps said (in Swahili) *Shauri la Liwali* (the *Liwali* was the senior Muslim authority in the village business), *Shauri la Police* (police business), *Shauri la Mungu* (God's business), and *Shauri lako* (your own affair). On a good day Cornell could use these four stamps to dispose of every single item that came before him.

Cornell was a bachelor and an immaculate dresser, always seen in a white suit and tie. He retired to a farm near Witu and died a heroic death. Learning one night that Somali *shiftas* (vicious bandits) were going to raid the village at dawn, Cornell set out for Witu to warn the inhabitants. For some reason he went unarmed. The *shiftas* caught and murdered him.

Coryndon, Sir Robert Thorne (1870–1925). Coryndon was a member of Cecil Rhodes's inner circle and one of the officers of the Pioneer Column that invaded Mashonaland in 1890. Later he was Rhodes's private secretary. In 1897 he became resident commissioner of Barotseland. The Barotse king, Lewanika, was not initially impressed by Coryndon, but the latter's personal charm and skill at hunting quickly won the chief over.

In 1900–1907 Coryndon held the post of administrator of North-East Rhodesia. He served as resident commissioner of Swaziland in 1907–1916, and spent a term at the same post in Basutoland. He later served as governor of both Uganda and Kenya.

One night while Coryndon was governor of Uganda in 1919, he was on safari and sleeping under the stars when some large animal seized his wrist and started pulling him away. Coryndon's sudden shout caused the animal to decamp. Coryndon dressed the wound and lay down again with his rifle at his side. A half-hour later he shot and killed the returning marauder, a large hyena. On another occasion, during his South African days, a known man-eating lion crept up to Coryndon's tent one dark and stormy night. The lion pulled at the tent, sending the whole structure, including fly, poles, and mosquito net, crashing down upon the man. Presumably smelling the human on the canvas, the man-eater ran off into the night, dragging the tent. It was found the next morning all chewed up and clawed to pieces. ROWLAND WARD 1928: HARTEBEEST, ELAND.

Cottar, Charles (1874–1940). Charles "Bwana" Cottar was a burly Oklahoman who first went to Africa in 1910 after reading of the Roosevelt safari. He bought a rifle and a minimum of equipment in Nairobi and spent the next year roaming the countryside on foot, shooting big game and having a hell of a time. He returned to the United States in 1912 to sell his various businesses and gather his family—his wife, Annette May (called Anita), and their nine children. He then built a house on twenty acres of land that he bought outside Nairobi (the family later moved to a ten-acre homestead near the Karura Forest).

Once settled in, Cottar left to hunt elephant in Uganda. He was returning with a fair amount of ivory when he fell sick with an obscure African disease called spirillum tick fever. This fever was often fatal in those days, but Cottar survived after spending several days in a coma, although he was to suffer from the debilitating effects of the illness for the rest of his life.

Over the next decade Cottar, who often displayed an American Wild West attitude toward regulations and laws, went on numerous extended poaching trips into the Belgian Congo. He took to making movies, acting as his own cameraman. In 1919 he even produced a commercially successful film called *Cameraring through Africa,* which was shown on both sides of the Atlantic.

A few years before that film, he had experienced his first mauling when a wounded leopard tore his face and scalp as it was bleeding to death. That incident was nothing compared to his next mishap. In 1917 Cottar wanted to make a motion picture featuring a captured leopard. Relying on his Wild West skills, he rode a big male leopard down on horseback and lassoed it. After tying its back legs together to hobble it, he turned to get his wife and twelve-year-old son Mike. The leopard was able to suddenly leap toward him, even with its legs tied. In seeking to escape, Cottar tripped in a warthog hole and fell. The enraged cat was instantly upon him, biting his face and raking his body with its claws. His wife was cranking the movie camera the whole time, but somehow the film snagged and didn't come out.

Cottar was somehow able to throw the leopard off him and shoot it, but the damage had been done. The wounds turned septic, and doctors begged him to allow an amputation of at least one leg, but Cottar refused. To the surprise of everyone except those who knew him best, Cottar made an almost full recovery.

In 1918 Cottar began operating the Cottar Safari Service, helped by his sons as they grew older. Typically American, the Cottars were one of the first companies to motorize their operation, importing four Ford automobiles in 1920. However, a fire broke out aboard a ship in Mombasa harbor (the *Berwick Castle*) and the crates containing the cars went to the bottom. The crates were retrieved from the wreck some three months later. Miraculously, the Ford company had packed the cars in so much grease that the salt water had barely damaged them, and they were up and running in no time. Try that with a modern Ford sometime!

Cottar settled in to running his safari business, making an occasional film, and writing magazine and newspaper articles. Occasionally he would go along on the hunts, but more and more often he left the actual hunting to his sons. In 1940 he accompanied his oldest boy, Bud, on safari to the Loita Plains so he could obtain film footage for a promotional picture he wanted to show in North America. The two men were armed with .405 Winchester rifles.

Bud wounded a black rhino and went to follow it up in the brush. Suddenly the animal appeared from a thicket not far from where Bwana Cottar and his gunbearer were standing by the camera. Cottar had long had a dramatic but dangerous habit of filming charging animals until the last possible second, then stopping the charge with a quick shot. Perhaps his reflexes were slowing down with age, perhaps he was just unlucky, or perhaps he just pushed his luck too far. At any rate, by the time he stopped filming and picked up his Winchester, the rhino was nearly upon him. He fired one fatal shot, but it was too late: As the dying rhino collapsed, it ripped its horns into the man's groin and thigh and then fell on his legs. An artery was torn, and despite tourniquets and other frantic efforts, Bwana Cottar bled to death within minutes.

Cottar, Charles "Bud" (1901–1960). Bud Cottar was the oldest son of Charles "Bwana" Cottar and was present at his father's death.

Cottar, Mike (1905–1941). The second son of Bwana Cottar, Mike was also a hunter for the Cottar Safari Service. Mike had an extremely high reputation as a woodsman and stood to become one of the best professionals of his time.

In 1940, armed with a .470 double rifle, he was guiding a United States Senator named Costello on a buffalo hunt in the Serengeti. The senator wounded a buffalo, and Cottar began trailing it up a steep hillside. The bull started charging down the hill at him, and Cottar gave it both barrels. They were effective shots—the buffalo died, but its momentum kept it hurtling down the hillside straight into Cottar, who was sent sprawling down the hill.

Cottar had some scrapes and bruises, that was all, and he laughed it off. But neither he nor anyone else realized at the time that the impact had ruptured his spleen, already damaged by seven episodes of blackwater fever. Months later, on 12 July 1941 Cottar died suddenly at age thirty-six. He was the father of highly regarded professional hunter Glen Cottar.

Courtney, Roger J. A. (1902–1947). As a young man in the 1920s, Roger Courtney sold goats for a living with George Adamson and Hugh Grant. Courtney was a major in the elite Royal Marine Special Boat Service before turning professional hunter. He was the author of *Claws of Africa* (1934), which told of his adventures as a professional hunter in Kenya, Uganda, and the Belgian Congo, and *Africa Calling* (1936), an odd but interesting account of what a 1930 white hunter did when he wasn't

In 1900 the SS Dunnottar Castle *carried a distinguished group home from Africa. Standing, left to right: Sir Byron Leighton, Claud Grenfel, Maj. F. R. Burnham, Capt. Gordon Forbes, Abe Bailey, unknown, unknown, the Earl of Warwick. Sitting on chairs: Maj. Bobby White, Lord Downe, General Sir Henry Colvile, Maj. Harry White, Maj. Joe Laycock, Winston Churchill, Sir Charles Bentinck. Sitting on deck: unknown, Col. Maurice Gifford.*

hunting. The 1930 EARB (see glossary) lists Courtney as residing in Londiani.

Courtney had a brother who was actively involved in the Temperance movement and thus was nicknamed "Sacred" Courtney. Inevitably, Roger, quite fond of the bottle and other earthly pleasures, became known as "Profane" Courtney. When he died of blackwater fever in the Northern Frontier District, a funnel was built into his grave so his friends could pour him a drink from time to time. The local Africans, whose religion forbade the use of alcohol, would pour in milk.

Cowie, Mervyn H. (1909–1996). Cowie, a professional hunter turned game warden, is generally considered the founder of Kenya National Parks. In the 1940s he led an imaginative conservation campaign by writing letters to Nairobi newspapers demanding the extermination of all wild animals in order to provide space for farmers. As he expected, the resulting backlash galvanized the public into demanding the establishment of national parks.

In 1946 he was named director of Nairobi National Park, the nation's first, and later he managed them all. He was also named director of European Manpower in the 1950s, a post that coordinated paramilitary efforts against the Mau Mau. As director, he still hunted game occasionally and prided himself on his ability to kill with only one shot. He considered it his obligation to patiently wait for the perfect shot, to minimize the possibility of a wounded animal escaping.

Cowie was a strong critic of the Adamsons' lion-rehabilitation program, fearing (with much justification) that they were creating potential man-eaters. He was the author of 1961's *Fly, Vulture* (published in 1963 in the U.S. as *I Walk with Lions*) as well as *The African Lion* (1966). He died on 19 July 1996. A fictionalized film based on his life, *Where No Vultures Fly,* directed by Harry Watt, was a Royal Film Performance presentation in 1951.

Mervyn Cowie was a twin; his brother was named Dudley. By 1928 civil aviation had become a popular fad, and the twins decided to take flying lessons. They hired Maia Carberry, the young wife of the well-known British baron and Kenyan settler John Carberry, as their instructor. On one spring day in March the boys met Maia for their lesson. She took Mervyn up first, and they did a few easy circuits of Dagoretti Field, just outside Nairobi. They landed and Dudley got into the cockpit. He and Mrs. Carberry took off for what at first appeared to be a routine lesson. Then something went terribly wrong, the result being Kenya's first celebrity air crash. The plane slammed into the ground as Mervyn Cowie watched, killing both his twin brother and Maia Carberry.

Cox, Sir Percy Zachariah (1864–1937). Cox was a British administrator who studied at Harrow and the Royal Military College. In 1884 he was commissioned into the 2nd Cameronians, based in India. He was early on drawn to political work and held minor posts in the administration of Kolhapur and Savantwadi in the late 1880s and early 1890s.

Cox was appointed assistant political resident at Zeila in Somaliland in 1893. A large part of his job was assisting British sportsmen, usually army officers who came to Somaliland to shoot lion. One hunter he helped equip was an American doctor, Donaldson Smith. In 1895 Cox led a successful punitive expedition against the Rer Hared clan of renegade Somali bandits. Captain Cox's force consisted of fifty-two Indian and Somali camel riders and fifteen hundred Somali irregulars. His decisive victory kept that part of Somaliland quiet for several years.

In the spring of 1898 Cox went on a long hunting furlough to India with Donaldson Smith. In 1898 and 1899 Cox was instrumental in organizing and then running an expedition to Somaliland, an official museum collecting safari under the auspices of an Indian prince, the Gaekwar of Baroda. Cox planned to take a two-year furlough to accompany Donaldson Smith on his second Lake Rudolf expedition, but at the last minute Cox was promoted to a post at Muscat and was thus unable to go.

Cox excelled at Muscat, the Arab government of which was under strong pressure from France for an alliance and concessions. Cox not only managed to thwart the French designs but also solidified the British presence. He is said to have got along well with the Arabs, who respected his honesty and quiet strength. Promoted to major in 1902, Cox became acting political resident for the Persian Gulf as well as consul-general in Fars, Luristan, and Khuzistan. His successful projects during this period included the erection of lighthouses along the Gulf coast, the construction of wireless facilities in the region, the suppression of the illegal weapons trade, and the establishment of friendly British relations with most of the Gulf states. He was also instrumental in obtaining a lease for a port facility in southern Iraq for the Anglo-Persian Oil Company.

In 1910 Cox was promoted to lieutenant colonel. During World War I he distinguished himself, first as political and intelligence officer for the army in Mesopotamia, then in active service under Major General Townsend. The appointment of Major General Maude, who didn't care for political and intelligence work, caused Cox a great deal of frustration. He would have resigned but for the intervention of Lord Curzon, who espoused Cox's cause in the War Cabinet.

In 1918 Cox was sent to Persia as acting minister. At this point he was grieving the loss of his only son, killed in action the year before. He negotiated an Anglo-Persian treaty to Britain's potential advantage, but the Persians backed out at the last minute. In 1920 the British faced a revolt in Iraq. Cox was sent to Baghdad by Curzon to take the necessary steps to resolve the situation. The intrepid agent supervised the formation of a provisional government, and by 1922 the country had returned to a peaceful state. Cox averted another crisis that same year when the head of the Iraqi provisional government, Amir Feisel, lapsed into a serious illness. Cox took over the reins of government, an act that was quite illegal but met with wide approval by the Iraqis, with whom he had great influence. The government remained stable, Feisel recovered, and in gratitude he signed a treaty of alliance with Great Britain.

Cox retired in 1923 and enjoyed himself the next fourteen years, serving as chairman of the Mount Everest Committee and as president of the Royal Geographical Society in 1933–1936. He never lost his health, dying suddenly while hunting near Bedford on 20 February 1937. Among the many honors Cox earned were the KCMG (see glossary) (1920), an honorary commission as major general (1917), and several honorary doctorates.

Craigie-Halkett. An elephant hunter in the Lado Enclave in 1911.

Crampel, Paul (1864–1891). Crampel was a French philosopher who was commissioned by the Ministry of Public Instruction to conduct a scientific expedition in the Congo. Arriving there in early 1887, he was detained by Commissioner de Brazza, who apparently felt that philosophy wasn't quite the proper training for African exploration. Brazza hired Crampel as his private secretary for several months, meanwhile teaching him the rudiments he would need to survive. In January 1888 Brazza finally allowed Crampel, who was bursting at the seams with enthusiasm and the thought of being a bona fide explorer, to begin his safari, but gave him strict instructions to take what was basically an easy route from the River Ogooué to the Benito River and thence to the coast. Crampel was presumably somewhat miffed at this condescension but set out on his big adventure. As was usual in those days, once Crampel and his men disappeared into the forest, no word was heard of them for many months. Eventually, he struggled out of the bush at the mouth of the Benito River, wounded by a bullet in the thigh and almost dead from malnutrition. Brazza shipped him back to France.

In France Crampel finally got the respect he had long craved. Despite his obvious inexperience, he had managed to collect a fair amount of valuable scientific and geographic information. He especially had a knack for charting the courses of rivers and their tributaries, a topic that was just ice cream to the armchair explorers of the Victorian Age. In December 1890 a letter from Crampel was read to the Paris Geographical Society on the subject of the Pygmies, filled with previously unknown details about their lifestyles and their relationship with other African peoples.

Lionized as an explorer, Crampel decided that his mission in life was to establish for France a great colony in the central Sudan that would link all of the French African possessions into one supercolony. That the British would go to war to prevent this didn't seem to faze Crampel at all. The hub of this great venture was to be a French settlement at Lake Chad. Crampel intended, in all seriousness, to build up a huge supply depot by the lake to replenish the colonizing expeditions that would set out from Chad in all directions like the rays of the sun.

His plan might seem far-fetched at this late date, but this was precisely the kind of bold scheme that so often succeeded in old Africa. Whether the British would have allowed it or not is another question entirely. The first step was to build this great depot, so in early 1891 Crampel launched an expedition from the Ubangi, heading north to the lake with enough supplies to begin the project.

Inevitably, however, Paul Crampel was brought down by his own inexperience. Along the Ubangi, Crampel alienated his porters and other African retainers, who all deserted. From there it was just a short time before Crampel was waylaid by bandits and murdered.

Cranworth, Lord (Bertram Francis Gurdon) (1877–1964). A veteran of the Boer War, Lord Cranworth (Bertram Francis Gurdon before he inherited the barony) arrived in Kenya in 1905, took one look around, and sent for his wife and family. It was a sportsman's paradise. He and Lord Wodehouse did a great deal of hunting in the Kenya Highlands. An early conservationist, he made a startling estimate that 795 lion (not counting poisoned animals and natural deaths) had been shot in Kenya in 1910–1911. His publication of this figure helped galvanize the wildlife protection movement in East Africa.

During World War I Cranworth fought with Berkeley Cole's unit of Somali Scouts, served as an officer in the East African Mounted Rifles, and then won a Military Cross and the croix de guerre on the Western Front. As a member of the House of Lords and 1929's Committee for a Closer Union, he was an advocate for the Kenya settlers, who often felt themselves at odds with the London government (after the early 1920s the official platform of the British government switched from promoting European settlement to developing African self-sufficiency). Later he was a founding member of EAPHA (see glossary). Cranworth was the author of *A Colony in the Making* (1912) and *Profit and Sport in British East Africa* (1919). ROWLAND WARD 1928: SITATUNGA, GRANT GAZELLE.

Lord Cranworth and Lord Wodehouse on their return from a hunting expedition in the Kenya highlands.

Craven, Charles (1879–1909) and Rupert Craven (1870–1959). The brothers Craven (a third brother was the earl of Craven) were aristocrats who attended Eton with Jim Elkington and moved to East Africa in 1904. The Cravens are frequently confused with the Brittlebank brothers (by me, anyway). In 1903–1904 the Cravens moved to East Africa and began hunting elephant with Quentin Grogan, brother of "Cape-to-Cairo" explorer Ewart Grogan. They conducted a particularly successful long safari to Mount Elgon.

Eventually the Cravens went to the Lado Enclave to hunt elephant. Charles was a former Royal Navy officer and Rupert an ex-Guards officer and a British army boxing champion. John Boyes once said that they were two of the bravest men he had ever met. Boyes once followed an elephant right into a camp and shot it next to a tent. The Cravens, who Boyes hadn't even known were in the area, came stumbling out of bed with the sleep still in their eyes. They had been looking for elephant with little success. Boyes happily pointed out that the early bird catches the worm.

Charles Craven was hunting one day early in 1909 near Mahagi on Lake Albert Edward, south of the Lado Enclave. He was in a ravine overrun with tall grass when he heard an elephant feeding very close. The grass was about fifteen feet high and very thick, but Craven could see the branches of a nearby tree waving where the animal was browsing. Creeping forward, he finally saw the elephant's head through thick bush just a couple of yards away. He fired and hit the elephant in the head but missed the brain. The animal started running, and Craven followed close on its heels.

Suddenly the elephant slipped on the side of a ravine, tumbled down a rocky slope, and landed upside down on the bottom, roaring wildly and waving its feet in the air as it tried to right itself. Craven was easily able to walk up and finish off the unfortunate animal.

Just a day or two later, Craven spotted two elephant in a marsh, again in thick vegetation. One was standing under a tree facing him, and the other was facing away, belly-deep in mud, about two hundred yards away. Craven was creeping forward when the closer elephant, the one under the tree, offered a head shot. Craven took it.

Both elephant bolted, with Craven in hot pursuit. Suddenly the ground went out from under him—he had run off a small cliff and fallen about twenty feet into mud. Picking himself up, he checked himself for broken bones and his rifle for damage. All things being in working order, he began trotting forward, less than optimistic he would find his quarry. Then he spotted the wounded elephant about three hundred yards away, just standing there. A quick stalk finished the animal off.

To his surprise Craven found that the fallen elephant had just one tusk, a large one. The elephant he had fired at under the tree had clearly had two big tusks. This one, he reasoned after a moment, must have been the other elephant, the one facing away.

Determined to finish off the wounded elephant, Craven took up the trail. Suddenly he came across the pachyderm lying dead on its side about three hundred yards from where it had all begun. The only problem was that this animal, too, had but one tusk. Craven began to wonder if he wasn't coming down with malaria.

The conclusion he came up with, after long deliberation and discussing it over a few drinks with his friends at the Harbour Lights saloon in Koba, was there must have been two elephant under the tree, each with one tusk, and some sort of optical illusion made him think there was just one animal. The elephant in the mud must have gotten away.

It was as good a theory as any, he decided, although in retrospect he might have given a bit more credence to the malaria scenario. It was certainly in his blood: Charles died of blackwater fever in Koba a few months later, on 19 July 1909. Rupert continued hunting for a while, but the fun had gone out of it, and he returned to England a dispirited man. He did return to East Africa briefly as an officer in the British army during World War I. He died at age eighty-nine in 1959.

Crawshay, Richard. Lt. Richard Crawshay of the Royal Inniskillen Regiment was an English sportsman who, while on a big-game hunting expedition to British Central Africa in 1889, joined up with Frederick Lugard, Harry Johnston, and Alfred Sharpe (who had also come to Africa to go hunting) for a military campaign against the Arab slavers. He was then appointed a vice consul for Deep Bay in the British Central Africa Protectorate. While so employed, Crawshay discovered a subspecies of waterbuck and another of puku. He served with distinction in the Boer War from 1899–1902, and in 1907 made headlines on the other side of the Earth by exploring Tierra del Fuego. He also wrote a respected book on that region's bird life.

Crofton, Richard. "Dickie" Crofton, a Kenya white hunter, was killed in action in Abyssinia in 1941. He was considered something of a lion specialist.

Cross, Alfred. Alfred Cross hunted Mashonaland with Selous, Goulden, Clarkson, and Wood in 1877–1878. He was a true professional elephant hunter of the South African horse-riding mode, on one occasion killing a herd of twenty-one elephant and later another of seventeen.

Crous, C. G. In the 1930s Crous was the game ranger responsible for the area of Kruger National Park just to the north of the Olifants River.

Cumberland, C. S. This British sportsman made his reputation hunting in Asia and in the Himalayas. Cumberland was the author of *Sport in the Pamir and Turkistan Steppes.* In 1911–1912 he hunted in British Central Africa.

Cumming, Roualeyn Gordon (1820–1866). A graduate of Eton, Gordon Cumming was the second son of a baronet (Sir William Gordon Cumming of Altyre and Gordonstoun) and a true Scottish laird. He served in India with the Madras Cavalry in 1839 but within a year his health curtailed his Indian army career. Rather than retire to the family estates, he joined the Royal Veteran Newfoundland Company.

Gordon Cumming freely admitted that he sought out this particular corps so as to get an opportunity to hunt North American game, such as the grizzly bear and the bison. His zest for hunting was keener than his sense of geography (there being remarkably few grizzlies in Newfoundland) and Gordon Cumming soon transferred to the Cape Mounted Rifles in South Africa. After serving in one brief punitive expedition, he resigned his commission and in the last half of 1843 began a five-year hunting trip that inspired a generation of British sportsmen.

Gordon Cumming roamed the interior of southern Africa from Cape Colony to Kuruman and the Limpopo and Vaal Rivers, meeting most of the famous missionaries, African chieftains, and Boer hunters of the day. He traveled trekker style, with several wagons and a large retinue of native servants. He was also invariably accompanied by a large number of dogs, seventy of which perished due to various reasons (crocodiles, leopards, baboons, and at least one was kicked to death by a zebra) during his days on the trail. Not an incredibly rich man by the standards of his class, Gordon Cumming collected hides, furs, and ivory in the hope of turning a profit from his expedition. The hides were cut up for use as the raw materials in *sjamboks* and riems, which were then sold to the Boers on their isolated farms. He also sold ivory. He received £28 to £40 per each 112-pound unit of ivory he brought in. On one trip he sold a mixed load of ivory and ostrich feathers at Grahamstown for £1,000.

His two-volume *Five Years Adventure in the Far Interior of South Africa* (later variably titled *A Hunter's Life in South Africa* and *The Lion Hunter of South Africa*) is well written and has aged well; the Scotsman's prose reveals a pungent wit. He has taken a beating from critics, however, on two counts. Some readers have felt that he had a tendency to exaggerate (or lie about) his exploits. This is certainly a common fault among sportsmen and is quite possibly true in his case.

In one definitely far-fetched story, Gordon Cumming tells about how he maneuvered a living, but wounded, hippo to shore by cutting hand-holds in its hide and pushing it while swimming. This anecdote was ridiculed from the start, being mentioned derisively in "Lion-slayers and Man-eaters," an article in *Harper's New Monthly Magazine* for July 1856. The press was simply full of the young Scotsman at that time; another article in the same issue, entitled "Negro-land and the Negroes," recommended that Gordon Cumming and Sam Baker venture to Africa's West Coast to take advantage of the rumored great herds of elephants.

In 1893 Henry Anderson Bryden took on the issue of Gordon Cumming's veracity in his *Gun and Camera in Southern Africa.* While hunting in Bechuanaland in 1890, Bryden had met a number of Africans who had known the Scotsman nearly forty years earlier. Among them were a Bakwena headman and even Khama himself. These eyewitnesses universally praised Gordon Cumming's strength and skill. Bryden, while mildly condemning Gordon Cumming for the sheer number of animals he had killed, came to the conclusion that as far as his truthfulness went, the old lion hunter "was assuredly wronged" by his critics.

Bryden's guarded criticism brings us to the other point. The second, more widespread, point against Gordon Cumming was that his own words reveal, if not an absolute bloodthirstiness, then certainly a zest for blood sports that is appalling to modern tastes; indeed, his bloodthirstiness even shocked many of his Victorian-era contemporaries. Author P. Jay Fetner (1987) aptly described Gordon Cumming's hunting technique as resembling "more or less, a war on all living things." His shooting was so indiscriminate that it bothered many of his Victorian fellows, who were accustomed to think of animals as being placed on Earth by a thoughtful God, purely for man's enjoyment.

Not that it is necessary, but in Gordon Cumming's defense it should be noted that not only was such profligate shooting common in South Africa (the Boers made a devastating environmental impact wherever they hunted), but even a century later Kenyan hunting professionals observed that many sportsmen coming from a land where hunting was restricted (particularly the United States) would go positively nuts when presented with huge herds of game animals. It is simply unfair to judge Gordon Cumming by modern standards. It should also be noted that American hunters of the same era did a pretty thorough job of wiping out the buffalo, the passenger pigeon, the sea mink, and numerous other species without the Scotsman's help. English and Icelandic collectors exterminated the great auk, and the large game of Europe (bears, aurochs, and wild horses among others) had either been harassed into extinction or forced to retreat to remote mountain enclaves. Gordon Cumming has been unfairly criticized for activities shared by much of his generation and their predecessors.

In addition, a careful reading of his work shows that he is sometimes misinterpreted. One of the passages most frequently quoted by Gordon Cumming's detractors concerns a wounded and immobilized elephant into which he fired shot after shot while making his tea; it is widely stated that he was torturing the unfortunate beast. What this interpretation fails to take into account is the poor lethality of the weapons of the day. The early elephant guns, although they fired a huge lead projectile weighing as much as four to a pound, didn't have anywhere near the penetrating power of a modern rifle. In consequence it often took an ungodly number of rounds to kill an animal as big as a rhino or an elephant. Gordon Cumming wasn't trying to torment the creature, he was trying to bring it down. What shocked readers was that he brewed a pot of tea in between shots, but that does not detract from the fact that he was doing his best to put the animal out of its misery. Later in the book, Gordon Cumming described the shooting of an elephant that he was most definitely not trying to torture, and that animal took fifty-seven bullets to finish off. It should also be noted that Gordon Cumming's contemporaries reported similar incidents in their own writings: William Cornwallis Harris, for example, wrote in *Wild Sports of Southern Africa* that he had cornered a black rhino in "an old stone enclosure," and shot it twenty-seven times "before it fell, dyed with crimson gore, and embossed with the white foam that rage had churned around its chaps." Yet Harris received nowhere near the amount of bad press that Gordon Cumming did, quite possibly because of simple snobbery, as the one was a British gentleman while the other was a wild Scots laird.

On the other hand, Gordon Cumming might legitimately deserve a measure of criticism in his lack of discrimination as to what he shot. He quite simply put a bullet into anything he could, be it buffalo, elephant, rhino with calf, or antelope. You didn't want to be sneaking through the woods when he was in the neighborhood. The elephants (he shot more

R. J. Cuninghame and one of Teddy Roosevelt's Robertsi *heads, 1909.*

than one hundred of them) were necessary to finance his travels, but time and time again he shot indiscriminately, killing many more animals than were needed for food or for trophies (he planned to open a museum when he got back to Scotland). On many occasions he would fire into the darkness at vague shapes, not caring what he shot, and then check it out in the morning to see if there were any good "heads" among the carcasses. Again, however, this behavior was not unique to the colorful Scot. As late as the 1920s French game warden Bruneau de Laborie was known to fire at distant rhinos and then not even bother to check out the result of his shot.

Gordon Cumming, a rough-and-tumble sort, presented a wild and unique appearance. He believed that a garish get-up helped ease his acceptance among primitive peoples, and it is evident from his memoirs that he also took an inordinate amount of pride in his eccentric image. Lt. Col. Napier described him (quoted in Williams, 1859) as wearing "a pair of rough Veldschoenen (shoes), white trousers and shirt without waistcoat or jacket; a leather girdle tightly encircled his waist, whilst on his head he wore a broad-brimmed hat adorned with jackals tails and surrounded by a magnificent plume of the finest ostrich feathers." His hair was bright red and worn long, and he loved to share stories and bottles. His daily appearance looked something like a Disney movie pirate of the 1940s.

After his return to Britain, Gordon Cumming spent the rest of his life making money from his African adventure. Not only did the ivory and other artifacts he had obtained bring a large profit, but he made a considerable sum lecturing, exhibiting his trophies in his museum along the Caledonian Canal, and selling his book. The flamboyant Scotsman went on shikar to India in the early 1860s where he shot up the local fauna with his usual gusto, killing seventy-three tigers in the Narmada River district between 1863 and 1864. His Indian adventures were recounted in *Wild Men and Wild Beasts* (1872), including another hunt along the Tapti River where he shot ten tigers in five days. It's nice to see that he hadn't lost his touch. He also published a descriptive catalog of his collection, with text cribbed from his books and magazine articles. Gordon Cumming died in Scotland in 1866, reportedly from the effects of drink. Two of his brothers died the same year.

Cumming, Walter Gordon. A relative of the famous "lion killer," British sportsman Walter Gordon Cumming went on vacation to Nyasaland in late 1895. (It was an immense clan—the lady explorer Constance Gordon Cummings listed more than fifty first cousins in her memoirs.) He was hunting big game with his friend Maj. F. C. Trollope of the Grenadier Guards when Sir Harry Johnston launched his punitive campaign against the Arab slaver Mlozi. With typical Victorian panache, the two hunters exchanged their black-powder Expresses for magazine rifles and joined the expedition, each taking command of a contingent of troops. After the execution of Mlozi in December 1895, Gordon Cumming led a detachment of soldiers that destroyed the remaining Arab fortifications on the northern end of Lake Nyasa. Early the following year he helped capture a renegade Yao chief named Mpembe, and then accepted a position as collector (district commissioner) of the central Angoniland district.

Cuninghame, Richard John (1871–1925). R. J. Cuninghame had a unique career for a graduate of Cambridge University. Early in life he worked on a whaling ship in the Antarctic. Arriving in Africa with £20 in his pocket, Cuninghame made a living for a while shooting buffalo for their hides near Beira and then running a Kimberly-to-Johannesburg mail coach. He did some early collecting work for the British Museum, and in 1889 won the Royal Humane Society's Medal for Life Saving, possibly the only white hunter to be so honored.

In the late 1890s Cuninghame moved to Kenya and became one of the first professional white hunters. He counted Lord Baden-Powell and Theodore Roosevelt among his clients. When opportunity beckoned in the Lado Enclave, Cuninghame took full advantage of it, joining up with Henry Darley for a few years in a poaching team the authorities called the "robbers of the north." This partnership lasted from about 1904–1907.

When World War I broke out Cuninghame was hunting deep in German Tanganyika with R. L. Scott, but the two evaded capture and got back to Kenya. Later he was an intelligence officer in East Africa and won a DSO (see glossary). Weak from fever and suffering constant headaches (which began when he was kicked by a zebra as a youth), Cuninghame was sent back to Britain to command a POW camp. His health was in tatters, and at one point he contracted meningitis. After his death on 23 May 1925, he was found to be suffering from a brain tumor that might have been operable had it been detected. Denis Lyell's *African Adventure* reprints a number of letters from Cuninghame, as well as the text of an amusing and

R. J. Cuninghame steering a big, bull hippo to shore, Kenya, 1909.

R. J. Cuninghame, Kermit Roosevelt, Teddy Roosevelt, Edmund Heller, and Hugh Heatley at Buffalo Camp.

informative lecture on elephant he gave in 1921. ROWLAND WARD 1928: KONGONI.

Cunningham, Teddy (xxxx–1929). Teddy Cunningham was an eccentric but adept white hunter who was raised (with his older brother Kenneth, also a hunter) on a farm east of Baringo. As a boy he learned hunting and trailcraft from the Wandorobo, the legendary forest nomads of Kenya. He grew up to possess amazing bush skills, and was an athlete as well—he once raced three Wandorobo trackers over a thirty-seven-mile course and beat them by forty-five minutes even though he was lugging a .470 double rifle. In 1920 Cunningham, who had a reputation for wild behavior, placed a pebble on the back of a sleeping rhino and then dared his friend to go and get it.

Cunningham was later attached to the game department as an honorary warden, shooting elephant on control. One night at a party his long-term girlfriend told him their relationship was over. Perhaps he was distracted, perhaps he drank too much, but the next morning Cunningham was not himself when he went to shoot some elephant that were raiding a farm near Rumuruti. With him was Engerua, a Wandorobo tracker who had been his friend since boyhood. Engerua had his head down, watching the trail, and Cunningham was distracted, as noted above. Suddenly a cow elephant burst from nearby brush. Cunningham had not spotted the animal. She grabbed him around the waist with her trunk and beat him against a tree. Engerua managed to frighten the elephant off and ran to get help for the fallen hunter, who was severely hurt and hemorrhaging. Cunningham was still alive when he was finally brought into the hospital but died a short time later.

Curtis, Charles P. and Richard C. Curtis. These two brothers arrived from Massachusetts with their father, Charles Sr., and Richard's wife Anita in Nairobi in May 1923 and went on a three-month safari, guided by Philip Percival. At the end of July, all but Charles Jr. continued to Portuguese West Africa, where, inspired by Colonel Statham's 1922 book *Through Angola,* they hunted the Angolan giant sable. Richard took a giant sable with a .303 while Charles Sr. bagged his with a .450 double. Anita kept busy by discovering sixteen new plant species. Their story was told in the 1925 book, *Hunting Africa East and West.* In the 1928 edition of Rowland Ward, each hunter is listed with a giant sable of 52½ inches.

D

Dafel, Kotje. A Boer elephant hunter of the nineteenth century, Dafel (also known as Danel) accounted for over one hundred lion.

Dalton, Jerry. He was a professional hunter employed by the firm of Safariland, Ltd., in the 1920s.

Daly, Marcus. This controversial sportsman and author wrote *Big Game Hunting and Adventure 1897–1936.* Daly was a Rhodesian PH and ivory poacher who began his career after his father and his older brother James had been murdered in the 1896 Matabele Rebellion. Early on he worked for Cecil Rhodes, trapping young animals alive for Rhodes's Kenilworth Zoo. At this time he also began hunting elephant, rhino, and buffalo, using a .500 Express given him by Fred Selous, a Martini-Henry, and a .303 sporting rifle. He stayed away from lion at first, admitting in his memoirs that he was afraid of them. Most of his early hunting was done in the company of his friend Tegwana, a young Matabele warrior.

It was Tegwana who helped Daly overcome his fear of lion. At first the young Rhodesian just couldn't bear to face the huge predators. Gradually Tegwana broke him in. Ironically, it was after a failed lion hunt had nearly ended in disaster that Daly realized he was no longer intimidated by the beasts.

Daly and Tegwana ranged far and wide, hunting in Matabeleland and down into Portuguese East Africa. They managed to get five hundred rounds for the .500 Express as well as a case each of .303 and Martini-Henry ammunition, and spent a solid year on safari in the Zambezi and Shangani River valleys. They were accompanied by a number of other Matabele hunters. One night lion tried to attack the zareba they had erected, and one Matabele youth, who had been picked to stand guard, killed five of the animals. Such was camping on the Zambezi in 1898.

Unfortunately, this idyllic existence did not last. The Boer War broke out in 1899, and two young men of such skills as Daly and Tegwana could not be expected to avoid it. They served as scouts for the British forces and were so efficient that the Boers put a reward of £500 on Daly's head. Shortly after, Tegwana was shot and killed during a skirmish in the Orange Free State.

At war's end Daly worked for a short time as a contractor, delivering supplies through the Kalahari Desert to German troops fighting the Herero natives. On this trip he first got to know and understand the Bushmen. According to Daly, some Angoli marauders had raided Bushmen kraals and slaughtered their women, as well as burning a few English and Boer farms. Daly went with a group of Bushmen that caught and wiped out one of the Angoli bands.

Daly spent the next several years variously working and hunting. In 1914 he was a captain in a territorial cavalry regiment. He resigned his commission and enlisted in a regular British unit because he wanted to see action and knew that the territorials were to be kept on security detail inside South Africa in case of a native uprising. He soon made sergeant and apparently served with distinction in the World War.

The Armistice found him in East Africa, and he spent the years from 1918–1926 hunting professionally in East Africa (especially Tanaland and the Serengeti) and the Congo. In 1927 he hunted Portuguese East with an American client, and then recreationally hunted along the Lake Tanganyika shores with Charles Grey (who was killed by a buffalo in a hunting accident soon after he split from Daly). After this excursion Daly was hired by the Harvard College Trans-African Scientific Expedition and helped Professors R. P. Strong and Harold Coolidge collect gorilla and other specimens in the Congo.

All along, he made side trips and sporting safaris into the Tana River area of Kenya, the Cameroons, Sudan, the Belgian Congo, and French Equatorial Africa. He had a lot of legal trouble with the French, who confiscated all of his kit. According to Daly, he was hassled, shackled, robbed, and deported under the fiction of legal proceedings, solely due to jealousy and greed by the authorities. According to the French, he was guilty of robbery and poaching and all sorts of mayhem. He was perhaps lucky to escape to British Africa when he did. The French hunter/writer Francois Sommer reported (1953) that Daly was treated harshly because the authorities were simply fed up with his boasting about breaking the game laws.

Once, on a poaching trip into French territory, Daly was pummeled by a wounded bull elephant and left for dead by his tracker. Daly spent the night unconscious and only yards away from hungry lion that were feeding on three elephant carcasses. In the morning the tracker returned and managed to get the badly injured Daly back to camp. Daly later wrote in a local paper an account of that night's events, claiming (undoubtedly just a literary expression) that "only the angels of God" had saved him from being devoured by the lion. One reply came from an ex-girlfriend, who wrote

Two lions shot by Marcus Daly. The one on the right died bravely in defense of its mate.

him "after many years of silence" to say that it wasn't the angels that had saved him but only the fact that lion dislike foul meat.

It's difficult to form a fair opinion about Daly. Virtually all the sources of information about him are biased, and not in his favor. The only exception is his own autobiography. He certainly violated a plethora of game laws, but that was not an uncommon event—so did many respected hunters like Grogan, Cuninghame, Darley, and Rushby. There is no doubt that Daly possessed considerable skill and bushcraft. He claimed to have collected a pair of tusks weighing 203 and 207 pounds in Ubangi-Shari, and he was one of the few early hunters to record killing a black panther. Yet again and again in the safari literature his name comes up as a source of controversy, not respect. He seems to have been almost insanely difficult to get along with: On numerous occasions unannounced visitors to his campsite found bullets whizzing by their heads. George Rushby wrote in *No More the Tusker* (1965), "Although I had some respect for Daly as a hunter, and for his toughness, I would not have trusted him under any circumstances." This opinion was widely shared.

Many other hunters recorded their skepticism about Daly and some of his tales. Temple-Perkins mentioned Daly twice in his memoir, *Kingdom of the Elephant* (1955). The first mention disparaged a story Daly told about killing an elephant. Temple-Perkins ripped apart Daly's account and made no bones that he thought the Rhodesian was a liar. In the second passage he called Daly "the greatest romancer on the subject of big game." Francois Sommer also used the word "romancer" in his 1953 *Man and Beast in Africa.* It is hard to tell at this date whether the writers were objectively stating their opinion or were motivated by personal dislike. Daly wrote in *Big Game Hunting and Adventure* how he had learned in the Kalahari to crawl under the belly of oblivious elephant without disturbing them, and bragged that he routinely performed this feat to get around cows for a shot at big bulls. It's safe to say that few, if any, of his fellow hunters believed this tale. It was, and is, generally recognized as nonsense. Yet Robert Foran wrote essentially the same thing, in *Kill or Be Killed,* about crawling under the bellies of an entire herd of elephant, and nobody called Foran a liar. Daly's reputation was such that everything he said was suspect.

His story about the elephant with 200-pound tusks needs closer examination as well. This is very heavy ivory. To put it in perspective, the biggest pair on record weighed 235 and 226 pounds when fresh; they were taken from an elephant killed by a slave on the slopes of Mount Kilimanjaro. After this spectacular pair, there is a huge gap. The 1928 Rowland Ward listed the Number 1 set at 198 and 174 pounds, shot by Powell-Cotton on the shores of Lake Albert. Not every animal ended up in Rowland Ward, however; Billy Pickering killed an elephant in the Lado Enclave with teeth of 191 and 193 pounds. Harry Manners shot one in Mozambique that carried 185 and 183 pounds, and Sam Baker (a reliable observer) saw a single tusk in a Khartoum market that weighed 172 pounds and another in London that rocked the scales at 188. His own personal heaviest weighed in at 149 pounds.

Most of the great elephant hunters never even approached the 200-pound mark. Pete Pearson's best was 155 and 153, Ionides had 126 and 123, Jim Sutherland 152 and 137, Pretorius 160 per side, Carr Hartley 164 and 167 pounds. Sir William Garstin shot an elephant with tusks of 135 and 159 pounds, and the modern Kenya record belongs to Mohammed Akbar, whose animal weighed in at 172 and 164 pounds. The American Museum of Natural History in New York used to own a pair that weighed 167 and 169 pounds, found by a lucky traveler near the Voi River in Kenya. More recently, Ray Petty took an elephant in Ethiopia in 1988 that boasted tusks of 145 and 121 pounds. So Daly's elephant, if real, would easily be among the very biggest trophies ever, judged by tusk weight.

But was it real? Let's analyze the story. According to Daly, it was during the late 1920s and he had just been released from a brutal captivity by the French in Ubangi-Shari. Charged with assault, spying, larceny, and sundry other crimes, he had been punished by the loss of his unrestricted hunting license and the confiscation of all his property, including his rifles, ammunition, and ten thousand pounds of ivory. Daly wrote that after the trial he went down to the capital, Bangui, to file an appeal with the governor. Finding no relief there, he took a job with two Frenchmen, Cornus and de Jardin, who were running a motorized transport business. He stated that he made a good deal of money maintaining and driving the trucks on long trips in all directions. Unfortunately, a deportation order suddenly came through giving him just one hour to leave the country, and he had to leave all his profits behind. Cornus and de Jardin gave him a canoe so he could make the thousand-mile trip down the Ubangi and Congo Rivers to Leopoldville, where he hoped to solicit the British government's help in reclaiming his property.

It was on this leg of the journey that he supposedly killed the record elephant. He somehow obtained a rifle and ammunition, probably from a trader on the river, and hoped to make some desperately needed cash. Drifting down the Ubangi, he heard an unseen elephant ashore and pulled in. After a stalk lasting less than an hour, Daly said, he came up to the bull and killed it without incident. The tusks weighed 207 and 203 pounds, and he quickly sold them and others he had gathered to a Portuguese trader on a passing steamer for fifty thousand Belgian francs.

That's the story. On the surface, it's plausible. Daly was obviously in need of quick money, having lost everything to the French. His arrest and rough treatment at the hands of the French authorities are an established fact—even the French admitted it. Still, there is no record of a pair of tusks weighing a total of 410 pounds appearing in Ubangi-Shari, the Congo, or anywhere else. This was the 1920s, not the 1880s, and surely people would have realized that they were a near record and thus merited a premium. The French government was still selling commercial elephant licenses at that time, so fear of the law should not have been an insurmountable factor. For that matter, how did Daly weigh the tusks, given the fact he had no equipment? We might assume that the Portuguese trader or the steamer captain had a scale, but Daly doesn't say that, and after all, this was a Congo steamboat, not the *Queen Mary*. Above all, if they knew what they had, wouldn't they have advertised the unique tusks? Extraordinary tusks routinely go for a much higher price than that warranted just by the weight of the ivory. All in all, given Daly's reputation, the story must be considered as very doubtful.

So much for how other sportsmen felt about Marcus Daly. For his part, Daly had little use for most of his fellow hunters. In his 1937 book he wrote, speaking of cannibals, "Several Belgians and French-European officials have finished up in those cooking-pots, and, if a few more of them that I know there did, the country would be much cleaner." Daly was an arrogant, insufferable man, but his talent for self-promotion and his undoubted stalking skills ensured him commissions as a professional hunter whenever he wanted them.

His reputation requires that you take his stories with a grain of salt, but some of Daly's anecdotes are too good not to repeat. One of his stories took place near a French station called Mbayo on the Ubangi River. The station had its own jail, and every morning the prisoners were shackled and marched down to the river to fetch their water. Each prisoner carried the water in a four-gallon tin pail, which he would balance on his head. They were shackled together by a chain running along their ankles. Under the bored eyes of the guards, they would enter the water single-file, each man filling his pail and then shuffling a few feet so the next man could go to the filling spot.

One morning the chain gang was made up of ten men. Nine had already filled their pails and were stretched out in a file leading back to the stockade when the tenth and last man stooped to get his water. Suddenly a crocodile lunged from the muddy shallows, grabbed the last man by the leg, and pulled him under. Like mountaineers roped together in an alpine slide, each of the ten men in turn was pulled into the water and disappeared forever. The stunned guards saw the entire episode but could do nothing, and as the last of the prisoners vanished, the guards' thoughts turned to how in hell they were going to explain this one. Finally they submitted a report up the chain of command that all

Marcus Daly with elephant tusks weighing 110 and 125 pounds, respectively.

ten men had escaped into the river, stealing the chain as they went.

Daly told the story in convincing detail, but it is only fair to state that other hunters gave different versions of the same or a similar event. John Boyes, for instance, in his 1927 *The Company of Adventurers,* recorded an almost identical incident that supposedly happened in Lake Victoria. He added another tale in which a rhino got his horn tangled in a chain that was holding several prisoners together, and disappeared into the bush with them. Boyes was not above stretching the truth (probably not to the extent of Daly, however), and it is only fair to acknowledge that Boyes's story is in a chapter called "Round the Campfire," a literary device used by several of the old hunter/writers to indicate tall tales. One of the major problems in investigating safari history is deciphering which story really belongs to which writer.

Darke, Grosvenor. A British hunter and adventurer who lived among the Zulus in the 1880s and took part in their civil wars.

Darley, Henry Algernon Cholmley (1870–xxxx). A blond, bearded man, Maj. Henry Darley was a big-game hunter and ivory poacher of some note. From about 1904 he hunted elephant in the Lado Enclave in a loose partnership with R. J. Cuninghame called "The Two Robbers of the North." They focused their activities in the Mongalla and Karamoja regions north of Lake Victoria and were very successful for a few years, but things began to slow down as the British administration expanded its authority in the district.

In 1907 Darley decided to try his luck in Menelik's kingdom of Abyssinia. He had worn out his welcome in Uganda (there was actually a Uganda warrant for his arrest until 1919) and saw an opportunity to trade and pick up some easy ivory. He also served as the British agent at the frontier town of Maji.

Serie, a local tribal chief from a people called the Shangalla, once tried to convince Darley to join him in rebellion and declare their independence; together they would rule the remote country. Serie promised Darley a hut full of ivory for his acquiescence. Darley refused, honestly noting in his memoirs that "I saw no way of leaving the country with my spoils."

Things went fairly well until the death of Menelik in 1908, when the traditional apocalyptic upheaval following a king's death split Ethiopia into savagely warring factions. After escaping from a variety of dangerous situations (including being charged with the murder of some thirty Abyssinian soldiers, a crime he claimed he did not commit), Darley led his followers (mainly Kikuyu, Swahili, and Luo porters and askaris) on an epic journey through western Ethiopia and into the Sudan. Conditions were such that at least two similar caravans disappeared entirely along the same route.

Darley relied on boldness and on his wits to successfully complete his escape. A reading of his book *Slaves and Ivory* (1926) gives a glimpse of what made the British so nearly invincible in those times. Time and again, when faced with disaster, some aspect of Darley's Imperial upbringing surfaced to save the day. Lost in the swamps of the Sudan, he came across a British expeditionary force led by officers who happened to be old schoolmates of his. On another occasion, an influential agent in Abyssinia turned out to be a fellow member of one of Darley's London clubs. All of these connections served to break down suspicion and procure necessary assistance. Perhaps the best example of the Victorian spirit occurred when Darley and his small safari were guests at a camp of tribal warriors who were plainly planning to murder them all. During the tense talks Darley kept his hand on the butt of his revolver "and decided, if the worst came to the worst, to let daylight into my chieftain friend sitting in front of me before anything else happened." Darley and his men managed to escape because the warriors did not realize they could speak the local language and so they talked about leading Darley into an ambush right in front of their intended victims. Darley and his men pretended to be fooled and headed off toward the trap, but once out of sight they simply killed their treacherous guide and swiftly escaped in another direction.

Once safely back in British territory, Darley became an aggressive champion for pacification of the frontier provinces. After serving in World War I, he guided Maj. L. F. Athill on a border-surveying mission back into Abyssinia in 1919. Athill credited Darley's skill and good reputation for the successful completion of the mission.

In 1926 Darley published *Slaves and Ivory,* both an account of his pre-war adventures and a ringing call for military protection for the loyal tribes of Uganda and the Sudan against the Abyssinian raiders. The call did not go unheard, and in the late 1920s the British government extended the road system in the Sudan to allow for a rapid armed response to Abyssinian incursions. Raiding, however, continued on a reduced scale well into the late part of the century.

From a historian's perspective, *Slaves and Ivory* reminds one of the formidable Abyssinian military reputation in the early twentieth century. We have long read about how Mussolini's modern military machine destroyed the medieval armies of the "Lion of Judah" in the 1930s. What is forgotten is that virtually nobody expected that outcome—the Ethiopians had handily exterminated one Italian invasion in 1896, and for the next forty years were considered an almost invincible fighting machine, at least on their own turf. The Fascist victory came as a shock to most military experts of the time. It is always interesting to note just how much of history is colored by hindsight.

Darter, Adrian (1867–1955). Adrian Darter was a twenty-two-year-old South African who in 1890 left a job as a clerk in his father's Cape Town music shop to answer the call for volunteers to invade Mashonaland. The powerful Matabele people, under their king, Lobengula, had long considered Mashonaland as a sort of subject province, a proving ground for Matabele warriors and a source of plunder and slaves. Lured by travelers' tales of mineral wealth and fruitful farmland, Cecil Rhodes and his confederates at the BSAC (see glossary) decided to grab the province and hoped to intimidate Lobengula (who was secretly receiving £100 a month from the BSAC) into allowing the annexation and restraining his young warriors, who were eager to come to blows with the British and Boer settlers.

The spearhead of this invasion was the so-called "Pioneer Column," of which Darter became a member. Led by Frank Johnson and guided by Fred Selous, the column consisted of about two hundred Europeans and a like number of African auxiliaries. The Pioneers were drawn from all walks of life and many different countries. They included hunters, soldiers, prospectors, missionaries, woodsmen, musicians, and politicians. There were many colorful and interesting characters in the column, including Arthur Eyre (a hunter who later killed the last white rhino in Rhodesia), Paddy O'Toole (who had won the Victoria Cross in the 1879 Zulu War), Fred Nesbitt (a soldier with several decades of experience in South Africa's Frontier Wars), and Robert Coryndon (a future governor of both Kenya and Uganda). Capt. Maurice Heany was a redheaded Virginian and a cousin of Edgar Allan Poe. In addition to volunteers, the column was made up of men culled from the Bechuanaland Police, the BSAC company police, and various other agencies. They were promised seven shillings, six pence per day, plus the rights to a Mashonaland farm and fifteen gold claims. The police were compensated at a rate of five shillings per day. The plan was for the Pioneers to construct a road to Mashonaland that would serve as a highway for the mass of settlers soon to follow. The BSAC police contingent would closely follow the Pioneers and guard the right-of-way against Matabele raiders.

Darter wrote an account of the superb equipment that the Pioneers were issued. Each trooper was given a blue overcoat, brown tunic, riding breeches, yellow leather leggings, wool jersey, leather belt with cartridge holders, socks, boots, blankets, a waterproof groundsheet, spurs, slacks, knapsack, canteen, and a sewing kit. They were armed with a Martini-Henry rifle, a Webley six-shot revolver, a shelter-half, and a small ax. The equipment was lavish and well made, which was not always the case in expeditions of this sort. The only complaint Darter ever lodged about the outfitting concerned the bandolier, which lacked loop-covers. The handier troopers soon manufactured these out of canvas. Darter's recollection of the equipment is confirmed in William Harvey Brown's *On the South African Frontier* (1899).

The invasion itself was relatively uneventful. Selous carefully chose a route that skirted Matabeleland proper, and the construction of the road proceeded at a pace that left the Matabele warriors guessing. Lobengula, impressed by the efficiency with which the British had destroyed the mighty Zulus just a decade earlier, managed to keep his rasher counselors and young warriors in check, and no Matabele impi (see glossary) descended on the watchful column. This is not to detract from the bravery displayed by the Pioneers—they expected a hard fight and were well prepared for it. The fact that it did not come off does not diminish their accomplishment.

The after-effects of the invasion of Mashonaland were significant. The region was not the treasure trove that had been anticipated, and three years later Rhodes and the BSAC rather treacherously attacked Matabeleland and destroyed Lobengula. This was followed by massive revolts in 1896 that rocked both Matabeleland and Mashonaland. Many of the original Pioneers perished in these conflicts, but most, like Darter, blamed Rhodes and the chartered company for the bloodshed, not the Matabele. They considered Lobengula an honorable foe who had kept his end of the bargain, refrained from killing them when it lay in his power to do so, and had been shabbily treated by the British. When the BSAC's activities in the area came up for review in 1914, Darter went so far as to write a book about the Pioneer Column that condemned Rhodes and his backers for their actions.

Pioneers of Mashonaland was Darter's only book. It is raw, choppy, grammatically flawed, and rather rambling, but its very flaws help to illustrate the type of men who served in the Column. One great attribute of the book is a roster of the entire unit, containing such biographical information as was known. Recent reprints have updated the roster, making it an excellent historical and genealogical source.

Darter himself remained in Africa long enough to experience blackwater fever, the 1893 and 1896 Matabele wars, and the Boer War, in which he served in the Rhodesia Regiment at the Relief of Mafeking. He moved to England sometime before 1910 and raised a family. During World War I he served as a rifle instructor, and he died in Southampton in 1955. Darter was one of the last surviving Pioneers. The last officer of the Column to die (in 1947) was the Protestant chaplain, the Reverend F. H. Surridge (there was also a Catholic chaplain, the Jesuit priest Father Hartmann), and the last-known enlisted man was Conductor H. A. Solomon, who died in Cape Town in 1963 at the age of ninety. The leader of the Pioneers, Frank Johnson, was the last surviving combat officer and lived until 1943.

Das Neves. Originally named Fernandes, Das Neves was a Portuguese sportsman who hunted elephant and traded for ivory in Mozambique and the Transvaal in the 1860s. He was the author of *A Hunting Expedition to the Transvaal* (1879).

Davis, Richard Harding (1864–1916). This American journalist and travel writer went exploring and hunting (mainly hippo) in Central and West Africa in the 1900s, especially on a trip to the Congo in 1907. He also covered the Spanish-American and Boer Wars. Davis was a close friend or at least an acquaintance of many interesting Africa-related figures, including Theodore Roosevelt, Frederick Remington, F. R. Burnham, and William A. Chanler, and was one of the founders of New York's Traveler's Club. He was the author of many books, including *The Congo and Coasts of Africa* (1907), and the subject of 1917's *Adventures and Letters of Richard Harding Davis* (edited by his brother).

Richard Harding Davis in South Africa, circa 1900.

Davison, Edward Hartley "Ted" (1906–xxxx). A Rhodesian game warden, Davison is one of those legendary wardens, like Stevenson-Hamilton, inextricably associated with the development of an African national park. In his case it was Wankie N. P. (now Hwange).

In September 1928 Davison became the first warden of the newly proclaimed Wankie Game Reserve. This huge area in southwestern Rhodesia was a barren, arid place inhabited only by wandering Bushmen. There were surprisingly few large animals for a national park, the district being both too dry and too heavily hunted for larger game populations.

Like many of the early parks, the Wankie area had been badly shot out. Zebra and tsessebe were rare, hartebeest extremely so, and no wildebeest had been seen there since 1926. No rhino had been spotted since 1925. There was at least a decent nucleus of giraffe, eland, sable, impala, elephant, kudu, and roan.

The area of Wankie was chosen for the reserve because the administration was under pressure to establish a park (Albert and Kruger national parks had been proclaimed in the previous few years), and Wankie was so desolate that it seemed to have no other potential anyway. Davison's initial responsibilities included road-building, rebuilding the stock of game, and controlling poachers in the five-thousand-square-mile reserve. To increase the numbers of grazing animals, he implemented a predator-control program, shooting lion and hunting dogs on sight. This approach had been tried in the Sabi Game Reserve and apparently had worked; game populations had risen. Researchers of predator/prey dynamics now believe that populations are most dependent on weather, human poaching, and land usage, not the number of big cats in an area, but in the 1920s this was not understood.

Whether it was predator control, the cessation of hunting, or just good weather for a few years, the game came back. In 1935 the first wildebeest returned, followed in 1942 by the first pair of black rhino, and zebra were fairly common by 1950. As in other parks, the predator-control policy was eventually lifted and looked back upon as an error. The lion in particular became one of the park's biggest attractions.

Davison was still in charge of Wankie when it achieved National Park status on 27 January 1950. The first real rest camps had been built in 1936, and increasing numbers of tourists took advantage of the park: 2,771 in 1949, 25,351 in 1965. Davison oversaw the boring of numerous water holes, which helped greatly to prevent overgrazing by the ever-increasing numbers of elephant. To a large extent, Davison's bore holes were the key to Wankie's success.

Water holes, of course, are a key component to the African ecosystem. Besides simply providing drinking water, they play a critical role in the food dynamic. All animals have to drink (except a specialized few that can get their required fluids from their food). It is only natural that they would tend to eat around their water source as well. The tendency of predators to congregate around water holes is well known. Less understood is the role water plays in the population dynamics of herbivores. Water holes are a major factor (often the major factor) in limiting the populations of elephant and other vegetation-eating animals.

Elephant provide the best example. During the dry season, when sources of water are scarce, elephant tend to remain near a water hole. The plants nearest the hole are devoured first, leaving a radius around the water that becomes barren of vegetation. This fringe area rapidly grows as the vegetation is eaten by elephant and other animals. If there is no rain and only a few water holes, soon the elephant are traveling twenty-five or thirty miles each day between their sources of food and their sources of water. In extreme cases, baby elephant cannot keep up and are eventually left behind to die of thirst, hunger, or predation somewhere between the two locations. During prolonged droughts this can cause a significant drop in the elephant population.

Hippo suffer from the same problem, to an even greater extent. Their skin cannot endure prolonged exposure to the sun, and during droughts they tend to cluster in groups in the middle of the shrinking water source, desperately maneuvering for a better position. Every sunset they have to leave the water hole, by now often just a puddle, to travel miles overland to find food. Elephant, at least, are smart enough to try to find a new water source. Hippo, and to an even greater extent rhino, will continue to try to use the same shrinking source until it is all gone. The rhino will not leave its home range; when the water source dies, so does the animal.

This connection between water and food was first realized by Davison, who pioneered the development of manmade water holes to assist the elephant herds and other plant-eaters. The more water sources there are, the more spread out is the impact of the elephant's appetite, and so Davison constructed dozens of bore holes in otherwise remote and arid sections of the huge reserve. The holes were created by either gasoline engines or windmills, and after some tinkering proved a great success. Davison found that the best design was to construct a shallow pool some distance from the pump, and then run a concrete trough from the pump to the pool. This provided wary wildlife with several different spots at which to drink; some would only drink from the trough, others from the hole itself. Various methods were used to prevent elephant from damaging the equipment. Soon Wankie-style bore holes began to appear in many African parks.

After transforming Wankie from a barren wilderness into a thriving national park, Davison was unexpectedly transferred to a desk job in 1961 and replaced by Bruce Austen. He retired in 1964. He was the author of *Wankie* (1967), a highly readable if somewhat rambling account of his years in the park. It's a good book but suffers from direct comparison to Stevenson-Hamilton's superb *African Eden.*

Davison, F. Trubee. Davison was a New York lawyer who inherited a fortune of $4,500,000 from his father, investment banker H. P. Davison. In 1933 he was named president of the American Museum of Natural History. In June of that year he led an expedition to acquire elephant specimens for the museum in East Africa. Noted military airman Pete Quesada flew Davison and his wife Dorothy from Cairo to Lake Victoria on a flying boat. From there they drove to Garissa on the Tana River, where they were met by professional hunter Al Klein and their friends Martin and Osa Johnson. Davison collected a total of five elephants for the museum's taxidermy collection. For public consumption the word was put out that the dead elephants were notorious crop-raiders, but that was not the case. In reality Klein had to find elephants of a precise size for Davison to shoot.

Davison later achieved a sort of notoriety, at least among the kind of people who think a secret cartel is really running the world. A member of Yale's Skull and Bones secret society (Class of 1918), Davison became the director of recruitment for the CIA in the 1950s. Modern conspiracy theorists credit Davison with the surreptitious installation of Skull and Bones alumni in key government positions.

Davison, Henry Pomeroy (1867–1922). Davison was an executive with New York's J. P. Morgan Company who rose to prominence after graduating from Yale, where he was a leader of the Skull and Bones secret society. After striking it rich on Wall Street, Davison served during World War I as a "Dollar-a-Day" man, working mainly with the American Red Cross.

Davison took a six-week hunting trip to Sudan in the early 1920s, shooting buffalo, hippo, white rhino, elephant, and plains game. He planned to write a book about his safari (at least a small privately printed edition for his friends) but died in 1922 before he could get around to it. A forty-four-page abstract of the manuscript was included as an appendix to *The Record of a Useful Life* (1933), a collection of his papers edited by T. W. Lamont.

Dawnay, Guy Cuthbert (1848–1889). Dawnay was a well-known English baronet and sportsman who had a long career in African hunting but came to a bad end. In 1872 he hunted the Zambezi Valley with a Natal hunter named Moore. Later he visited Victoria Falls and was a guest of the Matabele king, Lobengula. In 1876 Dawnay went on a hunting expedition with his friend Robert Russell that ended when Russell was killed by a buffalo.

Dawnay served in the 1879 Anglo-Zulu War as an officer in the Natal Native Contingent. Selous (1881) wrote that Dawnay had acquired a great reputation among the southern Africans for his athletic ability and skill. He also served in the 1882 Nile and 1885 Suakin campaigns.

In 1886 Dawnay was a member of the so-called Emin Pasha Relief Expedition Committee, a quasi-official organization that developed the plan and money to send Henry Stanley to "rescue" Emin Pasha in Equatoria. The EPRE committee was chaired by William MacKinnon (1823–1893), a Scottish businessman who was also the president of the IBEA (see glossary). Other committee members included James Augustus Grant, Sir Francis de Winton, and A. J. Kinnaird.

On 28 February 1889 Dawnay was hunting at Ngiri, near Kilimanjaro in East Africa. He wounded a buffalo and was following up in thick brush when the buff charged from close quarters. Dawnay apparently shot it once again with his .450 rifle but failed to stop the hulking creature, which killed him. Four months later, American William Chanler camped by a large acacia at Ngiri under which Dawnay was buried. His name and date of death were carved in the bark.

Dawnay was author of the privately printed *Campaigns: Zulu 1879, Egypt 1882, Suakin, 1885,* which was reprinted in the late 1980s.

Dawson, Alexander. Alexander Dawson arrived in South Africa from Scotland in 1870 and was trading in Bechuanaland by 1872. In 1872–1874 he hunted elephant in Matabeleland with Fred Selous, George Wood, and Fairbairn.

Dawson, James (1852–1921). The younger brother of Alexander, Jimmy Dawson hunted in Matabeleland with Selous in March of 1874. He was a trader with a long history with the Matabele. When the British wanted to make peace after Lobengula's death in 1894, it was Dawson who was sent to negotiate with the remaining tribal leaders. His mission was a success. Dawson commanded "F" Troop of the Bulawayo Field Force during the 1896 Matabele Rebellion. He farmed in Rhodesia for many years (marrying the ex-fiancée of Maj. Alan Wilson in 1896) and in 1915 opened a cattle ranch in Barotseland. He shot himself after an epidemic wiped out his herd.

Dawson, John. This white hunter was killed in a German ambush at Seki water hole near Bissell, southern Kenya, in 1916. Two British troopers were wounded in the skirmish, and the Germans stripped them of their weapons and left them. The two men had to listen to lion eating their own dead mules and horses before they were rescued that night.

Dawson, Richard. According to Frederick Seymour in *Roosevelt in Africa* (1909), Captain Dawson shot a white rhino in Kenya in 1909. The exact wording goes: "One of the lucky hunters to bring a white rhino to his game bag was Capt. Richard Dawson of the British Coldstream Guards, who made the shooting in July of 1909 in the Sotik district, northwest of Kijabe, where the Roosevelt party was operating at the same time, hoping especially for similar good fortune." If true, this would indicate that the 1909 range of the white rhino was substantially greater than otherwise believed.

In an attempt to verify the report, I checked the 1928 edition of *Rowland Ward's Records of Big Game,* which has thirty-four northern white rhino trophies listed, from a spectacular 45¾-inch horn all the way down to a fairly mediocre 22-inch horn. First, none of the records belonged to a man named Dawson. Second, and more telling, the kill localities are given as follows: Lado or Near Lado (11); Bahr el Ghazal (4); Belgian Congo (2); Rhino Camp, White

Nile (5); White Nile (4); French Congo (1); Uganda (2); Cameroons (1); Southern Sudan (1); and Mongalla (3). None of these places is anywhere near the Sotik or Kijabe. All, in fact, with the exception of the Cameroons, are pretty much just different names for the same general area. Put it this way: In the three world atlases in my library, all good ones, all the places mentioned above (except for the Cameroons are on the same page. As for the Sotik, there are no white rhino there, and weren't any in 1909. The map in Jonathan Kingdon's excellent *Kingdon Field Guide to African Mammals* indicates that the Sotik is not part of the white rhino's recent range. It does affirm, however, that native rock art and skeletal remains (presumably pre-fossil) prove that the white rhino inhabited the region some centuries ago.

I also checked the much lengthier list of black rhino in the 1928 Rowland Ward and found no Richard Dawson there. He's not listed in the 1899 Rowland Ward, but I haven't had an opportunity yet to check the appropriate issue of the British army list. I go into this at such length only to demonstrate just how careful you have to be with sources. Anyone reading Seymour's 1909 book and taking it at face value might think there were white rhino in Kenya and Tanganyika. This is how bad information gets passed on from source to source.

Deane, Walter (xxxx–1888). An officer of the Congo Free State, Captain Deane was assigned to Stanley Falls station in 1886. When the Arab revolt broke out, Deane and a Lieutenant Dubois found themselves surrounded by a small company of soldiers, most of whom promptly deserted because the station's ammunition was bad. After a four-day siege (during which Dubois was drowned), Deane and four loyal soldiers escaped under cover of darkness and fled through the jungle. It took them over a month to reach the nearest station, almost five hundred miles away, during which they were reduced to eating insects and bark. After recovering from his ordeal, Deane continued his career and was killed by an elephant while hunting in 1888.

DeBono, Andrea (1821–1871). This Maltese ivory merchant and slave trader hunted and explored the White Nile region in the 1850–1860s. His chief lieutenant, named Muhammad Wad el Mek, acted as a sort of field general for his chief, often taking large groups of men aside to plunder villages and raid for slaves and cattle. These men were known colloquially as the "Egyptian elephant hunters," although they were actually a ragtag assortment of Nubians, Egyptians, Turks, and African tribesmen. DeBono and Wad el Mek actually did have official Egyptian commissions to police the region, but instead terrorized the vicinity, not only shooting elephant but also raiding villages for slaves and cattle.

They operated on a large scale, with hundreds of irregular warriors accompanied by their women, living in tent cities around Gondokoro and Shooa for years at a time. Sir Samuel Baker once threatened to hang Wad el Mek if he did not refrain from raiding the country of a Baker ally.

For a time DeBono, author of *Annales de Voyage* (Paris, 1862), was accompanied by a French physician, Dr. Albert Peney. De Bono was by Peney's side at the latter's July 1861 death from blackwater fever on the Nile River near Fort Berkeley.

Decken, Karl Klaus von der (1833–1865). He was a German aristocrat from Kotzen in Brandenburg who left the army in 1860 and set out to find the snowcapped mountains of East Africa. He spent 1861–1862 in an exhaustive search of the Kilimanjaro region and was the first European to attempt to climb that eminence. In 1864 he led an expedition up the Tana and Juba Rivers and was killed along with most of his men by the Somalis while exploring the Juba. A total of eight Europeans were on this expedition. Baron von der Decken and five others were killed. The hulk of von der Decken's vessel, the *Guelph*, was found almost exactly twenty-seven years later by Commander Dundas of the Royal Navy—one side was gone, but the boiler was intact and the funnel still stood upright.

His notes were published posthumously in 1869–1870 as Karl Klaus von der Decken's *Reisen in Ost-Afrika.*

Decle, Lionel (1859–1907). A French adventurer, Decle first attracted attention by traveling overland from the Cape of Good Hope to the Victoria Nile in 1892–1894. In 1899–1900 he explored the Kagera River north of Victoria Nyanza. A few years later he went on a prolonged expedition through Nyasaland and Tanganyika, a trip partially financed by Cecil Rhodes. He was the author of *Three Years in Savage Africa* (1898).

De Crespigny, Sir Claude Champion. Major de Crespigny was a British soldier and sportsman who was active in horse racing, fox hunting, and hot-air ballooning. After the Boer War he went hunting in East Africa and in 1905 went on the Sotik punitive expedition. He and close friend Richard Meinertzhagen often went hunting together, as well as pig-sticking. On one of the latter occasions, De Crespigny and Meinertzhagen tried to run down a lion and kill it with their spears. These weren't proper pig-sticking spears like the specialist weapons found in India, but merely bayonets lashed to long poles. De Crespigny was better mounted and reached the lion first, but his horse balked at the last minute and the rider was thrown to the ground mere yards from the enraged lion. De Crespigny managed to pull out his service revolver and put a bullet in the lion's brain just as the big cat crouched to spring. At the same moment Meinertzhagen arrived and speared the lion with his makeshift lance. The pair were ordered to discontinue the lion-sticking as too dangerous. Meinertzhagen, for one, confessed he had no desire ever to try it again.

De Crespigny was the author of *Forty Years of a Sportsman Life* (1910). In the 1930 EARB (see glossary) he was listed as residing at Moshi in Tanganyika. ROWLAND WARD 1928: HARTEBEEST, LEOPARD.

Dedek, Georg. This German national hunted elephant in Portuguese East Africa in the 1930s.

DeFries, Louis. A hunter based at Chifumbaze, North-East Rhodesia, DeFries went on safari with Owen Letcher and Dillon Leonard in 1909. Some time before that he had been badly gored by a buffalo he had wounded. Failing to find the animal during the follow-up after his initial shot, DeFries was returning to camp when the bull ambushed him. It was thought unlikely that he would survive, but after an extended rest at Fort Jameson he resumed his hunting career, especially for buffalo.

Delamere, Lord (Hugh Cholmondeley) (1870–1931). The third Baron Delamere was a wild and reckless young man whose wasteful behavior appalled his parents and older acquaintances. In 1895 he went on a hunting trip to India, Norway, and East Africa, accompanied by Dr. A. Eustace Atkinson, a physician who was sent along at the insistence of Delamere's mother to keep him in one piece. The pair went hunting in what is now northern Kenya, collecting a substantial amount of ivory. Delamere fell in love with East Africa and made five trips there, largely to Somaliland, before finally relocating. He suffered numerous injuries during these expeditions and suffered from related aches and pains the rest of his life.

Africa changed the wild youth into a responsible farmer. Determined to make a success of his land, which was rich in beauty but unsuited for agriculture due to peculiarities of

Lord Delamere shortly before his death in 1931.

the soil, Delamere took to rising early in the morning and working at warp speed all day. He tried his hand at sheep, coffee, and other crops but finally settled on cattle and later wheat. He was a very wealthy man on paper, thanks to his land holdings in Great Britain, but was constantly bleeding his European estates to keep his African ranch going. His days were spent mending fences and tending to cattle and crops. All too often his nights were spent waiting up for stock-raiding lion. He is known to have killed about fifty lion single-handed. In 1903 he applied for the position of game ranger but was turned down by the provincial commissioner, J. O. Hope, because of his reputation for recklessness. Shortly afterward an appointment as assistant collector (district officer) and land officer was provisionally approved—but then rejected by authorities in London.

In December 1923 Lord Delamere was confronted on the steps of the Nakuru hotel by Capt. Jock Purves, the recently divorced first husband of Beryl Markham. Purves apparently felt that his marriage had been ruined by the machinations of Delamere's son, Tom, and their hired manager, Boy Long; Purves had, in fact, threatened to shoot Long. It is thought that Purves may have been waiting for Tom Cholmondeley when the father appeared. At any rate, he struck Lord Delamere a vicious blow, knocking the older man down the steps and putting him in the hospital for weeks.

Despite his periodic injuries at the hands of man and beast, Delamere's incredible energy and charisma soon made him the unofficial leader of the settlers, who increasingly found themselves at odds with the government back in London. His appearance was unconventional—he wore his hair, red but now streaked with gray, down to his shoulders to keep the sun from burning his neck. He generally wore a sweater and khaki trousers, often falling asleep exhausted in that outfit after a long day. Just as he worked hard, he preferred hard forms of relaxation, and his drinking and practical jokes further endeared him to the rowdy settler community.

The Galbraith Cole case helped cement Delamere's position as head of the settlers. Cole had been suffering from Masai stock thieves (the Masai historically consider all cattle as belonging to them) and had warned the tribe's leaders that he would kill the next man he found stealing his cattle. Given Cole's reputation as a straight-shooter in every sense of the word, it surprised no one when he shot and killed a Masai warrior who was caught in the act of rustling. Cole was deported and a law was passed in London limiting the settler's ownership of land to a twenty-one-year lease. The settlers, who considered

Lord Delamere (third from left) on a pigsticking expedition, Somaliland, 1897.

that Cole had only done what had to be done if they were to survive, were outraged. Delamere, an effective speaker, led the successful campaign to exonerate Cole and rescind the onerous lease law. The law was repealed. Cole, who had sneaked back into Kenya under an alias, gradually found himself rehabilitated during the confusion of the Great War, when government's attention was focused elsewhere.

In 1923 the British government provoked the settlers once again with a series of legal moves that seemed to presage British withdrawal from Kenya. Worse, from the settler's viewpoint, these moves seemed to be giving the country back to the Africans, not them. The country suddenly found itself on the brink of a full-fledged revolution. Arms were stockpiled and newspapers openly speculated which side the English officers of the King's African Rifles, most of whom loved Kenya and many of whom planned to settle there, would take. Delamere led a delegation to London to plead the settlers' case. Fortuitously, the telegraph line from Mombasa to Nairobi chose that moment to break down. The British colonial officials, who feared that the telegraph collapse might be the opening shot in a long, drawn-out colonial war, quickly backed down. A compromise solution was worked out that pleased no one but at least avoided war. In retrospect the compromise was fatal to the settlers' interests. In the space of a few short years, the British government had switched from a policy of encouraging colonization in Kenya to a commitment to prepare the country for independence under an African government.

By this time Delamere was the grand old man of Kenya politics. He had married twice, the first time in 1899 to Lady Florence Cole, the daughter of the 4th Earl of Enniskillen (making him, incidentally, a relative of Galbraith Cole). She died in 1914, and in 1928 he married Gwladys Markham, the daughter of the Honorable Rupert Beckett. Lady Florence Delamere, incidentally, had several hunting records in the 1928 edition of Rowland Ward's record book, including white rhino and elephant. Delamere died on his farm in November 1931. His son, Tom Cholmondeley, the 4th Baron Delamere, inherited his estates and married Diana Broughton, the widow of alleged murderer Jock Delves Broughton, in 1955. The mantle of "leader" of the settlers was passed, however, to Lord Francis Scott.

De Laporte, Cecil R. (1875–xxxx). Cecil De Laporte, a former intelligence officer in Rimington's regiment during the Boer War, was hired as a Sabi Game Reserve ranger in 1903. He took over a tough section of the reserve along the Crocodile River and patrolled it splendidly until about 1915. He then became Stevenson-Hamilton's assistant, and acting warden in his absence, including an extended stretch during World War I. De Laporte's wife went to France in 1915, and the ranger followed a year later, serving as an officer on the Western Front in the famous Ninth South African Division. De Laporte was badly wounded in France on 10 November 1918, the day before the Armistice. He returned to ranger duty in mid-1919 and resumed as acting warden, trying to clean up the administrative mess left by acting warden Fraser, and then continued his career as ranger, retiring in the early 1930s.

Delbande. Prior to World War II, Delbande was a professional hunter in the French Congo and Chad. He made his living supplying meat to the railroad crews. After the war he became the game warden of N'Dele National Park.

Delcommune, Alexandere. Delcommune was a young Belgian who fist came to Africa in 1877 as the manager of a French station at Boma, at the mouth of the Congo. In the 1880s Delcommune became associated with Albert Thys's Compagnie du Congo and led a survey team that explored the central watershed of the region, helping to map the navigable rivers and find likely locations for trading stations.

Delcommune led a major Compagnie expedition through Tanganyika and the Congo in 1891–1893. His was the second of four coinciding expeditions sent to Katanga. It consisted of a total of about three hundred fifty men. The expedition arrived at the Katangan capital of Bunkeya in fair shape, but Msiri, the king of Katanga, was cagily playing the Belgians against the British and refused to sign any treaties.

Delcommune then moved south into the region called Basanga. In 1891 he was the first European to visit Lake Kassali (Cameron had glimpsed it from a distance). One of his goals was to find the rumored Lake Lanchi in the Lualaba basin, but instead he established that the lake was a myth. He made valuable surveys of the Lualaba and Luapala watersheds, discovering impassable rapids that would hamper development in the area. By mid-1893 he was at Gongo Lutete and had hooked up with surviving members of the Bia expedition, namely Francqui, Cornet, and Derscheid. Delcommune was the author of *Vingt Annees de Vie Africaine* (1922).

Delegorgue, Adulphe (1814–1850). A French explorer and naturalist, Delegorgue arrived in South Africa in 1838. He traveled briefly in Cape Colony and then spent some years exploring and hunting elephant in Natal and Zululand. He was the first to record seeing the white rhino in the latter territory, in 1847. He was the author of *Travels in Southern Africa*.

Delporte (xxxx–1891). Captain Delporte led an 1890 scientific expedition along the Congo. His mission was to survey the river and take astronomic, geodetic, and magnetic readings at various points. The expedition, which also included another officer by the name of Gillis, began on 3 July 1890 at Antwerp and arrived at Matadi on 5 August. The travelers began their survey at a leisurely pace, but in February 1891 both officers developed dysentery. Delporte died of the disease near Matadi on 26 May 1891. Gillis survived to write up the expedition's findings for the Belgian Royal Academy. Delporte was the author of a small book entitled *Exploration du Congo,* published in Brussels in 1890.

Denham, Dixon (1786–1828). An English explorer who accompanied Clapperton on the 1822 expedition that discovered Lake Chad, Denham was a British officer with the rank of major. During the Napoleonic Wars he had fought with distinction under Wellington in the Peninsula and at Waterloo.

Denham is known to have tried his hand at elephant hunting, but his efforts did not reveal any great aptitude. According to Sir Harry Johnston in *Pioneers in West Africa* (1912), Denham and some African hunters near Lake Chad once crept up to within a few feet of a huge bull elephant (Denham estimated its height at sixteen feet, which would easily have been a world record). One of the Africans hurled his spear at the bull, and it stuck near the tail. The elephant roared powerfully through its trunk, from which came a huge blast of sand. Denham, who presumably was supposed to shoot the beast at this point, was blinded by the sand, and the angry elephant ran off. On several other occasions Denham is known to have shot at elephant with his musket but apparently never succeeded in bringing one down.

Denham returned to England in late 1824 and was widely praised and admired for his discoveries. The British public was keen on the idea of British officers infiltrating the "forbidden territories" of Arab Africa, and Denham had made a quite dashing exploration of Bornu, now in western Nigeria. In 1827 he was sent on an engineering assignment to Sierra Leone to build roads and design irrigation schemes. The following year, after a brief inspection mission to the island of Fernando Po, Denham was appointed lieutenant governor of Sierra Leone. He was only forty-two years old, and all indications were that he would have a long and successful career, but he got sick that same year and died.

Denhardt, Clarence (Clemens) (1852–1928) and Gustav Denhardt (1856–1917). The two Denhardt brothers were early German settlers in East Africa. They began trading along the Tana River in the 1870s and in 1885 signed a treaty with an African Sultan at Witu on the Kenya coast north of Mombasa. This act was greeted with great concern by the British authorities. A treaty in 1886 set the border between Kenya and Tanganyika at roughly what it is now but retained Witu in German hands as a Protectorate. The British found the German presence on both sides of Kenya so disconcerting that in 1890 they swapped the key strategic island of Heligoland, right off the German coast, for the obscure East

Adulphe Delegorgue in Boer costume.

African enclave. In the meantime, the Denhardts had been outmaneuvered by Carl Peters and forced into bankruptcy.

Dent, R. E. Dent was the solitary assistant game warden assigned to fish protection in Kenya in the 1920s and 1930s, and was stationed in Nairobi.

Derscheid, J. M. This Belgian accompanied the Akeleys on their 1926 expedition to the Kivu and Congo districts. Part of the trip's official purpose was to make a survey of the general situation in the Parc National Albert, with specific emphasis on the gorilla population. Derscheid was the Belgian representative sent along for this purpose. In 1926 he discovered a small pond, Lake Rukumi, on the slopes of Mount Karisimbi and built a ranger station there. In 1927–1928 Derscheid had to return to Belgium to meet his compulsory military obligation. While there he completed a report on the gorillas and corrected the government maps of the district. Derscheid's input was vital in the decision to keep the gorilla listed as a protected species, despite attempts (led by professional hunter Alexander Barnes) to add the animal to the hunting license.

Derscheid later became secretary for the International Bureau for the Conservation of Nature, established in Brussels.

Desborough, Lord (1855–1945). Born William Henry Grenfell (he became Baron Desborough in 1905), he graduated Balliol College, Oxford, in 1879 and was first elected to Parliament in 1880. Desborough was an extremely active man, constantly participating in local politics. During World War I he ran an organization that mustered more than one million men into military service. In addition to several terms as a member of Parliament, Desborough served with the Thames Conservancy Board, the London Chamber of Commerce, British Imperial Council of Commerce, chairman of the Home Office Committee on the Police, the International Navigation Congress, the Royal Agricultural Society, and many more organizations. It was estimated at one time that he was a member of some 115 committees.

A friendly, easygoing man, he was nevertheless a fierce competitor when it came to sports, excelling especially at rowing and fencing. His athletic feats were varied and legendary—he twice swam across Niagara Falls, climbed the Matterhorn three times by three different routes, and owned a stable of harriers that had once belonged to King Edward VII. Though he never served in the armed forces, he saw active military service when he came under fire in Burma as a newspaper correspondent. Desborough was once trapped behind enemy lines, alone and armed only with an umbrella.

The baron traveled the globe in search of adventure, fishing and hunting in Africa, India, and the Rocky Mountains, where one of his companions died from the hardships that Desborough routinely endured. He caught a hundred tarpon in the waters off Florida and shot a record-book Cape buffalo on the White Nile. Perhaps no one man better personified the myth of public service and sport so loved by the traditional British public. ROWLAND WARD 1928: BUFFALO.

Destro, John. John Destro arrived in East Africa as an employee of the wealthy American big-game hunter and soon-to-be expatriate William McMillan, working on McMillan's abortive Blue Nile expeditions of 1903–1905. After those failures he was manager of McMillan's Juja Estate, where Theodore Roosevelt stayed in 1909. John's address in the 1930 EARB (see glossary) is given as P.O. Box 283, Nairobi. His son Reggie went on to become a prominent white hunter.

Dhanis, Francis (1862–1909). Commandant Francis Dhanis led the Free State campaign against the Congo Arabs in 1891–1892. In 1890 he constructed a station at Lusambo, from which he was expected to keep the peace in a vast section of the Congo with just a few hundred workers in his command. In early October of 1892 he received the news of the death of the trader Hodister and the ensuing Arab-African uprising. He also received warning that a rebel force of ten thousand to fifteen thousand men under a chief called Sefu was coming to wipe out his little station.

Modern researchers disagree about Sefu's hostile intentions, but Dhanis and the European press of the time had no doubts. Allying himself with a friendly chief named Gongo Lutete, who supplied a decisive reinforcement of some ten thousand men, Dhanis defeated Sefu in a decisive battle that saw at least a thousand Africans killed (some estimates were treble that number), with the loss of just one European.

After the campaign Dhanis tried to intervene in the treacherous execution of his ally Gongo Lutete, but the emissary, Captain Hinde, arrived two days too late to save him. Dhanis's fate was more fortunate. He was made a baron and in 1895 was placed in command of a huge expedition that was to head toward the Nile headwaters and threaten Britain's hegemony on the region. The story for public consumption was that Dhanis was to liberate the Lado Enclave from the Mahdist warriors who had killed Gordon, but in reality the baron had orders to take Khartoum.

The expedition, one of the largest ever seen in West Africa, was an unmitigated disaster. The askaris mutinied at a place called Ndirfi and murdered most of their officers, including the baron's brother. The mutiny sparked a general revolt among African troops throughout the Congo. Dhanis himself narrowly escaped being butchered by his own troops and fled in a panic back to Stanleyville.

Dick, Andrew (xxxx–1895). In 1895 the Masai, provoked by insults to their women and cattle, massacred a thousand-man Swahili safari, killing five hundred fifty at a place called Ewaso Kedong. Dick, an English trader and early Kenya settler, tried to take advantage of the uproar by raiding a Masai kraal and stealing some cattle. In the ensuing battle he and a few African companions killed a large number of *morani* (some say over one hundred) before running out of ammunition. He was then caught and speared to death, the first Englishman to die under Masai spears since British rule had began. The fighting spirit he had displayed caused the Masai to erect a cairn in his honor over his grave.

Dickens. An elephant hunter in the Lado Enclave, Dickens was hunting with Knowles when their camp was attacked one night in 1908 by angry tribesmen. Dickens was wounded in the leg by an arrow but recovered.

Dickinson, W. V. D. Known as "Dicker." Maj. W. V. D. Dickinson, a Kenya PH, was employed by the firm of Safariland, Ltd. in the 1920s and often assisted Denys Finch Hatton on his safaris. Dickinson also worked with fellow professionals Sydney Waller, J. H. Barnes, and H. R.

Denys Finch Hatton and Maj. W. V. D. Dickinson with sable antelope, 1927.

Thomas Dinesen on Mount Kenya, 1923.

Stanton as white hunters on the 1930 MGM motion picture *Trader Horn,* providing protection from wild beasts and food for the film crew.

Dickinson hunted in the Lado Enclave with Boyes, Pickering, and Knowles around 1910, and he briefly worked for the Uganda Public Works Department. It is possible that Dickinson is the same man as Dickens, noted in the entry above.

Dinesen, Thomas (1892–1979). The brother of Karen Blixen, author of *Out of Africa,* Thomas Dinesen won the Victoria Cross fighting for England on the Western Front in World War I. The citation described how Dinesen had single-handedly killed twelve German machine-gunners with grenades and his bayonet, enabling the British to capture a mile of fortified territory. This feat helped put to rest the spurious speculation that the Baroness Blixen and her family were pro-German.

After the war Dinesen split his time between Denmark and Kenya, and married Jonna Lindhardt in 1926. He was involved with the business end of Karen Blixen's agricultural enterprise (the Karen Coffee Company). Dinesen was the author of a magazine article, "Lion-Hunting in East Africa," that was published by *Gad's* magazine in 1924, and the books *No Man's Land* (1929) and *My Sister, Isak Dinesen* (1975).

Dinuzulu (c. 1868–1913). A Zulu king, he was son of Cetshwayo and leader of the uSuthu faction. After being defeated by Zibhebhu and the Mandlakazi Zulus at Ondini in 1883, Dinuzulu made a pact with the Boers and, with their help, drove the Mandlakazi out of Zululand at the Battle of Tshaneni (1884). The Boers took much of the best farmland in the kingdom as payment. After the British annexation, Dinuzulu remained titular head of the Zulu (with the rank of regional chief, not king) until he was implicated in helping some of the insurgents in Bambatha's rebellion of 1906. Sentenced to four years imprisonment for treason, Dinuzulu was released in 1910 by Louis Botha, first prime minister of the Union of South Africa. He was allowed to live out his life on a small farm in the Transvaal, where he died apparently of gout and Bright's disease in 1913.

Dobson, D. D. Assistant magistrate at Ngara in Nyasaland in the early 1900s, Dobson was a graduate of Oxford (where he was a rugby star) and one of the few colonial officials who volunteered to work in areas known to be havens of sleeping sickness. He went out one evening to set a controlled brush fire and was surprised and killed by a rhino.

Dodson, Edward. Dodson was the young English taxidermist who accompanied Donaldson Smith on his 1894 expedition to Lake Turkana. He was also a member (with Carl Akeley) of the 1896 Somaliland expedition led by Daniel Elliott.

Doggett, Walter. Doggett was assigned to Sir Harry Johnston's small staff in Uganda in 1900 as a naturalist/collector. He accompanied Johnston on a trip to the Congo that resulted in the discovery of the okapi.

Doggett was eventually killed by a crocodile when a hippo overturned his canoe in Lake Victoria. There may have been more to the story, however, because Sir Harry was strangely reticent about the incident. In his memoirs he mentions Doggett only twice, and the accident not at all.

Dolman, Alfred (1827–1851). Born 19 September 1827 and schooled at Eton, Dolman went to South Africa at an early age and made several expeditions into the interior. He was fascinated with David Livingstone and made two trips in an attempt to visit the missionary. Dolman hunted profusely along the way, shooting buffalo, hartebeest, and springbok. On the second trip he was heading for Lake Ngami when disaster struck: His oxen ran away, leaving him stranded in the Kalahari Desert. His Bushman gunbearer returned to civilization but claimed that he had simply lost contact with the explorer. Dolman was never again seen alive.

When Dolman was first reported missing, it was assumed he had been killed by lions, but rumors began circulating that he had been murdered by his gunbearer, who had a checkered past. There was not enough evidence to convict the man, however, and legal proceedings were not initiated.

Dolman's diaries from his earlier expeditions, illustrated with his own superb artwork, were kept secret by his family until 1924, when they were published as *In the Footsteps of Livingstone.* Historians still disagree as to the cause of Dolman's death, many sources speculating that he died of exhaustion and exposure. Dolman's great-great-grandson, the controversial British historian David Irving, has stated his belief that Dolman was murdered and then eaten by the gunbearer.

Dominis. Dominis was a lieutenant in the German colonial army, stationed in the Cameroons. In the late 1890s he shipped a baby elephant back to Germany, the first to be exhibited there. The animal was probably obtained by shooting its mother.

Donald, Ronald. A British civil servant and a noted hunter in India, Donald came to Africa as Nairobi's Town Magistrate in 1904. He would hunt for birds with Foran in the mornings before court. The two were once treed for hours by a black rhino. Angry at being late for court, Donald went back at day's end and shot the rhino.

Doran. A man named Doran worked constructing telegraph lines in the Congo in the 1900s but quit to become an elephant hunter. He once gave John Boyes a free .303 magazine rifle with one hundred cartridges, but warned the former "King of the Kikuyu" that the rifle was cursed. Whenever somebody had used the weapon, apparently some disaster had befallen him, including the death of one hunter and the serious injury of another. Doran himself had had some close calls while hunting with the rifle, and although it fired perfectly in practice, he had yet to hit anything with it in the field.

The very first time Boyes went hunting with the rifle, he was charged by an angry elephant from close quarters. The gunbearer carrying it was trampled to death and Boyes was almost shot by a bullet accidentally discharged when the rifle hit the ground. Boyes gave the gun to his partner, Selland, who was about to leave on a long safari and was unimpressed by superstition. What kind of luck he had with the rifle Boyes never learned, for Selland died of blackwater fever before returning.

Dorehill, George. In 1872 Dorehill, an elephant hunter in southern Africa, had the unique distinction of blowing up Frederick Courteney Selous. While the latter was handling gunpowder, Dorehill dropped a lit pipe into it. The explosion severely burned them both, and Selous had trouble with one eye for a long time. Another hunter, Sadlier, rubbed a mixture of oil and salt on their badly burned faces. Selous credited this painful treatment with preventing any scarring.

It is perhaps a tribute to Selous's good nature that he continued to hunt with Dorehill. Or maybe he was just grateful that in December of 1872 Dorehill shot a crocodile that was trying to kill Selous's favorite dog, Bill. In the 1880s Mrs. Dorehill was perhaps the first Englishwoman to enter Mashonaland.

Douglas, John. Douglas, the one-armed manager of a sisal estate near Lake Naivasha, frequently hunted buffalo at a place called Hell's Gate with a .500 double rifle. When Eddie Grafton, a hunter for the Safariland Company, was killed by a buffalo in the 1920s, Douglas followed up the wounded beast and put it down.

Douls, Camille (1864–1888). Douls was born at Bordes in the Aveyron department of France, and as a teenager visited the Caribbean, Central America, and Morocco. In Morocco he learned to speak Arabic and became familiar with the traditions and customs of Islam. In 1885 he began exploring the interior of the Sahara disguised as an Arab. He was captured by bandits and spared, on the condition he convert to their religion. Upon his return to Morocco he was jailed on the order of the Sultan, and was released only after the British minister interceded. Douls then traveled to England, where a narrative of his adventures was printed in the Times and where he spoke before the Royal Geographical Society.

In June 1888 Douls left Paris with the intention of traveling to Timbuktu, again disguised as an Arab. The noted French explorer Henri Duveyrier warned Douls that he would never be able to pull off the disguise, despite his fluency in Arabic, Duveyrier pointed out that Douls's gait, mannerisms, and complexion would betray him as a European and that the consequences could well be fatal. Of particular concern was Douls's intention to portray himself as a hajji, or Moslem who had made the pilgrimage to Mecca. Duveyrier reminded Douls that even in Europe a German caught wandering around in disguise in, say, France would likely be considered a spy. The young Douls laughed off these concerns.

He did, however, make sort of a trial run by traveling with a group of returning Moslem pilgrims from the Sinai to Morocco. His masquerade held up—they did not detect his real identity. Once in Morocco he started out for Timbuktu, but this time it wasn't long before the local people began to suspect that he was a Frenchman. As Duveyrier had predicted, Douls's pretensions to hajji status was a major miscalculation. Had he donned a disguise as merely a simple Arab, he might have escaped with his life after being detected. As it was, the Arabs decided he had committed a major act of sacrilege, and in late 1888, somewhere in the desert between the oases of Alouef and Aklabi, Camille Douls was murdered by his guides.

Douville. Douville was a Frenchman who supposedly explored deep into the Congo interior around 1830. Many felt that his 1832 book describing his adventures was actually a work of fiction, and a poor one at that.

Dove, George. Kenya white hunter of the 1940s–1960s era.

Dower, Kenneth Cecil Gander (1908–1944). Kenneth Gander Dower was a big-game hunter and noted amateur cricket player who in 1933, with Raymond Hook, organized a safari to try to find the cryptid spotted lion. They reportedly found feline tracks too small to be a lion and too big for a leopard. In 1937 Gander Dower published *The Spotted Lion.* Two years later he went on a photographic safari with his friend James Riddell, experimenting with trip-wire night photography in the Aberdare Mountains and the Congo. This venture was curtailed by the outbreak of war in 1939; Gander Dower was posted to Force Headquarters in Nairobi and served in the Middle East in 1940. He was killed in action a few years later. The photos and stories of his last safari were published by Riddell in 1946 as *In the Forests of the Night.* Gander Dower also wrote *Amateur Adventure* (1934), *The King's African Rifles in Madagascar,* and *Into Madagascar.*

Gander Dower was an interesting man. In addition to his big-game hunting, photography, and cryptozoology pursuits, he also experimented with domesticating various wild African animals. In the early 1930s he brought some tame cheetahs back to England and timed them against well-known racing greyhounds. Skeptics scoffed at his reports that the cheetahs were running better than thirty miles per hour. (The cheetah can actually run at about twice that speed over a short distance.)

Downey, Sid (1905–1983). Downey was a respected safari hunter and businessman. He first arrived in East Africa in 1924 and conducted his first long hunting trip three years later, to the Masai Mara. After working for Safariland under the tutelage of Philip Percival, he formed the Ker and Downey Safari company, one of the most prestigious of the East African firms. Downey went on to become one of the mythic figures of the postwar hunting boom.

Downing, Tim. Starting his working life as a bank clerk, Tim Downing quickly moved on to more exciting occupations. After a painful love affair, he decided to escape civilization and became a professional hunter with Joe Dubbin. Dubbin was attempting to establish his own kingdom in the Congo at the time. Later Downing was employed doing animal-control work for twenty years in the Belgian Congo. He is said to have once killed twenty-one buffalo with twenty-one shots. It was thought then that exterminating the buffalo would help stop the spread of the tsetse.

In World War I Downing guided the expedition that cleared Lake Tanganyika of German gunboats. He later moved to Tanganyika, where he was involved in mining and, once again, banking. Regretting the bloodletting of his past, he ended his hunting days by throwing his favorite .404 into the Congo River. Considered a great hunter of both buffalo and elephant, Tim Downing never shot a lion.

Dracopoli, Ignazio Nicolas (1887–1923). Of Italian heritage (he became a naturalized British citizen in 1914), Ignazio Dracopoli was born in France and educated at Malvern College and University College, Oxford. In 1908 he moved to Arizona, where he worked as a cowboy for a year. With his younger brother he went on a big-game hunting trip in 1910 to British East Africa, and two years later explored the Sonoran Mountains of northern Mexico.

In October 1912 Dracopoli returned to East Africa, where he went on a grueling safari through the Lorian Swamp. During this harrowing affair he explored a lot of unknown territory and corrected the charts left by previous travelers. He was the only European in the expedition.

After the usual preparations (during which Dracopoli was assisted by Provincial Commissioners R. E. Salkeld and A. T. Reddie, and District Commissioner K. R. Dundas), the safari left Kismayu in December. Initially the party consisted of Dracopoli, headman Dahir Omar, interpreter Hassan Mohammed, one gunbearer, a syce, a personal servant, a skinner, a Swahili cook, six Swahili porters, seven camel syces or handlers, four Somali askaris, and a Herti guide. Livestock consisted of eighteen camels, five of which were devoted solely to transporting water. The seven syces and the askaris were armed with rifles, but it was a pathetically small force for that turbulent region. At night the tiny caravan built three-foot-tall hedges from thornbush around their tents, and an askari always stood guard at the only entrance.

Dracopoli almost immediately fell sick with dysentery and didn't recover until the second half of January 1913. Marching west along a small river called the Lak Guran, and then north and west to the Dera River and toward the Uaso Nyiro, Dracopoli hunted gazelle, topi, hirola, and small game such as civet cat and wild birds. Soon the safari began meeting up with the nomadic peoples who lived in the region—Somalis, the Galla, and finally the Boran. Dracopoli's interactions with the locals were occasionally tense but generally peaceful. He seems to have had a knack for tact and diplomacy and, unlike most European travelers in that area at that time, he had little need for his weapons except for hunting.

The biggest threat to the expedition was the constant danger of running out of water. Pools and water holes were few and unmarked, and even the rivers such as the Dera dried up during the summer. Frequently Dracopoli and his men survived only by drinking from filthy puddles fouled by animal wastes.

The main accomplishment of the expedition was geographic. By the time Dracopoli and his men reached Meru, he had accurately charted parts of Jubaland, the Dera River region, and the Lorian Swamp. While pleased with the sporting prospects of the district, Dracopoli warned sternly that this was a dangerous place and not one to be entered lightly. Nevertheless, in his subsequent book he included a small map detailing the whereabouts of the prevalent game animals of the region, a device sure to appeal to British hunting enthusiasts. The main map he made on this trip was printed in the *London Times* atlas in 1922.

I.N. Dracopoli with topi, Jubaland, 1912.

Wracked by illness, Dracopoli recuperated in England and then returned to Kenya in early 1914. When the war broke out later that year he was rejected for front-line service due to his poor health, but managed to secure an administrative (non-flying) post in the fledgling Royal Flying Corps. He served in RFC staff positions in both England and Egypt, and was awarded an MBE at the end of the war.

His health ruined by African microbes, Dracopoli married in 1914 and had two sons. He died on 7 January 1923 from what the *Monthly Notice of the Royal Astronomical Society* termed "a cruel disease" contracted while in the Lorian Swamp—quite possibly from the fetid drinking water. He was the author of the excellent *Through Jubaland to the Lorian Swamp: An Adventurous Journey of Exploration and Sport in the Unknown African Forests and Deserts* (1914). The book is short on excitement—no large-scale battles were described, like the ones that Baker and Stanley were always fighting, and Jubaland's lion and elephant largely behaved themselves. But the book is detailed and very well written. Its only aggravating feature is Dracopoli's reluctance to mention the date—almost every reference is "the following day" or "after a few days"—a feature shared by many early travelers/writers in Africa. This makes it hard to track his progress but does not detract from the book's overall value. ROWLAND WARD 1928: HIROLA.

Drayson, Alfred Wills (1827–1901). An early British sportsman and an officer of the Royal Artillery, Captain (later General) Drayson was the author of *Sporting Scenes among the Kaffirs of South Africa* (1858), about his adventures fighting and hunting with a party of Boers in South Africa. He also wrote *Tales of the Outspan* (1862), *The Adventures of Hans Sterk* (1869), and numerous classic books on billiards.

Driscoll, Daniel "Jim" (1861–1934). A British colonel, Jim Driscoll fought in the Boer War, and in World War I commanded the 25th Battalion of the Royal Fusiliers, a distinguished unit whose ranks included Selous, Alan Black, Cherry Kearton, and James Outram. After the war Driscoll grew coffee near Nairobi.

Drummond, Henry (1851–1897). He was a naturalist who traveled in Zululand and what is now the Umfolozi Game Reserve in Mpande's days in the late 1860s. He hunted eland, bushbuck, impala, elephant, buffalo, hippo, and especially both species of rhino.

Drummond was of hardy stock. He recorded how he and his few companions once marched for thirty hours with no water. He was one of the first to report the rhino's tendency to charge a campfire. Drummond's preferred method of hunting was to set up a blind by a water hole.

In his book *The Large Game and Natural History of South and Southeast Africa* (1875), Drummond gave his opinion that there were four species of African rhino. The book recounts his sporting adventures in Togoland, Zululand, and Swaziland in 1868–1872. Revealing a touch of the sentimentality that oddly affected many early English hunters (who were not known for their mercy), he wrote, "I cannot leave this subject without adding my protest against the wanton and wasteful wholesale destruction of these animals . . . merely for the purpose of supplying Europe with ivory ornaments and billiard balls."

In 1883 Drummond, an affable man but no intellectual giant, returned to Africa for an expedition to the Zambezi River and Nyasaland. On this trip he is credited with discovering the first fossils to be found in sub-Saharan Africa. He was also the author of *Tropical Africa.*

Duff, Sir Hector Livingston (1872–1954). Duff was a civilian in London in 1896 when, one snowy evening, he was visited by his friend, Maj. A. B. Thruston. Thruston was on leave from military duties in Uganda, where he had helped lead the survivors of Emin Pasha's Equatoria province garrison to new posts in British East Africa. Duff was so entranced by Thruston's tales, particularly his hunting adventures, that Duff promptly sent a letter off to the Foreign Office requesting a post in Uganda or anywhere near there. In October of 1897 he was visiting Bengal when he received an offer of a position in the administration of British Central Africa, otherwise known as Nyasaland. Duff accepted and within a month sailed to Africa aboard a German steamer, the *Safari.*

The first news he heard upon disembarking in Mozambique was of the death of his friend Thruston, who had been murdered by his own Sudanese troops during a mutiny. After waiting a week for a proper tide aboard one of the legendarily filthy and cockroach-infested African coastal steamers, Duff ascended the Zambezi to his new post.

He arrived at the capital, Zomba, on 8 January 1898. For six months he was retained at the capital as an extra officer and to become acclimated to the country. In July 1898 he was assigned as assistant collector (district officer) at Fort Lister, Mlanje district, taking over from a man who had died from malaria. In October Duff was reassigned first to Blantyre and shortly afterward to Nkata Bay as assistant collector for the district of West Nyasa.

After a brief return home to England, Duff became collector for Zomba in August 1900. In 1903 he published *Nyasaland under the Foreign Office,* a better-than-average example of the typical "district officer" memoirs that most of the survivors felt compelled to write. In this book Duff touches on the history, tribal organizations, missionary activities, politics, and, of course, big-game hunting and natural history of the area.

Duff was an avid hunter and seems to have spent most of his time in British Central Africa roaming the woods carrying a Gibbs-Metford Express, with a .303 in reserve. His book is full of what passed for natural history at the time. Almost everything that was known about wildlife in those days was discovered by hunters, and Duff was one of the more observant sportsmen to put pen to paper. Not until after World War II was hunters' information replaced by scientific observation. In his book Duff paid particular tribute to Harry Johnston and Alfred Sharpe for their foresight in protecting wildlife by setting aside the famous "Elephant Marsh" and the Lake Chilwa section of the Shire Highlands as game reserves.

Duff was the author of several other books, including *This Small World of Mine, Ivory Graves, African Small Chop,* and *The Sewells in the New World.*

Dugmore, Arthur Radclyffe (1870–1955). One of the first big-game photographers, A. Radclyffe Dugmore was born in Britain but moved to the United States as a young man. Dugmore got his start taking pictures of North American birds. Previously, naturalists had relied almost exclusively on drawings and paintings to study birds. Dugmore felt that these drawings were tainted by being seen through the artist's eyes, believing that a more objective record could be made by a photographer. He tried photographing stuffed birds, but they lacked the necessary lifelike quality. Finally he pioneered the photography of wild, live birds. His photographs soon appeared in Smithsonian Institution publications. He then graduated to other animals.

Dugmore first went to Africa in 1908 on a commission from the U.S. magazine *Collier's Weekly*. The idea was to photograph the game animals stalked by President Roosevelt, whose upcoming safari had already been announced. Dugmore was accompanied by the young taxidermist James L. Clark, who resigned from the American Museum to make the trip. Clark's job was mainly to protect the photographer from charging animals while he exposed his plates. Clark's excellent 1928 memoir, *Trails of the Hunted,* has several photographs of the first cow elephant that had to be shot as it went after Dugmore.

Dugmore made several other trips to Africa, and brought his camera to the wilds of North America and Asia as well. He was the author of *Camera Adventures in the African Wilds* (1910), *Wild Life and the Camera* (1912), *The Wonderland of Big Game* (1925), and *African Jungle Life* (1928) and also contributed four articles on African wildlife to *Wild Life the World Over* (1947). He was the first of the photo-safari pioneers to use an effective telephoto lens.

Maj. Arthur Radclyffe Dugmore in the army, 1917.

Duke, Thomas. Born in Ireland, Duke grew up in South Africa and was a member of the Cape Mounted Police, a detective in the Orange Free State, and a distinguished Boer War veteran of a British unit called Rimington's Guides. At just over forty years old, he became one of the first rangers of the Sabi Game Reserve. He was bushwise, courageous, and spoke various useful tongues including Xhosa. He had a distinguished career as a ranger, retired after World War I, and ran a small native store selling beads and cloth. His farm became a central clearing house for all the gossip of the district—the Transvaal version of the old Southern barbershop. He died in the 1930s.

Dundas, Anne. The wife of Charles Dundas, Anne was the author of *Beneath African Glaciers* (1924), an excellent account of the day-to-day affairs of an administrative family.

Dundas, Charles Cecil Farquharson (1884–1956). Dundas was an administrative officer in Kenya from 1908–1920, and a provincial commissioner in Tanganyika Territory in the late 1920s. He served as governor of Uganda 1940–1945. Legend has it that Dundas obtained his first African posting, that of district officer, Kitui, by accosting Winston Churchill over a few drinks at a Paris hotel.

Dundas, Frederick George, RN. Captain Dundas conducted a survey of the Tana River in April 1891, commanding the steam-powered stern-wheeler *Kenia*. Accompanying him on his venture were C. W. Hobley and Bird Thompson. They took the *Kenia* up to the farthest navigable point (the village of Hameye) and then continued overland to Mount Kenya. The party consisted of the three Europeans, a boat crew of eighteen Swahilis, and seventy Zanzibaris. The safari was memorable chiefly because Dundas was crossing ground that had just been swept by a major Masai raid. Burned villages and corpses were scattered everywhere, and among the dead Dundas saw broken figures squatting with their heads in their hands, mourning miserably. At one point Dundas and one European, ten askaris, and fifty porters were spotted by a group of about seven hundred Masai. Dundas deployed his few men in a skirmish line, but the Masai, for reasons of their own, declined to attack and moved on. The local inhabitants told Dundas that the Masai had stolen some two hundred fifty women and large herds of cattle.

The mission up the Juba, which started on 25 April 1892, was more problematic. Dundas's force this time consisted of twelve crewmen, a Goanese engineer, one Chinese carpenter, one Hindu, twelve askaris, and fifteen porters, again aboard the *Kenia*. They expected trouble, for no Europeans had sailed up the Juba since Baron von Decken's expedition had been massacred in 1865 (the American Chaille-Long had purportedly been in the area once but only briefly). Indeed, the *Kenia* was stopped at the mouth of the Juba and had to wait two weeks for permission from the local Sultan to proceed.

The entire trip was hazardous. On one occasion the Somalis rushed the boat at night in shallow water. The crew panicked, and Dundas deterred the attack only by firing off some signal rockets, the likes of which the Somalis had never seen. It was doubtful the same trick would work twice. At all times the *Kenia* was followed by bandits on foot who were just waiting for the vessel to run aground and give them a chance to make short work of the British expedition. As if to remind Dundas of his peril, he discovered the wreckage of the *Guelph*, Baron von Decken's ship lost twenty-seven years previously, upstream from the Somali village of Logh.

Still, by a combination of luck, pluck, and bribery Dundas managed to appease the major Somali warlords along the river, including the sheik of Bardera, a major town of some twelve hundred souls. This particular potentate cost Dundas the gift of his sword and an armchair. After ascending to the rapids some four hundred miles from the river's mouth, Dundas turned back and by the end of September was back at the Indian Ocean.

The main goal of his expeditions, to reconnoiter the two rivers for the IBEA (see glossary), had been achieved. Dundas, a dedicated sportsmen, also took time out for hunting whenever he had the opportunity. Among the species he mentioned successfully hunting on the two trips were topi, hippo, kongoni, wildebeest, and a rhino. On the Juba Dundas shot two "very large" crocodiles measuring fourteen and sixteen feet, establishing that the naval officer was an honest man. In that day less meticulous hunters would brag about twenty-five- and even thirty-foot crocs.

Accounts of Dundas's expeditions were published in *Proceedings of the Royal Geographical Society,* August 1892, and in the *Scottish Geographical Magazine* in March 1893.

Dunn, Alexander Roberts (1833–1868). Alexander Dunn was the son of a wealthy Toronto family. In 1856 he was a lieutenant in the 11th Hussars and participated in the "Charge of the Light Brigade" in the Crimean War for which he became the first Canadian recipient of the Victoria Cross. A tall (6'3"), well-built, good-looking man, Dunn was a bit on the arrogant side and created a scandal by bedding a brother officer's wife in the Crimea.

By the 1860s Dunn was a colonel in the British army and took part in the 1868 invasion of Ethiopia. He died at the very start of the campaign, the victim of a double shotgun wound in the chest. The official story was that he shot himself accidentally while hunting partridges; he was supposedly balancing his gun between his knees while uncorking a flask of brandy, and the weapon discharged. His last words, according to his valet, were "Run for a doctor." There were persistent rumors, however, that Dunn committed suicide or was murdered, either by a jealous husband or by his valet, who had recently been included in his will.

Dunn was buried along the army's route of march and his grave was forgotten. In 1945 a patrol of the Eritrean Mounted Police, led by a man named Reg Rimmer, stumbled across the grave, which had apparently been found and restored by the Italian army in the 1930s when Ethiopia was under Italian jurisdiction. In 1982 the grave was again restored by the Canadian government and is now visited every two years for maintenance purposes.

Dunn's Victoria Cross was put up for auction by Sotheby's in 1894. This caused an uproar in Canada, where patriotic citizens demanded that the country's first VC be kept out of foreign hands. Accordingly the Canadian government made arrangements to purchase the medal. It is currently displayed in a museum.

Dunn, Bill. Dunn was a swashbuckling member of the so-called Stellaland Brigade group of mercenaries.

After the Brigade was dispersed by Sir Charles Warren's expedition in the early 1890s, Dunn tried to establish himself in Mashonaland but was deported to the Transvaal as an undesirable (deportation at that time entailed being escorted to the frontier at gunpoint). He sneaked back into Mashonaland under the cover of working as an interpreter for a band of missionaries, but they soon tired of his ways and fired him. Dunn joined Maj. Allan Wilson's Mashonaland Border Police at the outbreak of the 1893 Matabele War and so distinguished himself in action that he was promoted in the field.

Dunn needs a detailed biographer: He was typical of a certain class of man—unconventional, almost criminal, but capable of great heroism when given a warrior's task requiring courage and action. If he had been born to a more socially prominent family, he may well have been another Richard Meinertzhagen.

Dunn, John Robert (1833–1895). Dunn grew up playing with Zulu kids in the bush near Beira. In 1847 his father, the trader Robert Newton Dunn (1796–1847), was trampled to death by an elephant; in a spirit of revenge, young John shot his first elephant later that same year. In 1853 Dunn and his pal George Cato killed the last wild elephant ever seen near Durban.

As a young man Dunn made his living wandering through Zululand, shooting game for food and bartering the meat and hides for other necessities. He formed many friendships with the local Zulus. His close relationship with the tribe was recognized by the British government in 1854 when he was appointed assistant border agent. During the Zulu Civil War of 1856 he supported the iziQoza clan against the victorious uSuthu of Cetshwayo, but afterward he changed sides and became a trusted advisor to his former enemy.

In 1861 Dunn was tasked by the Zulu king Mpande to shoot six hundred buffalo to supply meat for the Zulus. In return for this and other favors, Mpande gave Dunn the ownership of a large amount of land along the Tugela River. Within ten years, 10,000 Zulus lived in his territory. Dunn settled down and married 49 recorded wives, fathering an incredible 117 children. Clearly the rewards of African outdoors life were sometimes more than just philosophical.

Dunn tried to stay neutral during the 1879 Anglo-Zulu War, but finally threw his lot in with the British, serving as chief of intelligence. More than two hundred Zulu warriors from his district joined him in fighting against their homeland.

Dunsany, Lord (1878–1957). Born Edward John Moreton Plunkett, he became the 18th Baron of Dunsany in 1899. The title, an Irish one, stems from the fifteenth century. A relative of Sir Richard Burton on his mother's side, Dunsany grew up in both Kent and County Meath and acquired many of the characteristics of both England and Ireland. He attended Sandhurst and was commissioned into the Coldstream Guards in 1899, serving in South Africa during the Boer War. When the war ended he returned to Dunsany Castle in County Meath and devoted himself to hunting, fishing, chess, and cricket. He made several trips to Africa in pursuit of big game, a practice he would continue throughout his life.

After a few years of this idyllic existence he took to writing and in 1905 published his first book, a collection of short stories called *The Gods of Pegana.* His first play, *The Glittering Gate,* was performed in Dublin in 1909, and he produced many other works, mostly with fantasy themes. During World War I he served as a captain in the Royal Inniskilling Fusiliers in France, and was wounded and captured by the Irish rebels during the Easter Rebellion in 1916.

After the war his plays became popular in the United States, and he began writing novels (*The Chronicles of Rodriguez,* 1922; and *The Blessing of Pan,* 1927; and many others) and short stories. He wrote a series called the "Jorkens" stories that was inspired both by his African hunting experiences and his love of fantasy. He continued to visit the Dark Continent, filling Dunsany Castle with a magnificent assortment of trophies. The German blitzkrieg found Dunsany in Athens in 1941, lecturing in English literature, and he fled back to his homeland, where he served with the Home Guard and as a radio broadcaster.

Dunsany was an odd character. He dressed quaintly, wrote almost all of his works with a quill pen, and despised modern food. A strikingly tall and athletic man, he was a skilled hunter and a sharp observer of natural history, making many insightful observations that eluded other hunters who spent more time in the field. He died in Dublin on 25 October 1957. ROWLAND WARD 1928: NILE LECHWE.

Dutreuil de Rhins, Jules (1846–1894). Born at St. Etienne, Dutreuil de Rhins became a French naval officer and by 1870 held the rank of captain. After a long period spent surveying Annam, he produced a book and a map of Southeast Asia that was considered the finest of its time.

In 1882 Dutreuil de Rhins was assigned as geographer to de Brazza as the latter led an expedition along the

Ogowe River in the Congo. Once again he produced a fine map of the area, later published by the French Ministry of Instruction. He was then assigned to update the existing maps of Central Asia and produced his greatest achievement, a twenty-four-map atlas entitled *L'Asie Centrale.*

In 1891 Dutreuil de Rhins began an expedition to Tibet, accompanied by one Monsieur Grenard. It is known that the two men visited Tashkent, Kashgar, Khotan, and Ladakh. Dutreuil de Rhins was on his way back in June 1894 when he was waylaid and murdered along the trail.

Duveyrier, Henri (1840–1892). He was a French explorer who traveled among the Tuareg in 1859–1861. He was the author of *The Tuareg of the North* and in 1864 was awarded the prestigious Gold Medal of the Paris Geographical Society for his splendid map of the western Sahara.

Dybowski, Jean (1856–1928). Dybowski, a lecturer at the French Agricultural College at Grignon, led an expedition from Loango in the Congo into Chad in 1892. He had two goals—to find the best route between the Congo River and Lake Chad, and to ascertain the fate of the missing explorer Paul Crampel. The first mission was relatively simple, albeit physically difficult. Dybowski explored the River Kemo and then went two hundred miles on foot in the rainy season to the Shari, which flows toward Chad.

The second half of his mission was more problematic. Eventually, though, the intrepid Dybowski not only confirmed that Crampel had been murdered by Arab bandits ("Mohammedans" was his term) but also discovered the current location of the band. Surrounding the bandits, he attacked them at night, killing several and scattering the rest.

After that successful skirmish, Dybowski crossed the Shari but found himself unable to feed his men—a result, he claimed, of the depredations of the Mohammedan bands. When he came down with a serious illness, he decided to turn back.

Dybowski wrote of his adventures in the book *La Route du Tchad, du Loango au Chari* (1893). In addition to the factual account of the expedition, he also described fully the local inhabitants, flora, and fauna, and recommended that France arm the local people against the Mohammedans

E

Eastman, George (1854–1932). The founder and owner of the Eastman Kodak company, George Eastman first became interested in Africa in 1924, when he was prevailed upon to finance Martin and Osa Johnson's cinematic ventures. He put up $10,000. Two years later he visited the Johnsons at their camp at Lake Paradise, accompanied by PH Philip Percival. Two of Eastman's friends, Daniel Pomeroy and Audley Stewart, also came along, bringing their own PH, Pat Ayre.

Eastman was by then an elderly man in his 70s. In deference to his age (and wealth), Percival allowed him to chase lion with a motorcar, leaving the car only to make the shot. Eastman considered this grand sport while Percival secretly detested the practice. Kenya game regulations had prohibited the pursuit of game from motorcars since November 1923, but this was liberally interpreted by Percival to mean only that you couldn't actually fire from the car. Or perhaps the law just didn't apply to millionaire Americans. At any rate, it wasn't until the mid-1930s that a definitive regulation was passed banning shooting within two hundred yards of a vehicle.

Eastwood, Benjamin. The chief accountant and later general manager of British East African Railways, Eastwood was hunting one day in 1902 near Baringo on Lake Victoria when he spied two black rhino. He shot one, but the other charged. He put three bullets from his .577 cordite rifle into the beast but could not stop its charge. He tried to run, but the rhino easily caught up to him, goring him badly. Being alone, he was not found until several hours later when someone came out to investigate a mass of circling vultures. It took two days for a doctor named Falkner to arrive from Nakuru. Eastwood survived but was never the same man.

Edward VIII (1894–1972). The son of George V, Edward VIII was the British monarch who abdicated due to the uproar over his proposed marriage to an American divorcee, Mrs. Wallis Simpson. The abdication occurred in 1936. Taking the title of the Duke of Windsor, Edward spent most of the ensuing war years in Bermuda and lived much of the rest of his life in Paris. This sequence of events may have been a fortunate one for the sake of history—given that the Nazi leaders considered Windsor "somebody they might be able to deal with," it's probably just as well that he abdicated when he did.

Many biographers have written about the king and his politics. Here we will confine ourselves to his experiences as the Prince of Wales in East Africa. After his brother, the duke of York (1895–1952), enjoyed a successful safari in 1924–1925, the prince decided to visit the region in 1928. By royal standards his entourage was relatively small, consisting of his youngest brother Henry (the duke of Gloucester), Brigadier General Trotter, Lt. Col. Piers Legh, Edward Brook, John Aird, and the prince's chief aide, the long-suffering assistant private secretary Sir Alan "Tommy" Lascelles. It was Lascelles's almost impossible job to make sure everything went smoothly. The white hunters assigned to the group included Denys Finch Hatton, Alan Black, Andy Anderson, Bror Blixen, Monty Moore, Sydney Waller, and Pat Ayre.

Both the prince and the duke hunted northeast of Mount Kilimanjaro before splitting up. Henry then hunted in Tanganyika with Blixen and Moore while Edward went to Uganda. To their credit, neither man was obsessed with trophy heads or breaking records—they were content with the relatively carefree life they could enjoy away from the crowds and photographers of Europe. Edward in particular valued his privacy. It was known that film that caught him in an unflattering pose was confiscated from the cameramen and destroyed. Above all, they enjoyed the women—more on that in a bit.

In Uganda disaster was narrowly avoided when the Prince of Wales was charged by an angry elephant at close range. The combined rifles of game wardens J. D. Salmon and Pete Pearson managed to stop the animal just twelve feet from where Edward lay helplessly caught in a thornbush. Later the prince himself shot and killed a charging lion near Babati. Despite all this excitement, or perhaps because of it, Edward vowed to come back to East Africa as soon as his duties would permit.

The return visit was two years later. Prince Edward met Blixen and Finch Hatton in a railway car at Maungu in eastern Kenya in January 1930. First they went to Kasigau Hill, a well-known hunting ground for elephant, but struck out. After checking out some other popular locales with the same results (elephant hunting is a notoriously hit-or-miss business), the team went into Tanganyika. There they came across the fresh spoor of a huge bull and set out to trail the animal on foot, assisted by a couple of African trackers. Blixen, who knew that elephant ordinarily rest in the shade during the heat of the day, suggested that they stop for an hour to make lunch. That short respite was all the tusker needed to make its escape.

Bror Blixen (left), Edward, the Prince of Wales, and Denys Finch Hatton.

Hindsight is twenty-twenty vision, however, and Blixen, Finch Hatton, and the prince had no way of knowing this was no ordinary elephant. Hour after hour they tracked the bull through the steaming, arid bush of northern Tanganyika. Blixen and Finch Hatton had to keep one eye on the prince, who, although athletic, was slightly built and had no cross-country experience and unknown stamina. To their satisfaction, however, Edward showed no real signs of distress, though he was parched, sunburned, and growing great blisters on his feet. That night they camped in the open on a grassy plain.

The following morning they got an early start and resumed the chase. It seemed the elephant had halted for the night too, for the spoor looked fresher than it had the day before. This day's travels took them into rough country strewn with jagged volcanic rock that cut their shoes. Even so, they made over forty miles, and by sunset the tired hunters thought they were getting close and were optimistic about their chances on the coming dawn.

The third day, however, was just like the second. Again the spoor looked even fresher, and they expected to come across their quarry every time they turned a corner in the bush or topped a ridge. Water was running low, and all three Europeans were having trouble with their feet, which were so swollen that they struggled to get their boots on. Still they kept going and again camped in the open, believing that the fourth day would surely see the successful result of their long stalk.

And so it seemed, at least for a few minutes. At about two in the afternoon on day four, they finally came upon the elephant in a patch of dense bush. The bull was well hidden, and they sensed and smelled it more than saw it. Finch Hatton crept closer to get a good look and confirmed it was the animal they wanted. A huge bull—"Big as a house" according to Blixen, with tusks that must have weighed close to two hundred pounds per side—was standing there unaware and half asleep. Quietly, carefully, the trio mapped out their plan of attack. The prince inched forward but suddenly, disastrously, stepped on a dry twig. At the crack the bull immediately threw up its head and ran off in the opposite direction at nearly forty miles an hour. The chase was over.

The prince had several other interesting adventures during the 1930 expedition. Coaxed on by Edward, Finch Hatton and Tanganyikan game ranger Ray Hewlett allegedly sneaked up to a dozing rhino and slapped a postage stamp—bearing an image of the prince's father—on the beast's rump. Some weeks later the safari, guided by J. D. Salmon, was traveling across Uganda to Fort Portal when, to Salmon's intense embarrassment, they got lost and had to spend the night in the bush in pouring rain. Again to Edward's credit (he seems to have been a hardy soul at least, if not quite kingly material), he made the best of the situation and the men spent the night telling lion stories and passing around a bottle of whiskey.

Two points concerning the so-called "Royal" safaris warrant amplification. The first is the nature of the press coverage. If you read any of the contemporary accounts of the day, be they Blixen's ghost-written memoirs or the sycophantic *Sport and Travel in East Africa* (1934, by Patrick Chalmers), you may have been amazed at the way the prince and his brother were treated. It was like reading the authorized biography of some medieval king. There was not a hint of criticism. Everything the prince did was described in glowing terms, with constant parenthetical tributes to his noble character. Even Bror Blixen went so far as to call the prince the toughest sportsman he had ever met. Edward may have been athletic and aerobically fit, but the cattle ranches and safari camps and kraals and gold mines of East Africa were filled with tougher men. That's no knock on the prince, just the truth.

The second point (sort of made possible by the first) is the sheer sexual excess that went on during these safaris. It would not be far off the mark to state that the royal princes fornicated their way across Africa. On the first trip prince Henry struck up an affair with the promiscuous aviatrix

Beryl Markham. This affair, which continued after the duke returned to London, led to Markham's divorce and created questions about the paternity of her only son, Gervase (1929–1961). After Beryl's husband threatened to name the prince as a respondent in a divorce suit, the royal family gave Beryl an annuity that paid her a small sum each year until the end of her long life.

At least Henry restricted himself to committing adultery quietly. Henry's peccadilloes were as nothing next to those of his big brother. Edward groped every attractive female he could find, from cultured aristocrats to common prostitutes. His trysts included the wife of Viscount Furness, who delayed the prince for two hours on a trip from Tanganyika to Nairobi; the wife of a colonial official, who passed the time with him in the bushes at Lord Francis Scott's estate; and two young typists at Government House in the colony's capital. Edward's nightly revels led to him being a late riser, so a diagnosis of "insomnia" was circulated to explain why he frequently got out of bed at noon.

While at the Muthaiga Club he combined his carousing with a Valhalla-style alcohol intake, and may have taken illegal drugs. One offer of cocaine, by Frank Greswolde Williams, was aborted only when game warden Archie Ritchie bodily threw the burly dealer out of the club.

The man who bore the brunt of Edward's dalliances was his assistant personal secretary, Tommy Lascelles. This harried man had to not only arrange the prince's affairs and cover up the assignations but also had to constantly shift schedules to accommodate Edward's late nights, usually because of drinking and womanizing but sometimes for more sedate reasons. On one occasion Edward held up the entire party for five hours while he played an impromptu game of squash. Lascelles constantly considered resigning but held onto his post out of a sense of duty, vainly attempting to make his employer fit to someday be king.

Like his brother Henry, Edward slept with Beryl Markham. He also disappeared for several hours with Glady Delamere, the wife of Lord Delamere from 1928–1931. This latter assignation took place while various high-ranking guests were waiting for the prince to appear at dinner. Things got so bad that on safari Finch Hatton had to have the prince's tent set up some distance from everyone else's so that Edward could conduct his amours with some degree of privacy. Potentially the most dangerous event occurred when Edward, after a clandestine meeting with Beryl at Government House in Nairobi, tried to leave unobtrusively by sliding down a drain pipe. The prince was spotted by a guard and actually arrested as an intruder before his horrified aides could identify him and set him free.

All this tends to portray the prince in a bad light, and maybe it should. It must be remembered, however, that there was something about Kenya that seems to have encouraged this type of behavior in certain social circles. The activities of the notorious "Happy Valley" set were legendary, and safari hunting was well known for its tendency to heighten the senses and lead to adulterous affairs. Viscount Furness, for instance, once threatened to shoot his favorite white hunter, Andrew Rattray, for eloping with his teenage daughter, and even the staid John H. Patterson was allegedly involved in an adulterous affair that led to the death of Lord Blyth. Not to mention the fact that having Beryl Markham around was a certain antidote for a dull night.

To put it into perspective, consider the night Prince Edward camped in the Tanganyikan bush with Blixen and Finch Hatton, on the trail of that long-lost bull elephant. Edward had slept with Beryl; so had Blixen and Finch Hatton. Blixen, of course, had been married to Karen Dinesen, who'd had a legendary affair with Finch Hatton and who wrote letters about how much she loved the prince. The two hunters had shared other women as well. What stories might have been told around that campfire, had not the men been tired and blistered from their long stalk!

Edwards, Sam H. (1827–1922). Known as "Far Interior Sam," Edwards was a legendary hunter and woodsman of the nineteenth century. He was born on the Bechuanaland frontier, the son of missionary Roger Edwards (Edwards senior had traveled extensively with Livingstone in 1841). In 1851 Edwards was traveling south of the Zambezi with trader J. H. Wilson and naturalist John Leyland. The trio joined up with Livingstone and his family on an arduous expedition to see the Batawana chief Sebituane. Three years later Edwards visited Matabeleland with Reverend Robert Moffatt, the two being the first Europeans to visit that country.

In 1869 Edwards guided the London and Limpopo Mining company expedition under Sir John Swinburne to Tati. Later he went on hunting expeditions with such notables as Fred Green, C. J. Andersson, and Professor Wahlberg. By 1890 Edwards was managing director of the Tati Gold Mining Company and an unofficial advisor of great influence to both Lobengula and Khama. In that year he presented Fred Selous, another old friend, to Lobengula.

Perhaps the best epitaph for Far Interior Sam was written in 1973 by Bill Finaughty's modern editor, Edward

C. Tabler. In a footnote for *The Recollections of an Elephant Hunter,* Tabler called him "heads and shoulders above anyone then in the country in character, moral worth, and bushcraft, with the exception of Thomas Baines."

Eedes, Harold (1899–1975). A British colonial administrator, Eedes was resident commissioner of the Kavango region of South-West Africa from 1932–1946. Thereafter he replaced the legendary Cocky Hahn as resident commissioner of Ovamboland. Eedes did in Namibia at the age of seventy-six.

Egerton, Lord (1874–1958). Egerton (officially Lord Egerton of Tatton) was an eccentric recluse who built a "castle" near Njoro, Kenya, in the 1930s. Just before World War I he opened the Egerton Farm School (or Egerton Agricultural School), which expanded after 1945 to accommodate ex-servicemen immigrating to East Africa. Lord Egerton once found an extinct mammoth tusk in Alaska that weighed 157 pounds. ROWLAND WARD 1928: BUSHBUCK, KONGONI, LELWEL HARTEBEEST, WHITE-BEARDED GNU, KIRK DIK-DIK, RED-FRONTED GAZELLE, BUFFALO.

Egmont, Lord. Egmont was a British sportsman who went hunting bushbuck in Natal one day around 1910. He was loaded with buckshot and wounded a large male that escaped into dense bush. As he followed up, he was amazed when the bushbuck charged him at close range and tried to rip him open with its horns. Egmont felt the impact in his stomach and thought he was done for. A local dog had been following Egmont and snapped at the bushbuck, which turned to deal with the new threat, giving Egmont the opportunity to kill the animal with his second barrel. When Egmont looked down to assess the damage, he found that the animal had only succeeded in ripping open his waistcoat. His life had been saved not only by the dog but also because the bushbuck had a broken horn and had been virtually blinded by the first shot.

Eliot, Sir Charles Norton Edgecumbe (1862–1931). A well-educated man (you could call him a scholastic superstar), Eliot was fluent in Sanskrit, Syriac, Russian, Finnish, Turkish, Pali, Hindustani, and sundry other languages. Before coming to Kenya he held diplomatic posts in Bulgaria, Serbia, Samoa, and the United States. His work in Samoa earned him the KCMG (see glossary). Commissioner for East Africa from December 1900 to June 1904, he was responsible for moving the capital from Mombasa to Nairobi. As commissioner, he helped increase immigration, and his easing of land restrictions for Europeans created a farming boom. Ironically, he hated hunting. Eliot was also the consul general in Zanzibar 1900–1904. He resigned his posts in 1904 after a dispute with the Foreign Office.

After he left Kenya in 1904 he wrote *The East Africa Protectorate* (1905), served as vice chancellor of Sheffield University from 1905–1911, and held the same post at the University of Hong Kong from 1912–1918. After World War I he returned to public service, serving as British high commissioner to Siberia (1918–1919) and ambassador to Japan (1920–1926). He was appointed GCMG (see glossary) in 1923, and was the author of *Letters from the Far East* (1907), *Hinduism and Buddhism* (1921), and *Japanese Buddhism* (1935).

Elkington, Jim. An early Kenya settler, Elkington had attended Eton with the elephant-hunting Craven brothers. Moving to East Africa in the early 1900s, Elkington was perhaps best known for running the fox hunt called the Masara Hounds. A very big man, he once saved the young Beryl Markham from a tame lion. He was the owner of Elkington's Farm by Kabete station on the border of the Kikuyu Reserve near Nairobi. ROWLAND WARD 1928: ELEPHANT (130 AND 124 POUNDS, KENYA).

Elliot, Daniel Giraud (1835–1915). Elliot was the curator of zoology at the Field Museum in Chicago in the late 1890s. In 1896 he led a scientific expedition in Africa, starting at Berbera on the Gulf of Aden and moving overland via camels and ponies into Somaliland. Accompanying him was the young taxidermist Carl Akeley and an Englishman named Edward Dodson, who had been on the Donaldson-Smith expedition to Lake Rudolf. The expedition spent some five months collecting in Somaliland.

Akeley, who seems to have done most of the collecting for the group, shot and killed specimens of wild ass, greater kudu, oryx, spotted hyena, striped hyena, cheetah, hartebeest, and dibatag. While he was hunting for ostrich, Akeley had his famous hand-to-hand combat with a wounded leopard.

Elliott, Francis (xxxx–1916). An administrative officer in Kenya from roughly 1914–1916, Elliott was the district commissioner at Serenli in Jubaland. A former police official, he kept a "sleeping dictionary," a Zubair mistress who instructed him on local language, history, and customs.

Because of this nocturnal education, Elliott considered himself the ultimate expert on Somalis and Somalia—apparently he was pretty obnoxious about it. It was with some satisfaction that his successor discovered that Elliott had most of his facts wrong. Apparently the young lady, in an effort to keep him happy, had just been making things up and telling Elliott what he wanted to hear.

In January 1916 Elliott received several warnings that Serenli was about to be attacked by a Somali clan called the Aulihan. The Aulihan had been raiding along the frontier and had killed at least nine friendly tribesmen in the previous weeks. Elliott dismissed the warnings out of hand, at one point smashing an egg before the eyes of his concerned African companions and proclaiming, "Somali plots break up like that. They will do nothing." He refused even to let his men keep their rifles by their side—except for those held by the few sentries, all rifles were locked up in the arsenal. That very night five hundred Aulihan raiders rushed the unprepared outpost, sacking the *boma* (fenced enclosure) and killing Elliott and those of his men who could not escape into the night. For a few weeks tension and terror (but no fighting) reigned along the Jubaland frontier; then the raiders melted away in front of the inevitable punitive column.

The surviving askaris reported that Elliott had been wounded in the head at the first rush, had managed to shoot and kill the first Somali to rush at him, but then was stabbed and hacked to death by the others. The Aulihan claimed that Elliott had shot the first two to enter his house and then turned his gun on himself. His Zubair mistress ran off with the leader of the Aulihan.

Elliott, Grant. Captain Elliott replaced Dr. Peschuel-Loesche as leader of the Free State Niari expedition in 1882. His assignment was to find a route from the Atlantic to Stanley Pool by going along the Niari and Kwilu Rivers (the existing Congo route was troubled by rapids and required several portages). Elliott's safari was a small affair, just him, two other Europeans, and a small African contingent. After founding stations at Stephanieville and Franktown, all three Europeans collapsed with fever. Although eventually Elliott had to be rescued and carried back to the coast by Lieutenant Vandervelde, his was an important step in solidifying Free State control over the Congo.

Ellis, George. Corporal Ellis worked on Capt. Bertram Sclater's road-building team in 1895. Later he manned the British bullock depot near the stream called Nairobi, with a small force of askaris under his command. He is considered by many to have been the first European to live inside the boundaries of what is now Nairobi.

In January 1897 he was visited by the hunter Carl Schillings. Ellis warned the German to beware of the lion swarming the area. Attracted by the oxen and not used to firearms, the local lion were a particularly aggressive breed. Ellis himself had killed a big lioness near the corral the night before. Schillings admitted later (*With Flash-Light and Rifle* (1905) that he was a "little skeptical"—lonely soldiers had a tendency to exaggerate the dangers of their post. Schillings's skepticism soon disappeared, however: On his very first walk around the camp he ran into two lion. He wound up shooting four of the animals on his first day there and several more the following week.

Elton, Frederick (xxxx–1879). The consul at Mozambique, Captain Elton led an 1878 safari to Lake Nyasa to investigate the slave trade. He was accompanied by H. B. Cotterill, Captain Hoste, and Herbert Rhodes, who was elephant hunting in the area. Elton's expedition was the first to accurately map the northern end of the lake. He died shortly afterward in Wanyamwezi en route to Zanzibar.

Eltz, von. Von Eltz was the German officer in charge of Herrmann von Wissmann's 1892 attempt to bring a German steamer to Lake Nyasa. With twenty Sudanese askaris and a Hotchkiss gun, he came to the rescue of Harry Johnston and his officers at Zomba, where they were temporarily besieged by Arab slavers. Von Eltz later commanded the German garrison at Moshi in northern Tanganyika. He liked to hunt and was said by Schillings to have killed some sixty rhino while stationed there.

Emin Pasha (1840–1892). Born Eduard Schnitzer in Oppeln, Silesia, Emin was a scholarly German who graduated with a medical degree from Berlin in 1864. His father was Ludwig Schnitzer, a merchant, and his mother Pauline Schnitzer (died 1889). Both parents were Jews, but Eduard was baptized a Christian at age six. After graduation he went to Turkey, where he got a post as a medical officer to Vali Mushir Divitji Ismail Hakka Pasha, and traveled in that capacity through Turkey, Syria, Armenia, and Arabia. It was around this time that he changed his name to Emin, to encourage xenophobic Muslim patients to seek his medical services. After Hakka died in 1873, Emin practiced medicine in Constantinople until 1875, when he returned to Germany for a few months.

In 1875 he went to Egypt and procured a position as medical officer to Charles Gordon, governor of Equatoria province in the Sudan. Gordon used the enterprising German doctor on a variety of missions to places such as the Congo, Kordofan, the Lado Enclave, and Lake Victoria, and when Gordon left the Khedive's employ in 1878, Emin succeeded him as governor. At some point he converted to Islam, although he probably just put on the appearance of conversion for politics' sake. He was an able administrator but excelled in the more scholarly pursuits, taking valuable meteorological and climatic readings and amassing zoological and botanical collections. He also allegedly collected some seventy-five tons of ivory.

When the Mahdi revolt began in the mid-1880s, Emin retreated up the Nile with about ten thousand soldiers and their dependents, holding out against the rebels in several remote strongholds. Public sentiment in England, deeply disturbed by Gordon's fate, demanded Emin's relief, and a force of seven hundred men under Henry Morton Stanley was sent to effect his rescue in 1888. Stanley made no secret that he was also very much interested in saving the rumored seventy-five tons of ivory.

By the time Stanley's force struggled up the Congo to Emin's garrison at Lake Albert—fighting the Pygmies and the elements every step of the way—there was considerable question as to who was rescuing whom. The survivors of Stanley's column, maybe three hundred strong, were stretched out for some seven hundred miles. Hundreds had perished from starvation, disease, and hostile natives, while Emin's men were well fed and well uniformed and had at least a surface veneer of proper military discipline. Their only real shortage was ammunition, and Stanley had brought only a very small amount of that with him.

Last known photograph of Emin crossing Duki River, 17 August 1890.

Emin and Stanley did not hit it off (among the points of contention was that Emin turned out to have only a small stock of ivory), but eventually the Pasha was prevailed upon to leave with the reporter-turned-explorer. Stanley had several agendas, being beholden to Leopold of Belgium and also to British commercial and political interests. For his part, Emin was an odd man. Superficially courteous and almost courtly, he was dreamy and indifferent to the sufferings of others. One source even claimed that he had some deep-rooted sexual problems.

Only a portion of Emin's men agreed to go with him. After waiting for Stanley's stragglers, the combined forces left toward the southeast, discovering the Semliki River and passing the Mountains of the Moon. They encountered a German rescue party at Bagamayo in Tanganyika. At a dinner in his honor at Bagamayo, Emin (who was very nearsighted) walked out onto a second-story balcony, only to discover that there was no balcony. He fell fifteen feet and hit hard, fracturing his skull.

In 1891 Emin returned to Equatoria with a German force. He met up with some survivors of his old garrison at Lake Albert, but they refused to recognize his authority. Treating his safari as a scientific expedition, he entered the Congo, where his force was decimated by smallpox. In October of 1892 he was murdered by assassins commissioned by Arab slaving interests.

Erasmus, Abel (1845–1912). Erasmus was a leading Boer citizen of the Transvaal and a native commissioner in the late nineteenth century. He was a formidable man—Harry Wolhuter wrote that the Swazis respected and feared him more than any other man. In the Boer War Erasmus sided against the British. Wolhuter and other members of Steinacker's Horse once managed to steal a large herd of cattle belonging to him.

In 1881 a price was put on Erasmus's head (£500) by the British due to his questionable activities during the rebellion of the Sekukuni, a Basuto clan led by a chief named Mapoch. His chief accuser was a British general, Sir Garnet Wolseley. That did not stop the British from allowing him to serve as the Transvaal's native commissioner in later years.

His wife was a hard woman, hated by the local Africans for her brutal nature. She eventually went blind, and the local witch doctors took the credit.

Eriksson, Axel Wilhelm (1846–1901). As a young man Eriksson was traveling with Charles John Andersson when the latter died of peritonitis by the Kunene River in 1867.

Eriksson buried his older friend and read services over the grave. He later went on to become a highly regarded hunter and trader in South-West Africa in his own right. Eriksson married Fanny Stewardson in 1871. Their son, also named Axel Eriksson (1878–1924), became one of South-West Africa's premier artists.

Erlanger, Carlo Freiherr von (1872–1904). A German hunter who traveled through Somaliland in the 1890s, Erlanger had the distinction of being killed in an auto accident in Salzburg, Austria, a rare event in 1904.

Erskine, George Saint Vincent (1905–xxxx). Mr. Erskine was born on 24 October 1905 in Transvaal, South Africa, a fourth-generation white African. His grandfather was an explorer in the 1870s, and his father was a big-game hunter and gold miner in South Africa. At age two (1907), his parents took him to pioneer in Rhodesia, where he attended St. George's school in Bulawayo, which is now in Harare. He lived there for eleven years until his father, Charles Howard Erskine, died in 1918. In 1919 he returned to South Africa where he attended St. Andrews College in Grahamstown, Cape Province. In 1921 he and his mother immigrated to California, where Mr. Erskine studied electrical engineering.

His professional life took him to Liberia where he was the electrical engineer for the architects building the extension to Roberts International Airport near Monrovia. He married twice, once in 1936 and again in 1968; his second marriage occurred while working in Vietnam for a construction firm. He hunted in South Africa, Kenya, Rhodesia, Botswana, Ethiopia, and Portuguese East Africa, mainly for antelope and marauding elephants.

As a contributing author for Safari Press's African Country Series, Erskine wrote stories for *Hunting in Botswana, Hunting in Ethiopia, Hunting in Kenya, Hunting in South Africa,* and *Hunting in Zambia.*

Everett, Frederick (1920–present). The first of five children, Fred was born on 1 January 1920 in the dusty settlement of Mafeking, the capital of Bechuanaland, a landlocked British protectorate in Southern Africa. His father, a colonial official, took the family by oxwagon and donkey cart through vast stretches of wild country to outposts where Fred's first playmates were black children and those of the San peoples, the Bushmen. By the time most children can dress themselves, Fred already spoke several indigenous languages, rode with skill, could identify plants and trees, track, hunt with snares, throw sticks, use a bow and arrows, skin prey, and prepare food in the veld. The die was cast for his life as a hunter.

After several miserable years at school in Bulawayo, Southern Rhodesia, young Fred finally rebelled against the despotic teachers, bullies, and regimented life of boarding school. He walked out at age thirteen, never to return, his uncaring family then propelling him into the wilds for good. Thus, from about 1933 until he retired in the 1980s, Fred made the African wilds his home. Proficient in firearms, Fred hunted his first elephant before he was even a teenager and had taken the Big Five by the time he turned sixteen. Fred's mentor from boyhood was Agatauwa, a remarkable member of the Matabele tribe of Southern Rhodesia. He and other tribal peoples imparted their knowledge to Fred, helping hone his hunting skills and, at the same time, giving him insight into other cultures of a now vanished world.

The ensuing decades saw Fred live through a world war and experience firsthand the wind of change that began gusting through the continent soon after peace in 1945, altering irrevocably a whole way of life. He spent protracted

Fred Everett.

periods in countries from southern Africa to Somaliland as he hunted, explored, traded, and lived, surviving severe injury and periods of great privation. Elephants and ivory dominated his life as he traveled from Bechuanaland to Angola, the Rhodesias, Mozambique, Nyasaland, the Belgian Congo, Tanganyika, Uganda, Kenya, and southern Somaliland. It was a pristine world where 100-pounders existed and horizons were limitless.

Fred Everett's writings have preserved with admirable clarity and directness an astonishing life in Africa's wild places before and after World War II. Together with Sue, his gallant wife of almost sixty years, they raised three children in the bush. Fred eventually worked as tsetse fly field officer in what is now Zimbabwe where he hunted six species, including elephant and buffalo, reputed to be host to the deadly tsetse fly. After much hardship, the Everetts moved to South Africa in 1985, where they reside today.

Everett is the author of two books, written in the grand tradition of African hunting literature and covering the varied experiences of a lifetime in the bush. *Heat, Thirst and Ivory* was published by Safari Press in 2002 and was well-received. It was followed by a sequel, *Tuskers in the Dust.*

Eyre, Herbert (xxxx–1896). The brother of Arthur Eyre, Herbert served as a scout during the 1893 Matabele War. After the conquest he settled on a farm in Mashonaland. In 1896 the Matabele revolted, but Mashonaland seemed peaceful. Eyre was home one day when a group of local Shonas came to his door, ostensibly asking for work. As he sat on his verandah talking to them, the men suddenly pulled out knives and hacked him to death. This signaled the start of a general rising in the territory, but it was doomed to failure, coming too late to coordinate with the Matabele Rebellion.

Eyre, T. Arthur Page (1859–1899). In September 1892 Arthur Eyre, a former member of the Mashonaland Pioneer Column, went on a hunting trip to the hills northwest of Salisbury, Southern Rhodesia. He was accompanied by his brother Herbert and an American, William Harvey "Curio" Brown. Eyre shot a female white rhino and captured its calf, but like most captive animals in those days it soon died from malnutrition and disease.

The cow rhino had been escorted by a large bull when Eyre shot her near Rhodesia's Mount Domo. He made several trips to the region in pursuit of the bull, but didn't finally kill it until 1895. That animal is believed to have been the last white rhino killed in southern Rhodesia—at least until additional animals were transplanted from South Africa in the late twentieth century. Arthur Eyre died in Salisbury in 1899.

F

Fairbairn, James (1853–1894). Scottish trader who visited Lobengula in 1874 and obtained two wagonloads of good ivory. His partner was named Dawson. During the 1870s, he had a home in Matabeleland, called "New Valhalla," where he often entertained Selous during the hunter's trips to that country. Fairbairn had apparently lost a fortune in the gambling halls at Kimberley.

Fairbridge, Kingsley (1885–1924). Rhodesian outdoorsman and writer. Born at Grahamstown, Fairbridge moved with his family to a new farm at Umtali in Rhodesia. Growing up on the fringe of the wilderness, he acquired a tremendous reputation as a woodsman and writer, producing an autobiography that is considered one of the seminal books of Rhodesian history.

Fairweather, R. G. Captain Fairweather started out in the Rhodesian police and served in the King's African Rifles in the 1914–1918 war. He then became a game warden in Tanganyika and, in 1933, that country's senior game ganger. At that time Blunt described him as tall, thin, and wiry, and as having hunted elephant for thirty years. For a while he ran Tanganyika's Elephant Control Scheme.

Falkenstein, J. Dr. Falkenstein was a German explorer on the 1876 German Loango Expedition. He brought the first living gorilla back to Europe, a juvenile called M'Pungu. M'Pungu was exhibited at the Berlin Aquarium for nine months, then died.

Farquhar, William (xxxx–1871). A Scottish sailor, Farquhar joined Henry Stanley's 1871 expedition to find Livingstone. The idea was that Farquhar's nautical skills would prove invaluable during the anticipated river travel. Unfortunately, the river travel proved unfeasible, and Farquhar, who was a bit of a sea rogue, proved unfit for making long tropical marches. He quickly caught elephantiasis and died, unmourned by Stanley, in the Tanganyikan village of Mpapwa on 26 May 1871. He left a sister in Edinburgh.

Faulkner, Henry. An avid hunter, Faulkner joined Lt. Edward D. Young's 1867 expedition that was searching for the lost Dr. Livingstone. Faulkner made no secret that his primary motivation was to seek out new hunting opportunities rather than old missionaries. Young happily took him along to provide extra meat and defense. Upon their return from Nyasaland and Zambezia, Faulkner wrote a classic account of the expedition, *Elephant Haunts* (1868).

Fawcus, A. E. F. Lieutenant Colonel Fawcus of Elburgon, Kenya, a member of EAPHA (see glossary) from 1935, was killed in an accident in the Royal Auxiliary Air Force a year later. ROWLAND WARD 1928: LION.

Fenwick, George (xxxx–1884). A lay member of the Church of Scotland Mission in Nyasaland, Fenwick was, in the words of Sir Harry Johnston (1897), "a headstrong, lawless man who inspired fear and admiration alternately in the minds of the natives." Fenwick quit the mission and set himself up (with his wife) as a trader and elephant hunter. He had several ivory dealings with a Makololo chief called Chipatula, who lived at Chiromo.

One night in 1884 the two men were drinking and got into an argument about money. Fenwick felt Chipatula owed him some, which the chief vehemently denied, insulting the former missionary in the process. Fenwick shot him dead. As astonished natives gathered around, Fenwick shouted, "Your chief is dead—I am chief now!" But, seeing the men reaching for their weapons, the "new chief" fled to a canoe and escaped across the Shire to an island. There he tried to hide. For three days the natives stalked him, finally caught him, and cut his head off. A Makololo warrior was then sent as emissary to the British consul, a man named Foot, demanding money and Mrs. Fenwick as reparations. Foot demurred, and the situation was touchy for a while. The Makololo went on the warpath. A small lake steamer was sunk and shots were fired at unwary passersby, but eventually the affair blew over. But Consul Foot soon died of stress, and relations with the Makololo were never the same.

Ferguson, J. D. Ferguson was a British captain and a surgeon attached to Herbert Austin's 1898 Lake Rudolf expedition. Near Mount Elgon Ferguson shot an elephant with tusks of 110 and 108 pounds. One of the many places where Austin and his men were attacked by angry Turkana spearmen was at an inlet on the lake's western shore. The inlet was later named Ferguson's Gulf after the surgeon.

Fergusson, Vere Henry (1891–1927). Born 25 July 1891, Captain Vere Fergusson fought in the First World War with the West Africa Regiment in the Cameroons before transferring to the Egyptian army in 1916. He became an administrative officer in the Egyptian Sudan in 1919.

Fergusson was serving as the district commissioner for Bahr el Ghazal when the British government decided to send a man into the West Nuer district to try to convince the warlike Nuer people to stop raiding their neighbors. Fergusson volunteered for the job.

He was probably not the right man for the task. The Nuer were a proud, martial clan, one of the few tribes in Central Africa that had managed to defend themselves successfully against the Arab slavers of the nineteenth century. Theirs was a cattle culture and much of their social system revolved around raiding other tribes, especially the Dinka, both to steal cattle and women and to acquire status by killing human beings. Due to their nature as well as the inhospitable swampy terrain that they inhabited, the Nuer had had little exposure to the British or other Westerners. For his part, Fergusson was tough and rather tactless, and not one to brook any nonsense. He was a rugged man who enjoyed hunting buffalo and elephant, but he was inflexible in his outlook. He was a firm believer in the use of force for political ends. The combination of his stubbornness and Nuer independence quickly led to trouble. Fergusson decreed a stop to the raiding, and he antagonized his charges by ordering them to return a number of stolen Dinka cattle and to wear European clothing. The Nuer balked at this, and Fergusson had to send for troops.

There were several armed clashes in the mid-1920s, including at least one pitched battle in which dozens of Nuer warriors were killed while charging Fergusson and two hundred men of the Equatorial Battalion. The British were armed with modern rifles and machine guns while the Nuer wielded sharp spears and wooden shields. The tribesmen were slaughtered. Fergusson admired their bravery but welcomed the massacre, writing "I must say I am awfully glad they attacked as they did, for never again will any of them try to be truculent with me, and I ought to have them feeding out of my hand." He was wrong. The Nuer, showing better tactical sense than did the Zulus and Matabele, switched from mass attacks to guerrilla methods, and sporadic fighting continued throughout the 1920s.

Fergusson maintained his district headquarters aboard the *Kereri*, a beat-up old side-paddle steamboat. The West Nuer District was often flooded and the *Kereri* gave him great mobility over the otherwise impassable landscape. The steamer also provided him with a mobile fortress. In 1927 Fergusson was lured away from the safety of the *Kereri*, and was speared to death by some Nuer warriors who had been stalking him.

He was replaced by a calmer man, H. A. Romilly, who soon reached an understanding with the Nuer: They would stop their tribal raiding and the British wouldn't interfere with their internal affairs. Under Romilly's guidance (and that of his successor, Wedderburn-Maxwell) the West Nuer District soon became a relatively quiet outpost of the Empire.

Excerpts from Fergusson's letters and journals were published in 1930 under the title *Fergie Bey.* He was fairly well known in his day, and a fledgling writer named Frank Weber wrote a book about hunting with Fergusson titled *A Novice on the Nile,* in which Fergusson played the role of the experienced guide. ROWLAND WARD 1928: NILE LECHWE.

Fernbach, Balint. Fernbach was a Hungarian sportsman who in 1910 was guided by Kalman Kittenberger on a safari from Lake Victoria through the Rift Valley and on to the Indian Ocean coast. The safari was a large one, consisting of about one hundred forty, necessitating the shooting of at least one buffalo or three or four zebra or the equivalent per day just to satisfy the meat ration. During one hunt Fernbach's gunbearer, a man named Osmani, was bowled over by a cow buffalo. The incident happened after Fernbach had mistaken the cow for a bull. Fernbach, although frequently referred to as a "famous big-game hunter," doesn't seem to have possessed superior bush skills. For instance, on another occasion he mistook a troop of baboons for a herd of buffalo. Osmani was bruised and a bit sore but not seriously hurt, and two years later he traveled with Kittenberger to Budapest. Fernbach died shortly after this safari.

Fey, Jim. Fey was a Kenya professional hunter who was definitely not a fellow to mess with, especially if you were a stock-raiding lion. Fey's parents (Ernest and Mary, both of whom died in 1936) built a farm on the slopes of the Aberdare Mountains in 1906. On this farm they produced cattle, sheep, horses, honey, and, later, pyrethrum. Jim grew up roaming the woods with his relatives and Kikuyu friends, and learned to hunt at an early age, protecting the farm's livestock from lion and other predators. The family lived there until the late 1950s, when a government scheme appropriated all the land in the district for distribution to African small-farmers.

One night in 1922 lion killed four donkeys belonging to Fey. Setting up a bait the next evening, he killed fourteen lion in less than two hours. Fey also took up professional hunting and guided the maharaja of Datia on safari in 1921.

With two other men shooting as well, the party accounted for thirty-four lion and two leopard in one night.

Finaughty, William (1843–1917). One of the best, and scariest, of the early South African elephant hunters was Bill Finaughty, who didn't begin his elephant hunting until 1865 and still managed to bag some five hundred before Boer-style hunting stopped around 1870. Finaughty was born in Grahamstown, South Africa, the son of a blacksmith. He made his first trip into the interior in 1864, going on an impromptu big-game expedition in the Transvaal. The area was already bereft of elephant, however, and Finaughty soon tired of shooting the vast herds of wildebeest and antelope. By the Vaal River he came across a wagon train led by a trader named Edward Chapman. Chapman owned a store in Kuruman and was in the habit of making a yearly trip to Bechuanaland and Matabeleland. Finaughty accompanied him and William Francis, another experienced hunter-trader, on the 1864 trip. They visited Khama, king of the Bechuanas, and hunted buffalo in Bechuanaland, where Chapman had a close call when he stumbled across a buffalo bull in the bush. In his shock Chapman threw his rifle at the charging animal and managed to distract the bull enough to escape. Finaughty had a similar experience soon afterward, coming up unexpectedly on a lioness, but showed his presence of mind even at his young age by shooting the animal.

The caravan finally reached Mzilikazi's kraal at the end of July 1864, and Finaughty got his first look at the legendary Matabele king. He described him years later as a "physical wreck," old and paralyzed. Chapman and Francis conducted their trading business and the whole party returned to Kuruman, where Finaughty spent the winter of 1864–1865 working in Chapman's store.

When Chapman went on his 1865 trip, Finaughty followed him, but this time with his own stock to barter. When the older man returned to Kuruman, Finaughty stayed behind to do some further trading. He returned to Kuruman in March 1866 and two months later went on his first elephant hunt.

Finaughty started out in May 1866 with Chapman, Richard Clarke, and a well-known Griqua hunter named Haws (Hans) Hai on the usual trading expedition to Matabeleland. They ran into another party composed of several famous elephant hunters: The Hartleys (Henry and his sons Fred and Tom), George Phillips, James Gifford, Thomas Leask, Phil Smith, Cap Wilkinson, Tom Maloney, Christian Harmse, Karl Mauch, and a man named Frank.

Bill Finaughty in his old age. Circa 1913.

All except Chapman and Clarke decided to go on an ivory hunt in Mashonaland in July.

Finaughty had found his calling. He soon had shot nine elephant, more than anyone else in the party, which according to Finaughty apparently caused some resentment (though we cannot dismiss the possibility that Finaughty was being paranoid—he was not the most stable character, and suspicion was definitely part of his psychological makeup. Thomas Leask's account, *South African Diaries,* does support Finaughty, however). Finaughty split off from the main group, with just himself and two African servants and their horses. He quickly added eight more elephant, all cows, to his total.

When Finaughty went off alone with his two servants and his string of horses, he began a storied four-year stint of elephant hunting that was still being discussed more than a century later. He crisscrossed the region, hunting mainly in a remote area north of the Shashi River that was essentially his own private reserve, but also in Mashonaland and even occasionally in Matabeleland, where a fee had to be paid to the king.

The elephant hunters of that time and place grouped and regrouped like a giant amoeba, forming brief partnerships, splitting up, and forming again. The same names appear in different combinations, as if drawn from a pool of hunters. The Hartleys, Finaughty, Jan Viljoen, Leask, and others would gather together for a season and decimate the elephant herds, the roster changing only when a young newcomer appeared or an old-timer met with an accident. Henry Hartley accounted for some twelve hundred elephant in his career, but that total was enhanced by his "family-style" hunting, meaning that Henry and his sons would all blaze away at the same target. It was a business, not a sport. Bill Finaughty killed five hundred elephant during his five-year career, by himself with old-fashioned rifles.

Finaughty's account of these years—published first as a newspaper serial and then in an American press run of two hundred fifty books in 1916 as *The Recollections of an Elephant Hunter,* 1864–1875—is unmatched for its excitement and flavor. Narrating the story many years after the fact, Finaughty was unreliable on names and dates, frequently putting things out of chronological order, but true to form he remained brutally honest about his deeds and opinions. It's a small book, only two hundred forty pages in its 1980 Books of Zimbabwe reprint (with a superb introduction and notes by Edward Tabler), but definitely belongs on any African hunting bookshelf.

Finaughty was a hard man, not easy to get along with, but he must have had some charm—otherwise it is hard to understand why nobody ever put a bullet into him. In his memoirs he took great pains to rationalize everything he did, but the truth filters through. Finaughty sold guns to the Matabele and other tribes, primarily because it was a way to make a buck, but as a secondary motive, he privately detested the Boers. He wasn't crazy about the Africans either (I'm not sure he even liked his own people), and in one chapter of his book he recounts how he tracked down a Bushman who had stolen one of his oxen (later the ox had to be killed because the thief had hamstrung it). The Bushman fired first at a range of one hundred yards, the bullet striking the ground directly in front of Finaughty's horse. As Finaughty recalled in his old age, "Then the Bushman commenced to run, but he did not go very far . . . They [Finaughty's associates] were very curious to know what had happened to the Bushman. I told them he had run away—and so he had."

By 1870 the elephant were gone from the fly-free zones and Finaughty and the other hunters noted above were unwilling to follow the great beasts on foot. It wasn't that they were too lazy to walk. The truth is that the percussion rifles and ammunition of the period were not reliable or powerful enough to kill African dangerous game with one shot. It often took a dozen or more rounds to bring down an elephant or a rhino (Gordon Cumming once put fifty-seven shots into a bull elephant before it died). A horse would help you to escape the animal's charge, but hunting on foot was virtually suicidal. Later, in the 1880s, it was made possible by the advent of modern magazine rifles and more powerful cartridges.

Finaughty and his brother Harry set up a store at Shoshong, which he ran until 1875. He then found himself in hot water with the Boers (they almost hanged him) because they rightly suspected him of trying to sell a cannon to a hostile chief named Sekukuni. He did sell two other cannons to Mzilikazi's successor, Lobengula.

After living at Kimberley in 1877–1879, Finaughty opened another store in Mamusa. Tabler believes that about this time he married Elizabeth Krause. The couple had ten children, ranging from John (died 1910) to Gladys (died 1959). At least one son, William Jr., followed his father into the hunting business as a professional guide and was killed in a gun accident while hunting lion sometime after 1917.

In 1878, while Finaughty was running the store at Mamusa, he and J. B. Taylor went on a hunting and trading trip. Taylor was eighteen years old while the famed hunter was thirty-five. Early in the journey the two men had just crossed the Hartz River when they were approached by an African warrior on horseback, a messenger from one of the local chieftains. The chieftain demanded brandy and gunpowder as a toll to travel through his lands. Finaughty may have been retired as an elephant hunter, but he had an immense amount of experience in dealing with these situations—and was a violent psychopath to boot. Silently and calmly he loaded the rifle he had been cleaning, took careful aim at a small black-and-white bird perched in a tree some fifty yards away, and squeezed off one shot. After the bird transformed into a little ball of fluffy feathers and blood, Finaughty told the warrior, "Go, boy, back to your master and tell him that is my answer." They were allowed to pass unmolested—but later turned back when Lobengula denied them entry into Matabeleland. The Matabele would have taken Finaughty up on his challenge.

When the Boer War of 1880 broke out, Finaughty moved away from the area, but soon returned to the Transvaal, living on a farm from 1883–1887. In 1887 he was apparently involved in some bizarre scheme to launch a coup d'état in the Portuguese colony at Delagoa Bay and claim it for England. The scheme failed badly. Then Finaughty traveled to Australia as one of a counterfeiting gang, which passed their bogus bills at racetracks. The choice of locale was unfortunate for Finaughty: He was a compulsive gambler, and any money he made from the counterfeiting he soon lost on the horses.

Back in Africa, Finaughty took his family to Rhodesia in 1894, settling on a farm. His pattern was to vanish for weeks at a time, either working on some scheme or spending the profits and coming home periodically for a rest when the money ran out. At some point he added diamond smuggling to his resume. When the Matabele revolted in 1896, slaughtering settlers and burning their farms, Finaughty responded in classic Finaughty style: He sent Elizabeth and the children to safety in Bulawayo and occupied himself in looting his neighbors' homesteads.

After the rebellion had subsided, he started a cattle ranch on the Umguza River, but his herd was wiped out in the rinderpest epidemic. He continued to live on the Umguza farm until 1914, when his son William Jr., the professional hunter, took him in at his home on the Kafue River. Healthy and erect until the end, Finaughty died in 1917.

Firmin. In 1872, at the Ramaquabane River in Matabeleland, Selous found the grave of an Englishman named Firmin, who had been killed by an elephant, "the first he had ever seen" (Selous, 1881).

Fischer, Gustav A. (1848–1886). Dr. Fischer was a German physician with a penchant for African exploration. In 1876 he settled in Zanzibar. His first expedition was in 1877, when he traveled the Kenya coast from Zanzibar to Witu. In 1878 he went up the Tana River as far as Massa and spent some time poking around the village of Kau on the Osi River. Toward the end of 1882 he set out from Pangani, headed for Lakes Victoria and Samburu. He got as far as the Rift Valley and Lake Naivasha (and was considered their European discoverer) before the Masai forced him to turn back. In August 1885 he again struck out from Pangani, this time leading an expedition funded by Wilhelm Junker's brother. It was believed that Junker was with Emin Pasha and Fischer was to rescue him. This time he got as far as Lake Baringo before illness and privation forced him to turn around. Fischer also encountered opposition from the Kikuyu, who continually tried to raid his column.

Dr. Fischer died in Berlin soon afterward, on 11 November 1886, probably from the effects of malnutrition and the variety of African diseases he had encountered. He was the author of *Das Masai Land (Land of the Masai)* and *Mehr Licht im Dunklen Weltteil (More Light for a Dark Part of the World).*

Fischer, Hans. According to Sir Harry Johnston in *The Story of My Life* (1923), Capt. Hans Fischer was a German explorer in coastal southern Angola in 1882. The circumstances of the first meeting between Johnston and Fischer are remarkable. Johnston and Lord Mayo had just begun their epic hunting safari when they came across a European lying unconscious on the sun-baked ground. The two British sportsmen carried the man into shade and revived him. He identified himself as Captain Fischer, a German officer, and said he was on an expedition exploring the Koroka and Kunene Rivers. Johnston spelled the name "Visher," but he was probably mistaken—a Visher was a German administrative officer in the Cameroons at the time Johnston was writing, and it is my belief that he got the names confused. Fischer (or Visher) was alone, with no porters or any other entourage. Johnston and Mayo made sure he was OK and helped him on his way. Some years later, Johnston recalled in his memoirs with some amusement, the Germans made a claim for ownership of the Kunene area, basing their claim on the explorations of the German officer that Mayo and Johnston had found face-down in the dirt.

Fitzpatrick, Sir James Percy (1862–1931). Percy Fitzpatrick was born in Cape Colony and educated in Bath, England. He returned to South Africa in 1878 when his father died, and tried to support his family by working in a bank. He was a restless youth, and in 1884 he quit his job and moved to the gold fields at Barberton in the Transvaal, where he worked as a dispatch rider and edited a newspaper. He took to following the gold miners and moved with the bulk of them to a new strike at Witwatersrand in 1889.

An experienced hunter and a raconteur, Fitzpatrick guided Lord Randolph Churchill and the wealthy South African businessman Alfred Beit on a safari through Bechuanaland and the Transvaal in 1891–1892. Both men were impressed with the younger man's bushcraft and his store of wilderness yarns. Fitzpatrick was later to put his gift of storytelling to good use.

In 1892 Fitzpatrick joined the Hermann Eckstein company as director of intelligence, a position he held until retiring in 1907. He was arrested as a conspirator after the Jameson raid and sentenced to two years, but was released in May of 1896 provided he stay out of politics for a time. In 1899 his first book, *The Transvaal from Within,* was published; it was a dry but influential defense of the Rhodes faction.

The start of the Boer War found Fitzpatrick in London, where he soon set himself up as an unofficial government adviser on South African affairs. At war's end he returned to South Africa and became an important figure on the new scene, working with both the government and the mining industry. He was probably the leading proponent for the importation of Chinese laborers to work in the mines.

Despite his success in other endeavors, including a spell as a member of Parliament and a KCMG (see glossary), Fitzpatrick is best remembered today for his novel, *Jock of the Bushveld* (1907), a hugely popular fictional account of South African bush life. The tone of the book is humorous, and the protagonist is a dog, yet Jock's portrayal of the period's hunting scene is more accurate than those in most nonfiction works. It is still an excellent read. He also wrote *Through Mashonaland with Pick and Pen* (1892), *The Outspan* (1897), and the posthumously published *South African Memories* (1932). Fitzpatrick spent the last years of his life helping establish the South African citrus industry and died in 1931.

Fitzwilliams, Gerald H. L. (xxxx–1969). Dr. Fitzwilliams was a medical advisor to the Imperial Austrian court in Vienna before the Great War. He purchased the famous "Brussels Tapestries" from the abdicated Emperor Karl in 1918 and sponsored their display in a museum until his death nearly fifty years later. Dr. Fitzwilliams hunted elephant for seven years in Ubangi-Shari under the African name "Maderi."

Flatters, Paul Francois Xavier (1832–1881). Flatters was a French military officer (colonel) who was sent with a column to make a survey of a possible trans-Sahara railway. His second in command was a Lieutenant Dianous. In the Ahaggar region Flatters and a few troopers separated from the column to scout for water. They were ambushed by Tuaregs and slaughtered to a man. Dianous led the rest of the expedition back toward the Grand Erg Oriental, but repeated Tuareg raids and thirst killed almost everyone. Flatter's death was very similar to that of Stigand thirty-eight years later—a small party suddenly rushed and overcome by African spearmen.

Flegel, Robert (1855–1886). Flegel was an 1880s German explorer in the Cameroons who was turned back by local warriors before reaching the town of Tibati. He was renowned for his explorations of the Lower Niger (1875–1880) and the upper courses of the Benue and the Adamawa Highlands. He died on 11 September 1886 at Brass, a station at the mouth of the Niger.

Fleischer. An Austrian elephant hunter in the Lado Enclave, 1900s, he was one of the first to capture a baby white rhino—in his case more or less as an afterthought after he'd shot its atypically aggressive mother. When he was killed by an elephant in the Congo in about 1908, John Boyes, who knew him well, was camped just a few miles away. See entry on "Bucheri" for additional information.

Fleischmann, Max C. (1877–1951). A wealthy American (Fleischmann's Yeast and Nabisco), Fleischmann took an early photograph of a female black rhino being pulled into the Tana River and killed by a crocodile. The photo and accompanying description were the sensation of their day and found their way into numerous books. Selous wrote President Roosevelt about the incident. Fleischmann's life is the subject of *Gentleman in the Outdoors* (1986). ROWLAND WARD 1928: LELWEL HARTEBEEST, GREATER KUDU, LECHWE, BUFFALO.

Fletcher. A man named Fletcher, having arrived in Natal in 1853, was hunting with a Lieutenant Clifton of the Rifle Brigade on the Tugela River when he was killed by a cow elephant. Like the previously mentioned Mr. Firmin, it was the first elephant he had ever seen, and the last.

Florian (xxxx–1861). Florian was a German blacksmith and trader specializing in hippo-hide *kibokos* (whips) and zoo animals. Together with his partner, Johann Schmidt, he eked out a living on the banks of the Atbara River in Ethiopia. Florian went elephant hunting with Sam Baker during the latter's Abyssinian expedition in 1861. Florian was killed by a lion shortly thereafter.

Foa, Edouard (1862–1901). Edouard Foa was born in Marseilles, France, in 1862 and first visited Africa in 1880. His first years on the Dark Continent were spent hunting sheep and lion in the French territories in North Africa. From 1886 to 1890 he concentrated on West Africa, visiting and hunting in the Congo, Dahomey, the Ivory Coast, and along the Niger. In 1891 Foa was commissioned by the French ministry of Public Instruction to collect geographical information and zoological specimens in south Africa and the Zambezi Valley. He spent two years on this expedition, and the ministry was well satisfied with the results.

In August 1894 Foa, still operating under the auspices of the French government, undertook an expedition that would cross the African continent. He started out from the Chinde mouth of the Zambezi on foot (only the final leg of the journey, down the Congo to the sea, would use transport) with 355 porters, 25 askaris, and two French assistants, Bertrand and de Borely. Foa's personal weapons were two Express rifles, a .303 magazine rifle, and two shotguns.

Foa and his men followed the Zambezi for a few months and in late September reached Chiromo on the Shire River, where they camped for a few months to wait out the rains. At Chiromo Foa gathered many of the men from the Zambezi area who had worked with him on his previous safari. From Chiromo they walked to the region by the Kapoche River, north of where Lake de Cahora Bassa is now. There they set up another camp north of Makanga for nearly a year, with de Borely remaining in charge at the camp while Foa and Bertrand roamed far and wide, hunting and collecting specimens. The district was relatively deserted by humans, well stocked with game, and perfect for their goal of making a collection.

Satisfied that he had a representative sample of the district's fauna, Foa eventually led the safari northeast to Lake Nyasa. There Alfred Sharpe, the newly appointed commissioner of British Central Africa, loaned him the gunboat *Pioneer* to make a nine-day tour of the lake. While at Nyasa Foa made detailed astronomical readings and de Borely quit the expedition.

From Lake Nyasa the expedition moved north to Lake Tanganyika, surveying the Chozi and Chambezi Rivers along the way. Foa borrowed another boat at Lake Tanganyika and mapped that lake as he had Nyasa. He also made a collection of seashells at the lake. At Tanganyika Bertrand also quit the expedition. In the reports he sent back to Paris, Foa lauded the work of the Catholic White Fathers in fighting the slave trade while criticizing the German administration, which he saw in action at Ujiji.

The plan now was to cross over to the Kasai River, a north-flowing tributary of the Congo. To do this, Foa and his men had to cross the Mitumba Mountains. It was a rugged, hard passage of some seventy-five miles, and it took all their strength and resources to surmount the heavily forested hills. Once on the other side, however, they found themselves in the middle of a raging African war and had to retrace their steps to save their lives.

Back at Tanganyika, the new plan was to strike a course farther north, traveling the Manyema country to the Congo. Foa hired a contingent of Wanyamwezi warriors to help guide them through. The Wanyamwezi were a martial people and in fact contributed a large number of troops to the King's African Rifles. Again it was an arduous trek, through country said to be full of cannibals, but this time they made it through successfully. In addition to the Wanyamwezi, Foa and his men had the assistance of a column of Congo Free State soldiers sent out by Baron Dhanis to meet them.

The Congo leg of the expedition was much easier. Foa met with the Pygmies, then he and his men took canoes to the station at New Antwerp and from there a steamer to Stanley Pool. Near the mouth of the Congo they piled aboard the newly built Congo railway (a legendarily dangerous piece of transportation) and ended their journey at Matadi on the Atlantic Ocean.

Foa returned to Paris to hand over his collections and to write his account of the expedition, *Chasses aux Grands Fauves* (1899), which was later translated to English under the title *After Big Game in Central Africa.* It's an interesting book. Foa had a tremendous amount of hunting experience, spread among many different species and many different areas, unlike a lot of English-speaking hunters. The bare outline of the safari as given here above doesn't begin to convey the depth to which Foa was able to portray his adventures. It is also well illustrated; Foa was a proficient photographer and artist as well as a hunter and writer. The book's one real flaw is that it is somewhat confusing—Foa lost all sense of the narrative as he went along. Thus the book starts out with a fairly detailed chronological account of the beginning of the expedition, then jumps almost randomly from incident to incident in no particular order and finally goes off on a dozen tangents describing the hunting of certain species, snakes, insect life in the Congo, and whatever popped into the author's mind, without ever really picking up the thread of the expedition again. All in all, however, after reading this book you have to wonder why his other works have never been translated.

The various geographical societies of the late-Victorian period were extremely chauvinistic and nationalist in character. In 1895 the *Scottish Geographical Magazine,* journal of the Royal Scottish Geographical Society, published a review of Foa's *Mes Grandes Chasses dans L'Afrique*

Centrale. The book covered Foa's exploits in South Africa and the Zambezi region. While British hunters like Bell (a Scot) and Neumann were exterminating the elephant herds of East Africa, the Scottish reviewer wrote of Foa: "Monsieur Foa's total bag in three years was 704, of which 319 were big game. He records that a Boer expedition, about the beginning of the century, returned with the spoils of 93 elephants in a single season, and laments that the times are changed. We should think that such fell shooting as Monsieur Foa's must go far to sustain the record of the exterminators." The review neglects to mention that Foa was hunting largely for museum specimens. Fifteen years later, the great Anglo-Saxon hero Theodore Roosevelt was to cut a bloody swath through the wildlife of Kenya and Uganda, and was much lauded in the press for doing so.

Foa was a pioneer in the use of an electric torch for night hunting. From 1892 to 1896 he spent an average of thirty-seven nights a year staking out a water hole with a rifle and a primitive electric light. Foa may have excused this by pointing out that he was trying to make a collection for the Paris Museum, but it was actually more sporting than it sounds. The light was notoriously unreliable (attempts to align the beam along the gun barrel were an almost total failure), his hide was generally on the ground, not in a tree, and he had several close calls from the larger of his intended quarries. Night hunting in 1895 wasn't all that successful anyway—of those thirty-seven nights, he saw nothing on sixteen, saw something but not well enough to shoot on six, lost whatever he shot at on seven, and made a kill on only eight nights.

Foa died in 1901 at his home in Villers-sur-Mer in Normandy, France, from the accumulated effects of various African diseases. His other works included an 1895 work on Dahomey, a book about his 1891–1894 Zambezi expedition, a more scientific account of his 1894–1897 trip published in 1900, and a posthumous book published in 1908 containing the scientific findings from his explorations.

W. Robert Foran in Kenya.

Foran, W. Robert (1881–1968). Born in England, Foran was a veteran of the Boer War and the 1902 Waziri campaign on India's Northwest Frontier. He arrived in East Africa from Johannesburg in 1904 to take a post with the East African Police, one of the first four white officers of the EAP. In 1909 he left the police and Nairobi (he didn't return to Kenya's capital until 1929) to go elephant hunting in the Lado Enclave, at which he was extremely successful. His best elephant had tusks of 159 and 155 pounds, and he took another that carried 148 and 146. He also covered the Roosevelt safari as a correspondent for the Associated Press. Moving to America in the 1910s, he founded Chicago's Adventurer's Club.

A Sandhurst graduate, Foran fought in World War I and was badly wounded in the face, leaving him permanently disfigured. After the war he owned a farm in Mashonaland for several years in the 1920s, then served a spell as editor of the *Straits Times* newspaper in Singapore. He then returned to England, where he lived from 1933–1947. In World War II he served in the War Office and with the Home Guard. He spent his last years back in Nairobi, one of the last great figures from Kenya's colonial days. In his old age he befriended the noted hunter Tony Sanchez-Ariño.

During his long career Foran hunted in Africa, Burma, India, Ceylon, Mexico, Canada, and the United States. Foran was also a prolific writer, the author of some twenty-two books. These included *Kill or Be Killed, Hunters' Saga, Breath of the Wilds, A Cuckoo in Kenya,* and *Elephant Hunters of the Lado.* He died in August 1968.

Forbes, Colonel A. Game warden of the Sudan, mid-twentieth century.

Forbes, David. A Scotsman, Forbes arrived in Natal in the 1850s and immediately went on an eight-month elephant hunt. He did well for a novice, not only surviving but also bringing back enough ivory to show a substantial profit. He discovered a cave-riddled kopje called Hunter's Rock, and every August he and three other British hunters would rendezvous there to trade and swap yarns.

Forbes and his fellow hunters kept that rendezvous for seven years. All the big ivory had been shot out of that immediate area, so Forbes began ranging far and wide. He discovered a region of South Africa that came to be known as New Scotland and, with Alex McCorkindale, started a settlement there in 1867.

His son, also named David Forbes, became a rancher and one of the largest landowners in the Swaziland area.

Forbes, William Alexander (1855–1882). This British naturalist went on collecting expeditions to America (1880) and West Africa (1882). He drowned in the Upper Niger River in 1882.

Foster Brothers. Brothers Bob (killed by a lion in 1920), George, Fronny, and Hugh were well-known hunters, farmers, and poachers in Uganda in the 1920s. They were not related to the Bob Foster who was a postwar hunter for the Safariland firm.

Fothergill, Edward. He explored the Blue Nile and the Belgian Congo and wrote *Five Years in the Sudan* (1910).

Fotheringham, Low Monteith. Fotheringham was an agent of the African Lakes Company in Nyasaland in the 1880s and the early 1890s. A severe, righteous man, he acquired great influence and trust among the Nyasaland tribes, the Nkonde, the Mambwe, and the Atonga. When hundreds of Wankonde were massacred by the Arab slavers under Mlozi at the Kambwe lagoon on Lake Nyasa, Fotheringham gathered the remnants of the tribe around him and helped lead a successful defense of the British post at Karonga. Years later he turned down a post in the government of the British Central Africa Protectorate in favor of his career in the Lakes Company. He was the author of *Adventures in Nyasaland* (1891).

Fountaine, Margaret Elizabeth (1862–1940). She was an English artist–naturalist who gave up painting after a heart-breaking love affair in 1890. Thereafter Fountaine traveled all over the world collecting butterflies, accompanied after 1901 by her Syrian lover, Khalil Neimy (born 1872). Together they visited Turkey, Algeria, Spain, South Africa, Rhodesia, the Caribbean Sea, and India. In 1913 the couple immigrated to Australia, but Fountaine left her lover and moved to the United States and then in 1919 to New Zealand. She later visited Asia, East Africa, West Africa, and South America, and died in 1940 of a cerebral hemorrhage while chasing a butterfly in a Trinidad field.

Fourie, Ben. A professional hunter employed by the firm of Safariland, Ltd., in the prewar years. He was a member of EAPHA (see glossary) from 1937.

Fowle, Andrew. Fowle was a founding member of EAPHA (see glossary) in 1934. He had a listing in the 1928 Rowland Ward record book for black rhino, a bull with a 24-inch horn, shot in Kenya. His Nairobi mailing address in the 1930 *East African Red Book* was c/o the Standard Bank of South Africa, Limited.

Francis, William C. Francis was a hunter and trader in Bechuanaland and Matabeleland for many years. In 1864 he participated in William Finaughty's first real hunt, in company with Edward Chapman. After bringing trade goods to Matabeleland, they were allowed by Mzilikazi, the king of the Matabele, to hunt but not to prospect. They had a considerable amount of trouble convincing him they were not Boers, for whom he had a strong dislike. Their first sighting of Mzilikazi's kraal included a view of two women who had been hanged for some infraction or other, so they decided it would not be politic to be on his bad side.

In 1868 Francis again hunted Matabeleland, this time with Finaughty's brother, Harry. By the 1870s most of the elephant in Bechuanaland had been destroyed. Francis eventually became senior partner in the firm Francis and Clarke, based in Shoshong.

Francois, Curt Von (1852–1931). He was a German explorer who traversed much of the southern and central

Congo in the 1880s and 1890s. His name pops up continually in the geographical literature of the day but is almost forgotten now.

In August 1885 Captain von Francois accompanied George Grenfell aboard the missionary steamer *Peace* on a two-month exploration of some Congo rivers. Other members of the safari included Mrs. Grenfell, the little Grenfell girl, and eight mission children who were both on a field trip and used as interpreters. The *Peace* ascended the Lulongo, Busira, and Juapa Rivers, among others, and underwent a heavy attack by African archers (the Peace was equipped with metal-mesh arrow guards, so the poisoned missiles just bounced off). At one place Grenfell and Von Francois unsuccessfully tried to ransom a man being held by cannibals, and at another the cannibals offered (also unsuccessfully) to buy a robust *Peace* crewman as an item of food.

Von Francois went on safari to Lake Ngami (January–March 1891) and the Kalahari (1891–1892) and reported on it to German geographical and sporting societies. He hunted hartebeest and interviewed the Bushmen, later claiming to have established that those people had earlier lived much farther east. He also complained about the snakes, particularly the cobras and puff adders. He served as governor of South-West Africa and had numerous other important posts.

Fraser, A. A. (xxxx–1937). Fraser, formerly of the Bedfordshire regiment and an experienced Indian big-game hunter, was appointed as a South African game ranger in 1903. Originally assigned to the Pongolo Reserve, a separate area between Zululand and Swaziland, he was attached for a time to Stevenson-Hamilton's overall jurisdiction at Sabi Game Reserve. Fraser was quite a character—a very tall Scotsman with a gigantic red beard and a predilection for having dozens of dogs close at hand. He was an expert rifleman, a better shot even than the old Transvaal farmers of the district, and dismayed the old Boers by being able to drink them under the table, imbibing huge quantities of whiskey with no apparent effect.

Fraser was a terrific outdoorsman but an appallingly bad civil servant. He hated paperwork and would often pay his African staff out of his own pocket rather than write out requisitions and receipts. As an older man, Fraser was left in charge of the reserve for a two-year stretch in 1917–1919, during the war-related absences of Stevenson-Hamilton and Cecil De Laporte. When these gentlemen returned from duty, they found the reserve an administrative nightmare, with no reports filed, fines and fees piled in a strongbox without any documentation, and a labor crisis brewing because Fraser had refused to carry out his duties as acting native commissioner. While they started to sort out the mess, Fraser happily went back to his section in a remote part of the reserve, with his dogs and unlimited opportunities to hunt warthogs and other vermin.

Upon his retirement around 1930, Major Fraser was awarded a small plot of land adjacent to the reserve. There he built a mud hut and lived contentedly with his dogs for the remaining seven years of his life.

French, R. (xxxx–1879). French was a British hunter in South Africa, a member of the Selous-Clarkson-Collison-Wood circle. He seems to have been a pleasant and popular companion. Henry Stabb, who knew him well in 1875, included French on a list of traders he described as "gentlemen by birth but Bohemian by nature."

In March 1879, French was present when Matthew Clarkson was killed by lightning. Seven months later, while hunting between the Chobe and Zambezi Rivers with Selous, French and two servants (his gunbearer "Boy" and another African named Nangora) went off by themselves tracking a wounded elephant. They got lost and slept out in the bush, draining the last drop from their canteens that night. The next day, out of water, the three men struggled to find their way back to camp. Boy pleaded with French to head in one direction, but the Englishman swore at him and insisted on going the other way. French began spitting up blood and finally collapsed, with his last vestiges of strength scribbling a note to Selous: "I cannot go any farther; when I die, peace with all." When he died, Boy and Nangora were free to go in the right direction and eventually returned to Selous, still carrying French's rifle.

Dying of thirst is a horrible death; it is not some simple slide into sleep. It is very painful both physically and mentally. The rate of decline is affected by such things as temperature, humidity, and the individual's level of fitness. As a general rule, humans lose about 1.2 liters of perspiration per hour in the hot, dry conditions that typify the Kalahari. Once a man has lost a little more than 4 liters—about 5 percent of the normal body weight—he starts to lose his sensory perception and his cognitive ability. When the weight-loss due to perspiration reaches about 12 percent, his blood becomes so deprived of water that it can no longer dissipate heat from the inner organs to the skin, and the person dies of heat stroke.

This can happen in as short a time as four to five hours under desert conditions, even less if the person was sick or insufficiently hydrated to begin with. In French's case, he had drunk the last of his water the night before and then had walked all day under the southern African sun before succumbing. This is a fair indication that French was a tough and physically fit individual, but lack of water will eventually do in even the strongest man.

French-Sheldon, Mrs. May (1847–1936). May French-Sheldon was an American woman who went on a tour of East Africa in the early 1890s. Apparently not a believer in roughing it, she went in high style. The British India Company delayed her steamship an entire day so her palanquin (en enclosed litter carried by men with the aid of poles) could be brought onboard. She wore an elaborately regal costume complete with sword, and haughtily refused to pay *hongo* (see glossary) to the chiefs of the countries she passed through. She even brought a gross of specially made "French-Sheldon" rings to pass out to those Africans who pleased her. Small wonder that the puzzled natives began to refer to her as the "White Queen." It was also her opinion that many European safaris got into trouble with the Africans largely because of their pronounced military appearance. She felt that a dignified safari without the appearance of a military column could travel much more freely.

Her approach worked, and it seems that everyone in East Africa bent over backward to kiss her butt and help her on her way. One gets the impression that she was good-looking and could be charming—even no-nonsense types like the rugged Canadian William Grant Stairs went out of their way to be helpful. Yet her book, *From Sultan to Sultan: Adventures Among the Masai and Other Tribes of East Africa,* is not merely a story of a spoiled rich American being carried Cleopatra-style by the heathen. French-Sheldon possessed an inquisitive and discerning eye and was not without humor.

She certainly was courageous. When faced with Lake Chala, a crater lake that no European had touched in twenty years, she didn't hesitate to tackle the heavy thickets and dangerously steep slopes, even though they had deterred no less than Joseph Thomson a few years earlier. Not only did she negotiate the descent to the lake, she also managed to bring a pontoon boat with her, spent the rest of the day being the first white visitor to sail Lake Chala, and flew the American flag.

In some ways French-Sheldon was ahead of her times. She was intensely interested in the lives of African women and campaigned mightily to get a female interpreter for her safari. Alas, the cultural prohibitions were too strong and she failed in that quest.

Unlike many early explorers, she did not ignore the local people—in fact, she missed no opportunity to interact with them, and her observations of their lives form some of the best parts of her book. But she wasn't a pushover, and, unlike many modern Westerners, she wasn't gullible or condescending, either. She was not above enforcing strict safari discipline, and one of her boasts was that she'd had to resort to flogging a porter on only ten or fewer occasions. Before you judge French-Sheldon on that, be mindful that this was still a time and place where disorganization or insubordination in the bush might mean death for all concerned. Examples were everywhere—on her own expedition, one of her porters lagged behind one day, looking for water, and was eaten by a lion. Her safari's discipline was almost military in nature. It was not unusual for recalcitrant porters to be severely punished, and during roughly this same time period many travelers, including William Astor Chanler, Henry Stanley, and Herbert Austin, actually had porters executed for desertion. One wonders if her men weren't testing the resolve of this strange woman. Tellingly, the female stereotype of the time was such that American newspaper editors refused to believe her admission that she had actually flogged her porters herself; the report was too unladylike to be credited.

In the end Africa began to catch up to Mrs. French-Sheldon. First, her men were afraid to enter Masai territory. Then, crossing a Tanganyikan bridge in her palanquin, her porters either slipped or threw her into the ravine below, and she was so busted up that she was a virtual invalid for weeks. Finally, back aboard ship and theoretically safe, a sudden roll of the ship pitched her deck chair against a railing, fracturing her skull. At that point she was done with the continent. She sailed to Naples, where she met her family and recovered fully.

Mrs. French-Sheldon returned to Africa in 1904, commissioned by King Leopold of Belgium to report on conditions in the Congo Belge. World opinion had been shocked and horrified by the atrocity reports of the reformers Morel and Roger Casement, and French-Sheldon was paid to refute those allegations. She obligingly produced a report claiming that her detailed, on-the-spot investigations of the situation revealed nothing but dedicated Belgian civil servants and happy, industrious Africans. Any discontent was rooted, she said, in a local cultural bias against hard work. The truth, of course, lay between the two extremes—the Belgian Congo was neither a demonic hellhole nor a heaven on earth. It was a rough colony, in many places corrupt, exploitative, and cruel (even vicious) but in others stable and calm.

Frobenius, Leo (1873–1938). An anthropologist and the leader of the 1910–1912 German Interior Africa expedition in Angola and South-West Africa, Frobenius was the author of *The Voice of Africa* (1913). He was one of the first Westerners to recognize the historical richness of African civilization.

Frost, H. E. F. Frost held the post of assistant game warden in Kenya, 1919–1921.

Fuchs, Felix Alexandre (1858–1928). Governor general of the Congo Free State, 1891–1892 and 1912–1916.

Fuchs, Sir Vivian (1908–1999). Fuchs was a throwback, a British explorer active up to the last years of the twentieth century. More famous for his feats in the Antarctic, in the 1920s and 1930s Fuchs led a series of scientific expeditions into remote areas of East Africa, including a 1931 safari to Olduvai Gorge with Louis Leakey. A 1934 expedition to Lake Turkana ended in tragedy—two men, Martin and Dyson, were lost when their small boat capsized in Turkana's ferocious winds. Unknown to Fuchs and would-be rescuers, the men found themselves stranded on that lake's desolate South Island. Nothing more is known of their fate. Apparently they were drowned or killed by crocodiles in an attempt to reach the mainland. Twenty years later game warden George Adamson discovered whiskey bottles and other refuse at their island campsite. He believed that the bottom of their light canvas boat had been torn by the sharp rocks surrounding the island. Others have speculated that a hippo may have overturned the boat. Either way, the men fell victim to the lake's legendary crocodiles.

G

Galton, Sir Francis (1822–1911). Galton, from a prominent Quaker banking family in Birmingham, England, was training for the medical profession when his father died in 1844, leaving him enough money to abandon medicine for a life of geography, sport, and science. He immediately went up the Nile River to Khartoum and then traveled to Syria. From 1845 to 1850 he concentrated on hunting, visiting South-West Africa and exploring the interior with Karl Andersson. His *Art of Travel* (1855) was considered an essential work for late nineteenth-century explorers.

Galton was perhaps best known for his scientific work on heredity and is considered the founder of "eugenics." He was general secretary of the British Association from 1863–1867 and worked in meteorology, natural history, and psychology. He was a pioneer in the field of fingerprint identification, publishing three works on the subject. His many-faceted works earned him numerous awards, including medals from the French and British Geographical Societies, the Darwin and Copley Medals of the Royal Society, the Darwin-Wallace Medal of the Linnean Society, several honorary doctorates, and a knighthood in 1909. He was the author of *Tropical South Africa* (1853), *Arts of Campaigning* (1855), and many works of scientific interest. He was active until about 1905, when his health began to fail rapidly, but his mental acuity remained sharp until his death from bronchitis on 17 January 1911. Galton had married Louisa Jane Butler in 1853; she passed away in 1897. They had no children. Galton left his estate of £45,000 to the University of London for the endowment of a chair in eugenics.

Galvin, George E. (1872–1951). Although just seventeen years old when they started out, George Galvin of Red Hook, New York, proved to be an able assistant to W. A. Chanler on his Kilimanjaro safari in 1889. Three years later Galvin accompanied Chanler and Ludwig von Hoehnel on their perilous trip through the Northern Frontier District. Chanler, a loyal employer (as witness the annuity he paid to von Hoehnel when the Austrian fell upon hard times late in life), treated Galvin well after their African days were over. For some years Galvin managed Chanler's horse-breeding farm in Virginia and later worked as a travel agent at New York's Vanderbilt Hotel (Chanler was a part owner of the hotel). Galvin died at age seventy-nine in Jamaica, New York, in 1951.

Gano. An American named Gano served with the Boers during the Anglo-Boer War in 1901. Gano was said to be a former detective of the Brooklyn, New York police force. He persuaded a twenty-three-year-old Boer lieutenant named Hans Cordua to join him in a conspiracy to assassinate the British commander, Lord Roberts. The conspiracy failed. Cordua was captured (apparently while drunk) and shot by a firing squad; Gano escaped and disappeared.

Garden, George. Garden lived at Mlanje in Nyasaland in the early 1900s. He often went lion hunting with Denis Lyell and was an early amateur wildlife photographer. Several of his photographs were used to document Lyell's book, *Memories of an Elephant Hunter* (1923).

Garden, J. L. John L. Garden and his brother Peter, a lieutenant in the British army, came to the Zambezi Valley for a shooting vacation in 1874. Peter had been in Matabeleland before, in 1869 with David Hume and Robert Douglas.

The Garden brothers were accompanied by an English servant named Tofts and a number of native servants. At Tati on 6 May 1874 they hooked up with Selous and George Wood who were hunting elephants professionally. Since they were all going in the same general direction, Selous agreed to let the greenhorns ride with him.

On 27 June 1874 they saw Victoria Falls for the first time. J. L. Garden, who had visited Niagara Falls, ranked Victoria Falls "superior in grandeur and magnificence" (Selous, 1881), while Niagara had a greater volume of water. After they followed the river for a while, J. L. Garden shot a female waterbuck for lunch. The meat of the waterbuck is traditionally greasy and marbled with an unpalatable fat, and most Western hunters eschew it, but Selous reported that they ate only the liver "and made short work of it."

They stayed on the Zambezi for two days and then held a council to determine the next step. Wood wanted to search for elephants along the Gwaai River, so he took fourteen of the accompanying Africans and went off in that direction. Selous, the Gardens, and the rest of the expedition (Selous had ten Matabeles and two Bushmen with him) headed upriver.

They had an interesting trip, visiting the Chobe River and shooting puku, kudu, buffalo, lions, and another waterbuck. (This time they ate the bone marrow: Selous pronounced it "exceedingly good.") After meeting up with two African hunters who worked for George Westbeech, they finally met up with some elephants. Selous shot an old bull with tusks of sixty pounds per side, but Garden had to be content with a buffalo and some guinea fowl. Even Tofts caught the hunting fever and tried to stalk a puku, but made so much noise saying hello to Selous that the antelope got away.

For the next few weeks or so the party remained in the vicinity of the Chobe. Lieutenant Garden (now promoted to captain), succeeded in shooting a few elephants, and Selous would continually sneak away from his companions and down the odd tusker. Selous was feeling cocky and, having wounded a black rhino, finished it off with an assegai, a feat that greatly impressed his African servants. Toward the end of August, they ran into George Wood, who had struck out in his search for ivory along the Gwaai. J. L. Garden finally nailed a couple of elephants, including a fine bull with tusks of seventy pounds each. Sometime in September the Gardens finally called it a day and set back off to the British settlements in South Africa. Selous had been away hunting by himself when they left and came back to find the camp empty.

Garner, Richard Lynch (1848–1920). R. L. Garner was a scientist from Virginia who went to West Africa to study gorillas and other primates in the early 1890s. He was convinced that certain monkeys, chimpanzees, and gorillas were capable of speech, based upon a boyhood experience at a zoo where he was certain that the monkeys were talking to each other. In 1892 he traveled to Africa to prove his theory correct.

Drawing upon the writings of Paul du Chaillu and other sources that depicted the gorilla as an aggressive and violent animal, Garner was perhaps overly concerned about his personal safety. He had a steel cage built, much like the cages now used to observe great white sharks. He sat in his cage for days at a time, often accompanied by a pet chimpanzee that he was trying to teach English. The cage was placed in areas known to be frequented by gorillas, and Garner took careful notes of what he could see (which was rather little, given the circumstances).

In 1896 Garner published his first book, *Gorillas and Chimpanzees.* Despite its many flaws, the book was a great leap forward in mankind's knowledge of the higher primates. Garner fairly easily came to the conclusion that gorillas were shy and harmless if unmolested, and on his later expeditions he discarded the cage. *Gorillas and Chimpanzees* is an odd work, focusing on the animal's speech capacity. About twenty photographs show dead gorillas and their skulls and the like. Garner managed to include a lot of speculation on gorilla and chimpanzee morality, and the book is filled with Biblical and literary references. Anyone who can work both Moses and Othello into a natural-history book is OK with me.

Garner made three more trips to Africa (in 1894, 1911, and 1919) and wrote another book, *Apes and Monkeys: Their Life and Language* (1900). He died in 1920 on his way back from Africa.

Garstin, Sir William (1849–1925). Born in India, Garstin joined the Indian Public Works Department in 1872. In 1885 the department detailed a small group of engineers to Cairo to modernize the irrigation system throughout Egypt. Garstin was one of those engineers and worked in the Nile Delta for the next seven years.

In May 1892 Garstin retired from the Indian Civil Service to succeed Col. Justin Ross as inspector general of Irrigation for all of Egypt, and six months later became Egyptian under-secretary of state for Public Works. He was charged mainly with supplying water for the entire country. His main accomplishment was converting the Nile irrigation matrix from a seasonal one dependent upon the flooding of the river to a permanent system that flowed all year. He oversaw the construction of the first Aswan dam, which was finished in 1902.

After the British victory at Omdurman in 1898, Garstin began the effort to clear the Bahr el Jebel and the Bahr el Ghazal of sudd, the thick, choking vegetation mat that gave the Sudan its name. In 1902–1903 he traveled up the Nile all the way to Lake Victoria, assessing and reporting on the watershed. In the course of his travels he indulged himself in a lot of hunting and took an elephant in the Sudan with tusks of 135 and 159 pounds. Its feet were 63½ inches in circumference. In 1908 Garstin retired after a triumphant tour through lower Egypt that saw him receive the kind of adulation later reserved for rock stars and sports heroes. The Egyptian government gave him a gift in gratitude for his work of £15,000 in 1905.

On his trip back to England, Garstin—who had been widely considered too old for the Sudan—was congratulated while onboard ship by the Anglo-American adventurer Frederick Burnham, who commended him for disappointing his enemies by not dying in the desert. Garstin worked for the Red Cross during the Great War and died in London on 8 January 1925.

Gatti, Attilio. This Italian sportsman went to Africa often in the 1920s to make films and to shoot specimens for the museum in Florence, Italy, and other institutions. Gatti wrote more than a dozen books about Africa and made several films, including *Siliva the Zulu* (1927). He was known for shameless self-promotion and required everyone accompanying his ventures to sign an agreement that they would not publish any accounts of the expedition—the only record would be written by Gatti. Hunters and assistants who traveled with Gatti were lucky to find themselves even named in the ensuing book.

One of these books was *The King of the Gorillas* (1932). Except for a few decent photographs, it's one of his worst—even given that English was his second language. Commander Gatti (as he was called) was, shall we say, rather full of himself. As witness: "My good boys had surrounded me, squatting on the ground as a sign of respect, their eyes full of faith and affection as they murmured *Ja Baaba* (O Father) . . . [one] old man looked at me with the clear eyes of a faithful dog." There's a lot more like this, but you get the idea. It makes the book almost unreadable. For the record, the book covers lots of gorilla hunting and adventures with pythons and cobras, capturing elephant for the Belgian Congo training program, and the obligatory chapter on how to outfit a safari. But mostly it's about Gatti and how fearless and wonderful he was.

Gedge, Ernest (1862–1933). Ernest Gedge graduated from university in 1879 and took a job as an assistant manager of a tea estate in Assam. After nine years in that position, he tired of the drudgery and joined the IBEA (see glossary). His first African adventure was a safari into Uganda with Frederick L. Jackson to inspect the chartered company's interests in that country. Gedge remained in Uganda as a company official when Jackson returned to the coast. He worked with the Gerald Portal expedition when that party reached Uganda in 1893.

In addition to his company duties, Gedge got a commission to report for *The London Times.* He filed numerous articles from Uganda in 1892–1893 and from Matabeleland in 1893.

An enthusiastic hunter, Gedge is mentioned several times in Portal's diary, almost always in a hunting context:

- 21 March 1893. In the evening Mr. Gedge arrived from Buddu. He and Williams had shot 24 Speke's antelopes.
- 11 April. Gedge accompanied [Berkeley], shooting elephants at Chagwe.
- 27 April. Gedge returned from Chagwe; got 9 elephants. Asked leave to accompany us to coast.

In August Gedge was sent ahead to Kenya with Portal's official dispatches. Portal and his men were suffering from jiggers, hunger, and general depression, and it was thought Gedge would get the letters out more quickly. He spent so much time hunting on the return trip, however, that he reached the British posts in Kenya only two days ahead of Portal.

In 1898–1899 Gedge joined the throngs of eager outdoorsmen searching for gold in the Klondike. By 1900 he was back in Africa, prospecting for gold in Rhodesia. During most of his journeys he was able to defray costs by making them part of a journalistic venture. Every man who has ever tried to put a hunting trip on an expense account owes a debt to Mr. Gedge. ROWLAND WARD 1928: BLACK RHINO, LION. ROWLAND WARD 1899: KLIPSPRINGER (NO. 4), UGANDA KOB (NO. 2, NO. 5).

Gelder, Herman. Gelder was a German sportsman who did a considerable amount of hunting in German East Africa in the early years of the last century. He preferred large safaris of more than a hundred men. One night in 1909, on the eastern shore of Lake Tanganyika, a rhino charged Gelder's campsite for no apparent reason. Possibly attracted by the campfire, the rhino gored and killed an askari who had been tending the fire.

Gerard, Jules (1817–1864). Cecile Jules Basile Gerard, known as Jules Gerard, was the French counterpart of the British hunters Baldwin and Gordon Cumming. Born at Pignans in the French province of Var on 14 June 1817, Gerard was stationed in Algeria in the 1840s, where he made a name for himself with his lion-hunting exploits. Lion hunting with the percussion muskets of that era was an extraordinarily dangerous proposition, and Lieutenant Gerard's bag of twenty-five was virtually unprecedented, although easily surpassed by later hunters armed with modern magazine rifles. Gerard estimated that each Algerian lion cost the herders and ranchers of that territory some $45,000 during its lifetime, not counting any human victims the animal might have taken. Whenever a particular lion was causing unreasonable damage in an Algerian district, Gerard would be called in to terminate the animal. He drowned in West Africa in 1864. Gerard was the author of *La Chasse au Lion* (1855), *Le Tueur de Lions,* and other books.

Gessi, Romolo (1831–1881). An Italian explorer and soldier, he surveyed the Nile above Dufile and circumnavigated Lake Albert, acting on the orders of Gordon Pasha. It was

Gessi who determined that Lake Albert Nyanza belonged to the Nile watershed. He resigned in protest at Gordon's remark, "What a pity you are not an Englishman!" Gordon was angry because he had dispatched two British officers, Watson and Chippendall, on the same mission but they had not yet returned; therefore the glory was going to Gessi, apparently a rather dark-skinned Mediterranean type.

Returning to Italy, Gessi was treated as a hero and awarded the Italian Geographical Society's Gold Medal. He prepared an expedition to the Nile with two officers, Giacomo Morch and Riccardo Buchta. That trip fell apart when his stores were destroyed in a warehouse fire at Suez. He then explored the Sobat with Pellegrino Matteucci.

Gessi led a successful military expedition (1878–1879) against rebels near Khartoum, during which he captured and executed a notorious rebel leader called Suleiman. As a reward Gessi was promoted to governor of Bahr el Ghazal. He died in Suez in 1881.

Gibbons. John Boyes once had a partner named Gibbons, who arrived in South Africa sometime before 1890 and eventually wandered up to Kenya. There he worked with Boyes as a trader at Liombasa and later led a fifty-man ivory-trading safari into Kikuyu territory. When a price had been agreed upon, Gibbons sent ten askaris to pick up the ivory. They were ambushed and massacred, and then the Kikuyu then attacked the main body. After a long fight Gibbons and a few others escaped. The rest, including a white partner named Findlay, were killed.

Gibbons then established himself as an elephant hunter in Uganda and the Belgian Congo, and in later years he also grew coffee near Fort Portal. Boyes (1927) considered him an adequate hunter but too easygoing and relaxed to exert himself much. Gibbons remained in Uganda until the mid-1920s, then returned to England and died a short time later.

It is possible that this was the same Gibbons who later went on to set himself up among the Embu tribe southeast of Mount Kenya. He had a retinue of about thirty armed Swahili askaris and a harem of fourteen native girls. He collected ivory and food from the Embu as "taxes," but the British authorities soon got wind of this and sent Richard Meinertzhagen down to deal with him.

On 14 November 1903 Meinertzhagen and his troops surprised Gibbons and his men and took them captive. The local Embu chieftains were shocked because they had believed Gibbons to be a government representative. Meinertzhagen released the fourteen young concubines near the Tana River and none too gently brought Gibbons in to Fort Hall.

Gibbons, Alfred St. Hill. St. Hill Gibbons was a British soldier with the rank of major, a big-game hunter, and the author of *Exploration and Hunting in Central Africa 1895–1896* (1898) and *Africa from South to North Through Marotseland* (1904). In 1900, while waiting for a steamer on the banks of the Nile in the Lado Enclave, Gibbons shot a rhinoceros with strange characteristics. To his amazement he realized that it was a white rhino, a creature until then known only in the southern extreme of the continent.

Renowned for his energy, Gibbons's native name translated as "the man who walks so fast no one can keep up with him." He was the first European to visit and map the Lozi district in 1895–1896, and conducted a major ethnographic and commercial survey of the same region two years later under the auspices of the Royal Geographical Society.

In 1905 he led a three-man commission (the other members were Alfred Kaiser and a Russian engineer named Wilbushwitz) that investigated conditions on the Uasin Gishu plateau, in accordance with a Foreign Office scheme to open the area up as a Jewish homeland. Gibbons was the head commissioner and thought the plateau was probably unsuitable for cultivation, while the two other men felt that the area could sustain about five hundred families. At any rate, the scheme was rejected by the World Zionist Congress, meeting in Switzerland in July 1905. The Uasin Gishu was later settled by a group of wandering Boers.

Gibbons's life contained the usual excitements and adventures of an early African pioneer and hunter. On

Capt. A. St. H. Gibbons, an illustration from his 1898 book.

the Zambezi River, for instance, a huge crocodile once rammed his aluminum boat trying to knock him out of it. Stevenson-Hamilton of Kruger National Park fame was also in the boat.

Gibbs, Alastair. A professional hunter employed by the firm of Safariland, Ltd., in the 1920s.

Gibson, Lenny. Professional hunter in Nyasaland in the early part of the twentieth century.

Gide, Andre (1869–1951). This French author went on a tour of French Equatorial Africa in 1925. Gide submitted a report on the colony to the ministry of the Colonies in which he established that the concession system, which had been damned by Brazza in a sealed report in 1905, was still engaging in brutal and corrupt practices. He was the author of *Travels in the Congo* (1927) and was awarded the Nobel Prize in Literature in 1947.

Giesecke (xxxx–1880). Giesecke was a German ivory trader who in 1880 was killed by an African at Tabora, Tanganyika in a dispute over money. The Germans hanged an Arab (purportedly the wrong man), causing Siki, the chief of the Wanyamwezi, to revolt and plunder the German stores in the town. Two years later Emin Pasha retook Tabora for Germany at the head of 130 men.

Gifford, James. A South African ivory hunter who chased elephant with Big Phillips and William Finaughty in the 1860s, Gifford (also spelled Giffard) was one of the very earliest "professional" hunters, guiding visiting English sportsmen to the Zambezi as early as 1863. All of the South African elephant hunters preferred to hunt on horseback, and many of them, Gifford included, gave up hunting on a large scale around 1870, when the elephant had been shot out of the non-tsetse-fly areas. The horses couldn't survive in the tsetse belt, so the men gave up their profession rather than hunt on foot.

Gifford, Maurice. Gifford was an American adventurer who worked for Cecil Rhodes. In 1890 he was in Palapye as a district manager for the Bechuanaland Exploration Company, an offshoot of the British South Africa Company. He assisted H. A. Bryden with hunting arrangements during the writer's trip there, which is the subject of *Guns and Camera in Southern Africa.* Gifford had previously spent eleven years on America's western frontier and was a veteran of Reil's Rebellion in Canada. He served as a cavalry scout in the 1893 Matabele War and was considered one of the most effective rangers in the British army.

Gifford was in Rhodesia when the Matabele Rebellion erupted in 1896. He promptly pitched in to help organize the town's defenses, and when the Bulawayo Field Force was formed from the combination of the Rhodesian Horse Volunteers and local recruits, Lieutenant Colonel Gifford was named as the second-in-command under Col. Jack Spreckley. Gifford was badly wounded during a skirmish on 7 April 1896, and his right arm had to be amputated at the shoulder in order to save his life. He returned to England in 1900 on the same ship that carried Frederick Burnham, Winston Churchill, Abe Bailey, and Sir Henry Colvile back from the Boer War.

Last photograph of Col. Maurice Gifford, an American adventurer in British service.

Gilkison, Thomas Train. Gilkison was a British administrative officer in Kenya (1890–1911) and the provincial commissioner of Kikuyu province (1907–1910). He had a weakness for spirits.

While he was the district officer at Fort Smith in 1895, one of his responsibilities was to forward supplies to more remote outposts. In November of that year he sent a large safari off to the station at Eldama Ravine carrying food, ammunition, and mail. Contrary to the usual practice, the caravan was led not by a European (apparently no one was available) but by a young Swahili headman who showed great promise despite his inexperience. The safari was made up of one hundred Swahili askaris and about a thousand Kikuyu porters. They dutifully carried the supplies to Eldama Ravine and camped at a place called Ewaso Kedong on their way back.

There had already been some tension between the safari and the local Masai over the traders' attempts to seduce some Masai girls. Accounts of what happened are confused, but what follows is the generally accepted version. As the caravan was preparing to move on, the Swahili headman leading it ordered his askaris to kidnap the aforementioned girls; in the attempt, one of the askaris shot and killed a Masai cow. The Masai went berserk over this assault on their women and cattle, and when it was over at least 550 porters lay slaughtered, the rest streaming in terror back to Eldama Ravine.

The place of the massacre was known for decades afterward as the Plain of Skulls or the Plain of Skeletons. When Robert Preston of the Uganda Railway visited the scene a few years later he wondered why so many ostrich eggs were clustered about in one place. Closer examination showed the white spheres to be human skulls.

Gillett, Fred. An American from Philadelphia, Gillett was a friend of A. Donaldson Smith, who invited him to join his 1894 expedition through Somaliland. Gillett wanted the hunting opportunities while Smith looked forward to having some company. Gillett contributed to the expedition by bringing along a few additional men as well as twenty camels.

Gillett frequently left the main safari for a day or two to hunt elephant. In early 1895 he received word that his father had died and his presence was needed in America to settle the estate. Accordingly, on 25 January he set out for the coast and home.

Gillmore, Parker. Captain Gillmore was a British officer and a friend of Lieutenant Grandy, the man who led a futile expedition to rescue David Livingstone in 1873. Gillmore accompanied Grandy to South Africa in October 1875 but separated in Cape Town in order to go hunting in the Zambezi Valley. Gillmore spent most of the late 1870s on official business in Bechuanaland.

Gillmore went on an extended elephant hunt and gold-prospecting safari through coastal Mozambique in the 1880s, and spent several years hunting in South-West Africa. He was the author of *Through Gasa Land* and the *Scene of Portuguese Aggression* (1890). The July 1890 edition of *Scottish Geographical Magazine* carried a review that applauded Gillmore's hunting accomplishments but scathingly mocked his political pretensions: "His narrative of adventure and sport, which in places recalls the fictions of Rider Haggard, will appeal to those who are like-minded. It is interesting enough in itself, and therefore one cannot but regret that the author should have thought fit to introduce extraneous matters of a political character, on which he discourses with more confidence than intelligence. He tells us, on page 329, that 'without the assistance I afterward rendered the Bechuanas against the freebooting Boers, their country would not be British territory, nor the trade route from the Cape of Good Hope to the interior of tropical Africa open to our commerce.' Among the 'many thousands of my own countrymen' who are supposed to know this, we regret not to have been before included. Whatever Mr. Parker Gillmore's political services may have been, there is no doubt that he is a successful sportsman."

Glave, Edward J. Glave was one of the first English explorers to penetrate the Congo forests in the 1880s. He worked for the Congo Free State and is mentioned several times in Henry Stanley's *The Founding of the Congo Free State*.

Glave was once stalking a herd of buffalo in the Congo when a wounded bull charged him. He killed the beast with an expert shot at close range. Glave had given his pith helmet to a gunbearer to carry. The man, frightened out of his wits by the charge, climbed a tree and, with the helmet still in his hands, refused to come down. It took some time before Glave could get another man up the tree to fetch the helmet, and by that time it was nearly too late. In the opinion of the Victorians, who greatly feared the direct rays of the tropical sun, Glave's head had been exposed for too long. That exposure was blamed for a severe fever that struck him that night. For a while it seemed that he would die, and several burly porters had to physically restrain him in his delirium.

In the early 1890s Glave traveled to Nyasaland, working as a reporter for an American magazine, *The Century.* In the book *British Central Africa* (1897) Sir Harry Johnston described how Glave volunteered to fight in Johnston's 1893 antislavery campaign against the Yao chief Makanjira. Although a civilian, Glave fought as an officer, commanding Sikh and African troops. At the end of the campaign he put his journalist hat back on and went on a fact-finding tour up the Zambezi to the Congo River and finally down the Congo to the Atlantic Ocean. Since he had started from the mouth of the Zambezi River, this journey made him only the sixteenth European to cross Africa.

His articles in *The Century* magazine (1896–1897) alerted the international community that things were not right in King Leopold's model state. Glave was one of the first to report witnessing atrocities in the Belgian Congo. While waiting for a steamship to take him back to Europe, Glave had another attack of fever and died at the home of missionary Rev. Lawson Forfeitt's home at Old Underhill on the lower Congo. His untimely death is the main reason Glave is forgotten while other Congo reformers like Morel, Casement, and Morrison are still remembered today.

Glenday, Sir Vincent Goncalves (1891–1970). Vincent Glenday was assigned as assistant district commissioner at Fort Moyale in Kenya's Northern Frontier District in 1913. A powerful, stocky man, Glenday was eminently cut out for the job, which largely entailed curbing the activities of Abyssinian raiders and slavers. The raiders' pattern was to attack a Somali or Boran village at dawn, massacre everyone except the young girls, who would be sold as slaves, and escape back across the border with their captives and the defeated village's camels. Chasing them was hot and bloody work. In addition to his frequent antiraiding measures, Glenday carried out all the usual chores of a DC, such as holding trials for minor offenses and mediating disputes between tribes.

During World War I Britain withdrew most of her troops from the NFD. Glenday volunteered to stay behind and help the now-abandoned tribesmen to fend off the increasing raids. He carried out this duty with great credit to himself and helped alleviate the feeling among the Somalis and Borans that the English had left them in the lurch. The four years following 1914 were ones of constant skirmishing for Glenday and a picked group of soldiers he had kept with him.

After the war Glenday continued his duties, becoming a virtual legend in the Northern Frontier District. He was considered the epitome of what a colonial officer should be and rose to become the province's officer-in-charge from 1934 to 1938. He received a knighthood and eventually rose to other posts such as British resident in Zanzibar 1946–1951 and a position in Saudi Arabia. He lived to an old age, retiring to the so-called "white highlands" near Nairobi. Glenday and his successor, Gerald Reece, along with George Adamson, were the men who earned the NFD its reputation as the home of tough, rugged, honest, and efficient colonial officers.

Glynn, Henry. This pioneer in the Transvaal area hunted largely between the Sabi and Olifants Rivers and in Portuguese East Africa. He was considered one of the greatest hunters of that time and place, and would make long annual trips seeking ivory and hides. In 1880 he brought a British sportsman, Col. G. E. Pennefeather, along with him into the Transvaal. Glynn died in the early 1890s of fever while returning from a poaching trip into PEA. He had two sons, Henry and Arthur, who followed in his footsteps, hunting buffalo for the Beira railroad crews in 1894 and then in the lowveld for some years after. Henry Jr. was known to prefer a .303 and was the author of *Game and Gold.*

Goddard. Letcher reported that a hunter named Goddard, with about one hundred elephant to his credit, was killed by his quarry in about 1908 in North-East Rhodesia.

Goering, Heinrich Ernst (1838–1913). Dr. Heinrich Ernst Goering was a politically connected young man who fought for Prussia in the 1866 Austrian War and the Franco-Prussian War of 1870–1871. Catching the eye of Otto von Bismarck, Goering was assigned as imperial governor *(Kaiserlicher Kommissar)* of the newly established German colony of South-West Africa in 1885.

Unlike most of his associates in the Imperial German colonial service, Dr. Goering did not carry out his duties with an iron hand. Indeed, his administration of the German colony in South-West Africa was marked by comparative peace and prosperity. In a culture dominated by bloodthirsty men like Karl Peters and Lothar von Trotha, Goering stands out as perhaps the most moderate and reasonable of Germany's colonial civil servants. After leaving South-West Africa, Goering served as consul general in Haiti until his retirement from government service in 1896.

Years later, Ernst's son became an ace fighter pilot and a high-ranking politician. Unfortunately for the family name and for the world at large, Hermann Goering retained none of his father's penchant for moderation.

Goetzen, Adolf Graf von (1866–1910). Count von Goetzen led an 1894 expedition to Rwanda, where he climbed several mountains and explored the Lake Kivu region. He left Dar es Salaam in October 1893 and arrived at the mouth of the Congo in early 1895. During the course of this safari the count became one of the first Europeans to traverse Africa from east to west. At the outset of the expedition von Goetzen had bought some cattle for provision purposes from the Masai and was very fortunate in avoiding the tsetse—the last cow was eaten just as they reached the Congo. They faced some hardship at that time, but a Lieutenant Simon, a Congo Free State officer based at Kirundu station, had heard of their plight from local people and led a supply column out to meet them.

As governor of German East Africa (1901–1906), he put down the 1905 Maji-Maji revolt with typical Imperial German ferocity. An estimated 250,000 natives died, most by a method devised by von Goetzen called the "famine strategy." While offering a pardon, except to the rebel leadership, he had almost all the food crops in the country either confiscated or burned. Thus, the technically pardoned rebel rank and file could consider themselves forgiven as they starved to death.

Von Goetzen was more moderate when it came to wildlife matters—in fact, the officials of German East Africa were among the first colonists to show an awareness of conservation. Von Goetzen and von Wissmann were responsible for the first effective game laws and regulations in the region.

Goldfinch, G. H. A big man, Goldfinch was a Kenya hunter and, from 1907–1923, an assistant game ranger. One of the first Kenyans to try lion hunting on horseback, he was also one of the first to demonstrate its dangers—he was badly bitten on the thigh and limped for the rest of his life. His companion, Lucas, was killed. Goldfinch got the lion, though.

Goldie, Sir George Dashwood Taubman (1846–1925). From a prestigious Scottish and Manx family (his father was a lieutenant colonel in the Scots Guards), George Goldie-Taubman (he dropped the suffix in 1887) obtained a commission in the Royal Engineers in 1865 but resigned just two years later. Between 1867 and 1870 he toured Europe, dedicating himself to the pursuit of pleasure and cavorting in the company of a variety of women, in particular an Arab mistress.

The Prussian invasion of France in 1870 found Goldie trapped in Paris, besieged with Mathilda Elliot, a family employee. By the time the siege was lifted, Mathilda was pregnant and the two were returning to Britain to get married. He then roamed around North Africa for a number of years, visiting West Africa in 1877 with his brother. The two men planned to traverse Africa from the Niger to the Nile, but the idea was abandoned when Goldie's brother took sick.

Goldie saw that the Niger delta was ripe for development—only a few independent, poorly managed trading stations were scattered through the area. His family bought control of a West African trading company and sent Goldie to manage it—this was a common Victorian cure for free-spirited and wayward sons. Over the next two years he gained control of most of the competition, forming them into the United African Company in 1879. He applied for a royal charter in 1881, but because of accounting concerns was forced to found a new organization called the National African Company. The delay temporarily cost Goldie his charter, for two French stations had begun operating in the area and the European claim to the district was hence in dispute.

In 1886 the British government finally granted the charter, which was seen as the only way to keep the French and, increasingly, the Germans out of the area. Lord Aberdare became the first governor of the Royal Niger Company (as it was now called), and he was succeeded by Goldie in 1895. The area under company control gradually began to be called Nigeria, as distinct from the British Protectorate of Niger. Goldie pioneered the technique of "indirect rule" (later associated with Lugard), whereby existing African institutions were retained to form the first tier of government. This system, plus Goldie's efficient administrative technique, enabled the colony to be run without being a drain on the British treasury.

As did Rhodes in southern Africa, Goldie in Nigeria sometimes resorted to force to achieve his ends. In 1897 he led an army of eight hundred men against the emir of Nupe. He won a crushing victory against fifteen thousand African cavalry at Bida and deposed the emir. Goldie then suppressed a similar independence movement at Ilorin, west of the Niger, in a lightning two-day campaign.

Goldie was now at the height of his fame and power, but his glory was to be short-lived. On 1 January 1900, the British government officially took over control of Nigeria from the chartered company. Goldie was presented with a specially commissioned portrait of himself as "Founder of Nigeria," and the country became a Crown Colony.

Goldie doesn't seem to have minded much. He was nowhere near as addicted to the trappings of power as was Rhodes, and in fact he declined an opportunity to rename Nigeria "Goldesia." Goldie went on an Asian tour, visiting China in 1900–1901, and then served on a Royal Commission reviewing the British army's performance in the Boer War. He visited Rhodesia in 1903–1904 to report on the possibility of government control of that country (Rhodesia remained under the chartered company BSAC (see glossary) until the 1920s).

A slight, fair man with startling blue eyes, Goldie was elected president of the Royal Geographical Society in 1905. He spent the rest of his life involved in local politics, serving on the London County Council and on the finance committee. After World War I his declining health forced him to move to the Mediterranean. Goldie died in London on 25 August 1925.

Gongo Lutete (1860–1892). Gongo Lutete was a Manyema African who provided decisive assistance to the Belgian military when they were driving the Arab slavers from the Congo in the early 1890s. A former slave, he had risen to become a powerful warlord in the Lomami River region. When the Arab war broke out in 1892 after the murder of Hodister and Michiels, Gongo Lutete and his ten thousand warriors sided with Dhanis and the Belgians in defending the Free State. Many felt that his intervention was decisive in determining the outcome.

Gongo Lutete soon fell victim to European ingratitude, however. A Free State officer named Lieutenant Duchesne, for reasons of his own, brought trumped-up charges of conspiracy and treason against him. Gongo Lutete was sentenced to be shot and unsuccessfully tried to hang himself. He was cut down alive from the rope and dragged before the firing squad. Harry Johnston felt that his judicial murder was one of the most reprehensible acts in the European scramble for Africa.

Gordon, Charles George "Chinese" (1833–1885). Charles Gordon was an exemplary figure in the world of Victorian adventure. His first action was in the Crimean War in 1854–1856. He fought in China from 1860–1864, from 1863 commanding a Chinese force called the "Ever Victorious Army" against the Taiping rebels. He was the Egyptian governor of Equatorial Central Africa in 1874–1876, and then governor of the Sudan, Darfur, the Equatorial province, and the Red Sea. In this post he led a vigorous campaign against slavery.

After more service in China, Russia, Mauritius, and the Cape Colony, Gordon was sent by the British government to the Sudan in 1884 to oversee the withdrawal of Egyptian troops in the face of the Mahdi rebellion. Contrary to orders, he tried to hold out in Khartoum, sending increasingly desperate messages back to England for troops to break the siege. It almost worked: The British relief force reached Khartoum just hours after Gordon's death in January 1885. The failure to rescue Gordon provoked a major political crisis and goaded future British politicians into reluctantly taking military action whenever similar cases arose.

Gordon, R. W. Known as "Little" due to his short stature, Gordon, an administrative officer in Nyasaland in 1914, had the bad luck to be touring Germany at the outbreak of war and spent

General Charles "Chinese" Gordon.

the next four years in an internment camp. Upon his release he became the officer in charge of translating captured German records in Tanganyika, and later a district commissioner. He was an avid student of insect life and had a deceptively mild appearance, yet David Blunt considered him one of the better elephant hunters of his day. ROWLAND WARD 1928: LION.

Gosling, G. B. (xxxx–1905). This British officer, zoologist, and big-game hunter accompanied Capt. Boyd Alexander on his 1904–1906 expedition to northern Nigeria and Lake Chad. The expedition was ill-starred: Captain Alexander's brother Claud died of fever in November 1904, and Gosling expired from blackwater fever some months later at Niangara on the Welle River. ROWLAND WARD 1928: GIRAFFE.

Goss, Charlie (xxxx–1963). Charlie Goss was an almost legendary character who hunted the remote areas of Kenya, Tanganyika, the Ituri Forest, the Sudan, the Belgian Congo, Ubangi-Shari, and Rwanda for forty years. A friend of J. A. Hunter, Goss had a professional license in Kenya from 1926–1940. With over a thousand elephant to his credit, he preferred a .600 Jeffery double rifle. He once fired a single shot with this rifle through two adult buffalo bulls.

At this distance in time it is impossible to know Charlie Goss, but one gets the clear impression that he was quite a character. He had a William Tell act that he would perform in bars for drinks. This ended when he shot the ear off his accomplice.

Gowers, Sir William (1875–1954). Gowers was the governor of Uganda from 1925 to 1932. In addition to hunting elephant, he fancied himself a student of the great pachyderms. Among his theories were that the rumbles associated with elephant were not stomach gases or a means of communication but rather snoring. His contribution to the "elephant graveyard" debate was to suggest that many older elephant drowned swimming big rivers like the Nile, and that's why elephant skeletons were rarely found.

Graetz, Paul (1875–1954). A lieutenant in the Imperial German Army, Graetz attempted a transcontinental safari with French cinematographer Octave Frere in 1909. The plan was to use a motorcar to travel from Dar es Salaam to the Zambezi River, then up to the Congo and down to German South-West Africa. The men planned to make a feature film documenting the epic journey.

They didn't get far. While following up a wounded buffalo, Frere was killed and Graetz was gored in the face, leaving him horribly disfigured for life. Graetz, a well-known public critic of the missionary movement, was nursed back to health by two friendly missionaries (Malcolm and Marie) at Serenje.

Grafton, Eddie. A professional hunter employed by the Safariland firm in the 1920s, Grafton was hunting buffalo with his friend Sheila Herne one day near Lake Naivasha. He was killed following up a wounded buffalo after three slugs from his .470 failed to stop the animal's charge. Grafton was gored through the face. Herne's brother-in-law, John Douglas, later killed the buffalo.

Grandy (xxxx–1877). Lieutenant Grandy led one of two expeditions sent by the British to relieve Livingstone in 1873 (the other was under Verney Cameron). Grandy started from the west coast. Unfortunately, he was stopped at Tungwa (apparently they were a tough people to pass—Comber and Grenfell were stopped there in 1878, and Comber was shot there in 1880) and forced to turn back.

Grant, Hugh (xxxx–1946). An administrative officer in Kenya, 1930–1946. As a young man in World War I Hugh Grant won the Military Cross, and for years afterward he displayed a native knife with a silver stud on the handle representing the life of an enemy officer killed in hand-to-hand combat, and several brass studs for common soldiers. In the 1920s Grant was a partner in a goat-selling business with George Adamson and Roger Courtney. Later he was widely known for selling his guns and restricting his hunting to what he could kill with the bow and arrow. When war broke out again in 1939 he organized and led an irregular partisan band against the Italians in Somaliland. George Adamson was one of his irregulars.

After the war, Grant was the district commissioner at Narok, in the Masai Reserve about seventy-five miles west of Nairobi. He had a reputation as being somewhat high-handed. One of his duties as DC was to act as magistrate. In one relatively minor case in 1946, Major Grant ruled against a Masai warrior and fined him a number of head of cattle. The warrior begged the district commissioner not to take a particular cow, offering to substitute as many as ten other cattle. Various versions of the incident describe the beast as either a white cow or a black bull. The Masai apparently looked on the cow as a pet and had hand-reared the animal as a calf. Grant was obstinate and had the special cow confiscated. The infuriated Masai confronted Grant and stabbed him to death with his spear.

The warrior was tried for murder in Nairobi. He disdained any plea for mitigation and refused to claim that he had acted in anger. It was proven, though, that he had greased his spear before stabbing Grant, a premeditated act that the Masai only did when intending to spear a human enemy. The young warrior was convicted and hanged.

Grant's son, who apparently held no grudge against the Africans for his father's death, was a Kenya police officer during the Mau Mau insurgency. He was stationed at Manyami Detention Camp inside Tsavo National Park, where, because of his fluency in local languages, he was responsible for interrogating incoming prisoners and separating the leaders from the followers.

Grant, James Augustus (1827–1892). Born in Scotland, like a surprisingly large number of African explorers, Grant was the son of a minister. He received a well-rounded education at Aberdeen schools and at Marischal College, studying chemistry, natural history, mathematics, and botany. In 1846 he was commissioned as a lieutenant in the 8th Bengal Infantry, part of the so-called "Company" army that garrisoned India until after the mutiny of 1857.

Grant spent twelve years in India and fought at the Battle of Gujarat and both sieges of Multan. In late 1858 he fell sick with fever and was invalided back to England. There he learned that an old friend of his, John Hanning Speke, had just returned from Africa and was preparing for a second expedition to try to determine the source of the Nile. Grant and Speke had first met in India in 1847 and had often gone hunting together.

Speke was delighted that his old friend wanted to go to Africa with him, and signed Grant on as his second-in-command. Grant proved to be the perfect subordinate: steady, uncomplaining, loyal, and efficient. The team arrived in East Africa in early 1861. Speke went ahead with a quick-moving spearhead while Grant followed with the bulk of the expedition's supplies. Reuniting on 26 September 1861 in the then unknown area between Lakes Tanganyika and Victoria, the two friends then moved north and reached Karagwe near the equator in November.

Grant fell terribly ill at this time and the expedition rested until January; Speke then left him at Karagwe to recuperate while he took most of the expedition north to Uganda. This has been judged rather heartless of Speke as he could easily have arranged to have his junior officer carried in a litter, but Speke was possessed with an almost pathological desire for "priority," to be the first to discover new places. He had similarly run off on Richard Burton on his first expedition and was to do the same thing to Grant again in the future.

Grant lingered at Karagwe until January, unable to walk more than a few feet without fainting. He finally got frustrated with just waiting around and set off to follow Speke in a litter in April. By that point, Speke had arrived in Uganda and was parlaying with Mutesa, the Kabaka or king of that country, and Grant caught up at the end of May. The two British officers became a familiar sight at Mutesa's court, drinking palm wine and flirting with the local belles. Both Grant and Speke were smitten by the charms of some of the village women and a persistent rumor has it that Speke fathered a child during this time.

In July 1862 Speke and Grant finally left the court and moved on to look for the Nile. On 19 July Speke made a decision that must have broken Grant's heart. Native guides reported that the Nile was but two or three days' march to the east; Speke ordered Grant to continue north with the safari while he and a few picked men went off to find the river. Grant quietly followed orders, and, thus, it was left

James Augustus Grant.

to Speke to be the first Westerner to see the Nile near its source, a feat he accomplished on 21 July 1862.

The rest of the expedition was anticlimactic. Speke and Grant slowly moved north and finally met Samuel Baker near Gondokoro. By March of 1863, they were in Khartoum and on their way to Alexandria. Upon his return to England in July 1863, Grant continued to play the role of the dutiful subordinate. Grant had kept valuable scientific journals during the expedition and dutifully allowed Speke to use his data for his book *Journal of the Discovery of the Source of the Nile.* Grant had not intended to write his own account of the expedition, but the success of Speke's book and the public encouragement that Grant received caused him to change his mind. The result was *A Walk across Africa* (1864), and its sparse prose and clear sense of narrative makes it one of the better-written books produced by the Victorian explorers.

Grant later went with Lord Napier on the Abyssinian Expedition in 1868, serving as an intelligence officer. He retired from the army later that year with the rank of lieutenant colonel. He enjoyed his remaining years in quiet comfort at his home in Nairn, Scotland, where he died on 11 February 1892.

A steady, reliable sort, James Grant was well thought of and highly regarded by virtually all of his contemporaries. He got along well with the difficult Speke, and somehow managed to avoid becoming tainted with the charges of pettiness and jealousy that so dogged his commander. Grant was able to keep his good reputation even during the contentious Speke-Burton and Speke-Petherick controversies, and was still so respected that even James Macqueen, a coauthor of Burton who wrote a libelous attack on Speke in 1864, suggested that Grant be chosen as the leader of a hypothetical large-scale expedition to civilize Uganda. Incidentally, the Grant gazelle was named after him.

Grant, T. A. The son of James Augustus Grant of the Speke-Grant expedition, T. A. Grant went with Joseph Thomson on an 1891 expedition from Nyasaland through the Barotse country to the kingdom of Msiri.

Grant, William G. S. British administrative officer, an employee of the Imperial British East Africa Company or IBEA. Grant was one of the first civilian officials in Uganda in the early 1890s, assisting Frederick Lugard in his successful attempt to establish British hegemony over the country.

From Lugard's Uganda diary it is apparent that Grant was an immensely helpful assistant. He was a tremendously efficient bookkeeper, maintaining meticulous records of ammunition, food supplies, and the like, and a tireless worker, even when sick with fever or what was diagnosed as a persistent liver problem. He was also handy with a rifle: When Lugard was sick in his tent in May 1891, Grant borrowed his .577 rifle and shot two badly needed antelopes for the pot, hitting them in thick brush at an estimated two hundred yards. When war broke out later that year with the Bunyoro in the north of Uganda, Lugard tried to keep Grant doing his invaluable administrative work, but the junior man begged to be allowed to join the fight. Lugard, who wrote that Grant was "very keen" to get into the battle, finally allowed him to lead a company of some fifty Sudanese soldiers into action.

Grant later served as the provincial commissioner at Jinja in the early 1900s. According to C. W. Hobley, a British official who collected cryptozoological stories, Grant once reported seeing a mysterious creature swimming in the Napoleon Gulf of Lake Victoria. From the sparse account given by Hobley, it can be surmised that the animal was big and swam with its head out of the water, but was otherwise too far away to see any detail. This is the same area and the approximate time where Alexander Johnston spotted a sea serpent. ROWLAND WARD 1928: GREATER KUDU.

Grauer, Rudolf (1870–1927). Grauer was sent to the northwestern section of German East Africa in 1908 to collect specimens for the Vienna Museum. During the next three years he shot and sent back to Europe at least eight and possibly as many as eleven gorillas, plus many other animals.

Gray, "Gaza." Captain Gray, known by the African name M'stulela, was born around 1850 in the Eastern province of Cape Colony. For many years he lived in the Transvaal as a labor recruiter, hiring there and in Portuguese East Africa for the mines. In the course of his travels he gathered an encyclopedic knowledge of the fauna, flora, and peoples of that region. Gray was considered by the local Africans as a sort of wizard or medicine man.

During the Boer War Gray received a commission in Steinacker's Horse. While still serving in that capacity in 1902 he was approached by the new warden of the Sabi Game Reserve, James Stevenson-Hamilton, who was seeking local knowledge. Stevenson-Hamilton was so impressed that he appointed Gray as an honorary ranger, in return for which Gray retained the right to graze his livestock in the Reserve. Gray was placed in charge of policing the entire section of the reserve east of the Selati railway and between the Sabi and Crocodile Rivers. He performed in this capacity until late 1903, when he accepted an offer from the Witwatersrand Native Labour Association to do his old job—recruit Portuguese East Africans for the mines. He was replaced at his post by Thomas Duke, and on the rolls by Cecil de Laporte.

Gray, Prentiss N. (1885–1935). Gray was a well-known American sportsman and the editor of the Boone and Crockett record book. He became president of New York's Schroder Banking Corporation in 1923 and quickly made enough money to devote much of the rest of his life to sport.

In 1929–1930 he was the leader of the Gray African Expedition, a museum-collecting safari that went to Kenya, Rhodesia, and Angola. Team members included professional hunter Philip Percival, ornithologist Wilfred Bowen, and Gray's wife, Laura. They collected antelope, more than five hundred fish, a huge variety of African birds, and two specimens of the very rare Angolan giant sable.

Gray was the author of *African Game Lands* (1929), an account of his experiences hunting on the Dark Continent. It has been reprinted several times, including a few very expensive deluxe editions. Gray was killed in a boating accident in the Everglades in 1935.

Green, Frederick Thomas (1829–1876). Fred Green (sometimes identified as Frederick Joseph Green, which is incorrect) was a very successful elephant hunter in the mid-nineteenth century. He was one of three Canadian brothers from Montreal, sons of a British military officer (apparently a general), who came to South Africa in the late 1840s. Frederick and at least one of his brothers, Henry, saw action in the so-called Kaffir Wars. By the 1850s Fred Green was elephant hunting in the area known as Ngamiland. In 1858–1860 he explored much of the Okavango region.

Green hunted in the Chobe River and Lake Ngami areas with the legendary "Far Interior" Sam Edwards and with the unfortunate Swedish scientist Dr. Wahlberg. He was there when Wahlberg was stomped to death by an elephant. A third man died of thirst on that same arduous safari. Green also teamed up with Charles John Andersson in several trading ventures, and is known to have provided the Swedish naturalist with detailed maps and notes of the interior. He spent twenty-five years in the bush, with the exception of one brief 1864 trip to Cape Town, during which he met his wife.

Green's elephant-hunting technique was noteworthy. In a time and place where virtually all elephant hunting was done on horseback and thus restricted to areas where the tsetse fly did not exist, Green preferred to hunt the huge pachyderms on foot. This was considered suicidal with the unreliable rifles of that period, but Green suffered no known major accidents and was phenomenally successful—he is thought by some to have killed more elephant than any other South African hunter of that period. He had success with lion as well and killed one notorious man-eater that had taken the lives of more than one hundred Africans.

Green was also accomplished as an explorer. He claimed to have been the first white man to see Victoria Falls, before David Livingstone, and is known to have been the first European to visit many remote areas, particularly along the Kunene River. Some of his discoveries were more ephemeral. He wrote about a shining lake called Onondava—apparently it dried up or otherwise disappeared before anyone else saw it. He spent years searching for a mysterious snow-peaked mountain somewhere in South-West Africa that still hasn't been found. Green seems to have been a somewhat romantic and generous soul, given to extravagance and to blowing his ivory profits during uncontrolled spending sprees.

He accompanied a missionary, the Rev. Hugo Hahn, into Ovamboland in the 1850s. Hahn was seeking to establish the first mission in the district. Their efforts were not well received. They were attacked by warriors under the command of the hostile chief Mandume, and only Green's rifle allowed the men to escape, after a running two-hour fight.

Green's daughter, Mary E. Stroud, born on 4 November 1865 and nicknamed Chikongo after her African chief godfather, was still alive in the late 1940s and provided author Lawrence Green with much information on her father's career. Mrs. Stroud recalled that her father kept a journal and wrote an autobiography. Sadly, the journal has disappeared and the memoir was lost in an 1870s wagon fire. His only known writings are a few adventure stories that were published in Cape Town magazines. Fred Green died of fever and an abscessed liver while on the trail in 1876, his twenty-seven-year-old wife by his side.

Gregory, John Walter (1864–1932). He was a British explorer and geologist who visited East Africa in 1892–1893 and wrote *The Great Rift Valley* (1896), which disparaged British East Africa as a place of little mineral wealth and poor agricultural prospects. While traveling in the Naivasha district after the rinderpest epidemic, he didn't see a single buffalo in an area that a few years before had boasted herds containing many thousands.

Gregory, who also made extensive explorations of Tibet, South America, Australia, New Zealand, Russia, South Africa, and the Arctic Circle, visited West Africa in 1912 and returned to East Africa seven years later. He wrote prolifically, publishing twenty books and more than three hundred papers and articles, and was an expert on paleontology and geologic formations. He was drowned in the rapids of the Urubamba River in Peru on 2 June 1932.

Grenfell, George (1849–1906). A British missionary (Baptist Missionary Society) and explorer stationed in the Congo, Grenfell was also honorary British pro-consul for the Upper Congo from 1897 to 1906, during which his principal residence was at the mission station of Bolobo. He first came to Africa in 1876 accompanied by his first wife, who died in childbirth a year later. Aside from five return trips to England (each a year or so in duration), Grenfell spent the rest of his life working for the missions and exploring in the Congo and the Cameroons. His duties included administrative work, preaching, and traveling through the bush looking for prospective sites for new missions. Grenfell was the first European to see many parts of the Congo basin. He married a second time in 1879.

Grenfell was a meticulous naturalist and cartographer and in 1886 was awarded the Gold Medal of the Royal Geographical Society. A man who spent much of his life in the bush and always had to provide for hungry staff, Grenfell was an experienced hunter. Johnston (1908) quoted a letter from Grenfell dated 12 August 1905, in which the missionary reports having shot a gorilla by the Motima River: "It was not a very tall one, only four feet high, but it was very thickly built and immensely strong." Grenfell shot the ape out of a tree at a hundred fifty feet. His men ate it.

Grenfell was one of the most prolific and successful of the Congo explorers—his list of accomplishments is astonishing. He was the first European to ascend the Ubangi, and is one of those few about whom it can be said he literally rewrote the map of Africa. It is inexplicable that he is almost forgotten today.

Col. George Grey shortly before his death.

Grey, Charles (xxxx–1928). The youngest brother of George Grey and the British statesman Sir Edward Grey, Charles Grey was wounded at Kisii at the start of the 1914 war and lost his left arm. He was an intelligence officer, working with Jim Sutherland, at the time. Rigby made a special rifle so Grey could hunt with just his right arm. Grey hunted along the shores of Lake Tanganyika with Marcus Daly for several months in early 1927.

He had a listing in the 1928 *Rowland Ward's Records of Big Game* for a 48-inch buffalo he shot in Rhodesia. In 1928 Grey was killed by another buffalo.

Grey, George (xxxx–1911). Grey was a highly respected colonial officer and hunter. During the Matabele Rebellion of 1896, he distinguished himself by raising and commanding a small company of irregular horse soldiers made up of about twenty-five experienced woodsmen called Grey's Scouts. After a noteworthy administrative career in Rhodesia, Grey went to Kenya, where he shot the first mature bull bongo ever taken by a European. Grey got the elusive beast his very first day of hunting it, taking it down at twenty-five yards with a shoulder shot after tracking it for several hours through dense cover.

Colonel Grey was hunting with Sir Alfred Pease, Howard Pease (Alfred's cousin), Clifford Hill, and Philip Percival one day in early 1911, chasing lion on horseback. Hill was new to this style of hunting and got too close to a pair of males. One of them charged, and Grey leaped from the saddle (you can't shoot effectively from a nervous horse) and got off two shots with his magazine rifle before the lion knocked him to the ground. Pease and Hill killed the lion (the other lion escaped), but Grey was badly injured. He managed to say, "I alone am to blame for what has happened" before losing consciousness. Grey was rushed to a hospital in Nairobi, but sepsis set in and he died five days later, on 3 February 1911. He was the brother of Charles Grey and Sir Edward Grey (1862–1933), head of the Foreign Office from 1905–1916.

Grimes (xxxx–1906). Grimes was a British farmer in Rhodesia who caught sleeping sickness in 1906. He returned to England for an experimental treatment in which the patient was placed in a refrigerator for extended periods of time. The hope was that the cold would kill the virus. It worked, sort of—the virus presumably died when Grimes did.

Grixoni, Matteo (1859–1940). Captain Grixoni was an Italian officer who went along as second-in-command of Vittorio Bottego's 1892 Jubaland expedition. Unable to cope with the difficult conditions, Grixoni deserted in February 1893, after threatening to shoot Captain Bottego.

Grogan, Ewart Scott (1873–1966). Born in London, Ewart Grogan first visited Africa in 1895–1897 and came to stay in 1903. He served in the 1896 Matabele Rebellion as a captain of the 4th Royal Fusiliers, receiving a medal. At war's end Grogan went to New Zealand to recuperate from malaria. Sick with fever and tired of army rations, Grogan actually shook his fist at Africa as his steamer left Beira, vowing never to return again. Little did he know that not only would he come back in just a bit more than a year, he also was destined to become one of the outstanding men of the colonial era.

Grogan returned to South Africa in February 1898, starting out with his friend Arthur Sharp on an expedition to the Ruwenzori Mountains and Tanganyika. Once they reached their goal, they had to decide whether to go east to the coast or continue up the Nile River, thus becoming the first Europeans to walk from the "Cape to Cairo." This was a concept much ballyhooed by staunch British Imperialists like Harry Johnston, who cherished the thought both for its strategic value and as a vivid symbol of Victorian supremacy.

One morning early in the trip the two men, each armed with a .303 magazine rifle, decided to go fishing in a croc-infested river. They walked too close to a dense thicket wherein lay an irritable bull buffalo, which charged. Having seen these beasts in action before, Grogan chose the crocs instead and dove into the river. Having had no experience with African big game, Sharp began calmly firing round after round of .303 softnose bullets at the charging animal. By all rights he should have been killed, but one of his bullets miraculously shattered the bull's jaw and another broke its leg. Finally able to finish the buffalo off, Sharp expressed his admiration at the animal's staying power and admitted that next time he too would take to his heels rather than fight it out.

The men made their momentous decision, and the first stage of their epic journey to the Zambezi River was largely routine and uneventful. They did a great deal of hunting, generally plains game, and shot seventeen lion during this part of the trip. They also captured five lion cubs, three of which were successfully shipped back to a London zoo.

Grogan and Sharp left the Zambezi in October 1898, moving up the Shire River into British Central Africa. After taking a steamer up to the northern end of Lake Nyasa, they split up for a short time, Grogan exploring the Chiperoni Hills and Sharp moving on to Tanganyika to make some logistical arrangements. Sharp went to Ujiji, and Grogan, after recruiting some porters, followed him on the famous Stevenson Road.

Grogan found his friend in a hut in the town of Mtowa, delirious and bedridden with fever. Sharp had collapsed in Ujiji and been brought to Mtowa to be cared for by a Dr. Castellote, the medical officer for an expedition led by Mohun, the American consul in the Congo, who was surveying the region for likely telegraph routes. Sharp felt better after a couple of days, and the team moved to Ujiji, where they were put up by a hospitable German commandant, Hauptmann Bethe. Now the main part of the safari was to begin.

After hiring about a hundred thirty porters of the Manyema tribe, Grogan and Sharp left Ujiji and headed up the coast of Lake Tanganyika by land. Sharp, who seems to have had more than his share of bad luck, suffered from a mild case of sunstroke while Grogan's old malarial fever returned. Once again the German colonial officers helped out. The officer commanding the garrison at Usambara, Lieutenant von Gravert, gave them cattle and arranged to have Grogan carried in a machila (a hammock slung on a pole) to the Kivu highlands district (Victorian artists generally didn't picture their stalwart African explorers being carried around the Dark Continent in a hammock). Grogan repaid the German kindness by collecting a form of military intelligence, alerting the world in 1900 that the Germans had taken advantage of the ongoing slaver wars in the Congo Free State by inching their border stations some forty miles westward into Belgian territory.

At Kivu Grogan noted the two vastly different tribes that together formed the Rwandans (or, as he called them, the Waruanda)—the tall, elegant Watusi and the Wahutu, who formed the working class. He also explored the great Ruwenzori volcanoes and observed the local wildlife. Grogan went hunting elephant, the first herd he and Sharp had seen on their adventure. The Rwandan elephant were a wary, elusive breed, and it took a week of hard stalking through incredibly tangled forests before Grogan literally stumbled into a bull and shot at it (with a double-barreled four-bore) at a range of two yards. Nonetheless he seems to have missed—one of the most spectacular examples of bad marksmanship in all of history. At most the animal was lightly wounded, for by the time Grogan had picked himself up off the ground from the impact of the rifle's bone-breaking recoil, the bull had run off at high speed and showed no signs of stopping (Grogan wrote a year later, "I believe he is still running").

One would think that the local elephant would have by now dismissed Grogan as laughably harmless. But the very next day he was back at it again, and he had wounded another bull at least three times when the angry elephant charged him and knocked him some ten feet into a thorn tree. While Grogan lay stunned in his tree, the elephant went berserk, wildly throwing around other trees and logs in a frenetic display that gave Grogan nightmares for years. Finally the injured beast ran off. Bruised, bloodied, hungry, and cold, Grogan followed the animal for nearly a day but never caught up to it. Faced with the mounting evidence that he just wasn't cut out for elephant hunting, he temporarily decided to call it quits. His companion, Sharp, who himself had lost nearly thirty pounds stalking the elephant for some weeks but had never even seen one, heartily agreed.

The two Englishmen were dissuaded from exploring to the west of Rwanda by an aggressive people called the Baleka, reputed to be cannibals. Instead they headed north, along the eastern shore of Lake Albert Edward. Here they found only a few scattered Africans living in primitive huts and subsisting largely on fish, sweet potatoes, and the occasional hippo that was unfortunate enough to fall into a game pit. Entering what is now Uganda, both men were incapacitated by another virulent attack of fever and rested for a spell at what was then called Fort Gerry. The station was lightheartedly named by Harry Johnston after Sir Gerald Portal, the British officer who had died after an 1894 expedition to Uganda. The name was soon after changed to Fort Portal, "Fort Gerry" being considered too frivolous. Sharp, having had enough adventure for one trip, decided to return home and left for the east coast of Africa to catch a steamer. Grogan opted to continue on.

Apparently the optimistic type, Grogan bought an elephant license for £25 at Fort Portal and went hunting once again. With thirty porters he struck out for Wadelai on the west bank of the Nile, taking his time and shooting as he went. It's hard to say whether he was smarter than he had been, or Sharp had been a jinx, or the Wadelai elephant were dumber than the Rwandan ones, but Grogan was markedly more successful this time around. To the west of the town of Mboga, on the Semliki River, he shot two one-tusked elephant on the same day, one single tusk weighing 98 pounds and the other 86 pounds. These were the best tusks of the entire safari. His description of the tusks in a 1900 paper for the American Smithsonian Institution makes it clear that these animals were members of what's now called the forest elephant subspecies—their long, straight, hard ivory hangs directly down from the head. The forest elephant generally has somewhat smaller tusks than the savanna elephant, so these animals were phenomenal indeed.

Grogan continued northward, shooting elephant as he went. Although the area was British territory, it had recently been plundered by askaris of the Congo Free State and the local people first treated him with suspicion. He convinced them he was English by showing them a photograph of Lugard, in whom they had great trust, and soon they followed him in huge crowds, eagerly scrambling over the elephant meat he inevitably provided for them.

At the British post at Wadelai Grogan went over to the Nile's east bank in a dugout canoe and then meandered through the bush to Fort Berkeley and Kero, riding for a time in a steel whale boat provided by the Belgians. He was nearing his goal of becoming the first known human to cross the continent from south to north.

Possibly the most dangerous moment of Grogan's great safari came toward the end of his journey when he was nearing Bohr on the eastern bank of the Nile north of Rejaf, accompanied by only thirteen porters. Grogan was accustomed to the curious Dinka warriors who came by the hundreds to investigate his camp on a daily basis, poking through his stuff and mocking him in a vaguely threatening but hitherto benign fashion. Early one morning, however, Grogan noticed that the hundred or so spearmen who had come to visit were crowding him and his men somewhat more closely than usual. Suddenly the Dinka spears flashed and cut down Grogan's headman, and two others had their skulls crushed by clubs. The ten surviving porters broke for the woods, among them a young boy who was carrying Grogan's revolver. Fortunately, the Englishman was holding his double-barreled rifle, armed with exploding "dum-dum" bullets, and he promptly shot and killed the Dinka chief and another leader. A nearby Dinka tried to spear him, but Grogan slipped in another round and cut the man down.

Afraid of the rifle, the other warriors ran off but stopped to regroup some three hundred yards away. They seemed to believe that was a safe range, so it is likely that their only previous experience with firearms was with short-range muzzleloaders. Grogan took careful aim at an enormous and energetic Dinka (Grogan estimated the man at six feet, six inches in height) who was trying to whip up his fellows into a charge, and toppled the warrior. After killing one more man at long range, Grogan held his fire—he had only a few cartridges left. His porters returned from the bushes, and Grogan and his men force-marched out of the territory, followed at a safe distance by the angry warriors. One porter straggled behind and was never seen again.

Once past the Dinka territory, Grogan and his remaining men had just one leg ahead of them. Under the hot African sun they struggled for ten days along the Zaraf River, a region of sun-baked mud infested with mosquitoes and crocodiles, living on dried hippo meat and pelican steak. The men were failing fast when, unexpectedly, they ran into a European safari. It was a Major Dunn, a member of Malcolm Peake's sudd-cutting expedition, who had gone up the Zaraf to do a bit of hunting. From there it was an easy, almost luxurious trip down the Nile via steamer to Egypt.

Grogan returned to New Zealand, where he married Gertrude Edith Watt. His book *From Cape to Cairo* (1900) and the accompanying lecture tour brought him a great deal of renown in sporting and exploration circles. During the Boer War Grogan joined the British army as a captain but was hospitalized with another bad case of malaria. In hospital he met a Kenyan who had plans for a paper mill, and so Grogan moved to Kenya and tried his hand at timber farming. He then spent several years traveling through Europe and the United States.

In 1907 Grogan was back in Kenya, serving as a justice of the peace. He was a stern man with a definite sense of British superiority—modern biographers have accused him of being anti-Asian and anti-Semitic. In February of 1907 he made an official inspection of the Nairobi jail and vigorously denounced the appalling conditions there. Little did he know that he was soon to experience that fetid squalor first-hand.

On the night of 13 March 1907 three drunken Kikuyu rickshaw drivers insulted two women passengers, a Miss MacDonald and a Mrs. Hunter. Unfortunately for the Kikuyus, Dorothy Hunter was Ewart Grogan's sister. Beside himself with fury, Grogan went looking for the drunkards the next morning. He sent a request for assistance in the matter to Russell Bowker and a friend of Bowker's named Capt. Thord Gray. They soon found Grogan, who had already caught and manacled the rickshaw drivers. The three Europeans, surrounded by an enthusiastic crowd, marched the shackled Kikuyus to the courthouse. Despite an attempt by magistrate E. R. Logan to stop the proceedings, Grogan, Bowker, and Gray each grabbed one of the rickshaw men and gave him twenty-five strokes with a *kiboko* (whip). Then the three men were taken to Nairobi hospital, where their wounds were washed and dressed. One of them apparently had been flogged almost to the point of death.

The affair caused an uproar in Britain, but the Kenya press was generally supportive of the three Englishmen. They were charged for some reason with conducting an unlawful

Ewart S. Grogan.

assembly—and since five people were needed to constitute an "assembly," two innocent reporters were charged as well (and later released). Grogan was sentenced to serve one month in jail and pay a 500-rupee fine; Bowker (arrested while on safari days later and brought back by an armed guard) and Gray had to serve two weeks and pay 250 rupees. They were immediately locked in the foul Nairobi jail.

Word of the jail conditions spread like wildfire through the community, and settlers began to pour into Nairobi, armed with hunting rifles and *kibokos*. The colony seemed on the brink of revolt. In short order Acting Commissioner Frederick Jackson ordered the sentences changed to house arrest. Thus the men served their sentences in rather easy confinement, the only real hardship being a prohibition on tobacco. Grogan even beat up a servant he felt treated him disrespectfully. The convictions were later overturned on appeal, due to irregularities in the conduct of the trial.

In 1909 Grogan went to the Lado Enclave to hunt elephant, taking advantage of the lack of civil control in the district, and remained there for three profitable years. He served in World War I, rising to the rank of colonel and receiving a DSO (see glossary). He worked in the Intelligence section under Richard Meinertzhagen.

Between the wars Grogan lived mainly in Nairobi. During World War II he was sent to the West Coast of the United States to serve as a liaison officer for British troops stationed there. Grogan and his wife (legend has it she was the girl who had inspired his Cape-to-Cairo walk by telling him she wanted him to prove himself; they were together more than fifty years) later owned a farm near Taveta on the Tanganyika border. He played a substantial role in Kenya politics for many years and lived to be considered one of the last surviving legends of the pioneer days. By the time of his death he owned more than 500,000 acres in Kenya.

One example of his business acumen will suffice. In 1906 Grogan and an Indian partner, Sharif Jaffer, purchased a ninety-nine-year lease on the so-called Gertrude Swamp for a few hundred pounds. The swamp consisted of one hundred twenty acres close to the center of Nairobi and was generally considered useless. Grogan hired a surveyor and drained much of the acreage, and bought his partner out in 1910 for £3,000. For many years he sublet small parts of the swamp to Indian stockmen to graze their cattle, and they soon built a veritable shantytown of tiny vegetable gardens and corrugated iron shacks. In 1929 the Nairobi Municipal Council approached Grogan to buy the swamp. When he demanded £60,000 with a straight face, the Council retaliated by assessing the property at the absurd price of £300,000 pounds for tax purposes. Grogan paid the taxes but silently vowed revenge. His turn came in the late 1930s when Nairobi property values skyrocketed. The council came back and offered him the £60,000 he had asked for; Grogan joyfully refused. He wound up selling the lease to a private party in 1948 for £180,000.

Grogan, Quentin (1883–1962). Ewart's brother Quentin hunted in the Lado Enclave in 1909–1912. In the 1920s he owned a farm near Molo where he indulged himself in his hobbies of botany and horticulture. In 1928 he sold the farm to Mansfield Markham, the husband of Beryl.

Guest, Winston "Wolfie." Winston and his brother Raymond, the sons of 1920s air minister and sportsman Freddie Guest, were frequent safari clients of Bror Blixen. Winston Guest was a world-class polo player and a gifted hunter. His sister Diana (born 1911) had a torrid affair with Bror Blixen in 1934.

In addition to skill, Winston possessed the quality that Napoleon Bonaparte ranked above all others—luck. On one occasion he traveled to Jaipur, India, in an attempt to bag his first tiger. He arrived at one in the afternoon and went with game warden Kesri Singh for a brief acclimatization hunt through the neighboring fields. Almost immediately the beaters spooked a tiger and by 3:30 Guest had got his trophy, an exceptionally fine ten-foot male.

Just a few days later, Singh and Guest were out shooting partridge when they received word of a horrific incident that had taken place just a couple of miles away. A villager was walking through a cornfield when he stumbled across a sleeping tiger. The animal awoke and killed the farmer. Then, its instincts aroused, it killed three other men one by one as they tried to remove the first body. Singh and Guest grabbed their heavy rifles and hurried to the scene. The game warden spotted the tiger lying underneath a bush, and Guest put a bullet through its neck, killing the cat instantly.

H

Haardt, Georges Marie (1889–1932). A racing driver and the managing director of the Citroën automobile company, Haardt led two African expeditions in the 1920s. Their long-range purposes were to prove that it was possible to cross the continent by automobile and to blaze a connecting route between the French colonies in West Africa and the Indian Ocean ports.

The first safari, called simply the Citroën Expedition, was a 1922–1923 affair intended to establish way stations between Algeria and Timbuktu. Two separate columns were sent out across the Sahara, one led by Haardt and the other by Andre Citroën. Haardt reached Timbuktu in January 1923, and plans were made immediately to run regular commercial and tourist caravans to that exotic city from Algeria and Morocco. Civil unrest in Morocco in January 1925 caused the scheme to be abandoned.

Planning for the second expedition lasted over a year. It was a much grander affair, utilizing eight specially made Caterpillar-tracked trucks to cover some twelve thousand miles, with a number of supply caravans being sent out to meet them along the way. The trucks were made of duralumin and carried (in addition to men and supplies) some three hundred liters of gasoline and sixty liters of water. Each truck pulled a small trailer in which were carried the men's beds, tents, and camping equipment.

The Citroën Central African Expedition left Colomb-Béchar on the Moroccan-Algerian border in late October 1924. The eight trucks were divided into two groups, one led by Haardt and the other by Audouin-Dubreuil. Other significant members of the expedition included photographers Leon Poirier and Georges Specht, medical officer and naturalist Bergonier, military and political officer Commandant Bettembourg, engineer Charles Brull, and anthropologist and artist Alexandre Iacovleff. There were some ten or so French driver/mechanics and a small number of African servants.

The scientific and educational results of the expedition were significant. Artist Iacovleff made more than a hundred paintings and sketches, while the photographers Poirier and Specht exposed some six thousand still photos and twenty seven thousand meters of movie film. The naturalist Bergonier collected over three hundred mammal specimens, eight hundred birds, and about fifteen thousand insects. Haardt collected many of the large mammals, quite a few of which found their way into the Rowland Ward record book.

Haardt was author of *The Black Journey* (1927). It's a difficult read, at least in the English translation. The book is written in the present tense, and the prose is rather overblown. Still, it gives a detailed account of the day-to-day operation of a typical expedition of the 1920s, and contains the obligatory big-game hunting and ethnological chapters that distinguish the genre. Both expeditions were also described in a series of *National Geographic* magazine articles, the first in 1926 and the second in 1931–1932. Rowland Ward 1928: Lelwel hartebeest, elephant (from the Dongou River, Congo), white rhino (Belgian Congo), Lake Chad buffalo.

Hadow, Patrick Francis (1855–1946). When it comes to great natural athletes of the past, people tend to think of the likes of Jim Thorpe, Babe Didrikson, Christy Mathewson, and Jesse Owens. These people are associated with skill, grace, and a natural physical aptitude that transcends mere training and experience. The artistry of Bobby Orr skating on the ice at Boston Garden will long outlast the legacy of his statistical accomplishments.

Several natural athletes became successful African hunters. We're not talking here about a sporting figure who went on an occasional safari but rather men who truly distinguished themselves both in traditional sports and in the hunting field, reaching top rank in both arenas. Jim Sutherland and John Burger, legendary stalkers of the elephant and buffalo, respectively, were outstanding amateur boxers, and Citroën's Georges-Marie Haardt was successful both at the Grand Prix and in Rowland Ward. There were others. One of the more interesting of these athlete-hunters was an obscure Englishman named Frank Hadow.

Born in Regent's Park on 24 January 1855, Patrick Francis Hadow in his early twenties took a job managing a Ceylonese coffee estate. The custom at that time was for colonial workers to get both "short leaves" and "long leaves." The "short leave" was the standard two- or three-week vacation, often used to go hunting, sailing, or indulge in some other recreational activity. Some men just rested and drank. The "long leave," on the other hand, was a six-month affair, granted every few years. The idea was to allow the colonist to return home to England and visit his loved ones in those days before the telephone and quick international travel.

Frank Hadow became eligible for his first long leave in 1878 and dutifully returned to England. Presumably he was a bit bored, and somebody introduced him to the sport of lawn tennis. He took to the game with a vengeance, practicing diligently and showing extraordinary natural ability. Tennis had just entered a period of surging popularity. The first Wimbledon Championship had taken place the year before, in 1877, and had been won by a man named Spencer Gore. Hadow entered the tournament and, incredibly, beat the experienced Gore to become the second-ever Wimbledon champion. He then dropped his racquet and, his long leave over, returned to the coffee estate in Ceylon.

Having tasted glory, Hadow was not content with the sedate life of a colonial planter. He began to take longer and longer trips away from the plantation, hunting throughout India. Eventually he quit the coffee business and devoted himself to full-time shooting.

Hadow traveled widely, hunting across the world but especially in Africa. His best days were after the turn of the century in 1900. The 1899 Rowland Ward doesn't mention his name, but the 1927 edition has numerous entries, including buffalo, eland, sable, and various other antelope. He hunted in Kenya, Rhodesia, and Uganda.

Like many great sporting figures, the memory of Hadow faded after his retirement. He lived until an advanced age, dying virtually forgotten at the age of ninety-one on 29 June 1946. ROWLAND WARD 1928: TSESSEBE (NO. 2, 17½ INCHES, BELGIAN CONGO), BUFFALO, UGANDA KOB, WHITE-EARED KOB, PUKU, RED-FRONTED GAZELLE, ELAND, BUFFALO, LICHTENSTEIN HARTEBEEST, SABLE, IMPALA, GERENUK.

Hagenbeck, Carl (1844–1913). He was a German animal dealer and zookeeper who revolutionized the zoo concept. From the 1870s on he had agents scouring the world for captive creatures. Hagenbeck operated on a huge scale—a single East African safari in 1911 brought back eight giraffe, thirty-four ostrich, eleven hippo, two rhino, and a large variety of antelopes and smaller mammals. Shipments like this one were continually streaming back to Hamburg.

Hagenbeck's interests did not stop at the animal kingdom. In 1884 he was exhibiting human "oddities" such as Pygmies, Eskimos, Laplanders, and Somalis. (He was not alone in this endeavor—the New York Zoological Park displayed a Pygmy named Ota Benga in 1906). By the 1890s Hagenbeck had won international acclaim as both a dealer and a trainer, providing lion, tiger, and elephant acts.

In 1900 Hagenbeck decided to apply his principles of animal training and treatment (considerably more humane than what was otherwise current then) to his own menagerie. He purchased a potato farm near Hamburg, Germany, and converted it into the world's first modern zoo. Bars and cages were replaced by hedges and moats, and every effort was made to avoid the "concrete prison" look so typical of early zoos. The new zoo was a great success, and eventually his ideas were copied by most of the animal-keeping world.

While his zoo concepts gave the captive animals much more freedom than did traditional zoos, it should not be forgotten that many thousands of animals died en route to Hagenbeck's collecting pens. At the time it was generally felt more important to have wild animals represented in zoos or even as stuffed skins in museums than as free-ranging specimens. Zoos and museum taxidermists would compete to get the last members of an endangered species rather then attempt to safeguard its status in the wild. One of the best illustrations of this attitude was a letter written by Fred Selous to the magazine *The Field* in 1892, in which he first lauds the fact that the British occupation of Mashonaland saved "the few white rhinoceroses still alive" and then offers to obtain a skin and skeleton of same for the British Museum.

Haggard, Henry Rider (1856–1925). H. Rider Haggard was born the eighth child in a family of ten in Norfolk County, England. Trained as a barrister, Haggard in his late teens traveled to South Africa, where he took a post as an unpaid deputy to Sir Henry Bulwer, lieutenant governor of Natal. There Haggard acquired early experience in African hunting and bush life. He put this knowledge to good use in 1885 with his third novel, *King Solomon's Mines.* This rousing adventure tale sold 650,000 copies in his lifetime and catapulted him into the front rank of popular novelists. In all he went on to write more than forty books, including the novels *She, Allan Quartermain, Cleopatra,* and *Montezuma's Daughter,* and the nonfiction work *Cetywayo and His White Neighbors* (1882). Haggard is notable as the first major British or American author to develop well-rounded and admirable African characters in his fiction. First editions of his more popular novels and his nonfiction books are highly sought by collectors.

Hahn, Carl Hugo Linsingen (1886–1948). The region called South-West Africa or Namibia was transferred from German to British control in 1919. The German administration had been harsh and severe. The father of the Nazi leader Hermann Goering, Heinrich Ernst Goering (1838–1913), had been one of the few benign German rulers. The others were men like General Lothar von Trotha, whose campaign against the Herero people in 1904 was characterized by a brutality rivaled in the twentieth century only perhaps by the Russian Front in World War II. Between 1902 and 1911 the Hereros were reduced from approximately eighty thousand to fifteen thousand people, and an allied tribe, the Nama, was reduced from an estimated twenty thousand to about ninety-eight hundred. A number of Hereros—maybe ten thousand—had fled across the border to South Africa or Angola, but in the main the missing people had been killed or died in the desert.

The British invaded the place during World War I and were granted a formal Protectorate by the Treaty of Versailles in 1919. South-West Africa was a strange colony, divided among English administrators, Afrikaner settlers from South Africa, the remaining Germans, and the surviving original Africans. It was an arid and underpopulated place and definitely one of the "poor sister" colonies of the British Empire, with little investment or interest coming from the mother country. The German influence remained strong, to the point that there was a significant Nazi problem in the 1930s. The major industry was agriculture, including the production of Karakul wool, a gruesome business wherein newborn lambs were slaughtered for their pelts within hours of their birth. The ewes often would bleat piteously for weeks afterward, a distressing fact that is said to have deterred even many of the hard-bitten Boer farmers from pursuing the profitable industry.

The poverty of South-West Africa caused severe restrictions in the colony's administrative budget, and the few Imperial officials were underpaid and overworked. Nevertheless, many of these men did an outstanding job, and a few became virtual living legends. One of the latter was Carl Hugo Linsingen Hahn, known to everyone as "Cocky" (he also acquired the nickname "Shongola," an Ovambo word meaning "the whip"). Hahn was born to an old colonial family in 1886. His grandfather was the Reverend Hugo Hahn, the missionary who traveled with Canadian hunter Fred Green to Ovamboland in the 1850s. The Hahns were the first white family to settle in the Grootfontein district. Cocky grew up a healthy, energetic youth and was part of the invading British army under General Botha in 1915.

In 1917 Hahn served as intelligence officer for a punitive expedition against an Ovambo clan led by a rebellious chief named Mandumi, who had taken to raiding villages across the border in Portuguese Angola. The Portuguese were Britain's ally on the Western Front, and it would not do to allow these raids to continue. The British column of some seven hundred men, chiefly from the South African Mounted Rifles, was ambushed by the Ovambos and fought off the attack only because of Hahn's timely warning and the judicious use of three machine guns. Hahn remained in Namibia after the war as an assistant commissioner and in 1921 was posted as resident commissioner of Ovamboland, a job he held until shortly before his death.

Like all such officers, Hahn was woefully under-equipped for the immense territory he had to cover. In the late 1930s there were 117,000 African inhabitants in the 17,000 square miles of Ovamboland, and only one major road. Hahn was responsible for tax collection, agricultural assistance, jurisprudence, and myriad other tasks such as collecting botanical specimens for the British Museum, but he was almost literally a one-man show. He had no soldiers or policemen to back him up, and the total white population of the district consisted of seven other colonial officials and a few Finnish missionaries. This was "indirect rule" with a vengeance. But through force of character and an incredible sense of self-assurance Hahn managed to keep the district one of the calmest and indeed happiest in Britain's African Empire. His first major challenge was a serious famine that was crippling the countryside even as he took office. Through astute rationing, pressure on hoarders, and forceful negotiations with the territorial government, he managed to abate the worst consequences of the famine and thereafter maintained Ovambo agriculture on a sound footing. It has rightly been said that his work during the famine established Hahn as a man to be reckoned with.

Hahn lived in a small house he built north of Etosha Pan but spent most of his time on the road, riding a horse or donkey along the dusty trails that passed for highways in South-West Africa. He lived off his rifle, supplemented by an occasional gift of a chicken or goat from an Ovambo village. Like many of the best DCs, he was fearless to the point of recklessness. Early in his tenure he held a meeting to which some two hundred Ovambos were invited. Seemingly as a test, the Ovambos defied his order to come unarmed, and each one of the attendees conspicuously brought a rifle. Hahn went berserk, charging into the crowd, grabbing rifles, and smashing their stocks against the rocks. The meeting could easily have ended in tragedy but instead ended in farce as the two hundred men picked themselves up and made a frantic dash for safety to avoid damage to their priceless weapons. Nobody ever came armed to a Cocky Hahn meeting again.

In the late 1930s the American writer Negley Farson visited Ovamboland while researching his book *Behind God's Back* (1941). Farson accompanied Hahn on one of his usual patrols through the district and witnessed a dramatic confrontation wherein Hahn convinced an old Ovambo chief to confess to the murder of a servant girl some eighteen years previously. Hahn had been investigating the incident, which had happened while he was in the immediate area hunting for elephant, for all that time. He finally found a few witnesses who were willing to come forward, and the eighty-year-old chief knew the game was up. Apparently the crime, since it had happened so long ago and there was still some confusion as to who had struck the actual blow, was punished only by the confiscation of fifty or so cows.

Hahn stayed at his post throughout World War II and then retired in 1946. He was succeeded by Harold Eedes and died in 1948.

Haines, Stafford Bettesworth (c. 1801–1860). As political agent in Aden, Stafford Haines was only peripherally involved in Africa, but is included in this book to demonstrate the vagaries of British colonial administration. An exceptionally able man, Haines negotiated the sale of Aden to Britain by the sultan of Lahej in 1837. He then took the town by force, preempting its occupation by the Egyptian governor, Muhammad Ali Pasha. Haines remained as British agent—and virtual ruler—until 1854 at a salary of £2,400 per year.

Haines built Aden into a major commercial center. By the 1850s it boasted a population of twenty-five thousand (up from six hundred in 1840) and was the hub of a trade route that connected India, Arabia, and East Africa. Haines was woefully understaffed, however, and virtually unsupported by the London government, and his constant requests for assistance were ignored. Not until the early 1850s did the foreign office finally send out a team of officials to ease Haines's burden.

That team proved to be his downfall. Haines had been running the affairs of Aden out of his own pocket for over a decade. He kept few financial records and little other paperwork. He had not taken a leave in fifteen years because there was no one to take his place, even temporarily. The new administration found nearly £28,000 unaccounted for out of tax and custom receipts. Nobody believed that Haines had been dishonest. It was widely known that he had been overburdened and had simply failed to keep the proper records. Nevertheless, the money was technically missing and Haines was ordered back to India to stand trial. He was acquitted of fraud and embezzlement, but the East India Company had him thrown into debtor's prison in 1854. There he remained for the next six years, until pardoned by Governor Sir George Clerk in June 1860. He died a week later, in Bombay harbor aboard the ship that was to take him back to England.

In retrospect, that was certainly a shabby way to treat a man who had given his all in the furtherance of Queen and country. Haines was a colorful character—quick-witted, practical, even devious at times, and much respected and even loved by the Arabs in Aden—but something of a misfit in British society. His fate was extreme but not unique. Other—lesser—men profited greatly from careers in colonial administration, but many of the great Victorian figures were handled unfairly. Sir Richard Burton, for example, felt badly served by the British government, and Harry Johnston was meanly cheated out of most of his pension rights. It is ironic that Victoria's Empire, constructed largely not by design but by accident and built almost piecemeal by a cadre of strong, independent men exercising personal initiative, should have been so unforgiving to nonconformists.

Hale, William "Willie." An amusing, sociable man, Hale was an administrative officer in Kenya, 1930–1949. In 1938 he was the assistant district commissioner of the Turkana district. By 1942 he was a full district commissioner at Garissa on the Tana River. He succeeded Ritchie as chief game warden of Kenya in 1949. His wife's name was Morna. Hale was a close friend of George Adamson and often went hunting with him. In the late 1950s Hale retired to a hops farm in Kent, England.

Hall, Frank G. (xxxx–1901). An administrative officer in Kenya, 1893–1901. Frank Hall had been a British soldier, farmer, teacher, and big-game hunter in South Africa before coming to East Africa. In 1893 Hall was posted to Fort Smith at Machakos as DC. His position there—indeed, his life—depended on asserting his authority over the constantly bickering and skirmishing Masai and Kikuyu. The record of his first few years is a list of one punitive expedition after another. By the late 1890s the region was pacified. In 1897 Hall responded to the Sudanese mutiny by rushing troops to quell uprisings at Naivasha and Eldama Ravine. The next year he went home on leave and returned with a wife named Bee. Hall died in 1901 from dysentery. Fort Hall was named after him.

Hall was one of the administrative officials responsible for the arrest of the hunter John Boyes on charges of "dacoity" and impersonating a government. Boyes was for a brief period a paramount political figure among the

Kikuyu tribe. Since Boyes had begun his association with the Kikuyu in an attempt to find a convenient food source for the British troops and officials in central and western Kenya, including Hall, it is difficult to understand why these same men had him arrested and his operation shut down. Boyes's theory—that his authority with the Kikuyu might lead the London government to offer him official status and thus threaten several civil service careers—seems as good as any. At any rate, Boyes was soon acquitted and even got an apology from the judge. In his second book, *The Company of Adventurers*, Boyes got a measure of revenge against Hall by referring to him as "the presiding genius" at the trial.

Hall was an enthusiastic hunter and had the usual misadventures common at the time. In December 1894 he wounded a black rhino that objected to the point of tossing Hall several times through the air and trying to impale him with its horn, but instead smashed him with its nose and trampled him. Hall recovered after a long convalescence. A little over a year later, in March 1896, he wounded a leopard that took similar umbrage (one wonders what kind of rifle Hall was using). Hall's gunbearer killed the leopard before fatal damage was done, but Hall was left with nasty cuts that soon turned septic. He was delirious with pain for weeks. After twenty-two days the old rhino wound burst open, allowing a mass of pus to be removed, but only a quick operation by a traveling surgeon the next week saved Hall's life. He was left with a permanent limp.

Hall, Priscilla. The young Miss Hall accompanied Carl Akeley and Herbert E. Bradley on their 1920 Lake Kivu district safari. Priscilla killed an elephant and a lion.

Hallier, Mervyn. Hallier was a policeman in Tanganyika and a good friend of George Rushby. Rushby was moving to a new area, so he told Hallier of a legendary elephant that he had been tracking for several years, a huge, secretive beast. Hallier hunted the elephant down and collected its tusks, which weighed in at more than 140 pounds per side.

Hannington, James (1847–1885). Hannington was a British churchman from the Church Mission Society who was sent to Central Africa in 1885 as the first Bishop of East Equatorial Africa. Affable but devout, he disregarded warnings that his approach to Uganda was considered by many to be the dangerous fulfillment of a prophecy that would destroy the Baganda tribe. Specifically, Baganda legend had it that their kingdom would be destroyed by an enemy force invading eastward over the Nile at Busoga. Hannington was warned to approach by canoe over Lake Victoria instead. He laughed off the warning, crossed the Nile, and was seized by assassins sent by the chief, Mwange, and thrown into a vermin-infested hut. At first he thought his assailants were robbers. For eight days he was held prisoner, uncertain why he was being held, with only his sketchbook and his Bible to comfort him. An endless stream of curious African women came by to gawk at the tall, gaunt, bearded white man. On 29 October he had just finished his last entry in his sketchbook ("A hyena howled near me last night, smelling a sick man, but I hope it is not to have me yet") when his captors came and led him off, telling him he would soon be free. Suddenly they turned on Hannington, stripping him naked. They allowed him a few seconds to kneel and pray, and then hacked the first bishop of East Equatorial Africa into bloody pieces. Miles away, missionary Alexander Mackay wrote in his journal, "What an unheard of deed of blood!"

Hannington, Paul. The son of Bishop Hannington became the district commissioner at Koba, on the east bank of the Nile across from the Lado Enclave. Koba was a center of the ivory trade as long as the enclave was the focal point of elephant hunting in central Africa. Hannington, a tall, blond man, kept things in control with a judicious but firm hand. Once the ivory from the Lado stopped flowing, Koba disappeared. Hannington eventually retired to England.

Harding, Colin (1863–1939). A British officer with the rank of colonel, Harding was acting resident of Barotseland from 1898 to 1899. From 1900 to 1901 he was the acting administrator of North-West Rhodesia, as well as the commander of the Barotse Native Police. Harding lost his lucrative post with the BSAC (see glossary) when he publicly admitted that Barotse's King Lewanika had been tricked into signing the Concession of 1906, thus becoming one of the few colonial officials (of any nationality) to speak out against cheating the Africans. He was the author of several books, including *In Remotest Barotseland* (1904). ROWLAND WARD 1928: ELAND, LECHWE.

Hardwick, Alfred Arkell (1878–1912). Some texts list this name as Arkell-Hardwick, Alfred. Alfred Hardwick was born in London in January 1878, the son of businessman Alfred James Hardwick and his wife Louisa Hannah Green. Alfred was one of six children. He seems to have had a normal schooling but went off to sea as a young boy, about 1892. He had long been begging his parents to let him become a sailor, and when he reached his fourteenth birthday they finally agreed. Alfred spent three years or so at sea and then turned up in Cape Town in 1896. When the Matabele Rebellion erupted in the spring of that year, he made his way to Rhodesia and joined the British South African Police serving in Mashonaland. During this period he may have worked under the command of BSAC official Colin Harding.

When the rebellion was over, Hardwick went back to South Africa for a short time and then found his way to Cairo. Toward the end of 1899, he embarked on an expedition to the Galla country in northern Kenya and southern Abyssinia. There he hunted elephants and traded for ivory, hunting with George Henry West, another Englishman called "El Hakim," and occasionally in association with Dr. A. Eustace Atkinson. Hardwick hunted on the Uaso Nyiro for buffalo, hippo, giraffe, and rhino, and collected rhino and kongoni in western Kenya. He visited the Rendille and other tribes and had some trouble with hostile Kikuyus.

Hardwick returned to London about 1902, and produced a book about his adventures titled *An Ivory Trader in North Kenia* (1903). For some reason he created a nom de plume by adding his middle name to his surname and throwing in a hyphen: "A. Arkell-Hardwick." This is a device he used only on a few other documents, for he generally signed himself simply "Hardwick." The book tells of his hunting experiences and also of his interactions with the inhabitants of the region,.

Hardwick then traveled to West Africa where he operated as a trader for a spell. He periodically returned to London, and on one of his trips home he married Adeline Kate Dorington, the daughter of a pawnbroker. Hardwick continued to travel and promote his business interests; he is known to have visited Morocco in 1907–1908 and the United States most likely in 1910.

The visit to America was in connection with his profound interest in aviation. Hardwick, who habitually listed his occupation as that of "engineer," was fascinated by flying and went to the States to participate in some aeronautical experiments. Upon his return to England in 1911, he secured a position as the assistant manager of the Handley-Page Aeroplane Company, a fast-growing concern that a few years later produced the first British night bomber that was capable of reaching Berlin.

In late 1912 Hardwick's business duties took him to Constantinople, where Handley-Page hoped to sell warplanes to the Turkish army. He was back in London by December. On the 15th of that month he was flying as a passenger in a plane flown by a famous military pilot by the name of Wilfred Parke. The plane crashed at Wembley Field and Hardwick was killed. He was thirty-four.

Harmse, Christiaan (xxxx–1868). Harmse was a Boer elephant hunter who traveled with the likes of Bill Finaughty, Big Phillips, Thomas Leask, and Henry Hartley. He was sometimes accompanied by his brother Baart. In 1868 Harmse and his family were in Mashonaland hunting elephant when the entire party was stricken with fever. Harmse, three older daughters, two small children, three African retainers, and an English hunter named Thomas Wood all died in a matter of days. Only his wife and a young son survived.

Harnier, Baron Wilhelm von (xxxx–1860). A Prussian nobleman of the nineteenth century, Harnier was probably the first independent, nonprofessional hunter to travel the White Nile headwaters. He visited the district around 1860, bringing with him two German servants, both of whom died from fever in short order.

Harnier was killed shortly afterward. He wounded a buffalo, which charged his African tracker and knocked him down. Harnier, his gun unloaded, tried beating the animal off his man with the butt of the rifle. The buffalo left the tracker and turned on the European, goring him and stomping him to a pulp. The tracker ran away, making no effort to assist.

Harnier was buried at Saint Croix, an Austrian mission station on the Upper Nile run by a discouraged Roman Catholic priest named Morlang. The mission, consisting of twenty grass huts on the banks of the Nile, had been founded in the early 1850s. In 1862 Father Morlang abandoned Saint Croix, selling the station in its entirety to a Sudanese merchant named Koorshid Aga for 3,000 piastres (the equivalent of just £30), and selling Harnier's horse to Samuel Baker for 1,000 more. Harnier's grave was unattended and overgrown with weeds at the time of Baker's visit.

Father Morlang's sense of futility was understandable: Despite years of effort and a high death rate among the Austrian priests, the missionaries of Saint Croix had failed to make a single convert. More than fifty years passed before the missions returned to the area. The 1937 publication *A Tribal Survey of Mongalla Province* noted: "The introduction of organized Christianity dates only from 1917, the heroic but short-lived Roman Catholic attempt in the fifties having left no visible traces."

Harris, Rutherfoord (1856–1920). Dr. Rutherfoord Harris was the secretary of the BSAC (see glossary) in Kimberley in the late 1880s, and thus one of Cecil Rhodes's most important henchmen. A garrulous, untrustworthy man (the historian Robert Blake called him a "born gas-bag"), Harris played a shady part behind the scenes in the Jameson Raid and was noted for his propensity to spy on other BSAC officials for Rhodes (not that he was very loyal to Rhodes either). During the buildup to the invasion of Matabeleland in 1893, Harris was responsible (if that's the word) for the most egregious propaganda against the king, Lobengula.

After the occupation of Mashonaland Harris moved to Salisbury to oversee the administration of the chartered company. He took to bathing every day at a pool near the town limits and one day was bit on the rear end by a crocodile. His pride was more severely hurt than his body, and he spent the next several weeks having the pool blasted with dynamite in an effort to kill his assailant. Adrian Darter (1914) pointed out that the injury could not have been too bad, for Harris later took a seat in Parliament as the member for Dulwich.

Harris, William Cornwallis (1807–1848). An engineer officer for the East India Company, Harris was granted a two-year medical leave of absence in 1836 and decided to spend it hunting in Africa. Striking out from Port Elizabeth, he roamed the interior into Matabeleland, going as far as the Limpopo River. At first he was kind of a greenhorn—he made the rookie mistake of paying his African retainers with cash and muskets before the initial departure of the safari, with the inevitable result that the cash was quickly spent, the muskets pawned, and the men spread out all over Port Elizabeth in various stages of intoxication.

Harris gradually gained experience, dealing successfully with both the Matabele potentate Mzilikazi (who he called Mosilikatse) and the Boer trekkers. As a military engineer Harris was a gifted artist, and his books *Wild Sports of Southern Africa* (1839), especially the fifth edition of 1852, and *Portraits of the Game and Wild Animals of South Africa* (1840) are blessed with superb prints of native and animal life. He also wrote *The Highlands of Ethiopia* (1844). ROWLAND WARD 1928: GIRAFFE.

Harrison, Edgar G. Captain Harrison shot a five-horned black rhino in East Africa in 1897. Describing his unique trophy in that year's Christmas issue of the sporting newspaper *The Field,* Harrison reported that the largest of the five horns was a bit more than 15 inches long (the first measured 14 inches). The second horn was nearly straight and pointed off to one side. In 1905 Harrison, now a colonel, commanded the force sent to suppress the rebellious Nandi. ROWLAND WARD 1928: KONGONI, HIROLA.

Harrison, James Jonathan (1858–1926). Lieutenant Colonel Harrison, late of the Prince of Wales Yorkshire Hussars, was one of the leaders of the 1899–1900 Harrison-Whitehouse Expedition through Ethiopia and the Lake Turkana region. He was a veteran of several hunting expeditions to South Africa and Mozambique. The other members of the party included the American William Whitehouse, a Scottish sportsman named Archibald Butters, a surveyor named Donald Clarke, a taxidermist named Perks, and, for a few months, hunter P. H. G. Powell-Cotton. Harrison was somewhat pushy and overbearing, and Powell-Cotton, one of the great sportsmen of his time, quit after two months in disgust over the shooting of a number of adolescent elephant. Harrison wanted to present Menelik, the Ethiopian king, with a gift of ivory, and so he, Whitehouse, and Butters shot nine young bulls with an average tusk weight of only seventeen pounds apiece. Even Menelik was disturbed by the waste.

The expedition succeeded in one of its goals, to place a British flag on the northern shore of Lake Turkana. It also produced some interesting specimens for British museums and natural-history collections, including a spectacular albino topi that had originally been spotted the year before by Welby and was shot by Archie Butters. Unfortunately, the maps that Clarke made of the area between Turkana and the Nile, eagerly awaited by the Royal Geographical Society, proved to be less than accurate. In addition, the party had engaged in the old-fashioned indulgence of naming mountains, lakes, and other landmarks after themselves and their loved ones, producing maps showing a Mount Clarke, a Whitehouse Range, and a Lake Edith, among others. Custom had long since viewed such obnoxious behavior as inappropriate, and the Society had recently sent out a circular reminding its members about this and urging them to find and use local names whenever possible. The affair had the effect of making Harrison and his team—who were, for all their faults, courageous explorers in a dangerous land—look foolish and pretentious.

Harrison returned to Africa in 1905, this time hunting extensively in the Congo. Like several others, he became entranced with the forest people known as Pygmies and brought several back to England for exhibition. In 1910 he married a rich Illinois widow, Mary Stetson Clark, and began cutting back on his foreign exploits. When he died he left a huge sporting collection that can still be seen at the Scarborough Borough Council Wood End Museum of Natural History. ROWLAND WARD 1928: ELEPHANT (MOZAMBIQUE).

Hartley, Diana (xxxx–1960). During World War II Diana Hartley served in the British army in Kenya, where she met and married her husband, white hunter Lionel Hartley. The couple had two children, a boy (professional hunter Lionel Jr.) and a girl. After Lionel's death in a 1950 plane crash (there was a vicious and unfounded rumor that Diana had been having an affair with the pilot, Bob Astles, who survived the crash with a broken back), Diana went into the animal trapping business with a man named Heini Demmer. She was a guest at the farm owned by her mother and stepfather Gray Leakey on the night of 13 October 1954, when the Leakey farm was attacked by Mau Mau terrorists. Both of the Leakeys were murdered, but Diana escaped by hiding in the attic and was able to raise the alarm after the raiders had left.

Diana married Eddie Knodi, a prominent hotel chef in Nairobi, and continued her animal capture business. In November 1960 she was killed by a tame lion during the filming of the John Wayne movie *Hatari.*

Hartley, Henry (1815–1876). Hartley was one of the greatest of the nineteenth-century South African elephant hunters and the patriarch of a renowned hunting family. Known as the "Oud Baas," Hartley hunted the interior from Cape Colony to the Zambezi to Lake Ngami. He first ventured into the interior in 1834 and guided artist Thomas Baines on several lengthy expeditions. His preferred technique for elephant was to chase the herds on horseback with several others, such as his sons Fred, Tom, and Will, all blazing away at the same animal. Often friends such as Big Phillips and Tom Leask came along too.

The history of elephant hunting provides a great example of how conditions dictate tactics. Hunting techniques, like military tactics, are a function of the available weapons and other prevailing conditions. The "elephant guns" of Hartley's day, from the late 1830s to the 1870s, were large-bore, relatively low-velocity rifles firing unreliable ammunition (a classic example is the Boer *roer*, a 4-bore percussion smoothbore weighing about sixteen pounds). Though lethal against plains game like wildebeest and kongoni, these rifles were chancy against heavier game—you just couldn't be sure of stopping an angry rhino or tusker. Thus tactics evolved that minimized the risk to the hunter while enhancing his chance of success. Since one round couldn't be counted on to kill an elephant, several hunters took to firing together. And since there was a real risk the rifle would be unable to stop the charge of a wounded elephant, these hunters generally worked on horseback. That way, even if you couldn't thump the elephant hard enough to drop it in its tracks, you could at least ride away and set up for another shot.

The prevailing conditions in those years also dictated the need for a well-stocked but portable base. Hartley and the other South African pioneers would trek with their wagons deep into the interior, encamp at a likely spot, and then hunt the district on horseback. Once the place was hunted out, or if the weather turned bad or other problems came up, they simply moved on to a new locale. Again, the reason for this system can be traced back to the available technology: A group of hunters obviously required more food, ammunition, and other sundries than a solitary man; this necessitated a base (the wagons). The base also served as a warehouse for the various tusks, hides, and other trophies gathered by the hunters, as well as providing a position that could be defended against attacks by hostile locals. The need to follow the elephant herds meant that the base had to be portable.

Men like Henry Hartley understood full well the connection between technology and tactics. Many books have noted the virtual cessation of Boer elephant hunting once the herds retreated to the tsetse-fly zones in the late nineteenth century. Most of these books mention that the hunters gave up their profession once the elephant could no longer be worked on horseback (the tsetse fly is dramatically lethal to horses and oxen). The modern reader may wonder, however, whether the hunters were too lazy or too mired in tradition to hunt thereafter on foot.

The answer, of course, is neither. The great South African hunters quite wisely decided that the rewards no longer warranted the risks. Without oxen, there could be no laager, or sizable encampment; without a laager, the hunting party had to be kept quite small, its size determined by the provisions that could be carried manually. And small groups of hunters simply would not survive for long with the rifles of the 1870s. Without the capability to drop a charging elephant with one or two shots, elephant hunting on foot was a suicidal endeavor.

As with most things tactical, this situation soon changed. When modern rifles and ammunition began to appear in the 1880s and 1890s, it became plausible for one man to hunt African big game safely and profitably. Almost immediately a new breed of hunter emerged, capable of dropping the heaviest game with one well-placed round, and the tsetse-fly zones were no longer a safe haven for elephant. Instead they became vast killing grounds as tireless, hungry men began stalking them on foot with just a few trackers and porters.

Henry Hartley was gone then, of course, but his sons carried on the family tradition. Indeed, his descendants are still hunting Africa today—Hartley's Safaris is led by his great-great grandson, David Hartley. Henry is remembered today largely for his fortuitous discovery (with the German, Mauch; see below) of the Rhodesian gold reefs, but he was locally famous for his explorations and his hunting prowess long before that singular event. Hartley was in at the deaths (singly or with other hunters) of over twelve hundred elephant. As he got older, Hartley became chronically ill and was quite often shaky and took to riding instead of walking, even for short distances, but he never gave up hunting. His illnesses were compounded by being injured by a white rhino and by a club foot. According to Selous, this latter affliction did not normally interfere with his mounting and dismounting a horse (Darter, 1914), but it certainly restricted him even further once arthritis began to set in.

In 1867 Hartley fell in with German explorer Karl Gottlieb Mauch, and on 27 July of that year the odd couple made an historic gold strike north of Bulawayo. A persistent legend has it that Hartley shot an elephant that staggered off and died right on top of the spot where the gold reef was exposed on the surface. Within a short time they made other strikes, including the gold fields at Tati. By 1869 the area was sprinkled with parties making for the reefs. Transport costs and the low grade of the ore caused the rush to peter out (for the time being) by 1872, but it was resurrected a few years later and gold mining became a permanent part of the Rhodesian economy. In the 1950s Southern Rhodesia was consistently supplying about 3 percent of the world's gold.

Zimbabwe's Hartley Hills were named after Henry. Another spot, recorded by Selous as "Hill of the Stump-Tailed Bull," was named by Hartley for an elephant of that description that he had shot at its summit. Henry Hartley died on 8 February 1876.

Hartley, Lionel (xxxx–1950). Brother of Carr Hartley, Lionel Hartley took a job as a professional hunter at Mac's Camp, a pub and hotel owned by former warden C. G. MacArthur. He was killed in a plane crash at Voi in 1950. A rumor circulated that the pilot of the Tiger Moth, the unpopular Bob Astles, had deliberately staged the accident due to his infatuation with Lionel's wife, Diana. The fact that Astles, who later became a top advisor to Idi Amin, received a broken neck in the crash did little to stop the rumor. Hartley had also been a hunter at Treetops Hotel in the 1940s.

Hartley, Thomas Augustus Corke "Carr" (1910–1992). A strongly built man, Carr Hartley was a natural for wrangling wild animals. He started out as a white hunter while a teenager but soon achieved prominence as a "catcher" of wild animals for zoos and for translocation efforts. By 1926 he was manager of a twenty-six-thousand-acre farm near Mount Kenya. Like many young men of his time, he supplemented his income by shooting his two legal elephant a year and selling the ivory. One of his bulls had monster tusks that tipped the scales at 164 and 167 pounds. His hunting prowess quickly got him a job doing control work for the game department.

In 1934 Hartley bought a ranch at Rumuruti. He began to specialize in trapping game alive and shipping them out to zoos and circuses. That business expanded until Rumuruti was being used as a quarantine station plus a great place to obtain a tame animal for movie footage. The biggest stars of Rumuruti were some white rhino that appeared in many Hollywood films. Hartley started out with two but at one time had as many as five. Life on the ranch wasn't always easy, however. Hartley was twice gored by rhino and once went hand-to-paw with a wounded adult male lion. He claimed to have no fear of lion but admitted being terrified of snakes.

Harvey, Bill. A game ranger and friend of C. J. P. Ionides, Harvey was assigned to the Masai area of Tanganyika. In his spare time he was a noted ornithologist.

Harvey, Gordon. Harvey was a game ranger at Ngorongoro Crater in the 1950s, and a friend of John Hunter. Harvey was once on safari in Masailand when he spotted two gazelle grazing some distance ahead. He wanted to shoot one for the pot because his porters had had no meat for days and were becoming surly and uncooperative. After a short but careful stalk he fired a shot, and the bullet went through the first gazelle and killed the second animal as well. Shouldering his rifle, Harvey started toward the two carcasses when two lionesses appeared and each started running off with a gazelle in her mouth. The lionesses may have been stalking the gazelle at the same time as Harvey. Harvey hollered and ran at the cats, hoping they might drop one of the antelope, but instead one of the lionesses turned and looked as if she were going to charge. Harvey put a bullet into her, but after a quick tumble she recovered and started the charge. He was ready to squeeze the trigger again when the lioness just dropped dead in mid-charge, the earlier bullet apparently having nicked an artery or something. The second lioness escaped with the other gazelle.

Harvey, Sir Robert (1856–1931). A British explorer and hunter in Kenya, he accompanied Sir John Willoughby and H. C. V. Hunter on an 1886 safari around Taveta, near Kilimanjaro. This hunting trip was guided by James Martin of Thomson expedition fame. ROWLAND WARD 1928: KONGONI, BUFFALO, LORD DERBY ELAND, TSESSEBE, HIROLA.

Hassan, Ikram. Ikram Hassan's father, Dr. Syed Gulam Hassan Shah, came to East Africa in 1905. He was a veterinarian, and it was perhaps inevitable that his three sons became infatuated with hunting. After two years of study at veterinary school, Ikram became a professional hunter and started a family safari business in Mombasa called African Hunting Safaris just before World War II. The company specialized in what was advertised as "poor man's safaris."

Hassan's career had its ups-and-downs. He took an elephant with tusks of 146 and 144 pounds, but also suffered a massive goring from a wounded buffalo. He was one of the few non-Europeans to achieve success as a PH in British East Africa.

Hastings. In 1903 a man name Hastings was the agent for the British Central Africa Company in Katunga on the Zambezi. He got it into his head one day to reload some black-powder cartridges using the new cordite propellant. His Express rifle exploded on firing, taking off several fingers of his right hand.

Hatton, Denys Finch (1887–1931). Eternally linked with Bror Blixen and Isak Dinesen (Karen Blixen), Denys Finch Hatton was the son of the earl of Winchilsea. A resident of Kenya from 1912, Finch Hatton was equally at home at a London club and a Tanganyikan swamp. Though not as handsome as Robert Redford, he nonetheless possessed a distinctive charm that never failed to impress those who met him. One of those who fell in love with him was his friend Blixen's wife Karen, and their affair constituted most of the plot of the movie version of *Out of Africa.*

Finch Hatton was an unusual man, wealthy, witty, highly educated, and magnificently connected. His ephemeral charm especially captivated females. His appearance helped—he was tall (six feet, three inches), well-proportioned, exceptionally fit, and had a dazzling smile. Much has been made of his baldness, which was supposedly self-inflicted (a late-Victorian recipe for thick hair was to shave the head and rub the scalp with ammonia—Denys tried it and his hair never grew back), but he covered that up by always wearing a hat. Above all, he gave an impression of intelligence and physical vitality that awed his contemporaries and left future generations wondering what all the fuss was about.

Finch Hatton's first professional safari (he had done a great deal of hunting for himself previously) was in late 1924, when he guided a client named Maclean. He threw himself into his new profession with passion and dedication and soon became one of the most-sought PHs in East Africa.

A 1928 book, *African Adventures,* by Frederick Patterson, is an interesting and well-photographed account of a safari conducted by Finch Hatton and his assistant hunter, W. V. D. Dickenson. Both men worked for Safariland, Ltd., a company formed in 1921 to fill the void left by the dissolution of Newland and Tarlton two years earlier. Patterson spent six months roaming East Africa with Finch Hatton and wrote a book that foreshadowed Robert Ruark's treatment of a later white hunter, Harry Selby.

Denys Finch Hatton and bull elephant, Kenya, 1927.

Finch Hatton, who liked to scout new game country in his "Gypsy Moth" biplane, died in a tragic air crash along with his Kikuyu servant Kamau (who was afraid of flying) at Voi airfield on 14 May 1931. The crash was witnessed by several local people, including District Commissioner Vernon Cole, an American safari client named Lee Hudson, and Hudson's PH, J. A. Hunter.

Once he had split from Karen Blixen, Finch Hatton lived with friends and in various camps and clubs. After his death there was some difficulty in accounting for his estate, since his possessions were scattered about the residences of several friends, usually females. For instance, Beryl Markham had his combs (which could not have seen much use), an ivory-handled knife, and two well-used hunting rifles, a Gibbs Mauser and a .256 Mannlicher.

Finch Hatton was buried just outside the boundary of the Southern Game Reserve in Kenya. A well-known story tells how Mervyn Cowie, a game warden later to become director of Kenya National Parks, went to check the upkeep of the grave and found two male lion lying by it, as if in tribute. Some years later the reserve's boundary was straightened out and it was found that the grave was now inside the reserve. The game department pledged to correct its mistake, but then documentation surfaced indicating that the original intent had been in fact to place the grave in the reserve—meaning that they had inadvertently corrected the error.

Haws Hai. Also called Hans Hai or Haans Hai, Haws Hai was a Griqua hunter active in Matabeleland in the second half of the nineteenth century. Frequently working for William Finaughty, he comes across as a serious, quiet man.

On one occasion in 1869 Finaughty rudely berated him for letting vultures get at the corpse of an ox that had been killed by lion. Finaughty had set a gun trap at the scene and thought the vultures had set it off. Haws Hai (who Finaughty constantly referred to as an "old man") patiently allowed the irascible elephant hunter to rant. When he finished, Haws quietly explained that vultures had nothing to do with it—a lion had set off the trap and, indeed, been killed by it. Finaughty refused to believe him until he walked over and saw the lion's corpse.

On that same trip Finaughty sent Haws to the kraal of a chief named M'Tibi with orders to trade £80 to £100 worth of goods (six muskets, ten bags of powder, lead, percussion caps, beads, blankets, hats, jackets, shirts, and some brass wire) for cattle, sheep, and grain. M'Tibi robbed Haws at gunpoint. After twelve days the old Griqua returned to Finaughty's camp empty-handed. Finaughty, a violent man at the best of times, was in his own words "almost too furious to speak, but I soon saw that something was amiss for poor Haws was obviously in a state of great distress and nearly starved to death" (1916). There was no time to seek revenge right then, but a year later Finaughty and seven others raided M'Tibi's kraal and rustled a large herd of cattle.

Finaughty also blamed the Griqua for overturning his ox wagon on a trip in 1875. Finaughty, who could not always be trusted to apportion blame appropriately, wrote that Haws caused the accident by impatiently pushing the oxen too hard through a swampy area. Two young native boys were killed in the mishap.

Hayne, R. H. R. Lieutenant Hayne was an officer of the 6th Battalion of the KAR (see glossary), stationed in Arusha in the 1920s. ROWLAND WARD 1928: LICHTENSTEIN HARTEBEEST, LESSER KUDU, MOUNTAIN BUSHBUCK (NO. 1, 44 INCHES, LAKE ZWAI).

Healy, G. R. (1881–1916). Healy was born in Ireland and immigrated to South Africa as an Irish militia lieutenant in the Boer War. Subsequently he stayed in Africa, joining the South African Constabulary. By 1904 he was a game ranger at the Sabi Reserve, where he served with distinction until 1914, when he joined the King's African Rifles as an officer. He was killed in action in early 1916.

Healy was a very effective ranger, especially known for his good relations with the local Africans. He also erected a granite monument near the Sabi Bridge that has been the cause of some confusion over the years. The stark memorial is inscribed "Erected by G. R. Healy in memory of Mary, aged 3 years." Tourists have been seen shaking their heads over the monument in sadness and at the folly of taking young children into the wilderness to live. Their sympathy is somewhat misplaced—Mary was Healy's dog, which died of heat stroke on that spot.

Heany, Maurice (1856–1927). Born in the United States, Captain Heany was a cousin of the writer Edgar Allan Poe. Heany joined the U.S. cavalry and was a member of the 1876 Black Hills campaign that saw the destruction of General Custer and much of the 7th Cavalry. In 1878 he immigrated to South Africa, where he served in the Basuto war and the 1885 Charles Warren expedition into Bechuanaland.

Heany spent several years prospecting in Matabeleland and hunting and trading in Bechuanaland before joining

Hugh Heatley on a buffalo path, 1909.

Frank Johnson's syndicate, which was trying to expropriate Matabeleland and Mashonaland from King Lobengula. According to a story told by Johnson, a plan (backed by Cecil Rhodes) was afoot whereby Johnson, Heany, and their partners Henry Borrow and Ted Burnett would lead a small column of scouts to Bulawayo, where they would kidnap or kill Lobengula as a prelude to the invasion of Matabeleland. The plot was foiled, the story goes, when Heany got drunk and blurted details of its existence to a British missionary named Hepburn, who told the British government of the plan. Modern historians feel there may be a kernel of truth in this legend but that there was undoubtedly more to the story.

Heany was an officer of the Mashonaland Pioneer Corps in 1890, commissioned as the captain commanding "A" Troop. Adrian Darter, who always misspelled his name as "Heaney," described him (1914) as "a red-headed and red-bearded Virginian, quiet of demeanor and deep of thought." He was a reluctant participant in the Jameson Raid (detailed to either delay or prevent it, he went along when he realized Jameson wouldn't be stopped). After serving in the Matabele wars (commanding a relief column in 1896), he lived out his life in Rhodesia and died in Bulawayo on 25 June 1927.

Heatley, Hugh H. He was a Kenya settler who owned a sixty-eight-square-mile ranch called Kamiti. Kamiti Ranch contained large herds of cattle, a dairy, and hundreds of acres under cultivation. About 1910 Heatley captured an all-black leopard in a trap. Keeping the animal alive, he donated it to the Zoological Society at the Regent's Park Zoo in London, where it was displayed for several years. Theodore Roosevelt later hunted buffalo with Heatley at Kamiti during his great safari.

Heck, Lutz (1892–1983). Lutz Heck began working at the Berlin Zoo in 1921 and succeeded his father, Ludwig, as director in 1931. Along with his brother Heinz (1894–1982), who was director of the Hellabrunn Zoological Gardens in Munich, Lutz made many innovative changes in the way animals were kept and displayed. Lutz, like Hagenbeck before him, had a network of animal collectors throughout the world, especially in Africa. Lutz was often assisted by his English wife, Eva Lutz-Maclean.

The Heck brothers spent considerable time and resources on a pet project, trying to re-create both the extinct European aurochs (an oxlike animal) and the tarpon (a primitive horse) by selective breeding. Their work and their philosophies played well with Nazi racial theorists, and the brothers did very well under the Third Reich. They even participated in and profited from the Nazi plundering of Europe's zoos.

After the war, Lutz fled the advancing Russian armies (they wanted to question him in connection with the rape of eastern Europe's zoological gardens), finally surfacing in Wiesbaden. He made some postwar trips as an animal collector, being careful to stay out of Communist hands, and wrote several books, including *Animal Safari: Big Game in South-West Africa* and *Animals: My Adventure.* Heinz also continued as a zoo director for years and passed away in 1982. Lutz Heck died the following year.

Their father, Ludwig Heck (1860–1931), was a well-known naturalist and zoo director in his own right. He was the author of *The Animal Kingdom* (1896) and a friend of the hunter-photographer Carl Georg Schillings.

Heller, Edmund (1875–1939). An American, Heller was perhaps the greatest example of the museum curator turned hunter. A listing of his scientific expeditions reads like an

Edmund Heller preparing Roosevelt's trophies for shipment, 1909.

itinerary for a trip around the world: Galapagos Islands, 1898; Alaska, 1900; Africa, 1907; Africa, 1909–1912 (Roosevelt and Paul Rainey expeditions); northern Canada, 1914; Peru, 1915; China, 1916; Russia and Siberia, 1918; Africa, 1919 (Smithsonian "Cape to Cairo" expedition); the Congo, 1924.

Most curators relied upon professional hunters to obtain most of their animals, but Heller was thrilled to pursue his own quarry. He started out collecting for Chicago's Field Museum and the Smithsonian, and then became director of the Milwaukee Zoo. Later he held the same post in San Francisco. Among curator/collector, only Carl Akeley was comparable to Heller. Interestingly, one of the last nights of Akeley's life was spent in an old bamboo hut in the Congo that had been built by Heller years earlier. In 1914 Heller coauthored a book with Theodore Roosevelt, *Life Histories of African Game Animals.*

In 1924 Heller represented the Field Museum in a gorilla-hunting expedition to the Kivu District of the Belgian Congo, with Philadelphia naturalist Alfred Collins. They were accompanied by PH Alexander Barns, who grew frustrated with the pursuit and gave up. Heller and Collins kept at it and collected two specimens. Heller spent the last years of his life as director of the Milwaukee Zoo (1928–1935) and the Fleishhacker Zoo in San Francisco (1935–1939).

Hemans, Herbert Nassau (1871–1935). An administrative officer in Rhodesia who liked to hunt, Hemans was the author of *The Log of a Native Commissioner: A Record of Work and Sport in Southern Rhodesia* (1935).

Hemeleers. A Belgian game warden active in the Belgian Congo from at least 1906, he became first warden of Albert National Park in 1925, a post he held until the late 1930s. He was succeeded by Colonel Hoier.

Hemingway, Ernest (1899–1961). The legendary American writer had two famous African safaris. The first, in 1933–1934, was immortalized in his *The Green Hills of Africa* (1935), a rousing and thoughtful tale of a hunt for big game and especially a greater kudu. Hemingway was at his best during this safari, tough and frank despite being intensely jealous of the shooting success of his companion, Charles Thompson. Hemingway's saving grace at this period in his life was that he knew when he was being jealous and unreasonable; he was still Hemingway, not the parody he became in later years. He suffered, with a minimum of complaining, from a vicious attack of dysentery that forced him to go to the bathroom a hundred fifty times a day and caused his lower intestine to protrude three inches outside his body. During his seventy-two days of hunting he killed a buffalo, three lion, and twenty-seven other large game animals, and then capped it all off with a week of sport fishing at Malindi in January 1934.

Much speculation has whirled over which African professional was the model for Robert Wilson, the fictional white hunter in *Hills.* Critics are split between Blixen and Philip Percival. There is little argument over the inspiration for the story *The Short Happy Life of Francis Macomber.* Although one of the Percival brothers once claimed that it was entirely fiction and nothing like that had ever happened, the episode was rather obviously based upon John Henry Patterson and the so-called Blyth affair. The villainous Margot Macomber was based on Hemingway's paramour, Jane Mason.

Hemingway's second African safari, in 1953–1954, showcased the writer in the middle of his tragic deterioration. He seems to have been trying to recapture the glories of his youth, visiting Africa, Spain, and his other scenes of triumph. By the time he arrived in Kenya in August 1953, Hemingway was drinking heavily and his behavior was increasingly erratic. Philip Percival came out of retirement to guide him, backed up by Denis Zaphiro and Safariland hunter Roy Home. Just as he had been jealous of his 1933 companion Thompson, the writer was resentful of the success of his 1953 partners, *Life* magazine photographer Earl Theisen and especially Mayito Menocal.

Percival was shocked at Hemingway's appearance and behavior, constantly telling friends that he was simply not the same man. Hemingway grew an intense dislike for backup hunter Roy Home and accused him of padding the costs of the safari. Home took the abuse as well as could be expected. Hemingway picked a bad time to decide to "go native"—the middle of the Mau Mau insurgency. He shaved his head, insisted on dying his clothes the rust color preferred by the Masai, tried hunting with a spear, and shacked up with an African prostitute named Debba. "Shacked up" might not be the correct phrase, given that he was apparently impotent at this time, but at any rate she was his constant companion and slept in the same hut with him. His wife Mary, who was with him on this trip, tried to ignore his bad behavior. Above all there was the booze. Hemingway had entirely lost control by this point and was drinking constantly.

In January 1954 Hemingway chartered a Cessna 180 to do some aerial sightseeing over East Africa. On January 23 the plane, piloted by Roy Marsh, dodged a flock of birds near the Nile and struck a telegraph wire with its tail. They crashed near Murchison Falls, Hemingway spraining his right shoulder. They were some distance from help (a rescue plane spotted the wreckage and actually reported them dead), so Hemingway, his wife Mary, and Marsh spent the night in the bush next to a herd of elephant, surviving on Hemingway's cache of whiskey and beer. The next day they shouted down a boat and were taken to Butiaba, on Lake Albert. That very same day, 24 January 1954, they accepted a proposal from a pilot named Reginald Cartwright, who had been searching for them in his H-89 deHavilland Rapide, to fly them to Kampala.

The overloaded flight went no better than the previous day's flight. Cartwright was buffeted by a strong wind on takeoff, and the plane promptly crashed. Mary and Marsh quickly escaped, but Hemingway, with a much larger body, found himself stuck. He finally had to batter a passenger door open with his head, giving himself a concussion. The writer was seriously hurt—in addition to the concussion, he had cracked two vertebrae, fractured his skull, dislocated his right arm and shoulder, and ruptured his spleen, liver, and right kidney. The vertebrae were particularly troublesome, for they compressed the nerves in his spinal cord and caused all kinds of long-lasting subsidiary problems such as sciatica and a loss of control of his sphincter muscles. He was also badly burned on his face and hands.

Shades of the old Hemingway returned as he joked and made light of his injuries during a fifty-mile car trip to the hospital. He told one man that the loss of brain fluid was actually relieving the pain in his skull, and another that along with the sciatica he was now cursed with a permanent erection. But the injuries were serious and potentially life-threatening and the facilities in Uganda were ill-equipped to deal with them, so he bravely got into yet another small plane and was flown to Nairobi, where he spent weeks in the hospital. He greatly enjoyed reading the premature accounts of his death and obituaries in the world's newspapers, and saved the clippings in a pair of scrapbooks bound in zebra and lion hide.

Ironically, the two brushes with death restored some of Hemingway's old vitality. Africa, however, was not quite done with him. Just out of hospital in late February 1954, he went fishing again on the Indian Ocean shore south of Mombasa. Spotting an out-of-control brush fire, he insisted on joining the fire brigade and was badly burned once again after tripping and falling into the flames.

Hendrick. One night in 1847 Hendrick, a Hottentot working for Gordon Cumming, was snatched from the fireside by a lion and eaten. His coworker, John Stofolus, grabbed a firebrand and tried to fight the lion off but to no avail. Gordon Cumming found Hendrick's remains (just half of one leg with the shoe still on the foot, plus a pea coat) and shot and killed the lion two days later.

Henriques, Robert David Quixano (1905–1967). British sportsman and soldier; served in the Royal Artillery 1926–1933 and then became a professional writer. Henriques was descended from a Jewish family that had fled from Spain to England in the sixteenth century. He traveled extensively in the 1920s and 1930s, visiting the world's premier hunting locations, especially Africa. He also served in Egypt and Sudan in the 1920s. During the Second World War, Colonel Henriques served with the British commandos and as a staff officer with Gen. George Patton; he was decorated with both the Bronze and Silver Stars.

A respected novelist *(Red Over Green, A Stranger Here,* and *Too Little Love),* in 1938 Henriques wrote the nonfiction *Death by Moonlight: An Account of a Darfur Journey* that includes chapters on the hunting of lions and leopards. Henriques also wrote several books on Jewish topics including a best-selling history of the 1956 Sinai campaign titled *One Hundred Hours to Suez.* He retired to a farm in Gloucestershire in the 1950s.

Hepburn, Alonzo Barton (1846–1922). A Wall Street businessman, financier, and New York state legislator from

1875–1880, Hepburn hunted in East Africa and then wrote about his trip in *The Story of an Outing.* A man of diverse interests, he also wrote *A History of Currency* (1924). Hepburn is the subject of a fawning biography entitled *A. Barton Hepburn: His Life and Service.*

Herbert, Elsie Diana "Agnes" (c. 1880–1960). In 1907 two young British women decided to tackle the "man's world" of safari hunting in a sort of a half-lark, half-suffragette-protest adventure. Agnes Herbert and her cousin Cecily Herbert meticulously planned and organized their expedition, and when they set out southward from the traditional jumping-off spot of Berbera in Somaliland with forty-nine camels, they were better equipped than most traditional safaris—in fact, the only piece of equipment they later regretted not packing were bathing suits. Both in their early thirties, Agnes and Cecily adapted readily to bush life, and the account of their adventure (published by Agnes in 1908 as *Two Dianas in Somaliland*) establishes the pair as the equal of any other first-time hunting team. In fact, several other hunting parties were in the area, all consisting of veteran British officers with many a day in the bush, and the two Ladies Herbert incensed them all by frequently outhunting and outshooting them. The women came to view the men as the "Opposition" (one old officer referred to them as "duffers"), and it is one of the more amusing aspects of Agnes's journal that the local Somali gunbearers and trackers were immensely enjoying the discomfiture of the Englishmen at being shown up by these two.

It wasn't all fun and games, of course. A camel driver died of dehydration when they ran out of water, and Agnes's gunbearer was killed by a rhino she had wounded. The women, frequently tested, revealed great inner courage and strength. When a disgruntled Somali butler deserted, taking with him a precious Winchester .350 rifle, Agnes pursued him and brought him back at gunpoint after a long chase complete with warning shots.

Viewed as a whole, however, the safari was a smashing success, and Agnes and Cecily both enjoyed themselves and most certainly proved whatever they set out to prove. They hunted plains game for the most part, oryx and kudu, and occasionally went after rhino, lion, and even jackal. Unlike Mary Kingsley, who had insisted on dressing like a Victorian lady during her trips to Africa, the Herberts dressed practically in trousers and heavy-duty tunics with a lot of pockets. Photographs of the pair show them to be distinctly feminine when they wanted to be, however. Agnes brought home an excessive bag of animals, typical of the period, but predicted in her writings that photography would soon replace shooting in the field. That didn't stop her from bringing home a rhino table—rhino hide can be polished to a transparent amber look, and it was the centerpiece of her social teas and sundowners for many years afterward.

Not content with proving that women could survive in Darkest Africa, the Herberts went on several other adventures together. In addition to her African book, Agnes wrote many others, including *Two Dianas in Alaska* (1908), *The Life Story of a Lion* (1911), *Casuals in the Caucasus* (1912), and *Elephant* (1916).

Heuglin, Theodor von (1824–1876). A German explorer and ornithologist, von Heuglin traveled all through Somaliland, Abyssinia, Arabia, Kordofan, and Galla-land in the years 1850–1864. A superior scientist and linguist, he collected specimens and gathered collections that are still being used today. Of all the German explorers of his time, von Heuglin made by far the largest contribution to science. He was the author of seven major works on his expeditions and African birds. After a trip to the Russian Arctic in 1871, he visited Africa one last time in 1874, touring the shores of the Red Sea.

Hewitt, G. H. Hewitt was a hunter and trader operating in Bechuanaland in the early 1860s. He had a contract with a German museum to collect insect specimens.

Hewlett, J. R. H. "Ray." Major Hewlett was a professional hunter who was one of the first to join the Tanganyika Game Department, taking over the Serengeti when it was still a reserve. He backed up Denys Finch Hatton and Bror Blixen on the southern leg of the 1930 "Royal" safari, and helped Finch Hatton affix a postage stamp on a sleeping rhino for the Prince of Wales's amusement. Hewlett was the first warden for the Serengeti when it achieved national park status in 1950.

Heyer, Charles. Charles Heyer operated the first gun and safari equipment shop in Nairobi. He also ran a safari operation, frequently employing John Hunter as his PH.

Hichens, William (xxxx–1944). Capt. William Hichens was assigned to the Intelligence and Administrative Section of British East Africa in the 1920s. He liked to hunt and often volunteered to do control work, shooting man-eating lion and leopard. In the course of his travels he developed an interest in what is now called cryptozoology, and collected stories of weird animals from the local inhabitants. He published some of these as reports in several magazines, some written under a pseudonym because of the secret nature of his military work.

Among the mystery creatures described by Hichens was the Ngoloko, a Bigfoot-like cryptid from Tanganyika; the Chemosit or Nandi bear; the Mngwa, a ferocious, giant man-eating feline said to terrorize southern Tanganyika; the Lau, a giant aquatic reptile said to be found in the swamps of the White Nile; the unpronounceable Isiququmadevu, another giant reptile from the waters of Barotseland; and the Mokele-mbembe, a creature that some have claimed is a remnant dinosaur hiding in the recesses of the Congo (Hichens theorized that it was a surviving chalicothere, a slothlike mammal that's been extinct for many thousands of years). Perhaps the most intriguing of Hichens's reports described the Agogwe, tiny, furry, manlike beings that Hichens claimed to have personally seen in the Simbithi forest.

Hichens reported that he had been hunting a marauding lion in the Simbithi, in central Tanganyika northeast of Tabora, and was sitting in a blind overlooking a forest glade. Suddenly two small creatures walked into the glade. They were about four feet tall, walked upright, and were covered in short red-brown fur. They walked through the opening and then disappeared into the bush. Hichens, who later searched the area in vain for another glimpse of the creatures, reported that the African scout with him was shaken and terrified by the encounter.

Hichens was the author of *On the Trail of the Brontosaurus: Encounters with Africa's Mystery Animals,* published under the pseudonym "Fulahn" in the 1 October 1927 edition of *Chamber's Journal*, and "African Mystery Beasts," published in the December 1937 issue of *Discovery* magazine. Any study of African cryptozoology must begin with Hichens and his fellow administrative official, C. W. Hobley.

Hildebrandt, Johann Maria (1807–1881). A German explorer and botanist who first came to Africa in 1872–1873, traveling through Somaliland. In 1875 he went on safari between Mombasa and Mount Kenya, and in 1879 he reached Madagascar, where he died two years later in the Ankaratra Mountains.

Hill, Clifford and Harold Hill. Clifford and Harold Hill were a pair of South African cousins who moved to Kenya in the early 1900s. They established a farm at Machakos and began to raise ostrich. This endeavor was greatly appreciated by the local lion, which took to raiding the Hill farm at such a rate that the cousins, out of economic necessity, soon became expert lion hunters. Both of them went on to kill nearly two hundred lion each during their lifetimes.

Word of their skill traveled far and wide, and the Hills began guiding others on lion hunts. One of those who approached them was the American Paul Rainey, who wanted to film a lion hunt with hounds. When the cousins refused his offer as too dangerous, Rainey hired Fritz Schindelar, with tragic results.

Maj. Clifford Hill went on to lead the East African Rifles in World War I.

Hillier, Nobby. Nobby Hillier hunted elephant as a teenager with Bill Finaughty in 1870. Finaughty called him a "greenhorn." Apprenticed to his uncle, a merchant skipper, Hillier had jumped ship at Cape Town and made his way north to the Transvaal. On his first chase Hillier almost ruined the hunt by falling off his horse five hundred yards from the nearest elephant. He got none in the ensuing affray, while Finaughty and two other hunters managed to kill eight of the beasts. His first rhino hunt went no better—he was knocked off his horse and butted around by his intended quarry.

Finaughty, not an affectionate man, seems to have liked the greenhorn. In his *Recollections of an Elephant Hunter* (1917) he remarked that despite all of Hillier's troubles, "It was astonishing, however, how quickly he picked up shooting." When Hillier finally managed to shoot a giraffe and a couple of sable, "There was no holding him after this. If he told me once how he did it he told me a dozen times." A careful read of Finaughty's book, however, doesn't show that Hillier ever managed to down an elephant.

Hilton-Simpson, Capt. Melville William (1887–1938). Captain Hilton-Simpson was a medical officer who specialized in tropical medicine and spent much of his career in North Africa, except for a period in the early 1900s when he was in the Congo with the Hungarian Emil Torday. He was a contributor to the Lonsdale Library volume *Big Game Shooting in Africa* (1932), and was eventually killed by an elephant in the Congo.

Captain Hilton-Simpson had an entry in the 1928 Rowland Ward record book for Lake Chad buffalo, an "owner-measured" bull with 25-inch horns taken from the Kwilu River district in the Belgian Congo. He also ranked with a 15-inch cow from the same area. The unique specimens were given subspecies status as *Syncerus nanus simpsoni.* This subspecies is not now generally recognized.

Hinde, Sydney L. (1863–1930). A medical doctor, Captain Hinde served in the Congo Free State and Kenya Colony. Another British official once referred to him as "rather of the Congo Belge type, a bit of a brute to natives" (Trench, 1993). He was the medical officer attached to the Congo Free State's military force under Commandant Dhanis, campaigning against the Arabs in 1891–1892. Harry Johnston (1908) wrote that Hinde was one of the heroes of the campaign.

Captain Hinde wrote a book about the campaign called *The Fall of the Congo Arabs* (1897) in which he was one of the first to mention Belgian atrocities inflicted on the inhabitants of the Congo. After being hired by the Congo government, Hinde had originally landed at Boma in 1891 and went to the Stanley Pool. He spent four months living at the pool, just hunting and exploring the countryside, before he was ordered to the Lualaba River, where he was assigned to an expedition being outfitted to explore toward Katanga. The column consisted of three hundred fifty regular soldiers, one Krupp cannon, and several hundred African porters.

En route to Katanga the column was attacked by slavers under the command of Tippu Tib's son, Sepu. The raiders were fought off, but at the cost of heavy losses. At that point in time a general revolt of the Muslim population along the Upper Congo broke out. The resulting campaign saw the destruction of the Arab slave trade in equatorial Africa.

In 1892–1893 Hinde set out to survey those areas of the Congo that had not been covered by Stanley or Joseph Thomson, thereby providing the first comprehensive map of the region. This meant months of hard travel along the Lualaba and Lukuga Rivers. In 1894 Hinde was joined in these explorations by the American Consul, a man named Mohun.

Moving east, Hinde was a member of the Kenya administration from 1895–1915, including subcommissioner from 1902–1907 and provincial commissioner 1907–1915. He served as the provincial commissioner of both Wakamba and Kenya provinces. In the 1928 edition of Rowland Ward, Hinde has the record male black rhino horn of 47 inches, taken in Kenya. Only Painter's 53½-inch female rhino beat him out at that time. A photograph of the horn is reproduced in the record book, which is not nearly as lavishly illustrated as later safari record books. Hinde also had other listings, such as hippo.

Hindlip, Lord Charles (1877–1931). Hindlip, originally named Frederic Ernest Allsop, was the author of *Sport and Travel: Abyssinia and East Africa* (1906). In 1902 he hunted for ten months in Ethiopia with William Whitehouse. ROWLAND WARD 1928: BUFFALO (46 INCHES, KENYA).

Hippel, Erich von. Professional hunter von Hippel was hired in 1939 by a commercial fishing interest to eradicate the crocodile population at Lake Kyoga in Uganda. A literate, intelligent man, von Hippel made careful scientific observations of the crocs he killed. For instance, he noted that 24 percent of his specimens had empty stomachs at the time of death. This kind of stuff is academic gold. Compare his 24 percent with the 14 percent empty stomachs found by Hugh Cott in Northern Rhodesia and the 48 percent reported by Alistair Graham and Peter Beard in Lake Turkana. Von Hippel published his findings in the 1946 *Uganda Journal* in an article entitled "Stomach Contents of Crocodiles."

Hiram. Hiram was a rich American sportsman who met up with Daly in Nairobi for some big-game hunting. They spent an enjoyable evening planning the safari over dinner and drinks, accompanied by Hiram's wife. Before they could meet up in the bush, however, Hiram went lion hunting with some friends. Daly blamed the resulting tragedy on the inexperience of the entire party—they quite simply, he believed, underestimated the beast. Hiram wounded a lion, which took to cover with a broken shoulder. It was decided that Hiram would approach and draw the lion out while other members of the party stood by and took photos. They got what they wanted, and provoked a charge. Hiram shot the lion with his heavy double-barrel rifle, but it wasn't enough. The animal had enough strength to complete the charge and killed the rich American before anyone else could shoot it off him.

Hobley, Charles William (1867–1947). A geologist for the East Africa Charter Company, Hobley arrived in Kenya in 1890. Joining the civil service, he was assigned to the wild frontier province of Kavirondo, holding the rank of sub-commissioner from 1902–1907 and provincial commissioner from 1917–1921. With Sir Frederick Jackson, he founded the East African and Uganda Natural History Society. Hobley was a member of Kenya's

Legislative Council from 1912–1920. In the 1930s he was semiretired as secretary of the Society for the Preservation of the Fauna of the Empire. Harry Johnston (1923) called him "one of the few really remarkable men I encountered in the administration of Uganda." Hobley had a listing in the 1928 Rowland Ward book for an elephant with tusks of 163 and 161 pounds.

Hobley was very interested in natural history and spent years gathering information about the flora and fauna of East Africa. One of his more interesting pursuits was an attempt to track down those elusive animals called cryptids. A cryptid (from cryptozoology) is a mystery animal, not conventionally known to exist. These can be mythical creatures like the Unicorn, persistent legends such as Bigfoot or the Loch Ness Monster, extinct animals that might still exist like the thylacine, or very real animals that are eventually discovered, such as the okapi. Sometimes animals move from one category to another, like the coelacanth, an ancient fish that was presumed extinct but turned up in a fisherman's net in the 1930s. A convention of cryptozoological writing requires that the name of a suspected cryptid that has not been officially discovered is capitalized ("Bigfoot"), but lower-case letters are used once the creature is proven to exist ("bigfoot").

In the early 1910s Hobley began soliciting accounts of cryptozoological experiences from hunters, settlers, and especially British district officers stationed in the remote parts of East Africa. The responses give an interesting glimpse of the shadow animals that populated the darkest regions of the Dark Continent, if only in local folklore or the writer's mind. Many of these letters were reprinted or at least summarized in Bernard Heuvelmans's classic *On the Track of Unknown Animals* (1959), the seminal work of cryptozoology.

The major cryptid of the region has been called the Nandi bear or Chemosit. Legends of a bearlike creature roaming East Africa have persisted since the beginning of European settlement. There are no bears in East Africa. (The Atlas bear became extinct in Morocco in 1870.) However, according to Daniel Mannix, a sensationalistic and popular writer of the 1950s, records of the ancient Romans indicate that they imported something called a "bear" from Africa for their famous circuses. The Roman animal catchers would find the bear's den and then provoke a charge after placing a net around the entrance.

Many of the sightings collected by Hobley concern the Nandi bear. The first of the reports reprinted by Heuvelmans was by a farmer on Kenya's Uasin Gishu plateau, Major Toulson. It described an animal that had been hanging around Toulson's kitchen. The second report was from N. E. F. Corbett, a district commissioner at Eldoret who had helped with the Roosevelt safari in 1909. In a letter dated March 1913, Corbett told of a strange animal, slightly larger than a hyena, that he spotted near the banks of the Sirgoi River. Corbett regretted not having his rifle with him—he had been hunting in the same spot just a half-hour prior. Heuvelmans dismissed both Toulson's and Corbett's reports as being a misidentified ratel or honey badger, and stressed that Corbett was nearsighted and not wearing his eyeglasses (Corbett wrote "The place was overgrown and I was without my specs so could not get a very good view, but I am certain that it was a beast I have never seen before"). The sighting was in the brightness of midday, a half-hour past noon.

Heuvelmans next cited letters to Hobley from a man named Schindler, who drew a picture of strange tracks he had found, and one Hickes, who on 8 March 1913 saw a bearlike animal near the Magadi Railway. Hickes's report is interesting because he mentioned that several other settlers had seen the same mystery creature in that district. He was carrying a .350 Rigby at the time of the sighting but unfortunately did not get a shot off, which would have settled the matter. Hobley also received a description from a Mr. Rule of a six-foot-long sheep-killing animal that had been harassing the flocks of the Pokomo tribe. It was fierce—one of the Pokomo reports even alleged that this animal had killed a rhino.

Hobley was unable to track down the Nandi bear, and even Heuvelmans, writing nearly fifty years later, was unable to come to any firm conclusions except that at least some of the sightings were actually of honey badgers or possibly hyena. This latter possibility acquired some credibility when a strange skull and skin were discovered in Uganda in the late 1920s. Naturalists were hesitant to classify the animal, and some felt it might be the remains of a cryptid called the Ntarago, supposedly an animal resembling a cross between a leopard and a lion (large leopard and small lionesses have been successfully interbred in captivity). This controversy had its day but was put to bed when District Commissioner E. A. Temple-Perkins concluded that the remains were a hoax, the intentional combination of a leopard skull and a large hyena skin.

Although hoaxes are all too prevalent in cryptozoology, that does not necessarily mean that strange animals don't exist. Many African tribes certainly believed so: Uganda game warden Pitman wrote, "Anyone who has lived in a

Nandi bear atmosphere cannot doubt the reality of the dread the brute inspires." The Nandi bear was only one of many mysterious creatures. Hobley cited several accounts—including reports by Sir Clement Hill and Provincial Commissioner W. Grant—of an aquatic cryptid inhabiting Lake Victoria.

Besides Hobley's correspondents, many big-game hunters reported seeing unknown animals in Africa's trackless wilderness. John Alfred Jordan claimed to have seen a fifteen-foot aquatic animal with scales, spots, two long fangs, and a long, broad tail. Foran and Alex Johnston, Sir Harry's brother, each reported seeing a sort of sea serpent on Lake Victoria in separate incidents. Owen Letcher collected numerous reports of an amphibious animal resembling a horned hippo from Rhodesia in the early 1900s, and Harry Wolhuter of Kruger National Park similarly recorded tales of a 100-foot-long mystery snake called the Muhlambela. Both Bill Buckley, the first elephant hunter to operate in the Lado Enclave, and William Hichens, a magistrate in Tanganyika, reported seeing strange beings that resembled a cross between an ape and a man. Hichens also told of a vicious predator called the Mngwa, a huge beast said to look like a giant furry lion that terrorized remote villagers in the Tanganyikan forests.

Perhaps most tantalizing, the Hungarian naturalist Kalman Kittenberger, who hunted for years in the remotest reaches of Uganda and Central Africa, touched on the subject of cryptozoology in his *Big Game Hunting and Collecting in East Africa.* After mentioning the standard cryptids like the Nandi bear and a "water elephant," he wrote, "Once in the vicinity of Disappointment Camp on the Ngare Dowash I saw something just for an instant, which often returns to my memory, and I would give anything if I could get some certainty about what I saw there! And then?"

Hobley was the author of *Bantu Beliefs and Magic* (1922).

Hodister, Arthur (xxxx–1892). Arthur Hodister was an intriguing figure in the early history of the Congo Free State, and one of the main inspirations for Conrad's *Heart of Darkness* villain, Major Kurtz.

By 1892 Hodister had been roaming the Congo for several years trading for ivory, often with only a small entourage for protection. He was friendly, bluff, and weird, and strangers invariably fell under his charm. His policy was to encourage the local Arabs of the north Congo hinterlands to collect ivory for trade—a system that has been called the "forward strategy" of ivory trading. He ran into conflict with King Leopold, who mistrusted him and who wanted to keep the remote parts of the Congo off-limits as a sort of reserve to be exploited by the Belgian government in the future. When Hodister went on a major trading trip early in 1892 with a party of eighteen Europeans and several hundred porters, Leopold went so far as to assign an official spy, Lieutenant Michiels, to accompany Hodister and report back on his progress.

Hodister split the caravan in two. He led one half along the Lomami River, and the other took a parallel course some two hundred miles to the east. Michiels was assigned to the second group. The Arabs in the region were in an ugly mood, having recently suffered large losses at the hands of the Belgian explorer van Kerckhoven. They warned both Hodister and Noblesse, the leader of the column Michiels was in, not to try to establish any trading posts and to leave the area as quickly as possible. The Arabs were led by a famous ivory trader named Mohara and his chief aide, Nserara.

Nserara warned Noblesse and Michiels one last time not to raise the Free State flag in their territory. Michiels defied him, saying he could raise an army of one thousand riflemen to defend that flag. It quickly became apparent that Nserara was not a man to threaten. On the morning of 10 May 1892, at a place called Riba Riba, Nserara had Noblesse flogged to death. Lieutenant Michiels fled into the jungle but was caught two weeks later and suffered the same fate. The story spread among the Belgians that the bodies of both men had been butchered and eaten.

Hodister, unaware of this turn of events, had left his column with just three companions and was riding on horseback to Riba Riba to try to calm things down. Meeting a party of Arabs on 15 May, he dismounted to greet them. In his years in Africa Hodister had charmed the natives time and again, but no personality was going to win this party over. Hodister was cut down and beheaded before he knew what was happening, as were his three friends. Allegedly these four men were eaten too.

The rest of the Hodister safari simply melted away. In small groups they struggled to avoid the Arabs and make their way back down the Lualaba River to the security of the Belgian forts. Several of the Europeans died of fever or committed suicide.

The murders of Hodister, Noblesse, and Michiels marked the beginning of the Arab-Belgian war that solidified Leopold's hold on the Congo.

Hodson, Sir Arnold Weinholt (1881–1944). Born in England, Arnold Hodson took an early interest in shooting and hunting. In 1900 he traveled to Australia where he worked as a shepherd, and later that year he enlisted with the 7th Australia Commonwealth Horse, arriving in South Africa just in time for peace to break out in 1902. After the unit was disbanded, Hodson stayed in Africa, taking odd jobs in Durban and Pretoria. He became a subinspector with the Bechuanaland Protectorate Police in 1904, and an assistant resident magistrate for western Bechuanaland in 1905.

He did well in his new posts, patrolling the borders, collecting taxes, levying fines, and doing general police work. He had several special assignments, such as escorting Resident Commissioner Ralph Williams in 1906 on a sort of "farewell" tour. This period of Hodson's life was described in his popular book, *Trekking the Great Thirst,* which was published in Britain in 1912. The book is a fascinating account of hunting and travel in the Kalahari Desert and is illustrated by excellent photographs for its time.

In 1912 Hodson was transferred as a district commissioner to Somaliland, and in 1914 he took a consul's job in Ethiopia. In 1926 he became governor of the Falkland Islands and in 1930 governor of Sierra Leone. He was made Sir Arnold Hodson in 1932 and followed that with the position of governor of the Gold Coast from 1934 to 1941. Negley Farson interviewed Hodson for his 1941 book *Behind God's Back* and praised him very highly—Farson compared Hodson to Mahatma Gandhi for intelligence and stimulating conversation.

Hodson was an exceptional man, possessing talents and gifts in greater abundance than most colonial officials, who on the whole were a pretty impressive lot. His outstanding characteristics were integrity and courage—not flashy bravado but a quiet resolve to do what's right.

A story told by Wilfred Thesiger is typical of the man. As a boy, Thesiger was a student at Saint Aubyns, a boarding school near Brighton. Hodson, who had served with Thesiger's father in Abyssinia, was a family friend and would sometimes visit the boy. On one such occasion he was discussing school with young Thesiger and made an offhand remark, "I don't suppose you get beaten at school nowadays, not like we were in my time." Wilfred loosened his clothes and showed Hodson some half-healed scars, inflicted by a sadistic schoolmaster as punishment for a trivial offense. His brother had similar marks.

Hodson thereupon took it upon himself to drop in on the headmaster at Saint Aubyns. He confronted the man with the knowledge of his brutality, and sternly warned him that if he touched either boy again he would go to the police and have him prosecuted. The beatings stopped, but what is perhaps most telling about the matter is that Hodson didn't make a big deal about his intervention; in fact, it was many years before Thesiger even knew about it. He didn't want credit, he didn't want gratitude, he simply wanted to prevent an injustice, and he achieved his goal as usual in his quiet but effective way.

In addition to his Kalahari classic, Hodson was the author of *Seven Years in Southern Abyssinia* (1927) and *Where Lion Reign* (1929). He also wrote a grammar of the Galla tribes. Hodson married Elizabeth Hay in 1929, and they had two daughters, Jean (born 1930) and Elizabeth (born 1934). He died in New York City in 1944.

Hoefler, Paul (1893–1982). Hoefler led an extensive motorized safari through Kenya, Uganda, Tanganyika, the Sudan, the Congo, and Nigeria in the late 1920s. The ensuing book and film, both titled *Africa Speaks,* were very successful.

Hoehnel, Ludwig von (1856–1942). Von Hoehnel was an officer of the Austro-Hungarian Imperial Navy who accompanied Count Teleki on his historic Lake Rudolf safari, and later went with the American Chanler. Von Hoehnel was the author of *Discovery by Count Teleki of Lakes Rudolf and Stephanie* (1894). Von Hoehnel's private papers were destroyed by the Nazis after his death. His wife, Valeska von Hoehnel, died in 1947. For details of his career see the entries on Teleki and Chanler.

Hoey, Arthur Cecil (1883–xxxx). Born in England, Hoey explored the Uasin Gishu plateau in 1904. He established a farm in the bush, with the Wandorobo as his neighbors. He was one of the first professional white hunters, working for Newland and Tarlton and, later, Safariland. In 1908 Hoey and Bill Judd guided the American writer and preacher W. S. Rainsford on a long safari that ended with Judd's gunbearer being badly mauled by a wounded lion.

Hoey had a reputation as a "lion man," being involved in early experiments in hunting lion on horseback and killing many others on foot. In 1908 he guided American W. S. Rainsford on a lion hunt. His favorite weapon was a .450 double rifle. For a lion man, he was a pretty good elephant hunter too, taking one bull with tusks of 131 and 128 pounds per side.

Hoey's address in the 1930 *East African Red Book* is given as simply Hoey's Bridge, Kenya. He is listed as the justice of the peace for Uasin Gishu. ROWLAND WARD 1928: LEOPARD.

Hoier. Colonel Hoier was chief game warden, Albert National Park, 1939. See entry for Commandant Hubert.

Holmberg, Emil. An early Kenya settler, Holmberg and his wife Olga (died 1962) owned a farm in Thika. Along with fellow Swedish immigrants Bror Blixen, Erik von Otter, Helge Fagerskold, Ture Rundgren, and Nils Fjastad, Holmberg served with the British forces in World War I. He later was a founder of the Selby and Holmberg Safari Company. He was the father of professional hunter Andrew Holmberg.

Holub, Emil (1847–1902). A Czech surgeon, Dr. Holub opened up a practice by the Kimberley mines in 1872. He visited Victoria Falls with George Westbeech as early as 1875 and produced the first good map of the region, published in his book *Seven Years in South Africa* (1880).

His next major safari took place in the Lake Nyasa and Shire River districts, ending in 1879. In 1883 he embarked on a proposed "Cape to Cairo" expedition accompanied by his wife Rosa and a few friends. Setting a leisurely pace and exploring much of south-central Africa as they went, the group crossed the Zambezi in June 1886. They lost a few men and much of their cattle to illness but continued on, heading into the territory of the Ila people. There they were attacked, losing all of their goods and the life of one of the Europeans. Holub led them back south across the Zambezi in August of 1886, and, with the help of Francois Coillard, they struggled home. Holub died of malaria in Vienna in 1902. Rosa survived until 1958, when she passed away at the age of ninety.

Honeybone, Pat. The area east of the town of Keetmanshoop in southern Namibia boasts one of Africa's more intriguing cryptids. In the early 1940s several sightings, mostly by Ovambo shepherds, were reported of a huge carnivorous snake that could roll itself into a ball and also fly. The reptile (known as the Keetmanshoop Flying Snake) was said to be as thick as a man's thigh and more than twenty feet long, and could leap or fly at least fifteen feet into the air.

The most detailed sightings were by a sixteen-year-old farm boy named Michael Esterhuise, who on three occasions in 1942 saw the reptile hanging around a particular kopje (rock outcropping). He described the snake as having fins along the side of its head. On the third occasion the boy allegedly was actually attacked by the creature, which rolled itself into a ball, hurled itself at him, and tried to lash out at him with its tail. The boy fled and was later found by his father hiding in a patch of brush.

Police officer Pat Honeybone led a posse formed to hunt the snake. Although they found numerous tracks, animal bones, and other traces of the animal, the creature eluded discovery and reportedly has never been seen again.

Hook, Raymond (xxxx–1968). Raymond Hook originally came to Kenya in 1912 with his father, a painter named Bryan Hook, who relocated that year to a farm at Nanyuki. Raymond fought in World War I and afterward established a name for himself collecting animals for zoos. He had a great deal of success catching cheetah and selling them to British game parks and Indian maharajahs. He also conducted experiments in crossbreeding, successfully mating zebras with horses ("zebroids") but failing in his attempts to breed cattle with buffalo. As a professional hunter Hook specialized in mountain safaris around Mount Kenya.

Raymond Hook had a brother named Commander Logan Hook, formerly of the Royal Navy. Commander Hook owned the Silverbeck Hotel in Nanyuki and was known, inevitably, as Boat Hook. In the 1930 *East African Red Book* an advertisement for the hotel extols Nanyuki's virtues: "Unrivalled climate, dry and bracing . . . no fog, fever or insect pests . . . Elephant, rhino, giraffe, buffalo, hippo, lion, leopard, lynx, cheetah, serval cat, koodoo, Grant and Thompson gazelle, eland, oryx (beisa), waterbuck, reedbuck, bushbuck, bongo, kongoni, klipspringer, gerenuk, impala, colobus, etc., etc., within easy reach. Also bustard, pigeon, spur fowl, guinea fowl and quail. Good trout fishing close-by. Rainbow and brown up to six pounds. Baskets of fifty in an afternoon . . . Electric light, medical practitioner in close call. Chrysler and Chevrolet spares."

The writer John Pollard authored two books about Raymond Hook's career as a hunter. They are *Adventure Begins in Kenya* (1957) and *African Zoo Man* (1963).

Hop, Hendrick. Capt. Henrdrick Hop was an early Boer elephant hunter and explorer. He commanded a large and well-equipped expedition of seventeen Europeans, sixty-eight Africans, and fifteen wagons over the Orange River into Namaqualand in 1761–1762. The expedition was an official one, sent out under the auspices of the Cape government, and its journal was published in Amsterdam in 1778.

Hope, J. O. W. Hope was an administrative officer in Kenya, 1899–1928. He was DC in Kiambu near Nairobi around

1910, and a provincial commissioner in Kenya, 1921–1926. In 1903 he was an acting provincial commissioner (then called sub-commissioner) when the young Lord Delamere applied to him for assignment as a game warden. Hope rejected the application due to Delamere's reputation as a wild, ungovernable youth. Harry Johnston, discussing the matter in a letter to a friend in the Foreign Office, wrote, "Hope won't make Delamere a game ranger as he will make himself a confounded nuisance in any capacity. I wouldn't trust him. He and that other blackguard Dr. Atkinson are thick as thieves" (Trzebinski, 1985).

While stationed at Kiambu, Hope accompanied Robert Foran and District Officer H. R. McClure on a hunt in which Foran narrowly missed bagging a rare black leopard. The leopard was trapped alive a few days later by settler Hugh Heatley and went on to a thriving career at the London zoo.

Hopkins, J. G. Hopkins was a member of the Kenya administration from 1917–1938 and district commissioner of Embu in 1930. Chenevix Trench (himself a DC) called him (1993) a "good DC of the practical sort—not given to anthropological theorizing, but sound on roads, buildings, taxation, law and order; and respected by the tribesmen, who liked a character." Something of a loose cannon, Hopkins was very much into elephant hunting for a profit. The ivory of elephant that he shot on control in his own district belonged to the government, so he frequently took out licenses (signing them himself) to hunt elephant in neighboring districts.

The need to get a dead elephant on the profitable side of the boundary line caused him once to move a guidepost identifying the border between his own district, Meru, and the neighboring district of Samburu. In order for him to own the ivory it was necessary that the carcass be found in Samburu territory, and it was easier to move the marker than the elephant. This one act led to thirty years of dispute over where the proper boundary lay. Hopkins later was provincial commissioner of the Rift Valley. ROWLAND WARD 1928: ELEPHANT (165 AND 145 POUNDS, KENYA).

Horne, Edward B. Ted Horne was an administrative officer in Kenya, 1904–1934, and served as district commissioner in Meru, Kenya, as well as being a well-known amateur hunter. He hunted with the Roosevelt safari in 1909. He was appointed to the post of senior commissioner in 1924. Horne was the younger brother of District Commissioner H. H. Horne, known as "Long" Horne, and was therefore known as "Short" Horne. ROWLAND WARD 1928: PATTERSON ELAND, BLACK RHINO, BUFFALO.

Horne, H. H. Known as "Long" Horne, H. H. Horne was a Boer war veteran who had previously been vice consul in Mexico and a rancher in Wyoming. He was an administrative officer in Kenya from 1903 to 1927. Horne served as district commissioner at Karungu on Lake Victoria in 1904, district commissioner for Rumuruti in 1905, and later was district commissioner at Lamu.

Hotchkiss. A man by this name hunted professionally in Portuguese East Africa before World War I, providing buffalo meat for the Beira railway teams. He later opened a trading post in the Transvaal, which failed, and was last heard of hunting in Rhodesia.

Howard, Percy S. (xxxx–1890). British hunter who was killed by a Cape buffalo along the Lundi River in Mashonaland, 29 December 1890.

Hubbard, Wynant D. (1900–1961). Hubbard was a Harvard University student (born in Kansas City, Missouri) who nursed a yearning for adventure by training as a geologist and miner. From 1917–1919 he worked as a jack-of-all-trades at a mission in Labrador, exploring the wild inland rivers of that territory in his spare time. He then worked as a silver miner in Ontario and as an asbestos miner in Quebec, where he apparently had a wild time, somehow managing to get himself excommunicated from the Roman Catholic Church despite the considerable handicap of not being Catholic.

In 1922 he took his wife Carson Hubbard and infant children (the oldest boy drowned at age four on a trip to Provincetown in 1925) to Africa, where at first he worked at the Pretoria Zoo. Despite his inexperience, he convinced the zoo officials to send him to Rhodesia and Portuguese East Africa to collect young animals for display.

Hubbard wrote a book about this job, which lasted from 1922 to 1925. In September 1923 he joined up with the experienced Walker brothers of Southern Rhodesia who taught him the rudiments of elephant hunting and animal capture. When Rhodesia banned live collecting in early 1924, Hubbard and the Walkers moved their operations to Portuguese East Africa. Hubbard told the story of this venture in his 1926 book *Wild Animals* (rather boastfully subtitled *A White Man's Conquest of Jungle Beasts).* Well-illustrated with over forty photographs, the book is a fairly interesting account of a young American learning to function as an African outdoorsman. The bombast of the subtitle is offset by some of the chapter headings: "I Try to Catch a Hippo in the Kafue River" is something of a record for modesty in a hunting book.

Hubbard was also the author of *Ibamba* (1958) and *Wild Animal Hunter* (1958). He died in Miami, Florida. His 1933 film *Untamed Africa* has been digitally remastered and is shown occasionally on cable television. It's better than the Frank Buck movies, but still dated in its portrayal of Africans and in its overall concepts.

Hubert. Hubert, also known as Huberta, was one of the few vegetarians that earned a listing in this book. Hubert was a famous hippo, if you can believe that, which in the early 1930s wandered into parts of South Africa where hippo hadn't been seen in a century. Newspapers daily charted his progress, which was peaceful. Hubert tolerated people well and had a special fondness for munching expensive garden flowers. Hubert calmly and happily grazed in city parks and flowerbeds, and peacefully plodded along well-traveled waterways. He left Saint Lucia in Zululand in 1928 and wandered for three years through Natal and Cape Province, walking over a thousand miles before some dastard shot him in April 1931. Only then was it discovered that Hubert should properly have been called Huberta. The hiking hippo, which allegedly had caused several observers to swear off the bottle, was the subject of *Huberta Goes South* by Hedley A. Chilvers (1931).

In May 1931 a farmer, his two sons, and a family friend were arrested and confessed to shooting Huberta. The farmer, who was illiterate and thus able to claim that he had never heard of the celebrity animal, said that he and his friend were investigating giant footprints in his vegetable garden when the friend saw the hippo in a nearby river and shot it. The four men were sentenced to a £25 fine or three months in jail for killing royal game.

Hubert, L. E. Commander Hubert was a Belgian game warden in Ruindi Camp in 1939 who appeared with his compatriot, Colonel Hoier, in several hunting-and-travel books, including Riddell's *In the Forests of the Night* (1946) and Farson's *Behind God's Back* (1941). Contrary to the dark days of King Leopold and the Congo Free State, the Belgian administration of the Congo and Rwanda in the 1930s had the reputation of being enlightened and progressive. This viewpoint applied both to the civil administration and the game department. In the civil administration, for example, district commissioners were allowed to stay in the headquarters town of the district only ten days each month; the remainder of the month they had to be on the road somewhere else in the district. On the wildlife end, Belgium had very strict game laws in place at the time. Several hunters, including Attilio Gatti (an Italian who had a permit to collect precisely one gorilla specimen for the Florence Museum), were warned of dire consequences should they kill an unauthorized animal, even in self-defense. Gatti claimed in *The King of the Gorillas* (1932) that he'd had to wound a female gorilla in the hand in order to deter an attack. If his story was true, he was very lucky indeed that the gorilla wasn't fatally injured. Jail time for such an offense was not out of the question, even for a European, and he would invariably have received at least a heavy fine and been deported.

Hubert and Hoier were depicted as amiable, somewhat eccentric gents who would sooner chase crop-raiding elephant away with a shout than use the English method, which was to shoot them. Hubert in particular had a knack for reading the body language of animals and could take great liberties with them. He once brought writer Negley Farson and Farson's wife Eve up uncomfortably close to a lion in the knowledge that the lion had eaten and was more interested in napping than attacking. On the same trip Hubert guided Farson to within a few yards of a hippo so the latter could snap a photograph, and then chased the startled hippo off by bouncing a well-aimed chunk of clay off its head.

In the 1930s and 1940s Commander Hubert did an exhaustive survey of wildlife densities in Albert National Park and published some interesting figures. According to him, the district contained 1 lion to every 3–5 square kilometers; 3 buffalo per 2 square kilometers; 3 hippo to every square kilometer; 1 warthog per 6 square kilometers; 1 elephant per 8 square kilometers; 1 waterbuck, 12 topi, and 24 kob per square kilometer; 1 hyena per 4 square kilometers; and 1 leopard per 12 square kilometers. He was the author of *La Faune des Grands Mammiferes de la Plaine Ruindi–Rutshutu* (1947).

Hudson, Lee. Hudson was an American safari client who traveled to Kenya in 1931. On the night of 13 May he and John Hunter, his professional, stayed as guests of the district commissioner at Voi. Other guests included a family of four named Layzell and Denys Finch Hatton. The following morning Finch Hatton offered to take Mrs. Margaret Layzell up in his Gypsy Moth aircraft, but her little daughter Katharine unaccountably made a scene and begged her not to go. Finch Hatton shrugged and said "Another time" and took off with only his Kikuyu assistant Kamau on board. As the plane gained height, the engine seemed to stall and the small aircraft plummeted to the ground. Finch Hatton and Kamau were both killed. Hudson and Hunter delayed the start of their safari to bring the remains back to Nairobi.

Hughes, J. E. A settler and elephant hunter in Northern Rhodesia in the early 1900s, Hughes was the author of *Eighteen Years on Lake Bangweulu* (1933). ROWLAND WARD 1928: LION, ELAND, PUKU (NO. 6).

Human, Chris. Human was an elephant hunter in Portuguese East Africa in the early 1900s, and is featured by Peter Rainier in *My Vanished Africa* (1940). Human got his apprenticeship as a hunter by working with Fred Selous. As a young man he tried his hand at cattle ranching, but after East Coast Fever killed off most of his herd he took to professional hunting, shooting several hundred elephant in the course of his career.

Human owned a roadhouse in Massakessi in the years before World War I. He was married to a former Austrian actress, described by Rainier as "a shapeless mess of an old woman."

Hume, David (1796–1863). An early ivory trader based at Grahamstown, Hume made many trips into the interior, including Mashonaland and Matabeleland, in the 1830s. Hume's son, also named David, once in 1869 persuaded Bill Finaughty to guide him on an elephant hunt. Finaughty reluctantly agreed, but the boy made too much noise and spooked the elephant. The psychotic Finaughty "promptly lost a little bit of my temper" (1916), which must have been a sight to see. After Finaughty yelled at them, they went giraffe hunting instead.

Hunt, A. T. As a young man in the mid-1890s, Royal Navy Lt. A. T. "Mike" Hunt commanded a gunboat on the Zambezi River in British Central Africa. According to Maugham in *Africa As I Have Known It* (1929), Hunt was out hunting for the pot with a Lee-Metford service rifle near Chiromo in 1894 when he spied a lioness peering at him around the side of an anthill. Hunt fired and the lioness dropped. A second later, however, the lioness's head reappeared, still peeking around the corner. He fired again, and the same thing happened. And again and again. Hunt fired a total of five times (he was using softnose bullets), and each time the lioness's head reappeared. Finally Hunt maneuvered his way past the anthill and saw, to his surprise, five dead young lion. It seems that each time he fired and killed one of the young, virtually maneless, lion, another from the curious pride would take its place and look around the fatal corner.

Variations of this tale are told about several different hunters in different times and places. The victims are sometimes lion and sometimes elephant. It's not out of the question that something like this happened more than once. Maugham's version seems the most authoritative.

Lieutenant Hunt later went on to become a vice admiral of the Royal Navy. He had a listing in the 1928 edition of *Rowland Ward's Records of Big Game* for a trophy hippo, shot in the Shire River, with "malformed" tusks of over 37 inches.

Hunter, John Alexander (1887–1963). From his early days as an undisciplined rogue to his elderly role as ancient adventurer with a twinkle in his eye, John A. Hunter (known variously as Jack, John A., or, most commonly, J. A.) arrived in East Africa at a tender age in 1905, after having disgraced his godly Scottish family by having an affair with an older divorcee. His father wasted no time in emotional farewells but instead sent him off with a practical parting gift, a fine Purdey shotgun. Young Jack spent his first few months in British East Africa working on his parsimonious cousin's farm. Tiring of that, he got a job as a train guard on the Uganda railway. These were still the days when an attack by primitive spearmen was a distinct possibility. Hunter would sit atop the coal car or lean out a window with a .275 army rifle and shoot plains game for the pot, as well as lion and leopard. He worked out a scheme whereby the engineer would whistle twice for a lion and thrice for a leopard. Lion skins were selling at £1 apiece, and the two men split the profit. The living was good.

At this time in Kenya the hunting industry was just beginning. Hunter got onboard early, leading two American clients on the first-ever safari to Ngorongoro Crater. The two American hunters were highly competitive, and when they missed a shot at a record impala, killing its neighbor instead, they suggested that Hunter stretch the horns to record size by steaming them. Hunter disdainfully refused, and the Americans, once their competitive juices had cooled, eventually admitted he was proper to do so.

Hunter went on to become one of the foremost safari hunters operating in East Africa. He was a crack professional and also a respected raconteur, equally at home with gun and bottle. As an honorary game warden, he frequently took commissions from the game department. One of these commissions was the notorious Makueni rhino hunt (see below) of the 1940s, an affair that unjustly left Hunter's reputation somewhat sullied in the eyes of later readers.

At the request of the Masai, Hunter was once sent to thin out the predators that were raiding the tribe's cattle herds. In three months he killed eighty-eight lion (another source says ninety-eight) and ten leopard. The Masai were so pleased with these results, the story goes, that they offered to buy Hunter from the game department for five hundred cows—as much as it would cost to purchase several dozen wives. The game department, possibly reluctantly, declined the offer. All in all, Hunter shot about sixteen hundred rhino and more than a thousand elephant in his career. He was still doing control work for the game department in the late 1950s.

In 1930 his mailing address was Post Office Box 525, Nairobi. Hunter and his wife Hilda had four sons and two daughters. He recalled in his 1957 *Hunter's Tracks* that because of his profession as a hunter, he was on hand at only three of the births. When his son Dennis was born in 1925 he was on a "grand elephant shoot." When David was born in 1927 he was hunting a particular killer elephant with Sidney Waller, and when little Sheila Hunter came into this world in 1923 her father didn't return from safari until she was nearly a week old. Many of those who lived off their guns in the old Africa came to regret the inevitable separations from their family.

Hunter wrote several books, *White Hunter* (1935), *Hunter* (1952), *Tales of the African Frontier* (1954), and *Hunter's Tracks* (1957). The first book is a straightforward account of Hunter's days as a PH. The second book was a colossal seller and made Hunter's name familiar to generations of British and American readers. It is truly essential reading for fans of the genre.

Unfortunately, he couldn't keep it up. It is all too apparent that by the time the third book came out, Hunter was under a lot of pressure to repeat the success of his earlier work. The writing of *Hunter's Tracks* (in which he was assisted by Alan Wykes, who did a similar book with Ionides) shows signs of embellishment, and some of the exploits recounted there are frankly unbelievable. Built around the device of a hunt for a fugitive poacher, every other segment or so is a tangential account of some exploit, often far-fetched and lacking the raw taste of realism present in Hunter's earlier stuff. It is easy to imagine Wykes urging Hunter to please the publisher by adding more "color" to the stories. The result is a substandard book that cannot be relied upon as a work of nonfiction.

John A. Hunter returning from safari.

Interestingly, few if any safari writers have come right out and challenged Hunter's veracity (he was an extremely likable, avuncular old scoundrel who no doubt would have winked and offered you a shot of whiskey if you stopped by, but also a tough old bastard you might not want to anger). On the other hand, you never see any of the stories in *Hunter's Tracks* repeated in other works. Guggisberg, for instance, cites dozens if not hundreds of croc anecdotes in his *Crocodiles* (1972), and even ridicules some of the more outrageous tales (by Alexander Lake, for instance), but never mentions Hunter, who told a few incredible croc stories in his third book. Even Peter Capstick, in his collection of animal-attack stories, shied away from the unlikely parts of *Hunter's Tracks.* It's as if nobody ever wanted to hurt the old guy's feelings—or tick him off.

It must be stated that Hunter's fourth book, *Tales of the African Frontier,* is again an excellent book and nearly as well written as *Hunter.* It contains short biographies of early East African hunters, settlers, poachers and other sundry characters.

No description of J. A. Hunter's career would be complete without a mention of the Makueni rhino. The "Great Makueni Rhino Hunt" has attracted negative attention ever since Hunter wrote about it in his autobiography, *Hunter,* in 1952. The bare facts are simple. In the 1940s Kenya authorities wanted to clear fifty thousand acres of bush at Makueni in the Kamba Reserve to clear away the tsetse fly and make the land available for African farming. However, the bush was full of rhino that made the clearing job extremely hazardous. Under the supervision of David Christie-Miller, J. A. Hunter was brought in to eradicate the rhino. As it turned out, there were an awful lot more of them than anyone had thought: 1,078, all duly shot and recorded by Hunter. The project tarnished Hunter's career in the eyes of many, perhaps unfairly. Dozens of conservation books have brought up Makueni, generally not mentioning Christie-Miller but excoriating Hunter. Peter Beard's excellent *The End of the Game* creates an emotive and eerie effect simply by reproducing Hunter's diary showing the daily numbers of rhino kills.

As always, the reality is a bit more complex than the popular legend. First, J. A. Hunter was obviously just doing his job (after all, he was a professional hunter engaged in control work with the game department), and the blame, if any, for the affair should be attached to the desk-bound bureaucrats who made the decision to clear the district. Second, the animals were dangerous—they were so numerous and aggressive that the local workers purposely wore no shoes, so they could scamper up trees faster when charged. Third, far bloodier and larger-scale schemes—such as the annual slaughters in the name of tsetse control—were taking place throughout the continent without any protest and with little or no scientific justification. In 1952–1962, for example, 60,000 antelope in Uganda were shot in the name of tsetse control, and in the 1920s the government of Natal shot over 500,000 animals. It has been estimated that between 1932–1959 more than 550,000 large mammals were destroyed in Rhodesia due to the senseless program, yet there was little public outcry and this slaughter is almost never mentioned in the books that wax poetic over Makueni. Fourth, and most important, the plan (judged necessary by the government) worked. Makueni was no "groundnut scheme" (see glossary) like the Tanganyika fiasco of about the same time period. The land inhabited by the rhino was choice farmland right smack in the middle of the poor, hungry, overpopulated Kamba Reserve. By 1962 there were 2,187 families who had settled into productive farms in the former Makueni bush.

Many well-intentioned and well-fed Westerners are doubtless still horrified at the Makueni rhino hunt as they sit in their homes built on land that was once habitat for cougars and grizzly bears. The Makueni affair was unfortunate, but infinitely less so than the extermination of the millions of animals in the great bison herds to make way for the Americans on the Great Plains. You just can't condemn things like this until you solve the eternal dilemma that ultimately is behind every wildlife problem—competition for space between man and beast.

Hurst, George (xxxx–1923). A professional hunter from Arusha, Hurst hoped to obtain the lease rights to Ngorongoro Crater after World War I, made available when the British government confiscated all German property in Tanganyika. He squatted for a year on property formerly owned by the Siedentopf brothers, and estimated the herds of zebra and wildebeest in the crater at some fifty thousand animals. His efforts were in vain, however, for the Enemy Property Commission finally sold a ninety-nine-year lease to Sir Charles Ross.

Hurst guided the American taxidermist James L. Clark on several of his collecting hunts, and was with Kenyon Painter when the latter shot the world-record rhino. He was later killed by an elephant near Dar es Salaam in 1923.

Hurt, Roger. Colonel Hurt was a Kenya game warden in the coastal district, where he specialized in elephant control. A Sandhurst graduate and a WWII veteran of the KAR (see glossary), Hurt was the father of professional hunter Robin Hurt.

Hutchinson, Horatio Gordon (1859–1932). British golfer, author, and sportsman. The old British class system produced a group of men who were wealthy enough not to have to work and were not required to do anything for society. Basically they had their social obligations to worry about and that was it.

Horatio Gordon Hutchinson was one of that class. From an early age this son of a major-general could devote himself to playing golf and other sports. He was a sickly boy and had to leave school frequently for health reasons, but he was a smart kid as well and dabbled at law studies and sculpting before settling down to the less strenuous sports and to writing books. He excelled at golf and billiards while attending Oxford, and in 1886 published his first book, *Hints on Playing Golf.*

He wrote most of the volume on golf in the Badminton Sporting Library and in the 1890s produced a number of sporting books as well as popular novels with sports themes, for instance Peter Steele, *The Cricketer* (1895), and Bert Edward, *The Gold Caddie* (1903). He helped popularize golf in the United States as well.

Hutchinson wrote numerous articles and essays on natural history and hunting, and was the author of the 1905 book *Big Game Shooting*. On one hunt in Kenya he wounded a big bull elephant that escaped into the bush, wounded in the head. Hutchinson followed the spoor for three days, and suddenly the hulk burst upon him at close range. He got two shots off from his .450, both hitting the elephant in the head (this thing must have had one massive headache), but failed to stop the charge. The elephant grabbed the hunter with its trunk and swung him around like a doll, then threw him on the ground and knelt to tusk him. As the bull closed in, Hutchinson managed to dodge under its front legs, and somehow wrapped his arms around a hind leg. Once again the elephant got Hutchinson with its trunk and once again slammed him to the ground. At this point Captain Hutchinson lost consciousness. Fortunately for him, one of his African staff members now hurled a spear into the bull. Forgetting Hutchinson, the bull chased the African for a bit and then stumbled off into the underbrush. It was found dead three miles away. Hutchinson was laid up for six months.

Always prone to illness, Hutchinson spent the years after 1914 as a semi-invalid at his home at Forest Row in Sussex. When his last illness began in 1932, he had himself moved to London, where he died on 27 July 1932.

Hyatt, Stanley Portal (1877–1914). Hyatt was a popular novelist who spent his younger years on the African frontier. During the 1890s he worked as a teamster in Rhodesia and had the usual exploits in the field of hunting, trading, and mining. Several of his books are autobiographical in nature and deal with his African days, including *Diary of a Soldier of Fortune* (1910), *The Old Transport Road* (1911), and *The Northward Trek (1911).*

I

Ichac, Pierre. Leading French wildlife photographer in the 1930s and 1940s.

Ingram. Ingram, an English sportsman, was hunting on horseback in Somaliland in the late 1880s, accompanied by a friend named Lort Phillips. They were following up a cow elephant that Ingram had wounded with a black-powder .450 rifle. The cow charged, and Ingram tried to maneuver but was surrounded by thorny vegetation that his horse refused to enter. Rather than leap off the horse and run, or shoot again, Ingram tried to sting his mount into action by smacking it with his rifle. The horse remained frozen, and the elephant arrived and knocked Ingram out of the saddle with her trunk. The wounded beast then killed the hunter by driving her tusks straight through him. The pony was also killed. Years later, Lort Phillips was present at the death of another elephant hunter, Frank James.

Samuel Baker in 1890 blamed Ingram's death on inadequate firepower. Baker and many others considered the .450 black-powder rifle grossly inferior for elephant. On the other hand, Norman Smith disagreed in a letter to Denis Lyell nearly forty years later. He attributed Ingram's death to his unsportsmanlike act of shooting from the saddle and his folly in not dismounting when the elephant charged. This is an interesting example of how individual perspective can sway a man's opinions. In 1890 it was not considered unsportsmanlike to hunt on horseback (the "rule" against it more or less evolved in Kenya twenty or so years later). By the 1920s, however, shooting from the saddle "just was not done," and any .450 or similar-caliber rifle then being produced was more than powerful enough to stop an elephant. Baker and Smith, superb hunters both, let their preconceptions draw them to opposite conclusions about the same event.

Ionides, Constantine John Philip (1901–1968). C. J. P. Ionides, a strongly individualistic fifth-generation Englishman of Greek descent, was universally known as "Iodine" from the time he first went to public school. Wherever he went, his fellows seemed to consider him a foreigner. After a checkered school career, Ionides went into the army in India as a lieutenant in the South Wales Borderers. He was unconventional, getting into trouble over a pet bear and horrifying his senior officers by preferring to shoot pigs rather than stick them. In 1925 he wangled a transfer to the King's African Rifles (his superior officers were not sorry to see him go), frankly because he felt the hunting opportunities would be better.

He was right. Once he shed himself completely of his military uniform (that took two years), he made a name in the ivory-poaching business, working mainly in the Belgian Congo. What with license fees and special taxes, the Belgians had made legitimate elephant hunting prohibitively expensive, so the crafty Ionides figured out a way around the law. He simply shot elephant in the Belgian Congo at will and paid a kickback of 15 percent to the local African chiefs, who claimed the ivory as theirs. Since the Africans were exempt from the special ivory tax, the scam worked well. The business was lucrative enough and Ionides was respected (and violent) enough that the chiefs scrupulously kept their end of the bargain. At the start of the Great Depression, however, the ivory market crashed and Ionides found himself stuck with a lot of tusks that he had to sell at discount rates. He was left with a profit of just £150 for five months of backbreaking work.

Since crime wasn't paying, Ionides decided to find a legitimate way to live off his rifles. First he went into the white-hunter business with a partner, a skilled but alcoholic professional named McDougall. McDougall blew the company profits on women and booze, and the partnership folded. Ionides, responsible for debts incurred by his partner, found himself £600 in the hole. This was an enormous amount in the 1930s—government statistics for 1936, for instance, reported only 493 people in the entire Territory with incomes of more than £600 a year, and 334 of those were high-ranking administrative officials. Ionides had no choice but to go back to poaching for a couple of years to pay the debts off. He had his first serious mishap at this time, being battered by a cow elephant. The incident left him permanently deaf in his left ear.

In 1933 Ionides, newly out of debt, started another new career: assistant game ranger for the Tanganyika Game Department. The pay was just £40 a month, less than he could usually make poaching ivory, but the work was steady and legal, and he could live in the bush year-round and live the life he wanted. The job was certainly exciting—in addition to shooting over thirty man-eating lion and a rogue elephant called Lihogoya that had killed nearly thirty villagers, he had to contend with crop-raiding elephant, control tsetses and locusts, and deal with sick buffalo, marauding leopard, and troublesome locals. He threw himself into it with a passion.

Two factors set Ionides apart. One was his eccentricity. He was kind of a nut, hard on others and Spartan on himself. He actively cultivated a reputation for wizardry and magic among the Africans in his district and was not above treating them harshly, even brutally if he felt it necessary. On one occasion he had all the males of a village flogged for one infraction or another. The Africans generally responded with respect, if not affection. They recognized his management style as a type of leadership with which they themselves were long familiar, whether the autocrat was a black man or a white man. It was certainly preferable to the woolly-headed condescension that many European authorities adopted. The second distinguishing factor was his work with snakes. Ionides became a recognized expert on herpetology, discovering new species and profitably supplying the museums of the world with dangerous reptiles. Legend has it that he was not above shipping a live mamba in a packing box without any precautions or warning about the contents. He was often in trouble with the postal authorities.

Ionides spent much of World War II in Somalia, helping to keep the peace among the more remote and wild tribes. Once again his simple "my way or the whip" style paid dividends. After the war he continued his snake collecting and also set out on some famous collecting expeditions for various museums, supplying them with mountain gorilla, addax, bongo, and other rare trophies. He was always the consummate hunter.

By the 1960s Ionides was a legend, frequently featured in magazines and the subject (or author) of several books. No travelogue was complete without some visit or at least a reference to the eccentric hunter, who habitually wore a battered old hat that was stained through and through with the venom of a thousand snakes. His health failed in the 1960s, and poor circulation in his legs restricted his ability to walk. He often had to be carried in a *machila* (platform on poles) to places where a snake had been reported, and would leave the litter only to capture the serpent.

Ionides died in 1968 after an operation that amputated both legs. He is buried on a hillside in the Selous Game Reserve, which is just where Ionides would want to spend eternity. He was the author of *A Hunter's Life* and *Mambas and Man-Eaters* (with Dennis Holman).

Isaac, Francis W. Isaac was chairman (mayor) of Nairobi in 1907–1908, and a provincial commissioner in Kenya from 1914–1923. As a forestry officer at Eldoma Ravine in April 1902, he shot an antelope that proved to be not only the first bongo ever found in East Africa but also the first of the subspecies *Tragephalus euryceros isaaci.* He caught the animal with the help of a pack of hounds and donated the skin and horns to the Kensington Museum. Despite a lot of effort to repeat the feat of taking this rare animal, by Acting Governor F. J. Jackson and others, only four others had been shot by 1910, including one by Kermit Roosevelt for the Smithsonian Institution.

Isaacs, Nathaniel (1808–1872). Isaacs was a young Jewish trader who arrived in Natal from Saint Helena in 1825 and quickly became a friend and confidant of the Zulu leader Shaka. He was often associated with fellow traders Francis Farewell and Henry Fynn.

The term "trader" is often misleading when referring to those Europeans who interacted with the Zulus and their cousins, the Matabele and the Angoni. The original impetus was trade, it is true, often in the form of bartering guns, beads, and manufactured items for ivory and other animal products, but a large number of these traders settled in to become a part of the Zulu community. They often held rank in the native social system and even became a quasi-official arm of the government. Many led dual lives, keeping a European home in Durban or Port Natal while also owning villages in the tribal areas. Thus we read of men like Henry Fynn and Robert Biggar owning kraals in the countryside.

Isaacs carried his allegiance over to Shaka's successor, Dingaan, and was alleged to have obliged the despot by surreptitiously supplying him with firearms. By the early 1830s the relationship had begun to sour and Isaacs grew more and more distrustful of his royal friend. Afraid that Dingaan was planning to have him killed, Isaacs finally left Natal on 24 June 1831. Isaacs was the author of *Travels and Adventure in Eastern Africa* (1836).

Ivens, Robert (1850–1898). Portuguese naval officer and African explorer. The great-grandson of American diplomat Thomas Hickling, Ivens was born at Sao Pedro on 12 June 1850. He studied as a naval officer and made his first trip to Angola in 1872. In 1875 he traveled to South America, and then visited Philadelphia a year later, displaying Portuguese artifacts at that city's Universal Exposition. In 1877 he returned to Africa and explored Angola and Mozambique with Capello. Ivens made one more visit to Africa, to Mozambique in 1885, and died near Lisbon on 28 January 1898. Virtually forgotten in the United States, Ivens is well remembered in Portugal, where there are streets named after him in at least ten cities.

J

Jack, Evan MacLean (1873–1951). Maj. E. M. Jack hunted in Uganda, Rwanda, and the Congo in the early 1900s. He was the author of *On the Congo Frontier: Exploration and Sport* (1914).

Jackson, Sir Frederick George (1860–1938). Born at Alcester in Warwickshire on 6 March 1860, Frederick Jackson attended Denstone College, then spent three years on a cattle ranch in Queensland before finishing his education at Edinburgh University. In 1887 Jackson spent a season on a whaling ship in the Greenland Sea and then began making plans for an expedition to the North Pole. He tested his equipment and stamina with an overland trip in northern Norway in the winter of 1893–1894, and in the spring of 1894 launched the Jackson-Harmsworth Polar Expedition (Alfred Harmsworth was his patron). The venture fell far short of the pole but did succeed in mapping the previously uncharted western coasts of several arctic islands, and in rescuing the explorers Fridtjof Nansen and Fredrik Hjalmar Johansen. For this latter act Jackson received the Norwegian Star of Saint Olaf in 1898.

With the outbreak of the Boer War, Jackson enlisted in the Manchester Regiment, serving with the mounted infantry from 1899–1902. During World War I he fought on the Western Front.

In 1925–1926 Jackson went on a long safari through central Africa, hunting big game in Mozambique, Nyasaland, Rhodesia, Tanganyika, Rwanda, and the Congo. He was the author of *The Great Frozen Land* (1895), *A Thousand Days in the Arctic* (1899), and *The Lure of Unknown Lands* (1935).

Jackson, Sir Frederick John (1860–1929). A British civil servant, Jackson was an administrative officer in Kenya from 1902–1907. A former student of Jesus College, Cambridge, Jackson arrived in East Africa in 1884, having previously hunted in Kashmir. In 1884–1885 he roamed the area around Lamu on the Indian Ocean coast north of Mombasa, hunting and learning African ways. In 1886 he organized a hunting safari to Kilimanjaro, but financial difficulties forced him to curtail the trip and join the government service.

He signed on with the IBEA (see glossary) in 1888 and the following year was sent with Ernest Gedge, James Martin, and Archibald Mackinnon on a long journey into the interior to inspect the company's domains and establish a presence with the local tribes. They were also to look out for Henry Stanley, who presumably was coming to East Africa after "rescuing" Emin Pasha. Jackson had been instructed by the IBEA's directors to avoid any involvement in African politics, so when he received an appeal from the Kabaka of Uganda, who was seeking allies to help him crush a rebellion, he instead led the safari up to Mount Elgon to do some innocuous exploring.

The German explorer Carl Peters, however, was under no such restrictions and, after hearing of the Kabaka's request (apparently after stealing and reading Jackson's mail), hastened to Uganda to sign an alliance with the beleaguered monarch. Jackson quickly moved to intervene, but Peters's treaty was made moot by the Anglo-German agreement of 1890, which gave the North Sea island of Heligoland to the Kaiser in return for concessions in East Africa.

After the IBEA withdrew from Uganda in 1893 and Sir Gerald portal proclaimed the region a British Protectorate, Jackson was appointed the Foreign Office's "administrative assistant" for the country. The British government was reluctant to spend much money on its African possessions, so Jackson raised official funds by hunting elephant and selling the ivory. In 1895 he was upgraded to vice consul and then to deputy commissioner a year later.

The Sudanese soldiers garrisoning Uganda for Britain were becoming increasingly disgruntled. Most of them had been away from their homes since 1892, and their rations and pay were always late and always insufficient. They finally mutinied in 1897, and Jackson was deeply involved in efforts to convince the mutineers to peacefully ask for redress of their grievances. When that effort failed, he joined Maj. James MacDonald's military campaign

Frederick J. Jackson and buffalo in East Africa.

Frederick J. Jackson makes treaties with Kikuyu chiefs, 1889.

to suppress the revolt. Jackson was badly wounded in a battle against the mutineers near Lubwa Station on 19 October 1897.

After recovering, Jackson served as political officer in a punitive campaign against the Nandi tribe in 1900. In 1902 he was appointed deputy commissioner of the East Africa Protectorate, serving under commissioner Sir Charles Eliot, who resigned in 1904—the two men despised each other. Jackson's duties as deputy seem to have largely involved hunting and overseeing hunting. In 1907 his title was changed to deputy governor, and as acting governor he personally escorted ex-President Theodore Roosevelt from Mombasa to Nairobi in 1909. He became governor of Uganda in 1911 and spent six years in that post, retiring in 1917.

A friendly, charming man, Jackson constantly took advantage of his official postings to hunt and to study natural history. His personal collection of bird skins was said to number 12,000 specimens representing some 774 species, all of which he collected himself. An engaging writer, he was author of the East African chapter in 1897's *Big Game Shooting* volume of the Badminton Library. He also wrote *Notes on the Game Birds of Kenya and Uganda* (1926) and the posthumously published *Early Days in East Africa* (1930), as well as numerous magazine articles. He was the foremost expert on East African birds of his time.

Jackson designed a unique uniform for bongo hunting. The bongo is a famously elusive creature, and Jackson would blacken his face and hands and don a special dark suit. He wore this outfit on numerous occasions, stalking the wary animal through the thickest bush. The camouflage didn't help. Although he spotted one or two, in the end Jackson never got his bongo.

The very picture of a monocled English sportsman, Jackson hosted old friend Rider Haggard at his home near Lake Naivasha, where the writer purportedly got his inspiration for the character and adventures of Alan Quartermain. Jackson, along with C. W. Hobley, was the founder of the East Africa and Uganda Natural History Society, the institution that founded the Coryndon Museum in 1911 (now National Museum of Kenya). He married Alice Louise Cooper in 1904; the couple had no children.

Jackson died in France on 3 February 1929. ROWLAND WARD 1928: KONGONI, WHITE RHINO, BUFFALO, HIPPO.

Jacobs, Petrus (1802–1882). Petrus Jacobs (also known as Piet Jacobs) was perhaps the foremost of the Boer ivory hunters of the nineteenth century. Finaughty considered him "tough and skilful" (1916), while Selous, who knew Jacobs well, acknowledged him as "the most experienced elephant hunter in South Africa" (1881).

We first hear of Jacobs in the 1850s, hunting in the Transvaal with Jan Viljoen. Together they accounted for ninety-three elephant. An 1858 expedition to Bechuanaland had to be aborted when all four of Jacobs's salted horses (see glossary) were either eaten or run off by lion. Several years later, in 1865, Jacobs and Viljoen were reportedly the first white men to hunt Mashonaland, coming back with over two hundred pairs of tusks.

In 1869 Jacobs hunted for a short time with Bill Finaughty. Finaughty, not an easy man to get along with, does not appear to have thought too highly of the old Boer. First, he claims (1916) that Jacobs invited himself along on Finaughty's hunt without being invited. Then he accuses the old-timer of spooking an elephant herd by needlessly shooting a zebra. He rounds off his account by claiming that Jacobs wound up begging off the hunting trip because he was afraid to follow Finaughty into tsetse country. All in all, Finaughty seems to disparage Jacobs's abilities, even though during their short association Jacobs brought down six elephant to Finaughty's five, not including one huge bull that they shared, with Finaughty paying Jacobs £10 for his tusk. It bears remembering that Jacobs was about sixty-seven years old at the time and Finaughty only twenty-six.

Finaughty aside, Jacobs is remembered as a tough and adroit hunter. Estimates of the total number of elephant he dispatched range from four hundred up to a thousand, and as many as one hundred ten lion. His son David also became a famous hunter.

James, Frank Linsly (1851–1890). One of the forgotten hunters of the nineteenth century, Frank James was born in Liverpool and graduated from Cambridge University in the early 1870s with a master of arts degree. He and his brothers, William and Arthur, came from a well-to-do family and, with their similarly inclined friends Ethelbert Lort Phillips and G. Percy Aylmer, dedicated their youth to traveling the world from one hunting adventure to the next.

They were attracted to Africa both by the lure of exploration and by the hunting opportunities. In 1877–1878 Frank and his younger brother William traveled up the Nile to its junction with the Atbara River, then up the Atbara and the Bahr Setit, returning via the Kassala-Berber-Dongola-Nile-Cairo route. In 1880–1881 Frank James went on an expedition through Eritrea, starting in Massawa and going through Keren and along the Khor Baraka, producing an excellent map of the latter region.

In the winter of 1881 the James gang embarked on their most ambitious adventure yet, with a slightly larger than usual crew consisting of the three brothers, Lort Phillips, Aylmer, R. B. Colvin, and a medical doctor from London. They were supported by three European servants (one from England and two from Switzerland) and a varying number of Swahili, Arab, and Sudanese staffers. Their plan was to start at the Indian Ocean and travel west along the Sudanese-Abyssinian border, hunting elephant and other large game while mapping the region for the Royal Geographical Society. They went mainly on foot, with their supplies carried on a number of rented camels.

The expedition was relatively uneventful, but only in comparison to the dramatic happenings that marked similar ventures. One of the European servants, a Swiss named Jules, died of dysentery at the very start of the safari, and Lort Phillips and Aylmer were later robbed of their rifles by a band of some hundred Abyssinian bandits. In the latter incident Mahomet, one of their trackers, was speared by the raiders and mortally wounded. The local Egyptian authorities (the Sudan was nominally part of Egypt) vowed to retrieve the rifles and punish the killers, but the Abyssinians slipped silently back across the mountainous border.

The rest of the trip was more or less peaceful. There was some hunting (James and the others bagged a large number of buffalo, kudu, and antelope but missed out on the elephant) and a lot of exploring. The Englishmen had brought along a consignment of fireworks and a magic lantern show, which greatly facilitated making friends with the primitive local people, many of whom had never before seen a European. William James drew a superb map of the district that became the official map of the RGS, and Frank gathered enough material for his first book, *The Wild Tribes of the Soudan.*

From Berbera they sailed down the Nile and eventually reached Suez, where the expedition officially ended in April 1882. From there the party returned to England, where they rested while planning a visit to the Americas.

James's book about this trip, *The Wild Tribes of the Soudan,* was well written and very popular in its day, although it is almost forgotten now. James had a knack for observation and strange detail. One of his most amusing passages concerns the selection of the expedition's physician. Not knowing a suitable candidate, James placed ads in several prominent British medical journals soliciting a doctor or at least a male nurse who would be willing to suffer the anticipated hardships. He was "inundated" with replies, and reprinted some of the funnier ones in the book's first chapter. *Wild Tribes* also includes numerous high-quality woodcuts made from photographs taken by Aylmer and William James. There is a wealth of information about Sudanese tribes and customs, and the hardships of camel travel through that arid region.

In 1882–1883 James made a trip to Mexico, where he again went shooting with Aylmer, Lort Phillips, and his brother William. He then returned to Africa and sailed along the Somaliland coast in an Arab dhow in an attempt to investigate the possibility of using light craft to sail far upriver on his expeditions. At that time Somaliland was a remote and dangerous place. The coastal regions were fairly well known, but the days of British officers taking leave from India to go lion hunting in the interior were ten or fifteen years in the future. James decided to make another excursion inland, despite the fact that the last few Europeans to do so had been either murdered or robbed and were lucky to escape with their lives. As usual, William James, Lort Phillips, and Aylmer went along.

They left Berbera on 21 December 1884 and by the end of February had reached their goal, the Webi Shebeli (Leopard River, also known as the Shebele River). There was some friction with the locals, but the risks were outweighed by the rewards. The hunting was superb—the area was replete with elephant, leopard, rhino, antelope, and, of course, lion. Lort Phillips shot the then-record Abyssinian buffalo (40-inch horns), and Frank James killed the No. 4 animal of the same species (32-inch horns). The party arrived back in Berbera on 16 April 1885 and was widely praised in Britain for the successful completion of a task that many had deemed too risky. It could well be said that James and his ensemble made possible the traditional lion-hunting safaris of Indian army officers, noted above. Three years later he published his account of the trip, *The Unknown Horn of Africa: An Exploration From Berbera to the Leopard River* (1888). This book firmly established his place in the front rank of the Victorian hunter/explorer hierarchy.

The delay in publication was attributable to James's active life. In the years 1885–1890 he expanded his travels to the far corners of the earth, visiting India, Norway, Spitsbergen, Novaya Zemlya, and the Kara Sea. The end of the 1880s saw him back in Africa, this time on the west coast, where he went after ivory in the Cameroons and along the Niger. On 21 April 1890 James was killed by a wounded elephant on the San Benito River in the French Congo. He was accompanied on this last safari by Lort Phillips, who a few years earlier had witnessed the death of the hunter Ingram under similar circumstances.

A passage in *The Wild Tribes of the Soudan* illustrates a common problem in the old hunting books—a tendency to let preconceived ideas about wild animals take precedence over actual observation. In the twenty-first century we are so exposed to wildlife documentaries and scientific studies that it is startling to recall how little was known about how animals lived before, say, World War II. Back then researchers simply did not go out into the wild to observe nature—what passed for scientific knowledge were hunter's anecdotes and zookeepers' observations. That was all well and good, but hunters and curators see only certain aspects of animal behavior. A captive animal is an unnatural animal, and the stories told by hunters often create a picture of unusual ferocity. This fact allowed an incredible amount of misinformation to creep into the literature. Once there, these stories were inevitably repeated time and again until they became universally accepted.

One of these tall tales concerned the method of the Nile crocodile's attack. After describing a narrow escape from a "very large" croc on the Setit River (they are always really big, aren't they?), James wrote, "Probably, if my brother had not seen the crocodile when he had, it would have tried to knock me into the river with its tail." Nowadays, every ten-year-old kid with cable TV knows that's not how a crocodile attacks—the creature lunges forward with its

Frank L. James's hunting camp, Sudan, 1882.

teeth, not sideways with its tail. Yet the tail-swipe story pervaded the old African adventure literature.

Examples are legion. For purposes of this discussion, the classic tail swipe is differentiated from cases in which tail contact is either accidental or incidental. To qualify for the "TS" attack, the croc must deliberately use its tail to propel the victim off the bank or boat and into the river. While this tactic by the croc seems to have become much scarcer since the invention of video, dozens of famous early hunters and writers commented on it. A sample:

- Cherry Kearton, *In the Land of the Lion*, 1930: "Then, instantly, the tail will be lifted and swung around to knock the victim at one blow into the river . . ."
- Marcus Daly, *Big Game Hunting and Adventure,* 1937: ". . . their quick lightning-like spin near the bank where the water is deep enough, and a blow of their great tail, is quick and strong enough to knock a buffalo clean into the water and kill any human being."
- James Stevenson-Hamilton, *Animal Life in Africa,* 1912: "Should an animal be on the bank, close to but not actually in the water, it may be overbalanced and knocked in by a deft blow from the crocodile's tail. I have known both white men and natives to have very narrow escapes in this way . . ."
- E. A. Temple-Perkins, *Kingdom of the Elephant,* 1955: "The crocodile has tremendous power in its tail, which it commonly uses to catch its prey. With a single flick it knocks its victim unconscious or into the water, and then seizes it and drags it away."
- Count Byron de Prorok, *In Quest of Lost Worlds,* 1935: "The natives told us that, on average, they lost about twenty people by death among the crocodiles each year. Not that the crocodiles caused them any fear when they went for them; they had a delightful little trick of lassoing them and dragging them to a convenient spot to be skinned. It was the unsuspecting people who suffered, blissfully ignorant until a flail-like tail sent them spinning into the stream."
- Sir Samuel Baker, *Wild Beasts and Their Ways,* 1890: "Should a crocodile be unable to reach an object with its jaws, it will frequently strike with the tail so suddenly that the animal or person is tripped up, and knocked into the water, to be instantly seized by the teeth and carried off."
- Oskar Koenig, *Pori Tupu,* 1954: "He had been standing unsuspectingly on the bank when a crocodile smashed him down into the water with its mighty tail, grabbed him at once and dragged him along under water to the larder" and "Few would even venture near it, for the attack with a crocodile's tail at some victim on the bank was a well-recognized danger."
- William Holmes, *Safari RSVP,* 1960: "The crocodile's jaws contain row after row of wicked teeth. But these are not, oddly enough, the biggest danger. The tail is the most deadly weapon, and can be used to great advantage in an attack. The force of the crocodile's tail can smash a canoe or crush a man senseless with one blow."

It's enough to add that the story of the tail swipe appears in at least 75 percent of pre-1970 safari books that discuss crocodile attacks. It's probably the single most-repeated "fact" about crocodile behavior in the old hunting books.

The stories are so similar that at first blush they seem to have copied one another. But is it even true? Any ten-year old who has ever watched the Discovery Channel could point out some of the holes in the above excerpts. Baker's statement, for instance. Videotape makes it clear that if a croc cannot reach its prey with its jaws, it will either continue to wait patiently or it will rush forward to shorten the distance and catch the victim in its teeth. Can you imagine a situation where a crocodile could not reach you with its jaws but could reach you with its tail? Unless it was snared by the head, I just don't see how that could happen. And where are the videos of crocodiles casually "flicking" a zebra off the bank, such as Temple-Perkins described? Why were the pre-video crocs so rapacious in their tail attacks while modern crocs rely on the direct jaw approach? What reptilian Rommel dictated this change in tactics? Or were all the early writers just casually repeating bad information that they just didn't bother to check out?

This latter theory has distressing consequences for a safari historian. Men like Frank James and Stevenson-Hamilton are continually relied on as primary sources. If the tail swipe thing was fudged, how much of their other stuff was fudged? Come to think of it, Stevenson-Hamilton also repeated the old and inaccurate saw about a croc's jaw being hinged on the top instead of the bottom, like every other animal. This is a simple biological fact that could easily have been disproved by simple observation, and Stevenson-Hamilton must have seen the living proof (a croc's skull) many hundreds of times. But he never caught it. He was so convinced that a crocodile's jaw was hinged at the top that he was blind to what was right in front of his eyes. And so it was, I believe, with the "tail-swipe" legend.

Almost all accounts of the tail swipe are secondhand. Let's take a look at the Count Prorok example cited above. Secondhand, to be sure, and there is no way of knowing just how the "natives" actually described what happened to the "blissfully ignorant" souls who went down crocodile gullets at the rate of twenty per year. Prorok mentioned the "flail-like tail," but what words or gestures did the natives use to convey this? I strongly doubt they used those exact words. Isn't it at least possible that they, in discussing victims plucked off a bank, assumed that Prorok knew how a croc attacks—that is, with its jaws—while Prorok assumed that they must be talking about a tail swipe? Alexander Lake, in *Killers in Africa,* cited at least two firsthand instances, but there is ample reason to discount virtually everything that Lake wrote about anything. His stories in large part are simply unbelievable, for reasons that have nothing to do with crocodiles. In *Kingdom of the Elephant* E. A. Temple-Perkins, a sober observer and a staunch believer in the swipe (who incidentally scoffed at Alexander Lake's story of using softnose .303 bullets on elephant), cited two examples. In one, the croc chased a young man out of a canoe and onto an island, then knocked him down with its tail as he tried to run away. The other story is of a boy being swept off the steps of a barge. Both are secondhand, the first attributed to R. de la B. Barker, the second to an unnamed policeman. Several knowledgeable people have disparaged the first story on grounds unconnected to the tail swipe—suffice it to say that the anecdote does not have the ring of truth and is generally regarded with a jaded eye. Even Temple-Perkins, the published source of the story, was uneasy about it because in his experience even the initial form the attack took was unlikely (he was of the opinion that crocodiles won't attack boats; tell that to Richard Leakey and Mary Kingsley). Add to that the obvious fact that any situation involving a running person (or animal) and a croc might simply involve tripping, not a tail swipe.

David Roberts, a crocodile hunter with vast experience in the animals at Lake Baringo, where he virtually wiped out the population by clubbing the reptiles to death (not somebody you want to mess around with), was an outspoken critic of the tail-swipe legend. Colin Willock, in his excellent 1964 study *The Enormous Zoo* (page 124), describes Roberts as the "man who has probably caught more crocodiles legally and on license than anyone in Africa today." Willock goes on to state that Roberts believed the swipe was "utterly impossible . . . the mechanics of the croc's body were against the possibility. What earthly sort of leverage, he argued, could it get to lift half its body and swing it as an offensive weapon? Anyway, a croc's tail was not all that flexible."

I have seen proponents of the tail swipe respond to that last comment by waving photographs showing crocodile tails in all sorts of positions. That's great. But what people forget is that we are not talking about extremes here. Roberts (via Willock) did not say that the tail was rigid. He did not say that it was stiff. What he did say was simply that it wasn't "all that flexible." In other words, the crocodile tail is not whiplike in its speed and flexibility.

Roberts, by the way, challenged Willock to produce an eyewitness to the tail swipe. C. A. Guggisberg jumped all over this in *Crocodiles* (1972). "Well, here is the answer," he wrote triumphantly, and proceeded to quote a passage written by Dunbar Brander in which an Indian mugger (a freshwater crocodile of Southeast Asia) rushes onto the bank and, in turning, knocks some pigs into the water with its tail. He also cites a drawing (!) by Hugh Cott and an episode that happened to herpetologist Raymond Ditmars at a zoo involving an American crocodile being let out of its crate. Surely the drawing can be discounted out of hand, and an assessment of the Ditmars situation would depend on the relative positions of man, crate, and captive crocodile. Even the mugger incident may easily have been just a result of the pigs trying to escape the reptilian predator. But note how not one of the examples used by crocodile expert Guggisberg to support the hypothesis that Nile crocodiles use the tail swipe to knock their prey into the water involves a Nile crocodile. None. That's not evidence. It must be judged that Roberts's challenge to produce a firsthand account of the TS theory went unanswered by Guggisberg.

The simple fact is that gradually, as people have seen more and more video footage of crocodile attacks, the tail swipe has faded from the stories. It is all too easy to forget just how much television and video have changed the way we learn and how we view the world. Fifty years ago only a few Westerners had ever seen a lion pull down a zebra or a cheetah go after a gazelle. Before video, scientists weren't even sure how a cheetah caught his prey. Most of them who discussed the matter wrote that the cheetah would run alongside the antelope and suddenly lunge at its throat with its teeth. Now every little kid in America and the rest of the electrified world has seen how a cheetah trips its prey, and they've seen how a crocodile attacks. Every nine-year-old boy in my town has seen what happens when a crocodile tail hits a person—the victim might trip or be bruised, but he is certainly not flung into the air. And the tail-swipe legend has suddenly faded into oblivion.

Even as late as the 1970s, as mentioned above, the naturalist Guggisberg could insist that the swipe was an actual crocodile tactic. More recent books correct this fallacy or, more often, simply don't mention it. One of the better post-video books is 1991's *Crocodiles and Alligators of the World,* by David Alderton. The writer, a prominent herpetologist involved with CITES, stated unequivocally, "Although it has long been stated that crocodilians also use their powerful tails to knock potential prey off balance, there appears to be little real evidence to support this view." That old legend is unequivocally a myth.

James, William D. Younger brother of Frank Linsly James, William was a respected hunter in his own right. William drew the map that accompanied his brother's book *The Wild Tribes of the Soudan.* At least some of the trophies in the 1899 Rowland Ward listed under his name may have belonged to his brother, who was dead by that time. The book lists the owner of the trophy, who was not necessarily the actual hunter. ROWLAND WARD 1899: CARIBOU, TETEL HARTEBEEST, SWAYNE HARTEBEEST, WATERBUCK, SPEKE GAZELLE, SOEMMERRING GAZELLE, ROAN, BEISA ORYX, ABYSSINIAN BUSHBUCK, GREATER KUDU, LESSER KUDU, ABYSSINIAN BUFFALO, HIPPO.

Jameson, James Sligo (1856–1888). Jameson was an extremely wealthy sportsmen, the scion of a Dublin distilling firm. He used his great wealth to finance numerous big-game hunting expeditions in America and Africa, including one in the late 1870s when he hunted the Zambezi Valley and Mashonaland with Selous and his friends Wranksley, Sketchly, and Crook. Selous described him as a honorable and decent fellow, but it's not out of the question that the hunter was seeking to ingratiate himself with a wealthy young patron who would in all likelihood return to Rhodesia for future hunts.

Unfortunately for Jameson, both personally and for his place in history, he used his money to buy his way onto the Emin Pasha Relief Expedition in 1886. A gift of £1,000 was enough to procure for Jameson one of the highly coveted "officer" spots in Henry Stanley's massive safari. The Irish distiller seems to have been a sporting and basically decent man, but his association with Stanley was to cause both of them disgrace and tragedy.

Despite his money and his penchant for throwing it around, Jameson was no spoiled high-society type—he genuinely enjoyed the outdoor life and does not seem to have shirked the harder and more onerous duties. When Stanley decided to split his expedition into a flying column (which would rescue Emin Pasha) and a Rear Column (which would follow from Yambuya with supplies as soon as enough porters were recruited), Jameson was left with the Rear Column under the command of the difficult Maj. Edward Barttelot.

Jameson attempted to make himself useful with his hunting skills and add to the provisions of the struggling camp, but an early stalk with Barttelot almost ended in disaster when the two men narrowly avoided the charge of an angry rhino. Barttelot was injured just a few days later by a wounded buffalo while hunting with another officer, Bonny, not with the experienced Jameson. Bonny, in fact, went on to do most of the hunting for Yambuya camp, even shooting a large bull elephant that provided several tons of badly needed meat.

A troubled man, Barttelot saw conspiracies everywhere and developed the habit of sending those officers he didn't like—which amounted to most of them—out on needless missions that involved long absences from Yambuya. Thus Herbert Ward, who the major really despised, was sent on a ridiculous three-thousand-mile trip to send a pointless telegram. Jameson, likewise, was given several insignificant tasks, and after one of these—a visit to the Free State governor, Tippu Tib, in August 1888—he suddenly took sick and died.

His death has been the subject of some controversy. Stanley's European officers had a habit of never returning from Africa. The official verdict was fever, but rumors were rife. Tippu Tib himself was certain that Jameson had been poisoned by Belgian agents who believed the Irishman had too much influence on Tippu Tib. The Free State needed the Arab slaver's strong hand in the Congo, and Jameson had nearly convinced Tippu Tib (with the promise of a huge payment backed by his personal fortune) to abandon his gubernatorial province and personally go in search of Stanley and Emin. There is no doubt that Jameson, a man with long experience in tropical Africa, had been in fine health on 9 August but was stone-cold dead nine days later.

In one sense he could not have timed it better. Jameson had led a privileged life, but his reputation was about to go down the tubes. Shortly before his death, he became aware that stories about an unfortunate incident in his life were becoming public knowledge. The rumors involved an allegation that he had not only witnessed but arranged the murder of a slave girl by cannibals so that he could satisfy his intellectual curiosity and witness the deed firsthand.

There was a kernel of truth in the story, as shall be seen below. Some writers have speculated that the emergence of the tale might have caused Jameson to fall into a depression that led to his death.

The story had been publicized by a dismissed interpreter who wanted to besmirch Stanley's reputation, and thus was not directly directed at the wealthy Irishman. It was more of an attempt to reveal what was going on under Stanley's watch than an attempt to hurt Jameson, who was soon beyond hurting anyway. At first the story was widely dismissed, and it is entirely possible it might have been relegated to the status of myth had not the person who loved Jameson the most made an incredible miscalculation. Tippu Tib denied the tale, which meant nothing, for as an official of the Congo Free State he could hardly admit having either cannibals or slave girls in his camp, and the press had a field day alternately attacking and defending the dead Jameson.

Then Jameson's young wife (they had married on 4 February 1885) released a letter written by her late husband in which he described the events underlying the story. Apparently she believed that it would help clear his name, but the effect on the public was the reverse. In the letter Jameson revealed what had really happened: He had been discussing cannibalism with Tippu Tib and expressed the opinion that it was a myth. Tippu Tib laughed and offered to arrange a demonstration, and Jameson, believing him to be bluffing, agreed. For the price of a small piece of cloth, a young slave girl was obtained and given to some African cannibals in Tippu Tib's employ, who promptly stabbed her to death and butchered the body. Jameson, who apparently thought the whole thing a hoax until the very last second (or a scam to relieve him of his cloth), stood there shocked and dumbfounded as the murder was committed. Before his death he drew a series of pictures showing the sequence of events, which were published in several books including J. W. Buel's *Heroes of the Dark Continent* (1889).

Buel sensibly pointed out that the mere fact of drawing the incident did not mean that Jameson condoned the killing. Jameson's story was plausible and in keeping with human nature. Doubtless many other Europeans have witnessed—and committed—far worse, and with premeditation. But the now-indisputable fact that a British gentleman on an officially condoned expedition stood there and watched as a little girl was butchered blackened Jameson's name, and Stanley's, for generations. ROWLAND WARD 1899: GEMSBOK (NUMBER 1), CAPE HARTEBEEST, LECHWE, REEDBUCK, SABLE, AMERICAN BISON (MONTANA), WHITE RHINO (MASHONALAND), ELEPHANT.

Jameson, Leander Starr (1853–1917). A doctor from Edinburgh and a close associate of Rhodes's, Jameson agreed to lead a column of some three hundred fifty armed men into the Transvaal once an anti-Boer uprising had begun. The uprising, engineered and supported by Rhodes, was to be carried out by British and other emigrants who worked in the Transvaal mines and farms, the so-called *uitlanders*. The *uitlanders* chickened out at the last minute, too late to warn Jameson, and he and all his troopers were surrounded by hordes of angry Boers and captured after some bloodshed. There was some sentiment among the Boers to execute the raiders, but President Paul Kruger prudently decided to show lenience. Jameson was jailed for fifteen months, and Rhodes had to resign his premiership, but the BSAC (see glossary) was allowed to retain its charter.

Though still a popular figure in South Africa, Rhodes had lost much of his political power. He played a relatively small part in the events leading up to the Boer War and died a fairly young man in 1902. Jameson survived his disgrace to become the Cape Colony prime minister in his own right a few years later, and helped orchestrate the Act of Union in 1909. He served as opposition leader in the South African Parliament from 1910–1912. After retiring due to poor health, he was made a baronet in 1913.

Jameson has not received his full due in British colonial history. To a large extent he was the instrument that transformed Rhodes's policies and ambitions into action. He may have failed with the raid, but his machinations delivered both Mashonaland and Matabeleland to the control of the BSAC (see glossary), and, given a little luck and some cooperation from Harry Johnston and others, he no doubt would have added Mozambique and Katanga to the Empire as well.

An eminently practical man concerned above all with the bottom line, Jameson personally stopped one of the two known lynch mobs in early Rhodesian history. In 1893 a servant from South Africa called Zulu Jim was arrested for the brutal murders of a pioneer family, including a woman and a child. Zulu Jim had been arrested and jailed on suspicion of stealing cattle from his employer, a Mr. Grady. On the day of the murders Zulu Jim had managed to escape his confinement. He grabbed a rifle and shot Grady, hitting him in the spine. Grady pleaded with him to spare his wife and infant child, but Jim shot them both and then shot and killed another man, an invalid named MacKenzie who was staying with the family. Zulu Jim escaped into the woods, to be betrayed for a £30 reward some days later. Grady died of his injuries after spending several days in agonizing pain.

After Zulu Jim's capture, the settlers at Salisbury decided to skip the formality of a trial and hang him outright. Considerably fortified by alcohol, they gathered in a mob and moved on the jail, only to be confronted by the chief of police, a Captain White. They were about to overpower White when Jameson appeared on the scene. Like a movie sheriff, Jameson faced down the mob, but with his words not his gun. He pointed out that such a barbaric act as hanging the man without trial would ruin the budding Rhodesian economy in the eyes of the world. "We are on the eve of a financial boom," he repeatedly emphasized. Grudgingly, the settlers began to back down. Jameson then bought a round of drinks for the chastened mob. Zulu Jim was hanged a month later after a trial.

Jamieson, Crawford Fletcher (1905–1947). Fletcher Jamieson was a highly regarded Rhodesian hunter who agreed to provide photographs for John Taylor's books, *Big Game Rifles* and *African Rifles and Cartridges,* which was due to come out in 1948. The deal, a personal arrangement between Jamieson and Taylor, called for Jamieson to be paid a total of £50.

Jamieson was eminently qualified to provide these pictures. His father had come to Rhodesia in 1895, buying a farm sixty miles from Bulawayo he called Hillocks. He would make infrequent trips to Scotland to visit his wife, during one of which Fletcher was born in 1905. In 1911 Jamieson senior finally brought the entire family out to Hillocks.

Fletcher Jamieson grew up a young woodsman, fishing and hunting and playing with the Matabele kids. When he was thirteen he took over the farm when his father had to go to South Africa to work and raise some desperately needed cash. That same year Fletcher fell out of a tree, permanently damaging his left wrist. For the rest of his life he had to balance the stock of his rifle atop his forearm because his wrist was held together by pieces of steel and had no flexibility.

As head of the household, Fletcher hunted plains game daily for food and extra cash. By 1928 he had saved enough to outfit himself as an elephant hunter. He roamed the Zambezi Valley throughout the 1930s shooting elephant and buffalo and generally impressing everyone with his character and ability. He also assisted his brother, who was a building contractor.

Jamieson was scrupulously honest and listed every elephant he ever shot—all legally—in a journal. The total came to 134, all of them bulls. Jamieson was also an avid photographer. Unfortunately, most of his photos were "borrowed" from the family by a man who professed to be working on a biography of Fletcher after his death, and have disappeared. He also did some game department work for the government. For instance, in 1944 he was contracted to wipe out the elephant in the Sabi River valley as a tsetse control measure.

In 1947 Jamieson entered into the above-noted arrangement with John Taylor to provide photos for his books. Fletcher held up his part of the deal, providing excellent photographs. On 17 September 1947 Jamieson, just returned from a hunting trip, lowered himself on a bucket into a newly dug well with an electric light to judge the progress of the work. The light was not properly grounded, and when he stepped from the bucket he was immediately electrocuted. He left a wife, Joan, and two small children. John Taylor never coughed up the £50.

Janssen, Christiaen. A Dutch settler at Cape Town, he was described in contemporary documents as the colony's best hunter in 1659.

Januarie, Gert (xxxx–1934). Januarie was one of the original game rangers of Kalahari Gemsbok National Park when it was proclaimed in 1931. Both the senior ranger, Johannes le Riche, and Januarie died of malaria in 1934.

Jeary, Bertram F. Jeary was a wildlife photographer from Cape Town, the first man to photograph the aggressive buffalo of the Addo bush (and had a letter from game warden Harold Trollope to prove it). He spent a lot of time photographing the animals in Kruger National Park—Stevenson-Hamilton called him a "constant visitor" (1937). In 1933, after a conversation he had with Stevenson-Hamilton concerning the effect of the current drought on the park's animals, Jeary began a newspaper publicity campaign called "Save the Game" that quickly raised over £5,000, an enormous sum for the time. The money was used to drill water holes for the animals, and the campaign was the model for many subsequent fundraisers. Jeary was the author of *Pride of Lions* (1936), a neat photographic history of a family of Kruger lion that anticipated hundreds of books in the 1960s and 1970s.

Jenner, A. C. W. (xxxx–1905). Jenner was a provincial sub-commissioner in Kenya 1893–1900. In 1905 (some sources say 1900) he set out to explore and map Jubaland and the Lorian Swamp, following a trail that led between the villages of Afmadu and Liboyi. One night during a heavy rainstorm he collected the rifles from his askaris and placed them in a tent to keep them dry. Some Zubair bandits who had been following him took advantage of the opportunity to rush the camp. Jenner and nearly all of his men were speared to death, only three escaping to bring back the tale.

During his tenure as a government official, Jenner had often complained about the uncivilized nature of so-called "punitive expeditions" and half-seriously recommended that each British officer posted to East Africa be awarded some medals in advance, then have one taken away each time he participated in such a campaign. Ironically, Jenner's murder prompted one of the largest punitive expeditions ever seen. The culprits, however, escaped.

Jennings Family. They were a Transvaal family of elephant hunters, including the father, James Jennings II (a settler from 1820), and his sons Jeremiah, James III (known as William), John, and George. The sons were hunting in Matabeleland and Mashonaland in the 1860s and 1870s. They frequently teamed up with George Wood, Thomas Leask, Henry Hartley, Bill Finaughty, H. Biles, J. Giffard, and the other famous elephant hunters of that day, and quit around 1870 when the elephant had been driven into areas where horses couldn't follow. The boys seem to have been on the boisterous side. A granddaughter of one of the brothers, Stella, married Maj. C. Court Treatt, a hunter and wildlife photographer of the 1920s.

Jephson, Arthur Jermy Mounteney (1858–1908). The son of a vicar, Jephson became an officer in the Antrim Regiment of the Royal Irish Rifles in 1880 but resigned in 1884. In 1887 he joined the Emin Pasha Relief Expedition under Henry Stanley. Jephson stayed with the main body until it was nearing Lake Victoria. He was then sent ahead to meet Emin and assist in preparations to leave. Emin reluctantly agreed to go, and while preparations were being made, Jephson traveled through Equatoria Province rounding up Emin's troops and telling everybody that they could come if they wanted to. The retreat was unpopular, and Jephson spent nine months trying to convince Emin's people to come. Most of them were Sudanese soldiers who had taken wives and settled down and were reluctant to leave their homes. In August of 1888 both Jephson and Emin were held prisoner at the village of Wadelai by disgruntled soldiers. Only the approach of a Mahdist army in October began to convince the men of the wisdom of the move.

The rebel officers at Wadelai planned to execute Jephson and Emin, but in February 1889 Jephson reached Stanley and they were able to free Emin. Jephson then went along with the column to German East Africa and back to civilization.

Returning to England in 1890, Jephson obtained a posting as Royal Messenger under both Queen Victoria and King Edward. He was given a medal by the Royal Geographical Society in 1890 and died at Sunninghill, Ascot, on 22 October 1908, leaving one son. His writings included *Emin Pasha and the Rebellion at the Equator* (1890), *Stories Told in an African Forest by Grown-Up Children of Africa* (1893), and *The Story of a Billiard Ball* (1897).

Jeppe, Julius (1859–1929). One of the first European settlers of the Transvaal, Jeppe started with one mine and rose to become one of the leading mining magnates and landowners of his day. He was deeply interested in education and financed the construction of several South African schools. The first, an elementary school, was opened in Johannesburg in 1897; the neighborhood around it came to be called Jeppestown and the school the Jeppe Grammar School. Jeppe High School began operating immediately after the Anglo-Boer War.

A dedicated sportsman, excelling in athletics, polo, and cricket as well as shooting, Jeppe threw himself into his affairs with an enviable energy: He was the founder of the Witwatersrand Township Estate and Finance Corporation, the chairman of the Wanderers Club, vice-president of the Transvaal Cricket Union, and the dominant member of the Witwatersrand Council for Education. From 1910–1918 he became the honorary Japanese consul at Cape Town, fighting to have Japanese citizens excluded from the Union's increasingly restrictive immigration laws.

He was the holder of an incredible seventy-five listings in the 1899 edition of *Rowland Ward's Records of Big Game;* he died in London on 2 September 1929. Rowland Ward 1899: hartebeest, topi, bontebok, blesbok, tsessebe (#5), brindled gnu, white-tailed gnu, common duiker (#2), blue duiker, red duiker (#1), Somali dik-dik, oribi, Livingstone antelope, grysbok, steenbok (#5), klipspringer, waterbuck, sing-sing waterbuck, buffon kob, Uganda kob, lechwe, puku, gray rhebok (#4), reedbuck, mountain reedbuck, springbok, dorcas gazelle, Speke gazelle, Pelzeln gazelle, Loder gazelle (#3), Thomson gazelle, Grant gazelle, Soemmerring gazelle, dibatag, sable, roan (#4), gemsbok, beisa oryx, addax, bushbuck, nyala, sitatunga (#2), greater kudu, lesser kudu, eland,

BUFFALO, WEST AFRICAN BUFFALO (#2, NIGERIA), WARTHOG, BLACK RHINO, WHITE RHINO, ELEPHANT, LEOPARD.

Johnson, Frank W. F. (1866–1943). Johnson was a young adventurer with bush experience when Cecil Rhodes approached him in 1889 with an offer he couldn't refuse: Raise a volunteer corps of five hundred men and invade the Matabele king Lobengula's vassal state of Mashonaland. For this work Johnson would receive an operating budget of £87,000 and a reward of 100,000 acres of land in Mashonaland (other sources give different figures). Johnson fell to his task with zeal, raising the famous Pioneer Corps. With a volunteer rank of major, the twenty-three-year-old Johnson recruited as daring and bold a group of white men as southern Africa had ever seen. Guided by Frederick Selous, himself commissioned a captain in the unit, the Pioneers spearheaded the first real challenge to Lobengula's authority that the Europeans had ever raised.

Lobengula was assured by various emissaries that the British did not wish to offend him, that they merely wished to build a road around his kingdom to the new mines and farms they would build in Mashonaland. The Matabele king was not happy with the idea, but longed to avoid a fight with the Europeans. He had heard what the British had done to the Zulu armies a scant ten years before. Lobengula stated, "There is a wall built around the word of a king," meaning he would respect the Europeans' wishes provided they did not traverse his own lands. Still, he was under great pressure from the military caste of his people, particularly the younger warriors, to crush the impudent Europeans, and the British themselves were certain he could not resist the bait that was the Pioneer Column. When the time came, however, Lobengula was able to restrain his young men, and although the Pioneers were shadowed every step of the way as they built their road, no attack took place.

Trooper Adrian Darter wrote a memoir of the Column, published in 1914. In it he praises Lobengula for keeping his word and not attacking the Pioneers in 1890, and criticizes the chartered company for orchestrating the invasion of the king's lands just three years later. Darter goes on to tell a story of how he, Major Johnson, Trooper Fred Langermann, Capt. Ted Burnett, and a police captain named Heyman went hippo hunting one day to provide meat for the troops. They "fired incessantly" at numerous hippo along the reedy banks of a river, and because they were hunting for food for several hundred men, they did not wait to see if the animal was hit before going on to the next one. Hippo, of course, sink when they are fatally shot and take several hours to refloat. At one point Major Johnson, negotiating his way through the reeds, actually stepped on a hippo that was sleeping on its side in the shallow water, and as the equally surprised beast lumbered up and plunged into the water, Johnson was knocked over. Darter and Burnett were waist-deep in the water when Johnson fired a bullet near them, and when they asked, "What are you doing, Major?" he replied, "Potting a big crocodile." It was a joke, for they had seen no crocodiles all day and were beginning to think that the reptiles were absent from that stretch of the river.

The next day when the men returned to the river, several hippo carcasses had floated to the surface. When Johnson and Darter swam out to recover one of them, Burnett hollered, "Look out, Johnson, a crocodile near you!" But Johnson simply swore at him, thinking it was revenge for the previous day's prank. When they finally towed the carcass back to shore, some of the African trackers pointed out the crocodile teeth marks on the hippo's hide. Darter later wrote, "The Pioneers had hippopotamus bacon for days and excellent fare it is."

Johnson died on the Channel Islands during World War II.

Johnson, Martin and Osa. Martin (1884–1937) and Osa Johnson (1894–1953) were a husband-and-wife team of documentary filmmakers who traveled the world filming primitive societies and wildlife in the Pacific, Borneo, India, Java, and Africa. Best known for their African films, they packed movie houses in the 1920s and 1930s. The couple logged more than sixty thousand air miles over Africa and many more over Asia.

Martin was the cinematographer, pointing the camera and turning the crank. Osa was billed as the white hunter, firing a warning shot at the last minute to turn a raging rhino or shooting a lion within feet of her husband. In press releases she was said to be possibly the best female shot on the African continent, although the Johnsons took care always to have a second professional hunter standing in the wings. She benefited from skillful editing: A sequence in the film *Simba* shows her shooting a charging rhino, but the same footage, unedited, was also included in *Congorilla,* and it is clear that Osa did not kill the animal. Nevertheless Osa was certainly an effective shooter in her own right.

She hadn't started out that way. A pretty, small-town girl from the Midwest, she was smitten by local photographer Martin Johnson's true tales of roaming the South Seas with the legendary novelist Jack London and his wife Charmian. After a brief courtship the two married in 1910. Martin, who let Osa sing at his lecture show, liked to say "I couldn't afford to hire her so I married her." For several years the Johnsons eked out a living by alternating adventure travel and displaying the resulting photographs and films on the vaudeville circuit (a struggling humorist named Will Rogers sometimes shared billing with them).

Their first big expedition together, a 1917 visit to the South Pacific where they were in very real danger of being killed by headhunters, resulted in several silent pictures with titles like *Cruising in the Solomons* and *Saving Savages in the South Seas.* Most of the 1920s were spent filming in Africa. Gradually their films of the Solomon Islands and East Africa won them a following, and by 1930 the Johnsons had achieved both financial and critical success. Their financial backers included George Eastman of Eastman/Kodak, and the American Museum of Natural History.

In the 1920s the couple made several extended visits to Africa, making popular wildlife and "tribal" silent movies. Their first African safari, in 1921, was poorly organized and the porters were unhappy to the point that Martin Johnson had to order his headman to whip the more recalcitrant men. In later years the Johnsons were more prepared and set up a permanent camp at a remote lake near Marsabit, having been shown to the spot by Blayney Percival. The camp became the center of their activities when in Africa. The Johnsons called it Lake Paradise and in their books and films gave the impression that they were the first to see the pristine location, let alone settle it. This irked many of the old Kenya hands because not only was the lake an established safari area, but there had been a government outpost nearby since 1910.

Using Lake Paradise as a base, the Johnson's traveled on short safaris of various lengths, bringing along a number of cameras and returning to the lake to develop the results. A large water purification system had to be built on the site in order to filter out the sediments and tiny creatures inhabiting the lake water so as to prevent them from ruining the film. When the system was in full operation, over eight hundred gallons of water every day were hauled up from the lake by mule-power and filtered through layers of charcoal, sand, and cotton. The Johnsons built a number of other bases as well, and in 1928–1929 they stayed near Leslie Simpson's old camp on the fringe of the Serengeti.

Their films included *Jungle Adventure* (1921), *Trailing African Wild Animals* (1923), *Simba* (1928), *Wonders of the Congo* (1931), *Congorilla* (1932), *Wings over Africa* (1934), *Baboona* (1935), and *Borneo* (1937). The Johnsons tended to be more authentic than many documentary filmmakers of their day, and modern researchers consider their pictures to be important cultural records. *Congorilla* was the first talking film made entirely in Africa. Martin Johnson reportedly made a tasteless short film called *African Golf,* in which the mouths of dead hippos and crocodiles were used as golf holes and an elephant carcass as a hazard; fortunately, perhaps, the film was never released and it seems likely that the footage has been lost.

The Johnsons also published books (eighteen between the two of them), often with the same name as the corresponding film. Many of the books were written by ghostwriters, and it is difficult to tell at this point which parts were written by the Johnsons and which by the hired help, except that those sections produced by the ghostwriters generally have a more polished and professional style. For example, *Lion* (1929) was written almost entirely by ghostwriter Fitzhugh Green, while *Safari* (1928) was penned largely by Martin Johnson, with Green simply adding a professional touch-up.

Martin always displayed a tremendous amount of energy, all the more impressive when you consider that

Martin Johnson as a young man.

he suffered from severe diabetes for most of his life. He constantly had to be attentive to Osa who, while she had a genuinely sweet nature, was prone to drinking too much. Their last great adventure together was an expedition to Borneo in 1936.

Martin Johnson was killed in a plane crash near Burbank, California, in January 1937; Osa was badly hurt but recovered quickly. Within a year she was romantically involved with her manager, Clark Getts (1893–1982), a brilliant showman who transformed her image from being just Martin Johnson's rifle-toting wife to a media superstar in her own right. Osa dropped the frumpy safari outfits and adopted a dazzling array of beautiful dresses and expensive furs, and in 1939 she joined Bette Davis on the Fashion Academy's Twelve Best Dressed Women's list. She marketed her own clothing line, which included exotic colors like Kenya Blue, Masai Bronze, and Uganda Flame. So well dressed did Osa become that when she lost a $700,000 lawsuit for negligence against the airline involved in Martin's death, courtroom veterans blamed her expensive clothing for the otherwise inexplicable verdict. It was felt that the rustic jurors just could not sympathize with a woman whose clothing cost more than they made in a year.

Osa, despite her popular fame and a certain degree of success in the business world, had difficulty maintaining a separate identity apart from her late husband. When in 1939, for instance, the Lippincott publishing company printed a book of animal stories under her name, the head of the company insisted the author be credited as "Mrs. Martin Johnson." Osa protested, but Lippincott remained inflexible. Finally her agent, Clark, suggested a compromise that would work both desired names onto the cover: *Osa Johnson's Jungle Friends,* by Mrs. Martin Johnson. Lippincott agreed and that is how the book was published.

Osa Johnson and George Eastman blowing an ostrich egg for a breakfast omelet.

The Legend with Osa Johnson standing guard, Masabit, 1920s.

In 1940 Osa produced a best-selling memoir of her life with Martin, entitled *I Married Adventure.* The book was actually written by ghostwriter Winifred Dunn, who specialized in radio scripts. It was a huge, popular success and more than 500,000 copies were sold within the first year. Dunn, who had ghosted the book for a flat fee on the assumption that it would enjoy only minor sales, tried to get more money out of Osa when the book hit the bestseller list but failed. In 1989 William Morrow and Company published a new edition put together by the staff of the Martin and Osa Johnson Safari Museum in Chanute, Kansas. This latest printing was blessed with minimal editing and contained a number of previously unpublished photographs.

By the mid-1940s Osa had run out of stories about Africa and the South Pacific and began a rapid decline. She married Getts in a secret ceremony in 1940 and divorced him nine years later. She tried her hand at acting but a lack of talent and her increasing alcoholism cost her a number of engagements. In 1950 some of her African films were converted into twenty-six half-hour episodes and shown as a television show called *Osa Johnson's Big Game Hunt.* The show was narrated by naturalist Ivan Sanderson, whose father Arthur B. Sanderson had been fatally injured by a rhino while working as a professional hunter for the Johnsons in 1925.

Osa Johnson was found dead in her New York apartment on 7 January 1953, the victim of a heart attack. Many of the mementos from her and Martin's exotic career were sold at auction to pay off her debts; they brought piddling sums, much to the disappointment of Osa's mother, Belle Leighty (1876–1976). In the 1960s, following the establishment of the Martin and Osa Johnson Safari Museum, Belle and other people associated with the museum were successful in recovering many of the items.

Johnson, Wally (1912–1990). Johnson began hunting in 1926 in Mozambique when he was fourteen. Mozambique at that time was so primitive that when he got his first driver's license a few years later he was assigned No. 59. In the 1930s all restrictions on elephant hunting were lifted because the animals were so numerous they were causing serious damage to farms and plantations. Johnson quickly made a name for himself as an ivory hunter.

Johnson later went on to work for Werner von Alvensleben's Safarilandia Company. His many adventures there included being gored by a buffalo and bitten by a gaboon viper (he is one of the few men to survive such a bite). He was the subject of Peter Capstick's book, *The Last Ivory Hunter* (1988).

Johnston. In November 1904 a North-East Rhodesian hunter of this name, operating on the Luangwa River, was literally ripped to pieces by an elephant that he had wounded ten times. In another book the same source (Denis Lyell) gives the man's name as Johnson.

Johnston, Alexander Keith (1844–1879). Born in Edinburgh, Scotland, on 24 November 1844, Keith Johnston was an accomplished geographer and map engraver by the age of twenty-five. From 1873 to 1875 he worked on the Paraguay Boundary Commission, and in 1878 he was selected to head the Royal Geographical Society expedition to Lake Nyasa. Six weeks into the safari he sickened and died, leaving the young Joseph Thomson to take command. Thomson went on to make history. Johnston was buried in Africa. Once the rising star of African exploration, he is all but forgotten now. Ironically, Johnston was dissatisfied with Thomson as his second-in-command, and there seems little doubt he would have fired Thomson soon if he had remained healthy.

Johnston, Sir Harry Hamilton (1858–1927). The man who coined the phrase "From the Cape to Cairo," Sir Harry Johnston had a unique career in British colonial Africa. His memorial in Sussex honors his service as "Administrator, Soldier, Explorer, Naturalist, Author, and Painter," and to this list might be added novelist, historian, hunter, and linguist (he spoke English, Portuguese, Arabic, and several African tongues).

He first visited the Dark Continent as a lad of twenty-one, studying art in Tunis (he had some talent as a painter). In 1882 he went on a shooting trip with Lord Mayo to Angola, doing some diplomatic and scientific work on the side in the manner typical of nineteenth-century upper-class Englishmen. Separating from Mayo, he traveled to the Belgian Congo and met Henry Stanley, the beginning of a lifelong friendship. Johnston was very young looking and slightly built for his age, and the local chieftains often thought him to be Stanley's son.

In 1883 the Royal Geographical Society joined with the Royal Society and the British Association to finance a "Natural History and Botanical" expedition to Mount Kilimanjaro. Johnston, though just twenty-five, was picked to lead it. Despite great expectations and hopes, the meager sum of only £1,000 was allotted to the expedition. In March 1884 Johnston left England. After a stopover in Egypt (and obtaining the needed porters and provisions from the ex-missionary Charlie Stokes, later hanged as a gunrunner), Johnston led his safari out of Zanzibar into the interior.

Right away he had difficulties. On the very first day, his Swahili porters decided to strike for higher wages. Johnston, who was short and thin and still looked like a schoolboy, beat the ringleader severely with a stout stick. Clearly the boyish artist schooled by Stanley was not a bwana to trifle with. Throughout most of his career in Africa Johnston was repeatedly challenged by older and unwise Arabs and Africans who were presumably deceived by his boyish looks and easy charm into thinking that he could be pushed around. They couldn't have been more wrong, for Johnston was cut from the same mold as Burton and Baker and never hesitated to use force when it seemed called for. He would even kill when necessary. Not intrinsically cruel or violent by nature (like Stanley was, for instance), Johnston was immensely practical—once he decided that violence was the best way to solve a particular problem, he did not hesitate to put that solution into effect. Given other circumstances, he was just as likely to cajole, bribe, or charm an opponent, if that was more likely to achieve his goal. More than anything else, it was Johnston's clear-sighted pragmatism in the service of the Empire that enabled him to accomplish so much.

Johnston set up base in an area near Kilimanjaro ruled by a native king called Mandara of Moshi. Mandara was something of a tyrant and continually extorted goods and services from Johnston. Most of Johnston's Swahili porters, paid in advance by the inexperienced explorer, deserted him and returned to the coast. Johnston bought a small parcel of land on the slopes of Kilimanjaro from Mandara for some gunpowder. There he built a farm. He seems to have had dreams of establishing an English–African empire around his small plot of land.

Mandara proved a difficult neighbor, however, constantly demanding gifts and attempting to embroil Johnston in tribal wars. Despite this, the young Englishman gradually explored Kilimanjaro and collected botanical specimens, including some unknown plants that were later named after him—*Crinum johnstoni* and the bananalike *Senecio johnstoni.* Johnston indulged his interest in hunting and the animal kingdom, shooting a charging leopard at close range and discovering a herd of elephant that lived at an altitude of thirteen thousand feet. Hoping to get guns and military assistance, Mandara held Johnston a virtual hostage on his Kilimanjaro farm. Finally, using a subterfuge, Johnston slipped away from his watching guards and, on his way back to the coast, deterred a Masai raiding party by convincing them his porters had smallpox. He returned to London with his specimens in 1885 and for a while was lionized as "Kilimanjaro Johnston."

After this episode Johnston was appointed Vice Consul for the Oil Rivers and the Cameroons in West Africa. In 1887 he underwent, as his brother later put it in *Life and Letters of Sir Harry Johnston* (1929), "another gruesome experience in the course of painting the map red." Visiting a local chief, Johnston was served a banquet, the main course of which he could not quite place. It was the flesh of the tribe's former chief, carefully preserved and served up only to guests of great distinction. This gave Johnston not only indigestion, presumably, but also a unique perspective when he published his treatise on cannibalism that same year.

In 1889 Johnston was appointed consul general for Portuguese East Africa. As such he was able to renegotiate with the Portuguese a settlement that gave Britain control of the Shire Highlands and much of what is now Malawi. This occurred despite feverish efforts by the Portuguese explorer Serpa Pinto to stop him. At one point Serpa Pinto managed to have Johnston captured and temporarily detained.

Upon his release, Johnston didn't hold a grudge against the Portuguese. On the contrary, he and Cecil Rhodes had a falling out over Johnston's refusal to back a coup d'état designed to steal the Portuguese colony of Beira or Lourenço Marques for Britain. Bucking Cecil Rhodes had a serious negative impact on Johnston's career. Rhodes, who through the BSAC (see glossary) had been subsidizing Johnston's administration in Nyasaland, immediately cut all cash, and Johnston suddenly found himself a marked man in the Byzantine British government. Johnston, like many eccentric but brilliant men, had the fatal habit of appearing to be condescending and arrogant even when he was trying to be pleasant. To make matters worse, he was considered an upstart and a prodigy of Lord Salisbury. Once, when Johnston was feeling rather full of himself, a permanent civil servant brought him down to size by drawling, "Remember, we are always here."

Appointed commissioner of Nyasaland, Johnston waged a ferocious anti-slavery campaign against Arab and African traders, using some sixty Sikh soldiers and a handful of highly trained Zanzibar askaris as a strike force. The English made a series of forced marches and surprise attacks that prevented the enemy from organizing against them. A story was circulated by the English press that Johnston would lead each attack under a white parasol. This was the type of idiotic gesture and image that the British penny press loved, revealing the eccentric yet courageous warrior. But it wasn't entirely accurate, and in several future writings Johnston mentioned the "white umbrella" in mocking terms.

Rhodes and the civil servants may have had it in for him, but the British press and public adored Harry Johnston. The *Pall Mall Gazette* gushed, "Commissioner Johnston is playing havoc with the slave raiders. Not only has he liberated hundreds of captives, but he has tried the raiders and sentenced them to terms of imprisonment. It would not have been Mr. Johnston, by the way, if he had not had some remarkable escapes. We wonder if he carried any arms except his customary umbrella." Johnston finally triumphed completely over the slavers, hanging their leader, Mlozi, in December of 1895 after an unorthodox legal proceeding. He then settled down to establish the new administration of the fledgling colony.

The newspapers found Johnston to be a popular topic. In one reported case, Johnston ordered a Sikh soldier to spare a wounded Arab. The Arab treacherously pulled a gun and killed the Sikh, and Johnston promptly put a bullet in the wounded man's head. The story may be apocryphal but was passed on as true by Johnston's secretary and biographer, his brother Alex. The campaign finally ended only when the most prominent slaver, a native named Makinjara, was defeated on the shores of Lake Nyasa and his town was burned.

After a spell back in England, Johnston returned to Africa in 1899 as special commissioner and commander-in-chief of the Uganda Protectorate. He set up base at Entebbe, then considered the healthiest spot on the northern shore of Lake Victoria. In early 1900 he was planning a pacification campaign into the Sudan when he was stricken with blackwater fever, an often-fatal illness. He quickly recovered, but was warned by his doctors not to enter the Sudanese provinces.

Johnston, who had put the colony of Nyasaland on solid footing, tried to do the same with Uganda. His surviving proclamations and letters reveal a lasting interest in sustaining what came to be called "indirect rule"—that is, allowing traditional African authorities wide discretion in domestic affairs under British leadership. He brooked no nonsense, however, from tribal leaders or visiting European sportsmen—one of his dispatches, dated 1901, warned against the flood of British hunters, missionaries, naturalists, and tourists who were becoming a drain on the colony's very limited resources. "No matter how wealthy some of these individuals profess themselves to be," he wrote, "they invariably end up living like parasites on one official or another." Under Johnston's leadership Uganda became virtually the only British colony in Africa that officially discouraged European settlement.

On the other hand, Johnston's tenure in Uganda was beset by difficulties, not just his poor health. Many of the native tribes were still not pacified and were given to raiding caravans and patrols—in June 1900 the Nandi alone killed some twenty-five people in various small raids and ambushes. In addition, Johnston was once again being hampered by the London government, this time in the form of Sir Clement Hill, the head of the African department at the Foreign Office. An unpopular military reorganization instituted by Johnston also caused some resentment, especially since the junior British officers in Uganda knew that Johnston's term was decidedly temporary.

Harry made cryptozoological history in 1900 by his discovery of the okapi. This strange, giraffelike beast had eluded the scientists for years. Vague rumors of a striped wild ass called the Atti had reached Stanley's ears, but no such creature had ever been seen. Johnston had decided to visit the Belgian Congo, in part to look for the Atti and in part to return some Pygmies he had saved from a German collector who wished to exhibit them in Europe. One of the Pygmies died while still in Uganda, and Johnston had him buried in an anthill so the skeleton could be sent to the Kensington Museum. Probably this move was not as offensive to indigenous sensibilities as it would be to ours.

Harry Johnston in 1888.

At Fort Mbeni in the Congo Free State the European officers freely discussed the rumors they had heard of the Atti. At this point the men still believed they were searching for some sort of wild donkey or horse. So when cloven hoofprints were pointed out by the Pygmies as belonging to the elusive animal, they were dismissed by the Europeans as being those of an eland. Mbeni was the first place where Johnston heard natives refer to the creature as an okapi. He was soon able to obtain two strips of okapi hide, which were being used as bandoliers by African riflemen. Then two officers in the Congo service provided Johnston with two okapi skulls and a nearly complete skin, missing only the hoofs. In his 1908 book *George Grenfell and the Congo* Johnston named the two officers as Lieutenant Meura and Lieutenant Eriksson of the Congo state government. It was Meura who had obtained the important items, but he died from blackwater fever before he could ship them. Eriksson, a Swedish officer in the Free State army, then dispatched the specimens to Johnston.

On 21 August 1900 Johnston forwarded the specimens to the London Zoological Society along with a letter in which he announced the discovery of the new animal. To this day the animal is known as *Okapia johnstoni.* The okapi is now the poster child for cryptozoology enthusiasts, being one of the more dramatic large animals discovered in the twentieth century.

Johnston donated most of his hunting trophies (in his later years his house was full of them, along with hundreds of his drawings and paintings) to British museums. He didn't call them trophies, and didn't really consider himself a hunter. He considered himself a scientist, and the elegantly mounted heads and horns were specimens. He was always on the lookout for new and interesting creatures, and while in Africa he often housed menageries of wild, half-tamed animals. He had a pet leopard in British Central Africa, and even in London he kept a mongoose as a pet. Despite all of his years of collecting specimens and hunting for "science" and for the pot, however, he once said that he had shot only one lion during his entire career. That animal, according to the story, had broken into Johnston's pigsty in Africa and tried to take a rare swine that he was shipping back to London.

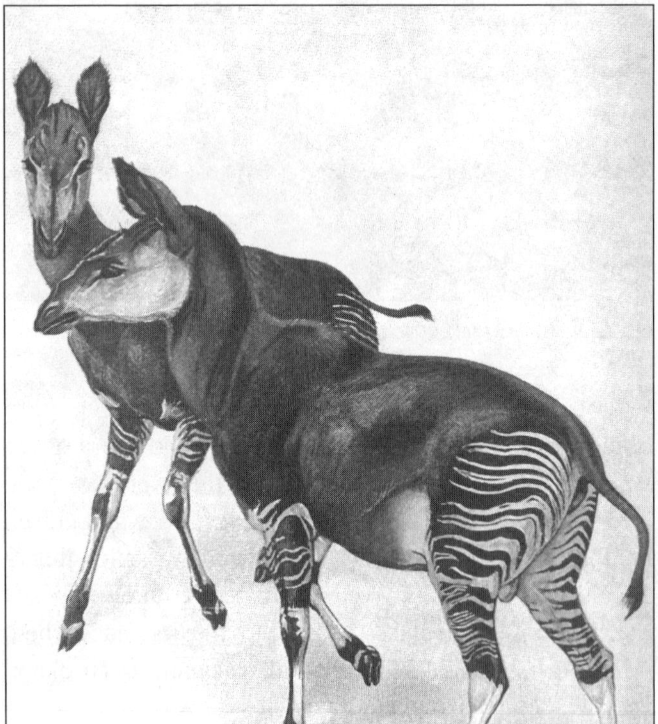

The okapi, newly discovered animal living in the African forests, sketched by Sir Harry Johnston, 1901.

Johnston continued as special commissioner for Uganda until September 1901. His health failing, he left that post and restricted himself to writing, finishing *The Uganda Protectorate,* a two-volume encyclopedic treatment of the country that came out in 1902. The book, like his *British Central Africa,* is an amazing accomplishment. The basic form of the civil administration that he established in Uganda remained intact until independence in the 1960s.

He also wrote a large number of profitable magazine articles and what we today would call think pieces. Frustrated by his efforts to find what he would consider a suitable diplomatic or colonial post, he retired from government service at a pension of slightly less than £500 per year. This was uncharitable, to say the least, considering Johnston's long service record and many accomplishments. The British treasury took the incredibly miserly position that since Johnston had been special commissioner for Uganda, the "special" part meant the job wasn't a regular government post and hence not creditable toward his pension. The amount was less than half what other officials with comparable careers were awarded. Sir John Kirk, a colonial official in Zanzibar of similar but less spectacular accomplishments, retired at £1,337 per year, while Sir Richard Wood, a contemporary consul general from Tunis whose name doesn't exactly ring through the history books, received an annual pension of £2,000.

As an aside, upon his return to England Johnston caused a bit of an uproar by writing an article for *Graphic* magazine on the Irish question. Though theoretically unopposed to Home Rule—the concept of permitting the Irish to legislate for themselves—Sir Harry was a bit out of touch. In all seriousness he recommended that animals once indigenous to Eire but now extinct, such as the elk, the wolf, and the bear, be reestablished to make the place "more interesting." His ideas might sound attractive to a modern audience schooled in conservation and ecology, but telling an Irish farmer of a hundred years ago that you wanted to put bears into his neighborhood woodlot, just to make the place "interesting," was simply crazy. These comments did not go over well, and public opinion was divided between those who thought Johnston was making fun of the Irish and those who thought he was losing his mind. Like many other public figures, Johnston at this stage of his life would have done himself an immense favor if he had just kept his mouth shut once in a while. Things like this kept him out of parliament and gave him a reputation as a loose cannon.

Always controversial, Johnston was a pronounced agnostic when it came to religious matters, and was known to become angry whenever one of his agnostic friends "found the faith" and joined a church. He studied many of the world's religions, large and small, but even his brother Alex admitted he could not discuss or write about them objectively. His friend Lady Percy Saint Maur, after listening to Johnston lecture on religion, remarked, "His trouble seems to be regret that he is not God." Harry once told his brother of his "readiness to become a Catholic if they would make him Pope."

Although a confirmed skeptic in matters paranormal, Johnston had his share of supernatural experiences. In one case that happened while he was stationed in the Cameroons, Johnston distinctly saw his African servant, Solomon, pass by him into his house at a distance of just a few feet. When he looked for Solomon later, Harry couldn't find him. It turned out that Solomon had drowned (or been killed by sharks) when his canoe capsized off a nearby beach at precisely the time Johnston saw his apparition. Similarly, Johnston's estate in Sussex, built around a twelfth-century monastery, was haunted by the faint sound of Gregorian chants—Harry heard them frequently, as did his wife and his brother Alex. The noises stopped when renovations were done on the old building. Another weird anecdote passed on by Alex Johnston had the famous journalist W. T. Stead telling Harry some years before his death that he had a premonition that he (Stead) would die in a panicked crowd. In 1912 Stead drowned on the *Titanic*.

Johnston spent the first years of the new century writing books, working as interim director of the London Zoo, and losing an election for member of Parliament for Rochester. In late 1903 or early 1904 he became a director for two companies seeking to develop the rubber and other industries in Liberia. Johnston profited greatly in this endeavor from his still-considerable connections in the British government. When Edward Grey became foreign minister in 1906, however, Johnston lost most of his influence and all of the financial backing. He also got himself embroiled in a public campaign against cannibalism, which further solidified his growing reputation as a loose cannon and an eccentric.

Johnston continued to involve himself in social issues, touring the Caribbean and the United States, where he struck up a friendship with Theodore Roosevelt. Among other things they discussed Roosevelt's upcoming hunting trip to East Africa. He met with Roosevelt a number of times and, when visiting Washington, was put up in the same room of the White House where Abraham Lincoln had signed the Emancipation Proclamation. Roosevelt saw in Johnston a kindred spirit, another twentieth-century "Renaissance Man" of action, with varied interests ranging from big-game hunting to simplifying English spelling. Both were deeply interested in the future of race relations, and Roosevelt helped introduce Johnston to noted black Americans such as Booker Washington and George Washington Carver. Johnston used much of the material provided by these men in his book *The Negro in the New World* (1910).

Age fifty-six when war broke out in 1914, Johnston offered to serve the government in any capacity but was refused. Thereupon he toured America as a private citizen, building up support for the British cause at lectures and fairs. He found time to complete a monumental grammar of the Bantu languages and made trips to the Western Front to talk to the troops and buck up morale. During one of these trips he got caught in a gas attack and was hospitalized for some time.

His long career of service to Great Britain, which had begun at Kilimanjaro and ended in Flanders, was nearing an end. Johnston published his autobiography, *The Story of My Life,* in 1923, and he is also remembered in *The Life and Letters of Sir Harry Johnston,* written by his brother in 1929.

Among his many books, *British Central Africa* (1897) is an absolute masterpiece of its genre, a comprehensive account of Nyasaland's geography, history, population, botany, zoology, and languages. That active men like Johnston and Baker found time to write such riveting books is both a testament to Victorian vitality and an indication of what can be done when you have servants running all of your errands. He was a unique man for a unique age. Anyone who can hang slavers, establish countries, be captured by cannibals, and get wounded in a German gas attack has led an interesting life. He deserves to be remembered more than he is.

Johnston, James. Johnston was a medical doctor from Jamaica who toured Africa in the early 1890s, traveling some forty-five hundred miles through Angola, Rhodesia, Nyasaland, and Mozambique without firing a shot in anger. He was the author of *Reality Versus Romance in South Central Africa* (1893).

Johnstone, Henry. Johnstone was a British diplomat in the early 1900s who held posts in Abyssinia, Zanzibar, and Nyasaland. According to a 1909 *McClure's Magazine* article, he was hunting in Nyasaland when he was charged by an enraged elephant. The source does not say whether the animal was wounded or not. At any rate, the elephant grabbed Johnstone around the waist with its trunk and threw him off a thirty-foot cliff. It then stomped his rifle, bending and ruining the barrel. Johnstone had serious injuries to his leg and foot and was one of the earliest beneficiaries of the new medical technique of skin-grafting. He recovered fully and was able to resume his African career.

Jones, Charles Jesse "Buffalo" (1844–1918). "Buffalo" Jones was an American stage cowboy billed as "The Last of the Plainsmen." He started his career as a bona fide buffalo (bison) hunter. In the 1870s he was based in Dodge City and made his living hunting the animals for their hides. Sometime around 1880 he settled down to open a ranch at Garden City, Kansas.

There Jones started experimenting with domesticating the bison. He began by capturing bison calves and having them raised by domestic cows. During 1886–1888 he captured some fifty calves and paired them with foster–cows. The animals got along well together and formed the appropriate bonds. This got Jones thinking of cross-breeding buffalo with cattle (the so-called "cattalo," a name Jones invented). Bison are hard to domesticate—as they grow up they become aggressive and even dangerous. As a general rule bison bulls are too hard to handle by their third year while cows are tractable a bit longer. Jones hoped he could combine the temperament of the domestic cow with the bison's ability to put on muscle and prosper in harsh winter conditions.

While technically successful, the cattalo experiments (conducted by various authorities besides Jones up through the 1940s) proved economically undesirable. There were problems with the fertility of the offspring, and the basic concept was fundamentally flawed. It's much easier just to grow a cow. Amateur geneticists always seem to think that crossbreeding two species will bring out the best qualities of each; it's often the reverse. Rather than emerging rugged and beefy like a bison and docile like a cow, the cattalo tended to be skinnier and more skittish than the respective parents.

There was one extremely beneficial result of these experiments, however: By gathering his bison stock, Jones was instrumental in saving the species from total extinction. By the 1890s he had a herd of some one hundred of the animals, one of the last significant reservoirs of the species. He sold parts of the herd to various other ranchers, and even sent five pairs of bison to England. The animals kept by Jones and a few other ranchers were the ancestors of today's remaining bison herds.

Around 1900 Jones turned to show business, specializing in rodeo-style lasso tricks. In 1910 he led a team of two expert cowboys (Ambrose Means and a man named Loveless), photographer Cherry Kearton, journalist Guy Scull, and Arusha white hunters Ray Ulyate and his son to East Africa in an effort to demonstrate that African animals could be captured harmlessly with a rope.

The Kenyans greeted Jones with a good-natured skepticism. The universal belief was that lassoes might be fine for roping steers and bucking broncos, but the dangerous game of East Africa would make fools of the hardened cowboys. The party left Nairobi with considerable fanfare, boarding a special train outfitted by the Boma Trading Company.

Contrary to Kenyan expectations, the expedition was a roaring success. They quickly demonstrated the efficacy of lassoing African animals by catching and releasing rhino, zebra, cheetah, hartebeest, eland, and warthog. They finished on 25 March by capturing a lioness at a remote location near Kijabe called the Black Reef. Unlike the other animals, which were let go, the lioness was sent to the Bronx Zoo. Contrary to some published reports, the lioness was the last animal roped, not the first.

Guy Scull wrote a magazine article about the expedition called "Lassoing Wild Animals in Africa" (*Everybody's Magazine*, 1910). Much of the memorabilia of this trip, and other Jones material from his careers as a rancher, hunter, showman, and Yellowstone Park ranger, is on display at the Buffalo Jones Museum in Garden City, Kansas.

Jones, Nicobar. A professional hunter from Ohio with fifty years of African hunting experience, he features prominently in Alexander Lake's *Killers in Africa* (1953).

Jones, Pitt. Jones was a Boer hunter from Arusha who guided Berlin zookeeper Lutz Heck on collecting expeditions in Tanganyika in the 1930s.

Jordan, John Alfred. A professional hunter and poacher, Jordan is a questionable character from a twenty-first-century viewpoint. There seems to be no question that he lived and hunted in the times and places he claimed he did—indeed, it is almost eerie how often his name shows up in other hunters' memoirs. Yet his stories seem to have a touch of, shall we say, blarney that just doesn't ring true to modern ears. For instance, in *Elephants and Ivory* he claims to have seen a bizarre fifteen-foot aquatic animal with scales, spots, two long fangs, and a long, broad tail. That's quite a sighting. It would be easy enough to dismiss this as an attempt to jump on the modern cryptozoological bandwagon. But if you read *In Closed Territory* by Edgar Beecher Bronson, you'll see that Jordan was making that same claim back in 1910. Not only that, but C. W. Hobley, in a 1912 edition of the *Journal of the East African and Uganda Natural History Society*, tells of several other persons who knew of this mystery beast. Like many of Jordan's claims, this one is impossible to either dismiss or verify.

Suffice to say that John Alfred Jordan was a good hunter and a fair writer (he usually had a coauthor) who might have embellished his stories just a wee bit. He married an American girl named Eva Mercer and produced several books, including *Mongaso* (1956), *Elephants and Ivory* (1956), and *The Elephant Stone* (1959).

Judd, Bill (1870–1927). A highly respected outdoorsman who first came to East Africa in 1899, Judd made his name as a hunter while running a coffee farm at Fort Smith and a ranch at Lake Naivasha. His hunting exploits were legendary. Selous told a story of how he and Judd were riding mules through rough terrain on the Mau Plateau when a lioness sprang from cover right at Judd. Judd's mule bucked and threw him. As he fell he got a shot off with his rifle. Scrambling immediately into a crouch, Judd looked for the lioness to complete her charge, but she lay dead on the ground. His snapshot, fired as he was being thrown, had hit the lioness in the right eye and penetrated the brain.

Bill Judd applies permanganate of potash to an African beater who was injured by a leopard.

Bill Judd and Teddy Roosevelt, Kenya, 1909.

A veteran of the Boer War, Judd was one of the first Kenya hunters to make a regular business of guiding amateur hunters. Among his clients were William Northrup McMillan, Sir Edmund Lechmere, Baron Rothschild, Congressman Tinkham, and the Roosevelts. Judd also hunted in the Lado Enclave. He was a literate man and wrote occasional articles for the British sporting periodical *The Field.*

Sadly, like a retiring cop in an action movie, Judd was killed on what was to be his last safari. On 20 December 1927, while hunting elephant with his son, Jack, Bill Judd was tusked and trampled to death by a bull elephant that was not stopped by four shots from his own .577 Westley-Richards double. Only after his father was dead did Jack Judd manage to drop the bull with a brain shot from his .350 Rigby Mauser. ROWLAND WARD 1928: IMPALA.

Junker, Wilhelm (1840–1892). Junker was a German scientist and explorer, born in Moscow in 1840. He collected botanical and zoological specimens in the Upper Nile area from 1879–1886. Junker traveled Africa from 1875 to 1886, mapping the Congo River and exploring the Nile sources. His first expedition was 1875–1879, his second 1880–1886. One of his major objectives was to solve the "Welle question": Did the river of that name form part of the Congo or did it run into Lake Chad? It seemed important at the time.

When the rise of the Mahdi made the district much more dangerous, Junker (who never traveled with a military escort) retreated with his collections to Europe, warning the world of Emin Pasha's plight and peril. He brought with him Emin's extensive journals as well, fostering an emotional movement to "rescue" the Pasha. Junker was awarded the Gold Medal of the Royal Geographical Society in 1887, and was the author of *With My Friends the Cannibals, African Travels* 1875–1886, and *Travels in Africa During the Years 1882–1886.*

Bill Judd and rhino.

K

Kabarega (c. 1843–1923). Kabarega was king of the country called Bunyoro, Uganda's northernmost kingdom. Ascending to the throne after a vicious civil war that followed the death of his father, Kamurasi, in the 1870s, Kabarega was an independent and formidable opponent of the British. Legend had it that Sam Baker's high-handed treatment of his father had fostered that antagonism.

He ruled with the help of an elite bodyguard called the *bonosoora*, recruited from escaped slaves. Kabarega believed that the men would fight to the death rather than return to bondage. The theory proved correct—the *bonosoora* seemed to have fought outstandingly well during the frequent rebellions against his reign, rebellions that were frequently led by his numerous brothers.

In the 1870s Kabarega fought first against Baker and then against Emin Pasha, both of whom served as governors of Egypt's Equatoria province. Emin wrote that the Bunyoro king was "hospitable and intelligent," but that did not stop the almost constant warfare between the two. When Emin sent his aide, Casati, to speak with Kabarega, the king had the Italian soldier tortured and imprisoned from 1886–1889.

The British finally drove Kabarega out of power by sending several expeditionary forces against him, led variously by Lugard, Frederick Jackson, and General Sir Henry Colvile. Forced into hiding with his few remaining warriors, Kabarega emerged from the swamps during the 1897 Sudanese Mutiny to ally himself with his former enemy, the Bugandan Kabaka Mwanga, in one last desperate effort to oust the Europeans. Their combined forces were smashed by the British, and both Kabarega and Mwanga fled to the Nile marshes for safety.

A bribed local chief betrayed them to a British force under Colonel Ewart. Mwanga was captured easily, but Kabarega was subdued only when his arm was shot off and the remnants of the *bonosoora* lay dead around him. Kabarega was sent into exile, first to the Seychelles Islands and then to East Africa. He died in May 1923.

Kabarega, one of the most successful African kings who ever fought against the Europeans, was the victim of a propaganda campaign similar to the one used to demonize Lobengula in the Western press. A photo in Hunter and Mannix's book *Tales of the African Frontier* (reproduced from Swann's *Fighting the Slave Hunters in Central Africa*) shows two Africans with mutilated hands, purportedly the victims of Kabarega's barbarism. The same photo can be seen in other books, where it allegedly portrays tortured rubber collectors from the Belgian Congo.

Kandt, Richard (1867–1918). This German explorer from Posen led an 1898 expedition to find the true source of the Nile. Kandt, well educated and a bit of a raconteur, has sometimes been compared to Sir Richard Burton. He reported in his book *Caput Nili* that he had indeed found the Nile's source, a tiny spring at the head of a tributary called the Rukarara. Geographers have argued the issue ever since. The Nile actually comes from several sources, and a case can be made for them all.

Kearton, Cherry (1871–1940). Kearton was an early wildlife photographer who started filming in Kenya in 1909. He helped train Paul Rainey in the filmmaking business, and was a member of the Buffalo Jones expedition. Kearton was often joined in his early film efforts by his brother Charles.

Cherry Kearton photographing birds from a blind.

During World War I Kearton served in the legendary 25th Battalion of the Royal Fusiliers, along with big-game hunters Frederick Selous, Alan Black, and George Outram, and was later attached to the Royal Naval Air Service. During his long career Kearton produced numerous travel and nature films. His 1920s documentary *Tembi* brought public notice to the famous tame crocodile Lutembe. Two of his outstanding original photographs graced the lobby of Ray Ulyate's New Arusha Hotel in the 1930s.

In his 1930 book *In the Land of the Lion,* Kearton describes how he spotted what would be the world-record crocodile if his estimate of its twenty-seven-foot length could be proved:

> Several crocodiles of normal size waddled out of the river with the painful-looking and apparently exhausting gait which the creatures always use on land, and threw themselves down on the sand among some crane and plover. There they lay, opening their huge jaws so that I could see their teeth and look down their horrifying throats. Suddenly the water of the [Semliki] River stirred, a scaly snout appeared, and then yard upon yard of body followed as the giant crocodile raised himself slowly on his legs till his body was two feet from the ground. He waddled about two yards away from the water and then flopped down on the sandbank, lying there, an abhorrent creature of evil, until after some minutes he slowly turned, waddled once more to the river, and sank out of sight.

You just don't see that "abhorrent creature of evil" stuff in today's nature writing.

In addition to *In the Land of the Lion,* Kearton was the author of various books including *Photographing Wild Life Across the World* (1924) and *Adventures with Animals and Men* (1936). He was credited as the coauthor with James Barnes of 1915's *Through Central Africa from East to West.* It was while on safari with Barnes that Kearton allegedly spotted the twenty-seven-foot croc.

Kearton's wife Ada was a world-class soprano and author of the memoir *On Safari.*

Kennedy J. T. Assistant livestock officer in the Uganda Veterinary Department and tsetse control officer of Uganda, he was mentioned prominently in Negley Farson's *Behind God's Back* (1941). Kennedy was a prolific buffalo hunter for thirty years.

Ker, Donald (1905–1987). Donald Ker arrived with his family in East Africa as a young boy in 1911. They lived just outside of Nairobi at Groganville, then later moved to Thika. Young Donald shot his first lion in 1919 and learned to hunt elephant with his boyhood friend Mike Cottar. In 1936 Ker guided the American businessman Ruli Carpenter on a highly publicized expedition to collect Cape buffalo specimens. After World War II he founded Ker and Downey Safari Company with his onetime archrival Sid Downey.

Kerr, Walter Montagu (1852–1888). Kerr was an early British sportsman and explorer who was remarkable for his habit of walking through Africa virtually alone. Unlike other pioneers who moved about with numerous porters and retainers, Kerr preferred to strike out into the interior accompanied by one or two friends or guides. He was the first European to travel overland from Cape Colony to the Lakes region of central Africa, crossing the Zambezi River at Tete and walking through the Angoni tribe homeland to Lake Nyasa. He was also a prolific explorer of the land south of the Zambezi.

In 1884 Kerr walked from the gold districts of South Africa to British Central Africa, and spent the winter of 1884–1885 recovering from dysentery at a mission by Lake Nyasa.

In 1886 he set out from Zanzibar to attempt to traverse the continent from east to west. His planned itinerary would lead him to travel through Masailand to the north of Victoria Nyanza, drop in on Emin Pasha at Wadelai, explore Lake Chad, and then paddle down the Niger to the Atlantic.

Kerr was the author of *Far Interior: A Narrative of Travel and Adventure from the Cape of Good Hope Across the Zambesi to the Lake Regions of Central Africa* (1887).

Kespars. Another noteworthy French elephant hunter of the inter-war years, Kespars was a poacher in the grand style, leading large expeditions into Belgian territory and returning with big ivory. His largest tusks weighed about 120 pounds per side, exceptional for French Africa. A solitary, unfriendly, moody man, Kespars was still hunting in the 1950s.

Khama (1837–1923). King of the Mangwato tribe who ruled Bechuanaland from 1875 until his death in 1923, he was the son and heir of Sekhowe and features prominently in some South African hunting books. Selous visited him in his capital of Bamangwato in 1879 and found him reasonable in granting permission to hunt on his lands. There is a good photo of him and Arnold Hodson in the latter's *Trekking the Great Thirst* (1912).

Khama was almost universally praised in the literature. His policies were often progressive, as witness his prohibition of alcohol in his domain starting in the 1880s. He was depicted as a man of character and foresight, although he wasn't a pushover—his warriors killed Jonathan Afrika for breaking his hunting laws. On another occasion men sent by Khama shot to death a trader named Grobelaar who had sold the king a large number of "supposedly" salted horses that had immediately sickened and died. There was the predictable uproar and call for revenge among the local settlers, but the British government realized that there was no actual proof of Khama's complicity, and even if he was responsible, he had not acted entirely unreasonably. The matter was quietly settled by bestowing a small pension upon Grobelaar's widow.

King, J. H. King was an American adventurer, apparently from California, who served with the Boer army during the Anglo-Boer War. His skill at blowing up railroad bridges (he is said to have destroyed every bridge and culvert around Barberton) earned him the nickname of "Dynamite Dick."

Kingsley, Mary (1862–1900). Mary Kingsley's father was Dr. George Kingsley, an unusual physician who specialized in recommending long foreign trips as a curative to his wealthy hypochondriac patients. Then he would accompany them on their long vacations as a doctor, friend, and hunting companion. In this way Dr. Kingsley got to travel to the Mediterranean, Spain, Egypt, Syria, North Africa, and the South Pacific, and was paid for making the trip. On one of his visits home, however, he got his thirty-five-year-old cook, Mary Bailey, pregnant. Dr. Kingsley did the honorable thing and the pair married in October of 1862. Four days later, their daughter, Mary Kingsley, was born.

Until her parents died, Mary Kingsley led a normal Victorian life, though she displayed somewhat strange reading tastes for the time (she was educated entirely at home). Both her mother and her father passed away within six weeks of each other in 1892. Mary was devastated. It has become fashionable to look upon Mary's impulsive decision to go to Africa as an act of liberation, the enterprising young woman finally freed from the shackles of Victorian domestic life. The truth, however, is less romantic and much, much sadder. Mary was depressed; she went to West Africa "to die," as she wrote in a letter to a friend.

But Africa, as it did for so many people, gave her life, at least for a time. In the same letter, quoted in Katherine Frank's *A Voyager Out,* Kingsley wrote, "West Africa amused me and was kind to me and scientifically interesting and did not want to kill me just then." Her questing intellect found a whole new world to explore, and she made the most of it. She was particularly interested in what she called "fetish"—that is, the magic and religious tradition of the native peoples.

From 1893 on Mary roamed the West African hinterlands, not on a guided safari or restricting herself to tourist spots but wandering the back country virtually alone. She refused to "go bush" and insisted on dressing like a Victorian lady because, after all, that is what she was. On at least one occasion, this attention to propriety may have saved her life. She fell into a cleverly hidden native game pit, but escaped death and injury on the sharp spikes below because her black silk dress and voluminous woolen skirt acted as a cushion or mattress. When necessary, however, Kingsley could be unladylike as well. Once a crocodile tried to climb aboard her canoe with felonious intent. She whacked the thing over the head with her paddle until it backed off.

Kingsley wrote two books that are now considered classics, *Travels in West Africa* and *West African Studies.* In 1899 she published a collection of articles written by her late father called *Notes on Sport and Travel.* During her last years in England, Kingsley wielded a tremendous amount of influence on the British government and public. She was generally considered the country's foremost authority on

Mary Kingsley (seated second from left) in Calabar in 1895. Roger Casement is standing on the far right.

West Africa and waged a long, hard battle for repeal of the "hut tax" in Sierra Leone. Despite her modern representation as a feminist hero, Kingsley was surprisingly conservative. She held conventional views on women's place in the world and opposed giving her sex the right to vote.

The following year she went to South Africa, both to work as a nurse and to report on the Boer War for the *London Evening News* and *Morning Post.* She had bought several new khaki uniforms for the nursing job. She was posted to the military hospital at a former barracks now called the Palace Hospital. There Kingsley cared for Boer prisoners of war who were ill from typhoid and measles, and some who had been shot attempting to escape. On her few nights off she often visited Rudyard Kipling, who was living a few miles away with his American wife Carrie. Then in May, after two months of nursing work, Kingsley came down with typhoid herself. She quickly weakened and died on 3 June 1900. She was thirty-seven years old.

After her death, her friends and fans back in England formed the African Society "in her memory." Lord Ripon was the first president of the Society but was soon replaced by Sir Harry Johnston. The ex-special commissioner of Uganda had mixed feelings about the society's adoration of Miss Kingsley. He felt, with justification, that Kingsley had less experience with Africa than many other people who had made the same sacrifices and received far less recognition in return. Johnston felt that if Kingsley had lived longer she may well have made significant contributions to Western knowledge and understanding of African ways, but that her achievements at the time of her death were not all that remarkable. As he wrote in his 1923 memoir, *The Story of My Life,* "I had an affection for Mary Kingsley, but no desire to create a Mary Kingsley myth, or to make her out as having written anything about Africa—as yet—worthy of serious remembrance or scientific discussion." Johnston, of course, lacked the historical perspective on the role of women in the Victorian Age that makes Kingsley so fascinating to modern readers.

Kinloch, B. G. (1920–xxxx). Major Kinloch was chief game warden of Uganda in the 1950s. Periodically the game department tried various programs to compensate ranchers and farmers for damage caused by wild animals. The programs were invariably short-lived, both because funds were short and the system was easily abused. In extreme cases, farmers would sell their crops and then report them eaten by wildlife. The decision about whether a claim was valid or not was left to the game warden.

Kinloch adjudicated one of the more unusual claims in 1956. An African farmer reported that a single wild animal had eaten much of his cotton crop. Game rangers duly went and trapped the culprit (identified as such by the farmer), but Kinloch was forced to reject the compensation claim. As he explained to the angry farmer, leopard just don't eat cotton.

Kirby, Frederick Vaughan. A British sportsman, taxidermist, and hunter, Kirby was hunting around Delagoa Bay as early as the early 1890s. He shot lion, buffalo, bushbuck, kudu, and leopard throughout Portuguese East Africa and the Transvaal, earning a great reputation among his fellow hunters. Arnold Hodson's *Trekking the Great Thirst* (1912) contains two chapters written by him. These relate how Kirby guided Lord Selborne on a 1910 hunting trip in Bechuanaland and also give some advice on the hunting of lion. Kirby was considered "the" expert on the subject.

He was the author of *In Haunts of Wild Game* (1896), *Sport in East Central Africa* (1897), and *Great and Small Game of Africa* (1899).

Kirk, Sir John (1832–1922). A Scotsman, Kirk was educated as a doctor and served as a civilian physician in the Crimea in 1856. In 1858 he joined Livingstone's second expedition as a naturalist and doctor, and worked with the missionary for the next five years. With J. C. Meller, Kirk explored the Shire River area in 1861–1862. Livingstone was a tough man to get along with: Kirk later wrote in a letter that the famous missionary was "as ungrateful and slippery a mortal as I ever came in contact with." After almost six years of loyal service, Kirk was dismissed by Livingstone without even a thank you.

In 1863 Kirk returned to England to recover his health, and then was appointed surgeon to the British Agent in Zanzibar in 1866. Kirk stayed in Zanzibar, becoming assistant political agent in 1868, consul general in 1873, and Agent in 1880. He retired from the diplomatic service in 1887, receiving an annual pension of £1,337. In 1889–1890 Kirk was a delegate to the Brussels anti-slavery conference, and in 1895 he was sent as a special emissary to the Niger. Kirk was also a member of the Uganda Railway Committee, an adept politician, and a highly regarded naturalist.

Kirkpatrick, Sir James Alexander. A half-brother of Beryl Markham, Kirkpatrick hailed from Limuru. He was a hereditary baronet and a handsome, hard-drinking bon vivant. In the 1930s he ran the Kenya Game Department's main office in Nairobi under chief game warden Archie Ritchie. After serving with the RAF in World War II, Kirkpatrick rejoined the department, becoming assistant chief game warden under Willie Hale in 1949. In 1954 he was found shot to death at Limuru. Despite rumors of adulteries and tangled love affairs, and despite some suspicious circumstances, his death was ruled a suicide. Modern writer Errol Trzebinski, probably the most meticulous researcher of this period, claims that Kirkpatrick died in a simple shooting accident while showing his wife how to handle a revolver.

Kisch, Daniel Montague (1840–1898). Kisch was a Jewish hunter and trader from England who operated in South-West Africa in the 1860s.

Kittenberger, Kalman. This Hungarian naturalist-hunter collector made numerous trips to British East Africa and Uganda. His first safari, under the auspices of the National Museum of Hungary, lasted from late 1902 to 1906, his second from late 1906 to the fall of 1907, and his third from December of 1908 through May of 1912. He came back in May of 1913, only to be interned as an enemy alien at the outbreak of war in 1914. Released in 1919, he came back to Africa for one last hunt in November of 1925, as a guide to several distinguished Hungarian sportsmen, including Eugene Horthy, a member of Hungary's ruling family.

Kittenberger was the author of *Big Game Hunting and Collecting in East Africa, 1903–1926.* Even in translation it is an excellent source. He was a thoughtful and careful observer as well as a practiced hunter. His skill at hunting bordered on professional status. Indeed, he frequently had to interrupt his collecting activities to guide safari clients or hunt commercially because the Hungarian authorities continually short-changed him in financing the collecting operation. To keep the expedition's financial head above water, Kittenberger hunted extensively for the pot and was not above selling surplus meat and hides to make ends meet. One unintended but fortunate result was that the Hungarian academic not only fulfilled his scientific responsibilities but also accumulated an unparalleled amount of big-game hunting experience.

In 1911 Kittenberger achieved the unique feat of performing an emergency Caesarian section on a black rhino. He shot a charging rhino without realizing that it was a female in the very act of giving birth. Always a scientist and a hands-on man, Kittenberger managed to extract the calf. Unfortunately, the animal died a week later. One wonders what Kittenberger was feeding it.

Kittenberger is remembered by Hungary's Kalman Kittenberger Botanical Park and Zoo, which opened in 1958.

Kirkman, R. H. Kirkman was appointed a game ranger at Kruger National Park in 1931.

Kleen, G. F. V. "Romulus" (xxxx–1990). "Romulus" Kleen was Bror Blixen's nephew, and the two men frequently went on safari together. On Blixen's last African hunt, in 1938, Kleen killed an elephant with tusks of 105 and 108 pounds. He was the editor of a book of Bror Blixen's letters.

Klein, Alfred J. "Al" (1883–1947). Born in New Jersey, Klein made a name for himself as a white hunter in East Africa. Armand Denis described him as a "small, dapper" man. He worked at the American Museum of Natural History before coming to Africa in the 1900s. Before World War I he worked for the safari firm of Newland and Tarlton; after the war he worked for Safariland. When Paul Rainey hunted lion with his pack of dogs in 1914, Klein came along to watch the fun. He kept a semi-permanent camp on the edge of the Serengeti, often shared with his compatriot Leslie Simpson. It was to this camp that Denys Finch Hatton came when he was bitten on the leg by a crocodile while guiding Frederick Patterson in 1927. Klein died in Kenya in 1947.

Professional hunter Eric Rundgren was the forestry officer at Karita in his youth. One day he was making his rounds through heavily wooded hills when he heard a shot. Investigating, he found a dead bongo, a snarling pack of hunting hounds, two American safari clients, an African game scout named Kumi, and professional hunter Al Klein. Everyone's eyes grew wide when Rundgren stepped into the clearing. Hunting bongo with dogs was strictly illegal. Klein stood to lose his license if reported, and the game scout would be at least fired and possibly jailed. Enjoying the moment, Rundgren cheerily said, "That's a nice bongo." Klein tried to bluff his way out. "Who are you?" he asked, looking Rundgren straight in the eye as if there was nothing in the world amiss. "I'm the forest officer, Karita," replied Rundgren and then calmly walked away. Rundgren, who knew a thing or two about breaking game laws, later speculated that Klein spent a nervous week or two wondering if the incident had been reported. The episode is probably atypical—Klein had a reputation as a naturalist and seems generally to have observed the game regulations.

Knoblecher, Ignaz (1819–1858). Well known in continental Europe but virtually forgotten in the English-speaking world, Knoblecher was born in Slovenia and originally went by the name Ignacij Knoblehar. Trained as a physician and as a priest in the Roman Catholic Church, he joined a missionary expedition to Khartoum in 1847. When the leader of the expedition, Father Maximilian Ryllo, died of dysentery on 17 June 1848, Knoblecher took over as expedition leader. He built a stone mission house (the only stone building in Khartoum) and planted a garden, the fruits of which were used to succor wandering European visitors like George and Andrew Melly and John Petherick.

Knoblecher was a brilliant, adventurous man who belies the image of the book-bound missionary. For starters, he liked to shoot. He made five trips up the White Nile, exploring new lands and investigating exotic tribes, and in the process he became an expert on the local languages (especially Bari). A small man with a reddish beard, he compiled huge amounts of data on Sudanese plants, animals, and geology, and sent the manuscripts and specimens back to the Vatican for safekeeping. Occasionally his travels became bloody: He was present at a fight at Libo where the Sardinian consul Vaudet was speared to death and Vaudet's nephews the Poncet brothers almost killed. The fracas seems to have started when a gun fired by Vaudet's crewmen as a salute to Knoblecher accidentally killed or injured a tribesmen standing on the bank.

Being a missionary on the White Nile in the 1850s was an incredibly dangerous business, and the majority of the priests who went to Khartoum and Gondokoro died from sickness shortly after arrival. Knoblecher lasted longer than most, but he was not immortal, and the microbes of Equatoria caught up to him eventually. He went to his reward on 13 April 1858, mourned by all who knew him and by a considerable portion of the scientific public. The mission he had created couldn't survive without him, and within a decade the Church had pulled out of the southern Sudan.

Knowles. A man named Knowles hunted elephant in the Lado Enclave in 1908, frequently working with Billy Pickering, an experienced hunter, and occasionally with Karamojo Bell. On his very first elephant hunt Knowles was charged by a bull. Pickering fired but failed to stop the charge, and Knowles tripped and fell as he tried to run away. The elephant tried to crush him into the ground, but Knowles managed to roll into some brush. He escaped serious injury but was bruised and had some broken ribs. He recovered after several weeks rest and became an effective hunter. According to Akeley (1920), Knowles shot a near-record 54-inch buffalo in Uganda.

Knowles took to hunting with a man named Dickens. In 1908 he and Dickens were camped near the Nile north of Lado. They had argued with the local Africans over buying some food, insulting the chief of the tribe. Dickens and Knowles were sitting quietly by the campfire one night when a shower of arrows rained down upon them. Dickens was wounded in the leg, and the two hunters barely managed to fight off the attack with their magazine rifles. News of the surprise attack caused mass desertions among the porters working for the Lado hunters.

Koch, Robert (1843–xxxx). Born in Klausthal, Germany, Professor Koch was one of the great early bacteriologists. He discovered the microorganisms responsible for both tuberculosis (1882) and cholera (1883) and in 1890 produced an early experimental treatment for the former disease. Koch accompanied the German expedition, whose purpose was to investigate cholera, to Egypt and India in 1883.

In *The Story of My Life* (1923), Sir Harry Johnston wrote that Koch, when "asked for a diagnosis when this malady [blackwater fever] was beginning to slay first hundreds then thousands in all Tropical Africa, offered the opinion that it was the result of overdoses of quinine." Johnston (along with the medical profession as a whole) dismissed that idea, stating, "It is sufficient to say that there are no grounds for such an explanation." Another thirty years or so would pass before Koch's speculation was validated.

Koenig, Oskar (1896–xxxx). Ossie Koenig was born in Germany and grew up on a landed estate in the Carpathian Mountains. His father promised him a trip to East Africa if he passed his Abitur, roughly equivalent to graduating from high school in the United States. World War I intervened, and young Koenig spent the best years of his youth fighting on the Western Front. After the Armistice Koenig just sort of drifted about, as did so many other German war veterans. In 1926 he decided to take the long-postponed African trip, which wound up being a three-month foot safari. Koenig enjoyed it so much that upon his return to Europe he

German PH Oskar Koenig.

immediately began saving for a second trip. He went back in 1928 and from then on made East Africa his home.

He settled down in Tanganyika. His first safari there was guided by Friedrich Siedentopf, the survivor among two brothers who had once leased the entire Ngorongoro Crater. By 1929 Koenig was a professional hunter leading his own safaris on the Tanganyika-Kenya border and in what is now Tanzania's Serengeti National Park. He was also made an honorary game ranger and in that capacity undertook elephant and rhino control when requested by the government. During World War II Koenig, who had fought against Britain in 1918, was so well thought of that the British authorities contracted his services on a number of occasions, including the jobs of supervising road construction and poaching control. He was an early member of EAPHA (see glossary) and the author of the *Pori Tupu* in 1954 as well as the *The Masai Story* in 1955. The first book is both a memoir and a look at the postwar safari industry, and is fairly well written and accurate.

Kolb, Johann Georg. Dr. Kolb was a widely known scientist and hunter of German nationality who came to a bad end. Kolb traveled through much of Kenya in 1894, taking lots of photographs. Some of these were printed in Arthur Neumann's *Elephant Hunting in East Equatorial Africa* (1898). Kolb had made an ascent of Mount Kenya and mapped the district. He was often accompanied by a fellow hunter named Von Bartineller.

Kolb is best remembered for his untimely death. Out collecting bird specimens with a shotgun one day, he was charged by a rhino. It was a large female, but no calf was seen in the vicinity and the attack was seemingly unprovoked. Kolb was chased to a large tree that had a hollow in its trunk. Around and around the tree he ran, the rhino snorting in pursuit, while his native staff climbed their own trees for safety. The unfortunate Kolb sought to end the stalemate by diving into the hollow of the tree, apparently thinking the rhino would give up. Instead the animal furiously jammed its horn into the hollow, skewering Kolb through the abdomen. Again and again the rhino gored the pinned man, leaving only a bloody pulp to be collected afterward. Even had he survived the initial attack, the state of medicine in those days was such that if the intestines were perforated, the resulting blood poisoning and infection were always fatal. But that point was rendered moot by Kolb's instant death.

Another version of his demise had the good doctor specifically gunning for rhino. He had killed one hundred fifty of the horned animals, but this one apparently avenged the others. Either way, some of Kenya's coarser sorts found Dr. Kolb's death a proper subject for jokes and wry commentary. The German was well known as a gourmet and purportedly had been very fond of fried rhino liver. Ironically, his penultimate rhino had impaled him directly through that same organ. Some found this accident amusing, others appropriate. Neumann named a lake after him. Harry Johnston wrote that each of Kolb's one hundred fifty dead rhino was "a far more interesting mammal than himself."

Kollmann, Paul. He was a German collector who made several trips around Lake Victoria to gather natural-history and ethnological specimens. He was the author of *The Victoria Nyanza* (1899), based on objects in his collection.

Krapf, Johann Ludwig (1810–1881). A German missionary and explorer, Krapf was the first-known European to sight Mount Kenya, in 1849. A theology student at Tuebingen and Basel, he joined the Church Missionary Society in 1837 and was sent on a mission to Abyssinia, where he stayed until 1842. In 1844 he founded an important mission at Rabai near Mombasa. Johann Rebmann joined him there in 1846, and Jakob Erhardt three years later. Krapf often explored

J. L. Krapf, December 1849.

Africa's interior, traveling as far inland as Kiambere Hill, on the Tana River near Embu. He returned to Germany in 1853 but came back to Africa as interpreter to the British General Napier on his 1868 Abyssinian expedition. Krapf died at Kornthal, Germany, on 26 November 1881. He was the author of an 1882 Swahili dictionary and the memoir *Reisen in Ostafrika* (1858). An English version was published in 1860 entitled *Travels, Researches, and Missionary Labours During an Eighteen Years Residence in Eastern Africa.*

Krieger, Carl. Krieger, a Boer elephant hunter in the 1850s, was considered fearless and a superior marksman. One day he wounded a bull and was following up with several friends on horseback, the usual Boer method. The elephant turned unexpectedly at close range and charged, focused on the man who had shot it. Krieger's friends panicked and fled. Upon returning to the vicinity the next day, all they found of Carl Krieger were a few bones, the elephant having "pounded the very flesh into dust." (Williams, 1859).

Krohnert, Otto (1888–1966). Krohnert was born in German South-West Africa and started hunting as a small boy tagging along with his father, a professional biltong hunter who also took the occasional elephant. When he became old enough, Krohnert moved away into Central Africa, where for many years he made a fine living hunting elephant. He also hunted the gorillas that were prone to raiding local farms. In his later years he traveled and hunted in the Congo and Angola. He retired to a farm at Akom in Spanish Guinea (Rio Muni) in the 1940s.

Kruger, Stephanus Johannes Paul (1825–1904). The president of the Transvaal from 1888 until its absorption by South Africa (with a few short interruptions), this Boer leader was a better hunter than a statesman, killing his first lion at age fourteen. An avid stalker of lion, buffalo, and other big game, he was once pinned to the ground by a wounded rhino, but managed to prop up his rifle and empty the second barrel into the beast. On another occasion he pulled off the admirable feat of outrunning a charging bull elephant. In his memoirs he estimated that during the course of his career he had shot some thirty to forty elephant, five lion, and five hippo.

If you look closely at portraits of Kruger, you will notice he was missing his left thumb. Some accounts say it was bitten off by a lion. Kruger himself said he had to amputate the digit when his rifle exploded. With no antiseptic, not even whiskey, he cut the finger and surrounding flesh off with his dull pocketknife. Some Boer women dressed the wound with, believe it or not, powdered sugar. I'm no scientist, but I think this would certainly increase the growth of bacteria and other microorganisms. It didn't help much in Kruger's case—he soon noticed black streaks running up his arm, indicating gangrene and blood poisoning. Then the women came up with another Boer folk remedy, this one more efficacious: They killed a goat, removed its stomach, cut it open, and made Kruger rest his hand in it. His hand began to heal, and thanks to the expenditure of several more goats over the next few months he was left with no permanent injury but the missing finger.

As a young man Kruger experienced the full tapestry of adventure in southern Africa. While he was leading a patrol in the Magapana country, for instance, one of his men knocked a black mamba from its perch in a tree. The snake, surrounded, began lashing out furiously, and when it was all over three of Kruger's men and two accompanying dogs were dead. The snake escaped.

Kruger, a tall, heavy man, liked to put on a sort of combination hillbilly and "Columbo" act, intentionally horrifying his staid British guests with his burps, dirty clothing, and atrocious table manners. He did this partly

President Kruger and his wife, Mrs. Paul Kruger.

on the theory that people would underestimate him (he could certainly turn on the charm when he wanted to), but I suspect his main motivation was that he simply enjoyed rattling their cages. Kruger was an effective negotiator and adept at domestic politics, but his inflexible attitude toward foreign affairs led to the destruction of his country. He died in exile in Switzerland in 1904.

For years after the Boer War, rumors abounded that $2 million in gold and specie—President Kruger's treasury—was buried somewhere inside the Sabi Game Reserve. Sometimes referred to as "the Kruger millions," the treasure had allegedly been buried by a Boer commando on the run from British forces. In his superb 1937 work *South African Eden,* game warden James Stevenson-Hamilton recounted details of some of the many quests for this alleged treasure. The first known retrieval attempt was in 1903, led by a former British intelligence officer named Captain de Bertodano. This was a quasi-official expedition with ample government support. Despite some months of searching, de Bertodano turned up nothing and the quest was called off. During the years 1904–1906 the peace of the reserve was regularly broken by eager search parties, including one made up of "Scientific Mystics" who apparently tried map dowsing to locate the gold. None of these parties met with any success. They did, however, provide employment for African laborers as well as numerous "treasure guides" who eked out commissions by hanging around bars pretending to have inside knowledge of the fortune's whereabouts.

Two locations in particular attracted a lot of interest. One, by the Crocodile River, actually yielded a buried heavy metal safe that created a firestorm of interest until it was blasted open and found to contain only worthless papers. The other popular spot, a kopje just north of the Sand River, gradually became the destination of choice for the treasure seekers. Over the next few decades the kopje was dug up time and time again, often by different teams led by the same professional treasure guides. The guides made a good but risky living—one overheard his two "partners" conspiring to murder him for his share when they found the elusive gold.

The quest subsided in the 1910s but revived in 1920, when the best-equipped of all the expeditions arrived to prospect the same old Sand River kopje. Stevenson-Hamilton saw a lot of this group, and they came across as just a step above the common gangster. They dug for six weeks before tiring of the game. The next group, in 1923, was of opposite legal and moral caliber—a group of policemen. They too ended up at Sand River kopje, and they too went home discouraged. The last known attempt was apparently made in 1931. Shortly afterward a fee of £25 was charged for a license to search for the millions, and few folks were still confident enough to pay it. Eventually the National Parks Board adopted a policy prohibiting the searches. It seems likely that the lost gold was but a chimera to begin with.

Kuhle, Bror. A professional hunter employed by the firm Safariland, Ltd., in the 1920s.

Kund, Richard (1852–1904). Lieutenant Kund was a German explorer assigned to the Noki Expedition in the Congo in 1886. He explored the Lukenye River in the Congo with Tappenbeck in 1885, and the Cameroons in 1887–1888. For details of the latter expeditions, see the entry for Tappenbeck.

Kuhnert, Wilhelm (1865–1926). German artist, specializing in oil paintings of African big game, especially elephant, lion, and buffalo. He was the artist for numerous hunting and natural history books including *Giants of the Forest* by C. S. Chadwick, *The Royal Natural History* by R. Lydekker, and *In Den Wildnissen Afrikas Und Asiens* by Dr. H. von Wissmann. Auction prices for his oil paintings of African wildlife are among the most expensive paintings on the subject matter from any artist in the world, alive or dead. Kuhnert often hunted with Bror Blixen.

Kylsant, Lord (1863–1937). The man who became Lord Kylsant was born Owen Philipps in Wales in 1863. Philipps started out in a low-level job in the shipping industry but rose to join the board of directors of the Royal Mail Steam Packet (RMSP) line in 1903. At age thirty-nine he was still a vigorous young man, and within three months he was elected chairman of the board.

The RMSP was a relatively minor shipping line, struggling in the face of major competition such as the White Star and Cunard companies. Philipps launched an aggressive policy of expansion, and RMSP quickly garnered a significant portion of the profitable South American trade. The outbreak of war in 1914 created huge opportunities for the company, and RMSP made a staggering profit during the next four years despite moderately heavy losses of shipping and personnel.

By the early 1920s Philipps's accomplishments were so highly respected that he was knighted and made Lord Kylsant. Perhaps the most significant indication of his success came in 1927 when the once-tiny RMSP purchased its formidable competitor, the White Star Line of HMS *Titanic* fame. Kylsant reveled in the public eye and, like American tycoons Rockefeller and Iacocca, was admired and consciously emulated by young businessmen all over Britain.

With his wealth came the opportunity to travel and enjoy himself. Kylsant went on numerous expeditions to Africa during the magnificent days when the nascent professional safari industry was transitioning from foot to motorcar. His hunting trips brought him to South Africa, Mozambique, Zululand, Rhodesia, Nyasaland, and Kenya. He earned a plethora of entries in the Rowland Ward record book, including bushbuck, waterbuck, reedbuck, kudu, roan, hartebeest, gemsbok, steenbok, and the No. 1 rhebok.

Lord Kylsant's world came crashing down in the early 1930s. When the Great Depression struck in 1929 the world economy was rocked—especially the travel industry since most people could no longer afford a berth. Desperately trying to weather the storm, Kylsant began to juggle the books, but he was soon found out. He was indicted for three counts of larceny in 1931 and forced to retire from the board of directors. Convicted on one count, he was sentenced to twelve months in prison. Kylsant was a broken man upon his release, and he died at age seventy-four in 1937.

L

Laborie, Bruneau de (xxxx–1930). A French big-game hunter and an explorer of the Sahara, de Laborie was appointed chief game warden *(inspecteur general des chasses)* of French Equatorial Africa around 1928. The creation of the post was prompted by the widespread destruction of the black rhino in the French colonies—over eight hundred horns were shipped out of Fort Archambault in 1927 alone. Naturalists and sportsmen alike applauded the establishment of the position. Awarding it to de Laborie, however, raised a few eyebrows. The explorer was considered a sort of crazy adventurer, a maverick. De Laborie promptly justified those apprehensions with his first official act as game warden—an extended hunting trip through the colonies.

Supposedly this expedition was aimed at getting a "feel" for the situation, but folks were skeptical. The game warden shot a number of elephant and rhino on the trail, killing nine of the latter on a single swing through Chad. Since these were the animals he was hired to protect, even some of his supporters began to have doubts about his suitability for the job. De Laborie added fuel to the fire by being a sloppy sportsman, wounding as many big-game animals as he killed. In his memoirs he noted one particular hunt during which he killed four rhino. He simply fired at two of them in the bushes without aiming, and when he killed the fourth animal he didn't even bother to go and look at it.

Fortunately for the history of conservation, if not for de Laborie, Mother Nature intervened in 1930. The chief game warden was hunting along the Middle Logone River when an African tracker attached to the safari fired a shot not far from the camp. De Laborie, rifle in hand, walked into the bush to investigate the shot. Little did he know that the man had wounded a male lion. De Laborie stumbled across the animal, which jumped him and tossed him to the ground like a sack of potatoes, the rifle falling away. By the time his staff rescued the warden, the lion had ripped him up pretty good.

It took four days to get the injured warden to the nearest medical station, at Fort Archambault. The doctor there was young and inexperienced and refused to amputate de Laborie's arm, which already stank and was turning green. For a moment de Laborie's luck seemed to change as two French explorers arrived, the Count de Sibour and his wife, who had just made an epic journey across the Sahara by automobile. The count agreed to drive the injured man to Bangui, where better medical facilities could be found.

The ride to Bangui took four more days. By this time de Laborie's condition was desperate. Several surgeons, including the noted sportsman and nature photographer Dr. Gromier, worked hard to save him, amputating the arm and trying to stop the gangrene. Their efforts were futile—to the great misfortune of Madame de Laborie but strongly to the benefit of the local rhino. After three surgeries, Bruneau de Laborie died of infection caused by the claws and fangs of one of his wounded charges. For another example of de Laborie's ability to offend people, see Frank Merfield's brief encounter with the warden in *Gorilla Hunter* (1956). De Laborie was the author of *Chasses en Afrique Française* (1929).

Labram, George (xxxx–1900). Labram was an American mining engineer who worked for Cecil Rhodes's DeBeers Company in Kimberley. When that town was besieged by the Boer army in December 1899, Labram constructed a large cannon pursuant to Rhodes's personal instructions. The twenty-eight-hundred-pound gun, built from scrap, was nicknamed "Long Cecil." Construction began on 27 December and the weapon began firing on 19 January 1900. "Long Cecil" fired a total of 255 rounds during the siege. The Boers were so concerned about the gun that they rushed their own heavy piece, "Long Tom" (a six-inch gun made by the Creusot Company of France), to Kimberley under the command of another American, J. H. King. One of the very first rounds fired by the Boer piece, on 19 February 1900, scored a direct hit on Labram's room at the Grand Hotel and killed him instantly.

Laing, Alexander Gordon (1793–1826). A British soldier who had served in Sierra Leone in 1822, Laing was sent on an antislavery and exploration mission to Timbuktu in 1825. He is believed to be the first Westerner to see that secluded city, but he was murdered there before he could report his findings. Laing was the author of *Travels in the Timannee, Kooranno, and Soolima Countries in Western Africa* (1825).

Lake, Alexander (1893–1961). An American, Lake hunted professionally in Africa throughout the first half of the twentieth century. He got his start in East Africa in 1911, working for a transport outfit. Lake would accompany the firm's wagons and shoot meat for the teamsters as they plied between Salisbury in Rhodesia and destinations in

Kenya, the Congo, and Tanganyika. He supplemented his meager income by shooting baboons for a bounty of five shillings a tail.

Lake went on to become a professional hunter in various capacities, taking out safari clients, filling meat contracts, and obtaining specimens for museums. At times his duties were more vague, such as a trip in July 1922 during which he protected Portuguese officials from wild animals as they spied on activities in British Rhodesia. On another safari, Lake claims (that word is going to come up a lot), his job was to shoot young hippo—and only young hippo—for a rich gourmet named L. Sam Marx. Marx apparently had a yen for hippo hams and sent Lake and a chef out to the Zambezi Valley in 1912 to obtain five hippo hams weighing eighty to a hundred twenty pounds each. The chef, a Scot named Stephens, went along to prepare the meat. He would smoke the hams, with the appropriate spices, inside the hollow of a baobab tree. Stephens was scared back to civilization by an encounter with a live hippo, but Lake filled the contract by himself.

The problem with Lake comes from his 1953 book, *Killers in Africa: The Truth About Animals Lying in Wait and Hunters Lying in Print.* This work is 290 pages of stories that frankly just don't ring true. Some of what Lake reported is flat out wrong. For instance, on page 123 he stated that the upper jaw of a crocodile is hinged and the lower jaw is solidly attached to the skeleton. As Guggisberg noted in his 1972 classic *Crocodiles,* "This can be disproved by anybody who cares to have a look at a crocodile's skull." Lake, of course, supposedly had seen hundreds if not thousands of crocodile skulls and was an expert on everything. Lake wrote that he was shown this particular anatomical feature by an expert taxidermist. However, quite a few of the old-timers made this mistake, even Stevenson-Hamilton, who certainly should have known better. So we'll give Lake a pass on this one.

But what about page 133? Here Lake told of running into "one of the great crocodile migrations I'd heard of." Crocodile migrations? Lake described watching some five hundred crocs slithering past his wagon, secure only because he had the wisdom to set up a wall of fire behind which he and his two companions sheltered. I need hardly point out that no modern wildlife photographer has ever been able to capture on film the thrilling spectacle of hundreds and hundreds of huge crocodiles marching together across the African plains, miles from any water. Lake even had their method of movement all wrong, portraying them slithering and crawling on their bellies at two miles per hour. Why wouldn't they have just walked to the new location? That slithering over dry land must have been painful.

My personal favorite starts on page 183. It was 1921, and Lake had agreed to take a British lad named Frankie on a photographic safari near the Sabi River. Frankie was the nervous type—like some character from a cheesy 1930s comedy, whenever he was touched unexpectedly he would lash out and hit or kick at whatever surprised him. Didn't Curly of the Three Stooges once have this problem? Anyway, the inevitable happened. A buffalo bull chased Frankie, who tripped and fell. The buffalo came up and sniffed the back of Frankie's neck. The minute the buffalo's nose touched Frankie, the young Englishman leaped to his feet and punched the beast right in the nose. The buffalo was stunned and young Frankie escaped.

I could quote example after example of this kind of stuff. Lake recommended softpoint bullets for bull elephant. He was commissioned by a billiard-ball manufacturer to shoot only elephant with ivory of a precise color. Lake traded one elephant eyelash to a Pygmy chief for 131 elephant tusks weighing 5,200 pounds. A baboon army forced a group of well-armed men to back down. Lake shot and killed a baboon at 840 yards (with aimed fire). A dead Italian hunter was stripped down to shiny white bone by ants in a matter of hours. It's just one whopper after another with this guy.

I can draw only one conclusion from all this. Remember that long subtitle to his book cited above—the part about "hunters lying in print"? Lake made a big deal out of this in his introductory chapter too. He protested so much about other hunters lying that this just has to be the key. Over and over Lake slanders other hunters, calls them blatant liars, and assures the reader again and again that only he will tell you the truth. Then he goes out and drops yet another ridiculous story. The tales he put in his book are the kind of stuff you would expect from an old-time comic-book writer who had never left Chicago. This cannot be serious—it just has to be a put-on. It might be significant that Lake's other book, *Hunter's Choice* (1954), also stressed "truth" in the subtitle—*Thrilling True Stories.* What was that about protesting too much?

Lamont, Sir James (1827–1913). A Scottish baronet and occasional member of Parliament from Bute, Lamont hunted in South Africa during the 1850s and 1860s, sometimes in the company of two friends named Burgess and Henry Reader. The missionary, Reverend John MacKenzie, met up with the three hunters along the trail in Bechuanaland in June 1860. Lamont also went on several hunting expeditions to the polar regions, which proved valuable from a geographic perspective, and traveled extensively throughout Egypt, Greece, and Turkey. He often based himself on one of his two yachts, the *Diana* and the *Ginevra*, and was the author of *Seasons with the Sea-Horses and Yachting in the Arctic Seas.* ROWLAND WARD 1899: BUFFALO, HIPPO (NO. 1, 51-INCH MALFORMED TUSK, FROM SOUTHEAST AFRICA), BLACK RHINO, LION (NO. 3 SKULL), POLAR BEAR (NO. 2, FROM NOVAYA ZEMLYA).

Lander, Richard (1804–1834). After accompanying Hugh Clapperton as a servant on the latter's last expedition, Lander was picked by the British government to explore the Niger Valley in 1830. He and his brother John Lander (1807–1839) checked out much of the river but were captured and held for ransom by Ibo tribesmen. After the money was paid, the brothers were released. Their return to the coast was a groundbreaking voyage down the Niger River.

Richard Lander returned to Africa in 1834 on a trading expedition but was ambushed and mortally wounded by a mob of several thousand natives; he died at Fernando Po a few days after the attack. The British government granted separate pensions of £70 a year to his widow and £20 to his infant daughter. His brother John died in London five years later from a tropical illness he had picked up in Africa.

Lane, C. R. W. Lane was an administrative officer in Kenya, 1894–1923, including sub-commissioner in Kenya 1904–1907 and provincial commissioner Naivasha 1907–1923. Lane was of the old school, somewhat rough-and-ready and handy with a bottle. The governor of Kenya in 1910, Sir Percy Girouard, described him in an official communication to London as "self-satisfied, pig-headed and highly unpopular." A short while later Girouard was complaining that Lane had said disloyal things while drunk in a bar. Though he didn't exactly stick up for Lane, it is only fair to state that the "second wave" of colonial officials tended to view themselves as professionals and their predecessors as drunken bums who happened to be available when the position was created. Like all stereotypes, there's some truth at the core of this one—the first district commissioners and collectors often were pioneer and outdoor types, while later officials were sent from London and had been trained specifically for the job.

Lang, Conyers. Lang was the author of *Buffalo: The Lone Trail of a Big-Game Hunter* (1934), about an extended safari that was supposed to be "Cape to Cairo." The adventure ended when Lang was pummeled by a buffalo in Kenya. He survived, crawled back to Nairobi, and wrote his book.

Lang, Herbert (1879–1957). This Lang was an American scientist affiliated with New York's Museum of Natural History. Between 1909 and 1915 he and associate James Chapin were allowed the use of facilities by the Belgian government to further their collecting work in the Congo. Together the two men shipped thousands of stuffed birds, mammals, and other specimens back to Massachusetts.

After the end of World War I Lang became interested in prehistoric art and made several successful expeditions to the Transvaal, where he discovered petroglyphs and cave paintings of rhino, mammoths, and other creatures that had survived some fifty thousand years in the arid conditions. He played a prominent role in the campaign to achieve national-park status for the Sabi Game Reserve.

Langford, Mrs. (xxxx–1896). Mrs. Langford was a young Englishwoman who married a doctor. The couple moved to Rhodesia just in time for the outbreak of the Matabele Rebellion in 1896. The Langfords and a friend named Lamon were heading toward their new home in the Insiza district when they were warned of the rebellion by an African servant and set out for a place called Rixon's Farm, where the locals were gathering to establish a defense. Two miles from the farm they were ambushed by the Matabele. Lamon and Dr. Langford were killed in the struggle, but Mrs. Langford escaped.

She ran first to the farm but found it deserted—the local settlers had found it unsuited for defensive purposes and had moved to another location. She then found shelter by crawling in a hole under a protruding bank at a nearby river. There she lived for several days, sneaking back to the farmhouse at night to rummage for food. Eventually she was discovered by some rebels and beaten to death with stones.

Larsen, Karl. A noted elephant hunter in Portuguese East Africa, Larsen, of Danish descent, was best known for killing seven lion in two minutes in Angola. Though an ivory specialist, he shot thirty-four lion in his career. He also made a living hunting buffalo for their hides, killing thousands. His favorite weapon was a .600 Jeffery Nitro Express double rifle.

Leakey, Louis Seymour Bazett (1903–1972). This noted anthropologist and paleontologist was born in Kenya in 1903 and grew up playing with the Kikuyu boys.

English was actually his second language. When he applied for university admission in Britain, the entrance requirements stated that he had to be fluent in two foreign languages. Leakey wrote down French (of which he had a smattering), and Kikuyu, and since there was nobody available in London to verify his claim, he was accepted. When he graduated with a degree in anthropology, the rules required that he pass an oral examination in both languages, so the university administrators asked the School of Oriental Languages to find a Kikuyu expert to give the test. The school could find only one qualified individual in all of England. So it was that Louis Leakey, student, received instructions to present himself to one Louis Leakey, Kikuyu expert, for the purpose of the final examination. He passed.

Leakey went on to make several great, if controversial, discoveries in the field of human prehistory. He was also curator of the Coryndon Museum in Nairobi for many years, from 1940–1945 as an unpaid honorary curator and from 1945–1961 as a full, professional curator. During the Mau Mau period he found himself in the unique and unenviable position of being distrusted by the British because of his intimate relationship with the Kikuyu tribe, and on a terrorist death list for the same reason.

Leakey, Mary (1913–1996). Originally Mary Douglas Nicol, Mary Leakey started as an employee, then wife, of anthropologist Louis Leakey and rose to become one of paleohistory's premier figures in her own right. She married Louis in 1936, and the couple had three sons and a daughter, the last of which died in infancy. In 1959 Mary discovered the fossil skull of the creature known as *Australopithecus (Zinjanthropus) boisei* in the Rift Valley.

Leary, Glen (xxxx–1925). Leary was the father-in-law of Sabi Game Reserve ranger Harold Trollope. The two men (along with C. A. Yates, who was an unarmed local scoutmaster and Harry Wolhuter's brother-in-law) were hunting leopard with hounds just outside the reserve in 1925. The dogs chased the leopard into tall grass, and Leary, who was in his seventies, walked right into the cat. He got one shot off before the leopard gave him a savage ripping. Trollope shot the leopard off him, but the wounds soon proved fatal.

Leask, Thomas (1839–1912). A South African trader who ran a store in Klerksdorp starting in the 1870s, Leask would often leave the counter in the hands of his partner, James Taylor, to go elephant hunting with Bill Finaughty, the Jennings boys, Henry Hartley, Big Phillips, and those guys. He was considered one of the premier South African elephant hunters, until the retreat of the elephant into the tsetse zones around 1870 forced an end to hunting them on horseback. Like most of his kind, Leask then retired from elephant hunting. He announced his neutrality in the Anglo-Boer War but was suspected by some of operating against the British. He subsequently retired to Scotland but kept commercial interests in South Africa. He was the author of the posthumously published *South African Diaries* (1954).

Lebombo Pirates. The "Lebombo Pirates" were an informal and unholy gang of bandits who terrorized Swaziland and the Transvaal in the 1880s. On the run from various jurisdictions, the pirates were used to living outside the law and probably aroused as much ire among the European population by living like "uncivilized" Africans than they did by their crimes. The three most notorious pirates were Charlie duPont and his friends Constable (a former Natal police officer) and Bob MacNab (also seen as McNab).

In 1885 duPont and a gang member named Joseph Sussens were shooting hippo and selling *sjamboks* (whips) made from their hides. The two argued over who had shot one particular hippo, and duPont suggested a shooting contest to settle the matter. Both men fired at a mark, and when Sussens, apparently the winner, leaned over to examine the target, duPont shot him in the back, killing him instantly.

A year later duPont met a widow named Howard, who was fleeing the interior with her few worldly possessions after her husband, a teamster, had died of fever. DuPont pretended to befriend her but wound up stealing everything she owned, including her wagon and two teams of oxen. MacNab and Constable were either fond of Mrs. Howard or wanted a share of the loot—the record is unclear. At any rate they confronted their erstwhile partner. DuPont shot and killed Constable and badly wounded MacNab. DuPont's mother, from all accounts a saintly woman, nursed MacNab back to health and convinced him to foreswear revenge. DuPont's ability to come out on top in a gunfight might have played a factor in MacNab's decision to forget the whole thing as well.

Because all this happened in Swaziland, the crimes fell under the jurisdiction of King Mbandeni, who apparently considered it just a European thing and took no official sanction. It is also unlikely that he felt compelled to intervene if these evil men wanted to kill each other. Though he didn't punish duPont directly, Mbandeni did allow the honest English settlers residing in his kingdom to set up a sort of vigilante police force.

From then on, duPont had to be considerably more careful. He built his next humble house in the Stegi district of Swaziland, close to the border of Portuguese East Africa—so close, in fact, that he could land in either Mozambique or Swaziland depending on which window he jumped from. This came in handy in escaping the arm of the law. The system worked well, it is said, until one day when both the Swazi and the Portuguese police showed up at the same time. His ultimate fate is unclear.

Lee, John (Hans or Jan). A trader and hunter of mixed Boer and English descent, he was the son-in-law of Carl van Rooyen. Lee from 1863 or so ran a trading post on the Mangwe River in Matabeleland and had great influence on Matabele leaders Mzilikazi and Lobengula. During the 1870s and 1880s European hunters visiting Matabeleland would invariably drop in. Lee was a personable character. Frederick Selous wrote that he was the picture of kindness and hospitality. Even William Finaughty, who had something bad to say about everybody, described Lee as pleasant and honest, if something of a blowhard.

In 1892 he guided Randolph Churchill on his safari to Mashonaland. His payment was the rights to two farms near Manica. Lee's son, who was known as Hans or Jan, was born in 1863 and became a respected "interior man."

Lefebvre, Theodore (1878–1955). A French elephant hunter known for using the small 8mm Lebel rifle, Lefebvre arrived in Africa about 1910. After a year of normal employment as a shipping clerk, he took to hunting and never turned back. For the next forty years he hunted Ubangi-Shari, with occasional excursions elsewhere. In the early days he hunted in the grand style, with large groups of natives assisting and traveling with him. On one such occasion Lefebvre positioned himself in the center of a "fire circle" while the natives burned the bush and drove a small herd of elephant toward him. From his vantage point he killed seventeen elephant in a few minutes, an act he later regretted, given the unsporting conditions. A true professional, his total bag consisted of at least one thousand elephant, several hundred rhino, and uncounted masses of buffalo.

Legendre, Sidney (1903–1948). Sidney Legendre was an American museum collector of the 1930s. Born in England and brought to the United States as an infant, Legendre graduated from Princeton University in 1925. Accompanied by his brother and his wife (Gertrude Sanford, the daughter of New York carpet manufacturer and sportsman John Sanford), he led the American Museum of Natural History Abyssinian Expedition in 1929, collecting numerous specimens including a rare nyala group. Sidney Legendre had previous experience hunting tigers in Indochina while Gertrude was a veteran of a safari through Tanganyika. In 1931–1932 the Legendres undertook an expedition to Indochina, in 1935 to South-West Africa, and in 1938 they led the Museum's Persian Expedition.

From the late 1920s the Legendres lived in southern luxury on the "Midway" plantation in Berkeley County, South Carolina. Legendre was the president of the Trinkomet Company, and served as a lieutenant commander in the Second World War. He died of a heart attack in 1948, leaving behind Gertrude and two daughters. Legendre was the author of several books, including *Okovango* (1939).

Lehrmann, Drag (1863–1918). Born in Austria of Croatian parents, Captain Lehrmann served the Belgians in the Congo from 1882–1896. He was considered an excellent officer and administrator, with a reputation for fair treatment of and good relations with the Congolese. In 1889 he was sent by the Free State on an expedition to open up cordial relations with a hitherto hostile people called the Bayaka, who were ruled by a hostile king called the Kiamvo. The expedition consisted only of Lehrmann and fourteen Swahili soldiers, for the expectation was that Lehrmann's superior diplomatic skills would prevent any violence.

Lehrmann was sick and being carried in a litter, but when the first Bayaka warriors came into view he abandoned his "ride" and approached them, armed only with a walking stick. One of the Bayakas threw a burning torch at him and another pulled a knife, whereupon Lehrmann dodged the torch, scrambled back to his men, and grabbed a shotgun from one of the Swahilis. The Bayaka with the knife came charging on, and Lehrmann shot him in the chest. The Swahilis and Lehrmann formed a square just as large numbers of warriors came out from hiding and attacked. The Bayaka had never faced disciplined riflemen before and came on in a rush. Volley after volley rang out, and when the smoke cleared the bodies of thirty Bayaka surrounded the untouched square.

The story had something of a happy ending. The chief of the Bayaka had been wounded in the wrist by a bullet. After the battle he came in peace to Lehrmann, who treated and dressed the wound. That particular chief became a firm friend of Lehrmann and later helped the explorer George Grenfell, but he warned the Croatian that the Kiamvo was resolutely hostile and would order other villages under his control to wipe out the expedition. Lehrmann was forced to abandon his mission.

The Bayaka continued to skirmish with the Free State for the next several years. At one point, after a show of strength by one Lieutenant Dhanis, the Kiamvo reluctantly agreed to allow the construction of a station near his capital. The station was manned by some seventy Swahili soldiers under two Belgian officers, Dunart and Vollont. The Bayaka continually sniped at the station, killing any of the Swahili who wandered from the safety of the stockade, and finally Dunart and Vollont (who had been threatened with death several times by the Kiamvo) decided that they had to break out. They launched a surprise attack on the Kiamvo's capital, killing some two hundred Bayaka while expending eighteen thousand cartridges (one wonders why the Belgians were stockpiling so much ammunition). They then reached the Belgian station at Popokabaka, but not before a final clash that wounded one of the officers and left many of the Swahilis dead.

The Kiamvo was apparently taken aback by the casualties he had suffered (primitive peoples were often stunned by how lethal a disciplined European army could be) and didn't push his advantage. The Belgians, meanwhile, contemplated evacuating Popokabaka but decided that the retreat would be too dangerous. In October 1892 they sent for help instead.

Help came swiftly, in the form of Capt. Drag Lehrmann and some four hundred askaris. This was truly an overwhelming force in the Kiamvo's eyes, and he sent the missionary, George Grenfell, a cryptic message of peace: "The caterpillar fell into the water, and his hairs came out." At this point most Free State officers would have simply massacred the Bayaka and burned their towns, but here Lehrmann displayed the wisdom that earned him the respect of both the missionaries and the local Africans. He marched on the Bayaka capital, sending messengers ahead to say that he would not fire the first shot but that any resistance would have catastrophic consequences. The Kiamvo reluctantly agreed to peace, and let the Belgians construct a new fort adjacent to his capital.

There is a photograph of Lehrmann in Harry Johnston's *George Grenfell and the Congo,* from which most of the above account is taken. It shows a lean, handsome man with confident eyes and bearing leaning against a hut. Add a six-shooter and you'd have the prototypical lawman of the Old West.

Leigh, William R. Artist and author of *Frontiers of Enchantment: An Artist's Adventures in Africa* (1939). He was a member of the 1926 Akeley-Eastman-Pomeroy expedition to Central Africa.

Lennox, George St. Leger (1845–1919). Generally known by the alias "Scotty Smith," Lennox was the illegitimate son of a Scottish aristocrat. He was born in Perth, Australia, and schooled as a veterinarian. After a spell as a gold prospector in Australia and as a prize fighter in New York City, Lennox served in the British army as the veterinary officer of an Indian cavalry regiment.

The story goes that his regiment was involved in a campaign against a rebellious Hill tribe on India's Northwest Frontier. His commanding officer was killed and Lennox seized command of the squadron, ordering it into a headlong charge at the enemy positions. The attack was a disaster, and most of the squadron's saddles were emptied by the rebel riflemen. Lennox was court-martialed and dismissed from the service.

He next showed up in South Africa in 1877, where he served as a trooper in the Frontier Armed and Mounted Police and fought as a soldier in the Gaika War. Bored of military life, he apparently deserted, stealing the papers of a dead comrade named Scotty Smith and assuming his identity. For the rest of his life he was generally known by his alias. Lennox (or Smith) moved to the Kalahari Desert, where he established himself in a variety of sinister pursuits.

Like that of Jesse James, Ned Kelly, and other famous desperadoes, Lennox's criminal career is shrouded in mystery and legend. He shot elephant, smuggled diamonds, robbed travelers, and ran guns to the Herero during their war against the Germans in the early 1900s. This master of disguise was captured several times, but he always managed to escape. On one occasion he was apprehended by a bounty hunter, but he managed to overcome the man, bound and gagged him, and then dropped him off at a police station as the notorious Scotty Smith. The most serious allegation against Lennox concerns the murder of a large number of Bushmen. According to the story, Lennox found an old Bushman skeleton and sold it to an agent for a European anthropological museum. This got him thinking, and according to the legend Lennox thereafter murdered dozens of natives in order to sell their bones.

Lennox lived for years on a farm near Witdraai in South-West Africa. Around 1892 he married a nineteen-year-old girl named van Niekerk. During the Boer invasion of South-West Africa in the First World War, he fought for the South Africans under Botha and apparently performed well as a scout and a guide. The law never caught up to him, and in 1919 he succumbed to the worldwide influenza epidemic and died at the picturesque Namibian town of Upington.

Leontiev, Nicholas Stephanovic (1861–1910). Described by author Pascal Imperato as a "scheming sociopath" (1998), Leontiev was a Russian reserve officer who accompanied Prof. Alexander Elisseiv (also seen as Yelisseieff) on his 1895 mission to Abyssinia. Leontiev had been selected for the mission by the Russian Geographical Society, whose members were impressed by a book he had written about his travels in India, Persia, and Turkmenistan. They didn't know, however, that not only had Leontiev been forced out of the army due to gambling debts but also that he had greatly embellished the story of his Asian travels. He seems to have been a bright, charming, persuasive rogue with much ability but little conscience or morals.

En route to Addis Ababa, Elisseiv fell ill and was replaced by Leontiev. The rogue quickly won the emperor Menelik's affection, but not his trust. One of Leontiev's tricks was to "promote" himself and all the members of his delegation in an attempt to impress the Ethiopians—he told Menelik that he was actually Count Leontiev, a colonel in the regular Russian army. When Leontiev, who was prone to bragging about his fictitious personal relationship with the czar and other notables, produced a phony letter from Nicholas II, Menelik saw right through the deception but didn't let on, hoping that Leontiev might prove useful in some way. At that time in history, during the so-called "Scramble for Africa," Menelik was looking for closer relationships with foreign powers, to obtain both arms and allies in case of European aggression.

When the mission returned to Russia in the summer of 1895, Leontiev brought with him a number of gifts from Menelik to the czar (jewelry, an illuminated Bible, a crown, and the Ethiopian Order of Solomon) as well as four Ethiopian ambassadors. He had absolutely no authority to invite this delegation or to promise that they would meet with the czar—that he managed to pull this off is proof of how shrewd the man was at self-promotion. Leontiev simply waited until the whole expedition was on the shore of the Mediterranean, booking passage for home, before sending word to the Russian foreign ministry that an Abyssinian prince, a bishop, and two generals were coming to meet the czar (here again he was pulling his old trick of promoting his associates—the bishop, for instance, was merely a priest). To send the delegation home at this point would have been a serious diplomatic insult to Menelik, and so the Russian government reluctantly authorized the mission, thereby also giving the conniving Leontiev access to the czar.

The mission was a success, and Czar Nicholas handed out decorations and orders to the Ethiopians and to Leontiev, whose stock soared as a result. Leontiev's past began to haunt him, however, and a Saint Petersburg newspaper even revealed his fraudulent use of the title "count" and the fact that he had tried to extort money from various Russian officials in connection with the Ethiopian mission. The newspaper even printed the fact that the Ethiopian "bishop" was drinking two bottles of champagne every morning at breakfast.

Governments are pragmatic, however, and soon the delegation was headed back to Addis Ababa loaded with gifts, including a precious consignment of modern rifles and ammunition. Leontiev was ordered to accompany them as far as Djibouti. After that he was to return to Saint Petersburg so that the newspaper allegations could be investigated. Leontiev, no fool and with a nose for profit, made a trip to Paris before returning and met with some arms dealers with previous ties to Ethiopia, discussing the establishment of a lucrative arms business in one of Africa's few independent countries. When he finally came back to Russia he received a slap on the wrist and then returned to Ethiopia in 1896, arriving at Addis Ababa directly after the catastrophic Italian defeat at Adowa.

Menelik seized the opportunity presented by Leontiev's arrival and commissioned him to solicit the czar's assistance in obtaining a peace treaty with Italy. As a humanitarian gesture Menelik allowed Leontiev to lead fifty Italian prisoners of war to freedom, a gesture that was reluctantly appreciated by Italy. With his characteristic gall, Leontiev then promoted himself to the post of Ethiopia's ambassador to Italy and sailed to Rome, where he promptly hinted that he—and peace—could be bought. He then made himself Ethiopian ambassador to Russia and met with the czar, who was on a state visit to Vienna. Peace between Ethiopia and Italy was signed in October 1896, and Leontiev, considered a close advisor to Menelik as well as to the czar, was at the peak of his career.

In gratitude, and wanting to keep this useful scoundrel around, Menelik appointed the crafty Russian governor of Equatoria province, the part of Abyssinia closest to Lake Rudolf. Leontiev was not content to be put on ice, however, and quickly began scheming with businessmen from most of the European countries to establish gold mining and other interests in his province. Because this was one of white Europe's traditional methods of ultimately obtaining political possession of an area, such schemes were not likely to gain Menelik's favor. Furthermore, gold mining in particular was traditionally the sole prerogative of the Abyssinian emperor, so Leontiev had to take great pains to keep his mining plans secret.

Upon taking office, Leontiev traveled to France to stock up on supplies for an inspection tour through his new land. Prince Henry of Orleans met with Leontiev and agreed to travel with him on the tour, which would transit some of the wildest regions of Africa, including the harsh and desolate Lake Rudolf (Turkana) area. By the time they set out in late 1897, Leontiev had bought a huge amount of modern weapons, but the ship was impounded during a routine stop in London. The British were concerned about the Africans obtaining such modern weapons and used the excuse that Leontiev had violated customs regulations by bringing them into a British port. The Russians and French were angered by the audacity of the British move and quickly helped Leontiev and Henry replace their cargo with even better weapons. These included twelve hundred magazine rifles and a pair of Maxim machine guns.

Fate intervened in Leontiev's fortunes on 30 June 1898, when he was seriously wounded at Harar while demonstrating the use of a Maxim gun. A minor scandal erupted when the Russian ambassador, a man named Vlassov, refused to allow Russian doctors to assist in Leontiev's treatment. Vlassov openly hoped Leontiev would die of his wounds and remove himself from the scene—he was considered something of an embarrassment to Russia by this time. Menelik sent his own physicians to nurse the governor back to health. The Ethiopian reaction to his stance was so negative that Vlassov eventually had to leave the country.

Fully recovered after a convalescence in Europe, Leontiev set out to explore his domain. With him were the Russians—Baron Chedeuvre, Ensign Babitchev, and Dr. Kahn—and a French lieutenant named Sebillou. (Prince Henry had returned to France after the machine-gun accident.) Also on the expedition were two Croatian scoundrels named Mirko and Stepan Seljan, who claimed to be doctors, one hundred thirty Senegalese askaris loaned by the French, and some two thousand Ethiopian soldiers.

Leontiev and his force moved along the Omo River establishing forts and stations, including a major center at Bako. He reached Lake Rudolf's northern tip on 21 August 1899 and cut down British flags that had been placed there by Austin the year before, replacing them with Ethiopian standards. Like Giorgis's expedition a short time before, Leontiev's men lived off the natives, pillaging their villages and robbing their cattle. The warriors retaliated, launching a major attack on the column and killing 216 of Leontiev's men in one battle.

A short time later, Leontiev suddenly received orders from Menelik to return to Addis Ababa. Leaving Baron Chedeuvre and Dr. Kahn (Kahn later deserted) to build an additional fort on Lake Rudolf, Leontiev returned to the capital. Menelik had ordered his recall to appease British protests against his hauling down of the Union Jack, and he was also concerned that the Russian was getting too powerful and/or was about to betray him to European interests (which may well have been true). Menelik was also reacting to atrocity reports that were reaching the European press and damaging the image of Ethiopia. The emperor was forced to promise the British that their flags overlooking Lake Rudolf would be replaced.

Precisely at this time Menelik received intelligence of Leontiev's prior efforts to interest European companies in gold-mining schemes in Equatoria province. The Emperor, not a man to trifle with, was furious. He stripped Leontiev of his rank and sent letters to all the European powers stating that the Russian was a criminal and a swindler. Leontiev was perhaps lucky to leave Ethiopia alive, which he did in late 1902.

Leontiev's dramatic career went into a swift and irreversible decline. The Russian adventurer surfaced in the 1905 Russo-Japanese War and later applied for permission to return to Ethiopia in 1906—it was denied. He settled in Djibouti and dabbled in farming and gunrunning, with little success. He then moved to Paris and died there in poverty in 1910. Leontiev was a cruel, greedy man, murderous to the African "warrior-herdsmen" of Turkana, and as faithless to his emperor as he was to his czar. Yet he has a certain fascination, as do all worthless but charming freebooters. His career is a monument to swashbuckling chicanery, with the bonus of an appropriately miserable finish.

Le Riche, Joep. Joep Le Riche was appointed as acting ranger for Kalahari Gemsbok National Park upon the malaria-caused death of the previous ranger, his brother Johannes, in 1934. He was soon made permanent and stayed in the post until 1970. His longtime assistant was Gert Mouton. In 1938 Le Riche was also put in charge of the Bechuanaland game reserve, which mirrored the Kalahari Gemsbok Park across the border.

Le Riche, Johannes (xxxx–1934). Le Riche, the son of a local trader, became the first game ranger of Kalahari Gemsbok National Park when it was proclaimed in 1931. His sole assistant was Gert Januarie. Both men died of malaria in 1934. Le Riche was replaced by his brother Joep.

Lerothodi (1837–1905). Grandson of Moshesh and chief of the Basuto, circa 1900.

Leslie, David. Leslie visited southern Africa in the 1870s and hunted along the Tugela and Pongolo Rivers, shooting rhino, buffalo, and elephant. He was the author of *Among the Zulus and Amatongas* (1875).

Letcher, Owen (1884–1943). Letcher was an interesting man whose hunting fame rests on his book *Big Game Hunting in Northeastern Rhodesia* (1911). Having studied at the Redruth School of Mines in Cornwall, England, Letcher came to the Transvaal at the age of twenty as a mining engineer. In 1908 he spent a month or so on the Mau Escarpment in British East Africa. In 1909 he walked from Tete in Mozambique to Fort Jameson, Northern Rhodesia, which was his home for the next few years.

Fort Jameson at that time had a thriving hunting community, including Martin Ryan and Denis Lyell, so it's not surprising that Letcher fit right in. Accompanied by his friend Dillon Leonard, Letcher went on a six-month *ulendo* (see glossary) through the Luangwa Valley, the Muchinga Hills, and the Tumbwa Swamps. This trip was the subject of his well-written and illustrated 1911 book, which has been deservedly reprinted. It differs from many similar accounts in that no incredible feats or even dramatic events occur—no one has ever accused Letcher of embellishing his achievements. It is just a simple and well-told story of a routine safari in 1909 Africa. His battery on this hunt consisted of a .375 magnum rifle, a Westley-Richards 12-bore, a .450 double rifle, and a Harrington-Richards .38 revolver.

Letcher went on to have a distinguished career. In World War I he served with the Nyasa-Rhodesian Field Force. He later became a Fellow of the Royal Geographical Society and a member of London's prestigious Institution of Mining and Metallurgy. He died in Johannesburg on 14 October 1943. Letcher also wrote *The Bonds of Africa* (1913) and nine other books.

Leth, Peter. Leth was a friend of Beryl Markham who in his youth had a job controlling the buffalo population on the Delamere estate at Soysambu. Many years later he worked for Markham as a rider during her abortive attempt to establish a horse-training business in Rhodesia.

Lethbridge, John. Jackie Lethbridge was a Boer War veteran who settled in East Africa in the early 1900s. He was notorious for keeping a full-grown pet lion on his front porch to deter visitors. An enthusiastic amateur hunter, Captain Lethbridge once, during a safari, rode thirty miles to get a doctor for a companion who had been badly ripped up by a lion. The first doctor he found was an Indian who was reluctant to make the distant house call (it was the middle of a monsoon), but Lethbridge forced him to come along at gunpoint. The doctor finally refused to cross a flooded river, collapsing and crying, "Shoot me!" So Lethbridge grabbed his medical supplies and swam the river on horseback. By the time the medical supplies arrived, however, his friend was fading fast, and Lethbridge and the dying man drank whiskey until the end. Lethbridge left Africa shortly after, in 1911. He was the father-in-law of professional hunter Tom Murray Smith.

Lettow-Vorbeck, Gen. Paul von (1870–1964). This German general led a brilliant defensive campaign against the British in East Africa during World War I. He was considered by his enemies to have fought a decent and clean war and was generally lionized by historians on both sides.

Levaillant, Francois (1753–1824). Levaillant was born in a French colony in South America but, contrary to a popular story, he was of pure French ancestry. A naturalist, he was stranded in South Africa when the British navy sank the ship he was traveling on. He spent the years 1781–1785 exploring and hunting in the Xhosa territories and along the Orange and Great Fish Rivers. Upon his return to Europe he wrote *Travels into the Interior Parts of Africa* (1790), one of the first books to combine exploration and hunting under one cover. The book tells of hunting elephant, kudu, and hippo. Levaillant was the first naturalist to describe the now extinct antelope called the bluebuck (blaauwbok or *Hippotragus leucophaeus*), of which there now exist only a few ragged museum specimens. He was also the author of the highly regarded *Birds of Africa.*

Lewanika (1842–1916). He was the paramount chief of the Barotse tribe from 1878–1884 and 1885–1916. Originally known as Lubosi, Lewanika spent the 1870s in a bloody political struggle that rivaled anything ever seen in Rome or Byzantium. After finally coming out on top, he was overthrown in an 1884 coup but regained his throne after a major battle in November 1885. At this time Lubosi took the name Lewanika, loosely translated as "the Conqueror."

Lewanika, who regained power just in time to meet the influx of the British, was a shrewd man. Using Khama as an example, he worked with the Europeans and avoided open conflict. Tricked in a series of treaties (the Concessions of 1890, 1906, and 1909), Lewanika fought for his people in the courts and in the meeting rooms. Thus he was more successful in maintaining at least some rights than were the more militant Zulus and Matabeles.

Lewis, Robert (1841–1894). Born in England, Lewis came to Africa via Walfisch Bay in 1858 and started hunting and trading in the Kalahari and by Lake Ngami. He was quite successful at this and became a favorite figure among the Hereros, to whom he traded guns and goods for gold, skins, and ivory. He also shot a great number of elephant and other game on his own. In 1875 he married a pretty Cape Colony woman named Mary Findon, and they raised five children on a farm near Windhoek. Lewis managed the famous Ebony Mine and worked for the James Todd and De Pass, Spence, & Co. trading concerns.

When the Germans began to establish themselves in South-West Africa in the 1880s, Lewis tried desperately to stop them, fomenting discord among the natives and petitioning the British government to intercede. By the latter years of the decade he had failed, and South-West Africa had become a German colony. The first German governor, Hermann Goering's father, was appointed in 1885 and Lewis was shortly thereafter declared an undesirable alien. In 1889 he was deported and some eight hundred head of cattle were seized from the family farm as punishment for his anti-German activities.

Lewis then received a commission from Cecil Rhodes to supervise the development of a British station at Rietfontein in Bechuanaland, directly across the border from the German colony. In late 1894 Lewis went into the bush near Rietfontein to follow up a wounded leopard and was badly injured. The leopard was killed and Lewis was rescued by some Herero workmen, who then refused to help cleanse his wounds because they were afraid they would be accused of poisoning him. The inevitable sepsis developed and Lewis died in great pain several days later.

After the Germans were expelled from South-West Africa in the First World War, Mary Lewis filed a lawsuit to reclaim a valuable gold-mining concession that had once been owned by her late husband. The concession had been given to Robert Lewis by a grateful Herero chieftain but had been voided by the German authorities during his deportation. Mary hired a top South African attorney named Leslie Blackwell to represent her in court. Things were looking good and it was believed that the restoration of the concession was merely a formality, but then it was discovered that Robert Lewis had actually sold his rights to the gold for a pittance back in the early 1890s when the concession seemed worthless. Mary Lewis and her five children were left without a penny.

Dr. Heinrich Lichtenstein.

Leyland, John. Leyland was an English naturalist who first came to Africa in 1848, shooting and preserving bird specimens for collectors. On his third visit to the continent he accompanied Livingstone and Sam Edwards on a trip through the southern Zambezi area in 1851–1852. Leyland was the author of *Adventures in the Far Interior of South Africa,* which included a very popular appendix on the skinning and preserving of birds and mammals.

Lichtenstein, Martin Heinrich Karl (1780–1857). A German explorer who traveled through the Kalahari area in 1803–1808, Lichtenstein in 1811 was appointed a professor of zoology at the University of Berlin. He was also the director of the Zoological Museum of Berlin. He wrote extensively about the Khoi and was the first to try to record their language. Lichtenstein was the author of *Travels in Southern Africa* (1810–1811). He died at sea at the age of seventy-seven.

Linant de Bellefonds, Edouard (xxxx–1875). A Belgian, Col. Linant de Bellefonds was the much younger brother of Adolphe Linant de Bellefonds (who had explored the White Nile in 1827–1829) and an officer of Charles Gordon's Anglo-Egyptian army in 1875. He was sent as an emissary to Mtesa, the *kabaka* of Uganda. While at Mtesa's court in April 1875 he met Henry Morton Stanley, who called the Belgian "very agreeable" and "intelligent and sympathetic" (1878). They went their separate ways on 17 April. Four months later, on 26 August 1875, Linant and thirty-six of his men were killed by Bari warriors at a place called Labore.

Lindstrom, Gillis (1882–1958). Lindstrom, a former lieutenant in the Swedish army, arrived in Kenya from Sweden in 1920 with his wife Ingrid (nee de Mare, born 1890) and four small children. The couple had married in 1911. Ingrid in particular was a close friend of Denys Finch Hatton, who would often invite her to Karen Blixen's house when he expected Karen to be upset over something. Ingrid's presence would act to calm the possessive Karen.

The Lindstroms bought a farm called "Sergoita" at Njoro near Lake Nakuru, where they tried to grow flax with little success. Gillis Lindstrom would sign on at other farms and ranches as a salaried manager for a season or two, particularly in Tanganyika. He also earned extra money by hiring out as a freelance professional hunter.

Livingstone, Charles (1822–1875). The brother of David Livingstone, Charles was a prominent clergyman and missionary in his own right. After preaching in the United States from 1840–1857, Charles joined his brother in Africa on the Zambezi expedition until 1863.

Charles's behavior on that expedition was appalling. He tended to take advantage of his relationship to the expedition leader by ordering the other officers around. When he discovered that Baines, the expedition's artist and commissary, and Thornton, the geologist, enjoyed an occasional drink with the local Portuguese traders and officials, it offended his Scottish Presbyterian sense of morality and he maneuvered to have both men fired from the expedition. It got so bad that Charles hired local Africans to spy on the two men, rewarding them profusely whenever they came up with something juicy. His behavior toward Baines was particularly bad—he fraudulently accused the commissary of stealing expedition materials for his own use.

To make matters worse, Charles was out of shape and couldn't keep up on the long foot journeys through the bush. David Livingstone was loath to criticize Charles and would abuse Baines and Thornton for wasting time and being lazy while ignoring his brother's insistence on frequent stops. Sir John Kirk, the expedition's naturalist, noted with disgust in his journal, "More than half the time is occupied allowing Mr. L. to have a little snooze every half hour."

Eventually Charles got so bad that he even had a falling out with his brother. In 1860 David Livingstone decided to take advantage of a lull in activities to return some thirty or so Makololo porters to their home village, in fulfillment

Karen Blixen (left) and Ingrid Lindstrom, Kenya, 1921.

of an earlier promise to their chief. Charles didn't want to make the trip and whined bitterly about it from the start. The first problem arose when the two brothers got into a sharp argument after Charles threw away an old pillow that belonged to David. The breaking point came when the unhappy safari was finally nearing Makololo territory. Charles lost his temper for some reason at the Makololo headman, a faithful worker who had never given any cause for concern. He started kicking the man savagely with his heavy, iron-nailed boots. David was incensed at his brother's stupid brutality, particularly since they were on Makololo ground and quite possibly subject to reprisal. The headman grabbed a spear and was on the brink of killing Charles when David was able to talk him out of it. All concerned, except Charles, agreed that the Makololo had shown great restraint.

The relationship between the two brothers was never the same and they barely talked to each other after this incident. David Livingstone was especially galled because he now realized that his brother had undoubtedly fabricated his charges against Baines and Thornton.

Charles returned to England in 1863 and coauthored the official narrative of the expedition with his brother in 1865. In 1874 he became British consul at Fernando Po. He died in Lagos at the age of fifty-two, just two years after the death of his famous sibling.

Livingstone, David (1813–1873). Born in Glasgow, Livingstone was missionary and doctor to the Bechuana people from 1840 to 1849. In the early 1840s he was living at Mabotsa Mission near Kuruman. On 16 February 1844 Livingstone was working in a ditch when he heard a commotion from a nearby pasture. A lion was attacking the village sheep. Livingstone had a double-barreled rifle and fired both barrels at the lion, wounding it twice but not stopping its ensuing charge. The lion grabbed the missionary by the shoulder and shook him like a rag doll. Some local Africans ran up to help, and two of them were bitten before the lion fell over, having bled to death from its wounds. Livingstone survived the injuries, including a badly broken arm and the inevitable infection, but he could never again lift his left arm higher than his shoulder.

Livingstone married Mary Moffatt, daughter of Robert Moffatt, on 2 January 1845. She would loyally accompany him on many of his expeditions until her death in 1862. Livingstone helped discover Lake Ngami in 1849 and then explored the Zambezi and Kuanza Rivers, discovering Victoria Falls in 1855. In 1858–1863 he led a government-sponsored expedition through Zambezia and the Shire River area, hoping to find a water route from the Indian Ocean into the interior, and "discovering" Lakes Shirwa and Nyasa. Nyasa had previously been visited by the Portuguese trader Candido, and Livingstone knew it, but he took credit for it regardless.

For the next several years he stayed on the move, visiting the Ruvuma Valley (1866); the Chambezi (1867); Lakes Tanganyika, Moero, and Bangweulu (1867–1868); and Ujiji (1869). The last was an Arab slave-trading center with a population of a few thousand. After a skirmish with the Manyema tribe in 1871, Livingstone retreated to Ujiji, where the famous meeting with Stanley took place in November of that year. By this time Livingstone's once-hardy constitution was seriously impaired. Stanley's visit revived him, and the two explored together for a while.

Returning to Chitambo's village by Lake Bangweulu, Livingstone died there of dysentery on 30 April 1873. His heart was buried under a tree and his body carried back to the coast by faithful retainers, from whence it was shipped back to England. Many people later took pieces of the heart-burial tree as souvenirs, including Denis Lyell, who donated one piece to the Scottish Geographical Society and kept others. The provenance of the Lyell pieces (all cut from one branch) is in some dispute, for he obtained them in a store in Fort Jameson in 1904 and had only the shopkeeper's word that the branch was from the Livingstone tree.

Livingstone's dream was to establish the Zambezi River as a great civilizing highway into the interior of Africa. He imagined missions and farms set up all along that waterway, receiving their supplies and shipping their produce via the Indian Ocean. The discovery that the Zambezi was not navigable past the Cabora Bassa rocks was a major setback. For a time he then looked to the Shire River as a similar conduit. His last major dream was an effort to tie the Congo watershed into the source of the Nile.

Livingstone was a tough man and an indomitable explorer but not necessarily a great hunter, although while living in the bush he did considerable shooting for the pot. He got along cordially with Gordon Cumming during the latter's hunting trips in the 1840s, but his later opinion of the Scottish hunter was not always a positive one. In a letter he referred to Gordon Cumming as "a mad sort of Scotsman" and later called *A Hunter's Life in South Africa* "a miserably poor thing." Livingstone did acknowledge that what Gordon Cumming wrote was largely accurate, writing that the "lion stories are true" and that the "book conveys a truthful idea of South African hunting." According to James Casada in the introduction of the 1980 reprint of Gordon Cumming, Livingstone read the book carefully and respected it. Much of the problem was that Livingstone held attitudes toward hunting and conservation that are positively modern: He was disgusted with Gordon Cumming's unsportsmanlike ways, calling the hunter's technique of building blinds by water holes a "sneaking cowardly looking thing." Few modern sportsmen would disagree with that judgment. Livingstone's beliefs, however, did not prevent him from "borrowing" a huge amount of gunpowder that Gordon Cumming had left in his care.

Livingstone was the author of *Missionary Travels* (1857), *A Narrative of an Expedition to the Zambesi* (1865), and *The Last Journals of David Livingstone* (1874). His nickname among the natives was Munali, meaning a superior strain of maize. The color of the grain was said to resemble his tanned skin. His wife Mary died at the Shupanga Mission station in Nyasaland in 1862.

Livingstone was an enigma. A courageous, unbelievably determined man, he possessed a rare quality that inspired respect and love among some of those who knew him. Yet he was also ambitious, sometimes dishonest, and almost insanely jealous of his celebrity. He treated his family poorly and yet complained that they lacked the proper devotion to him. His treatment of William Cotton Oswell, whose generosity saved Livingstone time and again, was petty and shabby. And his decades of missionary work in Africa produced exactly one convert, and that man recanted almost immediately. Yet Livingstone proved an enduring symbol of British courage and sacrifice that inspired generations of mission workers and civil servants to devote their lives to helping others.

Livingstone's behavior, as described by Sir John Kirk (who was on the 1859–1863 Zambezi expedition) and others, was often appalling. He needlessly alienated the Portuguese along the Zambezi, and was prone to discharging and defaming his assistants based on what can only be called a whim, or at least a neurotic overreaction to criticism or disagreement. Anyone who disagreed with him was fair game. An analysis of his correspondence done by his biographer, Tim Jeal, reveals a man who often lied in his letters, usually to make himself look good at another's expense. Livingstone intentionally misrepresented the difficulty of navigating the Zambezi, for example, in order to avoid revealing his earlier endorsement of that river as a highway for British settlement in Central Africa.

In the October 1891 edition of the *Scottish Geographical Magazine* there is a review of Harry Johnston's book *Livingstone and the Exploration of Central Africa* that is unconsciously ironic. The anonymous reviewer begins by acknowledging that no greater expert than Johnston could be found for such a book, but then states, "This volume is, we frankly admit, somewhat disappointing. There is too little of Livingstone and too much of the personality of Mr. Johnston in the pages of the book." He then takes Johnston to task for going on at great length about the flora and fauna of Central Africa (as always with Johnston, the best part of the book), essentially ignoring the religious aspects of Livingstone (the real source of the reviewer's dissatisfaction), and concentrating on the explorer. "He fails altogether, we think, in appreciating Livingstone the missionary-pioneer." Keep in mind that Livingstone made exactly one convert during his decades in Africa. Then the reviewer laments that these mythical religious accomplishments did not inspire the pen of Johnston, who "had seen for himself the practical results of Livingstone's life work." And that, I suggest, is precisely why Harry Johnston refused to portray Livingstone as the great martyr in whom the folks at *Scottish*

Dr. David Livingstone with a white rhino horn, 1857.

Geographical Magazine wanted to believe. A generation or two of Englishmen and Scotsmen were brought up to think of Livingstone as this Christlike (or at least Johnny Appleseed) figure wandering the African countryside healing the sick, converting the heathen, and, no doubt, teaching African kids to read and inventing crop rotation and building little cathedrals out of bamboo and cow dung. They didn't want to acknowledge the very focused explorer who abandoned his children and greedily claimed priority for every geographical discovery of his day. Johnston knew the difference between the man and the myth and chose to highlight the very real accomplishments of the flesh-and-blood Livingstone, and to tactfully ignore the hypocrisy of the image so beloved by Victorian Britain.

Lloyd. A game ranger appointed to the Sabi Reserve in 1919, Lloyd was posted to an area called Satara. An older man (age fifty-six), he was in great shape, frequently making long patrols and other feats of endurance that would have taxed a man twenty years younger.

After one such outing in 1923, Lloyd came down with a bad case of pneumonia. He was out in the bush miles from help, and no medicine and little medical knowledge were available, and Mrs. Lloyd, a much younger woman (Stevenson-Hamilton called her "a mere girl"), watched helplessly as the ranger sickened and died.

Lobengula (c. 1833–1894). The king of the Matabele whose name means "the Defender," Lobengula was a son of Mzilikazi. Unlike his father, Lobengula's name is usually spelled consistently in the history books and memoirs. Staunchly independent, Lobengula finally granted the British permission to develop Mashonaland in return for percussion firearms and ammunition. His regret over this decision, and the resulting Matabele anxiety over the extent of British development, led directly to the Matabele War of 1893.

Selous (1883) described Lobengula as a large man standing nearly six feet tall, strong but very stout, who for some years dressed in "greasy" European castaway clothes but who later reverted to his more impressive native garb. The accounts of his conversations show him to be a man of intelligence and humor. At his first meeting with Selous he good-naturedly chided the slightly built, boyish elephant hunter by asking whether he had come to shoot steenbok, a diminutive antelope. Like any primitive despot, however, Lobengula was not all peaches and cream. In 1883 he treacherously ordered the murder of his ally, the wizard Chameluga, who was speared to death with all of his retainers and family, except his youngest and prettiest wife, Bavea. It was from her that Selous later heard the story.

Lobengula was an almost classically tragic figure. He had the faults of his time and position—a despot in the true sense of the word, he was quite capable of ordering men, women, and children put to death on the slightest whim. But he was no bloodthirsty savage. He had seen what a British army had done to his cousins the Zulus and desperately tried to avoid a cataclysmic war against the Europeans. His neighboring monarch, Khama of the Mangwato, managed to keep the precarious balance between acquiescence and surrender, but Lobengula was sitting atop a powder keg. The Matabele heritage was one of war and conquest, so Lobengula was torn between two necessities, placating the English and keeping his own martial warriors satisfied. In the end he was ripped apart by the inability of his own people to avoid senseless battle, and the constant raids and skirmishes of the lesser Matabele chieftains gave Rhodes, Jameson, and other greedy Westerners all the excuse they needed to seize his kingdom.

The last great stand of the Matabele in the fall of 1893 was not without its glorious moments. After losing five hundred warriors in a pitched battle, Lobengula and his men surrounded and destroyed an overconfident British scouting party consisting of Maj. Allan Wilson and about thirty-five men. One trooper who narrowly escaped the slaughter was the young Bill Buckley, later a famous elephant hunter. Similar to the Sioux defeat of Custer at the Little Bighorn, Wilson's Last Stand (also known as the Shangani Patrol) became an iconic symbol of heroism and bravery and achieved a notoriety far beyond its strategic significance. Wilson was likewise similar to Custer in that his death was swiftly followed by the collapse of the enemy's war machine.

Despite some rather pathetic attempts to negotiate, the Matabele leader was forced to flee for his life from the British forces. Even in the final days, Lobengula hoped to achieve some sort of negotiated peace with the enemy. The few Westerners remaining at Bulawayo were left unmolested, something Lobengula hardly would have done if he had abandoned all hope. A large tribute of gold was sent to bribe the invaders into retreating, but the two English scouts who captured his emissaries stole the coins and kept them secret until it was far too late. Lobengula was unaccustomed to the hardships of life on the run and died of fever and exposure (or possibly smallpox or suicide by poison—the rumors were legion) in January 1894. Matabeleland, now renamed

Rhodesia, lapsed into an uneasy truce. The Matabele took up arms once more, in 1896, but it was rather a desultory affair, a series of uncoordinated massacres and atrocities on both sides, and was soon over.

Loder, Sir Edmund Giles (1849–1920). Loder was a celebrated English sportsman of the Victorian Age and the subject of *Memoir of Edmund Loder* by Alfred Pease. Loder's trophies are listed on almost every page of the 1928 edition of *Rowland Ward's Records of Big Game,* including a 184-pound elephant tusk. He used a Mannlicher magazine rifle almost exclusively and was regarded with great respect by the other British sportsmen of the day. Loder is best remembered today as a horticulturist. ROWLAND WARD 1928: SITATUNGA, LECHWE.

Loewenstein, Prince John. Loewenstein was a German prince who accompanied C. G. Schillings on safari to Mount Kilimanjaro in early 1903. Schillings was the expedition's photographer while Loewenstein hunted with a rifle. He had shot numerous antelope, a rhino, a buffalo, and a giraffe and was planning to climb the mountain when urgent business called him away to South Africa. When Schillings and two African porters capsized their canoe and were swept into the Rufu River, Loewenstein organized a party of askaris to fire at the encroaching crocodiles while he and another guard rescued the three men with a rope.

Longden, George Gerald (xxxx–1911). Commander George Gerald Longden, formerly of the Royal Navy, arrived in East Africa with his wife around 1910. He purchased some land in the Nairobi area and apparently did quite well financially with his first investments. After getting some pointers from John Boyes and becoming friendly with the Belgian administrators of the eastern Congo, he took to elephant hunting.

Longden shot an elephant with tusks of 139 and 141 pounds in Uganda, and was also listed in early editions of Rowland Ward for a trophy white rhino. After some initial success in the Lado Enclave, he was injured by an elephant and died after three days of intense pain.

Loring, J. Alden. Loring was the naturalist assigned to the Roosevelt safari.

Lucas. He was a Kenyan settler who went lion hunting with G. H. Goldfinch. This was an early experiment in shooting lion from horseback. The idea just doesn't work—the horses naturally tend to be jittery near the lion. Particularly if the quarry charges, it is almost impossible to get off a decent shot. Lucas was killed and Goldfinch lamed for life.

Lucy, Jack P. (xxxx–1950). A noted lion hunter, Lucy was one of the founders of EAPHA (see glossary) in 1934. He was associated primarily with the firm of Safariland, Ltd.

Luederitz, Franz Adolf Eduard (1834–1886). Luederitz was born in Bremen, Germany, in 1834, the son of a wealthy tobacco merchant. When he inherited the family business in the 1880s, he decided to personally expand the company's market. In 1883 he went to South-West Africa and, by a series of deceptive treaties negotiated by his unscrupulous agent, Heinrich Vogelsang (1862–1914), acquired land and mineral rights at Angra Pequena in Namibia. The most notorious of these documents was the so-called "miles treaty," which relied upon the difference in length between English and European miles to cheat the local leaders out of more land than they thought they were selling.

This action by Luederitz was the first officially recognized German acquisition of African land and began Germany's participation in the "African Scramble." Ironically, Luederitz saw little profit from it—its first shipment of ore went down when his company ship, *Tilly,* sank on 1 February 1885. A year later Luederitz attempted to travel in a small boat from the mouth of the Orange River to Angra Pequena, accompanied only by his pilot, a man named Steingroever. The craft was lightly built and patently unseaworthy, and neither man was ever seen again.

Lugard, Frederick John Dealtry (Baron Lugard) (1858–1945). Born in Madras, India, on 22 January 1858, Lugard was educated at Rossall School and the Royal Military College at Sandhurst. He was commissioned into the 9th Foot (the Norfolk Regiment) in 1878 and served in India for the next seven years. In 1885 he went to the Sudan, attached to the Khartoum relief expedition as a transport officer. A year later he fought in the Suakin campaign in Upper Burma, earning a DSO (see glossary) in 1887. After the close of the Burmese campaign, Lugard rushed back to England after receiving a message that his fiancée was deathly ill. The illness was of the heart—she had fallen for another man. The engagement was off.

The heartbroken Lugard joined the London Fire Brigade, apparently seeking a heroic death to relieve his pain. Much

Lugard leads a battalion of troops into the German Cameroons, 1916.

to his chagrin, he found that he was the perfect firefighter and even began to acquire some local fame for saving people from burning buildings and, no doubt, kittens from trees. This was hardly what he wanted, so Lugard returned to Africa in 1888 as captain of a small expedition sent by the African Lakes Company to defend Nyasaland from Arab-African slavers. In 1890 the Imperial British East Africa Company (IBEA) commissioned him to secure their interests in Uganda. He carried this out admirably, restoring order and convincing the Kabaka of Buganda to sign a treaty of friendship. When the IBEA withdrew from Uganda in 1893, following further unrest, Lugard returned to Britain to garner support for the occupation of that country. Lugard and Gerald Portal were the two key figures who persuaded the government to take on that responsibility.

In 1894 Lugard was sent by the Royal Niger Company to obtain treaties from the various West African potentates before the French could do so. He was largely successful, and was made a Commander of the Bath. He became commissioner of Upper Nigeria in 1897, and high commissioner of Northern Nigeria three years later. In 1902–1903 he led a campaign against the recalcitrant Fulani tribe, but his administration was mostly a peaceful one.

By 1905 officials at the Colonial Office were getting nervous about Lugard and what they viewed as his personal empire in Nigeria. Aligned against Lugard were the colonial secretary, Lord Elgin, and his formidable under-secretary, Winston Churchill. The latter even went so far as to recommend that large parts of Northern Nigeria be separated from the British Empire. Lugard brought matters to a head by insisting on a bizarre management scheme that he called "continuous administration" whereby he would spend half the year in England and the other half in Nigeria. The sole benefit of the plan was that it would allow him to spend six months each year with his wife Flora, whose health was considered too delicate for the West African climate. Not surprisingly, Elgin and Churchill turned the proposal down. Lugard gave up his post in protest.

Resigning in 1906, Lugard was appointed governor of Hong Kong a year later. The new post was much less strenuous and mostly urban in nature, but at least it could accommodate Flora's constitution. In 1912 he returned to West Africa as governor of both Northern and Southern Nigeria. When those two colonies were merged in 1914, he became governor of Nigeria until 1919. He was responsible for establishing "indirect rule," the principle behind most of the British colonial governments. As much power as was considered prudent was concentrated in the hands of African chiefs and headmen, with the most powerful British figures being the representatives to those chiefs, the provincial and district commissioners.

Lugard retired in 1920 and became a member of the Privy Council. He held a variety of posts in the 1920s and 1930s, including a member of the League of Nations Permanent Mandates Commission (1922–1936), and chairman of the International Institute of African Languages and Cultures (from 1926). He became Baron Lugard in 1928 and died at Abinger, Surrey, on 11 April 1945.

The dry summary of his career fails to project a real image of the man. Like Sir Harry Johnston, Lugard was a dynamic, inventive man of action. Unlike Johnston, he was diplomatic and tactful enough to sustain a career in the Byzantine world of British colonial politics. His early days in Uganda were fraught with danger, which suited him fine (he was still in his suicidal post-jilting phase then). Lugard was searching for death but discovered himself instead. He was a born leader, charismatic and fearless, with the ability to inspire his followers to great accomplishments. Uganda was the turning point of his life, and it transformed a desperate, uncertain, emotionally crippled wreck into a decisive and confident leader.

Lugard was the author of *The Rise of Our East African Empire* (1893), and *The Dual Mandate in British Tropical Africa* (1922). His wife, Flora Louise Shaw, was the author of a history of Nigeria, *A Tropical Dependency* (1905).

Lyell, Denis David (1871–1946). Born in Calcutta, Denis Lyell grew up in Scotland, where he devoured the works of Gordon Cumming, Baker, Baldwin, and the other great hunter/writers. At a young age he moved back to India, managing tea estates and making an occasional tiger hunt, but his real desire was to hunt in Africa. By 1900 he was working as a civilian for the British military at Zomba on Lake Nyasa. There he could hunt with the officers of the King's African Rifles, the likes of which included Stigand, Brander-Dunbar, and Piers Mostyn.

It was in partnership with Stigand that Lyell wrote his first book, *Central African Game and Its Spoor* (1906). Lyell also tried his hand at farming during this time, buying a ranch in Rhodesia, where he had Martin Ryan and T. Alexander Barns as his neighbors and frequent hunting companions. Lyell was a proficient hunter and successful at tackling all of Africa's big game, although he arrived a few years past the time when a man could make a good living off his guns. He therefore supplemented his income by writing, turning out seven books and numerous magazine articles. His *African Adventure* (1935), an annotated collection of letters from other big-game hunters, has been called "the nearest anyone had come at this stage to writing a history of hunting in the late Victorian and Edwardian period" (Brander, 1988).

Some years back, before I had read the book, a friend offered me a copy for free. I almost lost the opportunity because I didn't feel like making an eight-mile drive! To my

Denis D. Lyell

distinctly uneducated opinion, the book sounded extremely dull—letter after letter describing how somebody got his rhino. I could not have been more mistaken. Lyell's work is a well-thought-out collection of opinions on controversial subjects by some very opinionated and controversial men. An excellent work, and well worth my fifteen-minute trip. Lyell was also a contributor to *Big Game Shooting in Africa* (1932), part of the Lonsdale Library.

Like most of his generation, Lyell had some military experience. He was a veteran of the Boer War, having served in the Western Province Mounted Rifles. He wrote in 1923 that he "really had no wish to shoot Boers or be shot by one of them, but craved for excitement."

He was kind of a gun nut, writing in 1923 that his favorite weapons had been a .416 Rigby Mauser, a .404 Jeffery, a .425 Westley Richards, a Gibbs .505, a .318 Axite, a .350 Rigby Mauser, and a .350 Rigby Magnum. He also owned a 4-bore BP single-barrel and a .256 Mannlicher, among other guns, and for some time used a 7.9mm Mauser due to an increased availability of cartridges. It is a mystery how he managed to get by with such a paltry arsenal.

The most memorable thing about Lyell was the high regard he achieved in other hunters' eyes. Like Selous, Lyell was almost universally respected and admired—one of those people nobody ever seems to say anything bad about. I'm sure he had flaws, but if he drank too much or cheated on his wife, no one ever wrote about it. ROWLAND WARD 1928: WATERBUCK (NO. 1, 36½ INCHES), BLUE DUIKER, HIPPO.

Denis Lyell with kudo horns shot in North-East Rhodesia.

MAC, MC

MacArthur, C. G. MacArthur was an assistant warden for the Kenya Game Department starting in 1927. Months after Bror Blixen's safari client Winston Guest wounded and lost a huge bull elephant in what is now Tsavo National Park, a South African hunter brought MacArthur a pair of tusks totaling nearly four hundred pounds. Kenya game laws required that before a found tusk could be legally considered as the finder's property, an attempt had to be made to determine the original hunter. Seeking to circumvent this, the Afrikaner pretended that he had killed the elephant, even going so far as to smear antelope blood on it. MacArthur detected the ruse and confiscated the tusks, which weighed in at 198 and 186 pounds. Unfortunately, they were sold at government auction and carved up before Guest, who had returned home to America, was able to send in a claim for them.

After World War II MacArthur came out of retirement to work as a director of the hunting company Safariland. He also ran a roadhouse and hotel called Mac's Place, about halfway on the road between Mombasa and Nairobi. A photo of MacArthur in Peter Beard's *The End of the Game* shows a fierce-looking young man with a full goatee.

MacDonald, Freddie (c.1887–1958). Known as "Kalahari Mac," MacDonald made a living as a young man shooting lions in the desert and then selling their hides at Cape Town for £8 apiece. He also shot elephants for the ivory, and for several years lived a fugitive's existence as a poacher, hiding among the Bushmen and acquiring an unparalleled knowledge of their language and survival secrets. In the 1920s he lived in Spain and operated a private detection agency in Madrid.

MacDonald was one of the proponents of the "Lost City of the Kalahari" legend that has attracted treasure seekers since it was first reported by two Boer prospectors in 1885. The city is supposed to be a stone ruin somewhere in the southern Kalahari, a remnant of some lost civilization. MacDonald claimed to have visited the ruins in the 1930s while tracking a wounded elephant. He died at Upington in the late 1950s, still dreaming of returning to Abingero, his lost city.

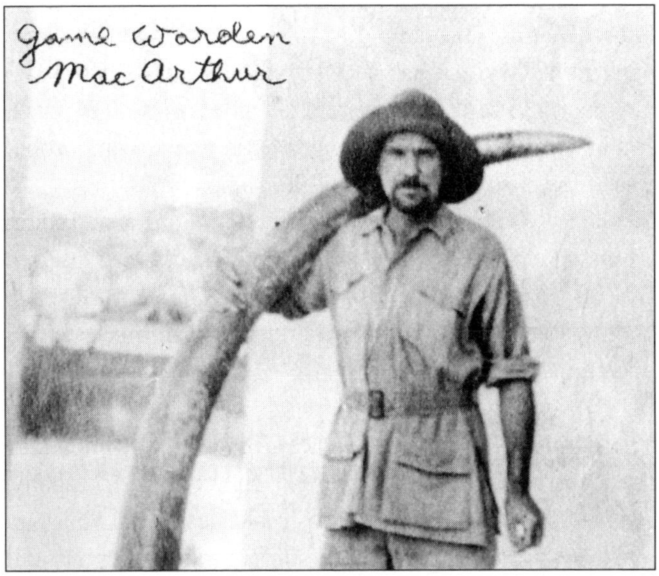

Kenya game warden C.G. MacArthur.

MacDonald, H. C. MacDonald was a big-game hunter who lived at Lilongwe, Nyasaland, around 1905. For some years his 48-inch buffalo was the world record, but once specimens of the larger buffalo from British East Africa started coming in, his record was soon eclipsed. In 1927 his buffalo head was in Lord Rothschild's museum at Tring. MacDonald did a lot of collecting work for museums. ROWLAND WARD 1928: GREATER KUDU.

MacDonald, James Ronald L. (1862–1927). MacDonald was a British officer with a good service record in India and Afghanistan from 1884. He supervised construction on the Baluchistan and Kabul railways and fought in the 1888 Hazara campaign.

He first went to Africa in 1891 as chief engineer for the Uganda railway project. Afterward he served in the campaign against the Sudanese mutineers in Uganda and as acting commissioner of the Uganda Protectorate in 1893. When French forces under Marchand threatened the British hold on Egypt in 1897, MacDonald was picked as leader of an expedition that would move up the Nile toward Fashoda. It was hoped he would reach that post before Marchand. MacDonald took as his assistant Capt. Herbert Austin, who later led his own fateful expedition around Lake Rudolf. MacDonald's expedition consisted of nine English officers, thirty Sikh soldiers, and five hundred porters, supported by three hundred pack animals and twenty-five oxcarts. In addition to French resistance, there was also the possibility of armed interference from the Abyssinian armies of the Emperor Menelik, who was becoming concerned about British designs in the Lake Rudolf area. The Abyssinians had recently slaughtered an Italian army at Adowa and were bristling with confidence.

Maj. James Ronald MacDonald.

The start of the expedition was delayed a few months because MacDonald had to contend with suppressing the 1897 Sudanese soldier revolt in Uganda. MacDonald had been ordered not to provoke the Abyssinians but disobeyed these instructions by sending one hundred eighty men under Austin toward Lake Rudolf while he led the main force toward the Nile. Five thousand Ethiopian troops were massed around the Omo River delta at the north end of the lake. Austin wisely skirted the enemy positions and avoided combat. MacDonald moved too slowly in his race with Marchand, and the French got to Fashoda first, in July of 1898. They were soon forced out by Kitchener, coming down from the north, but it is clear that the MacDonald expedition failed in its main objective. Much good political and geographical work was done, however, and the British government was not entirely displeased with the result. MacDonald wrote a book about the operation, but the government refused him permission to publish it.

MacDonald was promoted to major general in 1908 and later served as military commander of Mauritius, but retired from the service for medical reasons in 1912. When World War I broke out two years later, he was rejected for active service due to his health but served in a quasi-military capacity in Britain, and was promoted to colonel commandant of the Royal Engineers in 1924. MacDonald was the author of *Soldiering and Surveying in British East Africa, 1891–1894* (1897).

MacDougall, K. A provincial commissioner in Kenya from 1891–1907. As PC Tanaland, MacDougall was fined the enormous sum of £850 and transferred for having three Arabs—personal enemies of one of his drinking buddies—tied up and flogged. His district commissioner at Lamu, H. H. "Long" Horne, described MacDougall in a journal as a "low bred, uneducated, cunning Scot, who spits at table . . . an offensive beast . . . He is a hard drinker. He gets on your nerves so horribly by pretending to be a gent that you want to kick him . . . His chief aim is to draw travelling allowance" (Chenevix Trench, 1993). In the great literary tradition of bad-mouthing your boss, that's pretty good.

MacKinder, Sir Halford (1861–1947). MacKinder, an English sportsman, in 1899 led a team of mixed nationality that was the first party to climb to the summit of Mount Kenya. The other members of the team were mountaineer C. B. Hausberg, naturalist E. H. Saunders, taxidermist C. F. Camburn, and Alpine mountain guides Cesar Ollier and Joseph Brocherel. Their kit was carried by a crew made up of fifty-nine Zanzibaris, ninety-six Kikuyu, and two Masai scouts. This was the third attempt (earlier efforts were in 1887 and 1893) and was hotly contested by hostile African warriors. James Ramsey Ullman wrote in *High Conquest* (1941): "It is probably the only major mountaineering party in history that has had literally to fight its way to its mountain." Two Kikuyus were slaughtered in an ambush, and many of the supplies were pilfered by the Wandorobo. The safari also had trouble with rambunctious rhino. At one point the porters had to be forced forward at gunpoint. Ultimately, however, the mountain was climbed. Peter Beard's *The End of the Game* has a magnificent full-page photograph of Ollier and Brocherel at the summit, dated 13 September 1899.

MacKinnon, Sir William (1823–1893). MacKinnon was president of the Imperial British East Africa Company, 1887–1889. A canny Scottish businessman who had made his money largely from shipping and colonial mail contracts, MacKinnon's association with the company was sufficient to attract respectable investors. In 1886 he was the leader of the Emin Pasha Relief Expedition Committee, putting up £10,000 to finance the expedition. Uncharitable historians have speculated that he might have been more interested in saving Emin's legendary ivory hoard than in saving Emin himself. Previously he had shown little interest in East Africa.

Harry Johnston wrote about MacKinnon in his *Story of My Life* (1923). He described the wealthy Scot as a small, neat man "with an aquiline nose, side whiskers, a pouting mouth, and a strutting way of walking and holding himself." MacKinnon lived with his wife and her sister in a Spartan and very religious household. Daily services were held, presided over by a resident Minister but without the help of an organ, which was considered sinful. Johnston was fond of the sister, Miss Helen Fraser, who was "quite a nice-looking, amenable woman, but in terror of her sister and her sister's husband." On Saturday nights Lady MacKinnon would lock up the estate library and confiscate all the non-religious reading material in the house to prevent sin on the Sabbath. She once caught Johnston reading a secular magazine on a Sunday: "She hesitated and gulped, but decided to say nothing and let me go to my doom."

Sir Halford MacKinder, 1899.

Macleod, Olive (1886–1936). Olive Macleod was the fiancée of the British explorer Boyd Alexander. When Alexander was reported murdered on a 1910 expedition to Lake Chad, Macleod immediately left England for West Africa to investigate the circumstances of his death. Accompanying her were two friends, Mr. and Mrs. Amaury Talbot. Unfortunately, in her book on her travels (*Chiefs and Cities of Central Africa,* 1912), Macleod restrained herself to simple descriptions of the locales she went through, and thus what could have been one of history's great love-and-mystery stories reads like a simple travelogue. For instance, Macleod visited Fort Lamy to interview a French officer that Alexander had stayed with shortly before his death, but in her book made no mention of the man or any information he may have given her. Instead she simply gave physical descriptions of local housing and the resident Europeans.

There are no positive book reviews. Macleod was criticized for paying too much attention to social and cultural factors and not enough to her love story. Dozens of other writers, however, have been knocked for precisely the opposite. Many hunters wrote memoirs concerned only with their own personal adventures, the classic example being William Baldwin, who described an antelope hunt in some detail while ignoring a decisive Zulu battle taking place a few miles away. On the other hand, Donaldson Smith tried to mix everything into his *Through Unknown African Countries,* but no less a reviewer than Theodore Roosevelt criticized him for not giving enough space to his hunting exploits. You just can't win.

MacNab, Sandy. An American of Scottish ancestry, Colonel MacNab was a veteran of the United States Army and a frequent safari client of John A. Hunter. After a particularly thrilling lion hunt with Hunter on the slopes of Mount Kilimanjaro, MacNab switched to photo safaris, having "decided that he'd shot all the beasts he wanted" (Hunter, *Hunters Tracks,* 1957). One of his more intriguing photos, of an albino giraffe in Masailand, is reproduced in *Hunters Tracks.* Before he left Africa for Honolulu, MacNab gave Hunter both his .30-06 Winchester and .375 Hoffman rifles. MacNab died in America in the 1950s when he was in his eighties.

MacQueen, James. MacQueen, a hard-drinking but devoutly religious man, hunted elephant in the Lado Enclave. He was originally from Scotland and had spent his life prospecting in Australia and South Africa before arriving in East Africa in the 1900s. He became a hunter only after expending all his money looking for gold in Uganda and Kenya. John Boyes (1927) recorded that he first met MacQueen on the Kenya coast when he tried to return a horse that had strayed from MacQueen camp. MacQueen was digging a test hole in a dry riverbed, and gave Boyes "the rudest reception it had ever been my lot to experience in Africa." The Scotsman later apologized when he chanced upon Boyes in Nairobi.

MacQueen was a religious zealot and between safaris could usually be found in the Uganda town of Koba, the entry port for the ivory poached in the Belgian Congo. There he would frequently accost hunters for swearing and taking the Lord's name in vain. One time, while on his way to a new African church to hear the service, he overtook an African who was whistling a hymn—"Lead Kindly Light"—on the road. Outraged by such behavior on a Sunday, MacQueen thrashed the man before proceeding to the church. When he arrived there he found the place in much consternation because the minister had not yet arrived. The minister, of course, was the African MacQueen had beaten on the road. Unperturbed, MacQueen explained to the congregation what had happened and then led the service himself, lustily belting out the hymns while the parishioners accompanied him in their own tongue.

During MacQueen Lado days a "dead" elephant suddenly came to life and ripped his arm off with its trunk. Thereafter he took to carrying a tripod to steady his rifle. According to Boyes, MacQueen worked at the Kilo gold fields in the Belgian Congo for a while, and then by 1914 was lecturing in Rhodesia. When war came in 1914 he was commissioned as an officer in the transport department of the Rhodesian volunteer forces in East Africa, and he died of natural causes while campaigning in Tanganyika.

MacQueen, Peter. With his friend Peter Dutkewich, MacQueen took an extended hunting safari through British East Africa, Uganda, and up both Kilimanjaro and Kibo in 1908–1909. He wrote of his adventures in the book *In Wildest Africa* (1909).

McCabe, Joseph (1816–1865). McCabe was a hunter-trader operating in the Transvaal and the Orange Free State in the 1840s. He was something of a shady character, suspected of illegally selling guns to the Africans and of murdering stock-raiding Bushmen. McCabe was once fined for elephant poaching. He died at Molepolole in 1865.

McDonald, Hector. One of the new rangers hired when the Sabi Game Reserve became Kruger National Park in 1926, McDonald's name became associated with a variety of odd incidents that illustrate the vagaries of an old game ranger's life. One day early in his career he was involved in a lively gun battle with several white poachers. No one was killed, but the criminals escaped. Later, in 1929, tourism officials encouraged a daily excursion through the park via railroad. Tourists would take the train into the park, picnic in a little glade along the tracks, and return a few hours later. If a giraffe or an eland was seen along the railway, so much the better. On one such occasion, with McDonald riding shotgun, the train broke down and the passengers had to camp out overnight. Several caught malaria and all were frightened by lion, so the popular excursions were cancelled for a few years.

The lion back then were nothing to scoff at. At roughly the same time, a dedicated and respected native game scout named Mpampuni came limping up to McDonald's post. He had been badly ripped up by a lioness. McDonald hurried the man to a hospital in Barberton, but he died within a few days. Mpampuni was the first game department employee to be killed by a lion in the reserve, and only the second to be attacked (after Harry Wolhuter).

This may not have been just a coincidence. Not long after the death of Mpampuni, rumors started to surface that his wife had somehow been behind it. Considering that he had been killed by a lioness, most folks might have shrugged the rumors off, but McDonald was told by numerous earnest and serious natives that Mrs. Mpampuni had hired a local witch to kill her husband. Upon payment of a £5 fee, the witch would order her pet lioness to kill the chosen victim, or his cattle. It was known that the bride had visited the witch shortly before the incident occurred. Checking out the scene of Mpampuni's death, McDonald shot a lioness that was lurking in the vicinity. Whether the lioness was the guilty party, and/or connected to the witch, was unknown. The lioness got a bullet, the witch got her £5, the wife got her freedom, and Hector McDonald got an eerie story to ponder in his old age.

A few years later, McDonald figured in another odd lion story. A retired scout named Sakubona reported to McDonald, nursing a leg wound. He claimed that while stumbling home the night before, loaded to the scuppers with *pombe* (see glossary), a large lion had contested his right-of-way. Sakubona claimed that he rapped the lion on the nose with a stick. The lion supposedly bit him on the leg and ran off. Being a known raconteur, Sakubona was not universally believed. In fact, after seeing the old scout to the hospital, McDonald set out to verify the man's claim at the scene of the incident. To everyone's surprise, the spoor backed the old man up. Happily, Sakubona survived for several more years, cheerfully telling all and sundry how he had beaten *simba* with a stick.

McDougall, Ken. Ken McDougall was a skilled professional hunter who went into a partnership with C. J. P. Ionides in Tanganyika around 1930. The two operated a safari service out of Dar es Salaam. McDougall possessed a great amount of hunting knowledge but had a serious drinking problem. When under the influence he would fight and squander money, and he was always under the influence. The partnership broke up within two years. By that time McDougall had already managed to put Ionides £600 in debt.

McKenzie, Lady Grace. Lady McKenzie took some splendid motion pictures of big-game hunting in East Africa around 1920, particularly lion hunting.

McKinnie, Robert. McKinnie was a hunter and trader in Namibia in the late nineteenth century, often operating with his friends Robert Duncan and Robert Lewis. In 1894 McKinnie was arrested by the German authorities on suspicion of running guns to the local Africans.

McMillan, William Northrup (1872–1925). McMillan, a huge man with a sixty-four-inch waist, was a wealthy American (majority owner of the American Car and Foundry company of Saint Louis, among many other interests) who began his African life as a pioneer safari client. He loved the life and the country and decided to stick around. In 1902–1903 he started out on an exploration of the Blue Nile with Norwegian explorer B. H. Jessen. Their boats were wrecked and the men spent the time hunting instead of making discoveries. In 1905 McMillan financed Jessen in an expedition into the Sudan, but the hard-luck explorer once again had to turn back. Later that same year McMillan went on safari with John Boyes, and bought a twenty-two-thousand-acre ranch named Ju-Ja north of Nairobi. He owned other homes in London and Nairobi.

McMillan moved in exalted social circles, hunting with Selous and hosting Teddy Roosevelt during the ex-president's great safari. One day Kermit Roosevelt and McMillan went lion hunting, using beaters to drive the big cats out of a ravine. Instead a leopard came charging out at Roosevelt. The president's son shot the animal at six yards, whereupon the leopard sprang back into the brush. Unfortunately, the beaters had come up and the wounded cat leaped onto one of them. McMillan was able to shoot the leopard before it killed the beater, but the man was badly mauled. McMillan killed another leopard, an all-black one, in 1906 and for years displayed the skin in the trophy room in his house in London.

A highly respected man, McMillan was a member of Kenya's Legislative Council. He became Sir William in 1918. He is buried on top of El Donyo Sabuk Mountain in the Aberdares.

McClure's Magazine published a great article about McMillan in its March 1909 issue. Written by a fellow named T. R. MacMechen and entitled "Where Roosevelt Will Shoot: McMillan and his Ju-Ja Ranch," the article works on multiple levels. It is simply packed with information about McMillan's background, experiences, and African hunting in general. It is visually appealing,

W. N. McMillan.

containing numerous excellent photographs of McMillan and a lion, McMillan shooting with his shikaris, a leopard in a tree, rhino, and a party of Masai warriors standing around a wind-up phonograph. It is also unintentionally funny, the writer's sources obviously pulling his leg in a few instances.

For example, MacMechen writes that the rhino is so strongly armored in the front that no bullet can penetrate and only a shot from the side or in the eye can stop a charge. Buffalo are generally considered the most dangerous of the Big Five, for they intentionally track and ambush men, often unprovoked. Rhino are dreaded by hunters, but elephant generally are easy game, almost too easy. One wonders who MacMechen could have been talking to, but early articles like this one make it clear how certain fables about African animals and hunting started. Still, the article is well written and very entertaining, even after the passage of almost a century. ROWLAND WARD 1928: ELEPHANT (TUSKS: 110 AND 108 POUNDS, ABYSSINIAN SUDAN), SOUTHERN WHITE RHINO (NO. 3, SOUTH AFRICA), LELWEL HARTEBEEST, AND BLACK RHINO.

W. N. McMillan and rhino.

Baroness von Blixen and Sir W. N. McMillan.

McQueen Family. This pioneer family consisted of James (died 1942), Mary (died 1940), and six children—John (born 1896), Jean (born 1899), Madge, Minnie, Jim, and another. After arriving in Kenya from Scotland in 1896, the McQueens first settled in what is now a suburb of Nairobi. After a trip to Uganda to check out potential homesteads, they built a farm in the foothills of the Aberdares that they named Rhino Farm (later Rhino Park). James was a blacksmith and created all the nails, hinges, and other iron parts needed for the house himself. He specialized in growing potatoes, and made a good living by selling spuds to the men of the King's African Rifles.

No mean hunter, James once shot eleven elephant in one day and often fed his family with the products of his rifle. The McQueens were considered by many to be the essence of the hardy Kenyan settler and were immortalized by a chapter devoted to them in the Hunter and Mannix book, *Tales of the African Frontier* (1954). The kids were self-taught, grew up speaking Kikuyu better than they spoke English, and played with pet gazelle and hyrax. None of them had shoes until they turned ten. One of the sports they shared with the local kids was to steal beads from the corpses of dead Kikuyu women who were left in the bush for the hyena to dispose of—the Kikuyu took a very practical view of religion and often just went through the ceremonial motions. Only years later did the grownup McQueens begin to be bothered by that practice.

The McQueens would walk into Nairobi about twice a year to buy those few things they couldn't produce themselves. They presented a strange sight: Mary was a six-footer and much taller than her burly husband, and the kids were variously garbed in a mixture of homemade clothing and Kikuyu ornaments. James had sworn an oath never to shave again when his razor was stolen in 1896 and so had a thick black beard reaching to his waist. The family was unique in that they did not wear the sun-hats and spine pads considered so essential by other British settlers. Madge later married a man named McNaughten and lived at Rhino Farm all of her life.

M

Maguire, Cecil Montgomery (xxxx–1891). A captain in the Hyderabad Contingent Lancers who was seconded to the King's African Rifles, Maguire served under Sir Harry Johnston during the latter's campaign against the Nyasaland slavers. He arrived in Africa with forty Sikh Pioneers and thirty Muslim Lancers. The cavalrymen were quickly sent back to India because the tsetse promptly killed their horses. Captain Maguire was sent off in command of a small force to chastise a rebel Yao chieftain named Chikumbu, after which he joined Johnston at Zomba for the main campaign. That campaign was prosecuted successfully and was entering its "mopping-up" stage when Maguire got word that two valuable boats belonging to the slavers were hidden near Fort Johnston. On 15 December 1891, Maguire led twenty-eight Sikh soldiers to attack the enemy, but in the ensuing firefight Maguire and three Sikhs were killed. A stockade was later built in the district and named Fort Maguire.

Maguire, R. A. St. J. Maguire was an assistant district commissioner in Biharamulo, Tanganyika Territory, in the 1920s. He had a tremendous reputation as a hunter and a naturalist. When asked about the possibility of exterminating the elephant in the Addo Bush, he replied that it was impossible. His opinion, although wrong, was respected because very few sportsmen could boast a resume like his. Rowland Ward 1928: Buffalo, sable, lesser kudu, warthog, black rhino, Thomson gazelle, eland, Grant gazelle, greater kudu, Patterson eland, white-bearded gnu, gerenuk, kongoni, and a Tanganyikan elephant with feet 64 inches in circumference, just two inches shy of the record.

Magyar, Laszlo (1818–1864). A Hungarian explorer and adventurer, Magyar was a graduate of the Hungarian Naval Academy at Fiume when he sailed to Brazil in 1843. Obtaining a commission in the navy of the short-lived La Plata Republic, Magyar narrowly escaped execution when captured by the enemy Uruguayans. Released on parole, he spent some time casually exploring the ruins of the Incan Empire and trying to find financial support for a serious expedition into the Amazon jungle. Unsuccessful at this and despairing at finding another naval commission, Magyar shipped off to Africa in 1845.

For the next two years he found employment as commander-in-chief of the Royal Navy of King Dalabar of Calabar, a minor West African potentate. It is unknown when Magyar first met Dalabar or how he achieved such prominence in the African's eyes. The Royal Navy consisted of a schooner and 120 canoes, some admittedly very large. At this time he also made his first trip into the African interior, an 1848 expedition up the Congo to the Faro-Szongo cataracts. He later gave an account of this journey for the Hungarian Academy of Sciences. The account contained not only geographic and zoological information but also a blistering attack on the area's slave trade, then in full flood. Magyar not only barely escaped an ambush by cannibals but also sidestepped a possible assassination plot by the resident slave traders, who were deeply distrustful of all naval officers, Hungarian or otherwise.

Upon his return in 1848 he moved south to Benguela in Angola, where he hoped to set up a profitable trading operation. Soon (1849) he married Princess Ozoro, daughter of the African king of Bihe, Kaiaia Kajangula. Marrying an African woman was not unusual in Angola. Magyar blamed the poor health of most of the resident Portuguese on the sexual excesses they enjoyed with their several wives. Marrying the king's wife, however, was somewhat less usual and of course a brilliant commercial and political move. It was even more brilliant because it was at Kaiaia's insistence—he wanted Magyar's allegiance in a brewing intertribal war. It's generally a good idea to marry into the ruling family, particularly in a despotism. Fortunately for Magyar, Ozoro (whom he had never seen) turned out to be a charmer—elegant, educated, beautiful, and of a sweet nature. In a letter Magyar wrote later, he said, "We have lived in undisturbed family harmony." How much would his contemporaries—like, say, Abraham Lincoln—have given to say the same?

Magyar's chief wedding present was obtaining the use of Ozoro's personal slaves as his own private elephant and lion hunters—285 veteran woodsmen. By law anything they killed belonged to him and Ozoro. He used the money raised by the sale of the ivory and skins thus obtained to underwrite explorations of Katanga.

During these explorations he was often the first white man to enter a particular area. Near the Kasai River, Magyar encountered the ferocious Morupo people, whose king, Muata Jamwo, shocked the Hungarian by publicly executing hundreds of his subjects, including many poor souls that he ordered skinned alive. Magyar left the area as soon as diplomatically possible.

In 1851, armed with a Portuguese commission to map the rivers of the interior, Magyar set out to meet up with the English missionary, Livingstone. He also secretly desired to become the first European to cross southern Africa from west to east, a feat called the traversa. Efforts to obtain funds from his father (a rich farmer in Hungary) failed, and Magyar had to run things on a shoestring budget. Once again he traveled down paths never before seen by European eyes. In 1853 he was greatly disappointed when Livingstone avoided him—the British explorer, often pathologically paranoid about sharing credit for his discoveries, was reluctant even to acknowledge the presence of another white man in the interior of the continent. Magyar soon ran out of the funds and goods that were needed to pay tribute to the various native chieftains and was forced to cancel his expedition. It was left to Livingstone to complete the traversa.

Magyar returned to Bihe and continued his trading activities and minor explorations. In 1854 he was completing a successful hunting trip, loaded with ivory and skins, when he was attacked and robbed of everything by men of the Ganguela tribe. This same tribe defeated Kaiaia Kajangula in battle and forced a political crisis among the Bihe people. Magyar was ordered banished on penalty of death. He made one last furtive trip home to say good-bye to Ozoro, was spotted, and escaped execution only by the intervention of one Donna Isabel, a remarkable young woman of mixed blood whom he had met while hunting a few years previously. Her personal bodyguards rescued Magyar and allowed him to escape to Benguela, where he reached safety on Christmas Day of 1856.

He kept Benguela as his base for the remaining eight years of his life, leaving occasionally to hunt in the Lungo, Munda-Evambo, and Kapota areas. He also tried his hand at farming and collecting copal gum. Shut off financially by his father, he periodically petitioned the Hungarian Academy of Sciences for funding for another journey of exploration, but his pleas went unaided. He was, however, made a member of the academy in 1858 (mail service was such that he didn't receive his formal acceptance letter until 1861) and was encouraged to submit zoological and botanical reports. It was under the academy's auspices that his memoirs were released in 1859, for which he was paid a desperately needed 140 golden crowns.

After a letter to the academy in 1862, nothing more was heard from Laszlo Magyar. Eventually his fellow members of the academy—not his European relatives—became concerned enough to ask the Portuguese government for news of his whereabouts. The tragic truth eventually came out: The explorer had starved to death in Ponto de Cujo near Cape Santa Maria on 9 November 1864, surrounded by hunting trophies, maps, books, and other impediments of an explorer's life.

Magyar was the author of the books *A Short Resume of My Life* (1851) and *Explorations of the Zaire Delta* (1857). Unfortunately for his reputation, his works were published only in Hungarian and German. Had English, French, or even Spanish editions been issued, Laszlo Magyar would have received much more of the recognition he deserved—and quite possibly avoided his dismal fate.

Mahoney, Dan. From about 1891 through the early 1900s Mahoney was a professional hunter of immense experience in Portuguese East Africa. He hunted buffalo, killing hundreds and selling the meat to the railroad gangs for a handsome profit. He also made a significant amount of money from the hides. Mahoney was also considered one of the premier lion hunters of his day, having shot at least one hundred.

Mahuzier, Albert. A French cinematographer, Mahuzier made a series of successful black-and-white, Africa-themed films in the 1930s and 1940s. He returned to the continent in 1950 to film the story of a safari, this time in color. The project was only halfway complete when a lion killed his friend and guide, white hunter Marcel Vincent. Mahuzier wrote a book about the incident entitled *Tragic Safari.*

Maizon (1818–1845). Maizon (also spelled Maizen) was a French hunter-naturalist and naval officer who set out from Zanzibar to explore the Lakes region in 1845—one of the first attempts to find the lakes of Central Africa by moving westward from the Indian Ocean coast. Maizon's first mistake was to start during the rainy season, when foot safaris can proceed only at a crawl. In that situation of minimal mobility, disaster soon struck. Maizon was taken captive by hostile Africans at a place called Dege la Mhora (less than fifty miles from his starting point), tied to a tree, tortured, and beheaded. Reportedly the Africans were covetous of Maizon's lavish provisions.

Malewski, H. Fritz. A professional hunter employed by the firm of Safariland, Ltd. in the 1920s. He worked with Martin and Osa Johnson in 1933–1934. His address in the 1930 *Red Book* was Post Office Box 662, Nairobi.

Maloney, Thomas. Maloney was a South African elephant hunter of the 1860s.

Mandy, Frank (1838–1903). We first read of Mandy, born in Grahamstown, as a trader in Matabeleland in 1872. Nine years later he was running an ostrich farm near Port Elizabeth in the Cape Colony. The ostrich ranching business had its ups and downs. The farms boomed in South Africa in the 1870s, only to burst later in that decade as far too many people got into the racket. Mandy weathered the storm, however, and by the time Selous visited him in 1881 he was doing so well that it initiated a midlife crisis for Selous as he pondered his future prospects. The great hunter was pushing forty, after all, and there were no sports cars or Harley-Davidsons around back then to ease the pain. Happily, Selous snapped out of it, as men will, and was soon back where he belonged, shooting lion and elephant.

Mandy was one of the founders of modern Rhodesia, an officer with the rank of lieutenant in the "Pioneer Column" that Selous guided into Mashonaland in 1890. He died of natural causes in Kimberley on 28 June 1903.

Manley, James M. An elephant hunter and poacher, Manley was active in the Lado Enclave during the first decade of the twentieth century. He once watched the legendary marksman Karamojo Bell shoot fish with a rifle as they jumped from a lake to chase flies. Later Manley managed a safari firm that was a partnership of two branches, Bror Blixen's Tanganyika Guides and Philip Percival's Kenya Guides.

Margueritte, Jean. French general who distinguished himself in the Mexican campaign of the 1860s. Later he moved to North Africa, where he led huge organized hunts that virtually exterminated the ostrich population of northern Algeria. Margueritte is best remembered for a cavalry charge that he led during the Franco-Prussian War. The name is also seen as Marguerite.

Maritz, F. I. A South African professional hunter, Maritz, along with another hunter named J. J. Ferreira, bought a thirty-thousand-acre piece of land from the Swazi king Mbandeni in 1877. They paid a price of £180 in goods. Mbandeni was happy to sell the land, a parcel on the southwestern border of Swaziland, because it was his strategy to create a buffer zone between his people and the bellicose Zulus. Maritz and Ferreira cut the land up into farms. In 1886 the tract's seventy-two inhabitants declared themselves an independent state called the "Little Free State" (Klein Vrystaat in Afrikaans). One of history's smallest republics, the Little Free State was later (1890) voluntarily annexed by the Transvaal.

Markham, Beryl (1902–1986). She was a Kenyan socialite, racehorse trainer, writer, and aviatrix, also known as Beryl Clutterbuck, Mrs. Mansfield Markham, and Mrs. R. C. Schumacher. Born in England on 26 October 1902, the daughter of farmer Charles B. Clutterbuck and Clara Alexander, she was taken by her parents to East Africa when she was a toddler. Mrs. Alexander abandoned the family, and Beryl grew up believing that her father's mistress, Emma Orchardson, was her mother. Young Beryl led an exhilarating, tomboy life, roaming the woods with the Masai kids and being chased and knocked down by a neighbor's semi-tame lion.

After a successful period as a trainer of racehorses (her father's penultimate occupation—she was the first licensed female horse trainer in the world), she went to flight school, inspired by her friend and lover Denys Finch Hatton. She was tutored by Tom Campbell Black, the man who had rescued the German ace Ernst Udet from a lingering death in the desert. Once again she broke new ground, becoming the first woman to hold a commercial pilot's license in Kenya. From 1931 to 1936 she flew with a private air-transport business, the Blue Bird Flying Circus, and also flew her own charters, delivering mail, supplies, and an occasional passenger to remote locations in Kenya, Tanganyika, Uganda, Rhodesia, and the Sudan.

Markham frequently flew as an elephant scout for Bror Blixen, with whom she had an affair. She would not only locate the herds but would also fly low over them to try to spot big tuskers. In her memoirs she claimed that the cow elephant would try to hide the large-tusked bulls when they saw her plane approaching low overhead. These elephant scouting flights were called "reccies." Her scouting work for one client—Col. Leonard Ropner, a member of Britain's Parliament—was so successful that Ropner wrote an enthusiastic newspaper article about it when he returned to London. Ropner, guided by Bror Blixen, had been stalking the elephant herds for a big bull for three weeks without success. Markham and her plane joined the safari on Ropner's last day in the field and found what he had been looking for almost immediately.

A glamorous and engaging woman, Markham had a torrid affair with Denys Finch Hatton (after his death in 1931 she never attended another funeral) and was involved with the man third-in-line for the British throne, Prince Henry. In the 1930s the Royal Family bestowed an annuity upon her, payable for the rest of her life, as a way of keeping her second husband from naming the Prince as a respondent in a divorce suit. The sum put aside was

£15,000. Beryl received an annual check of £500 from this annuity up until she died. Another source claims that the capital sum was £10,000 and the yearly stipend £750. This was paid from 1929 until her death in 1986. Other celebrity lovers (she had dozens) included the conductor Leopold Stokowski, the sculptor Renzo Fenci, the boxer Jack Doyle, the earl of Erroll, and her flight instructor, Tom Campbell Black. George Adamson wrote, not necessarily of Beryl, "Two further pastimes, flying and adultery, quite often went together."

Beryl was married three times, and her excellent autobiography, *West with the Night,* is remarkable for not mentioning any of her husbands, except for an acknowledgment note to the third. The first spouse was Jock Purves, a former rugby player from Scotland whom Beryl married when she was just sixteen. The second was Gwladys Delamere's brother-in-law, the wealthy Mansfield Markham, whom she married in 1928. Her third husband was the American rancher and journalist Raoul Schumacher. Their marriage took place in 1942. Most historians now believe that Schumacher was the actual author of *West with the Night,* working with Beryl's notes and guidance.

In September 1936 Beryl flew solo from east to west across the Atlantic, taking off from Britain and crashlanding in Nova Scotia. Her flight time was 21 hours and 25 minutes. She was the first woman to accomplish this feat. Two men had previously laid claim to the accomplishment, but both were outdone by Beryl. One was Jim Mollison, the first person to cross the Atlantic solo from east to west, but he started in Ireland, not England, a shorter flight. The other man was John Grierson, who flew from England to Hudson's Bay, Canada, but landed in Iceland, where he had to wait for sparc parts to catch up. This was a much morc dangerous affair than it may seem to the modern reader—several fliers had died in the attempt, and Beryl herself miraculously escaped death when her carburetor iced over.

Beryl spent a considerable amount of time in the United States, including Hollywood. In 1940 she was able to tap several of her areas of expertise by working as a consultant to the Edward H. Griffith film *Safari,* which told the tale of an aviator turned white hunter, played by Douglas Fairbanks Jr. Markham advised about wardrobes, hunting, aviation, and especially the Swahili spoken by the extras, and she thoroughly enjoyed the experience. For most of the 1940s she considered the United States her home, and her friends included such well-known Americans as Burl Ives, Joseph Cotton, Frank Sinatra, and Joseph Kennedy. She left America in 1949 and never returned.

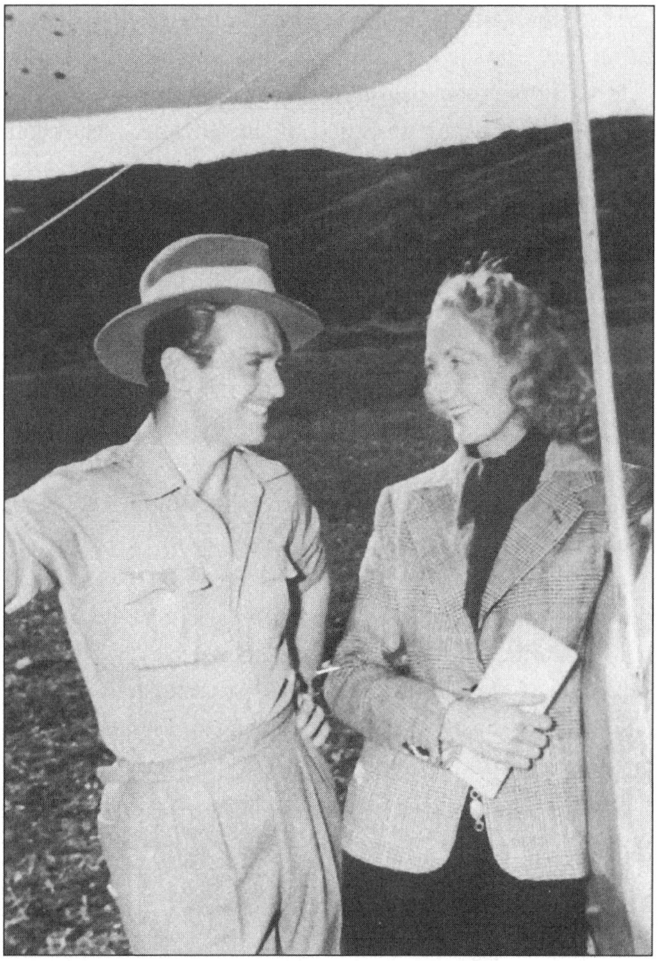

Beryl Markham and Douglas Fairbanks Jr. on location for Safari, *Hollywood, 1939.*

Like her father, who had been asked to resign his army commission due to the sorry state of his financial affairs, Beryl was a poor handler of money. Worse, she had a free and easy attitude toward other people's money as well as her own. Most of her friendships ended in bitterness when she used her friends to get easy credit or failed to repay personal loans. Once she was even caught trying to raise cash by submitting, in her name, short stories written by a friend of hers.

Beryl returned to Kenya and devoted herself to training horses. She was very successful at this, having a natural affinity for the animals. She was a fixture around Kenya's racetracks, and her horses regularly won the East African Derby, the Kenya St. Leger, and other major races. So successful was she at getting every possible effort from her horses that popular gossip alleged that she was enhancing their performance by use of powerful native herbs. One plant in particular was suspected—*seketet*, a bark that is crushed and drunk by the Masai to increase strength and stamina.

Adding fuel to the fire was the fact that Markham's horses often came down with a mysterious condition called the "Beryl Bloom" that caused them to grow massive muscles without a corresponding increase in strength. Markham attributed the "Bloom" to too much fluoride in the local drinking water.

After a series of debilitating incidents, including a savage mugging, being shot and wounded in a 1982 coup attempt (she was an innocent bystander), and finally a fall sustained tripping over her pet dog, Beryl Markham died in Nairobi in 1986. She was one of the last of her generation and, ironically, is probably more widely known now than when she was alive. *West with the Night* was rescued from obscurity by a North Point Press reprint in the early 1980s and has never been out of print since.

Martin, James (1857–1924). Martin was a Maltese sailor (born Antonio Martini) who accompanied Joseph Thomson on his second safari as Thomson's executive officer. Thomson had originally been reluctant to include another European in his party (the falling out between Burton and Speke was an ever-present reminder of how personalities can clash in the bush) but was so impressed with Martin's abilities that he changed his mind. It's a good thing he did—Sir Frederick Jackson later credited Martin with saving Thomson's life by his careful nursing when the Scotsman was stricken with fever.

James Martin (Antonio Martini)—sailmaker, explorer, and administrative official, 1885.

Illiterate but respected for his common sense and bushcraft, Martin later held numerous important posts. He was second-in-command of the Zanzibar army under General Mathews, a highly sought safari guide, and even became a district officer (one of the few who couldn't read or write) assigned to Baringo in Uganda. In that last capacity he made an estimated £12,000 to £15,000 profit in a shady ivory scheme, was caught, and quietly transferred to an obscure outpost on Lake Victoria's Sese Islands.

After resigning from the East African civil service about 1900, Martin managed the Mabira Forest rubber plantation in Uganda for several years. In World War I he served in the British and Belgian armies as an intelligence officer, a position shared by many of the region's outdoorsmen. In his old age Martin lived first in Tanganyika, then in Portugal, where he died in December 1924.

Mason, Alexander McComb (1840–1897). Alexander Mason came from a distinguished Virginia family (several generals, the author of the Virginia Bill of Rights, that sort of thing). His grandfather, Gen. John Mason, built a luxurious mansion designed to look like a Chinese palace on an island in the Potomac and dedicated his retirement to hosting scandalous parties. Young Alexander, with a feel for the wild side himself, ran away to sea in the early 1850s and became master's mate on the frigate USS *Niagara.* Accepting an appointment to the United States Naval Academy, he resigned at the outbreak of the Civil War to fight for his native state. He served at the actions of Drury's Bluff, Hampton Roads, and Charleston, and then went back to sea to become one of the South's leading blockade-runners.

In 1862 Mason was serving as secretary to his uncle, James Mason, who, along with another commissioner named Slidell, was sent to England to petition for British recognition of the Confederacy's independence. The three men were arrested and taken off the HMS *Trent* by the Union navy in the infamous Trent Affair. After furious diplomacy, the two Masons were allowed to reach England, but were unsuccessful in their ultimate goal of obtaining British intervention.

Mason resumed his blockade-running but was captured fighting as an infantryman at the Battle of Sailor's Creek and imprisoned for the duration of the war. Released in 1865, he drifted to Latin America, where he fought as a rebel in both Chile and Cuba. In 1870 Mason was recruited by an American agent named Thaddeus Mott, who was seeking professional soldiers to serve in an Egyptian force for a leader called the Khedive. Mason was one of about fifty Civil War veterans who agreed to go to Egypt.

The Khedive's chief-of-staff, another American named Lt. Gen. Charles Stone, assigned Mason to map the oasis of Siwa. The Virginian carried out his mission with dispatch and soon had a commission to survey Darfur and the Nile Valley. A romantic soul, Mason learned to speak fluent Arabic and enjoyed the drama of exploring strange and unknown places. After a couple of years in the wastes of the Sudan, Mason was appointed deputy governor at Khartoum. There he served under the iconic Victorian soldier, Charles "Chinese" Gordon. In 1879 there was a political shakedown in Cairo and many of the Civil War veterans were dismissed. Of the original fifty or so, less than half a dozen were kept on. Mason was one of those, and he assiduously carried out railway surveys and mapped the countryside. He liked the outdoors and hunting, and generally enjoyed his duties immensely.

The Egyptian government was grateful to Mason Bey, as he was now known, and was not shy about awarding promotions and honors. Mason became governor of Eritrea and was sent on a key diplomatic mission to Abyssinia. He had some hand in training the Egyptian troops and also served as director of Public Lands. All in all, it was a successful and enjoyable life for the boy from Virginia, the young rebel sailor who found his destiny in the desert. Alexander Mason died in 1897 while on leave in America. *The Washington Post* noted that he was "still in the service of the Khedive."

Mason, Jane Kendall (1909–1980). Mason, an American heiress and socialite, was a friend and lover of Ernest Hemingway and the inspiration for several of his characters. The adopted daughter of American millionaire Lyman Kendall, Jane was a glamorous debutante, often in the society pages, who sold Cuban folk art in a shop in Havana. She was married to airline executive Grant Mason when she met Hemingway during an ocean cruise in 1931. The two began a tempestuous affair after (according to Hemingway) Jane clambered through the transom of his hotel room to gain access to his bed. Always dramatic, Jane attempted suicide soon afterward by jumping off a balcony. Hemingway, with his usual charm, boasted to friends that the beautiful blonde had "really fallen" for him.

After her fling with the author, Jane Mason went on several safaris in Africa, hiring Bror Blixen as her professional hunter and romancing wealthy coffee planter Dick Cooper. It was at this time that Hemingway used Jane as the model for his character "Margot," the homicidal wife in the story *The Short Happy Life of Francis Macomber.* He also based two other unattractive characters on her, "Dorothy" in his play The "Fifth Column" and "Helene Bradley" in the novel *To Have and Have Not.* Hemingway, who could be remarkably petty and vindictive toward former friends, repeatedly referred to Jane in personal letters as "a bitch" and by other sordid terms.

Mason went on to live a long life and have three more husbands, politician John Hamilton, columnist George Abell, and *Esquire* magazine founder Arnold Gingrich. Late in life she became somewhat unhinged, believing herself to be possessed by demons and spending hours engaging in automatic spirit writing. She underwent an exorcism in the early 1970s and died of cancer in 1980.

Matana. Matana was a Matabele leader (Lobengula's older brother, according to Marcus Daly) who was considered the tribe's greatest general. In the 1830s or 1840s Matana led an army of twenty-five thousand north on a punitive expedition against the Barotos. At the Zambezi River he halted, hesitant to make a contested crossing against the Baroto army on the northern bank.

Matana kept five thousand men to hold down the Barotos, sent ten thousand to sweep south and look for a crossing, and personally led ten thousand toward the right flank to find another crossing point—the traditional three-pronged offensive of the Zulus on a grand scale. The southern horn crossed the Zambezi and successfully pillaged the Barotos, but the contingent under Matana entered the Mafungabusi forest and disappeared forever. It has been theorized that they followed the wrong branch of the river and died in a trackless waste. The survivors of the western flank, finding themselves worn out and far from home, settled down in Tanganyika and became the Angoni people.

Mathews, Lloyd (1850–1901). In 1877 the British consul in Zanzibar, Sir John Kirk, persuaded Sultan Barghash to dismiss his foreign bodyguard of Baluchi warriors and establish a modern fighting force of African troops under British guidelines, British discipline, and a British commander. For commander Kirk made a surprising but effective choice. Lloyd Mathews was only a young lieutenant in the Royal Navy, but he had a likable and winning manner. Barghash took to the young mariner, who was quickly seconded to the Zanzibari forces as major general and commander-in-chief.

Despite his inexperience, Mathews proved to be both hard-working and very effective. He trained and developed the African troops under his command into a crack fighting outfit. In the mid-1880s he twice led them on punitive expeditions into the interior of the mainland. Politically he proved extremely adept, his one possible "failing" being his faithfulness to Barghash—several times he seems to have put Zanzibari interests ahead of those of Great Britain.

He still acted to protect British prerogatives, however, if the situation did not create a conflict with his loyalty to Zanzibar. For example, when an American, William Astor Chanler, organized an expedition to Mount Kenya in 1892, General Mathews did everything in his power to obstruct him, despite being asked to assist Chanler by the British consul general, Sir Gerald Portal. Mathews felt that a successful safari by Chanler would strengthen American influence at the expense of Britain.

By the 1890s Mathews was one of the most influential men in Zanzibar, eventually even becoming *wazir* (first minister). From 1891 he was also the British commissioner for East Africa. He died in 1901, a victim, the doctors said, of malaria aggravated by overwork.

Mattenklodt, Wilhelm (1887–1931). Wilhelm Mattenklodt emigrated from Germany to German South-West Africa in 1908. He was looking for a chance to make something of himself, and was also attracted by the hunting possibilities. Almost immediately he enlisted in the local territorial defense force, every adult male having to undergo sixteen weeks of mandatory military training. As it happened, just one week after his training began in December 1908, his Schutztruppe (Defense Force) unit was sent on a punitive expedition against African rebels who had allegedly massacred ten German settlers. Mattenklodt and his fellow troopers were on patrol for five weeks. It was his first taste of active service, and ended only when another unit brought the suspected terrorists to bay.

His military obligation met, Mattenklodt set out to become a farmer at a place called Leipzig Farm near Grootfontein. Leipzig Farm cost Mattenklodt 16,000 marks (£800) and was about 12,000 acres in size. It came with 60 head of cattle, 40 sheep, and numerous chickens and ducks. The young German expatriate settled down to live off the fruits of the land. Meanwhile, he kept up his hunting activities, pursuing ostrich, antelope, hartebeest, gnu, oryx, and eland. His Boer neighbors taught him to shoot from horseback, a skill that was to provide unexpected dividends within a few years. As he wrote in his memoirs, "Shooting was my great recreation on the farm, and here, too, the Boers were my masters."

In 1911 and again three years later, Mattenklodt went on an extended hunting trip into southern Angola, accompanied by his Boer friends Piet du Plessis, Gert Lemmer, Ludwig Luesse, and Dirk Luesse. The big attraction there was elephant. The men made a substantial profit from the sale of the ivory.

Mattenklodt was still on his 1914 hunting trip, camping on the Okavango River, when the Great War broke out. The next four years were an incredible adventure for the young German. He was captured by the British and released on parole, took up arms again and was recaptured, escaped and was captured again, and escaped again. He lived an underground existence, staying with friends in South-West Africa and then disappearing on long safaris to his old Angolan hunting grounds when things got too hot. Finally the British declared him a guerrilla and put a price on his head—to be captured again would mean death by firing squad.

At the end of 1918 Mattenklodt found himself in a strange position. Hostilities had stopped in November; for many, the war seemed over. However, legally a state of war still existed (the Treaty of Versailles was not concluded for over a year), and Mattenklodt was still under summary sentence of death should he be caught. If he could evade capture until peace was declared, however, the British would have to let him go because the legal authority to execute a guerrilla would dissipate upon the signing of peace. That was how Mattenklodt understood the situation. So on Christmas Eve 1918 he helped his old friend Voswinkel and another man named Feuerstein escape from a British prison in Grootfontein. The three men fled back to the wilderness of the Omaheke.

It is ironic that the end of hostilities brought the greatest burden on Mattenklodt. Hotly pursued by the English, and realizing that even his phenomenal luck would someday run out, he devised a desperate plan that would put him beyond their reach for good. He and his two comrades would flee up the west coast of the African continent, through Angola, the Belgian Congo, and French Equatorial Africa to the

Spanish colony of Rio Muni. There they hoped to find safety and live out their lives.

The trip was epic. The trio evaded capture time and again, slipping past ambushes in the dead of night and occasionally exchanging shots with the local Africans. Once they reached Angola, they cagily decided not to shoot when confronted by regular forces, and to defend themselves only if attacked by irregular tribesmen working as mercenaries or scouts. The rationale was to commit no crimes in Angola unless they absolutely had to. For the same reason, the men paid for any food or other supplies that they requisitioned.

The strategy paid off. When the inevitable happened and they were captured by Portuguese soldiers, they were informed after an initial round of shackling and torture that if they had not committed any postwar crimes on Portuguese territory, they would not be tried there. And so it proved. Feuerstein and Voswinkel were extradited to British territory. Mattenklodt was able to convince the Portuguese authorities that he hailed from the right side of the Angola and German South-West Africa frontier—he did, after all, have considerable local knowledge of the district, retained from his prewar hunting trips. They let him go and provided him with passage back to Germany. Once there he was able to bring attention to the plight of his two comrades, and both Voswinkel and Feuerstein were soon released as well.

From Windhoek to his final place of capture at Fort Kalulu in Angola, Mattenklodt had covered about 2,035 miles. It was an appropriate epic ending to what was a remarkable career as a fugitive. Aided by the local populace and by his own knowledge of the terrain and local bush, Mattenklodt had eluded the best efforts of the not-inefficient British army to capture or kill him.

In the late 1920s he wrote his memoirs (*Verlorene Heimat,* 1928), published in English in 1931 by Little, Brown and Company as *Fugitive in the Jungle.* He was more of a fugitive in the desert than the jungle, of course, but the recent success of movies like *Trader Horn, Tarzan,* and the films of Martin and Osa Johnson had convinced most Americans that all of Africa was a jungle. Mattenklodt died in August 1931 at Swakopmund, Namibia, of sleeping sickness contracted while hunting big game in Angola.

Fugitive in the Jungle has never really received the attention it deserves. It belongs in any Africana library, whether the emphasis is on hunting, World War I, or simply social history. In it Mattenklodt includes only minimal information on ballistics and shooting, usually merely mentioning what type of rifle he was using at a particular time. But amidst all the patrolling and scouting and skirmishing, it is informative to see what an important part hunting played in the lives of early settlers, be they British, Boer, or German. Even when all hands were against him, when he was hiding out on his old farm and being sought as a spy and wanted for summary execution, Wilhelm Mattenklodt still risked exposure rather than giving up the simple pleasure of hunting springbok with his forbidden service rifle. Even though Mattenklodt never attained nearly the "bag" of his more famous British contemporaries, he deserves to be remembered right up there with J. A. Hunter, Alan Black, Pretorius, and all the others who wrote the rich history of African hunting.

Mattross, Abraham. Mattross was an African teamster and trader who accompanied James Chapman on his explorations in South-West Africa in the 1850s. He was still hunting near the Kunene River in the mid-1870s.

Mauch, Karl Gottlieb (1837–1875). This German explorer arrived in Durban, South Africa in January 1865. He toured the Transvaal and the Limpopo River valley, meeting up with Henry Hartley and traveling with him into Matabeleland.

On 27 July 1867 Mauch and Hartley discovered gold, inaugurating the first South African gold rush. Mauch profited little from his discovery—in fact, he needed a £173 charity draft from home to make ends meet. Then soon afterward he was captured by one of Mzilikazi's chieftains and held prisoner for six months. Only the intercession by, and ransom of, Adam Render, the discoverer of the Zimbabwe ruins, got Mauch released.

Mauch tried next to uncover the secret of the Zimbabwe ruins and also looked for more gold in that area, but was unsuccessful. Worn out and broke, he went home to Stuttgart, where he died a poor man, falling from a high window of his house.

Maugham, R. C. F. (1866–1956). A British administrator and sportsman, Maugham first came to Africa as a civilian official of the British Central Africa Protectorate (later called Nyasaland) in June of 1894. He was stationed at Zomba. In April 1895 Maugham transferred to Blantyre as acting collector. The job of collector in those days was what became known as district commissioner within a few years. He took part in the various antislavery campaigns in that region in the following few years. With the exception of a high-wheeler imported by fellow official Frederick Moir, Maugham brought the first bicycle to the Shire Highlands in 1895 (commissioner Harry Johnston later became a noted cyclist himself). He later had appointments as acting vice consul in Chinde and acting consul in Beira before finally transferring from the British Central Africa administration to the Consular Service, a section of the Foreign Office, in November 1898.

Maugham's first permanent consular post was as vice consul at Quelimane in Portuguese East Africa. In 1899 he became consul at Mozambique, the capital of Portuguese East. After three years it was decided to discontinue the Mozambique Consulate, and Maugham was transferred to Beira. He spent several relaxed years there, hunting and fishing (he was an accomplished yachtsman). In 1912 he was appointed consul general in Liberia. He was the author of several books, including *Wild Game in Zambesia* (1914), and *Africa as I Have Known It* (1929).

Maugham went on safari with Lieutenant Colonel Stevenson-Hamilton in July–August 1908, traveling through Portuguese Nyasaland. They had poor results, for the game had been shot out of the area by the many armed local villagers years before.

Maund, E. A. British sportsman and unofficial ambassador to the Matabele. Well educated and from a good family, Maund was a member of Warren's Bechuanaland expedition in 1885. Thereafter he spent a lot of time in the Zambezi interior as a representative of Lord Gifford's Exploring Company, visiting Lobengula's court at Bulawayo and spending months at a time as the Matabele leader's guest. After having worked vigorously for Gifford's concern, Maund then defected to rival Cecil Rhodes's British South Africa Company. He participated in the 1890 occupation of Mashonaland.

Maxwell, Marcuswell (1890–1938). Born in France and raised in Australia, Marcuswell Maxwell was an engineer who came to East Africa in 1919. Maxwell, who was interested in photography, was one of the first to realize that many wild animals could be approached very closely by the use of an automobile since they seemed not to associate the vehicle with human beings. By using this method, Maxwell was able to produce a series of superb photos of lions and elephants, many of which were published in the *London Times.* In 1930 the newspaper published the book *Elephants and Other Big Game Studies,* a collection of photos taken by Maxwell on two safaris in Kenya and Tanganyika while accompanied by professional hunter Clary Palmer-Kerrison. His pictures were the first to establish that adult African lions can climb trees. He was also the author of an article in the 23 April 1932 edition of *The New Passing Show* magazine titled "Lions Stalk My Car."

Maxwell visited the United States aboard the SS *Olympic* (sister ship to the *Titanic*) in 1913. The ship docked at Ellis Island, New York, on 1 October, and the passenger manifest still exists. The entry for Maxwell indicates that he was twenty-three years old, a student, was five feet, ten inches tall, and had a fair complexion, brown hair, and blue eyes. The form stated that the purpose of his trip was to visit his father in Schenectady, New York. His father was given as W. Maxwell of Boston. The form also stated that he had previously entered the country in 1901 and had visited Massachusetts. At the time of his 1913 entry he was a resident of Australia and listed someone named "B. C. H. Pookey" of Wahroonga district, Sydney, as his contact person in that country.

Maxwell was an honorary lieutenant colonel of the Royal Engineers and was married to Margaret Dorothy Pughe. He died on 21 April 1938. He is frequently confused with Marius Maxwell.

Maxwell, Marius. Marius Maxwell was a British-born naturalized U.S. citizen and early camera pioneer in East Africa. He was the first to produce true close-ups of live game. Previously a close-up of dangerous African wildlife was by necessity a photo of a dead animal. For his 1924 book, *Stalking Big Game with a Camera,* Marius Maxwell took his photographs accompanied by white hunter James Hugh Barnes. Marius wished to get close for the camera while Barnes wanted to keep a safe distance from the lion. This led to some interesting and intense conversations. Eventually the photographer got his way, and the resulting book was a big success.

The similarity in names between Marius and Marcuswell Maxwell has led to a lot of confusion. Author Jay Fetner, for example, in his otherwise excellent *The African Safari* (1987), clearly believed them to be one person, Marius "Marcuswell" Maxwell.

Maydon, Hubert Conway (1884–1944). Hubert Conway Maydon was the son of J. G. Maydon, Minister for Harbors and Railways of the Natal colonial government. The younger Maydon, described by John Taylor as a "very keen and observant amateur" (1948), was a sportsman and the editor of *Big Game Shooting in Africa* (1935). This book, published as one of the popular Lonsdale Library series, influenced an entire generation of African hunters, both amateur and professional. His rifle of choice was the 7.9mm Mauser action.

Maydon also had a distinguished military career, graduating from Sandhurst in 1904 and retiring with the rank of major in 1924. He served with the 12th Royal Lancers and the Egyptian Camel Corps. With the latter unit he was stationed at El Obeid in the Sudan, where he was able to devote much of his free time to hunting the elusive Barbary sheep and oryx of the Sahara. His own article in *Big Game Shooting in Africa* is about these hunts. In 1930 he married Virginia Tattersall. They had one child, a daughter named Sarah. Maydon died in South Africa in 1944. ROWLAND WARD 1928: ABYSSINIAN IBEX (NO. 1, 44 INCHES), MOUNTAIN BUSHBUCK (NO. 2), CHEETAH, BONGO.

Mayes, Walter. Mayes was an administrative officer in Kenya from about 1895–1905. An early district commissioner at Nandi, Mayes, originally a seaman from Glasgow, was not a likable man. Rumor had it he had deserted his ship in Madagascar before making his way to East Africa. Meinertzhagen described him in his diary as "uneducated . . . out to make what he can from his job." Provincial commissioner John Ainsworth wrote that Mayes had "as bad a character as can be" (both quotes from Chenevix Trench, 1993). Mayes was the man behind the repeated schemes to have Meinertzhagen cashiered for his killing of a Nandi leader during a truce.

In 1909 Mayes was charged with a series of rapes he had allegedly committed while on a tax-collecting safari, as well as embezzlement, but the administration, anxious to avoid a scandal, covered up the worst crimes. Mayes was simply dismissed from office and sent home.

Mayo, 7th Earl of (Dermot Robert Wyndham Bourke) (1851–1927). Lord Mayo was a British Guards officer about thirty years old when he organized an ambitious exploration of Angola and the Congo in 1881. Mayo proposed to explore the little-known banks of the Kunene River and beyond, with an eye to discovering potential settlement districts and even to clarifying the relationship between the Congo and Zambezi Rivers. He sought an English companion who was willing to pay his own way, and came up with a good one, twenty-three-year-old Harry Johnston. Not incidentally, the two men planned to get a lot of hunting in as well.

Johnston borrowed £200 from his father, and the pair left Liverpool for Africa in April 1882 on an old steamer named the *Benguela.* After stops in Niger and the Cameroons, they landed at Mossamedes in southern Angola. There Mayo organized sufficient trek wagons and oxen for a Boer-style hunting trip. They rescued a German explorer named Fischer (who had collapsed from fatigue—they found him sprawled in the mud) and spent six happy months hunting the prodigious native fauna. As Johnston wrote in 1923, "The shooting became better and better . . . the elephants, giraffes, rhinoceroses, zebras, buffalo, roan antelopes, palas, waterbuck, and ostriches were sufficiently abundant." At Humbe on the Kunene River, Johnston said farewell. Mayo hooked up with another friend of his from Britain, writer Henry Houghton Beck, and continued hunting and casually exploring for some months.

Prior to all that, Lord Mayo had conducted a similar hunting and exploring trip in 1879 along the Takaze and Atbara Rivers east of Khartoum in the Sudan and Abyssinia. It is amazing how important the sport of hunting was in mapping the interior of Africa. Some historians have termed this the "hunting frontier," a line on the map in advance of civilization that was the operating area of the professional hunters.

Mearns, Edgar A. (1856–1916). Lieutenant Colonel Mearns, a surgeon, accompanied the Roosevelt safari in the capacity of naturalist. He spent much of his time treating wounds, including those of several Masai who had been hurt spearing a lion to death. He spent a month (September–October 1909) doing a zoological survey of Mount Kenya, which is summarized as Appendix D of Roosevelt's *African Game Trails.* He was a member of the American Childs-Frick expedition to Angola in 1911.

Mecklenburg, Duke of (1873–1969). Duke Adolphus Frederick of Mecklenburg was a noted hunter and explorer of early Africa. He was that type of person, like Teleki, who had enough wealth and stature that he never had to leave his European estates, but a craving for adventure and sport took possession of the man and he went to share the hazards of the Dark Continent. Mecklenburg got what he was looking for—hostile natives, poisonous mambas, and charging elephant. In 1907–1908 he traveled to the Belgian Congo to hunt the furtive okapi. He never saw the living animal himself, however, and had to be content with trading for five skins and a skeleton from the Pygmies. The duke was the author of *In the Heart of Africa* (1910).

Meerhoff, Pieter (c. 1636–1668). Meerhoff was a Dane stationed at the Dutch East India Company fort at Cape Town in 1660 as a military surgeon. In November 1660 Meerhoff led an exploring party to the Olifants River in an effort to establish trade with the local Hottentots. On 14 January 1661 Meerhoff saw a strange creature in the river: "A live monster with three heads like cats' heads . . . and three long tails showing above the water." Meerhoff later married a Khoi girl named Eva. Eva Meerhoff had been helpful to the colony (established in 1652) and was working as a maid for the commander, van Riebeeck, at the time of their marriage.

Meerhoff was slain during a slave-trading expedition to Madagascar in early 1668. Eva was exiled for some offense to a penal settlement on Robben Island and died there, probably of alcoholism.

Meikle, M. E. and R. S. Authors of *After Big Game* (1915) and hunters in the Uganda railway area.

Meikle, Tom (1862–1939). One of a family that arrived in southern Africa from England in 1868 and settled on a farm along the Mooi River in Natal. In the early 1880s Tom Meikle and his brothers Stewart and Jack (1868–1949) were instrumental in the development of the Barberton mining district. The Meikles worked their own claims but became best known for the stores and taverns that they built. These eventually became the basis of a successful family hotel and department store business. (The famous Meikles Hotel in Harare is named after this family.)

Working a gold claim with a Russian partner, Tom discovered a nugget weighing fifty-eight ounces, the largest ever found in the Transvaal to that date. The Russian was badly burned in a brush fire while hunting and was laid out in the Meikle camp to recuperate. One day when Tom returned from hunting, he found both the Russian and the big nugget gone. Some days later, the Russian showed up back in camp, and Tom, who had a legendary temper, gave him a severe thrashing and threw him out again.

Tom considered the nugget lost for good, but one day he received a map and a strange letter in the mail. Pieced together with cut-out letters like a ransom note, the letter said simply: "Tree gold dig find." Tom followed the directions on the map and, underneath a large tree near the camp, found the buried nugget, which he promptly sold for £200. Months later he accidentally ran into his Russian ex-partner on the road and, characteristically, gave him £100 as his share of the sale.

Meinertzhagen, Richard (1878–1967). Born in London the scion of a wealthy banking family, Dick Meinertzhagen grew up fishing, shooting, and trapping small game around his family's rented estate at Mottisfont, Hampshire. From an early age he had a particular fondness for birds, and later achieved an international reputation as an ornithologist.

As an aside, Meinertzhagen was apparently convinced that Mottisfont was haunted by a ghost living in a small statue of Buddha that he kept with him throughout his life. Meinertzhagen was somewhat superstitious. He had reason to be. In 1897 his older brother Dan, the family heir, witnessed an apparition running across the lawn at Mottisfont. Family tradition said that whoever saw such an apparition would soon die. Dan told Dick about it and no one else, and six weeks later Dan was dead of appendicitis.

Dick joined the Hampshire Yeomanry as a cavalry officer in 1897 and transferred into the regular army as a lieutenant in the West Yorkshire Regiment a year later. Wanting to go hunting, he wangled a transfer to the Royal Fusiliers in India in 1899. In India he proved a superb hunter and naturalist but an indifferent peacetime officer. He also displayed a tough streak bordering on psychosis, once holding a .455 revolver to the head of a fellow regimental officer named "Bobby" Roberts. In 1902 he had an argument with his commanding officer over a snipe hunt and requested, and was given, a transfer to the East African Rifles in Kenya.

The next few years made his reputation. Given command of a company, Meinertzhagen drilled the men into shape while indoctrinating himself to the wonders of African hunting. He was especially fond of hunting lion and plains game, and many years later still had trophies listed in the 1928 Rowland Ward for cheetah, kongoni, and sitatunga. He and his men were stationed at Fort Hall in the heart of Kikuyu country. It wasn't long before he saw action.

Meinertzhagen was a born fighting leader, and a born killer. In July 1902 four African mailmen were slaughtered in a Kikuyu ambush. Many of the eleven wounded survivors later died. Meinertzhagen tended to the wounded and began planning a punitive strike. Before this happened, however, the Kikuyu ambushed and murdered an African policeman not a mile from Fort Hall.

Meinertzhagen attacked the village that had been responsible for the policeman's death. He lost three men to at least seventeen dead Kikuyu, and torched the place. This was to set the pattern for his responses to local strife in the future. It was an effective response.

For the next four years Meinertzhagen was almost constantly in action, fighting against the Kikuyu and the Nandi, though he did make one trip home to England. His actions were controversial—he would usually burn offending villages and several times gave orders to take no prisoners. His African troops, augmented by a picked force of Masai warriors, would attack with bayonets and show no mercy. On at least one occasion, Meinertzhagen shot five of his own men for insubordination when they disregarded his orders to spare a captured infant.

During all this military activity Meinertzhagen still found time to hunt. His bag included lion, leopard, rhino, buffalo, the rare bongo, and all kinds of plains game—a total of thirty-eight species. He is credited with bringing in the first giant forest hog, known forever afterward as *Hylochoerus meinertzhageni.* Meinertzhagen never completed the Big Five, though, because in all his long career he never could bring himself to kill an elephant. He considered the huge animals too intelligent and admirable to shoot.

The turning point of his East African career came in 1905. Something went wrong at a parlay with a disgruntled Nandi chief named Koitalel, and Koitalel and his entourage were shot and killed by Meinertzhagen and his men. Meinertzhagen claimed that Koitalel had treacherously tried to kill him. His detractors called it murder. Whatever it was, it effectively ended the Nandi rebellion. Meinertzhagen was three times exonerated by British military courts investigating the matter, but the rumors of impropriety eventually led to his recall.

To be fair to Meinertzhagen, his accusers in the Koitalel case seem to have been led by one Walter Mayes, a disreputable district commissioner from Glasgow. Mayes could not be trusted as a source. He was soon after dismissed from duty as a thief and a rapist. The British military authorities seem to have taken the view that while Meinertzhagen may not have been guilty of treachery in the Koitalel matter (indeed, many of his fellow officers thought Meinertzhagen should have been commended and even decorated for his role), the notoriety caused by the incident was damaging to British interests in the colony. Meinertzhagen always claimed that most of the native Africans respected him for his boldness and straightforwardness and bore him no ill will over the incident, but that is partially refuted by the fact that two young Nandi girls poisoned him with laced honey soon after his court of inquiry. One has to suspect, as well, that officialdom was

Col. Richard Meinertzhagen and buffalo in Kenya, 1904.

Richard Meinertzhagen in the uniform of the King's African Rifles, Nairobi, 1903.

more than a little nervous about the Meinertzhagen tendency to settle arguments by killing his opponent.

The poisoning incident was by no means the only injury suffered by Meinertzhagen. In 1905 he was one of seven men hit by poison arrows in an attack on a Nandi village—two of the seven died. Meinertzhagen recovered with no lasting effects.

In later years Meinertzhagen served with distinction in East Africa and Palestine during World War I. In charge of military intelligence along the Tanganyika front, he carried out his duties with dispatch. After capturing two Africans who were sabotaging communication cables, he promptly had them shot. On one raid he killed a German officer in hand-to-hand combat, crushing the man's skull with a knobkerrie. He ran a variety of intelligence and espionage schemes, including an elaborate scam to frame an Arab who was in fact working for the Germans. Meinertzhagen sent the man a congratulatory letter, thanking him for his services to the British Crown, and a large sum of money as a reward. He sent the dispatch via a bumbling African scout who was sure to fall into German hands. The letter was, of course, in an easily broken code. The Germans fell for the deception, and the Arab (and presumably the hapless scout) was promptly arrested and executed. True to form, Meinertzhagen showed no remorse over the fate of the unfortunate scout, who was, after all, working loyally if ineptly for the British cause.

Meinertzhagen also had African spies in the German camp who would collect and forward the contents of the enemy's chamber pots and latrines—well, not all of the contents, just the toilet paper. Meinertzhagen shrewdly realized that the Germans were short of real toilet paper and had to resort to using any source at hand. In this way he managed to collect a large number of important and informative documents, from personal letters to daily returns and even copies of orders. Meinertzhagen termed this the "dirty-paper method"—whoever first said espionage is dirty work had no idea how right he was.

Later in the war Meinertzhagen served as chief of Intelligence in Palestine and as a staff officer on the Western Front. He repeated the dirty-paper method against the Turks in the Holy Land and came up with a new stunt as well. The British propaganda experts had been showering the Turks with leaflets designed to make them yearn for peace. To ensure that the Turks would read them, the leaflets were contained inside packs of cheap cigarettes, which were dropped behind enemy lines. Meinertzhagen made up a special consignment of identical cigarettes and had them heavily laced with opium. This special batch was held until just before a surprise British offensive. The stratagem proved a success—when the attack took place, a considerable number of Turkish soldiers were found to be dazed, confused, and, well, sort of mellow. Meinertzhagen tried the doctored cigarettes himself and reported experiencing a blissful haze and vivid, fascinating dreams.

Postwar, Meinertzhagen was a strong supporter of the Zionist movement and worked with enthusiasm on his ornithological studies. He also worked undercover as a British intelligence officer, allegedly killing at least a dozen Bolshevik agents on a trip to Russia in the early 1920s. In 1934 he met with Hitler and Ribbentrop in an unofficial capacity to try to reach an understanding between Britain and Germany. A year later he met with Rudolf Hess for the same purpose, and met again with Hitler in 1939. He later expressed regret in his diary that he hadn't assassinated the Nazi leaders when he had the chance. It's interesting how history would have treated such an assassination, given that Hitler and his entourage would have been dead before the more widespread horrors of their regime had been committed. Say what you will of Meinertzhagen, his trademark method of solving problems by killing them was amazingly effective, if morally questionable.

Meinertzhagen married at least twice but was not fated to find domestic happiness. He divorced his first wife when he found out that she had been unfaithful. The second, Anne Constance Jackson, married Meinertzhagen in 1921 but died in 1928, when she apparently accidentally shot herself with one of her husband's handguns. She left him with two sons and a daughter. His oldest son, Daniel, was killed in action on the Western Front in 1944.

Meinertzhagen continued to champion Jewish causes, even fighting alongside Haganah soldiers as a civilian in 1948, when he killed seven Arabs in a firefight—nice to see he hadn't lost his touch. Fittingly, he lived to see Israel's stunning victory in the Seven Days War before dying on 17 June 1967.

Meinertzhagen is a tough one to figure. He was an unquestionably great hunter and an unparalleled fighting commander. He did a lot of good work in nature studies and ornithology, and provided valuable services to Britain in an undercover capacity, most of which we don't even know about. Yet he was an incredibly violent, murderous, and disturbed man. He was an artist, and violence was his medium. Leaving aside his killing of the Nandi chief, for at the very least Koitalel was no doubt planning treachery even if Dick beat him to it, he is still one of the most violent figures of modern history.

From Meinertzhagen's own writings it is possible to get some idea of the amount of personal violence and mayhem he inflicted during his long career. As mentioned above, in India he once pulled a revolver on his friend Lieutenant Roberts for insulting him one drunken night. Given his future behavior, there is no question that he would have shot Roberts if the man had not backed down. Also as noted previously, he is thought to have killed at least a dozen Communist agents during the inter-war years, and seven Arab militiamen in 1948. He executed at least two African saboteurs that we know about, and no doubt many more. He beat an Indian groom to death for mistreating his horse. On another occasion he killed a Russian spy in Greece, and during a British offensive on the Western Front in 1918 he slipped away from his staff duties long enough to join the attack and personally kill some twenty German soldiers. When you add the Africans that Meinertzhagen killed during his KAR days (numbering in the hundreds), the other Bolshevik agents, and the Germans in Tanganyika, he was clearly one of the most efficient killing machines of his age.

Violence seems to have been Meinertzhagen's first recourse in any difficult situation. Early in World War I he accompanied an Indian Rajput regiment in an attack on the German port of Tanga in Tanganyika. Meinertzhagen had warned against the plan, but his cautions were ignored. The Rajputs broke and ran during the attack, and Meinertzhagen shot and killed one of them in an attempt to stop the retreat. For good measure, when a Rajput officer protested by starting to draw his sword, Meinertzhagen shot and killed him, too.

An official trip to Iraq in early 1914 (still peacetime) was marred by several ugly incidents. On one occasion a

Meinertzhagen in disguise in southern Palestine, 1917.

mob of Arabs threatened his boat on the Tigris River near Tikrit. Meinertzhagen dispersed the crowd by opening fire with a shotgun, and when the local Turkish governor approached the boat later to demand compensation, the governor was bullied to the point that he dismissed all charges and fines and promised the crazy Englishman that the instigators of the mob would be harshly punished if only Meinertzhagen would please go away. History missed a great opportunity by not putting this guy together with Bill Finaughty in his prime. About the best that can be said for his lethal behavior is that most of the killings were at least arguably in a good cause and pretty much all were in "fair-chase" conditions.

In addition to violence, Meinertzhagen had more than a touch of dishonesty about him as well. Even his sympathetic biographer, Peter Capstick, in *Warrior* (1998), came to the conclusion that Meinertzhagen probably altered some diary entries before publishing his papers, for the sole purpose of appearing prescient about the Mau Mau rising and similar colonial troubles. And the 2002 cryptozoology classic *The Ghost with Trembling Wings,* by Scott Weidensaul, details the distressing fact that Meinertzhagen falsified many of his ornithological records as well. It's a sad tale that reveals much about the soldier's nature, although it's damn lucky for Weidensaul that Meinertzhagen isn't around to read it.

Over the years Meinertzhagen donated some twenty-five thousand bird specimens to London's Natural History Museum, each with a tag detailing where and when he had collected it. As early as 1910 or so he was suspected of stealing specimens from that and other museums, and relabeling the skins collected by others as his own. He would then donate the stuffed bird to a museum, spuriously claiming that he had collected it. In the files of the British Museum are several reports accusing Meinertzhagen of stealing specimens, but they could never quite prove it. Nobody wanted to confront him without proof because, well, would you? Apparently a trap was set up at one time, but the wily soldier avoided it. It wasn't until the 1990s that the handwriting on the labels and the individual techniques used to stuff the specimens were examined with an eye to proving authenticity. The conclusion was that Meinertzhagen had stolen and marked as his own hundreds if not thousands of bird skins.

One example of the kind of problem that Meinertzhagen's deception created involved an Indian forest owlet. For years this bird was thought extinct because no one could find it. The problem, however, was that the scientists and birdwatchers were looking in the part of India where Meinertzhagen claimed to have collected it. In reality the bird had never lived there. Once they realized that the specimen was falsified, the scientists started looking in other suitable habitats and quickly established the bird's survival. ROWLAND WARD 1928: CHEETAH (NO. 1, 7 FEET, 9 INCHES), KONGONI (NO. 3), SITATUNGA.

Melland, Frank H. Native commissioner in Northern Rhodesia in the 1900s, Melland preferred a .350 Rigby double rifle for his work as a dedicated elephant hunter in both his own territory and in Tanganyika. Melland shot an elephant in North-East Rhodesia with tusks weighing 119 and 110 pounds. The larger tusk was the record for all of Africa south of Tanganyika, and by 1909 Melland's elephant was one of only three that had come out of that country with tusks over 100 pounds per side.

Like many other big-game hunters, Melland had an interesting cryptozoological story to relate. While in the Jiundu Swamp area (where the borders of Northern Rhodesia, Angola, and the Belgian Congo converge), he kept hearing tales of some flying monstrosity called the Kongamato. As related in his book *In Witchbound Africa* (1923), Melland somehow got his hands on a picture book containing a drawing of a pterodactyl. When he showed it to some natives, they excitedly identified the pterodactyl as the mysterious Kongamato. Melland also wrote *Elephants in Africa* (1938) and *Through the Heart of Africa* (with Edward Cholmeley, 1912). ROWLAND WARD 1928: WARTHOG, LICHTENSTEIN HARTEBEEST, TSESSEBE, BLACK LECHWE, ELEPHANT (119 AND 110 POUNDS, NORTH-EAST RHODESIA), PUKU.

Melliss, Sir Charles J. (1862–1936). A captain in the 9th Bombay Infantry, Melliss was the author of the 1895 work *Lion Hunting in Somaliland.* The book tells of his adventures while on leave, including hunting lion and indulging in some pigsticking. Melliss was one of the first to go hunting in Somaliland during vacation, a practice that soon became the fashion among Victorian officers stationed in India (it's not unlikely that Melliss's book started the craze). Despite warnings about wild tribal raiders, Melliss ranged deep into the interior of Somalia to engage in his pursuits—in fact, he pretty much had to be ordered out for his own good. The treatise on pigsticking is one of the best available and captures something of the excitement that made it so popular among British officers of that day.

Melliss went on to have a brilliant military career. He served during the Asante War of 1900 and won the Victoria

Cross for bravery in action. He particularly distinguished himself by leading numerous bayonet charges and wielding his saber with great effect, despite being wounded several times. It was reported that when he was finally invalided back to England, the entire garrison at Cape Coast turned out in salute.

In 1903 he was on campaign in Somaliland when he was badly torn up by a lion. He made a complete recovery, served with distinction in World War I, and finally retired as a lieutenant general.

Melly, Andrew (xxxx–1850). Melly was a civilian from Liverpool who decided to vacation in the unexplored regions of the White Nile in 1849. Apparently something of a well-off nut, he brought his wife, two young sons, and a daughter along with him to Khartoum in a day when most men feared to make the journey by themselves. His main interest was apparently collecting natural-history specimens. Unfortunately, Melly had no idea whatsoever of how to survive in tropical and primitive conditions, and he died of fever at Shendi on the Nile in 1850.

His son, George Melly, published a book based upon his father's journals. George Melly later became a member of Parliament for Liverpool.

Mendose (xxxx–1872). Mendose was a native hunter who in 1872 was part of a group hunting elephant near the Gwaai River with Selous. Coming up on a herd of seven large bulls, the men opened fire. Mendose, who'd had some experience with elephant, was closing the range, but some of the less-experienced men opened fire from a distance. One of their bullets struck Mendose right in the middle of the shoulder blades, killing him immediately. Only one of the elephant escaped.

Merfield, Fred G. Fred Merfield hunted in the French Cameroons for many years, collecting specimens (alive and dead) for zoos and museums. Born in England, he first went to Africa in 1910 as a plantation manager but quickly gravitated to hunting. After a trip home to Britain to recover from the effects of blackwater fever, Merfield fought in Africa during World War I, spending two months as a prisoner of the Germans.

After the war he stayed in West Africa for over twenty years, never once leaving the continent. While he preferred his lucrative live-capture business, he acquired a reputation as a gorilla hunter, killing 115 of them for European museums. When French game warden Bruno de Laborie was assigned the job of obtaining a gorilla grouping for a Paris museum, he summoned Merfield to his office for advice on hunting the animals and preserving their skins. It was midday in the tropics, and De Laborie neglected to offer Merfield the traditional aperitif. Merfield, offended by this discourtesy, never mentioned to De Laborie the preservative that he used to avoid spoilage of animal skins. Months later he heard that all of De Laborie's skins had gone bad, and, irony of ironies, Merfield was offered the lucrative assignment himself.

Merfield also guided other hunters, including Major Powell-Cotton, to the great apes. He considered the wealthy British big-game hunter as a mentor who taught him respect for his quarry and the principles of fair chase as well as practical lessons on collecting for museums. During and after World War II Merfield worked as a functionary in the French colonial police. He was the author of *Gorilla Hunter* (1956), which, unusual for a hunting book, was praised by naturalists like George Schaller for providing accurate information on the then relatively unstudied gorilla.

Merker, Moritz. Captain Merker was a German officer stationed at Moshi at the base of Mount Kilimanjaro from 1895 to 1902. He became an authority on the Masai and authored a detailed book about them. When he returned to Germany in 1903 he was highly acclaimed in popular and scientific circles, which for some reason seemed to irk the military establishment. When Merker's leave was over, his superiors transferred him to run a training camp near Dar es Salaam. He died there of pneumonia in 1908. Kittenberger (1927), who on his first trip to Africa saw a room full of Merker's hunting trophies awaiting shipment home, accused him of not shooting his own animals but rather having native hunters shoot for him.

Metcalfe, Ralph (also seen as Medcalfe). The nephew of Walter "Karamojo" Bell, "Slim" Metcalfe was also a professional hunter in East Africa. In the 1940s he shot an elephant with tusks of 154 pounds per side on Balambala Island in the Tana River (see entry on van Rensberg).

Meyer, Hans (1858–1929). Meyer was a German explorer who, after early travels in America, Asia, and the South Pacific, reached 18,333 feet on Kilimanjaro in 1887. In 1888 he returned to the area but aborted his expedition after being kidnapped by Arab traders. Meyer was released only after the payment of a small ransom. The following year he reached the Kibo summit at 19,320 feet, the forty-ninth man to make the attempt and the first to succeed. He was accompanied by a Herr Purtscheller. It was Meyer's fourth trip to Kilimanjaro, and on it he discovered its crater and glacier. Meyer later sponsored Axel Eriksson Jr., the young artist from South-West Africa whose father was an elephant hunter and trader, arranging for the painter to live and study in Europe. Meyer was the author of *Across East African Glaciers* (1891).

Miani, Giovanni (1810–1872). An explorer from Venice, Miani's 1860 attempt to find the source of the Nile failed only because some locals gave him bad directions. As it was, he explored much of Uganda, the northwestern fringe of the Congo basin, and the Bahr el Ghazal. He died from sickness at Mangbattu in 1872.

Migeod, Frederick William Hugh (1872–1952). Migeod was a prolific world traveler and the author of numerous books. The two that concerned Africa were *Across Equatorial Africa* (1923) and *Through Nigeria to Lake Chad* (1924).

Miles, Arthur Tremaiyne "Tich" (1891–1934). A small man, short and weighing less than one hundred pounds, Miles came to East Africa in 1910 to find work. His first job was as a counter clerk for £8 per week, but when war broke out in 1914 he joined the King's African Rifles and served with distinction, opening up a spot for himself in the colonial administration. Decorated several times, Miles remained in the army after the war ended and was stationed in Jubaland, where he engaged in several bloody frontier incidents and quelled a mutiny among a disaffected KAR unit.

In 1923 Miles joined the Consular Service and was appointed Consul for Southern Abyssinia. At that time the job paid £800 a year with a transportation allowance ("horse allowance") of £50. His headquarters was at Mega, eighty miles north of Moyale, in a dilapidated ramshackle mud house he called "the Palace." His job was largely to keep tribal raiding to a minimum and to ensure that the rare water holes and wells were kept open to all who needed them. Most of the wells along the Kenya–Ethiopia border were on the Ethiopian side, but a 1907 treaty required the Abyssinians to allow access to herders from Kenya. Many of the Abyssinian tribesmen resented this, and there were frequent conflicts over this issue. The Kenyans were generally the losers in these battles because British law restricted them to spears while virtually every male Ethiopian had a primitive firearm of some kind.

Miles won the respect of the Abyssinians, however, by his strength of character and his earnest efforts to adhere to local custom. Miles was also fearless, unafraid to "mix it up" with bandits, and of all the British colonial officers stationed along the Northern Frontier District he was perhaps the most popular with both the Abyssinians and the Somalis. Although a very small man, as noted above, and afflicted by a weak liver caused by the tropical diseases to which he was prone, Miles made it a point of honor to match local leaders drink for drink during their festivities. The indigenous rotgut, a noxious barley wine called *tej*, had deterred most previous European visitors, but Miles could keep up with the best of them. His health often suffered as a result, but his reputation soared.

Miles stayed in the job from 1923 until his health collapsed in 1934, except for a two-year period during which he was seconded to Nairobi as an aide to Governor Edward Grigg. He was very much inclined to accept an offered post on the staff of the governor general of Canada but declined because it would have meant the forfeiture of his pension rights. Though highly popular and effective in his Consular position, Miles nevertheless suffered from recurring blackwater fever, liver problems, and sundry other African ailments. In the spring of 1934 he was rushed back to London for medical treatment but died within a month. He was forty-one years old.

Millais, John Guille (1855–1931). Millais was a noted British sportsman, artist, and naturalist. His father was Sir John Everett Millais (1829–1896), considered by some authorities to be the most popular artist of the Victorian era. As a young man John Guille Millais traveled extensively in the American West, later painting pictures of the great bison herds and their Indian hunters. He hunted all over the globe and amassed a noteworthy collection of trophies. In his travels he met many, if not all, of the legendary hunters of his day, including Oswell and Stigand, and was particularly close friends with Selous and Neumann. He once stated his opinion that William Finaughty was the greatest English elephant hunter of them all.

Millais had many sporting interests, including fishing, breeding hunting dogs, duck hunting, and, of course, big-game hunting. He kept alive the family tradition of popular, sentimental, competently executed art. Some of his paintings are quite evocative, and his rendering of Selous's grave, titled "They Cannot Break His Sleep," was

John Guille Millais.

used as a propaganda poster during World War I. Millais, at the time a British Consul in Norway, lost his eldest son (Capt. G. de C. Millais of the Bedfordshire Regiment) in that war. His other son, Raoul, achieved success as a big-game hunter.

John and Raoul Millais went on a successful but strenuous safari in the Sudan in 1924, shooting ibex, gazelle, kob, roan, giant eland, and buffalo, but were refused permission to hunt the white rhino. During this trip the elder Millais suffered from both dysentery and malaria, finally being hospitalized in Khartoum. His son bagged a buffalo that made the Rowland Ward record book.

Millais was the author of *A Breath from the Veldt* (1899), *Wanderings and Memories* (1919), *Life of Frederick Courteney Selous* DSO (1919), *The Wildfowler in Scotland, Far Away Up the Nile* (1924), and many other works. He is perhaps most remembered as an artist and author, but the listings in the 1928 edition of *Rowland Ward's Records of Big Game* are liberally sprinkled with his name. ROWLAND WARD 1928: SCOTTISH ROEBUCK, SCANDINAVIAN REINDEER, FALLOW DEER, GREATER KUDU, SIBERIAN ARGALI, GIANT SABLE.

Miller, Edwin. A young colonist and hunter, Miller worked for Selous in 1876. In 1879 he hunted with Selous "on halves"—Selous providing the guns, ammo, and rations, Miller turning over half of what he shot. This was a popular system among the Boer elephant hunters. On this same trip they were joined by a German named Sell. Miller also hunted with R. French shortly before the other perished of sunstroke and thirst.

Mills, E. C. A member of EAPHA (see glossary) from 1935, Mills died in 1946.

Minnery, Jock. An old army buddy of Ionides (and a recipient of the Military Cross and the Distinguished Conduct Medal), Minnery later became a Tanganyika game ranger at Arusha. In the 1930 *East African Red Book* he is listed as assigned to the Game Preservation Department at Shinyanga.

Mlozi (xxxx–1895). Mlozi was an Arab-African chief from Karonga in Nyasaland who was the chief slave dealer for the Awemba tribe. The Awemba captured the slaves, and Mlozi would buy the wretched souls from them. In 1889 Harry Johnston sat down with him and negotiated a peace: Mlozi would stick to legitimate trading, and Johnston wouldn't kill him. In 1895, however, Mlozi once again started raiding the countryside. Johnston went in person to Mlozi's fortress on the northern shore of Lake Nyasa to try to reason with the slaver, but Mlozi refused to see him and even threatened him.

Sir Harry, who didn't take well to threats, gathered a force of a hundred Sikh soldiers and three hundred African askaris, officered by the usual competent crew of Victorian officers, men with names like Maj. C. A. Edwards, Capt. F. T. Stewart, the Honorable Capt. W. E. Cavendish, Lt. H. Coape-Smith, and Lt. G. de Herries Smith. Two other men, the well-known hunters Maj. F. C. Trollope and Walter Gordon Cumming, came along as volunteer officers. They had come to Nyasa to hunt big game but couldn't resist the temptation to go after more dangerous quarry.

Borrowing an armed steamer from the German authorities, Johnston's little army descended on Mlozi's town toward the end of November 1895. The town was strongly fortified, with a peculiar but effective stockade consisting of a double fence plastered with hardened clay and roofed over with wood, thatch, and clay. Wood partitions divided the area between the double fences into rooms in which the garrison lived, with plenty of loopholes for shooting and gun pits dug so as to provide maximum protection. The walls were flimsy enough so that artillery shells passed right through without exploding, but admirably served the purpose of disguising just where the gun pits were. The fort's one weakness, however, was that for some reason Mlozi had built it a quarter-mile away from the nearest water source.

Johnston began shelling the town on 2 December. That night the Arabs attempted a sortie but were repulsed with losses. The next morning Mlozi asked to meet Johnston personally under a flag of truce, but a friendly African warned the Englishman that the Arab planned treachery. Johnston met Mlozi at a distance of some eight yards and demanded what was essentially unconditional surrender. As the two parties returned to their lines, Arab sharpshooters tried to pick off Johnston and his aide, Lieutenant Anston, but missed, and Johnston ordered the bombardment resumed.

During the truce some of Mlozi's slaves escaped from the citadel. One of them, described by Johnston as a Mhenga chief, told the British precisely where Mlozi had his headquarters. The English artillery commander aimed a nine-pounder at the house in question and quickly brought the roof crashing down. The British were graced with the amazing luck that so often assisted these shoestring Victorian campaigns: Mlozi was indeed in the building and was dazed by a beam falling upon his head. A rumor went out through the fort that Mlozi was dead, and the Arabs tried one last furious sortie in revenge. The ragtag English army shot them to pieces, and resistance quickly collapsed. The Sikhs and askaris, led by their British officers, entered the town.

The first concern was the safety of the numerous women in the town, both Arab and African, who were being held as captives. They had suffered remarkably few casualties and were swiftly put under guard. The second priority was to find Mlozi, who had seemingly disappeared. His house was searched, but no one was found and the search party moved on. One astute sergeant, however, an Atonga askari named Bandawe, craftily remained silently behind in the ruins of Mlozi's house. Before long he heard whispering from a secret room in an underground chamber beneath Mlozi's bed. The slaver had only one guard with him, armed with a spear. Bandawe flung himself on the spearman and killed him with his own weapon, then took Mlozi captive.

What happened next was somewhat out of the ordinary but not atypical for Harry Johnston, who was a distinctly no-nonsense type of guy. Some of the escaped slaves from the town claimed Mlozi had executed some hostages during the bombardment on 2 December. Johnston gathered a group of African chiefs as a sort of jury, and "under my superintendence" (1897) they sentenced the Arab to death. Johnston claimed later that he couldn't spare anyone to guard Mlozi, so he had him hanged right then and there. In his book *British Central Africa* Johnston made no apology for this questionably legal act, and at this distance one doubts that Mlozi was much mourned.

Moffatt, Robert (1795–1883). Arriving at Cape Town in January 1817, Moffatt was a Scottish missionary sent out by the London Missionary Society. He labored at Kuruman in Bechuanaland for the next fifty-three years with only occasional trips home, finally retiring to England in June of 1870. Moffatt made two long trips from Kuruman into the Transvaal in 1830–1835, and into Matabeleland in 1857–1861. In 1844 his daughter married David Livingstone. Among his published works were a Bechuana dictionary (1826), the New Testament translated to Bechuana (1839), the Old Testament translation (1857), and *Missionary Labours in South Africa* (1842).

Moffatt's memoirs give a good indication of the aggressiveness of African lion before the use of firearms became widespread. In *Missionary Labours*, for instance, he recalled an early visit to the Matabele in 1829. A pair of lion attacked his wagon team in broad daylight. The men went scrambling for their guns while the lion killed one of their oxen. The noise of a couple of hurried shots scared the lion away.

Mohr, Eduard (1828–1876). A German hunter and explorer, Mohr had traveled in Polynesia, Siberia, Alaska, and California before arriving in Natal in 1866. He spent the next five years roaming through Zululand, Matabeleland, and the Zambezi Valley. He died in Angola while recruiting porters for another trip into the Interior. Mohr was the author of *Travel and Hunting Pictures of the South Seas* (1868) and *To the Victoria Falls of the Zambesi* (1876).

Moloney, Joseph A. Lieutenant Moloney of the Royal Artillery was a member of Grant Stair's 1891 Congo Free

State expedition to Katanga. He was killed a few years later while serving in Uganda. He was the author of *With Captain Stairs to Katanga* (1893).

Moloney went lion hunting in East Africa in the early 1890s. He wounded a large-maned male, but not fatally; the lion charged Moloney and knocked him down, sending his rifle sprawling. Moloney covered his head with his hands and hoped for the best. The lion just bit him once in the back and walked off.

Monson, Ronald A. Monson was a journalist working for the *West Australia* newspaper when he answered an ad put out by one Edward Cooke in the late 1920s. Cooke was looking for a suitable companion to walk with him along the fabled "Cape to Cairo" route. A tough, healthy young man, Monson fit the bill precisely. They started out from Cape Town in September of 1928.

The first month was the worst, as the men's bodies adapted themselves to the grueling march. Their feet, particularly, caused a great deal of trouble, blistering and festering until callused. Cooke was forced to drop out after only 1,000 miles when it was discovered by the press that he had lied about being an Australian air force lieutenant when he was, in fact, only a former enlisted man. His place was taken by a South African accountant named James Hunter Wilson who managed to convince his boss to give him a year off. He apparently felt sorry for Monson who was valiantly trying to carry on alone after Cooke left the expedition. Wilson went through the same horrible experience with his feet, at times crying in pain as he struggled to get his boots on.

Monson, armed with only a .30-30 Marlin rifle, had some harrowing adventures with big game animals, including being slightly injured by a bull elephant in Kenya. Monson and Wilson completed the trek, arriving in Cairo in late December of 1929. Wilson's photographs were used to illustrate Monson's excellent book, *Across Africa on Foot* (1931).

Moodie, John Wedderburn Dunbar (1797–1869). Charles Williams (1859) told the frantic tale of Lieutenant Moodie and other members of a hunting party that went after a herd of elephant near the Gualana River. A large cow elephant was brought down with over 100 bullets in her. The next day, visiting the scene, Moodie was ambushed by a furious one-tusked cow from the same herd. His gun misfired, and the elephant knocked him down with her trunk and tried to tusk him. Moodie twisted and dodged while the elephant tried to crush him; fortunately, the elephant succeeded only in knocking him about. Other members of the party, including Mr. Knight of the Cape Regiment, Lieutenant Chisholm, Moodie's brother, and a Khoi-Khoi named Diederik, ran to the scene and fired at the cow, which kicked Moodie one or two more times and then lumbered off.

While these men were helping the badly bruised Moodie to his feet, another elephant, a bull, burst from cover and grabbed a soldier named McClane of the Royal African Corps in its trunk. The bull carried the soldier some distance, then tossed him to the ground and stamped upon him. McClane being obviously dead, the other men of the party drove the bull off with rifle fire, but the animal soon returned and stomped McClane's corpse again. Eventually a lucky shot (one gets the impression that these guys weren't the best of marksmen) anchored the beast by breaking its foreleg. When the bull went down, to the surprise of all the one-tusked cow that had originally beaten up Moodie came running out to the bull's rescue. A Mr. MacKenzie of the Royal African Corps finally killed the bull with a well-placed shot and mortally wounded the cow, which ran off into the woods and bled to death.

Moodie himself wrote a book about his days in Natal, entitled *Ten Years in South Africa* (1835). He followed that many years later with *Scenes and Adventures as a Soldier and Settler* (1866).

Moore, Montgomery S. A recipient of the Victoria Cross in World War I, Capt. Monty Moore was the game warden for the Serengeti region in the 1930s and was one of the professional hunters who accompanied the Prince of Wales on his African safaris. He later became chief game warden of Tanganyika. In this capacity he once explained his predator policy to hunter R. de la Bere Barker: Protect lion in one-half of the country and shoot them in the other.

Moore pioneered the tactic of attracting lion by dragging a dead zebra or other bait behind a truck. He used this trick to satisfy the aspirations of wealthy American hunters and photographers. Moore's wife Audrey was a respected animal photographer, notably of lion. The 1930 *East African Red Book* lists Monty Moore as attached to the Game Preservation Department at Kilosa. ROWLAND WARD 1928: STEENBOK, LESSER KUDU, SITATUNGA.

Morel, Edmund Dene (1873–1924). Born in France, Morel became a British citizen in 1896. From 1891 he worked in the office of the shipping firm Elder Dempster. Morel was a born radical, and his inquisitive mind noticed

Congo reformer E. D. Morel.

some oddities about his firm's trade with the Congo Free State. He began to write magazine articles out of financial necessity, and the first ones were largely about what he saw as the unfair trading conditions in West Africa and the unethical tactics of the French commercial companies and the British Royal Niger Company. In 1900 he expanded his reports to include attacks on the Congo Free State and the brutal methods used to collect rubber, palm oil, and ivory.

Morel soon lost his job as head of Elder Dempster's Congo division, but in 1903 he founded a newspaper, the *West African Mail.* A year later he joined with Roger Casement in forming the Congo Reform Association. Fueled by Morel's detailed knowledge of the Congo trade and reports from other journalists and missionaries, the scandal culminated in 1908, when Belgium took over the Free State and began a cosmetic reform program.

Morel next turned his attention to other causes, including the Moroccan Agadir crisis in 1912 and British neutrality in 1914. When the United Kingdom entered the war anyway, Morel formed the Union of Democratic Control (UDC), an anti-imperialist organization that called for a negotiated peace settlement. During the war he was jailed for six months for violating the Defence of the Realm Act. While in prison he suffered from bad health, which apparently hastened his death seven years later.

After the war Morel joined the Labour Party and defeated Winston Churchill in an election for a parliamentary seat in 1922. Morel, who had apparently been promised a seat in the cabinet as Foreign Secretary, felt bitter and betrayed when Ramsay MacDonald (a former member of the UDC) refused to appoint him to the office. Nominated for a Nobel Peace Prize, Morel died of a heart attack shortly after winning re-election in 1924.

Morlang, Franz (1828–1875). Morlang grew up in the Dolomite Alps, one of the few places on earth that boasted Latin as its native tongue—a handy upbringing for somebody destined to become a priest. He was sent to the Jesuit mission in the Sudan in 1855 and served for seven years at Gondokoro and among the Bari and Dinka tribes. Morlang made several important explorations of the area, including an 1859 expedition to the Nyam-Nyam district southwest of Gondokoro. He also traveled with the Baron von Harnier, and sold some of the latter's effects after the Prussian hunter was killed by a buffalo.

When the Gondokoro mission fell apart around 1863, Morlang despondently returned to Europe, where he taught for ten years in his native land. Morlang's sense of futility was understandable: Despite years of trying and a high death rate among the Austrian priests, the missionaries of Gondokoro and Saint Croix had failed to make a single legitimate convert. More than fifty years passed before the missions returned to the area.

Morlang got his calling back eventually and moved to Peru in 1873, where he tended to a parish of German immigrants. He died of typhus two years later. For some reason he has received less attention than other explorers of the White Nile. Parts of his Sudan diaries were published in German in 1863 but the entire journal was only released in its entirety in an Italian edition of 1972. Morlang was an excellent observer and an English edition is long overdue.

Morse, Ira H. Morse was an American sportsman who made frequent trips to Africa and other exotic places in pursuit of big game. He was always accompanied by at least a few family members, including his wife Lillian, his brother Dr. Richard Morse, and children Julia and Phillip. The family collected a wealth of trophies and produced several pamphlets about their adventures, including *On Safari* (1937) and *Big Game Hunting in Africa* (1934). They also wrote at least one full-length book, *Yankee in Africa* (1936).

In 1928 Ira Morse opened a roadside museum in the small town of Warren, New Hampshire. The museum was packed with trophies from the family safaris, including heads, full-body mounts, photographs, and cultural artifacts. Unfortunately the museum closed in 1992 and the contents were auctioned off. At last notice the building was now an ice cream parlor.

Moshesh (c. 1790–1870). First great chief of the Basuto people in southern Africa, he ruled from about 1818–1870.

Mostyn, Sir Pyers. Sir Pyers (also seen as Piers) Mostyn was a distinguished British soldier and sportsman. In 1903 he was a lieutenant in the King's African Rifles battalion at Zomba in Nyasaland, the same unit as Lieutenant Stigand. Shortly thereafter he was the commander of Fort Manning, where he would often hunt with Stigand and the civilian hunter Denis Lyell, who was making his first trip to Central Africa. The three men practiced hunting elephant with small-bore .256, .303, and 7.9mm rifles.

In later life Mostyn used his considerable influence (he was a baronet) to obtain special "elephant control" contracts throughout British Africa. He would eliminate problem animals for no pay, keeping the tusks. In the early 1920s Mostyn was one of the hunters who obtained a special Tanganyika control license, enabling him to shoot twenty-five problem elephant at the direction of the game department. Unlike many of the hunters who worked for this project (the precursor of the famous Elephant Control Scheme), his reputation was such that no one suggested he was selectively shooting big tuskers instead of bona fide problem animals. He did take some heat, however, for pioneering the use of a private plane to find the elephant herds, for many people mistakenly thought he was shooting the animals from the plane. ROWLAND WARD 1928: PATTERSON ELAND, ELAND, LESSER KUDU, FRINGE EARED ORYX, LAIKIPIA BEISA ORYX, GRANT GAZELLE, BOHOR REEDBUCK, KIRK DIK-DIK, ELEPHANT (80 AND 79 POUNDS, UGANDA).

Moubray, J. M. Moubray was an English mining engineer who spent six years in Rhodesia, 1903–1908. He worked mainly as a surveyor, traveling from district to district searching for suitable mining spots. He was also an avid hunter, and judging from his writings he spent more time pursuing game than gold. It is indicative of his priorities that on his mining surveys he carried a .500 double rifle by Westley Richards, a .375 Mannlicher, and a single-shot .360. This is not your standard geological equipment array. His 1912 book, *In South Central Africa,* is an excellent account of the budding Rhodesian mining industry along with observations on hunting and the various native communities. He manages to touch upon just about every aspect of Rhodesian life in the first decade of the last century.

Mouche, Florian. Of German origin, Mouche originally came to Africa as a mission worker on the White Nile. He found the life not to his liking and set up shop as a commercial hunter at Sufi, profitably hunting elephant and other animals in the 1850s and 1860s.

Msungo Appa. This Portuguese elephant hunter of mixed blood was based in Tete in the 1890s. Ho would equip native hunters on a conscription basis, as well as hunt elephant himself.

Muller, Diederik and Christian. The Muller brothers were well-known Boer lion hunters in South Africa in the first half of the nineteenth century. They usually hunted in tandem and were credited with saving each other's lives on many occasions. In one particularly close call, according to Charles Williams (1859), Diederik was "so roughly handled that he lost his hearing in one ear, the lion having dug his talons deeply into it."

Murray, Mungo. Mungo Murray was from Lintrose, Cupar Angus, Forfarshire, Scotland. In 1844–1845 Murray went on a prolonged hunting trip with William Cotton Oswell, during which the two men covered some four hundred miles of previously unknown South African territory. In 1849 the pair set out again, looking to enjoy the hunting but also to see if they could find a legendary inland lake deep in the interior. At the time rumors of the lake had brought much speculation and many men were contemplating making the trip, but Murray and Oswell were the first to actually set out. En route they met up with a party that included the missionary David Livingstone and an ivory trader named J. H. Wilson. In July of 1850 the combined party discovered Lake Ngami. Oswell and Murray were much more interested in the sporting aspects of the trip, so Livingstone was able to grab most of the credit for discovering the lake.

Mzilikazi (c. 1796–1868). Also known as Mosilikatse, Mzilikazi, and at least a dozen other spellings. One advantage of all these spellings is that you have a pretty good idea of how the name was pronounced. However you spell it, the name means "Great Road," and the man was the chief of a people called the Khumalo who volunteered his tribe as vassals to Shaka, the Zulu king.

From 1819 to 1824 Mzilikazi was a loyal vassal commander, but then decided to secede. Tradition records that Mzilikazi and his warriors defeated one of Shaka's enemies, but then Mzilikazi, rather than turning over the captured cattle of the defeated tribe to Shaka as custom dictated, used the opportunity to insult the Zulu king and declare his independence. He may have hoped to live peacefully side-by-side with the Zulus, but Shaka was not one to brook rebellion lightly. A Zulu impi (see glossary) attacked the Khumalo and killed or captured almost all of their women, children, and possessions. Mzilikazi was forced to flee with a surviving army of just a few hundred warriors.

That began an epic adventure of empire-building. Mzilikazi and his men, who eventually became known as the Matabele (or, more properly, Ndebele), for years went from place to place in southern Africa destroying the weaker Basuto clans and amalgamating defeated warriors and refugees from Shaka's army into their own society. Their superior morale and tactics guaranteed their success against everyone they encountered. They retained the weapons and battle formations of the regular Zulu armies and only gradually altered the decorations and markings that passed for a uniform. Mzilikazi and the Matabele eventually settled in what is now Zimbabwe. There he ruled with an army that numbered in the tens of thousands, secure against all enemies until the coming of the Europeans.

Mzilikazi led a long life and is remembered as one of the great military and political figures of his day. In the mid-1860s he underwent a marked physical deterioration as various diseases took their toll. He died in 1868 and was succeeded by his son, Lobengula, a man superior in appearance but weaker in character and force of mind.

N

Nachtigal, Gustav (1834–1885). Yet another competent German explorer of the Sahara area, Nachtigal first went to North Africa to ease the strain on his tubercular lungs. He became court physician to the bey of Tunis in 1863, a post he held for a few years. In 1868 he was sent by the king of Prussia to deliver presents to the Sultan of Bornu. He spent the next seven years exploring Chad and the Sahara before returning to Germany. During his travels he was the first to ascertain the fate of missing explorer Eduard Vogel, murdered by natives seventeen years before. For several years he wrote books and helped form business concerns that sought to promote commerce with Africa. After a short stint as consul to Tunis, Nachtigal became the first Imperial German commissioner of West Africa in 1884. He was instrumental in the German annexation of Togoland, Angra Pequena, and Cameroon. In 1885 he died of fever on board ship and was buried in Liberia.

Napier, David. Napier went on a hunting trip with William Finaughty in 1868 in the Tati River area. In the space of three days Napier was trampled by both an elephant and a black rhino, escaping with minor injuries. Finaughty noted that he was "very slow."

The rhino knocked Napier down but did not really hurt him. The elephant mishap occurred when Napier, on horseback, was charged from behind. The elephant bowled over both rider and horse and stabbed its tusks directly into the horse's thigh. The saddle came off and the elephant began stomping it. Napier, bruised on the shoulders and badly scraped on the face, took advantage of the distraction to crawl away. The horse also miraculously survived.

After a short rest to recuperate, Napier and Finaughty split up, planning to meet up two weeks later. Finaughty was at the rendezvous point on time, but Napier didn't show for sixteen days. His appearance was shocking: ". . . almost a living corpse, unable to walk and carried in a rude stretcher by four boys. He was simply wracked with fever . . . he had had bad luck with the elephant, getting only a few cows." (Finaughty, 1916).

One gets the impression that Mr. Napier simply wasn't cut out to hunt elephant.

Naude, Rudolph. Naude was an Arusha-based professional hunter in the first decades of the twentieth century. In 1913 he was guiding Kenyon and Maud Painter on a safari in Kenya, accompanied by an assistant named Thompson. Kenyon Painter shot a lion, which fled into a thicket. During the follow-up, Thompson was badly bitten on the chest and limbs. Thompson managed to shoot the lion during the mauling, and as he lay there in agony he asked Naude (whose name was spelled Noadi by Painter) if the animal was definitely dead. Naude fired another shot to make sure, and the lion surged to its feet and bit Thompson again.

Naude stayed in the hunting business and assisted John Cudahy's Milwaukee museum expedition in 1928–1929. At that time Naude was a tall, rangy man with an impressive physique and a full white mustache. He quickly helped the American collectors gather the animals they needed to complete their buffalo and rhino groups. In the 1930 *East African Red Book* Naude was listed as still living in Arusha.

Nero (37–68). Even as far back as the notorious Roman emperor Nero, who reigned from the years 54 to 68 CE, people were interested in the exploration of Africa. Nero sent an expedition led by two Roman centurions down the Nile River to find its source. They got as far as the place where the White Nile and Blue Nile come together (the site of present-day Khartoum) before they turned back.

Nesbitt, L. M. (1891–1935). Nesbitt was born in Italy, the grandson of a British officer who settled there in 1848. At the age of eighteen he left to study at the Camborne School of Mines and then served in the British army. After 1918 he began working as a prospector and geologist (looking mainly for gold and platinum), visiting Africa, Cuba, North America, Colombia, and Venezuela. In 1928 Nesbitt led an expedition exploring the remote Danakil region of Abyssinia. He and his companions claimed to be the first Europeans ever to explore the area, and Nesbitt was awarded the Murchison Medal by the Royal Geographical Society. He authored *Hell-Hole of Creation* (1934) before dying in a plane crash in Switzerland in 1935.

Neufeld, Karl A. (1846–1918). Neufeld was a German merchant and engineer who tried to complete a gum-buying trip to Sudan in 1887. He was captured by the Dervishes and kept as a captive at the Mahdi's compound in Omdurman. Almost alone among the various European prisoners at Omdurman (besides Neufeld, there were Slatin Bey, Lupton Bey, a few priests, a pair of Italians, and some twenty-odd Greeks and Syrians). Neufeld steadfastly refused to submit to his captors and, as a result, was kept in chains for virtually the entire twelve years of his captivity. He was set free by the British after the battle of Omdurman in 1898.

After his release he wrote *A Prisoner of the Khalifa* (1899). He then married a Kurdish teenager and settled in Aswan, where he managed a travel bureau. Sent back to Germany when war broke out in 1914, Neufeld dabbled in intelligence work and served as the interpreter for an abortive German invasion of the Sudan. He died shortly before the Armistice in 1918.

Neumann, Arthur H. (1850–1907). Born on 12 June 1850, the son of a church rector, Arthur Neumann was one of the most successful and yet oddest of the professional ivory hunters. As an explorer and elephant hunter he was a late bloomer. He went to Natal in 1868 at age eighteen and worked on a coffee plantation near Verulam, as well as growing cotton and tobacco with his brother, Charles. His other early careers included prospecting and trading with the Swazis. In 1879 he saw service in the Zulu War, first with a "native" contingent and then as an interpreter with the Swaziland Police.

In 1880 Neumann moved to Charles's farm near Maritzburg, and then spent several years hunting and trading in the region that is now Kruger National Park. Despite his years as a hunter in the Transvaal, it is thought that he did not shoot his first elephant until he was in Kenya in 1890—the huge animals had long been shot out in South Africa. He made a trip to Mombasa in the 1880s to check out the possibility of an elephant-hunting safari, but decided that he just didn't have the money to do it right.

In 1890 Neumann took a job for the IBEA (see glossary) supervising a work gang building a road from the coast to the station at Machakos. His supervisor was Frederick Lugard, detached from the army to company service. Lugard, who shortly would become a major Victorian hero and who would end his life in 1945 as Baron Lugard, disliked the older man. He wrote in his journal that Neumann was slow, stubborn, and impractical. Ordered to make the road as straight as possible to facilitate the erection of telegraph lines, Neumann instead followed a needlessly long and winding course through the East African countryside. As a metaphor for his life it was nearly perfect, but as public work the road was useless, and Lugard quickly tried to jettison Neumann by sending him back to company headquarters with a recommendation that he be replaced. Europeans of any competency were rather thin on the ground, however, and George Mackenzie, a director of the IBEA who was on site and who liked Neumann, assigned him to a survey team that was traveling to Lake Victoria. The team was led by Eric Smith and included James Martin of the Thomson expedition. If Mackenzie gave it any thought at all, he likely figured Neumann would function better under the eyes of more-experienced men.

After leaving Mombasa in December 1890, the survey went well and was relatively uneventful. On the way back to the coast, however, Neumann was camped at Loita with ninety-two men when the camp was attacked by the Masai. Thirty-eight of the men were killed and Neumann was speared in the arm while making his escape. The wound was not serious, and, immediately upon his arrival in Mombasa, Neumann accepted the offer of a magistrate position down in Zululand.

It is highly probable that even as he accepted the post, Neumann intended to raise just enough capital to return to East Africa and launch a proper elephant hunt. By December 1893 Neumann was back at Mombasa organizing a safari of fifty men armed with Snider rifles, a breechloading conversion of the old Enfield rifled musket that was already obsolete. Neumann's own weapons were a .577 double rifle, a .450 single rifle (both made by Gibbs), a .250 "rook" rifle, a Martini-Henry rifle, and a shotgun. The Martini-Henry, a Zulu War-vintage weapon, was used to finish off wounded elephant so as to economize on cartridges. Neumann later discarded the shotgun so he didn't have to carry its shells around.

His original intention was to hunt the area around Mount Kenya, and he met with William Astor Chanler in early 1894 to get his advice. Chanler had just returned to the coast after a semisuccessful safari marred by labor trouble (Chanler had a deserting porter shot by firing squad). The American gave Neumann many valuable tips, as well as a small dog named "Frolic." Frolic proved a brave and loyal companion but met his fate at the hands of a baboon early in Neumann's second safari.

Neumann left for the interior almost immediately after his meeting with Chanler. He shot his first elephant in February 1894, and by July had sent his first shipment of ivory back to Mombasa. The sophisticated ivory merchants of Zanzibar had a well-thought-out system in place, and wandering hunters like Neumann had little trouble getting their ivory either warehoused or sold by an agent and the profits deposited in the bank.

Neumann stayed in the bush for a year, mainly in the Uaso Nyiro region, and this is where he learned the craft and art of elephant hunting. With the help of African trackers he amassed a substantial hoard of ivory, necessitating several shipments to the coast. At the beginning of 1895 he finally returned to Mombasa himself, not to rest but to reinvest his profits in his next adventure, an ivory safari to Lake Rudolf. He had heard there were plenty of elephant up there.

He had heard right. Leaving Mombasa in May 1895 with a retinue of thirty-five men, Neumann struck out for the lake. On this trip his rifles consisted of a 10-bore elephant gun, the .450 Gibbs, the rook rifle, and a Lee-Metford .303 British service magazine rifle. Almost all his men were veterans of his first expedition, and they were armed with the same Snider rifles that, though obsolescent, fired a deadly .577-caliber lead slug that could tear a man's arm off.

Hunting all the way, Neumann reached Lake Rudolf in early December of 1895. He led his people along the entire eastern length of the lake, cheerfully mowing down the elephant herds, which had never before faced a skilled European hunter. By year's end he was at the Omo River on the very northern shore of the lake, where a horrible tragedy took place. Neumann had just finished bathing in the river on New Year's Day 1896 when his Swahili servant Shebane prepared to take a swim. Shebane, in all their travels together, had never bathed at the same time as his employer. Suddenly a huge crocodile surged forward, grabbed Shebane by the waist ("like a fish in the beak of a heron," Neumann wrote), and disappeared forever back into the murky river.

Any grief Neumann felt at the death of Shebane was superseded eleven days later when the Englishman had his own mishap. Neumann was out hunting elephant in an area where the animals were noticeably aggressive, armed with the Lee-Metford .303 magazine rifle and the Martini-Henry (a single shot falling-block rifle of .450 caliber). Neumann came across a herd, but it was mostly cows with disappointingly small tusks. He had wounded two cows with the .303 and dispatched another with the Martini-Henry but then went back to the Lee-Metford, even though that rifle had lately developed a habit of jamming or, more precisely, failing to slip another round into the breech after firing.

During the hunt Neumann had noticed one particular cow that seemed bolder and more aggressive than the others, but had so far spared her because her tusks were negligible. The cow was accompanied by a half-grown calf. Turning a corner in the bush, Neumann suddenly came face to face with three elephant, among them the aggressive cow—which immediately charged straight for him. Neumann whipped the .303 rifle to his shoulder and pulled the trigger—but heard only a click. The weapon had once again failed to rechamber upon working the bolt. Neumann, a very brave man by everyone's account (even Lugard's), turned and ran. As he put it later, he knew it was futile but could think of nothing else. He tried to work the bolt as he ran and fire backward over his shoulder, an act of desperation if there ever was one, but again the rifle did not go off. As the elephant closed on him, Neumann flung himself sideways into the bushes, vainly hoping the animal might rush on by. But the elephant wheeled ("like a terrier on a rabbit," he wrote) and straddled the fallen hunter, who lay face-up on the ground, his head propped up by a bush.

Now began what was every elephant hunter's nightmare. The cow kneeled over Neumann, its knees on either side of him, and made three lunges at him with her tusks, meanwhile butting his body with her head. The tusks went first through his right arm, then his chest, and the great elephant head thumped hard and crushed Neumann's ribs. The skin was scraped off Neumann's face by her hide, and the crushing pain in his chest made it difficult to breathe and almost impossible to remain conscious. After the three

Arthur Neumann.

lunges, the elephant stopped and walked away. Neumann later wrote, "Whether she supposed she had killed me, or whether it was that she disliked the smell of my blood, or bethought herself of her calf, I cannot tell."

The hunter's injuries were appalling. Several of his ribs were broken, and the tusk had gone through his arm and also clear through the side of his chest, although miraculously no arteries or major organs were ruptured. The bush that had propped him up undoubtedly saved his life by giving his body a little cushion when the animal tried to crush him. His gunbearers came back for him, having run when the elephant charged, and Neumann wondered idly why his gunbearer Squareface, who was carrying his 10-bore, hadn't risked a shot. But the Swahilis argued convincingly that, in flight themselves, they hadn't even realized that Neumann was caught.

Neumann's ordeal was actually just beginning. Unable to walk, he was brought back to camp. It immediately started raining, and Neumann, cold and trembling from the damp and shock, came down with a malarial fever on top of his wounds. For nearly a month he lay in a hammock unable to hunt, dependent on milk bought from local herdsmen for his sustenance. The days were tolerable, but darkness brought agony for he could find no position to lie in that didn't cause excruciating pain. The arm healed quickly, albeit somewhat stiff, but the chest wound was infected and oozed gruesome discharges of pus and other fluid. After about a month he was beginning to feel somewhat better and in early February had his men carry him to a new camp on the lakeshore. The exertion was too much, however, and he had a serious relapse of fever, combined with dysentery, that left him weak and barely alive. It was more than two months before he could walk any distance at all, although he eventually recovered nearly completely.

As he gained strength he began to hunt again, relishing the opportunity to obtain solid food, but was forced to rely on the treacherous .303 as his only weapon. The recoil from the other rifles was so powerful that it threatened to burst open his newly healed wounds. It wasn't until 17 April, however, that Neumann felt well enough to begin the long march back to the coast. On that same day the suppurating open wound in his chest finally healed over.

The march back down the shore of Lake Rudolf was relatively uneventful. Neumann was not fated to get back to civilization without further misadventures, however. After leaving the lake region he led the safari along the western ridge of the Lorogi Hills, where he had hunted once before with little success. The Lorogis were a haunted district, dark mountains dotted with tiny stone structures of some forgotten race. Neumann wanted to scout the area one last time to see if it might be worth coming back to. He also needed to kill some time while waiting for the bulk of his porters to return from a camp at Ukambani, where he had cached some ivory. Like Bell, Neumann was such a successful elephant hunter that finding a way to transport all his tusks was always a major concern.

The party Neumann led into the Lorogis was a small one—himself, Squareface, three or four Swahilis, and a Wandorobo guide named Baithai. The Wandorobo led them on a round-about route that, as night fell, found them in an open area. They set up camp around a single tree.

Neumann had been warned that there were dangerous lion in the district, and at any rate it was his normal practice to build a strong thorn *boma* (enclosure) around his campsites, undoubtedly a lesson learned from his earlier experience with the Masai at Loita. But on this night it began raining heavily just as they started to make camp, which hampered construction of the fence. Neumann even admitted that he didn't really respect the warnings about the lion. His earlier encounters with the great cats had been relatively benign, and he had developed a complacency that all too often proves fatal in the African bush. The *boma* was poorly constructed and had many gaps. As the rain stopped, Neumann tried to sleep in his tent while his men huddled around the fire trying to get dry. As he drifted off, Neumann's mind was plagued by the tiniest doubt, a vague concern that they were exposed in lion country. . . .

It happened in a flash. A few minutes after one in the morning Neumann was jerked awake by the growl of a lion and the cries of his men. Grabbing his rifle, he flew out of the tent, but the lion was already gone. In its jaws was Squareface, Neumann's interpreter and chief gunbearer. The next morning Neumann and a Swahili named Juma followed the lion's trail and found what remained of Squareface. They did not find the lion.

Neumann wanted to stay in the district and avenge his gunbearer, but his men vociferously protested. What was done was done, they said, and they wanted out of those accursed hills. Neumann reluctantly agreed. It is clear from his memoirs that he was troubled by his failure to protect his men, but in this case there was nothing for it but to wind up the safari. The caravan reached Mombasa on 1 October 1896, the men proudly bearing the great tusks that Neumann promptly deposited in a warehouse.

In 1897 Neumann wrote his monumental *Elephant Hunting in East Equatorial Africa* while staying at

Dunvegan Castle, home of the noted big-game hunter and Scottish chief Norman Mangus Macleod. Published the following year, it was his only book, and thus his first two safaris are by far the best known, but his career was far from over. He returned to South Africa when the Boer War broke out and served in a volunteer mounted infantry company, seeing action at Spion Kop (where he was nearly killed) and the siege of Ladysmith.

When the war ended he went back to East Africa to resume elephant hunting. His 1902–1904 safaris concentrated on the area around the Lorian Swamp, Lake Rudolf, and the Turkana district, and Neumann once again gathered several tons of ivory. By this time the British government had begun to place restrictions on hunting in general and elephant hunting in particular (much to Neumann's fury), and Neumann-style campaigns were becoming impossible. Given a grace period to return to the coast, he wrapped up his career in Mombasa in July 1906 and returned to England, selling his last load of ivory for £4,500, a profit of £1,500.

The end came in London on 29 May 1907. Accounts of his death vary. There seems no real doubt that he shot himself with his elephant rifle, but other reports feature an accidental discharge while cleaning his revolver, or even sickness. A 1909 *McClure's Magazine* article by an ivory expert named Mrs. Childs claimed that he died from influenza. John Guille Millais, who knew him as well as anyone, is one of the sources for the suicide version. Neumann was despondent over a young lady's rejection of his marriage proposal, and it is well known that the flu can be fatal in such circumstances.

More so than most of the great old elephant hunters, Neumann was a thoroughly sensitive and modern character. His personal complexity is fascinating. He could be cold. His writings display no great emotion toward the deaths of his assistants Shebane and especially Squareface (who had served him with tremendous good faith, courage, and loyalty), and he was certainly hell on elephant. Neumann never dealt well with people on a personal level and was frequently described as shy or aloof. He hated crowds and was horrified at the idea of shooting a giraffe, yet was furious at the game laws restricting the killing of elephant. Mrs. Childs described him after his death as "a handsome, modest, modish person; brave in the wilderness, but rather diffident in the haunts of men; manly, politic, courteous." Richard Meinertzhagen, hardly a poet, described Neumann as "a quiet, unassuming little man with a faraway and rather sad outlook on life" (Meinertzhagen, *Kenya Diary*).

He seemed to observe a moral code, a sense of right and wrong that elevated him far above the level of his peers. When the white doctor A. Eustace Atkinson and two other Englishmen murdered a group of Rendille Africans by blowing them up with a keg of gunpowder, Neumann (who could offer only hearsay testimony because he was not an eyewitness to the deed) was one of only three prosecution witnesses willing to testify at the murder trial. The remaining witnesses had all backed down, fearful of retaliation and social ostracism.

Neumann's motives for testifying are unknown. His personality was such that he may well have been driven by a sense of justice, but it is only fair to note that some white Kenyans believed that he perjured himself in his testimony. The Kenya historian Errol Trzebinski (1985) unearthed an intriguing letter from a trader who visited Neumann's old camp in 1907. Writing three months after Neumann's death, the author of the letter reported that he had spoken to the local Africans about the elephant hunter and uncovered some shameful information. The trader expressed wonder that Neumann hadn't shot himself long before, and writes to his correspondent that he will provide more information later. The story ends there, unfortunately. It has been speculated that the trader may have uncovered proof that Neumann perjured himself at the Atkinson trial. Or the allegations may have involved his sex life or ivory dealings. Whatever the case, the answer died with Neumann with that bullet in London.

His personal quirks have a decidedly modern flavor. He was inconveniently fastidious, considering that he lived in the bush for years at a time. He affected the wearing of white gloves and went through hundreds of pairs. He also was obsessed with food contamination and, uniquely, had his meat dried in porous cloth bags to keep the flies off. Anyone who has ever seen an open-air market in the tropics can appreciate the difficulties that Neumann's obsessions put upon him. His idiosyncrasies anticipated by nearly a century the recognition of conditions like Obsessive Compulsive Disorder and Attention Deficit Disorder.

Neumann was a thoroughly modern man in a wilderness setting, somebody who from today's perspective would seem more at home in front of a typewriter or word processor rather than being what he was—a supremely efficient executioner of wild elephant. Some men find themselves easily, while others take to the bottle or drugs or beat their wives in frustration at their own failures. Neumann could find himself, could relax, only with a rifle in his hand on a remote, windswept wasteland hundreds of miles from his peers and commanding the respect and obedience of primitive warriors. He could take anything the natural world could dish out—he had the inner strength to survive illness and fever and one of the most devastating animal attacks in history. He was superb in the bush. But when it came to the civilized world, the urban world of sophisticated people, he couldn't handle it—he lacked the social skills to deal with society's excruciating pressures. The man who could take all the punishment Africa could dish out couldn't survive a heart-wrenching rejection of the type that every high-school kid endures.

In the 1928 Rowland Ward book he still had the ranking for Neumann hartebeest and was listed in the giraffe category. He also had a high-ranking black rhino trophy (a bull shot on Mount Kenya with a 40-inch horn) and several ranking elephant. A butterfly collection of 170 species, brought back by Neumann from his second safari, was considered an important contribution to entomology. Strangely, it is remotely possible that his death was not the end of Arthur Neumann. His favorite goddaughter later reported that he had appeared to her several times in the form of a ghost. Neumann would not have been the first adventurer to return home from Africa in an unearthly form—Mungo Park was seen by his sister after his drowning in 1805.

Neumann, Oskar (1867–1946). Neumann was a turn-of-the-century German adventurer and naturalist who made some significant explorations in Abyssinia, Uganda, and the Upper Nile. He traveled between Masailand and Kavirondo in 1894, and went back and forth across Uganda north of Lake Victoria four separate times, each time at a different distance from the lake. On each leg he made a thorough survey and collection of the local wildlife.

Neumann focused primarily on antelope, predators, and monkeys on this 1894 trip. Because Uganda was heavily populated at the time (prior to the sleeping-sickness epidemic that depopulated entire districts), animal numbers were down somewhat. He noted large numbers of elephant, and near a place called Kwa Mtessa reported three herds of thirty to fifty animals each. He saw lots of hippo but no rhino. The buffalo had been wiped out by the recent rhinderpest epidemic, and Neumann saw only the tracks of a solitary animal. He also reported numerous zebra, a population of giraffe in extreme northern Uganda, and nine species of antelope, not one of which could be found in the coastal parts of Tanganyika. There were also a marmoset and two other species of monkey that previously had been known only in West Africa. In 1900 he explored between Lake Rudolf and the Akobo River, and from there to the Pibor.

Neumann was an avid hunter and donated significant collections of mammals and birds to European museums. He finished his days in the United States, working at the Field Museum in Chicago.

New, Charles (1840–1875). An English missionary, New in 1857 became the first man to reach the snowline of Mount Kilimanjaro. He also discovered Lake Chala, a crater lake southeast of the mountain, and took a bottle of its water for analysis. The steep, thickly tangled slopes surrounding this lake made it so inaccessible that after New's 1871 discovery no European actually reached the water for another twenty years. Even Joseph Thomson was deterred by the thickets and the slope and saw no safe way down to the water. It was left to an American woman, Mrs. French-Sheldon, to somehow work her way down to the water with a pontoon boat in 1891 and sail about the lake, flying the Stars and Stripes.

Newland, Victor M. Born in Australia, Newland relocated from South Africa to Kenya immediately after the end of the Anglo-Boer War. He and his friends, the brothers Leslie and Henry Tarlton, had been promised the opportunity to farm in the countryside near Naivasha. When they arrived in Kenya, however, they were informed that the Naivasha area was now a native reserve, so they settled near Kiambu instead. A popular man, Newland rose to become chairman (mayor) of Nairobi in 1921, and was co-owner of the Newland and Tarlton safari company.

Nicolls, James. Nicolls was a British hunter and author of *A Sportsman in Southern Africa* (1892). In 1889 he accomplished the singular feat, near Lake Ngami, of capturing a live sitatunga, which was displayed in a London zoo for some years afterward. At that time he was hunting Matabeleland and the Chobe River area with William Eglington. A year later Nicolls was reported to be hunting elephant with two men named Hicks and Strombom in the Queebe Hills.

Niemand, Berns. In 1876 Boer elephant hunter Berns Niemand was crossing the Crocodile River with companions named Solomon Veermaak and Pieter Swart. The three men stripped to wade across to see if the river was shallow enough for their ox wagons to negotiate. The water was shoulder-high. Veermaak and Swart had made it to the far bank when they looked back and saw the head of a huge crocodile approaching their friend. Niemand probably never knew what hit him—he was just turning in response to their frantic shouts when the reptile closed in and took him. His body was never recovered.

Nollet. Nollet was a French elephant hunter hailing from the rural forests of the Ardennes. He first came to Africa in 1918 with a French colonial infantry unit. Stationed at Fort Sibut, he began hunting in the Belgian Congo. Preferring a .475 Francotte double Express, Nollet is known to have killed more than four hundred elephant. He also did some trading and gold prospecting. In the 1940s and 1950s, as he aged and his body was wracked by malaria and sleeping sickness, he "got religion" and traveled through his old hunting grounds, preaching the Gospel and trying to convert the heathen. He was thus one of the few old-time professional elephant hunters to become a successful evangelist.

Northey, Sir Edward (1868–1953). Governor of Kenya 1919–1922. ROWLAND WARD 1928: LELWEL HARTEBEEST, BONGO, BLACK RHINO.

Norton, Maurice "Mickey" John (1873–1949). Mickey Norton was a huge red-headed Irishman, standing six feet, four inches tall and weighing in at well over two hundred pounds. He immigrated to the United States around 1886, and after working a number of menial jobs for seven years shipped off to South Africa in 1893.

Norton worked as a Cape Town policeman for several months before moving on to the Transvaal, where he tried his hand at prospecting. He was arrested as a British sympathizer after the Jameson Raid but was released in time to serve as a mounted infantryman at Bulawayo during the Matabele Rebellion of 1896. After hostilities ended Norton went to Portuguese East Africa where he found employment as a hunter.

His job was to supply meat for the railroad gangs, shooting buffalo with a Mauser magazine rifle. He also shot plains game and an occasional elephant. In 1898 he quit the railroad and set himself up as a professional ivory hunter in Blantyre, British Central Africa. Determined to make a good living, he jettisoned the Mauser (and a .303 service Enfield he had picked up) in favor of a .577 Nitro Express. In later years he also used a .404 Jeffrey magazine rifle.

When things got too hot for him in Mozambique and Nyasaland, Norton moved north; thereafter he centered his operations in German East Africa and the southern part of the Belgian Congo. For a few years he based himself on an island in the Ruvuma River. He also hunted in North-East Rhodesia, where in 1907 he was involved in a terrifying incident—an enraged elephant threw a tree trunk at him and then charged. A few weeks afterward he was reported as having killed a bull elephant with tusks of 84 and 86 pounds, big for the area. Burger (1957) tells a slightly different version of the tree trunk episode and places it in the Belgian Congo, but the Rhodesian version is backed by contemporary evidence, a letter from hunter A. L. Barnshaw.

Norton served in the British army during the First World War, operating as an intelligence officer in the East Africa campaign. Elephant hunter Jim Sutherland was in the same section, and by some reports was Norton's immediate superior.

When the war ended, Norton settled in Tanganyika and worked for the game department: The 1930 East *African Red Book* shows him as attached to the department at Rufiji in Tanganyika Territory. He also operated as a trader and did occasional for-profit elephant hunting, but most of his shooting in the 1920s and 1930s was for the purpose of elephant control. He retired from the department in 1940.

Norton was quite prolific: Burger credited him with killing over 4,000 elephants, although that seems a bit high. Norton himself reportedly put the total at about 2,000 bulls. He was one of the last of the nineteenth-century ivory buccaneers. His safaris were huge, often with hundreds of porters, and he would move from village to village in the remote bush, trading and making alliances with local kings. The natives were generally all too happy to assist him, both to get rid of the crop-raiding elephants and for the meat he provided.

A highly regarded woodsman with the reputation of never hunting female elephants, Norton had apparently completed a memoir of his sixty years of hunting and was arguing over the publishing contract when he died in 1949. The manuscript disappeared. John Burger, incidentally, lists Norton's death as taking place in 1946. I have gone with the date supplied by Tony Sanchez (2005).

Nurk, Carl. A professional hunter for Safariland, Ltd., Nurk was killed in action in Ethiopia in the early days of World War II. He was leading a charge of African irregulars when he was cut down by Italian machine-gun fire. Nurk was awarded a posthumous Military Cross.

Nyschens, Ian Reginald (1923–2006). Nyschens, who was born in South Africa, was of Danish descent. This rather sickly youth grew into a man of great physical fortitude. On the invitation of a friend, Faanie Joosten, he moved to Southern Rhodesia to hunt elephant for their ivory. This was in the mid-1940s, and Nyschens and Joosten chose the most difficult to reach areas of the Zambezi Valley to set up

Ian Reginald Nyschens.

their operation. It was a time when game laws were being enforced throughout Africa, yet these two feigned complete ignorance of the prevailing ordinances of the countries in which they hunted.

Nyschens set upon an elephant-hunting career that proved to be the equal of James Sutherland's and Walter Bell's, but he did it at a much later time and under much more difficult circumstances. Nyschens, with and without Joosten, roamed far and wide, almost always outside of the law, as far north as southern Tanzania and as far east as the coast of Mozambique. But his stronghold was the thick jesse bush of the Zambezi Valley, a place he loved more than any other. Visibility was so poor in the jesse that sometimes a hunter could actually be close enough to touch an elephant with his rifle barrel before he could see it.

His personal life stood in sharp contrast to the success he enjoyed in his hunting career. He was married for a time, but his lifestyle was not a domestic one and the marriage did not last. He had a son named Clive and a daughter, Cheryl. Unfortunately, Clive died in a car accident during the prime of his life, and this was a great personal tragedy to Ian who loved and admired his son greatly.

Once the Kariba Dam was completed in 1959, it flooded a great deal of his beloved Zambezi Valley, and Nyschens's world began to shrink. He continued to shoot elephant under a control scheme set by the Rhodesian authorities, but his footloose days were at an end. He joined the wildlife department as a game ranger for a while, but his unsociable character made for a short career. After leaving the game department, for a while he bred horses for a living, and he seemed to have enjoyed some success with this endeavor. After Zimbabwe gained independence, Ian became adrift, and his meager pension from the game department was eaten up by inflation.

To the end of his days, he remained irascible and, to a large degree, unknown to all but a few. Even though the world no longer held a place for the professional ivory hunter, Nyschens left a record of his elephant-hunting days in two books: *Months of the Sun* and *Footsteps of an Ivory Hunter.* Ian Nyschens died on 6 December 2006.

O

Oates, Frank (1840–1875). Frank Oates and his brother traveled to South Africa early in 1873. Starting their trek from Maritzburg, the brothers toured the Transvaal and Bechuanaland, and got into the area known as the Tati district. His brother returned to England at this point, but Frank Oates continued on to Matabeleland, meeting with Lobengula and later arriving, after much adversity, at Victoria Falls on the last day of 1874. He died of fever shortly thereafter. His notes and letters were published as *Matabele Land and the Victoria Falls* (1881).

O'Hara. Also seen as O'Hara. In 1899, near Voi, a lion crept into a tent occupied by a sleeping road engineer named O'Hara, his wife, and their two small children. The lion bit O'Hara in the head, crushing his skull and killing him instantly. The wife woke up, and her shouts woke the camp. In the confusion an askari fired at the lion and missed, but the lion dropped the corpse and made off into the night. Mrs. O'Hara and the askari dragged the body into the tent. The lion, recovering his courage, tried for the rest of the night to reclaim his prize but was kept away by shouting and erratic but loud gunfire from the askari. A different version has no askari and only Mrs. O'Hara to fire the shots.

Orgeich, William. Orgeich was the taxidermist who accompanied C. G. Schillings on his photographic safari to Tanganyika in the early 1900s.

Orleans, Duc d'. Also known as Prince Henry of Orleans, he hunted elephant in Somaliland. He planned to accompany the Russian swashbuckler Leontiev on his Turkana expedition in 1896, but Leontiev was wounded playing around with a Maxim gun and Prince Henry didn't deign to wait around for his recovery. Rowland Ward 1928: Gerenuk (No. 1), hippo, hirola.

Orpen. Described by Gordon Cumming as a "mighty Nimrod," Orpen was the Scotsman's companion on his final African hunting expedition in 1848. The team, which started from Colesburg, consisted of Gordon Cumming, Orpen, Khoi servants, a Bushman outrider named Booi, and an "immense pack" of mixed hunting dogs. They hunted successfully for almost six months. On 17 September, with Gordon Cumming confined to his bed with rheumatic fever, Orpen and a Khoi named Present went hunting on foot and wounded a leopard. While following up in thick bush, with the dogs inexplicably trailing rather than leading, the two men stumbled upon the leopard, which promptly jumped at Orpen's head. The Englishman had time to snap off one shot, but missed. The leopard severely tore up Orpen's face, hands, and arms before fainting from loss of blood from its earlier wound. Present, who was armed, had fired his weapon into the ground and climbed a tree, where he was joined by most of the other staff. Orpen and the leopard each staggered to their feet and went different ways, Orpen back to the tent of his sick partner. Gordon Cumming wrote that his wounds were "many and dangerous."

Osler, Henry Smith (1862–1933). Born in Toronto on 8 November 1862, Henry Osler followed the traditional occupation of his family and became a lawyer in 1886. He had a long legal career, including almost being sentenced to jail for refusing to violate the lawyer–client privilege during the Teapot Dome scandals of the 1920s. An expert revolver shot and billiards player and a connoisseur of fine art, he was also deeply interested in ornithology and hunting. In 1906 he became chairman of the board of Ontario Game Commissioners and was a member of the American Bird Banding Association from 1918. On one of his several trips to Africa in 1906 he collected 181 species of birds from the Sudan, which are still the property of Royal Ontario Museum of Zoology, as well as numerous mammals. He died in Montreal on 8 December 1933. Rowland Ward 1928: Buffalo, Nile lechwe, Grant gazelle, Lord Derby eland, sitatunga, white rhino, roan, impala, bohor reedbuck.

Oswell, William Cotton (1818–1893). An English sportsman, Oswell attended Rugby school, did well academically, and excelled on the very difficult Indian Civil Service examination. In 1832 Oswell went to India, taking a post as Collector and Judge and making a name for himself in the fields of tiger hunting and pigsticking. It is unknown how much collecting and judging he did, but he put a serious dent in the area's tiger and pig populations. After ten years in India malaria began to wear him down—in one short period he lost over sixty pounds from what had been a very muscular frame. His doctors told him that if he wanted to live, he needed a change of climate and suggested Cape Colony.

Africa revived him. Almost immediately upon landing there in 1844, Oswell took off hunting in the interior along with a Scotsman named Mungo Murray. Among other adventures, they encountered a starving tribe called the Baka. As a mission of mercy, Oswell and Murray shot a

William Cotton Oswell.

huge quantity of meat for them, mainly hippo. On their first foray of hippo hunting they shot one of the beasts and were dismayed when the animal sank. So they quickly shot thirteen more in an effort to supply the needed meat. They did not realize until later that these hulking animals resurface after they bloat from the intestinal gases. The Baka were left with a surfeit of hippo meat.

The next season Oswell went out hunting with a Maj. Frank Vardon of the 25th Madras Native Infantry. There were the usual adventures and misadventures on the trail. Vardon was taken in by the apparent docility of the white rhino and once pulled the tail of one of the beasts—only Oswell's quick shooting saved his life. Together he and Vardon shot eighty-nine rhino in that one season, a profligacy that Oswell came to regret in old age.

He didn't regret it in his youth. From 1844 to 1855 Oswell hunted regularly in Africa. He preferred to move in close to his quarry rather than using the prevailing method of peppering the animal with shots from a distance. His ideas came to be accepted as the way a true sportsman should conduct himself. Much of the "code" adopted by the professional hunters of East Africa stemmed from Oswell's ideas of sportsmanship.

Oswell's greatest fame came as a companion to David Livingstone. It was his 10-gauge smoothbore (later loaned to Samuel Baker) that kept Livingstone fed on the 1848–1849 expedition that discovered Lake Ngami. Time and again Oswell dug into his very deep pockets for funds to assist Livingstone and his family. It is a matter of record that Livingstone, who despite many great qualities, was often petty and jealous of his fame and celebrity, consciously minimized the part Oswell played in the Ngami and other expeditions. Livingstone's papers contain several instances where he blatantly misrepresented Oswell's role in things so as to reduce any chance that Oswell might steal some of the missionary's thunder. This was a great disservice to a good friend and a great blot on Livingstone's memory. Late in life Oswell came to realize how unfairly Livingstone had treated him, but even then, true to form, Oswell shrugged it off by simply acknowledging that fame was more important to Livingstone than to him. The simple fact of the matter is that if it weren't for William Cotton Oswell, few people today would recognize the name of David Livingstone. The legendary explorer might have lived out his life doing his futile mission work (he made only one true convert his entire career), or might very well have found an early grave along some dusty Bechuanaland track.

Oswell lived a long life, dying on 1 May 1893 after a short illness at his home at Tonbridge Wells. The illness was most likely a recurrence of his African fever. Unfortunately, Oswell never published a memoir or autobiography, despite the pleas of his friends and family. He was, at least, a contributor to *Big Game Shooting* 1894, part of the Badminton Library of *Sport and Pastimes,* and his son edited a two-volume collection of journals and letters that came out in the 1900s. Oswell was the recipient of the Silver Medal of the Paris Geographical Society, a rare honor for an Englishman. A daguerreotype that he took of Niagara Falls in July 1856 was one of the first ever taken (if not the first) of that natural wonder.

In the 1928 edition of Rowland Ward, Oswell is credited with the world-record domestic bull, a Ngamiland monster with horns of 81¼ inches. Whether this animal had gone feral or Oswell shot it at a rodeo is not recorded.

Otter, Eric van (1889–1923). A Swedish baron and officer, van Otter immigrated to Kenya Colony in 1914. When war broke out in 1914, van Otter, along with most of Kenya's Swedish community, sided with their adopted British homeland. Subsequently he served in the King's African Rifles. An avid hunter, he converted to Islam and was highly regarded by his predominantly Muslim troops. He died in Turkana from blackwater fever in 1923. Van Otter's African name was Resase Moja (One-Shot), a tribute to his marksmanship.

Oulten, J. T. Capt. Tom Oulten arrived in East Africa in 1899 as a telegraph linesman. He was assigned to the Kenya Game Department in the 1920s and 1930s, while in his fifties and sixties. A year later he and his wife started a dairy farm near Ngong. The birth of their son, Harry, was the first registered at Nairobi.

Oulten was an interesting man, a gifted storyteller with a lot of odd beliefs. For instance, he held to the theory that the dimensions of the pyramids can predict the future. He also wouldn't eat lamb or unfertilized eggs, and always slept with his head pointed north. Despite these quirks, he was a brave and efficient game warden. Oulten was the man who persuaded Adamson to apply for a job at the game department in 1936. He was also justice of the peace for Kiambu, Kenya.

Eric van Otter and Karen Blixen enjoy lunch in the field.

Outram, George Henry (xxxx–1922). An Australian professional hunter living in Kenya, Outram was in on the Paul Rainey hunting-lion-on-horseback scheme. Prior to that he had been a scout for the 1903 Anglo-German Boundary Commission. Outram was one of the first to penetrate the Masai Mara. For a time he worked for the Newland and Tarlton safari firm. In 1913 he was on a normal safari near Thika when he was mauled by an angry lion. He kept at it and in 1922, near the MacKinnon Road railway station, was killed by yet another lion that he was trying to remove from his gunbearer.

Overweg, Adolf (1822–1852). Year of birth also seen as 1813. A German explorer, geologist, and astronomer, Overweg accompanied Barth and Richardson on their Sudan expedition in 1850. At that time there was a popular misconception that the Sahara was below sea level, and Overweg's observations on this trip were the first hard evidence to disprove that myth. When the expedition split into three separate groups, one under each leader, Overweg traveled to Zinder before heading to the rendezvous point at Bornu. Like Richardson, who died at Bornu, Overweg never returned to Europe. He died near Lake Chad in September 1852.

Overweg was a gifted handyman and was constantly being called upon by the local people to fix little gadgets like clocks and watches. This was an invaluable method of making friends and even raising supplies, by trading services for food, but it tended to be time-consuming and distracting. It also annoyed the expedition leader, Heinrich Barth, a complete klutz who didn't much like Overweg anyway and who was annoyed at being given the African nickname of Faidansa Bago, which translates as something along the lines of "practically useless."

Owen, L. M. Owen was an Englishman "well known in the colonies as a splendid rider and a very daring leader of volunteers" (Selous, 1881). He accompanied Selous on an 1877 trip into the Zambezi hinterlands. They crossed the big river at Wankie's Town on 30 October, lion hunting as they went, and found themselves between two warring groups, the Batongas and the Shakunda, the latter made up of freed and escaped slaves well-armed with muskets and working closely with Portuguese traders.

After much skirmishing and a few deaths, the Batongas and Shakundas reached a truce of sorts. By this time, January 1878, Owen had come down with fever. Selous left him temporarily at a native village, well cared for, while he himself did some further hunting. When they met up again in March, Owen was in such a serious state that Selous, himself sick, had to leave him again and trek many days to Matabeleland to arrange a relief caravan to bring Owen out.

By July Owen was back in English hands and well on the way to recovery and Selous was off on an elephant-hunting trip in the Mashona country.

P

Pailthorpe, R. He was district commissioner in the Masai province in the 1920s. Part of the DC's job was predator control. Pailthorpe, more of an administrator than a hunter, was badly injured by a lioness on one of his first hunts. John Hunter was brought in to finish the job in the Masai district, his pay being the skins of the lion he killed. These were fetching from £3 to £20 in Nairobi at the time, depending on quality. With the help of a pack of trained mongrel dogs (the prohibition against hunting with dogs did not apply to control work), Hunter killed more than ninety lion in the next few weeks.

Painter, Kenyon V. (xxxx–1940). A rich American banker from Ohio and a personal friend of Theodore Roosevelt, Painter started coming to Africa on safari in 1907 and later settled near Arusha. He spent the rest of his life investing in East African businesses and going on extended safaris, a whopping thirty-one of them. Painter owned more than ten thousand acres of land around Arusha and established a coffee-planting research center near the town. He was a great public benefactor, donating the post office, a church, and a hospital, and was said to have invested an estimated $11 million in the area.

During his hunting expeditions Painter took many record trophies, including the all-time world-record black rhino with a front horn of 53½ inches. His top white rhino, shot at Bahr el Ghazal, had a horn measuring 38½ inches. In the 1928 edition of Rowland Ward he is also credited with the top eastern roan antelope, taken in Kenya, with horns of 29¾ inches, and one of the top leopard, which before skinning measured 8 feet, 7 inches. He also had a listing for an Indian buffalo, African buffalo, bushbuck, brindled gnu, Kirk dik-dik, leopard, and nyala, among others. On his fourth safari in the Shimba Hills, Painter shot the last Roosevelt sable to be legally hunted in Kenya.

His younger wife, Maud (born Wyeth), was a distinguished hunter in her own right, first coming to Africa on Painter's third safari in 1910. Painter often hunted with Arusha professional Ray Ulyate and seems to have financed Ulyate's New Arusha Hotel in the late 1920s. Painter's honeymoon expedition was guided by two Arusha hunters named Hamilton Twigg and Smith. Smith, who may have been Ulyate's brother-in-law, was badly injured by a wounded lion around this time. One of Ulyate's sons was named Kenyon after the American businessman.

Palat (xxxx–1886). Lieutenant Palat was a French officer who decided to find a route from Algiers to Timbuktu through the Sahara. He left Algiers in October 1885, accompanied by a few guides. At the oasis of Tidikelt, near Ain Salah in the Tuareg country, his own guides robbed and murdered him on 8 March 1886.

Palmer-Kerrison. Captain Palmer-Kerrison had a cushy job as an aide to Governor Coryndon of Uganda but gave it up in 1925 to join the Uganda elephant control staff. In 1926 he was hunting a herd that had been raising all kinds of hell in the countryside. As usual he was armed with a .318 rifle while a gunbearer carried a heavy .450 or .577 as a backup. Palmer-Kerrison had downed one or two of the problem animals with brain shots when another elephant unexpectedly burst from thick cover and charged him at very close range. He had just enough time to snap off one shot into the elephant's chest, but the bull impaled him through the abdomen with one tusk. For some distance the animal carried the hunter, stuck like a butterfly on a pin, before the man fell off. The elephant staggered and collapsed, dead, a few yards farther on. Palmer-Kerrison miraculously made a complete, if long and painful, recovery.

Palmer-Wilson, Clary (1907–1985). This Tanganyika hunter, born the son of a Uganda railroad engineer, holds the record for Cape buffalo (a cow), shot in 1946. This animal had a spread of 64 inches. Palmer-Wilson was actually guiding a photographer, Manuel Cabrera, when he spotted the cow, reportedly said, "Stop the camera—that's the world-record buffalo," and brought it down with his .375. The trophy was beset by controversy raised by hunters who felt that a cow buffalo should not be considered the world record, regardless of its size.

Despite the notoriety he achieved with the record buffalo, Palmer-Wilson was actually considered an elephant specialist. He shot and helped others shoot hundreds of bulls, including many carrying ivory of more than one hundred pounds a side. Palmer-Wilson also shot the legendary elephant called the "Crown Prince," a huge tusker that had been stalked through Tanganyika for decades. He accompanied Col. Marcuswell Maxwell on two photographic safaris in 1930, the results of which were published in the *London Times* and later in a paperback supplement. He died in Oregon in 1985.

Park, Mungo (1771–1805). One of the more adept Scottish explorers of his time, Park first attracted notice as author of a work on Sumatran fish that described eight new species. In 1795 the African Association of London commissioned him to trace the course of the Niger. He was the first to reach the Niger via the Gambia in July 1796, and ascended to Bammaku. During this expedition he suffered from severe fever and was imprisoned by Muslim tribesmen for several months. He returned to Britain thinking himself a failure but discovered that the public considered him a hero and a success. For several years thereafter he led a quiet life as a country doctor at Peebles in Scotland. In 1805 he returned to the Niger. Starting from Pisania on the Gambia in May 1805 with thirty-five Europeans and a number of Africans, he reached the Niger three months later with only seven companions. He sent his notes and journal back before proceeding further. In November 1805 he was drowned with four Europeans while fleeing an attack by natives. He was the author of *Travels in the Interior of Africa* (1799).

Like Arthur Neumann, Park's persona lived on. Documents in the possession of the Royal Commonwealth Society report that an apparition, said to be the ghost of Mungo Park, appeared to his sister, Mrs. Thomson, in 1805–1806.

Parke, Thomas Heazle (1857–1893). Born in Roscommon County, Ireland, Parke joined the British Army Medical Staff in 1881. He received the Queen's Medal and the Khedive's Star for his service in the Egyptian campaign of 1882. The following year, while an epidemic raged through Egypt, Surgeon Major Parke commanded the "cholera camp" at Tel el Kebir and subsequently was a member of the abortive attempt to relieve Charles Gordon in Khartoum. In 1887 he signed on with Henry Stanley for the Emin Pasha relief expedition, and is mentioned prominently in Stanley's *In Darkest Africa.*

On 10 September 1893 Parke was staying as a guest at the home of the duke of Saint Albans when he suddenly took sick and died that same evening. He was the author of *My Personal Experiences in Equatorial Africa* (1891) and *Guide to Health in Africa* (1893), with a preface by Henry Morton Stanley.

Partridge, J. W. Partridge was assigned to the Kenya Game Department in Nairobi in the 1920s.

Patterson, Frederick B. This American took a five-month safari in British East Africa in 1927. His professional hunter was Denys Finch Hatton. The safari was largely uneventful, but Patterson wrote a book about it, *African Adventures* (1928), which is mildly notable for both its portrait of Finch Hatton and about fifty good photographs. Not the worst of its genre, it successfully conveyed a taste of the 1920s Kenya-style safari.

Patterson, John Henry (1867–1947). Patterson hailed from Ballymahon in County Westmeath, Ireland. After service as a noncommissioned officer in India, where he learned surveying and engineering, he was sent to work on the Uganda railway (called the Lunatic Line or Lunatic Express by skeptical opponents) in 1898. Although he is almost always called Colonel Patterson, at the time of the Tsavo nightmare Patterson was a sergeant—he became a colonel only later in the Boer War. Many modern articles and films give the impression that Patterson was in charge of the entire project. In fact, he was responsible for only one section of the line. Specifically, he was to build a bridge over the Tsavo River.

The story of the man-eaters of Tsavo is almost too well known to bear repetition, but to briefly summarize, the British were building a railroad from Mombasa to Lake Victoria in the 1890s. The manual labor was done largely by Hindu and Swahili workers under British supervision. In 1898 a large workforce was gathered under Patterson at Tsavo, where they were building a bridge over the river of the same name. Tsavo means "place of slaughter." The area had seen a lot of warfare, disease, and famine in its time, and the local lion had a bad reputation to begin with.

Patterson arrived at Tsavo in March 1898. Already laborers and workmen had begun to disappear. At first Patterson and the other British officials tended to believe

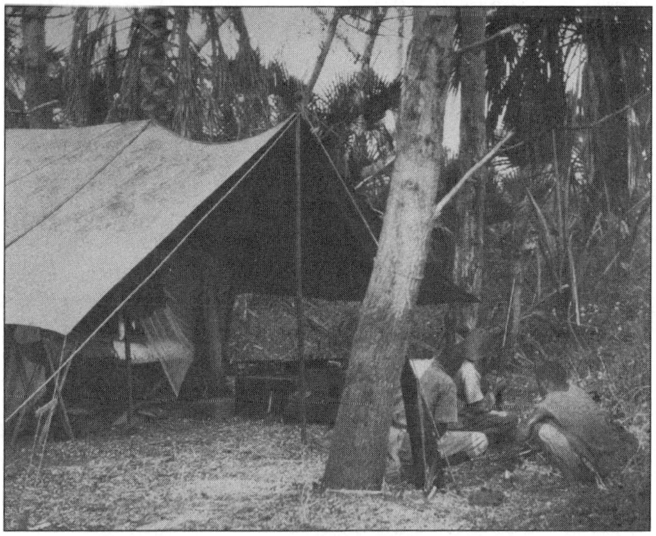

Frederick B. Patterson's safari camp, Kenya, 1927.

Frederick Patterson with black-maned male lion.

that the missing men were deserters or possibly had been murdered by other workers for their wages or over gambling debts. But about three weeks after his arrival a burly Sikh foreman named Ungan Singh, known personally to Patterson as a solid man, was dragged out of his tent and eaten.

Patterson set out to track the killers but soon realized that these were no ordinary lion. Presumably he had some experience hunting tiger in India, but certainly he had done nothing that would prepare him for what lay ahead. His classic 1907 book, *The Man-eaters of Tsavo,* chronicled a series of attempts, by Patterson and others, to kill or capture the lion—attempts that always seemed to be foiled by amateurishness, bad luck, or simply the amazing cunning of the man-eaters. The lion ranged over a wide area. For instance, one night they took two men from the railhead and a few nights later struck at a place called Engomani ten miles away. Throughout 1898 lion killed something more than 135 people (exact records of African victims were not kept). This voracity occurred despite increasingly desperate attempts to kill the beasts.

In one such attempt, Patterson constructed a cage trap divided into two secure parts. Bait would be placed in one half and the lion presumably trapped in the other half. The trap was an elaborate affair that took a lot of effort to build and was the subject of much scoffing by observers, who frankly didn't have any better ideas themselves. On 3 December 1898, Patterson set up the trap using Indian troopers as bait (if this seems cold-hearted, in fairness Patterson had himself sat up as bait on several occasions). At nine o'clock at night the trap door crashed shut—the trap had been sprung and a lion was caught in the second compartment across from the troopers.

Unfortunately, what happened next was exactly the kind of ill luck that had plagued Patterson from the start. The "bait" panicked, and instead of simply shooting the enraged man-eater they started firing indiscriminately in all directions. So bad was the fusillade that Patterson dropped to the floor in his tent even though he was at right angles to the line of fire. Amazingly, one of the troopers' .303 bullets knocked out a bar from the door of the trap. The lion was able to squeeze through and make its escape. Small wonder that the superstitious workers universally believed the lion to be more devil than animal.

The lion did not observe the proper social customs either. The night before the trap fiasco, district officer Whitehead had to spend the night in a tree, his back clawed, after one of the man-eaters tried to pull him down on his short walk from the railway platform to Patterson's camp. The animal sprang from a bank and knocked Whitehead down. Luckily for him (if not for his companion), the district officer was carrying a rifle and managed to get off a snap-shot, which missed but was sufficient to startle the lion. The beast backed off, shook its head, and then grabbed the companion, a sergeant of askaris named Abdullah, dragging him into the night. Whitehead fired again but missed, and the sergeant disappeared forever, saying only *"Eh, bwana, simba!"* ("Oh, master, a lion!") as he was taken to his death.

Unknown to everyone, however, the reign of terror was nearing its end. Patterson finally got lucky and managed to shoot the first man-eater when it stalked him as he sat up over a donkey bait in a machan. Morning light revealed the trophy—a large, nearly maneless male lion. The second man-eater continued to be a problem, snooping around the veranda of the English Permanent Way inspector a few nights later. Then it too finally fell to Patterson's bullets, again fired from a tree. The follow-up was more exciting this time. The lion was wounded, not dead, and it chased Patterson and his gunbearer up yet another tree. Patterson finally put the beast down with a slug from a Martini carbine.

Patterson's book is very well written, which no doubt accounts for some of the fascination that the lion of Tsavo have held for people, but it doesn't account for it all. The man-eaters were a sensation, discussed in Parliament and written about in *The London Times* and all the sporting journals. The Victorian upper class was a hunting class, and sportsmen spent countless hours in clubs, in bars, and around campfires speculating and bragging how they would have handled the situation. When the Prince of Wales and game warden Samaki Salmon got lost in the Congo bush thirty years later, and had to huddle together all night in the cold rain with only a bottle of whiskey to keep them warm, it was the story of the lion of Tsavo that His Royal Highness kept gleefully discussing. Movies have been made based loosely on the events *(The Ghost and the Darkness,* for one), and even today new books are being published with the man-eaters as a central theme (two of the better recent ones are *The Lions of Tsavo,* 2004, by Bruce Patterson, no relation, and Philip Caputo's *Ghosts of Tsavo,* 2002). Many modern hunters have criticized Sergeant Patterson's methods as amateurish and even bungling, but he was the man with the gun and on the spot. He didn't have a hundred years of discussion to guide him, and he didn't have much in the way of backup. He was faced with a unique situation and he dealt with it bravely and at great personal risk—and successfully.

After the bridge was finally finished, Patterson went on to new adventures. When the Boer War broke out in 1900 he was commissioned as a temporary lieutenant into the 20th Regiment of Imperial Yeomanry. He was mentioned in dispatches, a uniquely British honor equivalent to a decoration, on at least four occasions, and was awarded the DSO (see glossary) for gallantry. He returned to Britain in 1901 with the position of first adjutant of the Essex Yeomanry. He was soon recalled to South Africa, and given the rank of lieutenant colonel, in command of the 33rd Regiment of Imperial Yeomanry.

When the South African war finally ended, Patterson returned to the Essex Yeomanry and spent the next decade traveling, sometimes as an official observer (seconded, for instance, to the King's African Rifles) and sometimes on half-pay, a type of reserve status. In 1907 he was appointed the chief game warden of British East Africa, a position he held for two years. It was during this period that he was involved in a strange incident that was later the inspiration for an Ernest Hemingway short story.

In February 1908 Patterson went on an expedition to survey the northern border of Kenya. He brought along two friends, a married couple named James Blyth (1874–1908) and his wife Ethel. The Blyths soon became ill, and Patterson began to have second thoughts about bringing them along, for they were slowing down his survey. They set up camp one afternoon near a water hole called Lersamis in the Northern Frontier District.

James Blyth was very sick, so Mrs. Blyth (who had married James in 1903) slept in Patterson's tent. At least that's what they told the authorities later. Early the next morning a shot rang out. Patterson ran into James's tent and found the man dead with a gunshot wound to the head. Due to the hot climate and lack of transport, Patterson and Mrs. Blyth buried her husband in a shallow grave covered with stones. For some reason Patterson burned Blyth's tent, an act that encouraged suspicion later. The colonel then continued his survey, moving on to Marsabit.

Naturally, the case caused a scandal. Patterson and his defenders theorized that Blyth, who allegedly was in the habit of sleeping with a revolver under his pillow, had accidentally killed himself. Other, less-charitable people questioned the reason for Mrs. Blyth spending the night in Patterson's tent. Even then, adulterous affairs on safari were not uncommon, and later they became almost a standard feature of the safari business. Patterson was exonerated by both an inquest in Nairobi and an investigation in the House of Lords (the victim's father was Lord Blyth), and returned home to England on sick leave in 1909, suffering from an intestinal disorder. Another account claims that Patterson was acquitted in return for his resignation. Patterson gave his version of the incident in his 1909 book, *In the Grip of the Nyika.* The Blyth affair later was adapted by Hemingway for his story, *The Short Happy Life of Francis Macomber.*

Patterson survived the scandal with support from President Theodore Roosevelt, among many others, and took over command of an Irish Division in 1913. When the Great War erupted a year later, Patterson was assigned to command a regiment of Jewish volunteers, mainly exiles from Eastern Europe. For the rest of his life he was a stalwart defender of Zionism.

J. H. Patterson and C. Rawson.

Patterson's faulty lion trap.

That experimental unit was not a front-line combat outfit but rather a transport corps. Nevertheless, they were in the thick of the action and took many casualties. Patterson and his men served in the horrendous Gallipoli campaign of 1915 as the Zion Mule Corps, and his experiences were recounted in his book *With the Zionists in Gallipoli.* Patterson fought at Gallipoli for seven months before his health collapsed, and he was invalided back to Britain with enteritis and jaundice. After recovery he served in Palestine with the Australian Mountain Division and again commanded Jewish troops in combat. His health failed for good in 1919 and he again returned home, just before his beloved Zionist troops were transformed into the First Judean Regiment of the British army.

Patterson continued to fight for Jewish causes. He traveled the world in the 1920s and 1930s, lecturing and raising funds for the Zionists, an odd vocation for an Irish Protestant. In 1940 he was on a trip to South America, trying to unify Latin American Jews under the Zionist banner, when he once again got sick and had to visit the United States to convalesce. He wound up settling down at La Jolla, California, with financial help from a Jewish-American businessman. He died in Bel Air in 1947 at the age of eighty. His devoted wife Francie, who had married him in 1894, died from grief six weeks later.

The maneless character of the Tsavo man-eaters has led to much speculation over the years about the African lion and its subspecies. Many writers and researchers have claimed that the maneless lion should be considered a distinct subspecies. The modern consensus is that maneless-ness is an individual variation and that the African lion had only two subspecies, the Cape and Barbary. Both of these subspecies are generally considered extinct, but that too is in dispute—it is possible that purebred animals from these strains still exist in zoo and circus populations.

Patterson, R. R. Patterson was a British captain who was sent by Theophilus Shepstone as leader of a small ambassadorial group to Lobengula in 1878. Patterson was a tactless, headstrong man and quickly angered the Matabele king. Patterson and his companions vanished without a trace near Victoria Falls, no doubt murdered on Lobengula's orders.

Pearson, Pete (1877–1929). Pearson, a tall, well-built Australian, began elephant hunting in the Lado Enclave shortly after the start of the last century. The Lado, made famous after legal complications following the death of the Belgian King Leopold made it temporarily an unregulated no-man's-land, was a haven for ivory poachers even earlier. The district was simply too remote from communication lines to be governed effectively by any country except Great Britain, which controlled the Nile.

Leopold had uncontested legal dominion over the Lado from 1894, so far as the great powers of Europe were concerned. The armies of the Mahdi chased the Europeans out and kept them out until 1902, when Belgian troops reestablished stations throughout the territory. The arrangement between Belgium and Britain allowed for Belgian control via lease until a date six months after the death of King Leopold, at which time the province would be transferred to the British government. In fact, Belgium began to pull out about a year before the King's death in 1909.

The legend has arisen that the period between the 1908 Belgian withdrawal and the British occupation in 1910, a time that saw no effective government administration of any kind in the Lado, presented an opportunity to massacre the region's elephant, and this opportunity was seized upon by European ivory hunters. This legend is only partly true. About a dozen or so hunters were operating in the enclave years before Leopold breathed his last. In fact, the elephant hunters began trickling into Lado as soon as the Mahdist armies withdrew or were destroyed in the early 1900s. There was no need for them to wait for the king's death and the Lado's subsequent extra-national status. The Belgian forces were too few on the ground and too isolated from their bases to prevent elephant poaching, even in 1903. Any supplies, instructions, and reinforcements had to make the laborious journey up the Congo River and then overland through pestilential terrain before arriving in the enclave.

The eastern border of the Lado was the western bank of the Nile; the eastern bank was administered by Britain. A few of the early British hunters, like Karamojo Bell, took the trouble to obtain an unrestricted elephant-hunting license from the Congo Free State, but most of them simply lived on the east bank and slipped across the river to do their shooting. On those few occasions when the Belgian authorities posed a problem to the poaching operations, the hunters found that the Belgian officers were easily bribed and convinced to look the other way.

Pete Pearson was one of those early hunters in the Lado Enclave. Born in Australia on 16 January 1877, he joined with the veteran Bill Buckley on an ivory safari into the Lado Enclave in 1904. He used a .577 Nitro Express double rifle for his elephant hunting. He was very successful at this pursuit, killing hundreds of bulls in the Lado, including one with tusks of 155 and 153 pounds.

Pearson remained in the district for several years but left when the Lado became British territory (with British game laws). He then obtained so-called "commercial" elephant licenses in the Belgian Congo and Ubangi-Shari, the latter a part of French Equatorial Africa. These permits allowed him to continue hunting elephant on a scale that was no longer legally possible in British Africa (the French continued issuing commercial licenses until the late 1920s). In 1912 Pearson switched from his beloved .577 Express rifle to a Holland and Holland .375 Magnum magazine rifle that had been custom-made for him by the London gunmaker John Rigby.

After World War I Pearson hunted for a while in formerly German Tanganyika, then returned to Uganda, where he became one of the first elephant control specialists in the 1920s. Estimates of the number of elephant he shot in this capacity range from eighteen hundred to two thousand, making him one of the most experienced hunters of his time. One of the animals he was forced to shoot on control was the world-record cow elephant, shot near Munyoro, with ivory of fifty-six pounds per side. These tusks ended up in the Natural History Museum at South Kensington.

In 1924 Pearson and fellow game ranger Samaki Salmon guided the duke and duchess of York (later the king and queen of Great Britain) on a successful safari through the wilds of Uganda. Four years later Pearson and Salmon hunted with another royal party, the Prince of Wales (later King Edward VIII) and his younger brother, the duke

The railway camp at Tsavo.

Kermit Roosevelt, Sir Alfred Pease, and Theodore Roosevelt at the carcass of the first big lion.

of Gloucester. While following an elephant track near Uganda's magnificent Murchison Falls, the two rangers and the prince were surprised to see a large bull charging out of heavy cover at close range. Pearson grabbed the prince around the body and flung him to safety in a thornbush. Then Pearson and Salmon fired simultaneously at the elephant, which crashed to the ground just four yards from the heir to the throne.

Still a relatively young man, and one whose habits were largely healthy (except for a fondness for champagne), Pearson nevertheless took sick in the summer of 1929. Tests revealed that he was suffering from cancer. The prognosis was hopeless, and Pete Pearson died in a Kampala hospital on 10 September 1929.

Pease, Sir Alfred Edward (1855–1939). Pease, an early Kenya settler, was a close friend of Lord Delamere and the Percival brothers. Pease owned a ranch at Kitanga, raised ostriches, and hunted lion in his spare time. On one occasion he shot fourteen of them in one day on his ranch.

An episode in Pease's life illustrates the dangers inherent in butt-kissing. While visiting Washington, D.C., in 1908, Pease bragged to President Teddy Roosevelt about the tremendous big-game hunting that could be found at his luxurious Kenyan hunting lodge. Roosevelt, who had been planning to take a hunting trip to Alaska when he left office, impulsively changed his mind and invited himself to Pease's lodge. The unfortunate Pease, whose actual lodgings were less than impressive, had to hurry back to East Africa and begin construction of the camp he had so eloquently described.

Pease, a baronet, hunted with the Roosevelt safari and often acted as a guide for visiting sportsmen. In his younger days he had served in Parliament and had explored and hunted in South Africa, Ethiopia, the Sudan, and the Sahara. He sold his Kenya home in 1912 and returned to England, living at Pinchinthorpe House in Guisbrough, Yorkshire. Pease was the author of a biography of Sir Edmund Loder, *The Book of the Lion,* and the monumental three-volume *Travel and Sport in Africa* (1902). ROWLAND WARD 1928: TRANSVAAL LION.

Peddie (xxxx–1818). A British officer who led an expedition along the Gambia River in 1818, Major Peddie died on the trail, and leadership of the party was assumed by William Gray, who continued on into Senegal.

Peel, Charles Victor Alexander. Victorian sportsman and author of *Somaliland* (1906), largely concerning his hunting adventures there in 1899. He made a total of two expeditions to that country, hunting elephant, lion, rhino, and leopard. *Somaliland* is partially illustrated by Edmund Caldwell; Peel also wrote *Through the Length of Africa* (1927) and *The Polar Bear Hunt* (1928). ROWLAND WARD 1899: SCOTTISH RED DEER, EUROPEAN ROE, SWAYNE HARTEBEEST, SOMALI DIK-DIK, KLIPSPRINGER, SPEKE GAZELLE, PELZELN GAZELLE, SOEMMERRING GAZELLE, DIBATAG, GERENUK, GREATER KUDU, LESSER KUDU, DOMESTIC GOAT, BLACK RHINO, LION, AFRICAN LEOPARD, CHEETAH.

Peney, Alfred (xxxx–1861). Dr. Peney was a French physician who took a job in Cairo in 1840 as private secretary to an official named Clot Bey. Peney made several trips to Khartoum, the Blue Nile, and Kordofan and became fascinated with the idea of African exploration. For years he campaigned vigorously for a Franco-Egyptian joint expedition to find the source of the White Nile, the famous Mountains of the Moon. Peney finally got his wish in 1856 when the government of Egypt agreed to finance the venture. Unfortunately, the expedition was doomed from the moment its commander was named—Count D'Escayrac de Lauture, an émigré aristocrat, was a total incompetent. Much money and time were wasted and the expedition fizzled out, never leaving Cairo. The French were left out of the White Nile scene until the desperate Marchand expedition some forty years later.

Peney, who was to have accompanied D'Escayrac as medical officer, was made of sterner stuff than his elderly erstwhile leader. He arranged for leave from his private position and took matters into his own hands. For the next several years Peney roamed the White Nile and the Sudan, taking notes and catching on with whatever caravans he could find, be they Arab traders or elephant hunters or explorers such as Andrea De Bono. Peney made some excellent maps and was the first European to enter many localities near the Yei River and also east of Gondokoro. He finally died of blackwater fever in 1861.

Pennant, Douglas. A British army officer, Captain Pennant was stalking a wounded leopard in 1909 in the Sotik area of Kenya when the animal leaped at him from a tree, mauling him severely, breaking his jaw, and ripping one ear off. When Pennant left the hospital, his bed was taken by another man who had been chewed up by another leopard.

Pennefeather, E. G. British sportsman and officer of the Inniskilling Dragoons who hunted in the Transvaal with Henry Glynn in 1880.

Percival, Arthur Blayney (1875–1941). Blayney Percival, the son of Percy Percival and Emily Margaret Blayney, came to South Africa in the late 1890s as an ornithologist for the British Museum. In 1900 he decided to move to East Africa and, typically, walked there. He was appointed an assistant collector in June 1900 and given a special appointment in 1901 as Kenya's "Ranger for Game Preservation." This was an extra-departmental post. When the game department was officially created in 1907, the senior job went to John H. Patterson, with Percival as his assistant. Percival was responsible for drafting British East Africa's first comprehensive game laws.

In 1909 Patterson went back to Britain and R. B. Woosnam took his place. Together Woosnam and Percival enforced the game laws and carried out the predator control policies of the young colony until the start of World War I. When Woosnam left in 1915, Percival took over as game warden of Kenya (he was the first to have that title) until 1923.

During World War I Percival led a special scouting force of Wakamba hunters armed with bows and poisoned arrows. These crafty bush fighters struck terror into the hearts of German officers and their troops.

In 1925 Percival wrote a letter to Denis Lyell in which he recapped his exploits as a lion hunter. He stated that he had shot most of his lion, about forty, with a .256 light rifle. About twenty-five of the animals went down for good with one shot, while a number of rounds was required to kill the rest.

Percival was also Justice of the Peace for Machakos, Kenya, for many years and a founder of the East Africa and Uganda Natural History Association. He was one of the first to introduce trout into Kenya's cold-water streams and was the author of *A Game Ranger's Notebook* (1924) and *A Game Ranger on Safari* (1928). He died in January 1941.

Percival, C. J. This British officer (Royal Artillery) was on safari deep in Somaliland when the Donaldson Smith expedition passed by in 1894. The two groups were the only known Europeans who had penetrated that far into the country at that time. Just after he met Donaldson Smith, Percival entered a village that had been terrorized by a lion for weeks. The warriors of the village waited up one night until the lion made its usual appearance and then attacked the beast. The lion was speared to death at the cost of one man dead and two wounded. Captain Percival gave some medical assistance to the wounded (most likely permanganate of potash).

Percival, Philip Hope (1886–1966). The younger brother of A. Blayney Percival, Philip came to East Africa in 1906. On his first-ever lion hunt, he was out on horseback with his brother when he nearly rode into a lion hiding in the bush, and the animal charged. It was just about to leap up and pull him from the saddle when Blayney rode up and spooked the lion off.

Philip bought a farm in the Mua Hills and started ostrich ranching. He went along on the famous Roosevelt safari in 1909 and then decided to try his hand at being a guide. Percival's first professional safari client was an Englishman named Martin. In 1910 the pair hunted near the Lorian Swamp and enjoyed themselves immensely. His second client was Baron Rothschild. During his third safari, serving as an assistant to Flash Jack Riddell, they took out the duke and duchess of Connaught.

Philip Percival went on to escort many prestigious clients, including George Eastman, Gary Cooper, and Martin and Osa Johnson. He acquired the formidable reputation of being the best of the East African hunters,

Philip Percival and family, 1909.

commanding a reported $1,000 per month on safari. As he got older, he served as a mentor to a new generation of white hunters, including the legendary Sid Downey. Perhaps the best indication of the esteem in which he was held is the fact that he was elected to thirty-four consecutive terms as the president of EAPHA (see glossary).

Peschuel-Loesche, Moritz Eduard (1840–1913). Born near Merseburg, Germany, on 26 July 1840, Dr. Peschuel-Loesche (also seen as Pechuel-Losche) visited the Caribbean, the South Pacific, the Arctic, and Antarctica as a young man before setting his sights on Africa. In 1874–1876 he was a member of the German scientific expedition to Loango.

Peschuel-Loesche was commissioned by King Leopold in 1880 to find a shortcut from the Atlantic to Stanley Pool in the Congo, along the lines of the Niari and Kwilu Rivers. He possessed impressive scientific credentials and had done some African exploring as well, but he evidently wasn't the man for the job, for he quit and headed home after some petty bickering with the other officers assigned to his expedition. He was replaced by Grant Elliott.

Peschuel-Loesche returned to Africa in 1884 and worked for the German government in Damaraland. Harry Johnston (*Story of My Life,* 1923) wrote that Peschuel-Loesche was "very aggressive" in his attempts to subvert British influence on the continent in favor of Germany.

Peters, Karl (1856–1918). The founder of the German Colonization Society, Dr. Peters obtained via treaty huge tracts of land in East Africa in 1884 and arranged for them to become a German protectorate. His method was to bribe or scare chieftains into signing one-sided treaties. The sultan of Zanzibar himself got a £200,000 bribe. Peters spent many years in Africa exploring and intriguing, and was very good at it. In 1889 he even gave the Masai a beating along the Tana River.

In 1890 the *Scottish Geographical Magazine* published reports first announcing and then confirming Peters's death in Africa, which was untrue. On 26 July 1889 Peters led an expedition up the Tana River, ostensibly to rescue Emin Pasha. His actual motive was to bolster the German claim on the region. He reached Lake Baringo on 7 January 1890 and Kavirondo a few weeks later. No word of his expedition had reached European ears save some vague reports of heavy fighting, and it was widely believed that he had perished. When he finally returned late in 1890 he had a case full of treaties signed by African chiefs in East Africa and Uganda, which unfortunately (from his perspective) had been rendered moot by an 1885 agreement between Germany and Great Britain.

Appointed imperial commissioner for German East Africa in 1891, Peters was known for his brutal methods (his African name was Mkono-wa-damu, "man of bloodstained hands"). In 1897 those methods began to catch up with him. He was brought up before a colonial court and charged with "indiscipline." The indiscipline consisted of hanging his young African servant, a youth named Mabruk, for stealing Peters's cigars and sleeping with Peters's teenaged native mistress, Jagodja. Jagodja was hanged too, after a brutal, sadistic flogging. Note that the charge was not murder: In the eyes of the German government the offense was that the hangings had been done without even the pretense of a trial. To the surprise of many, the brutal official was convicted. The sentence, however, was merely dismissal from the colonial service and forfeiture of his pension. No criminal sanction was ever imposed.

The scandal caused an uproar in Germany. As late as 1906 the Peters case was still causing heated debate in the Reichstag in Berlin. Most of the German public felt that Peters had been treated unfairly.

For his part, Peters moved to England and lived there until 1914, lecturing and writing several books. He married a woman named Thea Herbers and then, on the eve of war, returned to Germany, where he was universally regarded as a hero. He died in 1918, just before Germany's collapse. When Hitler and the Nazis took over in the 1930s, Peters was lionized as a symbol of Germany's heroic past. Hitler personally ordered all three of Peters's books republished in new editions. The 15 September 1938 issue of the monthly Nazi veteran's magazine, *Deutsche Kolonial-Dienst (German Colonial Service),* ran a laudatory article called "The Ideas and Actions of Dr. Karl Peters." Column headings of this article, written in connection with the twentieth anniversary of Peters's death, included "Lebensraum for the Germans!" "Act, Don't Talk!" and other catchy phrases demonstrating just how neatly Karl Peters fit into the National Socialist scheme of things. He was truly a man before his time.

Peters, Wilhelm Karl Hartwig (1815–1883). A German naturalist and traveler, Wilhelm Peters was the brother of Christian Peters, a famous nineteenth-century astronomer. Wilhelm explored Mozambique in 1843–1847 and was the author of *Natural History Trips in Mozambique* (1852–1882). Many of his descriptions of Zambezi Valley reptiles and amphibians are still referenced today.

Petherick, John (1813–1882). A burly Welshman with the beard of a Biblical patriarch, Petherick joined the Egyptian civil service in 1845. A mining engineer, he spent several years prospecting for coal in Kordofan and along the Red Sea. In 1848 there was a change of regime in Cairo and Petherick quit the Egyptian service and set himself up as a gum and resin trader in Kordofan. Eight years later he decided to enter the ivory trade and began traveling along the White Nile.

A gifted naturalist, he was the first European to discover the antelope then called Mrs. Gray's waterbuck and now known as the Nile lechwe *(Kobus megaceros),* and the whale-headed stork *(Balaeniceps rex).* He was also probably the first European to visit many of the tribes of the White Nile and Sudan.

In 1858 Petherick was appointed the British vice consul in Khartoum. With his new wife Kate (who he married on a brief trip back to England in 1861) constantly sharing his hardships, along with an intrepid young English assistant named Foxcroft, he now did a good deal of exploring, hunting, and ivory trading in the west Nile area. His books, *Egypt, the Soudan, and Central Africa* (1861) and, with Mrs. Petherick as coauthor, *Travels in Central Africa* (1869), contain a good amount of hunting and natural-history information.

The turning point in Petherick's life came when he promised John Hanning Speke that he would meet him with supplies at Gondokoro at the close of the latter's Nile-source expedition. Speke was late for the rendezvous. The Pethericks, who relied on trading to supplement the meager consular salary, in the meantime made a short trip to collect some ivory. Speke never forgave Petherick for not being there when he staggered out of the equatorial wilderness. Petherick had been entrusted with money raised by subscription in England to buy supplies for Speke and Grant, and Speke felt strongly that Petherick should have held this duty sacred above all others. Neither Samuel Baker and Florence Baker nor the Pethericks themselves were able to smooth things over in this matter, although Speke (who was rather unstable at this time) did seem to relax a little and left the Pethericks a friendly note when he left the Sudan.

On Speke's return to England, however, he set out to ruin the vice consul, going so far as to accuse him of trading in slaves. Other members of the European community in Khartoum, many of whom had connections to the slavery industry themselves, were eager to back Speke up on this. For the most part their testimony has been dismissed as perjury designed to rid themselves of a conscientious foe. Petherick, in truth, seems to have been somewhat less than energetic in his antislavery campaign, at least by British Victorian standards. Part of his job as vice consul was to combat the slavers, and his efforts to do so have been termed sporadic and inconsistent. All that means is that he was no Harry Johnston or Sam Baker or Richard Burton; it

John Petherick.

does not necessarily follow that he was in cahoots with the slavers. Due to Speke's fame and influence, Petherick was publicly excoriated, and the vice consulate in Khartoum was disbanded. The abuse that Petherick and his unfortunate wife had to endure was almost beyond belief. Kate's fate, in particular, seems all the more unfair when you consider how Florence Baker was being lionized for doing much as Kate had done. Inevitably, however, a backlash set in and, particularly after Speke's sudden death in 1864, Petherick's good name was restored, to an extent.

Modern researchers disagree about whether Petherick was just ineffective at fighting the slaving interests or culpable to the extent of allowing his subordinates to engage in slave raiding. There was also an allegation that he fabricated some of his adventures by writing about places he had never actually visited, particularly in his 1861 book. Petherick's case seems to me to be an object lesson in how financial distress can pervert an otherwise decent man. He was always under the gun for money, always had to hustle for it. In addition to ivory trading, he collected birds and small mammals for the European pet and zoo markets. Like a bartender or department-store cashier who is desperate for money, the temptation to cheat a bit—just this one time only—must have been overwhelming. Even if he successfully fought off the temptation, the stress must have been enormous. If Petherick had had the financial resources of Baker, say, or Harry Johnston, or the backing that Henry Stanley could always rely upon, he could have devoted all of his considerable talents and energies to his official duties, and there is no doubt in my mind that he would be remembered as one more honorable, devoted servant of the Empire. As it was, those duties had to take a back seat to just keeping his head above water, and it is a shame that at the moment of his greatest success the whole Speke affair blew up in his face and virtually ruined him. Many of the glories of the Victorian Age arose from the fact that there was an entire class of people wealthy and privileged enough to never have to really work for a living, and they could dedicate themselves to art, science, literature, and the building of an empire without worrying about paying the mortgage or having the telephone shut off. It was Petherick's misfortune to be on the fringe of that group, connected and talented enough to gain entry but not rich enough so that money was never an issue.

Pettitt, Harry. Harry Pettitt and his brother were two young professional elephant hunters who built a trading station at Chiromo, Nyasaland Protectorate, in 1889. In 1892 Harry Pettitt presented Sir Harry Johnston with a pair of rhino horns he had "obtained" in Portuguese East Africa south of the River Ruo. The horns appeared to have come from a white rhino as opposed to a black rhino, but the southern white rhino was virtually extinct at that time and certainly hadn't been seen in Portuguese East Africa for decades. Recording this in 1897, Johnston isn't clear whether Pettitt picked the horns up in a trade or was claiming to have shot the animal himself—the words chosen seem to indicate a trade. The horns in question were apparently sent to the British Museum in time.

Phillips, Ethelbert E. Lort (1857–1941). British sportsman and naturalist who was a sort of "Jonah," at least on safari in Africa. In the 1880s he was hunting in Somaliland with a man named Ingram who was killed by an elephant that they were stalking. Lort Phillips was unhurt. A few years later, on 21 April 1890, Lort Phillips was again elephant hunting, this time in West Africa with his old friend Frank Linsly James. History repeated itself and James, a very experienced hunter, was killed; Lort Phillips again went unscathed. Lort Phillips had been a participant in James's expeditions to Somaliland and the Sudan in 1881–1882 and 1884. He was the author of several works on ornithology. ROWLAND WARD 1928: BUFFALO (ABYSSINIA). ROWLAND WARD 1899: SCOTTISH RED DEER, IMPALA, SPEKE GAZELLE, HEUGLIN GAZELLE, GERENUK, ROAN, GREATER KUDU, LESSER KUDU, ABYSSINIAN BUFFALO.

Phillips, George Arthur "Big" (1837–1896). An early South African hunter, Phillips was also known as "Elephant" Phillips and "The Playful Elephant." I suspect he was a big man. He first came to Mashonaland in 1864, hunting variously with Finaughty, Hartley, Gifford, Haws Hai, Leask, and Edward Chapman. In 1872 Selous found him acting as interpreter for Lobengula. At the time Selous apparently was a sorry sight. Lobengula mocked his request to hunt elephant, hinting that he was only a child (Selous was twenty), and Phillips gave the future legend a goat to eat. Phillips remained in Mashonaland until he retired to England in 1890. He died at sea six years later.

Phillips, F. G. Lort. The nephew of E. E. Lort Phillips, he had a peripheral role in the Donaldson Smith expedition to Lake Rudolf in 1894. He returned to Somaliland with his uncle in 1897 and thereafter spent many years hunting in the far corners of the world, shooting in Europe, Asia, and North America as well as Africa. In 1931 he published a book of his hunting adventures, *The Wander Years.*

Piaggia, Carlo (1830–1882). An Italian explorer and natural-history collector, Piaggia first came to Africa as a youngster. In 1856 he was in Khartoum, in 1860 Bahr el Ghazal, in 1871–1876 Abyssinia, in 1876 the Nile lakes. He was the first Westerner to meet the Nyam-Nyam tribes. After his death the Berlin Museum obtained his anthropological collection.

Pickering, William A. (1883–1914). Elephant hunter of the Lado Enclave in the 1900s. John Boyes called him (1927) "above the average as a hunter." Pickering was born in London and served in the British army until 1905, fighting in South Africa during the Boer War. Upon entering civilian life, he went to Mombasa where he accidentally shot and killed a Hindu bystander while carelessly handling a handgun. He spent three months in jail for this mishap and paid a heavy fine.

Pickering continued to have more than his share of bad luck, including being captured by Belgian troops about 1907 before the Belgians evacuated the Lado region. Held for poaching, he managed to escape and fled through the jungle, barefoot and almost naked. He finally reached safety in the camp of another hunter named Knowles. For a time he went legitimate, working for the Uganda Public Works Department. Pickering spent the better part of seven years stalking the elephant herds in Uganda, the Lado Enclave, the Belgian Congo, and Sudan, often hooking up with Bill Buckley, F. N. Clarke, and two friends named Knowles and Dickenson. By and large he was a successful hunter, displaying great skill and bringing in unusually large loads of ivory from his forays into the bush. Estimates of his total bag range from three to five hundred elephants.

Pickering is another one whose death has been told in a number of variations, the result of the evolution of the story as told over sundowners. The following is the most popular version. Pickering, age thirty-one, was hunting for ivory in the Lado Enclave. He had just shot one of the greatest elephants ever, a monstrous bull with tusks that weighed 191 and 193 pounds. His very next time out, Pickering froze up when charged by a male elephant; he was paralyzed and just couldn't bring himself to pull the trigger of his .577 Express (another version claims that his rifle simply misfired). The bull knocked him down, stepped on his chest, and pulled his head off with its trunk. Fellow hunter F. N. Clarke was camped a few miles away and was the first to see Pickering's body after his trackers brought the news. Months later Clarke was hunting elephant along the Semliki River when he, too, froze up in the act of shooting. Fortunately, his elephant didn't charge, and Clarke quit professional ivory hunting right then and there.

Piggott, L. In 1908 Piggott was a district commissioner at Neri in Kenya, where one of his duties was to eliminate a man-eating leopard that had killed at least six African children. While Piggott was stalking the marauder and setting gun traps, it attacked and killed a seventh victim but was in turn speared to death by two elderly warriors. The leopard was found to be an old beast, starving and with poor teeth. At the same time as the leopard attacks, Piggott's district was also plagued by a number of particularly aggressive rhino that had killed numerous people. He was forced to conduct an anti-rhino campaign similar to the later one by John Hunter at Makueni, although on a much smaller scale.

Pitman, Charles Robert Senhouse (1890–1975). C. R. S. Pitman came from a prominent family in Dawlish, England; his father was a city council member and chairman of the county education committee. The younger Pitman was commissioned as a second lieutenant in the Indian army on 8 September 1909. The following year he was assigned as the commanding officer of two infantry companies in the 27th Punjabis. He was promoted to lieutenant on 8 December 1911.

Pitman served in France during the First World War. He was promoted to temporary captain on 8 September 1915 (the rank was made effective on 1 September 1916). On St. Patrick's Day 1917, he was awarded the DSO for conspicuous gallantry in leading a raiding party that inflicted much damage and captured an enemy trench mortar.

After the war, Pitman moved to Uganda and became the country's senior game warden in 1924. His office was at Entebbe. His entire staff consisted of two English rangers and a number of African scouts. He was fortunate in that his two European rangers were Samaki Salmon and Deaf Banks, both excellent field men. It has been estimated that Pitman shot 100 crocodiles and nearly 4,000 elephants (with help from African rangers) while on control work.

Pitman was one of the first game rangers to take a scientific approach toward game management. He kept careful track of elephant mortality, noting in 1927 that the annual death rate from all causes, including sport hunting and control work, was still less than the yearly natural increase. One of his most significant accomplishments was his completion of a monumental game survey of Northern Rhodesia in 1931–1932, published in 1934 as *A Report on a Faunal Survey of Northern Rhodesia.* This groundbreaking study (five hundred pages and a second volume of maps) was used as a basis for wildlife and conservation decisions for the next twenty-five years, until superseded by a similar survey by F. Fraser Darling. Pitman made several critical recommendations, such as the formation of an independent game department, a revision of the hunting schedules, buffalo reduction, and formalized elephant control. He also advised that measures be taken to protect the vulnerable lechwe population and that a national park be established in the Kafue reserve.

Pitman was the chairman of the Uganda Society in the 1940s. For some years he was involved in the investigation of a mystery animal called the Ntarago, a mysterious cryptid that combined features of a hyena and a leopard. A skull supposedly from this creature was given by a villager to Capt. Tracy Philips; Provincial Commissioner Temple-Perkins, himself a big-game hunter and naturalist, investigated the object and concluded that the skull belonged to a misshapen hyena.

In memory of his father, Pitman once donated a breeding pair of black swans to his hometown of Dawlish. Their descendents are still living in local parks. Pitman was the author of many magazine articles and the books *A Game Warden among his Charges* (1931) and *A Game Warden Takes Stock.* ROWLAND WARD 1928: SITATUNGA, KLIPSPRINGER.

Pocock, Edward and Francis Pocock. The Pocock brothers, boatmen from the Medway, accompanied Stanley to Africa. Edward died of fever in 1875, and Francis drowned in the Congo two years later.

Pogge, Paul (1838–1884). A German explorer, he first visited Africa at Natal in 1864. In 1875–1876 he explored the Lunda country and then, accompanied by Hermann von Wissmann, started out from Angola in an expedition attempting to cross the continent. He returned to Loanda due to illness and died there in 1884, while Von Wissmann continued on to Zanzibar.

Pollock, A. J. A. Pollock, an officer of the Royal Scots Fusiliers and a noted international big-game hunter, was the author of *Sporting Days in Southern India* (1894). He frequently shot in Africa as well. ROWLAND WARD 1928: TOPI (NO. 1, 22¼ INCHES, ABYSSINIAN BORDER), LICHTENSTEIN HARTEBEEST, HIPPO, ELEPHANT.

Pollok, Fitzwilliam Thomas. A schoolmate of Charles Gordon, Pollok served for many years in India as an officer of the Madras Staff Corps. He married Agnes Campbell in 1859. Pollok was a prolific hunter and the author of *Wild Sports of Burma* and *Incidents of Foreign Sports and Travel* (1894). The latter book contains the usual material on shooting lions and tigers, but is particularly noteworthy for one sequence where Pollok claims to have killed a gorilla by punching it to death. The story goes that Pollok and his tracker were captured by a savage tribe and tossed into a primitive arena to fight to the death with the ape. The gorilla, an adult male, killed the tracker but was then killed by a body blow from Pollok. The author mitigated his remarkable claim by speculating that the gorilla may have been suffering from a previously incurred internal injury.

Polson, George and Arthur Polson. This set of brothers hunted and traded in the Zambezi Valley and South-West Africa around 1860. On one 1861 expedition George Polson and his partner (a man named Kenny) accumulated over three thousand pounds of ivory.

Poncet, Jules. Jules Poncet and his brothers operated elephant-hunting rings in the Sudan in the mid to late nineteenth century. Based in Khartoum, they hunted by themselves as well as having large numbers of "guns in the bush," and collectively were responsible for the destruction of large numbers of elephant, including twenty-eight in one day and seventy more over a two-week period. The Brothers Poncet had originally been invited to Khartoum by their uncle, a Piedmontese trader named Vaudet, who held a post as the Sardinian consul. Uncle Vaudet was killed by Bari tribesmen near Gondokoro in 1859. Jules Poncet was the author of an 1863 book, *Le Fleuve Blanc.*

Pooley, George. Professional hunter in Portuguese East Africa, early twentieth century. Known for hunting buffalo for rations and hides.

Pope, Saxton (1875–1926). An American doctor from Texas, Pope became interested in archery when he was treating a Native American named Ishi, the last surviving member of California's Yahi tribe. In 1925 Pope and his friend Art Young joined writer Stewart Edward White on a bowhunting trip to Tanganyika and the Serengeti. During this seven-month safari he and his friends shot fifty-two male lion. Pope wrote a book about the expedition entitled *The Adventurous Bowmen* (1926).

Port, Attila. Of German descent, Atti Port was a farmer and hunter in Rehoboth, near Windhoek in South-West Africa. He liked to keep game on his extensive farmlands and so was very active in predator control, killing his first leopard at the age of thirteen. He looked the part of a rugged outdoorsman—his twenty-fourth leopard managed to inflict serious and permanent facial scars on him before dying.

Port, a huge man, worked hard to protect his livestock and acquired a reputation for predator control. Thereafter he was often hired by other farms and ranches to reduce problem leopard, lion, and wild dogs. As his fame as a hunter spread, he was also hired to do collecting work for museums.

Portal, Sir Gerald (1858–1894). Portal was a British civil servant who was active in East Africa in the 1890s. He entered the diplomatic service in 1879. His first post was in Rome, and in 1882 Portal was transferred to the staff of Sir Evelyn Baring in Egypt, where he monitored the Arabi rebellion and the bombardment of Alexandria. For actions during this period Portal was awarded the Khedive's Star plus a British campaign medal with clasp. In 1884 Portal was assigned to the British Ministry at Cairo.

In 1887 Portal was sent on his first independent venture, a diplomatic mission to Abyssinia. He failed to achieve the mission's stated purpose (to mediate the dispute between the Ethiopians and the Italians), but it was obviously not his fault that the Italians decided to go to war, and he was made a CB (Commander of the Bath). He wrote a book about the expedition titled *My Mission to Abyssinia* (1892).

He was appointed commissioner and consul general at Zanzibar in early 1891. At the end of 1892 Portal was made a KCMG (see glossary) and sent into Uganda to report on the administration of the Imperial British East Africa Company.

The expedition was a large one. Officers included Portal, his brother, Capt. Raymond Portal, Col. Frank Rhodes (the brother of Cecil), Major Owen of the Lancashire Fusiliers, Lieutenant Arthur of the Rifle Brigade, consular official Ernest Berkeley, medical officer Dr. Robert Moffatt, and an IBEA (see glossary) representative named Foaker. Also in the group were a British officer on leave, Lieutenant Villiers of the Royal Horse Guards, who cancelled his plans for a hunting trip to Kilimanjaro to tag along as a supernumerary, and Portal's plucky servant Hutchisson, who had faithfully followed his employer through the Abyssinian wastes five years earlier. The African staff consisted of more than three hundred fifty porters carrying food, ammunition, tents, trade beads, tools, medical supplies, and the like, and a number of headmen, cooks, and "tent-boys," for a total of four hundred men.

There was also an escort of two hundred askaris from the Sultan of Zanzibar's army, commanded by Lieutenant Arthur. These men were picked for their physical fitness and were outfitted with khaki uniforms and Snider rifles. Portal recruited so many of them because he was unsure of the situation in Uganda. Some reports indicated that the entire British garrison, composed mainly of Sudanese troops and holdovers from Emin Pasha's army, had deserted upon the collapse of IBEA rule. As it turned out, Portal found the Zanzibaris, who cut a promising figure on parade, to be worse than useless. The Sudanese had not deserted, and there were enough soldiers in Uganda for occupation purposes. In his memoir of the campaign Portal expressed regret that he had brought the Sultan's troops along at all.

When he finally got there, Portal found the situation in Uganda to be deteriorating rapidly, largely due to the IBEA's lack of ready funds. The IBEA had already announced its intention to withdraw from the country. Concerned that the resulting instability might lead to a massive shedding of blood in Uganda's ongoing religious wars, Portal took matters into his own hand by declaring (without legal authority) the area to be a British Protectorate. A few months later the British Parliament promptly ratified his act by legalizing the Protectorate. In a time before instant worldwide communication, it was decisive action by men like Portal that often carried the day.

Portal left a memoir of the Uganda mission, half-finished at the time of his death, as well as a diary. They reveal him as an intelligent young man, not devoid of charm and humor, and a typical British imperialist in his thoughts and designs. Considering his ultimate fate and that of his brother, these are touching documents, and Portal's pain in writing about his brother's death is still heart-wrenching over a century later.

There are some humorous touches as well. When he first entered Uganda at the head of his column, Portal found his way blocked by the military guard of an African king, who was justifiably proud of their high state of drill and discipline. Portal inspected the impressive soldiers, who were drawn up in a line across the road, then indicated his satisfaction and, with effusive praise, told the king he had to move on. The king didn't understand and thought Portal was merely complimenting his men. Portal pointed several times to the troops, and again the king nodded thankfully at the praise. Even marching straight up to the soldiers, in the hope that they might part and let him through, only caused them instead to arch their backs even straighter and present arms with a flourish. Finally one of Portal's men who spoke the local language hollered out something incomprehensible, and immediately the guards performed a perfect about-face and proudly marched off. Portal later asked his man, "What did you say to them?" The reply was, "Get out of the way, you idiots!"

Uganda was a hard country in those days. Portal was originally impressed by its natural beauty and the educated inhabitants. After dealing with the primitive tribes of western Kenya, Portal was pleasantly surprised when the first man he met on the road in Uganda refused beads and trade goods as a present and asked instead for something to read, preferably in Swahili or the local language. Later experiences, however, caused him to despise the place. In his book he compared Uganda to a marble tomb, glorious and shining on the outside but rank and decaying on the inside. Because memoirs are written by survivors, it is easy to forget how precarious life was in the old Africa, and how much of the continent earned the name "white man's grave."

The sobriquet was appropriate in Portal's case. His older brother, Capt. Raymond Portal, who accompanied him to Uganda and carried out some important scouting work, died of malaria in May 1893. Portal's book contains a copy of a wrenching letter he wrote to their mother informing her of Raymond's death.

Gerald Portal himself, a pillar of the Empire and described by Charles Miller (*The Lunatic Express,* 1971) as "exceptionally brilliant and almost impossibly handsome"), lasted only a bit longer, dying on 25 January 1894, shortly after he returned to England. He was healthy and in good spirits on the ship home and for his first week or so in London. Then he suddenly took sick and faded fast. His death was attributed to malaria and typhoid fever. While still in Africa he had written to his mother that the one good thing that came out of the Uganda mission was that he and his dead brother had very much enjoyed their time together.

As mentioned above, Portal kept a daily diary during his Uganda expedition. Lengthy portions are reprinted in *The British Mission to Uganda in 1893.* It is worth reading from a sportsman's point of view if only because it shows just how important sport shooting was in the hearts and minds of the Victorian gentleman. Here's Portal in the midst of the most important, indeed the climactic, event of his life, his own brother and other men dying around him, so busy and often sick and tired himself that usually he can just manage a short journal entry at the end of each day. But he never forgets to comment on the day's shooting: For instance, 12 September 1893: "Remained in tent all day, to give chance of healing to sore feet, and also because no boots. Hutchisson mending one pair. Only one guinea-fowl between three of us all day." Between 26 August and 14 October, Gerry Portal, Frank Rhodes, and Hutchisson shot and killed (according to the diary) fifteen Kirk dik-dik (called by Portal the little Kirk's gazelle), seven impala, four waterbuck, three wildebeest, four Thomson gazelle, ten hippo, four hartebeest, one rhino, one bushbuck, one hog, thirty-six guinea fowl, seven partridge, three geese, two stork, two francolin, and two sand grouse. On 30 August Rhodes shot a twelve-foot crocodile "of enormous girth." Most of the animals and birds went to feed the officers and men, but Portal did skin the heads of the wildebeest, the rhino, and most of the larger antelope for his collection. Unfortunately, the trophies were lost when two careless porters capsized a canoe on 9 October 1893.

Portal, Raymond Melville (1856–1893). Gerry Portal's older brother and subordinate, Capt. Raymond Portal was educated at Eton and at Balliol, where he excelled at athletics. He then decided on a military career and attended Sandhurst, but due to an obscure army regulation he was too old (and therefore ineligible) for a regular commission and could only be commissioned into a colonial regiment. He became a second lieutenant in the First West India Regiment in 1881, and thereafter served in Ireland (seconded to the 52nd Regiment of Foot for training purposes) and Sierra Leone, his first taste of Africa. After a severe bout with a tropical fever, he exchanged into the 81st Foot, a regiment on the regular establishment.

By 1893 Raymond had risen to the rank of captain and the post of adjutant to the mounted infantry at Aldershot in England. At this point his brother Gerry, who had risen to prominence in the Colonial Office, arranged to get him seconded to the Uganda expedition of 1894. Raymond excelled as a sort of executive officer, and in April was sent along with a Major Owen to the Toro district, where they hoped to recruit some Sudanese askaris. Portal was stricken with fever, possibly complicated by sunstroke, but refused to halt the expedition to rest. By the time he rejoined his brother in late May, Raymond had a constant fever of 101 to 102 degrees. He died late in the afternoon of May 27 and was buried the next day. The sparse portrait of him in *The British Mission to Uganda in 1893* is of a quiet, hard-working, dutiful man, deserving of a better fate than a swampy grave in a desolate outpost of Empire.

Portions of his diary were printed in his brother's book. The entry for 14 April 1893, during the Toro excursion, reads: "One of our cows was killed by lion last night. Didn't know there were any."

Posselt Brothers. Harry and Willie Posselt were hunters in the Zambezi Valley in the last decades of the nineteenth century. They were among the first to visit the ruins at Great Zimbabwe. At least one of the brothers worked as a British scout during the invasion of Matabeleland in 1893.

Postma. This Boer teamster camped one night near Deepdale Drift in Kenya. No sooner had he inspanned early the next morning when a pride of about thirteen lion attacked his oxen. He jumped atop his wagon and cut loose with his .350 Mauser-action Rigby, killing seven of the animals (another account says nine). For this affair he was much feted by the company of hunters in Kenya. The evening before this incident, Postma had met Denis Lyell on the trail and had stopped for tea. Lyell later wrote (1935) that he always wondered what part Postma's Great Dane had played in the lion affair.

Potocki, Count Jozef Nicolas Xavier Maria Alfred Jacob (1862–1922). A great sportsman, Count Jozef Potocki was born in Lwow (Lemberg) on 9 September 1862. A lawyer by training (he studied law at Lwow and Vienna), he was a leading member of the Polish aristocracy and a breeder of fine racehorses, including the legendary Skowronek, one of the greatest names in the history of racing. Potocki was also a top-notch huntsman and hunted in Africa on many occasions, up until just before his death in the early 1920s. During his lifetime he was internationally famous for his hunting adventures on several continents. His other interests included running a railroad company, politics, and fine art. Potocki married Princess Helena Radziwill (1874–1958) in Berlin on 28 April 1892.

Potocki's holdings included a magnificent six-thousand-hectare game park known as Pilawin. The reserve was home to herds of American and European bison, wapiti, roebuck, and many other ungulates. The estate was described by Lydekker in 1908 in *A Trip to Pilawin*, an excellent book for anybody interested in the old European game parks.

Pilawin and the rest of the count's holdings were pillaged by Bolshevik mobs during the Russian Revolution. Most of the fine Arabian horses were butchered by the attackers, and the houses burned to the ground. Potocki himself was shot and killed by Red Army deserters on the steps of his mansion at Slawuta in 1922.

Potocki was the author of several books, but only *Sport in Somaliland* (1900) is available in English. His other works include a two-volume description of shooting in India and Ceylon. The Potocki family now runs a distillery that produces an excellent high-grade vodka. ROWLAND WARD 1928: KONGONI, LEOPARD.

Potter, H. B. Game conservator of Zululand in the 1930s, his headquarters were in the Hluhluwe Reserve and his bailiwick also included the Mkuzi and Umfolozi reserves. He deserves a lot of the credit for safeguarding the few remaining white rhino during their period of greatest peril.

Powell, E. Alexander (1879–1957). A popular travel writer of his day, Powell made several trips to Africa. He was the author of numerous books, including *Fighting in Flanders* (1914), *The Map That Is Half Unrolled* (1925), and *In Barbary* (1926).

Powell-Cotton, Percy Horace Gordon (1866–1940). A wealthy British sportsman who gained great renown as a hunter, P. H. G. Powell-Cotton was born in Kent in 1866. Highly regarded, courteous, and refined, he inherited a fortune and a lavish estate in Kent called Quex Park in 1894. Already an experienced sportsman, Powell-Cotton first tried Africa the next year, going on safari in Somaliland. In 1897 he did his hunting in India and Tibet, but every year thereafter (except during World War I) he took an annual safari in Africa. His last trip ended in 1939, when he was seventy-three years old.

The 1899–1900 safari was of particular interest. Powell-Cotton was one of several men, under the leadership of the Britisher James Harrison and the American William Whitehouse, who ventured into the Lake Turkana wilderness to hunt and to survey the terrain between Hawash Valley and the lake. The expedition had the blessing of the Ethiopian Emperor, Menelik, which ironically caused some friction. The men set out in November 1899. Powell-Cotton was under the impression that the hunting part of the program was to be carried out in the interests of science. Hence, he hunted only those rare or spectacular animals that he felt might make a real contribution to natural history. Harrison, however, a brash and somewhat bullying type, was much less selective in determining what animals to shoot. When Harrison and the others shot and killed nine immature bull elephant in the Awash Valley with an average tusk weight of only seventeen pounds apiece, Powell-Cotton was disgusted and left the expedition soon afterward, in

January 1900. Not comprehending the problem, Harrison presented the diminutive tusks to the emperor Menelik as a gift. The British agent in Addis Ababa had to apologize to the emperor.

In 1902 Powell-Cotton was hunting near Lake Turkana when he stumbled upon a rock-strewn area near a stream that was literally covered with elephant bones. The distinguished sportsman was certain he had found the legendary elephant graveyard. In time several more of these bone deposits were found. It was game warden Blayney Percival, however, who pieced together the puzzle. The elephant in these graveyards had not died natural deaths—they had in fact been poisoned by Turkana hunters and, driven mad with thirst from the poison, took the path of least resistance to the nearest water. There they had died, the natives taking their tusks and meat.

For his honeymoon in 1908 Powell-Cotton, a romantic sort, took his bride on safari in Uganda. During this trip he was mauled by a lion and survived only because a courageous porter battled the beast with a stick, distracting it long enough for an askari to come up and shoot it. Mrs. Powell-Cotton's thoughts on all this have not been recorded.

Powell-Cotton was the epitome of the upper-class, wealthy British big-game hunter. His civility and self-possession were universally admired, and he possessed the peculiar reserve and dryness that was one of the hallmarks of English aristocracy. On one trip to West Africa, Powell-Cotton was reading in his tent, his stomach a bit upset, while Fred Merfield went out to shoot some francolin with a .22-caliber rifle. Crawling through some bushes, Merfield came face to face with an equally surprised lion, and considered himself lucky to crawl back out the way he'd come. After breathlessly telling the tale to Powell-Cotton, Merfield was chagrined to be asked, "Why didn't you shoot the beast?" Merfield gestured to the .22 and said something about a peashooter. Powell-Cotton wasn't impressed, remarking, "I should have thought that a hunter of your skill could have shot him through the eye. Even a .22 bullet would have been fatal at that range if it were properly placed," before turning back to his book (Merfield, 1957).

Powell-Cotton devoted himself to creating one of the finest collections of its time, now the Powell-Cotton Museum of African Fauna and Ethnology at Quex Park. In it are over six thousand mammal specimens representing forty-one species and subspecies. One was the world-record tallest elephant of its time, at 11 feet, 6½ inches. Six Abyssinian ibex that he shot in 1900 were the only ones collected by a non-native until 1924.

Powell-Cotton wrote several books (see Bibliography for details) and was a contributor to *Big Game Shooting in Africa* (1932), part of the Lonsdale Library. ROWLAND WARD 1928: ELEPHANT (NO. 1, 198 AND 174 POUNDS, LAKE ALBERT), SPOTTED HYENA (NO. 1, 2, 3), ABYSSINIAN IBEX, WHITE ORYX, WESTERN ROAN ANTELOPE, GIRAFFE, VARIOUS HARTEBEEST, VARIOUS DUIKER, BUFFALO, LAKE CHAD RED BUFFALO, DORCAS GAZELLE, KLIPSPRINGER, BOHOR REEDBUCK, SITATUNGA, KUDU, BONGO, IMPALA, DAMA GAZELLE, GIANT ANGOLAN SABLE, LORD DERBY ELAND, INDIAN BUFFALO, ASIAN SLOTH BEAR, TIBETAN ANTELOPE, BROWN BEAR.

Preston, Ronald O. (c. 1870–c. 1951). Ronald Preston and his older sister were abandoned at an orphanage in India in the 1870s. Fortunately, his sister married a hard-working, decent British soldier who took it upon himself to educate his little orphaned brother-in-law. Trained as an engineer, Ronald Preston worked on the Madras Harbor and the Godavari Bridge until the opportunity came to go to Africa.

The nature of that opportunity was the Uganda Railroad, called the "Lunatic Line" or "Lunatic Express" by its critics. The hope was that a railroad from Mombasa to Lake Victoria would open up the interior of Kenya and the lush paradise of Uganda to settlement and development. It didn't really work out that way—the railroad provided no significant boost to the local economy. But it was all a part of the opening up of Africa, and a brilliant opportunity for a young engineer like Preston.

His biggest problems were the lack of labor and infrastructure. The local Africans were still too independent-minded to work on a railway crew. Their culture had no factories or assembly lines, and they frankly didn't understand the concept. They preferred instead to simply grow their own food and take it easy, a lifestyle that the Victorian English were determined to wipe out. For the time being, however, Preston and his men would have to rely on Indian labor, imported at great expense from Asia. The infrastructure problem was even worse. There was no contingency whatsoever to provide food and other supplies for the tens of thousands of men who would be needed for the project. Early on, even Preston was reduced to eating roadkill—steaks cut from the flesh of camels found dead on the trail.

A massive effort was made to get things going. The harbor at Mombasa, called Kilindini, was improved at great expense to accommodate modern ocean-going freighters. Teams of European riflemen, mainly young bucks with a taste for adventure like John Hunter, roamed the countryside shooting antelope for rations. Earlier railroad projects in Africa had relied on buffalo herds for food, but a great rinderpest epidemic in the mid-1890s had reduced the species to near-extinction.

Another problem was the local wildlife. The famous "man-eaters of Tsavo" ate hundreds of laborers and held up construction for weeks. Other lion terrorized the rail lines, including the ones that ate Ryall, the superintendent of railway police, and an engineer named O'Harra. Aggressive black rhino were prone to charging anybody who disturbed their rest. Dangerous animals came in all sizes, even microscopic—blackwater fever and malaria killed more laborers than all the lion and rhino of Africa combined. Of the approximately thirty-five thousand Indians who came to East Africa to work on the railroad, 2,493 died during the job and 6,454 others were permanently injured.

Some of the more aggressive local Africans caused problems as well. Several railway gangs were attacked by the Nandi near Lumbwa and massacred. The British prepared a punitive expedition but called it off when it was found that the Nandi had attacked out of anger over the molestation of their young women by the railroad workers. After a peace conference, the British and Nandi settled into an uneasy truce.

Work on the rail line began in February of 1897. The railhead moved forward in spurts and stops, dependent largely upon the nature of the terrain. Tsavo was reached in December 1897, and Kima a year later. All work at the Kima railhead was suspended for two weeks in December 1898 when horrendous rains caused washouts and train derailments.

After Kima, Preston and his crews were able to pick up the pace. Nairobi was reached on 31 May 1899, and the Mau Summit, highest point on the route at 489 meters above sea level, in early 1901. The last leg was completed in good time, and the final spike was driven in by Mrs. Preston at Port Florence on Lake Victoria on 19 December 1901. The story that Port Florence (now Kisumu) was named after Mrs. Preston is not true; it was named after Florence Whitehouse, who visited the area with her explorer-husband George Whitehouse in 1898.

Lauded for his success, Preston decided to settle in his adopted country. He bought a farm in the highlands near Nairobi and lived out his life there in relative quiet. The 1930 *East African Red Book* gives his address as a Post Office Box in Nairobi. He was the author of *The Genesis of Kenya Colony* (1948), and died in Kenya around 1951. ROWLAND WARD 1928: GRANT GAZELLE.

Pretorius, Philip Jacobus (1873–1945). P. J. Pretorius was a South African hunter from the Transvaal who led one of those storybook careers that are the subject of legend. A descendant of the great Boer leader Pretorius (for whom the city of Pretoria was named), he nevertheless rendered great service to the British Crown. As a sixteen-year-old boy he got a job as a teamster for Cecil Rhodes's British South Africa Company. Four years later he drove a wagon during the 1893 Matabele War, after which he continued working in transport until he enlisted to fight in the 1896 rebellion in Mashonaland (the Mashonas, in a classic case of bad timing, decided to revolt against the British just after the Matabele were defeated in their own uprising), distinguishing himself as a scout in that short but bloody campaign.

In 1899 Pretorius purchased a .303 magazine rifle and took to the woods. He began hunting north of the Zambezi River with just a retinue of African servants for company, and got his first taste of life in the bush. It was the usual difficult African wilderness baptism of thirst, hunger, and dysentery, but he soon mastered the business, staying in the wilds of Zambezia for more than three years, occasionally going to the town of Zumbo for ammunition and other supplies. He was in such a remote area that he never heard of the Boer War, raging several hundred miles to the south, until it was over.

Pretorius shot his first lion in 1899 and his first elephant (he was to shoot 557 during his career) a year later. At this time of his life it appears that he was at least reasonably scrupulous in obtaining the proper game licenses. Pretorius would roam from the Kafue River in Rhodesia to German Tanganyika and Portuguese Mozambique, setting up camp in each place and hunting the district for several months. He would shoot plains game for the pot, an occasional buffalo for meat and leather, rhino for their meat and horns, and the rare elephant. A short, wiry, restless man, he traveled to Beira sometime around 1904 (getting his first look at an ocean) and took a steamer to Mombasa, from where he struck out for Mount Kilimanjaro. After a month or two there he moved north to Lake Victoria and settled for a while at a German-held village on the lake's southern end called Mwanza, where he built a house and started raising a herd of cows.

In short order he tired of the sedentary life and moved westward to Rwanda, where he set up shop to hunt elephant.

Pretorius was now in his early thirties. Hearing of a herd that lived in a local valley, he went out to scout one day. He found the herd's fresh spoor but didn't see an elephant in several hours of tracking. It was nearing five in the afternoon when he decided to call it quits for the day.

He had just exchanged his .500 Express rifle with his gunbearer for an 8mm rifle when suddenly a bull elephant charged him from a nearby bush. The gunbearer and the trackers all fled. Pretorius put four bullets from the light rifle into the elephant's head with no discernible effect. He turned to run but felt the animal's trunk grab him around the waist and lift him into the air. The fifth and last round in the rifle went off more or less accidentally, startling the bull, and instead of being hurled hard to the ground and then stomped, Pretorius was merely tossed about fifteen feet into a tree by the stunned creature.

He lay there for a minute trying to get his breath back and clear the blood from his eyes—his face had been ripped open by the thorns of the tree. By this time a cow elephant had also arrived on the scene. Pretorius played dead, but when the cow's attention wandered, he managed to grab his rifle, which had fortunately landed a few feet away. Reloading, he killed the cow with a shot to the spine. The bull, which had gone on some distance, turned, but Pretorius was able to stagger into thick brush and avoid the subsequent charge.

His injuries were relatively minor, and such accidents were but a staple of sporting life in those days. After a brief recovery, Pretorius finally managed to take a large safari to the Congo, where he made friends with the Pygmies and did a bit of hunting and trading. By now he had tired of wandering in strange places and decided to head back eastward, still accompanied by his large African staff and by some Pygmies who were acting as guides. Along the Kagera River he camped near an unfamiliar village. He tried to give some presents to the chief, a traditional gesture of peace, but the chief sternly refused and warned him to get out of the country. Pretorius decided that the chief and his people were cannibals. Heavily outnumbered, Pretorius reckoned that discretion was the better part of valor and packed up, leading his men east toward Tanganyika. He was aided in his decision by the discovery of numerous dead bodies strewn here and there around the village, all of them cut up and mutilated. By the river he discovered a pile of some sixteen heads and a variety of body parts.

As he was entering the Ruwenzori foothills, Pretorius got word that he was being followed by hundreds of the cannibals. Reaching a defensible plateau on a hillside, he decided to make a stand. Despite being warned, the cannibals charged, led by a witch doctor. Pretorius promptly shot the witch doctor dead, and the rest of the attackers dropped back. At the top of the hill Pretorius found several more beheaded and mutilated bodies.

Finally Pretorius and his safari reached safety—of a sort—in a friendly village. The Pygmy guides were still with him. After the usual exchanges of greetings and gifts, Pretorius and his men settled down for the night. No sooner had he done so than he was disturbed by the noise of the Pygmies gleefully cutting chunks of meat off a living cow. Disgusted, he ordered the poor beast to be killed before it was slaughtered. He went back to bed, only to be awakened once more, this time by shouts and fierce war cries. The Pygmies, it seemed, had raided the village garden and were making off with armloads of pea plants. The villagers were incensed, and a bitter fight was about to start. Pretorius managed to calm everyone down, paying the villagers off with calico for their losses and yelling at the Pygmies to behave. The Pygmies decided it was time to leave, and Pretorius agreed to give them an armed escort. They left, still with their pea plants, but when the escorts returned to the village days later they reported that five of the Pygmies had died from intestinal distress caused by overeating the unfamiliar legume.

You'd think this would have been enough for any one safari, but the worst was yet to come. A day or two later, Pretorius and his men, after an arduous trek through a dismal swamp, camped at an empty village. Several men went down to a stream to fetch water but soon came running back, yelling that they had been attacked and several men killed. Suddenly a large number of African warriors came cascading out of the bush, spearing the porters and pillaging the camp. Pretorius grabbed the nearest weapon—a shotgun—and fired into the mob of attackers until the gun's seams burst. Disarmed, he threw the worthless gun down and ran for his life, behind those of his retainers who could still run.

Pretorius and five of his men got away into the woods, armed only with a Mauser pistol and seven rounds of ammunition. They slept in the forest that night but at daybreak crept back to a point from where they could see their ransacked camp. The attackers were still there, just waking up in the ruins of his safari. Suddenly Pretorius spotted a group of Africans approaching the village along a path. He recognized them as twenty of his porters who had been straggling behind the main group for days but was powerless to help them. The unsuspecting porters entered the village and appeared, from Pretorius's vantage point, to get a friendly greeting from the raiders. But it was a ruse—the attackers marked the porters man for man, and at a signal leaped upon them and stabbed them to death with their spears while Pretorius watched. He wrote that watching his men be murdered was "one of the most distressing moments of my life." He didn't explain in his memoirs why he didn't at least fire a warning shot with his Mauser, but since nobody ever questioned his courage, we can be sure it must have been impractical.

To top it off, when Pretorius finally got back to German territory he was arrested and tried for the alleged murder of forty-seven Africans during his disastrous safari. This raises an interesting problem in writing the history of African big-game hunting. All we have is the white man's version. The Africans never wrote any memoirs or books about their experiences. The account as given above comes from Pretorius, and he seems a reasonably reliable source, but the cultural environment in Africa in those days made it perfectly feasible to treat the local people in an atrocious or even murderous fashion and then just lie about it. It has been established that the British hunter Henry Cavendish did just that, and few of the contemporaries of the Rhodesian Marcus Daly trusted his word. Certainly the surviving porters of Pretorius's group backed up his account, but the German authorities sentenced him to twelve months of jail time nonetheless (apparently for being overzealous while acting in self-defense), starting a bitter feud they would come to regret. As Pretorius had already been held for over two years, he was released at the conclusion of the trial. They also confiscated his herd of cattle at Mwanza, which had grown to over seven hundred head, citing concerns about rinderpest. They gave Pretorius remuneration that was only a fraction of the value, and he found himself penniless, with his one possession being an 8mm rifle.

In retrospect, this was a turning point in the life of Pretorius. During the first thirty-three years of his life he had been more of a wanderer than a professional hunter. He had certainly done a lot of shooting, but it was largely for the pot. He had taken the occasional elephant (and rhino and buffalo) just to pick up an odd buck or two here and there. But now he found himself in his mid-thirties in a foreign country, his only assets a rifle and his incomparable wilderness skills. On 27 October 1906 he left Dar es Salaam heading to the Rufiji River for the express purpose of making money by killing elephant.

The Rufiji at that time was an elephant hunter's paradise. It teemed with the animals, separate herds of cows and bulls seemingly on every horizon. The bull herds, Pretorius found, generally consisted of ten or twelve animals of all ages, from teenagers to grand tuskers that must have been sixty years old. He took to his new profession with a passion, every so often sending men back to Dar es Salaam to sell the ivory and pick up supplies. His longest tusks were a pair 9 feet, 3 inches in length, each weighing 120 pounds, while his heaviest was a shorter pair, only 8 feet in length, that rocked the scales at 160 pounds per side.

In 1907 Pretorius was hunting along the Rufiji. Earlier that day one of his trackers had killed a snake, and his superstitious Africans warned that this would bring bad luck on them all. "Don't you know that one of us will be killed?" they cried, but Pretorius laughed it off. Two miles down the road he fired at some elephant. A wounded bull charged him and knocked him down. Pretorius was very fortunate that the enraged animal kept on going rather than stopping to finish him off. As it was, he had a badly sprained ankle and decided it would be impossible to travel farther that day.

As they set up camp, with Pretorius immobile in his hammock, his servant Juma went to fetch water. Suddenly the wounded elephant returned and chased Juma with murder in its eyes. Juma ran back toward camp but realized he was bringing the bull directly to the injured Pretorius. Selflessly, he swerved so that the elephant would follow him.

The elephant was too fast to escape. It reached out with its trunk, grabbed Juma by the neck, and smashed him against the ground. Juma lay still as the elephant first stomped him, then picked him up again and threw him into the brush. It is thought he died instantly.

Despite this tragedy and other hardships, Pretorius found his new career to be stunningly successful. On the safari on which Juma was killed, Pretorius was out in the bush for six months and upon his return to Dar es Salaam sold his ivory for £3,600 pounds. This was a huge amount of money in those days, as much as many men would make in a decade. His success caused a sort of ivory rush among the Germans in the neighborhood. Several of them quit their day jobs and went on safari to elephant country, but they lacked the South African's bush skills and generally came to bad ends, a couple of them dying of fever and malnutrition and one having to be rescued by a German patrol from Dar es Salaam.

You would think Pretorius had turned the corner by this time career-wise, but this was not the case. The Germans, either concerned about the status of the Rufiji herds or jealous of the foreigner's success, cancelled his hunting license. No matter: Pretorius moved his operations to

Portuguese Nyasaland and hunted legally there with his friend, a Captain Hemming. The Germans, in the person of an officer with the unusual name of Hauptmann Blake, offered Pretorius a paltry sum for a farm he had bought with his ivory profits. Pretorius refused to sell, so they confiscated the farm under the doctrine of eminent domain. That was it—enough was enough. Pretorius vowed revenge. He sent a letter to the German authorities coolly advising them that he would now poach elephant in their territory until he had made good all of the losses he had suffered at their hands. From now on, it was war.

Pretorius spent the next few years carrying out his threat, repeatedly crossing the Ruvuma River into German East Africa, slaughtering choice elephant, and recrossing with the tusks back into Portuguese territory. After an initial reluctance, Hemming joined him on these expeditions, lured by the fantastic ivory Pretorius kept bringing back. The Germans sent patrols out to capture them, but the local natives hated the German administration and liked Pretorius, so the patrols continually came back empty-handed. This went on until 1914, when the Great War broke out.

When news of the declaration of war reached Pretorius, he and Hemming were deep in German territory, resting and idly planning a hunting trip to Liberia. The Germans looked upon the pair as potential enemy spies and sent a company of two hundred askaris under German officers to catch them. This column was big enough to intimidate the local Africans from protecting them, and the two British hunters found themselves in a very precarious position. They moved carefully toward the Ruvuma River, on the other side of which was neutral Portuguese territory and at least a chance for safety. Somebody undoubtedly betrayed them, probably fearing a firing squad, and one morning the Germans rushed the camp. Hemming was captured (he was later executed for firing on the Germans as a civilian), and Pretorius, badly wounded in both legs, escaped only by hiding in the croc-infested Ruvuma River. He struggled to a patch of weeds and lay there quietly, waiting for the enemy to leave while a school of small fish nipped savagely at his wound.

When the Germans finally gave up the search, Pretorius began one of the most excruciating journeys on record. Unable to walk (his right leg was broken) and unarmed, he struggled to a nearby village on the other side of the Ruvuma, in Portuguese territory. His only hope was to somehow reach the British colony at Nyasaland, but getting there seemed impossible. A patrol of Portuguese askaris arrived and arrested him, telling him they had orders to turn him over to the Germans, some of whom were on their way. He lay in the village for days, despairing of life, and there is little doubt he would have died then and there if his gunbearer, Saidi, had not suddenly appeared at the village, having somehow escaped the German attack. Even better, Saidi still had Pretorius's .303 rifle and twenty rounds of ammunition. Hope surged within the hunter's breast.

Knowing you might get to safety and getting there are two different things, however. The rifle convinced the Portuguese askaris to release him, but Pretorius was still deep in foreign territory and unable to walk. He solved the latter problem by kidnapping some unfriendly Africans at gunpoint and forcing them to carry him on a *machila,* or litter. The reluctant men had to be tied to the litter to keep them from running away.

Pretorius eventually made it, after a variety of adventures including cutting the pus out of his infected leg with a knife and spending several days delirious, during which time he casually ordered Saidi to transfer him to a nice comfortable round bed without corners. But he finally arrived at a friendly mission, and the missionary, an old friend of his, helped nurse him back to health.

Once recovered, he had an easy trip (by Pretorius's standards) to British territory and from there to South Africa. On arriving in his native land he was surprised to get a message to report to Royal Naval headquarters. There he was commissioned to help discover the whereabouts of a German warship, the cruiser SMS *Koenigsberg.* The British knew the *Koenigsberg* was in African waters, but they didn't know where. As long as the warship was in the vicinity, it posed a deadly threat to the vital oceanic lifeline around the Cape.

The *Koenigsberg*, it turned out, was hiding out upstream in the Rufiji River, Pretorius's old hunting ground, and he soon found it. After a daring reconnaissance designed to chart the depths of the Rufiji, a British squadron sailed close enough to shell the *Koenigsberg* and pummel her into oblivion. One of those impressed by Pretorius's feat was Field Marshal Jan Smuts, who promptly took the elephant hunter under his wing as a scout.

Pretorius, now a major, fought with distinction in the East African campaign alongside other hunters like Fred Selous, who was killed in action in 1917 during an attack near the village of Behobeho at the ripe old age of sixty-six. Pretorius had actually been earmarked for the Behobeho mission, but Selous had replaced him at the last minute. Through a series of lucky twists like that, Pretorius survived the war and found himself both a military and a hunting legend in South Africa. Which was opportune, for the South African government was having a spot of trouble with a herd of animals called the Addo elephant.

The so-called Addo Bush was a rugged area of about one hundred square miles near Port Elizabeth, Cape Province, its primary feature being almost impenetrable scrub some fifteen to eighteen feet high. In many places visibility was about five feet. Native African legends claimed the place was cursed. A small herd of elephant lived there. Estimates of their number varied from two hundred to as few as one hundred twenty, and the fairly reliable almanac *Southern Africa: Today and Yesterday* (1956 edition) suggests a total of ninety-five. Pretorius himself wrote that between two hundred and three hundred elephant lived there to begin with, and that he killed all but sixteen (his math wasn't his strong point—according to his 1946 memoirs he started with two or three hundred elephant, shot a hundred twenty, give or take a few, and wound up with sixteen). These Addo elephant were intriguing animals. Many of them, especially the cows, were tuskless, and they had a tendency to be aggressive. Some scientists even considered them a separate subspecies. No matter what they were, by the turn of the century they had become an agricultural pest to the *shambas* in the surrounding district.

The Addo elephant were one of the last surviving populations in South Africa, the others being at Knysna and Tzitzikamma. The population had been relatively seldom hunted. Ever since the 1890s the government of Cape Colony, recognizing the animals' rarity, had charged a special fee of £20 to hunt them. That fee, plus their reputation for aggressiveness, had kept these last few surviving South African elephant alive. Even so, there was a growing desire after the war to clear the Addo bush for farmland. Due to the elephants' reputation and the tough terrain, however, those hunters who were approached were reluctant to take on the job. Experts like Fred Selous, Sir Harry Johnston, and Capt. R. A. St. J. Maguire gave their professional opinions that the mission would be impossible to carry out in that bush.

Finally in 1919 the provincial administration hired Pretorius to kill the Addo animals. He didn't want to do it—any experienced hunter could see that the task was insanely dangerous. But he felt that refusing would somehow damage his hard-earned reputation. The original idea was for Pretorius to just supervise the job, but he had trouble hiring help. So, despite thornbush that limited visibility to a few yards and a very small staff composed mainly of petty criminals, Pretorius finally agreed to do the actual hunting. Armed with a .475 Jeffery double, he first made a careful survey of the district and then began the job of eliminating the herd.

Assisted by just a few African convicts who agreed to help in return for time off their jail sentences, Pretorius went after the Addo elephant, shooting his first on the first day of actual hunting, about three miles into the bush. The trees of the Addo were really just shrubs, incapable of being climbed by a full-grown man, so he used a ladder to give him extra visibility. He killed whatever elephant he came across (except for a few calves that he captured), often shooting four or five at a time. The animals quickly realized they were being stalked and became even warier, hiding in ambush along the trails and retreating into the deepest parts of the bush during the day. The vegetation was so thick that in the whole campaign Pretorius never shot an elephant beyond a range of ten yards.

Toward the end of the assignment two British officers, General Ravenshaw and General Dawson, visited him in the bush on holiday. Both had recently been released from German POW camps at the end of the Great War. On the morning they arrived, Pretorius took them along on his hunt. Ravenshaw somehow became separated from the others and got lost. The bush was so heavy and dark that they were unable to find him despite a massive search, and despite the fact that Pretorius figured he had to be in an area only five hundred yards square. Late the next day they found General Ravenshaw, or rather his body. The old soldier had died of a heart attack. In a sad postscript, his friend General Dawson, who had gone to Tanganyika to hunt elephant, died a month or so later from blackwater fever.

Within a couple of years Pretorius had reduced the Addo herd to a score or so. This is all ironic, considering that within a few short years the government of Natal decided to create a reserve out of the Addo Bush and hired experienced ranger Harry Trollope to consolidate the last surviving elephant and restore the herd to health.

Pretorius lived long enough to serve in World War II, again with distinction, and was awarded the DSO (see glossary). He died in a hospital near Pretoria in 1945. Sadly, one of his daughters was murdered in 1987 in her home by African terrorists during the political turbulence surrounding the end of Apartheid.

Prittie, F. R. D. Captain Prittie hunted in Uganda and the Congo around 1910. He is featured in E. M. Jack's *On the Congo Frontier* (1914).

Prorok, Count Byron de. Prorok was an anthropologist and archaeologist who led some expeditions into underexplored locales in the 1920s and 1930s. Of particular interest here is his Ethiopian trip from Khartoum to Addis Ababa in 1933–1934. His memoir was called *In Quest of Lost Worlds* (1935). His thirst for hunting was almost obsessive. His expeditions were basically march a mile, shoot some wild goats, march three miles, shoot a gazelle, explore an ancient ruin, march a mile, stalk some antelope, that sort of thing. He took a detailed interest in the sexual practices of the primitive people he met—he was, after all, an anthropologist.

Pulitzer, Ralph (1879–1939). Pulitzer was a wealthy New Yorker who went on extended safari in East Africa in 1926, guided by noted white hunter Alan Black. He was the author of the privately printed *Diary of Two Safaris* (1927).

Putnam, Patrick Tracy Lowell (1904–1953). The American Pat Putnam was a Harvard anthropologist who arrived in the Congo in 1927. He had spent the previous two years on an expedition to the East Indies. His original mission in Africa was to conduct ethnological studies for Harvard's Peabody Museum, but he soon fell in love with the place and decided to spend his life in the Belgian Congo.

By 1930 Putnam was the lone white settler in the Ituri forest, running a sort of combination clinic-inn-zoo by the Epulu River called Camp Putnam, where he kept a pair of okapi as pets. Numerous other exotic animals graced his personal zoo during all his years in the bush. He made only a few trips to Europe or America during the rest of his life, but about 1945 he married an American artist. Putnam received a small salary from the Belgian government as a district health officer, but was allowed to conduct his affairs without supervision.

During World War II Putnam supervised the collection of wild rubber in the Congo, a strategically vital job. His health began to fail, and he came down with Malta fever and arthritis. By the end of the 1940s he was largely immobile and often confined to a wheelchair. He continued, however, to run Camp Putnam and provide medical services to the local people.

The brother-in-law of Amelia Earhart, Putnam was considered the foremost expert on the Pygmy people. They in turn looked on him as one of their own. Virtually every African travel book of the early 1950s has a paragraph in which the author states that he or she tried to look in on Putnam while visiting Ituri, but he wasn't home (away on business, hunting, or had just died).

Puttkamer, Jesko von (1855–1917). German explorer in the Cameroons, 1880s.

Puxley, Frank L. Puxley hunted Uganda, Kenya, Tanganyika, Nyasaland, Mozambique, Rhodesia, and South Africa during the first thirty years of the twentieth century. He wrote *Wanderings with a Rifle through Eastern Africa.*

Q

Quabeet (c. 1824–1878). Quabeet was a Zulu from the town of Inxoichin. Clues in the old books indicate that he was born around 1824 and then moved north into Matabeleland around 1836. He worked with most of the European hunters and traders who roamed that area throughout the middle of the century, and they universally spoke highly of him. In 1870 the kraals nearest Kuruman fought with the Europeans against Lobengula, and Quabeet received several wounds fighting against the Matabele.

In September 1878 Quabeet, who was about fifty-four years of age, was headman of Thomas Wood's *ulendo* (see glossary). They were hunting elephant with Cross and Selous. Quabeet wounded an elephant and was chasing after it when a second elephant burst from some brush. The Zulu was knocked to the ground, and the elephant pressed him down with its foot while ripping the man apart with its trunk. Quabeet was found in three pieces the next morning by Selous.

Quesada, Elwood R. "Pete" (1904–1993). A U.S. Army aviator, Pete Quesada piloted one of Martin and Osa Johnson's planes, *The Spirit of Africa,* on an East African expedition in the mid-1930s. The purpose of the trip was to collect and transport four elephant to complete an exhibit in the Akeley African Hall at the American Museum of Natural History. The hunt was carried out from a base at Garissa on the Tana River.

Quesada had achieved some fame earlier by being a member of the crew of the so-called *Question Mark,* a Fokker trimotor that set an endurance record of 151 hours, thanks to in-flight refueling over Los Angeles in 1929. His crew mates on that flight included Carl Spaatz and Ira Eaker, both legendary figures in the U.S. Army Air Force. During World War II, General Quesada was commander of the USAAFs Ninth Fighter Command, and in charge of America's tactical air power on the Western Front during 1944–1945.

Quicke, Francis Churchill (1867–1901). F. C. Quicke was a British officer and sportsman who went on an extended hunting trip through southern and eastern Africa in the late 1890s. While in Barotseland in 1899 he was bitten in the inner ear by a number of driver ants, an experience, he said, he would never forget.

Quicke, a captain of the King's Dragoon Guards, was sent to South Africa in 1901 for the Boer War. He was brevetted to major after capturing an enemy laager of some 65 wagons and 4,000 cattle on 2 August of that year. Quicke was shot to death in action near Harrismith on 26 October 1901. Rowland Ward 1899: Swayne hartebeest, blackbuck, Soemmerring gazelle, gerenuk, dibatag, beisa oryx, Asiatic ibex, wild boar, warthog.

R

Rainey, Paul J. (1877–1923). A coal-mining magnate from Mississippi, Rainey was a hunter and horseman and among the first to be taken with the idea of stalking lion on horseback. Helped by Alan Black, E. R. Shelley, and George Outram (and filmed by American cameraman John Hemment), Rainey put together a pack of dogs and started coursing lion on the Loita Plains. The men were not disappointed. The dogs would chase the animals, and the hunters followed on horseback. Hemment struggled to get it all on film. On one occasion a lion charged the cameraman and was brought down by Black and Rainey just three feet from Hemment. In one year Rainey's dog pack was in on the death of one hundred twenty lion. His method eventually had to be banned.

Rainey then concentrated on filmmaking and created several great motion pictures of African wildlife. His *Water Hole* (most of the footage was actually taken by a man named Lydford), *African Hunt,* and *Common Beasts of Africa* all drew critical acclaim, as did *Military Drill of the Kikuyu Tribes* and *Other Native Ceremonies.* He was not satisfied, however, with any of his scenes of charging lion. It was during an attempt to capture that act on film that famed white hunter Fritz Schindelar met his death in 1914.

Rainey, who stood 6 feet, 4 inches tall, was an expert car racer, polo player, steeple chaser, and yachtsmen as well as a hunter and photographer. He volunteered for active service when the United States entered the Great War in 1917 but was rejected due to his health. Undaunted, he purchased an ambulance and, at his own expense, began to operate a medical service on the Western Front. The Red Cross soon appointed him its official photographer in France.

There is an interesting story concerning Rainey's death in 1923. He was returning to the States from Europe on a passenger liner when one night he observed an Asian man dancing with a Caucasian woman in the ship's lounge. Rainey, born and raised in old Mississippi and long habituated to British Africa, was offended and ordered the man to leave. As the story goes, the Asian man complied but stopped at the lounge doorway and said, "You will not see the sunset on your next birthday." Rainey scoffed at the curse (or challenge) and remarked that the next day was his birthday and he damn well intended to see it through. Toward late afternoon of the following day he collapsed and died of a heart attack.

Rainier, Peter W. (1890–1945). Rainier was born in South Africa in 1890 and served in the British army during the Zulu Rebellion of 1906 and the South-West African campaign of World War One. A hunter, prospector, and rancher, Rainier was the author of *My Vanished Africa* (1940). The book contains a chapter on elephant hunting in Portuguese East Africa. Rainier spent the 1930s searching for emeralds in South America.

Rainsford, W. S. (1857–1933). Dr. Rainsford was an esteemed American clergyman and writer who was also an enthusiastic hunter with much experience of North American big game when he first started coming to Africa in the 1900s. His second safari, with a fellow American named J. J. White, Arthur Hoey, and professional hunter Bill Judd, began in 1908 and lasted nearly a year. The men hunted with Nandi and the Wandorobo tribesmen.

One unpleasant incident resulted in Judd's Kikuyu gunbearer, Momba, being mauled by a wounded lion. The seventeen wounds were painful but not life-threatening. Rainsford blamed Judd for the incident, sharply criticizing him (though not by name) in his 1909 book *The Land of the Lion.* Rowland Ward 1928: Lion, 10½ feet, Kenya.

Randall, Ken. During WWII, Randall had a contract to supply Italian POWs in Kenya with food. He and his brother-in-law, Carr Hartley, shot over a thousand buffalo to provide the meat.

Rankin, Daniel. Rankin was a British colonial official who first came to Nyasaland in about 1883 as private secretary to the British consul at Blantyre, Captain Foot. Rankin became a vice consul for Mozambique later in the 1880s. Since Livingstone's days, the conventional wisdom had been that the Zambezi River was impassable for any ship drawing more than ten feet or so. The sandbars at the delta prevented any deeper-drawing vessel from steaming upriver. This greatly reduced the opportunity for development and settlement along the Zambezi. Rankin heard from a Portuguese planter that the branch of the Zambezi called the Chinde channel allowed a substantially greater draft.

Obtaining a grant from the Royal Scottish Geographical Society in 1888, Rankin set out to survey the Chinde channel. To his delight he found that the water's depth was twenty-one feet at maximum and nineteen feet on average. The shallowest depth year-round at the time was seventeen feet (though by 1900 the river was a few feet shallower). Even this shallower depth would allow small steamships to travel all the way to the Shire. Shipbuilding technology at the time dictated that a vessel had to draw at least thirteen feet to be considered seaworthy. Viewed in that context, this geographical discovery was extremely important—it seemed to open up the possibility of creating a new America in Central Africa. In the words of Harry Johnston (1897): "In terms of far-reaching political importance, probably no greater discovery in the history of British Central Africa has been made than that of the navigability of the Chinde River from the Indian Ocean to the main Zambezi." The importance of the discovery is not diminished by the fact that the projected development never really took place—for a variety of reasons ranging from political to microbiological to climactic.

Rankin was the author of *The Zambezi Basin and Nyasaland* (1893), and therein lies a minor mystery. He dealt harshly with Harry Johnston in this book. In fact, the reviewer for the December 1893 *Scottish Geographical Magazine* states, "Its chief blemish is the unfair attack which the author makes against Mr. Johnston's administration, the obvious bias of which carries its own condemnation." Now, Harry Johnston was hardly a man to avoid a fight. In fact, one of the best features of his own writing is how artfully he was able to insert his own strong opinions on everything without seeming to be partial. Yet in his book *British Central Africa,* which came out a few years later, he treated Rankin well. Did he not read Rankin's book? Had they made up? I don't know enough of the personal relationship between the men to judge. But the matter speaks well for Johnston's objectivity.

Rattray, Jock. Rattray was a professional hunter based at Isiolo in the 1920s and working for the firm of Safariland, Ltd. Rattray was at the center of one of the many scandals that were constantly cropping up in the hunting business. Viscount Furness, like many of his class, enjoyed an annual big-game hunting safari in East Africa. Furness always brought along his wife and his teenage daughter, a tomboy named Averill, and always engaged Jock Rattray as his white hunter. The expeditions lasted six weeks and were cheerful, successful affairs, at least until 1934. That year a deep affection grew between Rattray and young Averill, and the two lovers ran off and eloped. Furness originally vowed to shoot Rattray on sight but then settled for disinheriting his daughter and placing an advertisement in the *East African Standard* that Rattray was no longer his professional hunter.

Rattray had a team of Grevy zebras that he trained to pull a buggy; he owned a farm and frequently caught wild animals and sold them to American zoos. He was badly injured by a wounded leopard in the early 1920s; the incident is described by Martin Johnson in *Camera Trails in Africa.*

Ravenstein, Ernst George (1839–1913). Ravenstein was the cartographer of the Royal Geographical Society and helped finish the maps of many of the Society's explorers. He made the large-scale maps for the Stanley-African Exhibition in London in 1890.

Rayne, H. A hunter who accompanied Karamojo Bell on safari to the Turkana region around 1900, Major Rayne was the author of *The Ivory Raiders* (1923).

Rebmann, Johann (1820–1876). A German missionary from Wuertemberg and an ordained minister of the Church Missionary Society, Rebmann came to Africa in June 1846 to join Johann Krapf at Rabai mission northwest of Mombasa. Like his brother missionaries Erhardt (who survived) and Wagner (who didn't), Rebmann promptly caught a savage dose of fever. This seems to have been the acid test for most nineteenth-century African explorers—if they survived that initial blast of microbes, they often lived long enough to make a name for themselves in history (only to succumb to Africa's slower illnesses later in life). Rebmann soon recovered and helped Krapf negotiate permission from the native Wanyika tribesmen to build the mission on a spot a thousand feet above sea level, the elevation being essential for the health of the Europeans. Like Krapf, Rebmann made some significant explorations into the interior of East Africa. On one of these safaris, in 1849, he became the first white man to see the snows of Kilimanjaro. Unlike Krapf, who returned to Germany in 1853, Rebmann stayed on in the so-called Dark Continent until 1875. For him that nickname was appropriate, for he went blind in the service of the Lord. Riddled by disease, he then went home to Germany, dying in 1876.

Reddie, A. T. Provincial commissioner of Tanaland. Reddie arrived in East Africa around 1890 and was the first European to visit the Lorian Swamp by way of the Tana River valley. In 1912 he helped outfit I. N. Dracopoli for his epic safari through Jubaland.

Reel, Basil. Basil Reel was a professional hunter based in Tanga, Tanganyika, during the 1920s. He took the biggest elephant ever shot in British Tanganyika, with tusks of 168 and 160 pounds.

Rees, Owen. A professional hunter (also seen as Omar Rees) employed by the firm of Safariland, Ltd., in the 1920s.

Render, Adam (1822–c. 1872). Render (also seen as Renders) was born in Germany but moved with his family to the United States at a very young age and considered himself an American. He immigrated to South Africa in 1843 and joined with the Boers, marrying Elsie, the daughter of Boer leader Andries Pretorius. Elsie was a special girl in her own right, carrying seventeen different assegai (spear) wounds on her body. Render fought alongside Pretorius for several years and then, in the early 1850s, started making long trips across the Limpopo River and hunting in what is now Zimbabwe.

He became a successful hunter of hides and ivory, and became well known and respected among the Matabele and the other tribes of Mashonaland. His expeditions lasted the better part of each year, and he was usually accompanied by three Boer hunters named Hendrick Roets, Marniwick, and Snell. In 1867 he became the first European to discover the mysterious ruins of Zimbabwe.

Render was much intrigued by the ruins and believed that there just had to be some fabulous treasure hoard contained therein. He returned several times to search the vast stone complex and tried to convince the government of Transvaal to annex the region. At one time he apparently brought his wife and children along, intending to settle there, but the story goes that Elsie Render took one look at the desolate citadel and demanded to go home. This may or may not have happened. Render's fidelity is in itself in doubt—at least one source claims that he took an African wife, the daughter of a chief named Pika.

Render used his friendship with the Matabele to obtain the release of Carl Mauch, a German explorer who was being held prisoner in 1870.

Render's end, like his obsession, is clouded in mystery. Sometime during the following few years Render was once again searching the ruins when he had some sort of dispute with the local people and was wounded in the shoulder by a poisoned arrow. He died within hours and was buried alongside the fortress that had captured his soul long before. Fittingly, Render left a treasure-trove legend of his own—he was believed to have stockpiled a large cache of ivory and gold that was never discovered.

Retief, Piet (1780–1838). This Boer leader was murdered by Zulu chieftain Dingaan in a spectacular 1838 act of treachery. Retief and sixty-nine other Boers (along with thirty or forty Hottentot servants) had visited Dingaan's kraal to negotiate a peace treaty. The document was signed on 4 February 1838, and the Boers then feasted with their Zulu hosts. On 6 February, at a farewell dance, each Boer was suddenly and treacherously seized by several Zulus, dragged to a nearby hill, and impaled. Retief was saved for last. The Hottentot retainers were also slain.

The treachery was the signal for a general Zulu attack against the Boers. In a ferocious onslaught, Zulu warriors slaughtered the unprepared and poorly defended Boer homesteads throughout Natal. It was recorded that on the first night 41 Boer men, 56 women, 185 children, and 250 Hottentots were killed in the surprise raids, and 10,000 head of cattle carried off.

Rhodes, Arthur Montagu (1859–1931). One of the Rhodes brothers, Arthur (like his brother Bernard but unlike Frank and Herbert) had a tendency to sponge on his rich and famous sibling, Cecil. Cecil set him up with a farm near Bulawayo in 1893. When the Matabele Uprising took place three years later, Arthur filed a fraudulent compensation claim with the BSAC (see glossary). Nervous claims examiners were afraid to deny it until Cecil Rhodes gave his own opinion, calling it "the most impudent claim which has yet been submitted."

Rhodes, Bernard Maitland (1861–1935). His rich brother Cecil called him a "loafer." Nevertheless, Bernard wound up living in Cecil's house after Cecil's death in 1902.

Rhodes, Cecil (1853–1902). Cecil Rhodes did more to build Britain's African Empire than any other man, often against the wishes of the government. The son of a vicar, Rhodes went to South Africa at an early age in 1871 to nurse his frail health. His arrival fortuitously coincided with the discovery of diamonds near Kimberley, and the ailing young man traveled north to try his hand at diamond mining. He was quite successful—eighteen years later he completed his takeover of the South African diamond industry by buying out his sole remaining competitor with a check for £3,338,650. As head of the DeBeers Mining Company, Rhodes could have easily used his health as an excuse to retire to a life of luxury. Instead, he set out to conquer the African continent for Great Britain. The "Cape to Cairo" concept, though the term was coined by Harry Johnston, was Rhodes's obsession.

By 1890 Rhodes was prime minister of Cape Colony. That same year, he engineered and financed the occupation of Mashonaland. Three years later, he led the invasion and conquest of Matabeleland, an act that was widely considered treacherous, even by many Britons. His British South African Company (chartered in 1888) agreed to finance the payroll for the administration of Rhodesia and British Central Africa (Nyasaland, now Malawi). When Harry Johnston, the commissioner of British Central Africa and a Rhodes ally, balked at Rhodes's plan to launch a sneak attack on Portuguese East Africa, Rhodes terminated their friendship and eliminated his subsidy to the country. The British government was forced to step in and pick up the tab. The Rhodesias, however, remained the private property of the BSAC (see glossary) until the 1920s.

Rhodes's lust for power was all-consuming. He was the consummate practitioner of realpolitik: the ends justify the means. The extent to which he was focused on practical matters is amazing. He never took the time, for instance, to visit Victoria Falls, the premier natural attraction of the country that bore his name. When a Captain Sapte brought orders from the Foreign Office to a Rhodes subordinate not to invade Mozambique, Rhodes demanded to know why the subordinate hadn't just falsely accused Sapte of drunkenness and had him arrested. His treatment of Harry Johnston was detestable and a clear warning to everyone that once Rhodes bought you (or thought he had), you had better stay bought.

His lieutenants were infected by his determination and the belief that, with enough money and daring, anything might be possible. The formula worked in Mashonaland and Matabeleland. It failed in Mozambique and, most importantly, in the Jameson Raid of 1895, in which a column under a Rhodes confidant, Leander Starr Jameson, failed to spark the desired rebellion in the Transvaal. The consequences of the raid were immense. Temporarily, at least, both Rhodes's and Jameson's careers seemed to be derailed. The Anglo-Boer War became inevitable, and the Matabele launched the revolt of 1896, taking advantage of the fact that nearly every white fighting man in Rhodesia was in a Transvaal jail.

Rhodes resigned the premiership of South Africa due to the fallout over the raid, but never really lost the base of his power. His personality underwent an almost Citizen Kane-style transformation. Where once he had been driven and electric, he now became dour, obsessive, and alcoholic. Long plagued by ill health (modern researchers speculate he suffered from a congenital heart defect), Rhodes died at the age of forty-nine and was buried in the Matopos Hills south of Bulawayo. While he added a lot of British red to the map, he did so at a cost. One of his most enduring legacies was the South African apartheid system. Rhodes was a fervent believer in white supremacy. Another, more benign artifact of his influence was the Rhodes Scholarship, originally designed to subsidize the creation of a cadre of tough, educated young men whose steady hands, in Rhodes's dream, would steer the course of the Empire.

Rhodes, Ernest Frederick (1852–1901). The Rhodes brother nobody ever writes about.

Rhodes, Francis Williams (1850–1905). Frank Rhodes, Cecil's older brother, went to Eton, then joined a British cavalry regiment. He was the chief hunter on the 1892 Gerald Portal expedition to Uganda. At the time, he was

Cecil Rhodes and Dr. Leander Starr Jameson.

military secretary to the governor of Bombay and held a commission in the Royal Dragoons. Portal's diary for August–October of 1893 records that Rhodes shot numerous guinea fowl, several hippo, and a twelve-foot crocodile "of enormous girth."

An accomplished hunter and cricket player, Col. Frank Rhodes served in India but was cashiered after his participation in the Jameson Raid. He accompanied Kitchener during the 1898 Omdurman campaign as a correspondent for *The London Times* and joined his brother's BSAC (see glossary) in time to serve in the Boer War. Frank Rhodes died in 1905 at his late brother Cecil's estate at Groote Schuur near Cape Town.

Rhodes, Herbert (1845–1879). Herbert Rhodes was Cecil's oldest brother. Herbert attended Eton and was considered one of the best cricket players of his time. He immigrated to South Africa at an early age and tried his hand at farming and gold prospecting before taking up hunting for a living.

In 1878 he went to Lake Nyasa to shoot big game. For companionship's sake, he fell in with Consul Frederick Elton and two other Englishmen (Cotterill and Hoste) as they were heading toward the lake to investigate the slave trade. Rhodes went along with Elton to the northern end of the lake and then returned to the Upper Shire, where he built a hut and set up camp.

He spent the next two years hunting elephant professionally (he shipped the tusks to a seaport via porters and had the money credited to his bank account) and is said to have established a reputation among the local Africans for his hunting skills, integrity, and bravery. In 1879 a barrel of rum exploded in his hut, and he succumbed to his burns after several days of intense pain.

Richardson, James (1809–1851). An English explorer, Richardson traveled through the Sahara and wrote a book about the land and the Tuareg people called *Travels in the Great Desert of Sahara* (1849). In 1850 he started for Lake Chad with the Germans Barth and Overweg but took sick and died not far from his goal. His notes were published as *Narrative of a Mission to Central Africa* (1853) and *Travels in Morocco* (1859).

Ritchie, Archibald Thomas Ayres (1890–1962). Born in County Kildare, Ireland, Captain Archie Ritchie arrived in East Africa in 1920 after winning the Military Cross and the French Chevalier de le Legion d'Honneur in the First World War. The French decoration derived from his service in the French Foreign Legion at the beginning of the war; later he transferred to the British Grenadier Guards. In 1924 he became the game warden of Kenya, a post he held until 1949 (except for a few years in the late 1930s when he was seconded to Malaya). He was the chief game official in the country during the period when it became the foremost destination for big-game hunters. Ritchie married Queenie Mary Falconier MacDonald in 1917, and was a founding member of EAPHA in 1934. While on control duty in the province of Tanaland in the 1920s, he shot an elephant with tusks of 124 and 116 pounds.

Cecil Rhodes (on left) in the field, 1896.

A tall, impressive looking man, with silver hair and mustache, Ritchie had a flair for the dramatic. His favorite automobile was a shocking yellow Rolls Royce with a giant hippo tusk mounted as a hood ornament. He famously kept a bongo-hide bag in his desk drawer that contained a bottle of very potent liquor. The bag and the bottle served two important purposes. First, Ritchie was in the habit of taking one (and only one) stiff shot every morning at eleven o'clock as a refreshment. Second, and more important, over the years he broke up hundreds of arguments with angry hunters, upset safari clients, and other incensed guests by offering them a touch of his private stock. Although everybody knew the trick, it was nearly 100 percent effective, and the argument or bad blood almost always dissipated with the alcoholic fumes. His hospitality had its limits, however. In October 1928, Ritchie was the man who ejected Frank Greswolde Williams from the Muthaiga Club after Williams had offered cocaine to the Prince of Wales.

Ritchie was not without his humorous side; one of his quips has become perhaps the most oft-retold joke of the safari industry. The story concerns the horn of a rhino and its purported powers as an aphrodisiac. The belief in Asia and Arabia in this property has been a driving force behind the near extinction of the animal. Ritchie was admiring the trophy horn collected by a safari client (in most versions of the story it was an elderly American) when the proud client asked the game warden how to best glean the desired effect from the lengthy article. "What should I do?" he asked, "crush it up and brew some sort of drink with it?" "I really don't know," Ritchie replied. "Perhaps you might begin by using it as a splint."

In addition to numerous magazine articles, Ritchie was a contributor to the 1932 Lonsdale Library volume *Big Game Shooting in Africa.* ROWLAND WARD 1928: GREATER KUDU.

Riddell, G. H. Jack. A Kenyan white hunter who had fought in the Boer War, Capt. Jack Riddell (nicknamed "Flash" due to his expensive and extravagant manner) guided the young Winston Churchill on his safari through the Thika country and Uganda in 1908. The two men had served together in India. Churchill endorsed Riddell's creation of the Boma Trading Company, an all-purpose outfitting company. The BTC went on to equip many famous safaris, including the Buffalo Jones Expedition. Riddell was outclassed, however, when he tried to compete head-to-head against John Boyes. Despite Riddell's best efforts, the "King of the Kikuyu" managed to monopolize trade with the medieval empire of Abyssinia. Riddell served with Richard Meinertzhagen in military intelligence in World War I. After the Armistice, he went to work as a professional hunter for the Safariland Company. ROWLAND WARD 1928: BLACK RHINO.

Riddick. A Captain Riddick claimed to have shot a twenty-six-foot crocodile in Lake Kioga in 1916.

Ridley, Mervyn. An early settler in Kenya, Ridley owned a farm called Kapsiliat. He kept a pack of foxhounds at Makuyu in the Thika area, and used to chase jackals and steenbok across the African plains. Ridley was a burly, friendly, popular man who also kept horses, purebred bulls, and sheep. His wife was named Sybil.

Rimbaud, Jean-Nicolas-Arthur (1854–1891). Arthur Rimbaud was born in France in 1854. He was a wild young man and frequently ran away from home to live as a vagabond and even a highway robber. Nevertheless, he was a brilliant poet and turned out a considerable amount of fine work before the age of twenty. His *A Season in Hell* (1873) is considered one of the first examples of free verse.

Rimbaud had a relationship (apparently homosexual) with the poet Paul Verlaine, which ended badly when Verlaine shot his young friend in the hand during a drunken argument. At the age of nineteen Rimbaud abandoned poetry (his future writing was confined to letters) and went to East Africa, where he scraped out a living dealing in trade goods, guns, and, possibly, slaves. He made several trips into the interior and was one of the first Europeans to visit Ogaden in Abyssinia.

In 1891 Rimbaud began to notice a pain in his leg. A medical examination revealed cancer, and despite a trip to Marseilles for treatment he soon succumbed to the disease. His posthumous fame was assured when his friend Verlaine arranged for the publication of his complete works in 1895.

Rimington, G. B. An officer in the Kenya administration 1920–1940, he was known as "Rim." Rimington was district commissioner at Kapenguria in the late 1920s, DC at Isiolo in the 1930s, and then sent to be DC at Wajir when it appeared that he was overwhelmed by the Ethiopian refugee problem occasioned by Mussolini's invasion. Rimington was formerly a member of the Royal Dragoons (Military Cross) and the Royal Canadian Mounted Police.

Long before the Adamsons found Elsa the lioness, Rimington was taming whole troops of wild animals, including chimpanzee, zebra, ostrich, and giraffe. One chimp, named Katalina, could ride the giraffe. Rim trained a Grevy zebra (bigger than the common zebra) to play polo at Nanyuki. The regular ponies were so frightened by the zebra that Rimington scored goal after uncontested goal. The club soon banned zebra from play.

Ringer, G. C. R. Major Ringer was an Englishman who came to East Africa on a hunting trip and liked what he saw. In 1904 he visited the Uasin Gishu plateau, the Athi Plains, and the Kavirondo region while hunting with John Boyes, Charlie Bulpett, W. N. McMillan, and a physician named Groat. Ringer was so taken with the country that he decided to settle and in December 1904 opened the doors of the Norfolk Hotel, a mile from the railway station in Nairobi. He did well financially, but some years later he fell overboard from the deck of his yacht in Falmouth Harbor and drowned. His body was never recovered.

Ringler Brothers. A pair of well-known German elephant hunters who practiced their craft in East Africa during the first decade of the twentieth century. One day the brothers fired at an elephant that crashed off into the brush wounded. Following up, they found the beast lying dead on its side. One of the brothers leaned on the animal, and unfortunately it turned out to be not the wounded elephant but only a sleeping one. The hulk promptly scrambled to its feet, grabbed the man with its trunk, and dashed him fatally against a rock. The surviving brother killed the elephant.

Ritchie, Archibald Thomas Ayres (1890–1962). Born in County Kildare, Ireland, Capt. Archie Ritchie arrived in East Africa in 1920, after winning the Military Cross and the French Chevalier de le Legion d'Honneur in World War I. The French decoration derived from his service in the French Foreign Legion at the beginning of the war. Later he transferred to the British Grenadier Guards. In 1924 he became the game warden of Kenya, a post he held until 1949. He was the chief game official in the country during the period when it became the foremost destination for big-game hunters. Ritchie married Queenie Mary Falconier MacDonald in 1917 and was a founding member of EAPHA (see glossary) in 1934. While on control duty in the province of Tanaland in the 1920s he shot an elephant with tusks of 124 and 116 pounds.

A tall, impressive-looking man with silver hair and mustache, Ritchie had a flair for the dramatic. His favorite automobile was a shocking-yellow Rolls Royce with a giant hippo tusk mounted as a hood ornament. He famously kept a bongo-hide bag in his desk drawer that contained a bottle of very high-powered liquor. The bag and the bottle served two important purposes. First, Ritchie was in the habit of taking one (and only one) stiff shot every morning at eleven o'clock as a refreshment. Second, and more important, over the years he broke up hundreds of arguments with angry hunters, safari clients, and other incensed guests by offering them a touch of his private stock. Although everybody knew the trick, it was nearly 100 percent effective—the argument or bad blood always dissipated with the alcoholic fumes.

His hospitality had its limits, however. In October 1928 Ritchie was the man who ejected Frank Greswolde Williams from the Muthaiga Club after Williams had offered cocaine to the Prince of Wales.

Ritchie was not without his humorous side. One of his quips has become perhaps the most oft-retold joke of the safari industry. The story concerns rhino horn and its purported powers as an aphrodisiac. That belief in Asia and Arabia has been a driving force behind the near extinction of the animal. Ritchie was admiring the trophy horn collected by a safari client (in most versions of the story an elderly American) when the proud client asked the game warden how best to glean the desired amorous effect from the lengthy trophy. "What should I do—crush it up and brew some sort of drink with it?" he asked. "I really don't know," Ritchie replied. "Perhaps you might begin by using it as a splint."

Toward the end of his life Ritchie felt somewhat remorseful about all the killing he had done. He still encouraged and directed the various control and game-management schemes in Kenya, but his personal revulsion toward hunting became such that he even tried to dissuade his son from shooting grouse. Perhaps he was not exactly the guy you want in charge of the game department when big-game hunting is your Number 1 source of foreign currency. In addition to authoring many magazine articles, Ritchie was a contributor to the 1932 Lonsdale Library volume *Big Game Shooting in Africa.* ROWLAND WARD 1928: GREATER KUDU.

Roberts, Austin. A British sportsman who hunted northern Mozambique with F. Vaughan Kirby around 1900. The two shot a group of four man-eating lion that had been credited with twenty victims per month over a period of years.

Robins, Herbert G. (xxxx–1939). Robins settled in the Wankie area of Rhodesia in 1914 between two streams called Big Toms and Little Toms. The Tom in these names was Tom Saddlier, a friend of Selous's who had hunted there thirty years earlier. Robins raised cattle and gradually began setting up a "game viewing" area on part of his spread. Invited guests would come from afar to relax and watch wild animals with Robins over a sundowner. One of these invited guests frequently was Kenya's Bob Foran. After 1928 Robins was frequently a thorn in the side of Wankie Game Reserve Warden Ted Davison. It was Davison's job to build up the reserve (he did so well that it eventually became Wankie National Park), while Robins tended to look at the reserve as a breeding place for his viewing area. By this time Robins had sold all his cattle except for one small group maintained as an "indicator herd" to monitor the spread of hoof-and-mouth disease. Robins bought an annuity with the cattle-sale proceeds and settled down to enjoy his viewing area and raise Great Danes. Considered a "character," Robins was frequently sought out by tourists and newspaper and magazine writers looking for an offbeat story. Upon his death the farm was incorporated into Wankie, becoming the Robins Camp area of Wankie National Park.

Rogers. An American prospector from California named Rogers was known to have poached ivory in the Lado Enclave well after the beginning of the British administration there. He would stick close to the border, slipping across when necessary. On one such occasion, in 1912, he was chased by troops from the King's African Rifles but slowed down once he had reached safety over the border. One of the askaris, either out of ignorance or because he was the type not to be stopped by a technicality, shot Rogers anyway. When the askari's British officer, a Capt. C. V. Fox, got to the scene, Rogers was lying wounded under a blanket. Rogers asked the Englishman if he had given the order to fire, even though he, Rogers, was safely over the border. Absolutely not, replied the officer, and implied that the border was sacrosanct. Whereupon Rogers, so the story goes, drew a cocked revolver from under his blanket and explained that he would have killed the officer if he didn't believe him. Another version has it that Rogers simply told Fox that he would shoot him if he, Rogers, could still move. At any rate, Rogers died from his wound a few hours later. Rumor had it that he had been one of Soapy Smith's criminal gang in Skagway, Alaska, during the Klondike gold rush.

Rohlfs, Friedrich Gerhard (1831–1896). Hailing from Bremen, Gerhard Rohlfs joined the French Foreign Legion and first saw Africa as a military apothecary and surgeon's assistant in Algeria in 1855–1860. Between 1860 and 1866 he explored Morocco, Tafilet, Tuat, and Chad, crossing Africa from Tripoli to Lagos via Lake Chad and Yoruba. In 1868 he began ten years of traveling in Abyssinia and the Sahara, finally settling down as German consul in Zanzibar in 1884. He was the author of several books, including *Travels Through Morocco* (1869), *Kufra* (1881), and *What's New Out of Africa?* (1886), and received the Patron's Medal of the Royal Geographical Society in 1868.

Roosevelt, Kermit (1889–1943). Teddy's son Kermit participated in the famous safari at the age of twenty. He did a good deal of the hunting and collecting, including shooting a rare bongo. Five years later he again went on a major hunting expedition with his father, this time in the Amazon jungle, a trip they both were lucky to survive. An Imperialist at heart, Kermit served in the British army during World War I as a captain in Mesopotamia. He was invalided back to the United States after a bad attack of malaria (it may have been a more mysterious fever that he had originally caught in the Amazon). After TR's death in 1919, Kermit founded a successful shipping firm, the Roosevelt Steamship Line. He also continued his big-game hunting in a grand way, hunting in China, Turkistan, Tibet, and other parts of Asia in the 1920s. With his brother Theodore, he was one of the first Westerners to hunt—or even see—the giant panda.

Plagued by an alcohol problem, he began to slip in the 1930s. When World War II started, Kermit Roosevelt again served in the British forces, but was soon shipped to a U.S. Army base at Fort Richardson, Alaska, where it was thought the climate might do him good. It didn't. Despondent, he killed himself there in 1943. Kermit was the author of *War in the Garden of Eden* (1919), *The Happy Hunting Grounds* (1920), *East of the Sun, West of the Moon* (1926), and *Trailing the Giant Panda* (1929).

Roosevelt, Kermit (Junior) (1916–2000). The son of Kermit and a grandson of Theodore, the "junior" in this Kermit's name was arbitrarily dropped by a bureaucrat in the U.S. Army. Kermit (Junior) was a Harvard graduate, a history professor, an oil executive, and a State Department–CIA official. He played an important role in the 1953 coup in Iran.

In 1960 Roosevelt was commissioned by *Life* magazine to re-create the famous Roosevelt safari. With his own two sons (Jonathan and yet another Kermit) hunting and

Kermit Roosevelt and leopard, 1909.

photographing alongside him, Kermit covered much of the same territory his grandfather and father had gone through fifty years earlier, meeting the surviving old-time hunters and even using many of the same guns and cameras. The trip was chronicled in *Life* and in a 1963 book called *Sentimental Safari,* which is actually pretty good.

Roosevelt, Theodore (1858–1919). It's a little difficult for a modern reader to comprehend the impact of President Roosevelt's decision to go on an East African safari. In the early 1900s Africa was still very much the Dark Continent. Most areas had been explored, at least in theory, but the vast majority of sub-Saharan Africa was still a wilderness inhabited by wild men and wilder animals. It was unheard of for someone of Roosevelt's stature to visit there—the so-called "royal" safaris of the Prince of Wales and the dukes of York and Gloucester were at least fifteen years in the future.

Roosevelt seems to have made the decision casually. He had long wanted to make an adventurous trip when he left the White House and had halfheartedly decided to go to Alaska. After talking to various Britons with African experience, such as Alfred Pease, Fred Selous, and Harry Johnston, he made up his mind to go to Kenya instead. He planned the trip with meticulous detail, even down to the books he would read in his leisure hours, some sixty or so specially made volumes called the "pigskin library," ranging from the Bible to Shakespeare to Dickens to Poe.

Teddy Roosevelt, Loring, Cuninghame, and bull elephant, Meru, 1909.

The financial arrangements for the expedition are interesting. The total cost was approximately $75,000. Andrew Carnegie underwrote most of this, and the Smithsonian Institution made a contribution. The Smithsonian was to receive the hundreds of specimens procured on the trip. President Roosevelt put up some of the cash, paying all the expenses for himself and for his son Kermit, but he got that all back with the money he made writing about the safari. A serialized version of *African Game Trails* was published in *Scribner's Magazine* in 1909, and the book form came out later that year. Roosevelt received $50,000 for the book plus a 20 percent royalty on sales.

The safari left New York on 23 March 1909 on the German liner *Hamburg* and switched to the *Admiral,* another German ship, at Naples for the final leg through the Suez Canal to Mombasa. Selous joined the party aboard the *Admiral* and spent many hours in conversation with the ex-president, going over plans and tactics and telling old hunting yarns. They reached Mombasa on 21 April 1909.

The party as originally constituted was made up of Roosevelt, his son Kermit, and the naturalists Edgar Mearns, Edmund Heller, and J. Alden Loring. Final preparations for the venture had been made by Selous and Edward North Buxton, an African hunter and photographer. At Mombasa they were met by their white hunters, R. J. Cuninghame and Leslie Tarlton.

Roosevelt was delighted at the reception he got and at the beautiful country he was traveling through. It was positively swarming with game in those days. In a memorable phrase, he termed the Uganda railway "a railroad through the Pleistocene." They left the railroad at the station at Kapiti Plains to begin the safari. All such expeditions were on foot in 1909. This was ostensibly a collecting expedition and thus was weighted down with a huge amount of equipment and supplies, including four tons of salt to cure the hides. They were also well armed, of course. Roosevelt brought an army-issue .303 Springfield, a Winchester .405, a Fox Number 12 shotgun, and a double-barreled .500-450 Holland heavy rifle. His son Kermit was similarly armed.

This is not the place to go into the details of the safari. For those interested, dozens of books have been written on it—in fact, the expedition spawned an entire sub-genre of hunting books. Suffice it to say here that the Roosevelts leisurely moved through Kenya toward Uganda, being treated like royalty and having a whale of a time. There was some unpleasantness behind the scenes, however. In his account of the trip, *African Game Trails,* Roosevelt railed against "game butchers," people who massacred indiscriminate amounts of wildlife, but in fact he and Kermit did just that. They embarrassed some of their British hosts (who tactfully kept quiet) by shooting large numbers of game animals, including seventeen lion, ten buffalo, eleven elephant, eleven black rhino, and nine of the already rare white rhino. Modern writers tend to state that the British were appalled at the slaughter, but this is clearly overstating the case. The British were not appalled: Other parties, including their own countrymen, did a lot more damage. There was just a vague feeling that perhaps the Americans were overdoing it a bit, that's all.

What did irritate the British, however, was the Roosevelts' tendency to have their snapshot taken over every dead animal. This was considered somewhat gauche and, well, touristy. Photos of the ex-president standing proudly over every single dead waterbuck or gazelle were frowned upon by the British, and were still being remarked upon in letters twenty years later.

All in all, however, the safari was a rousing success. It finished up on the Nile, at a famous banquet where Roosevelt saluted the elephant hunters of the Lado Enclave as "gentlemen adventurers." From there they steamed up the river to Cairo and then, after a triumphant tour of Europe, back home.

The East African expedition was by far Roosevelt's most successful (a subsequent trip to South America was marred by disease and cursed by bad luck). The venture had some scientific benefit as well—the three naturalists brought back a tremendous collection of East African fauna for the Smithsonian, including many rare specimens of small mammals. The most important result was undoubtedly the boost in interest in safari hunting in general and East Africa in particular. In the years after Roosevelt, hundreds of distinguished Americans and Britons flocked to Mombasa to embark on their own expeditions. As noted above, the publishing industry was flooded with books on African hunting and adventure, of all qualities. Among those inspired by the President's trip included the writer and spiritualist Edward Stuart White, Richard Tjader, Carl Akeley, E. M. Jack, and A. Radclyffe Dugmore.

Roscher, Albrecht (1837–1860). Roscher was a young German explorer from Hamburg commissioned by the king of Bavaria to find Lake Nyasa in 1859. Poorly equipped and with little money, Roscher dressed himself as an Arab and traveled with an Arab trading caravan. Despite a bad case of malaria and being robbed and beaten by the real Arabs, Roscher made it to the town of Lusefa on the lake's eastern shore. He reached the lake seventy-two days after his rival, Livingstone. On his return journey in March 1860 he was robbed again and murdered at a place called Kisoon-goonie. Ironically for a man whose expedition suffered constantly from a lack of equipment, the murderers coveted his only valuable possessions, some scientific instruments. His African murderers were later captured and executed at Zanzibar.

In his 1865 memoir, *A Walk Across Africa,* James Augustus Grant recalled witnessing the execution of two of the murderers on 23 August 1860. The execution was marred by an almost comic farce. Everyone was in their place, the two condemned men squatting on the sand outside the wall of the fort with hands and feet untied and guarded only casually by a few mocking musketeers, but no execution order from the sultan had arrived. One of the doomed men told Grant that he had committed his crime while unconscious, whatever he meant by that. A warder of the jail then asked Grant if the British consul, Colonel Rigby, could give the order to proceed with the execution. Grant went back to the consulate to inquire, but Rigby declined. Upon his return to the execution site, Grant was startled by the rapid approach of a lively group of Arabs, armed with swords and shields, who pushed their way right up to the prisoners. Grant thought it was a rescue attempt, but it turned out the Arabs only wanted a good view of the coming attraction. Everyone laughed heartily at the confusion. Finally one of the jailers asked Grant, "Might we proceed?" and he replied, "Yes, certainly, proceed." The executioner then cut off the men's heads with a sword.

Roscoe, John (1861–1932). A missionary, he was the author of *The Soul of Central Africa* (1922) and *Twenty-Five Years in East Africa* (1921).

Ross, Charles J. Maj. Charlie Ross, DSO (see glossary), was an elephant hunter based in Kenya and an assistant game ranger from 1907–1922. He hunted in the Lado Enclave before 1908.

Ross, Sir Charles Henry Augustus Frederick Lockhart (1872–1942). Sir Charles Ross, with Sir Northrup McMillan and Ewart Grogan, gave advice to Carl Akeley for his 1922 Kivu gorilla expedition. The inventor of the Ross magazine rifle, Ross purchased a ninety-nine-year lease on Ngorongoro Crater in 1922. He had first explored the crater a year earlier during a shooting safari with T.

Alexander Barns and Radclyffe Dugmore. Ross made no improvements on the old Siedentopf farm and started guarding the game herds. He played an important part in getting the crater declared a reserve in 1928.

A shooting champion at Eton, Ross made a fortune from the sale of his bolt-action rifle, which, however, proved to be too delicate for military use in World War I. He got himself into serious trouble with the Inland Revenue by his use of various "ingenious" tax dodges, including an attempt to have the family estate declared American territory.

Rossi, Aurelio (1898–1942). Rossi was born in Rome in 1898 and trained as a criminal lawyer. In the First World War he served as an officer, distinguishing himself in action against the Germans and Austrians on the Alpine front. He was wounded twice.

In 1921 Rossi went to Africa for the first time, as a member of the Milan Museum's expedition to Somaliland. Rossi was the expedition photographer and produced a documentary called *Hic Sunt Leones;* unfortunately, all his films have apparently been lost. He returned to Africa several times in the next few years, hunting big game and roaming into little-known parts of the tropical hinterland. He visited the Belgian Congo in 1922 and 1924. On the latter trip he shot four elephants (average tusk weight of about fifty pounds each) and a white rhino. He also spent several months living with a Pygmy tribe deep in the Ituri forest.

Rossi returned to Rome and the practice of law in 1926 but soon tired of the city life. In 1927 he went to the French colony of Ubangi-Shari and purchased a so-called commercial elephant hunting license, which allowed him to bring in unlimited amounts of ivory. Unfortunately for Rossi, the area had been worked over very extensively by previous hunters and he bagged only about forty animals before calling it quits a couple of years later.

Rossi went back to his law office and wrote a book about his African adventures called *Tra Elefanti E Pigmei* (1931). When Mussolini invaded Ethiopia in 1935, Rossi returned to his military duties and commanded the Ninth Eritrean battalion in antiguerrilla operations near Addis Ababa. He continued in the Italian army when the Second World War broke out, and held the rank of colonel when he was killed in action at the Battle of El Alamein in late 1942.

Rothschild, Sir Lionel Walter (1868–1937). The third baronet and second Baron Rothschild of Tring. A sickly youth, Rothschild was educated at home by private tutors. He was trained to work in the family banking business but early in life developed a love of natural history. In 1889 his father built a small house on the family estate at Tring to house his library and insect collections. By 1892 a large new building had been built and was open to the public as a museum. Sportsmen from all over the world sent their finest specimens for display at the Tring Museum, including Selous, Lyell, and many other African hunters. The museum published its own magazine, the *Novitates Zoologicae.* Rothschild became Baron Rothschild on his father's death in 1915.

A conservative member of Parliament from 1899–1910, Rothschild received many honors for his natural-history work. Among them were the Victoria Medal of Honor in horticulture, a trusteeship of the British Museum, an honorary doctorate from the University of Giessen, and a fellowship of the Royal Society. He died a bachelor in 1937 and left the collections at Tring to the British Museum and the rest of his estate, including the titles, to his nephew.

The description of the Tring Museum in the 1928 edition of Rowland Ward states that it "contains a very fine collection of big game trophies, birds, etc., and is one of the most complete private museums in the United Kingdom. The entomological and bird skin collections are noteworthy." Baron Rothschild was Philip Percival's second safari client. His mother, Baroness Rothschild, the former Emma Louise Rothschild (from a German branch of the family), was considered one of the best female rifle shots in the world. She used a .256 Mannlicher magazine rifle with a short barrel.

Ruark, Robert (1915–1965). Ruark was an American journalist who struck it rich writing about African hunting and the problems of East Africa. His *Horn of the Hunter* (1954), a classic account of safari life in the 1950s, made a star of white hunter Harry Selby, but it was his *Something of Value* (1955), a massive novel about professional hunters and the Mau Mau uprising, that really catapulted Ruark into fame. *Something of Value* was later made into a movie starring Rock Hudson and Sidney Poitier. Ruark made so much money off that one book that he was able to buy a castle in Spain and move there permanently.

Ironically, Ruark first went to East Africa not to write but to slow down his lifestyle and his drinking, which was affecting his health. His original newspaper job in the United States involved coverage of the celebrity and social beats, and Ruark had won the confidence of film stars and singers by his ability to drink them under the table.

With the publication of *Uhuru* and *The Honey Badger*—two early 1960s books that presented a raw and controversial look at settlers and Africans alike—Ruark became persona non grata in Kenya. He then moved his activities to Portuguese territory in Mozambique. There he hunted with Safarilandia's Werner von Alvensleben, Wally Johnson, and Harry Manners. Other Ruark books dealing with Africa were *Use Enough Gun* (1957) and *Robert Ruark's Africa,* a collection of magazine articles published more than thirty years after his death. The drinking finally caught up to the iconoclastic writer, and he died in 1965 at the young age of fifty.

Rueppell, Eduard (1794–1884). Also seen as Rupell. The author of *Reisen in Nubien* (1829), Rueppell was a German explorer and naturalist who popularized African natural history for the German-speaking world. He concentrated his efforts in Sudan and Kordofan. Harry Johnston (1903) compared him to William Cornwallis Harris and Gordon Cumming in his influence on the sporting public.

Rueppell might well be considered the first practicing cryptozoologist, insofar as he investigated reports of the "unicorn" in the hill regions of Kordofan. What separates Rueppell from earlier naturalists who discovered odd animals like the kangaroo or platypus is that they were not specifically looking for an animal believed to be mythological. Rueppell was. His search for the unicorn was the direct ancestor of modern searches for Nessie and Bigfoot. Unfortunately, it also had the same result.

Rumanika. King of Karagwe on the western shore of Lake Victoria around 1861, he kept a harem in which women were force-fed dairy products until they were fantastically obese. Speke measured the primary queen of Karagwe as having a chest of fifty inches and thighs of thirty-one inches. Speke was later widely criticized for showing an obsessive and not entirely scientific interest in this harem.

Rundgren, Eric (1918–1992). Rundgren was a professional hunter whose career fell mainly in the postwar years and thus is beyond the scope of this book, but his name comes up so frequently in old hunting stories that at least some description is merited.

Rundgren was one of those white hunters who might very aptly be described as a living legend. He was a fascinating man, combining superb bush skills with a dominant, at times even abusive personality. Born in 1918, he came from strong stock—his sturdy parents feature prominently in early accounts of Kenya Colony. He received a .22 rifle for his eighth birthday and started following the local Wakamba tribesmen on their hunts. At an early age he accompanied his father, Ture, on short buffalo-hunting safaris. The elder Rundgren would sell the hides to the Kavirondo tribe for use in making shields.

About 1935 Eric got a position as the forest officer in Karita. His job was to locate good sources of wood for the lumber companies, and to replant the cut-over areas with a variety of woods like American pine, cedar, and especially blue gum trees, which were used as fuel for the Kenya and Uganda Railway. Soon after taking his post he requested, and received, the post of honorary control officer from F. N. Clarke, acting head of the game department in the absence of game warden Archie Ritchie. Clarke commissioned Rundgren by sending him a handwritten note stating (according to Rundgren and Holman, 1969) "Look, son, if you think you can do it have a go, but don't blame me if you get killed."

With this encouraging endorsement, Rundgren officially began his long career as a professional hunter, in the sense of someone who gets paid to do it. Part of the reforestation program was allowing Kikuyu squatters to farm the timber cuts for a few years before replanting them. Rundgren was kept busy chasing elephant away from their shambas. He also tried his hand at other profitable endeavors in the name of game control, trapping some thirty-seven leopard in his first two years and selling their pelts for £20 apiece. He needed the income to supplement his meager salary of £18 per month. By way of comparison, game ranger Harry Wolhuter of the Sabi Game Reserve had been paid almost twice that amount thirty years earlier, and even Wolhuter's salary was considered a subsistence wage.

About 1939 Rundgren quit the forestry department and took a job running a seven-hundred-acre ranch at Mawingo for a wealthy American widow named Wheeler. His starting salary there was £25 a month. Mrs. Wheeler was the girlfriend of Percy Smith, a settler from Eldoret who had captured the first bongo to be taken alive. When Smith died in 1939, Mrs. Wheeler returned to America and Rundgren (after declining Mrs. Wheeler's offer to accompany her) started working for another American woman. Mrs. Gabriel Prudhomme bought the Mawingo estate and wanted to turn it into a game park. She emphasized that it was not to be a zoo—she wanted the various bongo, forest hogs, zebra, oryx, cheetah, and other animals to live in a natural setting that was accessible for public viewing. Rundgren supervised the construction of two parallel moats, each five feet deep, around the entire estate and led the capture team, composed of himself and two farmers named Maurice Randall and Noel King. Together they began capturing wild animals to stock the park, using traps and experimenting with the lariat. The outbreak of war in September 1939 terminated the game-park idea. It was obvious no tourists would be visiting Kenya in the immediate future.

Rundgren served in the war as a scout for the 11th Indian Division, serving in the Sudan and in Ethiopia. In 1944 he was released from the army at the request of Archie Ritchie to become a control officer at Nanyuki. His official career with the game department spanned the years from 1944 until 1952, when he quit and immediately became one of Kenya's best-paid white hunters. His years as a professional hunter are beyond the scope of this volume.

Suffice it to say that Eric Rundgren became one of the most popular, and controversial, white hunters of the glamour years of East African hunting in the 1950s and 1960s—a legitimate safari superstar, if you will. His hunting skills were exceptional, even by the standards of his peers, and he combined his talents with a colorful personality and a devil-may-care attitude that made him great copy. Rundgren was a tough man, capable of killing leopard with his bare hands, and he had incredible powers of endurance. He was also violent at times and prone to being a bully.

He had a deep-rooted problem with authority his entire life, and sometimes flirted with the wrong side of the game laws. On one occasion, after he had bagged an immense elephant with tusks of 178 and 174 pounds, Rundgren panicked when he learned that Tanganyika game warden Swynnerton was investigating supposed irregularities in Rundgren's license and might confiscate the tusks. Rundgren sold the ivory to a shifty dealer who cut the tusks into smaller pieces to disguise their origin. His no-nonsense persona and his frequent conflicts with authority repelled some but attracted more. If it can accurately be said of anyone that you either loved him or hated him, it can be said of Eric Rundgren.

Rundgren died in Australia on 18 August 1992.

Eric Rundgren (right) after his encounter with an angry leopard.

Rundgren, Ture. The father of postwar PH Eric Rundgren, Ture (who arrived in East Africa in 1904) tried his hand at coffee farming as well as being an occasional professional hunter for the firm of Safariland, Ltd. To help make ends meet he would shoot Cape buffalo and sell the hides to the Kavirondo people for £5; they would use the hides to make shields. His son Eric got his first taste of hunting on these buffalo stalks.

A friend of Karen Blixen, Ture served as a scout under the command of Blixen's husband, Bror, in the first months of the 1914 war. Using motorcycles and loyal African scouts, Rundgren kept the communications lines open between Nairobi and the British forces in the field.

Runton, George (xxxx–1935). Runton was a founding member of EAPHA (see glossary) in 1934. He died of malaria a year later.

Rushby, George (1900–1969). Rushby was a pilot in the Royal Flying Corps during World War I and moved to Africa in 1922. Rushby successfully poached elephant in Mozambique, Tanganyika, Northern Rhodesia, and the Belgian Congo in the 1920s and 1930s. He took it easy on Tanganyika because he hoped to retire there someday. As his headquarters he used an old Tippu Tib hideout some five miles over the Belgian border from Rhodesia. He was particularly successful hunting around Lake Mweru (once shooting sixteen bulls and two cows in a day there) but was finally warned out of the area by a Belgian official due to pressure from the Rhodesian government.

He later served as a Tanganyika game warden from 1937–1953, specializing in lions and elephant control. During the 1940s Rushby was responsible for eliminating the dreaded Njombe man-eaters, a pride of lion that had killed a possible one thousand people over a period of several years. This was another of those rare cases in which a particular group of lion not only develop a taste for human flesh but also operate with cunning and intelligence that baffle hunters and scientists alike. Rushby shot some fifteen members of the pride in 1941–1946.

Rushby was the author of *No More the Tusker,* and the subject of T. V. Bulpin's excellent biography *The Hunter Is Death.* It has been estimated that he shot roughly four hundred elephant as an ivory hunter and another fourteen hundred on control duty. He died in retirement in South Africa.

Ruspoli, Prince Eugenio (xxxx–1893). Ruspoli was an Italian aristocrat who explored Jubaland and the Boran territory up to the Omo River in 1893. He was killed by an elephant while hunting on 4 December 1893. The Amara tribesmen of Ethiopia told Donaldson Smith in 1895 that Ruspoli had crept to within thirty yards of the animal and fired one shot. The elephant charged, grabbed the prince in its trunk, and shook him vigorously back and forth before dropping him to the ground and stomping him to death.

Dudo Muhammud, Ruspoli's gunbearer, told a similar story to Carl Akeley years later. In his version, the elephant grabbed Ruspoli with its trunk and lifted the man into the air. The prince was punching the elephant in the face with his fists while the elephant was beating him against his tusks. Finally the elephant threw Ruspoli on the ground and rolled on him.

Russell, Robert (xxxx–1876). He was a British hunter who was killed by a buffalo while hunting in 1876. He was accompanied by the sportsman Guy Dawnay, who was later killed by a buffalo himself. Russell had shot his buffalo in an open field with no trees to climb and was unable to kill the beast before it reached him. By the time Dawnay reached the scene, both man and buffalo lay dead side by side.

Ryall, Charles Henry (1874–1900). Ryall was the superintendent of Railway Police for the Uganda Railway. On 6 June 1900 he was traveling on official business

Grave of Charles Ryall.

from Mombasa to Nairobi when the Wakamba people of Kima (Swahili for "minced meat") prevailed upon him to take a day off and try to rid them of a man eating lion. Accompanied by two other Europeans, an Austrian merchant named Huebner and Parenti, the Italian vice consul at Mombasa, Ryall pulled his private railroad car onto a siding. The plan was for the three men to take turns on watch all night until the lion made its usual appearance. Accordingly they ate dinner early and Huebner and Parenti went to sleep, Ryall taking first watch. Huebner crawled into the top bunk while the Italian bedded down on some blankets on the floor.

According to John Patterson, Ryall dozed off on the lower berth while he was supposed to be sitting up on guard. There was a slight grade to the railroad spur, so the sliding door of the car did not shut tightly. No sooner had Ryall fallen asleep than the lion nudged the door open with its paw and sprang at him.

All hell broke loose. In its lunge at Ryall, the cat actually stepped on Parenti. Huebner fell out of the top bunk, landing on the beast, and then managed to clamber through a doorway into the front of the car where the terrified Indian staff was trying to tie the door shut with their turbans. The lion grabbed Ryall in its mouth and jumped off Parenti and through a window, escaping into the night with its prey. What was left of Ryall was found the next morning. Some days later a lion presumed to be the killer was caught near Kima and displayed in a cage for a few days before being shot. The attacks stopped for a while, but no one was ever really sure whether the trapped animal was the one that killed Ryall.

That was the version John Patterson wrote in his *Man-eaters of Tsavo.* There are many other versions in the literature, ranging from drastically different accounts to merely the change of a few details. Virtually every writer from that era claimed to have got the inside story, usually from either Huebner or Parenti, both of whom seem to have spent the rest of their lives cadging drinks in bars. Foran, for example, heard the story from both men. Most of the secondhand accounts got their information from Parenti, but Denis Lyell obtained his version from Huebner.

Everyone seemed to have some version of the story to tell. Some were way off. John Taylor, for instance, wrote in *Pondoro* that John Henry Patterson was in the car with Ryall. Frederick Seymour (1909) described how the lion pulled a man from a slowly moving train that was passing by its lair. Alex Johnston (1929) had Ryall being chased through the railway car by the lion, only to find the door had been locked by his panicked servants. And German-born Kenyan hunter Ossie Koenig, in his 1954 memoir *Pori Tupu,* repeated the story he had heard—that two British railway engineers had been sleeping in the train and were dragged to their deaths by multiple lion. He may have got his information from another German, C. G. Schillings, who wrote of two engineers sleeping in an open car when the guy in the bottom berth was seized by a lion. Schillings, a contemporary, insinuated that it was the dreaded Tsavo man-eaters that performed the railroad stunt.

One slightly different version—more a detail—is rather convincing. Richard Tjader was an American sent to East Africa to collect animal specimens for the American Museum of Natural History in New York. His book *The Big Game of Africa* (1911) tells of his adventures. He was riding the same Mombasa-Nairobi stretch of railroad in 1906 when he heard his version of Ryall's death. It mostly agrees with the standard account, but offers this twist: Tjader clearly infers that the three hunters had drunk too much. This would explain a lot, and be in keeping with the social mores of the time and human nature. Ryall, after all, was only twenty-five (born 13 July 1874) and presumably quite full of himself—a young British civil servant with a prestigious position gone lion hunting. He grew up in India, so it is doubtful he had much experience with lion. There is no way of proving the case now, but Tjader's account would explain how a young man hunting a known man-eater could fall asleep so quickly in such a situation. He was drunk. The story has the ring of truth, and it is easy to understand why it was not public knowledge, given that Ryall's family was rather highly placed in society.

As a footnote, Ryall's main purpose for his trip through Kima was to mediate a labor dispute in Nairobi. As Charles Miller put it marvelously in *The Lunatic Express* (1971), Ryall became "the first and only official in the history of labor arbitration to be eaten by a lion."

Ryan, Bill (xxxx–1985). Ryan was an experienced Kenya professional hunter in the 1930s, and also undertook buffalo and elephant control for the game department. During World War II he fought in the Somalia campaign and took a security post as police commandant of Mogadishu. In one of those exotic gestures so beloved by the white-hunter community, he established a surprisingly efficient intelligence network by recruiting Mogadishu's prostitutes as spies. Their undercover work was a fine asset. Later in the war he led antiguerrilla forces in the Somali hinterland. After the war Ryan continued his hunting career, bringing out a lot of movie star clients like Robert Stack and John Wayne and working on films such as *Hatari.* Ryan also served in the anti-Mau Mau campaign.

Ryan, Martin (xxxx–1917). Martin Ryan lived in Ceylon, where he adopted the local sport (popularized by Samuel Baker in the 1850s) of hunting deer down with a pack of hounds and then closing in for the kill with a knife. Around 1900 he moved to Northern Rhodesia and worked for a time on a cotton plantation near M'Soro. He was then hired by the government to manage a state-owned cattle ranch at Fort Jameson. There he met fellow hunters like Denis Lyell and Thomas Alexander Barnes.

Ryan, a tall, rangy man nicknamed the "stork" by the Africans, became one of the premier elephant hunters of North-East Rhodesia. He went after the animals whenever his duties at the cattle ranch permitted. When word came in of elephant in the area, he would mount his bicycle and pedal off to the scene at high speed. The district was perpetually poor and every penny counted, so he and the other hunters were willing to try anything for a buck. Not only did they procure meat and ivory from their hunting, they also fulfilled numerous commissions from the world's museums that were looking for skins and skeletons for taxidermy displays. In addition to elephant, he hunted buffalo, hippo, kudu, sable, roan antelope, and lesser game like warthog.

In 1913 Ryan captured an elephant calf and was offered £25 by the Pretoria Zoo (£30 if it lived for six months), but his partner in the capture, a man named Fellowes, wanted to hold out for a better offer. After three weeks the calf took sick and died, leaving the two men with nothing.

Ryan originally used a .375 magazine rifle in Africa but later switched to a .416 Rigby. He habitually cut down his rifles to make the barrel shorter, finding them easier to sight. He was very interested in anatomy and was constantly dissecting animals to see how they were put together.

Martin Ryan.

Ryan served in the famous 25th Battalion of the Royal Fusiliers in World War I, commanding a troop of mounted infantry. He still managed to do some hunting, shooting a rhino and a buffalo while on a mission to Tanganyika. On 18 October 1917, he and his brother were killed in action in a firefight against a German patrol.

S

Sacchi, Maurizio (xxxx–1897). Sacchi was the naturalist and scientist on the 1895 Italian Ethiopian expedition led by Capt. Vittorio Bottego. His assignment was to collect and categorize the natural-history specimens and take meteorological readings.

Sacchi did not have a good trip. On 5 November 1895 he was speared in the shoulder during a skirmish with Somali raiders. He recovered, only to be killed in a skirmish against the Ethiopians on 5 February 1897 while he was leading a small patrol sent to pick up a stockpile of elephant tusks.

Sadlier, Tom V. Also known as Saddler, Sadlier was an American Civil War veteran who hunted the Zambezi Valley area in the 1870s. A friend of Selous, he hunted with him and George Dorehill in 1872 but left the group to go after elephant with the famous Boer hunter Jan Viljoen. Sadlier was unhappy with the Boers, whom he felt had cheated him out of a kill. He was also known to have had a hunting camp along the Deka River about 1875, at the site of what later became the Robins Camp area of Wankie National Park.

Salmon, Roy John Dugdale "Samaki" (1888–1952). "Samaki" Salmon was a legendary Uganda game warden and elephant control expert. He served in East Africa during World War I as a member of a partisan unit led by Capt. Tracy Philipps, and participated in several dangerous commando-style raids into German Tanganyika. Salmon was made a captain and awarded a Military Cross for his exploits.

When the Uganda Game Department was formed in 1924 (then called the Elephant Control Department, which should give you a sense of its priorities), Salmon was one of two European rangers, the other being Deaf Banks. They worked under the direction of the game warden of Uganda, C. R. S. Pitman. Salmon spent more than twenty years as a ranger and became one of the legendary figures of his time.

One of Salmon's noteworthy exploits came in 1930, when he was guiding the Prince of Wales to Fort Portal in western Uganda. This small safari was making its way on foot through dense bush. The prince had packed a bottle of whiskey as an emergency ration, despite Salmon's airy announcement that it was a rather short hike and there was plenty of whiskey at Fort Portal.

As they trudged along the trail, it began to rain heavily. Salmon, who hadn't been on this track for some years, became disoriented and lost all sense of direction. The men wound up huddled under blankets all night in a drenching rainstorm, thankfully sipping the whiskey, with the prince immensely enjoying the experienced ranger's discomfit at getting the heir to the British throne lost in the jungle. They made Fort Portal the next day.

When Pitman was seconded to Rhodesia in the 1930s, Salmon took his place as Uganda game warden. He continued his elephant control work, killing over a thousand by 1936 and a reported four thousand during his career (David Blunt recorded that Salmon stopped counting at one thousand).

Some animals went easier than others. Late one afternoon in 1939 Salmon went out after two bulls that had been causing a lot of trouble, raiding local *shambas* and chasing travelers. He dropped one with a head shot and the second with a bullet in the heart. But as he was closing in to finish off the second, the first elephant, a single-tusker, sprang to its feet and ran off into the bush. Salmon had been sick and was rather fatigued, and in the opinion of many experts should have called it a night and picked up the trail in the morning. Instead he tried to follow up in the gloom. As he worked his way slowly through a thicket, one of his two African gunbearers touched his arm in warning—the wounded bull was standing right next to them. Salmon fired both barrels with the rifle actually touching the elephant's head, but because he was firing almost directly upward, he succeeded only in blinding the animal on the tusk side. The bull wrenched the rifle from his hands with its trunk and then grabbed Salmon around the waist and began to beat him against the ground. The elephant then threw the hunter down and tried to gore him, but fortunately the tusk was so curved that it could be used only as a bludgeon, not a skewer. Still, Salmon was taking a beating as he desperately tried to roll away from the huge bull.

Salmon's first gunbearer, a brave man, crawled up on his hands and knees to try to give the hunter a rifle, but naturally approached on the side without a tusk, not knowing that was the only side the elephant could still see. The elephant slammed its trunk down on the gunbearer's head, killing him instantly, then walked to the corpse and sniffed him, as if to make sure he was dead. The second gunbearer, by no means a shooter, fired the reserve rifle into the bull's flank at that moment. Startled and hurt, the elephant finally ran off into the brush. It was found dead the next day. Amazingly, the only physical damage Salmon had sustained, besides one hell of a lot of bruises, was a broken wristwatch.

Salmon was the rare big-game hunter and naturalist who considered the African elephant to be not very intelligent. Writing in the British sporting magazine *The Field* in July 1951, he stated, "My outstanding impression is of the pathetic stupidity of the overwhelming majority of them. Between the fortieth and fiftieth elephants, the not-so-stupid one would turn up; and then the idea that the whole elephant race was pathetic would be in abeyance for an indefinite period."

Ill health eventually caused Salmon to retire from the game department after the end of World War II. He died in his sixth year of retirement on his farm in Natal in 1952.

Salt, Henry (1780–1827). Trained as an artist, Henry Salt toured India and North Africa with George Annesley as a young man. In 1809 Salt was sent to Abyssinia by the British government with orders to establish an embassy at Addis Ababa. He spent only a short time there before moving on to a consular post in Egypt, but his book *A Voyage to Abyssinia* (1814) is said to contain the first English-language description of a hippo hunt. In addition he collected the small antelope that now bears his name, Salt dik-dik *(Madoqua saltiana).*

As consul, Salt is chiefly remembered as a defiler of ancient tombs. Along with Giovanni Battista Belzoni, he is credited with smuggling out an incredible treasure in Egyptian antiquities. In 1821 the British Museum balked at his asking price of £8,000 for an assortment of artifacts that he had shipped from Cairo, and Salt was accused of neglecting his official duties in order to concentrate on his antique business. An extremely ambitious man, Salt's last years were marred by his bitterness at being passed over for promotion. When he died of an intestinal disease in late 1827 it was estimated he had made more than £20,000 from his tomb raiding, a considerable fortune in those days.

Sanderson, Arthur Buchanan (xxxx–1925). Sanderson was a distiller who became a professional hunter in Kenya in the 1920s. In late 1924 he signed on with the Martin and Osa Johnson expedition that was filming near Lake Marsabit in northern Kenya. Contrary to the publicity put out by the Johnsons, Osa wasn't the only person guarding Martin while he took his dangerous footage. In actual fact there was always a backup hunter, ready to drop a charging rhino or lion should the animal get too close to the cameraman. It was Sanderson's job to provide this extra layer of security. Although fairly new as a hunter, he already had a reputation as a cool and skilled hand in the bush.

One of the other workers on the Johnson safari was a seventeen-year-old American boy named Beverly Hecksher Furber, a wild rich kid who was the son of one of the expedition's backers. Furber's assignment was to help Sanderson and also tend to general camp chores. On 3 May 1925, Sanderson and Furber were directed by Martin Johnson to try to spook some rhinos out of a thicket just a quarter of a mile from the lake. They stumbled across three of the animals, one of which charged directly at them. Young Furber put two rounds into the rhino, but it managed to gore Sanderson in the thigh before dying.

Sanderson was brought back to the Johnsons camp at Marsabit, where he spent over a month recuperating. In need of further medical attention, he was then brought back to Nairobi in early June. Complications set in and he died in the hospital. Sanderson left a son, the best-selling naturalist and cryptozoologist Ivan Sanderson (1911–1973).

Sanderson, Bill. One of three hunting brothers from Scotland (Bob and Tom were the two others), Bill Sanderson hunted throughout the Lowveld of the Transvaal from the 1870s on through the next thirty years. He was known for his great horsemanship and woodcraft. Starting about 1873, he made annual expeditions into the interior using a Boer trek-wagon drawn by donkeys. The donkeys were a business expense because they would inevitably succumb to the tsetse fly in short order. The cost of replacing them every year was offset by the sale of the ivory, hides, and biltong (jerky) that Sanderson gathered.

Pioneer Bill Sanderson of Logogote, 1908.

This didn't leave much of a profit margin, but Sanderson and his brothers loved the life, and every spring found them heading into the bush with their donkeys, hoping to make the venture profitable by killing more animals than they had the year before.

In the 1890s Bill Sanderson was prospecting for gold in the Transvaal. By 1900 he had set up a trading station and cattle ranch near Sabie called "Ceylon" and later, with brother Bob, a farm at Logogote called "Peebles." Bob eventually established his own farm some miles away at Klip Koppies. In his spare moments Bill hunted everything except elephant, which had pretty much been shot out of the area. He is known to have shot just five lion in his career, however, being primarily a meat hunter. He once captured a fourteen-foot python, which he kept in a chicken coop, where, amazingly, it didn't molest the feathered inhabitants.

Brother Bob died during the Boer War of illness in the Barberton Hospital. Bill eventually died of an intestinal illness in Johannesburg. He is remembered as having possessed the finest horse stables and dog pack (used to hunt bushbuck and duiker) of his time.

Sapieha, Prince Eustachy (1881–1963). Sapieha is listed in the 1928 edition of Rowland Ward with several impressive elephant tusks, the best being a pair from the Ituri forest at 103 and 102 pounds. Sapieha also had listings in the Chad buffalo category.

Sapieha was married to the Princess Lubomirska (1888–1964). He served as the foreign minister of Poland, as well as the Polish ambassador to Great Britain. He narrowly escaped execution when captured by the Russians in 1939; instead, he was held captive in the notorious Lubyanka prison until released as a sop to the Polish resistance fighters after the German invasion of Russia in 1941.

After the war Sapieha moved to Kenya, where he took up hunting, eventually being joined by his namesake son. In 1959 the Polish government-in-exile awarded Sapieha the Order of the White Eagle, Poland's highest decoration, one of only six people (excluding presidents of the government-in-exile) to be so honored between 1941 and 1990. Sapieha wrote a small 1953 book called *Safari*, which I'm not sure has ever been translated from Polish. His son Stas moved to Africa in the 1940s and became a professional hunter. His son Lew was also listed in the 1928 Rowland Ward record book.

Saunders, W. A South African hunter active in Mashonaland and Matabeleland around 1870.

Sauer, Dr. Hans (1857–1939). Sauer was a Boer physician, a mine owner, and a member of the Rhodes circle. Trained as a doctor, he frequently served as a district medical officer; he was known for his outspokenness, which bordered on contempt for authority. In the 1880s he engaged in the so-called "smallpox war" against Dr. Leander Starr Jameson. A number of miners and their wives reported sick with skin lesions. Sauer diagnosed and publicized the presence of smallpox while Jameson, for reasons best appreciated by the shareholders of the British South Africa Company, claimed that the mysterious rashes reflected a harmless skin disease. The controversy caused a sensation in the press, and Rhodes and the other mine owners were terrified that their labor pool would suddenly dry up. A government doctor named Saunders was sent to investigate the matter. It was indeed smallpox, but by the time the truth came out the danger of a major outbreak had passed. Sauer was allowed to open up a vaccination clinic that stopped the spread of the disease.

Consistent with the spirit of the times, Sauer and Jameson later became good friends and even business partners. The two doctors once played a legendary poker game at the climax of which Sauer, with £800 in the pot, bet all of his possessions including his ox team, wagon, guns, and personal equipment on the strength of having four kings; Jameson had a straight flush and was the winner. Jameson allowed Sauer to keep his boots and surgical implements.

In 1894 Sauer discovered ancient ruins in Matabeleland, in company with two Englishmen named Captain Sampson and Mr. Bradley. The ruins, which were named by the men Fort Regina, consisted of an oval fort that was made of stone. Sauer, who was another of those South Africans present at an amazing number of important historical events, was at the famous conference in 1896 when Cecil Rhodes negotiated peace with the rebel Matabele leaders. Sauer was also arrested and tried as a traitor by the Transvaal government following the Jameson Raid. He was the author of *Ex Africa* (1937), an above-average autobiography that is distinctive in that it succeeds in painting both the big picture (international politics, the founding of Rhodesia, etc.) and the small (daily life on the veld, hunting, and communal Boer squabbles).

In 1886–1890 Sauer served as the district surgeon for Johannesburg under the Transvaal government. As such he was responsible for performing autopsies on every suspicious death; in the wild-and-woolly atmosphere of the mining days sudden death was commonplace, and Sauer (who received a fee of £10, 10 shillings for each postmortem) was constantly employed in this capacity. He made so much money from this practice that at one point he actually advised the government of the Boer republic that they were paying him too much. Monday was the busiest day, as the bodies of those miners and natives who died or were killed while letting off steam over the weekend had to be examined, sometimes as many as ten in a day.

In *Ex Africa* Sauer briefly noted the presence of a serial killer operating in the Transvaal. This person, who was never caught, murdered at least five men, three in downtown Johannesburg and two in the nearby Parktown district. He would waylay his victims—apparently an ambush—and stab them through the heart. In each case he also took a long, thin blade and inserted it between the base of the skull and the top of the spine, severing the spinal cord; it is unclear which injury came first. Sauer noted that robbery was not suspected as a motive, as two of the victims were poor white men and the others were native laborers. The killings took place roughly the same time as the much more famous "Ripper" killings were happening in London.

Not a man given to flights of fancy, Sauer reported an interesting cryptozoological story in his memoirs. As a schoolboy, he was once swimming with friends in the Orange River near Aliwal North. The boys fled from the water when they saw "what we took to be a very large black snake swimming steadily upstream, with its head out of the water." The beast was not unlike the popular image of a dragon or the Loch Ness Monster. Sauer's father and a neighbor armed themselves with rifles and pursued the creature but lost it among some rapids and islands. The British prospector Cornell saw a similar animal in the same river. ROWLAND WARD 1928: BONGO (KENYA).

Savage, Thomas. Dr. Savage, an American missionary and amateur naturalist, in 1847 visited a mission on the Gabon River in West Africa, where he got a good look at some gorillas. He published the first good description of that animal in the December 1847 edition of the *Boston Journal of Natural History.*

Scarborough, Earl of (1857–1945). Scarborough was an English aristocrat who went on a well-publicized safari to West Africa in 1890. He and his friends stayed aboard the steam yacht *Lancaster Witch,* making daily excursions along the coast and along the Niger and Gambia Rivers. One member of the shooting party was killed by an elephant—his ammunition had become wet, and he was unable to stop the animal's charge and took a tusk directly through the chest.

Schellendorf, Baron Bronsart von. An early hunter in German East Africa, he is known to have shot about sixty lion over fifteen years, a high figure for its day.

Schillings, Carl Georg (1865–1921). A German photographer, Schillings began exploring Tanganyika in 1896 and achieved distinction with his innovative use of flash powder to take photos of big game at night—at no small risk to himself. Given camera technology's then-primitive state, Schillings's was a dangerous business no matter what the hour. The cameras were large and bulky and difficult to move quickly. Ironically, however, the precision German optics were finer than those found in most modern cameras, and many of his photographs are of startling quality. His

German photographer C. G. Schillings.

Schillings's camera.

night photography, of animals coming to a water hole and lion attacking tethered bait, was exceptional.

His operation was a huge one—170 porters carried dozens of heavy chests full of chemicals, glass plates, and camera equipment as well as the normal safari impedimenta. His artistic success was a direct result of his painstaking preparation. Schillings often split his team into two separate camps so that he could be operating from one while the other was packed up and sent off to a new location. He was often accompanied by a taxidermist named William Orgeich and a friend named Alfred Kaiser, and was frequently assisted by German colonial officers and their askaris.

These were tough safaris. Schillings could never afford to get complacent, could never let his guard down. In January 1897 he nearly died from a severe case of malaria, surviving only after weeks of care at Fort Mumias by the British geologist C. W. Hobley and an English officer named Tompkins. His expeditions had problems with lion, hyena, and crocodile, and Schillings and his men were frequently charged by rhino. On one occasion one of his porters was badly gored and thrown a considerable distance. The man survived despite having his intestines hanging outside his body. Another porter was less fortunate. Having become separated from the column while drunk, he was trying to make his way back to camp along a trail at night when he was killed by a rhino. By the time Schillings found him, lion had eaten most of the body.

The rhino indeed seems to have been Schillings's particular nemesis. Modern readers who wonder why the early colonials considered the rhino as inimical to settlement would do well to read Schillings's memoirs. He had dozens of close calls with the huge creatures, some provoked and some not, and on several occasions barely missed being skewered. The black rhino that was so common in East Africa in those days is a nervous, aggressive animal that, through centuries of evolution, has learned the defense of blindly charging all enemies. That mechanism was tremendously successful until the invention of efficient firearms, after which the tactic became suicidal. East Africa, with its huge tracts of thick thornbush, was a perfect environment for the animal, and over the centuries countless people have fallen victim to black rhino.

Eventually Schillings's meticulous planning and hard work paid off. He returned to Europe with his specimens and a wealth of notes, and set about writing his book. After a successful German edition came out, in 1905 he published a two-volume English version of his work, *With Flashlight and Rifle* (introduction by Sir Harry Johnston), followed by a single-volume American abridgement.

The book greatly influenced future wildlife photographers. It's particularly interesting to an English-speaking reader with the benefit of historical hindsight. The narrative is naturally Germano-centric and shows signs of a proud Teutonic imperialism, almost to the level of the syrupy schlock-patriotism that Joseph Goebbels produced a generation later. Where British and French authors might write about the scenic beauty of Africa, Schillings always felt compelled to remind the reader that the Imperial flag was overlooking the scene—"the beautiful, the grand, the German Masai-nyika!" that sort of thing. And he tells an unconsciously funny tale about how he was almost nailed by a panicked elephant while daydreaming about the glorious Fatherland and humming "one of our beautiful folk songs."

In addition to his photography, Schillings made some valuable contributions to natural history. He was one of the first observers to note the existence of lion prides—he called them troops—and of adult male lion lacking manes, a topic that was still controversial in the 1990s. Schillings brought the first live white-bearded gnu back to Europe in 1900, two to his estate at Weiherhof near Dresden and another that he shipped to a British game park. He also had a species of hyena named after him, if only for a while. At the time of his first safari, zoologists believed that the striped hyena did not exist in East Africa south of Somalia. Schillings knew that an animal resembling the striped hyena of the Near East was rather common in Tanganyika and Kenya. In 1896 he trapped 121 of them and sent sixty-six sets of skins and skulls to Berlin for identification. In recognition of his accomplishment, the animal—a striped hyena—was named *Hyaena schillingsi.*

It is now known that the striped hyena *(H. hyaena)* shows a tremendous amount of individual variation, and the *H. schillingsi* classification is considered defunct.

Schindelar, Fritz (xxxx–1914). A colorful and controversial Kenya hunter of the immediate pre-World War I era, Schindelar's origins are cloaked in mystery. He gave all the outward signs of having had a high birth and a good education, and even today writers sometimes refer to him as an Austrian prince. Other rumors pegged him as coming from Germany or Switzerland. A photograph found after his death shows Schindelar in the uniform of a colonel of Hungarian Hussars, which would indicate that he was indeed of high birth. It was not unusual for aristocrats to seek a simpler life in Africa. Denys Finch Hatton, to cite just one example, was the son of a British earl. Schindelar is believed to have arrived in East Africa in 1906, but even this is disputed by some historians. He seems to have enjoyed creating an aura of mystery about himself.

Whatever his antecedents, Schindelar soon rose to the top rank of Kenya's professional hunters. He worked for the firm of Newland & Tarlton and was known for his strength and daring. He was also known for his love of the good life—Fritz was a common figure at Nairobi's best restaurants, bars, and gambling dens. Schindelar possessed a certain reckless charm that captivated his clients and fellow hunters, who would shake their heads in amusement over his latest crazy adventure.

It caught up to him in the end. When the American filmmaker Paul Rainey began looking for a hunter to help him film a lion hunt with dogs, all of Kenya's best lion hunters turned him down—except for Schindelar. Even Clifford and Howard Hill, probably the two best-known lion hunters of that time and place, declined to take on the assignment. Rainey envisioned filming the lion at bay, surrounded by snapping hounds, and hoped to film a head-on charge at the camera. *The Hills* (and others) pointed out that the lion, unable to escape, would surely charge at the first human it saw, leaving time for only one shot to try to stop the charge. Schindelar disregarded the danger, apparently believing that he could beat the odds by staying on horseback.

At first it appeared that he and Rainey would succeed. During the first two weeks of their hunt near Mount Longonot they killed fifteen lion, but Rainey failed to get the precise footage he desired. On 9 January 1914 the group set the hounds after a lion seen at the head of the Ngasawa Gorge. After a long chase the animal holed up in a thicket. Rainey set up his camera while Schindelar repeatedly tried to get the lion to charge out from the cover by riding his white horse ever closer to the thicket before wheeling away.

Suddenly the lion burst from the bush. It was too close—Schindelar had pushed his luck too far. The furious cat caught him just in the act of turning his horse and knocked him from the saddle. Schindelar showed his amazing dexterity by landing on his feet with his rifle in his hands. Just as the lion sprang for the kill, Schindelar fired one barrel directly into the animal's face.

Incredibly, he missed. There is no explanation, just the simple fact that his hasty shot went wide. The lion pushed him to the ground and gave him one horrible bite in the stomach. Then it jumped off him and charged the rest of the party, who brought it down with a volley of bullets. At first Rainey and the others thought Schindelar might be OK, given the short time the lion had spent over him. When they ran up to the fallen hunter, however, they saw that he had been virtually disemboweled by the attack.

Schindelar, still conscious, was rushed to Nairobi, reaching the hospital six hours later. According to a witness, Pop Binks, Fritz kept repeating, "My God, what a blow!" over and over. He died after two days of excruciating pain.

Schinderhutte, Stoffel (xxxx–1875). Schinderhutte was a German trader who spent decades hunting and trading in the Zambezi Valley. He was one of the first Europeans to see Victoria Falls, visiting there as early as 1873. Selous described him (1881) as a "fine handsome man, and, I have been told, a very agreeable and well-informed one when he was sober." That last remark may indicate where this is going. One of the items Schinderhutte had to trade, unfortunately, was brandy, and he was prone to sampling his own product.

Selous last saw him in November 1874. Shortly afterward Schinderhutte was making his way back to Cape Province when he suffered an attack of delirium tremens or some other neurological disorder brought on by drinking. He began shooting his own oxen and committing other mad acts. Fed up with this behavior, one of his African employees decided to quit and demanded his back wages. Schinderhutte, incensed that the man's contracted time had not expired, shot him dead.

Schinderhutte's mind was not entirely gone—once he sobered up he knew that the victim's friends, if not the authorities, would soon seek revenge. He decided never to leave his wagon without a loaded firearm. It didn't help. A few days later Schinderhutte vanished, and his hyena-chewed remains were found the next morning. A person or persons unknown looted Schinderhutte's wagons of all guns, powder, and other valuable items the day after his disappearance. It seemed likely that one of the murdered employee's friends or relatives had killed the German, but once the cause of the affair became known, the authorities had no interest in investigating the case.

Schmarsow, H. This man hunted in North-East Rhodesia and lived at Blantyre, Luangwa Valley, around 1910. His 1909 elephant kill consisted of four in North-East Rhodesia and a fifth in Nyasaland, the last having tusks of 93 and 97 pounds, very heavy for that time and place.

Schmidt, C. E. An official in German East Africa, Schmidt went hunting for hippo in the Rufiji River circa 1905. Schmidt and his men shot two and were towing the carcasses back to shore in a large rowboat when a huge hippo attacked the boat, spilling them all into the water. All the men could swim and were striking out for the bank when the hippo returned and bit one of the Africans nearly in half. The rest, including Schmidt, survived. Efforts to snag their rifles and cartridge bags from the riverbottom proved fruitless.

Schmidt, Johann (xxxx–1861). Schmidt was a German trader who made a living in Abyssinia, at Sufi on the Atbara River, where he shot hippo for *kibokos* (whips) and captured wild animals for zoos. He had a partner named Florian who was killed by a lion in 1861. Schmidt thereupon joined Samuel Baker's expedition as a sort of foreman, but died of illness that December.

Schoemann, David. Well-known Boer hunter in the Transvaal around 1880.

Schomburgk, Hans. This German wildlife filmmaker and collector in the 1920s had worked for Hagenbeck. He was author of *Wild und Wilde in Herzen Afrika* (1910) and *Mein Freunde im Busch* (1936).

Schultz, Bert (1900–1971). As an elephant control officer in Northern Rhodesia (1922–1960), he shot about 1,100 elephants and 29 lions on control. Schultz was a native of South Africa but moved to Rhodesia at an early age. He was based largely in the Luangwa Valley. His favorite rifles were a .450 Rigby, a .450 Westley Richards double, and a .30-06 for brush work. Schultz bagged his two best elephants in the space of 12 hours, each having identical pairs of tusks weighing 105 and 98 pounds.

Schuver, Juan Maria (1852–1883). Schuver explored both the White Nile and the Blue Nile 1880–1883 looking for a passage connecting the interior to the Indian Ocean. He was murdered by tribesmen when he entered the Dinka territory.

Schweinfurth, Georg August (1836–1925). This German explorer was born in Riga on 29 December 1836 (another source says 1838). In 1864–1866 he explored around the Red Sea, collecting botanical specimens. In 1868 he moved his activities to the Sudan and then to the Congo. In 1869 he was the first European to contact the Pygmies in the Akkas. On 1 December 1870 his safari and all his records were destroyed by a fire. He returned to Khartoum in July 1871 and then went back to Europe. In 1873 he did some explorations in the Sahara. In 1874 he founded a geographic society at Cairo and stayed there for at least twenty years, making occasional scientific forays into the continent. In 1890–1891, for instance, Schweinfurth went to Abyssinia, where he gathered a valuable collection of botanical specimens. He was the author of *Heart of Africa.*

Sclater, Bertram Lutley (1866–1897). A son of Philip Sclater and brother of William Sclater, Bertram was an officer (then a lieutenant) of the Royal Engineers who joined the staff of Harry Johnston in Nyasaland in 1890. He spent the next several years building roads and other infrastructure, with time out for big-game hunting. He returned to Britain as a captain in 1893. In 1895 Sclater was sent to East Africa by the Foreign Office to supervise the construction of a 130-mile road from Kibwezi to Kedong. Parts of the road are still used today.

Sclater, Philip Lutley (1829–1913). Sclater was secretary of the London Zoological Society from the 1850s to 1902, and an English naturalist who received an unusual pair of rhino horns from Harry Johnston in 1892 (Johnston had received them from a trader named Harry Pettitt). They were unusual in that they were quite similar to white rhino horns but came from near Lake Nyasa, where that animal had long been extinct.

Sclater, William Lutley (1859–1913). Son of P. L. Sclater and a fine zoologist in his own right, William did a lot of fieldwork in India and South Africa and succeeded his father as secretary of the London Zoological Society in 1902.

Scott, Lord Francis George Montagu Douglas (1879–1952). Lord Francis Scott was the fifth son of the duke of Buccleigh and lieutenant colonel of the Grenadier Guards. As a military man he served in both the Boer War and the Great War and was wounded in the latter conflict. He married Lady Eileen Elliot, daughter of the earl of Minto. Scott arrived in East Africa in 1920 and became a fixture in the Kenya Highlands social set. He became the acknowledged leader of the settlers after the death of the third Baron Delamere in 1931, retiring after an electoral defeat by Michael Blundell after World War II.

Scott, John. John Scott was born a British subject in Saint Helena. He married a Spanish girl and set up an illegal slaving station on the Congo. Despite occasional visits from the Royal Navy (during which Scott and his wife would simply go camping in the bush), it was an extremely lucrative operation. On one occasion Scott was alleged to have rid himself of forty unwanted slaves by tying them to an anchor chain and drowning them in the river. When the missionaries first started coming in the 1870s, Scott tried to ingratiate himself with them by being helpful with supplies and information. He was of some assistance, for example, to the Grenfell-Comber expedition of 1878. This worked for a time, but eventually Scott was found out. He escaped to Spain and died there some years later.

Scott, R. L. Scott was hunting deep in German East Africa with R. J. Cuninghame when World War I broke out in 1914. Despite German patrols sent out to intercept them, the two men managed to get back to British territory safely and enlist in the war effort. ROWLAND WARD 1928: SITATUNGA, BUFFALO, ROAN, KONGONI, LEOPARD, CHEETAH, ELAND, DAMA GAZELLE, ERITREAN GAZELLE, LECHWE, ORIBI, LICHTENSTEIN HARTEBEEST.

Scott-Elliott, G. F. Scott-Elliott was a Scottish naturalist who visited Uganda in 1893–1894 to collect zoological and botanical specimens. He made an accurate map of the Ruwenzori region and was the author of *A Naturalist's Wanderings in Mid-Africa* (1894) as well as "Africa as a Field for Colonial Enterprise" (*Scottish Geographical Magazine,* 1895).

Selborne, Earl of (William Waldgrave Palmer) (1859–1942). Lord Selborne was governor of the Orange Free State 1905–1907 and high commissioner of South Africa 1905–1910. An avid sportsman, he left the latter post in 1910 and went on an extended shooting trip in the Kalahari guided by Arnold Hodson and Vaughan-Kirby. A detailed account of this safari is related in Hodson's *Trekking the Great Thirst* (1912). The Barotse chief Lewanika gave Selborne a young hippo, which he in turn donated to the Transvaal Zoo.

Selby, Paul. Selby was an American mining engineer and enthusiastic amateur photographer from San Francisco working in South Africa. In 1924 he began taking pictures of the animals at Sabi Game Reserve, using a 500mm telephoto lens and experimenting with nighttime flash photography. In 1926 a portfolio of his photos was used in the campaign to persuade the South African government to grant the reserve national park status.

G. F. Scott-Elliott.

Selland. An elephant hunter in the Lado Enclave in the 1900s. He hunted with John Boyes in the Koba area in 1907 (Boyes's *The Company of Adventurers* places this safari in 1901, but other sources and internal evidence in the same book establish the later date), and both Selland and Boyes each came out with twelve hundred pounds of ivory. The two hunters made a second trip to the same area and took fifteen hundred pounds of ivory, including a pair of tusks weighing 150 pounds each. On this expedition Selland lost four of his porters, who wandered away from the camp one day to forage for food and were killed by local tribesmen armed with poisoned arrows.

Elephant hunting was a rough business in those days. In 1910 Selland established a camp on the banks of the Nile near Lado. Unfortunately, he had planted himself right in the middle of territory claimed by two rivals for the leadership of the Madi tribe. Warriors from one faction raided the camp, and Selland and his men were lucky to escape with their lives—all their weapons, ivory, and provisions were lost.

Boyes, who knew Selland as well as anyone did, did not believe Selland was his real name. He was of northern European origin, probably a Swede or a Dane. He was also a veteran of the United States navy and had served with the British in several African campaigns including the Anglo-Boer War. When that conflict ended, he eventually made his way to Kenya, where he asked Boyes for a job. Boyes refused, for he was always reluctant to take on partners or assistants with little experience in elephant hunting. But Selland, or whatever his name was, started pitching in around Boyes's camp and quickly made himself so useful that Boyes took him along on a trip to Abyssinia in 1906. Boyes booked Selland a third-class berth on the steamer taking them to Djibouti as a sort of character test—if Selland complained about the atrocious conditions in third class, Boyes was prepared to immediately cut him loose. But the Scandinavian endured the passage stoically, and Boyes realized he had found a good employee. Soon Selland was a full partner in Boyes's various hunting adventures.

They worked together for several years, occasionally taking breaks when one or the other would go into business by himself for a few months, but always getting back together in the end. Boyes found Selland to be an excellent pupil, a good hunter, and an outstanding rifle shot, as well as an honest and upright man. His only fault was said to have been an almost total lack of a sense of humor.

Boyes was in Britain on vacation in 1910–1911 when Selland, hunting in the Congo, contracted a bad case of malaria and returned to Kenya. Blackwater fever soon developed, and Selland died in the Nairobi hospital. Because his was an assumed name and he left no will, his estate of some £2,000 was left in a bank while the authorities tried to figure out who his next of kin was. They were unsuccessful, and the money eventually reverted to the state.

Selous, Edmund (1857–1934). The youngest brother of Frederick Selous, Edmund trained as a barrister and began practicing in 1881. From an early age he was interested in ornithology and in 1898 began concentrating on birds on a large scale. Edmund abhorred blood sports and collecting birds, and much preferred to simply observe them. Not only can he be considered the first modern birdwatcher, he even invented the words "birdwatcher" and "birdwatching." His books included *Bird Watching* (1901), *Bird Life Glimpses* (1905), *Thought Transference—or What?—in Birds* (1931), and several other works.

Selous, Frederick Courteney (1851–1917). Probably the most famous hunter of them all was Frederick Courteney Selous. The middle name is also seen as Courtenay and even Courtney, but Courteney is how it is printed on the title pages of his books. As a fifteen-year-old boy in 1867, Selous (pronounced *Sell-ooo)* survived a notorious disaster at Regent's Park Ornamental Water in London, a large pond used for skating and other winter sports. Park employees had cut a hole in the ice to help some ducks that had nowhere to swim, but cracks spreading out from the hole quickly spread, and some hundreds of skaters slid into the freezing water. The park was transformed into a nightmare scene of screaming children and parents. Young Selous escaped by spread-eagling himself on a slab of ice and carefully making his way to dry land. Many adults showed less presence of mind and drowned. It took weeks to recover most of the bodies. The official death toll was forty-nine, but there were no doubt many more fatalities.

Selous arrived in Africa in 1871 with £400 in his pocket. Nineteen years old, he had been studying medicine in Switzerland and Germany when, inspired by the works of Gordon Cumming and Baldwin, he suddenly decided to seek a life of adventure in the Dark Continent. Landing at Algoa Bay on 4 September, he set out for the diamond mines two days later. From there he planned on striking out into the interior in pursuit of Africa's legendary big game.

He reached the mines on 28 October 1871. Almost immediately somebody stole Selous's favorite rifle, a double-barreled breechloader made by Reilly. He was left with only a pair of inaccurate light rifles. Nevertheless, after buying a horse for £8, Selous set out for the Orange River to hunt and trade, accompanied by a young miner named Arthur Laing and an interpreter named Crossley who had a drinking problem.

The first trek was a brief one. Selous, Laing, and Crossley traded cattle, sheep, and goats along the Orange and Vaal Rivers and were back in Kimberley, capital of the diamond district, by early March, splitting a profit of some £145. Confident now that he knew what he was doing, Selous outfitted himself properly with wagons and oxen and added a Snider carbine to his arsenal, a breechloading conversion of the Civil War-era Enfield rifled musket. Toward the end of April 1872 Selous embarked on his first long-term hunting expedition with two friends named George Dorehill and T. V. Sadlier. In addition to Selous's three firearms, Dorehill carried a Martini-Henry and Sadlier an Enfield. These were all transitional weapons that few modern hunters would choose to use on elephant.

Thus began the first of the great hunts that were to earn Fred Selous undying fame. He had his rookie troubles. All of the horses ran away one night, for instance, and it took two weeks to gather them all up. He soon began to learn all about stalking and firearms. Along the trail he was able to purchase two proper elephant guns, Boer *roers*, smoothbore percussion muzzleloaders that fired enormous lead slugs weighing four to a pound.

As recounted in his 1881 book *A Hunter's Wanderings in Africa* and synopsized in dozens of monographs and other accounts, Selous's trail eventually carried him on big-game hunting expeditions all over the globe. In late 1872 he met up with the Bechuana king, Khama; shortly thereafter with the great Boer elephant hunter, Jan Viljoen; and a few days later with Lobengula, king of the Matabele people. Selous had come to Bulawayo, Lobengula's capital, to request permission to hunt elephant in Matabeleland. The powerful king scoffed at the slight, boyish-looking youth and teased him by asking if he had come to shoot steenbok, the small South African antelope. Selous thereupon shot seventy-eight elephant in Lobengula's territory, and the king teased him no more. The two, in fact, became friends, after a fashion.

Selous spent the next several decades hunting in southern Africa with remarkable success. He worked with a variety of friends and partners, frequently putting up other down-on-their-luck hunters by the system called "shooting on halves." On one trip with George Wood the pair shot ninety-two elephant, with Selous claiming forty-two. These totals were surpassed not that many years later by ivory hunters like Neumann and Bell, but those men had the benefit of using magazine rifles while Selous at that time was using roers and other black-powder weapons, a much chancier proposition.

During the late 1870s and the 1880s Selous hunted all over the southern African continent, ranging from Matabeleland down to Portuguese East Africa. He had his share of injuries, for example being knocked off his horse and trampled by an elephant in 1878, but always came through relatively unscathed if you don't count cuts and bruises. George Dorehill once dropped a lit pipe into a carton of gunpowder from which Selous was loading a gun, burning Selous's eyes and face, but again a quick bush remedy saved his eyesight.

Selous freely admitted that he was only a middling rifle shot. His great success and reputation came as a result of his superior bushcraft and nerves, and the publicity generated by his best-selling books. He also possessed a large share of what would today be called leadership qualities, his quiet and gentle strength fostering admiration and respect in nearly everyone who knew him.

Adrian Darter of the Pioneer Column met Selous in 1890 and left a Victorian-style portrait of the hunter at age forty in his book *Pioneers of Mashonaland:* "He has been described as slight and wiry—that is wrong. He is muscular,

Selous (right) and Roosevelt talking about strange adventures.

the thighs and legs are massive, but he is symmetrical, and that is deceiving, and, again, the shoulders are sloping. He stands about 5 feet, 9 inches, wears a fair pointed beard, and has fine blue eyes. The voice is musical and he is exceedingly modest. That was the Selous manner. The charm of his voice reminded you of a refined woman, and none but those who have looked into the great hunter's eyes can realize the beauty of those steady orbs . . . a water-drinker, a nonsmoker, a native linguist and a chivalrous gentleman."

In 1890 Selous was commissioned by Cecil Rhodes to guide the first settlers into Mashonaland. The territory was dominated by the Matabele, who frequently raided the Shona towns and kraals to carry off cattle and women and who looked at the region as a sort of advanced military training ground. It was widely believed that Lobengula would not tolerate any European excursion into his private reserve.

In consultation with Rhodes and Frank Johnson, the young commander of the so-called Pioneer Column, Selous advised taking a roundabout approach to Mashonaland. If the Englishmen were careful to avoid entering any Matabele territory—all the while showing a readiness to intervene if necessary by stationing armed columns in British land on the Matabeleland borders—it was just possible they might bluff Lobengula into inaction. As it was, Lobengula knew full well what the consequences of war against Britain would mean (his Zulu cousins had learned that lesson to their grief just eleven years earlier) and had no desire to attack the settlers. Though he did have some trouble restraining his younger and more aggressive warriors, Lobengula made no effort to intercept Johnson and his men. Guided by Selous, the column reached Mashonaland in safety.

A scant three years later, the British put an end to Lobengula's regime. A series of border incidents provided Rhodes with the excuse he needed to take over all of Matabeleland, tumbling Lobengula off his throne in the process. Selous again served as a scout and guide and was wounded in action. He convalesced in England, where he married Marie Maddy in 1894.

Selous now turned his energies toward international hunting. In 1894 he hunted in Asia Minor; the following year saw him stalking caribou and moose in North America. He fought in the Matabele Rebellion of 1896. He returned to Canada in 1900, shooting a record caribou in Newfoundland. By this time he was a successful writer as well as a hunter, having produced *Wanderings* in 1881, *Travel and Adventure in South-East Africa* in 1893, and *Sunshine and Storm in Rhodesia* in 1896. Other books, such as *African Nature Notes and Reminiscences* (1908) were to follow, as well as numerous magazine and newspaper articles and an 1894 contribution to *Big Game Shooting*, part of the Badminton Library of Sport and Pastimes.

By the 1890s Selous was using a .450 Metford Express rifle for his big-game hunting, but in 1898 he switched to a .303 Holland magazine rifle. When his favorite .303 wore out around 1904, he changed to a .375 Holland.

In 1906 he went on a trip to the Yukon, where he got six caribou, all of them at least near-record-book size. He also hunted moose and wolves on this expedition. Selous followed that with a 1909 visit to East Africa, where he hunted with President Roosevelt, and a late-1910 safari to the Sudan.

Despite his magnificent constitution, Selous was finally beginning to have some health problems, and underwent a serious operation (any operation was serious in those days) in 1911. He emerged as good as new, returning to East Africa to hunt on Mount Kenya, along the Uaso Nyiro River, and on the McMillan ranch in the winter of 1911–1912.

When the Great War broke out in 1914, Selous immediately volunteered, despite his advanced age. Still in excellent physical condition, he frequently performed better during the grueling East African campaign than men forty years his junior. He fought in his traditional role as a scout and intelligence officer against the German East African army, earning a DSO (see glossary). His son Freddy joined the Royal Flying Corps and was killed over France in 1918. The great hunter, however, was spared the pain of this loss. In 1917 Selous was scouting German positions when a bullet in the forehead killed him instantly at the age of sixty-five.

Serpa Pinto, Alexandre Alberto da Rocha (1846–1900). A Portuguese politician and explorer, Maj. Serpa Pinto was sent on a scientific expedition from Angola to the Transvaal in 1877–1879. In 1884–1886 he helped solidify Portuguese authority over Mozambique and for a time was a threat to British interests at Lake Nyasa. He was the author of *How I Crossed Africa* (1881), a chronicle of his cross-continental safari from Benguela to Durban in 1877–1879, making him just the fourth known European to traverse Africa (after Livingstone, Cameron, and Stanley).

Serpa Pinto had joined the Portuguese army in 1864 and saw his first action during a massive punitive campaign against rebellious tribes on the lower Zambezi River four years later. A resolute, forthright man who was admired even by his foes, he was awarded the Royal Geographical Society's Founders Medal in 1881.

Seth-Smith, Donald (xxxx–1950). A pioneer hunter in Kenya, Seth-Smith and his wife Kathleen established a farm at Makuyu early in the twentieth century. At the time of his death he was working on a history of Kenya hunting and had collected numerous manuscripts and accounts by old hunters.

Seth-Smith, Kathleen. Wife of Donald Seth-Smith and mother of Tony, in 1926 she was tossed by a rhino she had wounded. She suffered three broken ribs and some bad cuts on her head, and was saved only by quick action by her gunbearer.

Seth-Smith, Martin P. Brother of Donald, Martin Seth-Smith was a Kenya assistant game ranger, 1914–1918. ROWLAND WARD 1928: BUFFALO.

Shackleton, E. R. An officer in the Kenya administration 1927–1934, Shackleton was somewhat wild and erratic. As district officer at Isiolo, he challenged the DO Marsabit to a duel, each to be assisted by spearmen from their district. He would have Samburu helpers while the DO Marsabit would have men of the Rendille tribe. As often was the case in the Northern Frontier District, the dispute was over water holes. The proposed fight never came off. A few years later Shackleton was DO in Northern Turkana (where one of the main problems was Merille raids) when he disappeared. Scouts sent out to find him discovered that he had set up a *boma* (enclosure) in the Omo River delta north of Lake Turkana. Even though this was in Ethiopian territory, Shackleton had decided to set up a station here so he could act as an ad-hoc DO Merille (who weren't even British subjects) and prevent them from raiding the Turkana. Amazingly, the Merille thought it was great to have their own administrative officer in the neighborhood, but Shackleton was ordered out of Ethiopia and back to his own job before the Ethiopians could raise a stink about it.

Sharp, Arthur Henry. Sharp accompanied Ewart Grogan (which see) on much of his historic "Cape to Cairo" journey. ROWLAND WARD 1899: INDIAN SAMBAR DEER (FROM THE MOUNAR VALLEY), LION (ZOMBA).

Sharpe, Sir Alfred (1853–1935). Sharpe was an aristocratic big-game hunter who worked in the colonial administration of Fiji. When financial restructuring forced the abolishment of that position, he was offered a job as a district commissioner in the Gold Coast. Sharpe declined, however, preferring to spend some time traveling through Africa and hunting. In 1890 he was sent by the BSAC to negotiate some treaties with the African chiefs in northern Nyasaland and Barotseland.

Sharpe was recruited by Sir Harry Johnston in 1891 as a vice consul in British Central Africa. The circumstances of their first meeting are typical of both men. Sharpe was hunting in the thick brush alongside the Shire River. He had shot a splendid male waterbuck and had followed the blood trail after it plunged into the thickets. When he found the carcass, there was a strange man sitting nearby and sketching it. The man was short, slightly built, and in his early thirties but looking much younger; he had a rifle laying by his side. It was Johnston, the British consul and BSAC commissioner in the district. Johnston had been steaming down the river and gone ashore to investigate when he heard the shot. The two men fell to talking and before long Johnston had offered Sharpe a position in the administration.

In November 1891 Cecil Rhodes and Johnston sent Sharpe as a BSAC agent on a mission to Msiri (also called Mushidi), the king of Katanga, in an effort to secure Katanga's rumored mineral wealth for the charter company. Joseph Thomson had originally been selected for the assignment by the BSAC board of directors in London, but Johnston disliked Thomson and sent Sharpe on a competing expedition. Thomson's expedition only reached Blantyre before he collapsed from sickness. Sharpe made it to Katanga, but his credibility was undermined by his appearance; he loved hunting and roughing it, so by the time he reached Msiri's capital he looked like a scarecrow with a rifle. Msiri found it impossible at first to believe that such a bedraggled figure could be the ambassador from both Rhodes and the mythic British queen, so he scoffed at Sharpe and his presents of beads and calico. Sharpe continued his travels, covering much of the Zambezi valley with a safari of only fifteen to twenty men, obtaining such concessions as he could from other African chiefs and minor potentates, as well as seeking out new trade routes. A letter from Johnston to Msiri which might have established Sharpe's credentials was intercepted and burned by his rival, Grant Stairs, a Canadian who was working for King Leopold's Congo company.

After a leave of absence back in England, Sharpe returned to Nyasaland as a full consul and deputy commissioner to Johnston. He fought in the 1893 campaigns against the Yao chiefs Liwande and Makanjira, and he became acting commissioner when Johnston got sick in 1896. He remained fit and active all of his long life, going on safari to East Africa in 1924 and shooting seven elephants at the age of seventy. Sharpe was the author of *Backbone of Africa* (1921).

Sharpe had an extremely high reputation as a hunter among sportsmen of his day, which for some reason has faded considerably with time. One of the administrative officers who knew him, Hector Duff, wrote in 1903 that "Sharpe's practical knowledge of African game beasts is indeed probably greater than that of any man now living, with the exception of Mr. Selous. . . . Of elephants in particular he has had an almost unique experience, having devoted himself exclusively to the pursuit of these animals for several years after his first arrival in the country." While he is almost unknown to the current generation, it is worth noting once again that Sharpe and the vastly more famous Joseph Thomson set out on separate expeditions to Katanga at roughly the same time; Thomson turned back, Sharpe got there. Sharpe was the discoverer of the antelope known as Sharpe grysbok. ROWLAND WARD 1928: LICHTENSTEIN HARTEBEEST, ELEPHANT.

Shattuck, George. Professor of geology at Johns Hopkins and Vassar Universities, and photography director of the 1919–1920 Lowie anthropological expedition to Uganda and Kenya. ROWLAND WARD 1928: ELEPHANT, BUFFALO.

Shaw, John William (xxxx–1871). An Englishman, Shaw was a disgruntled sailor on the USS *Nevada* in late 1870 when he was arrested and tried for mutiny. Despite his acquittal, he was dismissed from the service and set ashore on the island of Zanzibar. His bad reputation nixed any chance of getting another sailing berth, so Shaw agreed to sign on with Henry Morton Stanley, the newspaper reporter who was about to embark on an expedition into the wilds of Africa to find the missing British explorer Livingstone. His salary was set at three hundred dollars for the year.

Shaw, along with the other hired European, William Farquhar, was a terrible choice to go on safari with Stanley. He blew his advanced salary in the bars of Zanzibar the night before departure, then whined constantly that he didn't want to go on the venture and didn't feel good. Citing illness, he refused to walk and was given a donkey to ride. He kept falling off the donkey, causing the native porters to laugh. Shaw responded by habitually beating the porters. Stanley, who had his own ideas about beating natives, disagreed with Shaw's but refused to intervene. Shaw also distinguished himself by bribing Arab slavers into letting him sleep with their female charges. Unsurprisingly, he soon caught a strange tropical venereal disease.

Stanley, not an easy man to work for, balked at these extracurricular activities and publicly chastised Shaw. The American responded by "accidentally" firing a bullet from an elephant gun through Stanley's tent. This event apparently enlightened Stanley to the validity of Shaw's illness, and he allowed the sailor to rest at the nearest village while the expedition struggled on. Shaw actually was sick, it seems—he died in the Tanganyikan town of Tabora late in 1871.

Sheppard, William Henry (1865–1927). Born in Virginia on 8 March 1865, William Sheppard ("The Black Livingstone") graduated from Booker T. Washington's Hampton Institute and the Tuscaloosa Theological Institute and in 1890 went to West Africa as a missionary for the Presbyterian Church. In 1893 he traveled to England to be received by Queen Victoria and from then back to America to marry Lucy Gantt (1866–1940?). The couple returned to West Africa and Sheppard's mission alongside the Kuba tribe.

Sheppard was known for his moral and physical courage. He was one of the first to attest to the outrages of the Congo Free State, where men were mutilated and killed if they refused to harvest rubber for the Belgian authorities. He was of the practical school of missionaries, more concerned with helping educate people than with some eternal reward. There exist pictures of him hunting buffalo and extracting a bad tooth from an African native. From his first days in the Congo he impressed others with his skill with a rifle—his first humanitarian act was to kill a hippo for some starving tribespeople. Like many men of action, Sheppard could be somewhat unrestrained in his personal affairs. He is known to have had at least one mistress during his missionary days (more likely several). It is only fair to state that his wife was away for more than two years during the time in question.

This wandering eye led to his departure from the Congo. Once the atrocities of the Free State became public knowledge, Sheppard became a hero on the world stage. People in a dozen countries idolized him and looked to him as an example of virtue. Sheppard's superiors in the church, aware of his adultery, were appalled at the prospect of exposure. They felt that supporters of the Free State regime might use Sheppard's peccadilloes to discredit him and the entire movement. Accordingly, in 1910 they recalled the man known as the "Black Livingstone" to the United States.

In the years left to him Sheppard worked as a lecturer and a preacher. He wrote some rather odd children's books about his experiences in Africa, including *The Girl Who Ate Her Mother*—yes, that's precisely what it's about. Cannibals kidnap a little African girl and force her to eat the flesh of her dead mother, prior to the girl's conversion to Christianity. In 1912 Sheppard became pastor of a church in Louisville, Kentucky. While comfortable financially, he was a poor fit in Louisville, which at that time was segregated to the point of apartheid. Still, the bills were paid and he and Lucy bought a very nice middle-class house in a Louisville suburb.

In 1926 malaria and other Congo diseases caught up to him and he suffered a debilitating stroke. Sheppard lingered as an invalid for a year before passing away at the age of sixty-two.

Shircore, John Owen (1882–1953). Shircore was a Scottish doctor and surgeon, a graduate of Glasgow and Edinburgh medical colleges. He was licensed to practice medicine in Kenya Colony and Protectorate. ROWLAND WARD 1928: BUSHBUCK (NO. 1, 21¾ INCHES, NYASALAND), UGANDA KOB, SUNI, PUKU.

Siedentopf, Adolph and Friedrich Wilhelm Siedentopf. These two German brothers obtained a lease on the entire Ngorongoro crater in the years before World War I. The Siedentopfs have long been the subject of intense interest and curiosity among students of East African hunting and colonial history.

They arrived at Ngorongoro crater around 1899 and built a farmhouse and outbuildings. Their land was home to a large number of wildebeest. According to different sources, they either set up an operation to kill the wildebeest and can their tongues for shipping (one wonders if this scheme seemed as reprehensible back then as it does now) or tried to drive the wildebeest from the crater to make exclusive grazing room for their cattle. At this time Adolph was said to be the leader of the two brothers. By 1908 they had about twelve hundred head of cattle and a flock of sheep and were experimenting with taming ostrich and planting citrus trees. Another source puts the size of their cattle herd at more than two thousand.

Shortly before the Great War, the brothers split their lease holding right down the middle of the crater and built separate houses some eight miles apart. They had a partner or foreman named Hartnung, who had a reputation as a brutal man. The Siedentopfs had a lot of trouble persuading the local Masai to stay away from their livestock—so much trouble that eventually Hartnung fatally shot some of the poachers. The Masai responded by killing Hartnung and some nineteen Wambula workers. Some sources claimed that Adolph Siedentopf was killed in the massacre (Adolph died many deaths in local legend), but it was Hartnung who fell to the Masai spears.

Just before the war some old burial mounds were found on the Siedentopf property that attracted scientific interest. Excavators found the skeletons of a man, woman, and child of Nilotic origin, and at least one expert dated the remains to the Neolithic Age. The outbreak of war in 1914 brought fierce anti-German sentiments to the fore, and local partisans burned what was left of the Siedentopf farms. All German property in Tanganyika was turned over to an enemy property commission and eventually sold to British settlers after the Armistice.

The brothers became professional hunting guides after being released from internment in 1918. Several sources state that Adolph Siedentopf was at some point killed by a lion. However, researchers recently uncovered convincing evidence that he actually died in the United States, probably in 1932 in Alabama, where he may have committed suicide by taking poison.

Friedrich went on to have a successful career. He took his countryman and future professional Ossie Koenig out on Koenig's first safari. Koenig (1954) wrote that Friedrich was "one of the best shots I have ever seen." Siedentopf also guided the director of the Berlin Zoo, Lutz Heck, on live-capture safaris in East Africa in the 1920s.

Friedrich escorted Ernst Udet, a famous World War I flying ace and later a top-ranking officer of the Luftwaffe, on a safari in 1930. One morning Siedentopf and another pilot took off from their base camp near Mtombu to scout for game. They were in an old war-surplus Klemm two-seater. Not far from camp, they spotted a rhino and dipped low to assess the size of its horns. The tip of a wing hit an anthill and the plane flipped over onto the ground, trapping the pilot and Siedentopf. Neither man was injured, but they couldn't climb out of the airplane, which was upside down. Udet grabbed the other plane he had on that safari and flew the mile or so to the accident. He tried to cut the men out of the canvas fuselage, but every few minutes the rhino would come back and charge, and Udet would have to dodge around the anthill. The men were trapped for an hour before the rhino finally got bored and Udet was able to rescue his comrades.

Sometime after 1930 Friedrich contracted a severe tropical fever that left him permanently impaired. He still hunted occasionally but did all of his traveling and stalking on the back of a mule. When he died he was buried at Mbulu in Tanganyika.

Siewert. A game ranger of the Sabi Game Reserve in the years before World War I. His performance seems to have been more than adequate. On one occasion in 1911 he and two African policemen shot it out with a large group of native poachers from Portuguese East Africa. He was discharged, however, during the war due to his German ancestry, became an alcoholic, and shot himself.

Siggins, A. J. An official and hunter in Portuguese East Africa and Rhodesia from about 1900 until the 1930s, Siggins had a reputation for disposing of man-killing beasts. In the late 1920s he wrote *Man-Killers I Have Known.*

Simpson, Leslie. Simpson (also seen spelled Simson) was a successful American mining engineer stationed in Johannesburg. Late in life he took up big-game hunting, killing his first lion at about age fifty. A quiet, reserved man, he arrived in East Africa in 1920, coming in on the first Model A Ford to be seen in the region. Simpson hunted Kenya and Tanganyika throughout the 1920s, killing up to three hundred lion with his own rifle in fair-chase conditions, not including hunts he took part in as a professional. Around 1927 he had a hunting camp on the fringe of the Serengeti in Tanganyika, from which he guided clients like Paul Selby, a skilled wildlife photographer from Johannesburg.

Simpson was a wealthy man, rich enough to donate "African Halls" of taxidermy to both the California Academy of Sciences in San Francisco and the Los Angeles Museum. He personally hunted each of the animals exhibited in these halls, and arranged for their preparation and shipment at his own expense.

Slaipstein, John. A mixed-race retainer of Frederick Selous, Slaipstein shot a hippo in Matabeleland in 1883 without having received Lobengula's permission. Lobengula charged Selous with the crime, and Selous was afraid to tell the truth because he feared for Slaipstein's life if the true facts were known. Lobengula fined Selous ten heifer cows, for which the hunter never forgave him. In his memoirs Selous referred to this as the "Sea Cow row."

Sleeman, Sir James. A British sportsman, big-game hunter, and wildlife photographer, Sleeman was active throughout the first half of the twentieth century. In 1938 he went on an extended photographic safari with Uganda game warden Temple-Perkins. He later wrote the preface for Temple-Perkins's memoir, *The Kingdom of the Elephant.*

Smart, Sammy. In 1900, during the Boer War, a hungry lion attacked a sentry at the Sabi Bridge in what later became Kruger National Park. The sentry's name was Sammy Smart, and he was a member of the battalion called Steinacker's Horse. The lion seized him while he was on guard duty and started to drag him away. His cries woke his messmates, who fired at the lion, missing but causing the animal to release the trooper. Smart died of his wounds a few days later.

Smidt. Large Boer family that hunted around Matabeleland in the 1870s.

Smith, Alfred Aloysius "Trader Horn" (1854–1931). Born in Scotland, Aloysius Smith went to Africa at the age of seventeen and began working as a trader. He scratched out a living and toiled in relative anonymity until the 1920s when he met a South African novelist named Ethelreda Lewis while selling mousetraps door-to-door. The two got to talking and Lewis quickly recognized that the old man's stories could sell in book form.

She gathered his material and it was published in 1927 as *Trader Horn.* Much to everyone's surprise, including Lewis, the book was a huge international bestseller. Reprinted dozens of times, the fictionalized biography was even turned into a popular motion picture by W. S. Van Dyke (as well as an atrocious 1970s remake that is best forgotten).

Smith, who apparently didn't make much money from the original book, exploited his newfound fame by publishing a second volume, titled *Harold the Webbed.* This rather bizarre sequel was actually a historical novel about the Norsemen, of all things, but nevertheless sold well and provided Smith with financial security for the rest of his life. He died in 1931.

Smith, Andrew (1797–1872). Dr. Smith, director general of the British Army Medical Department at Cape colony, led a scientific expedition into the interior in 1834. It consisted of Smith, hunter Benjamin Kift, trader David Hume, Robert Scoon of Graham's Town, draftsman George Ford, Captain Edie of the 98th Foot, surveyor John Burrows, artist Charles Bell, two men named Mintern and Hartwell, three English soldiers, and twenty-seven Hottentots.

Smith and his men worked their way up to the Kuruman River and the mission home of Robert Moffatt. Concerned about Matabele raids, particularly the attack on Andrew Bain, the expedition stayed in that general area for a while. Messengers were sent to the Matabele king, Mzilikazi, to ascertain his attitude toward the group. Four Matabele generals arrived to invite (read "command") Smith to visit the unstable king.

Mzilikazi was rude and inattentive but not hostile. Smith's people did a tremendous amount of hunting, collecting over a thousand scientific specimens of stuffed mammals, birds, and reptiles, while the artist, Bell, made valuable sketches of wildlife and the tribal people. The expedition returned to Graaff-Reinet on 4 January 1836. It was considered a great success, and Smith received a knighthood.

Smith, Arthur Donaldson (1866–1939). Arthur Donaldson Smith, M.D., was born in Pennsylvania on 27 April 1866. He was the third son of powerful Philadelphia socialites who traced their distinguished ancestry back to Revolutionary War days. Well educated at the University of Pennsylvania, Johns Hopkins University, and the University of Heidelberg in Germany, Smith (he dropped the name "Arthur" upon reaching maturity and was always known as A. Donaldson Smith or simply Donaldson Smith) inherited $69,000 upon his father's death in 1892. The modern-day equivalent would be more than $2½ million. Thus equipped to face the world, Smith decided to delay beginning his medical career (he earned his M.D. in 1889) and enjoy himself with sporting pursuits for a few years.

After an early 1893 hunting and fishing trip to Norway, Smith decided to go on safari in East Africa. He was accompanied by another Dr. Smith, William Lord Smith, not a relative but a friend. The two doctors hunted in the traditional area for vacationing British army officers, British Somaliland. They enjoyed themselves immensely, hunting lion, elephant, and rhino in the winter of 1893–1894. Donaldson Smith was intrigued by the stories he heard about Africa's interior and determined to make a full-fledged expedition to the remote and barbarous Lake Rudolf (now Lake Turkana).

Smith's plans were straightforward and admirable. He would hunt and explore and make a contribution to science by mapping the region and collecting zoological and botanical specimens. He even attended a course in London on "the many methods of laying down my positions accurately" (Smith, 1897), taught by John Coles, map curator of the Royal Geographical Society. Donaldson Smith drew a big distinction, both then and later, between his hunting trip with W. L. Smith and the later, bigger expedition. The former he always referred to as the "shooting trip," for he considered it mere sport compared to the scientific and geographic focus of the latter venture.

The June 1894 edition of the *Scottish Geographical Magazine* published the notice announcing Smith's intentions: "An American, Dr. Donaldson Smith, who has just returned from a journey of 200 miles into the interior of Somaliland, is about to start for Lake Rudolf. He hopes to explore the country around the northern end of the lake and between the lake and a point 200 miles west of Berbera."

The big safari set out from Berbera, the traditional jumping-off spot on the Indian Ocean coast, in late July of 1894. Smith had hired a British taxidermist named Edward Dodson to help with the specimens, and had also invited a Philadelphia friend named Fred Gillett, who was interested primarily in hunting. Smith seems to have brought Gillett along just for company. Gillett did defray expenses somewhat by hiring twelve additional men and buying twenty camels. Together with Smith's seventy Somalis, the caravan was thought to be large enough to deter any bandits. The Royal Geographical Society loaned Smith various scientific instruments like thermometers, compasses, and a six-inch theodolite, a surveying instrument. Along with these marvels of science, the eighty-four camels and assorted donkeys carried a collapsible boat, spirits to preserve zoological specimens, ammunition, and a 150-day supply of food.

The safari almost got off to a catastrophic start when, barely out of Berbera, a lion tried to make off with one of the donkeys. Smith fired and wounded the lion, which charged and almost nailed the good doctor, crashing into the zareba (protective enclosure of thornbush) behind which Smith was crouching. Only the increasing effect of the mortal wound caused the lion to get confused and dizzy and stumble away just inches past Dr. Smith. It lay down in some nearby bushes, and Smith and his Somali gunbearer waited quietly for the animal to die. The morning sun revealed a magnificent but very dead black-maned lion, a fine trophy. A photo of this lion appears in Smith's *Through Unknown African Countries,* and it is indeed an impressive animal.

The next obstacle came in the middle of September 1894, when Smith and his men first met up with Ethiopian raiders and soldiers who were terrorizing the region. The Ethiopians were generally affable so long as

Arthur Donaldson Smith with a lion shot in Somaliland, July 1894.

they were outnumbered, and they hesitated to take on a safari of this size. But much time was lost dealing with Ethiopian officers who refused to let Smith travel through the territory (nominally claimed by Ethiopia) unless the Emperor Menelik approved their passage. Not until November did word come from Menelik. The request was disapproved, and they were to return whence they had come. Smith decided to double-back on his trail and then proceed to Lake Rudolf by an alternate route that skirted Ethiopian territory.

At this time Fred Gillett received word that his father had died and left the expedition to return home. There may have been more to the story, according to Pascal Imperato's magnificent 1998 book *Quest for the Jade Sea,* from which most of this account is taken. Imperato unearthed evidence—in the form of a letter from Smith to the Royal Geographical Society—that strongly indicates the two old friends had had a serious falling out at some point. At any rate, Gillett left for the States, Smith and the others retreated and regrouped, and the newly revamped expedition set out for Turkana anew on 31 January 1895. The new route would take them south by way of the Juba River.

Instead of trouble with the Ethiopians, the expedition now ran into trouble with the Boran, the area's nomadic tribe. The Ethiopians still made their contribution, albeit indirectly. Their constant raids and depredations upon the Boran had whipped the latter people into a feverish state of armed hostility, particularly toward any strangers. Enter Smith and his folks. Again there was an inauspicious start: Smith and his gunbearer were both knocked unconscious by a bolt of lightning on a sparkling, clear day.

Things rapidly got worse. A group of Boran spearmen (the Boran have a cultural affinity with the Masai) ambushed two of Smith's Somalis. One escaped, but the other man, called Elmi, was speared to death, disemboweled, and castrated. The Boran practiced castration in a fashion similar to the North American custom of taking scalps. For several days the Boran harassed the expedition. Fortunately for his sake, Smith had been very careful during the hiring stage to recruit men experienced with firearms. The Boran were unfamiliar with modern weapons, and the Somalis' rifles took a terrible toll on the aboriginal spearmen, who could not conceive of the range of Smith's rifles until it was too late.

The Boran may have been primitive, but they were not stupid. Faced with overwhelming military force, and taking unacceptable casualties for no good reason, they quickly patched things up with Smith, returning cows they had stolen and letting him go on unmolested. For his part, the American was happy to make friends. He had come to Africa to explore and hunt, not to conduct a senseless war. Once again the Donaldson Smith expedition plodded on.

Discovery was a slow business in those days. It was fully a year—July of 1895—before the caravan finally reached Lake Rudolf. Smith and Dodson, the taxidermist, camped on one of Teleki's old campsites from 1888. Much affected by malaria, the safari marched along the lake's nearly endless shore looking for its source. One of the questions Smith had set out to resolve was whether the Nianamm River (discovered by von Hoehnel and Teleki, it flows into the north end of Lake Rudolf) and the Omo River (discovered by Jules Borelli many miles north) were the same river. They are, but somehow Smith, who had set out to prove just that, became convinced that the two rivers were separate and so managed to confuse the issue for many years.

At Lake Rudolf Smith enjoyed the best hunting of the expedition. Frequently prowling the barren terrain with taxidermist Dodson, he shot a number of rhino and a wide variety of plains game and had some harrowing adventures with elephant. One day he was nearly killed by a wounded bull that turned and charged him on a narrow path in thick thorn country. Smith and Dodson escaped with their lives by crawling through the thorns while the elephant stomped about, blindly trying to crush them. On the next day Smith killed another elephant, this one an enormous bull with the largest tusks of Smith's career, weighing in at 108 and

100 pounds. The ivory was later displayed with many of Smith's other trophies at the University of Pennsylvania.

Having completed the main goal of the expedition, Smith and Dodson decided to lead the safari homeward via the easiest route—south. They were the first white explorers to see Mount Marsabit and the lake later known as Paradise (the same Lake Paradise that Martin and Osa Johnson claimed to have discovered thirty years later). On Marsabit the caravan stopped for a bit so that Smith could administer a massive quinine treatment to try to rid himself of malaria. Feeling much better, Smith led the expedition over the Uaso Nyiro River and down to the coast at Lamu. They reached the Indian Ocean in October 1895 and promptly returned with their men via ship to Aden. Donaldson Smith sent a one-word telegram back to Philadelphia: "Successful."

Arriving in England on 30 November 1895, Smith and Dodson presented the fruits of the expedition to the Royal Geographical Society. These included twenty-four new species of birds, eleven new reptiles and amphibians, three hundred types of plants, thousands of insects, and two hundred mammal specimens. The new species were donated to the British Museum, and the rest of the specimens went to Philadelphia's Academy of Natural Sciences. Smith was much honored, but several things rankled. For one, no government or scientific society offered to help defray his expenses. It was well known that Smith had independent means, and the fact that he had spent at least ten percent of his inheritance on the expedition seemed to strike no one as unreasonable. Second, and more important, several important geographers raised doubts about Smith's conclusion that the Nianamm and Omo Rivers were separate entities. The consensus was growing strong that they were one and the same. Smith felt slighted by the controversy and immediately began making plans to return to Lake Rudolf in the near future.

After a return visit to the United States and hunting and collecting trips to China, Russia, and India, Smith and a friend, a British civil servant named Percy Cox, arrived in Berbera in late 1898 to set up a second expedition. After overcoming immense red tape and interference from the British government, Smith finally got moving in 1899 with a force of seventeen Somalis and seventeen Gurkhas (legendary fighting men recruited in India). Smith obviously was intrigued by the enhanced security provided by these Gurkhas. Unfortunately, he found them stubborn and almost mutinous.

The local British agent tried to sabotage the expedition because the Queen's government was apprehensive about

Arthur Donaldson Smith being attacked by an elephant at Marsabit, September 1895.

the political consequences of the venture. Still, having this time obtained Menelik's permission to cross Ethiopian land, Smith arrived on the shore of Lake Rudolf for a second time on 10 December 1899 after a relatively uneventful four-month trip. His new observations led him to modify his position on the lake's source (he was now willing to concede that the Nianamm and Omo Rivers were of equal importance in feeding the lake—not accurate, but better!). And he obtained a specimen of a hitherto unknown gazelle, *Madoqua guntheri smithii.*

This time Smith returned to civilization by going northwest, to the Nile River and then to Cairo. This time around, there was a great deal of tension between Smith and the Royal Geographical Society. Smith felt that the society had treated him shabbily and threatened to give his maps and detailed notes of the region to Belgium or Germany. The Society sought to appease him with the award of a medal and many promises, but to the end of his days Smith complained that it had cheated him of some $2,000 it had promised to help cover expenses.

Smith's later days were less eventful. Attempts to make a profit by lecturing on his adventures proved only modestly successful, largely because Smith was a quiet, shy man and almost pathologically afraid of speaking in public. President Roosevelt, who in 1905 called Smith's memoir *Through Unknown African Countries* "an excellent book of mixed hunting and scientific exploration," appointed him United States consul in Mersine, Turkey, in 1909. The job paid $2,500 a year, once a pittance but now an important consideration to the increasingly impoverished Dr. Smith. Smith became an alcoholic, and thereafter his erratic behavior frequently caused him to be transferred to such backwater posts as Patras, Greece, and Aguascalientes, Mexico.

During World War I Smith was commissioned a captain in the U.S. Army and stationed in Georgia. He finally opened his long-delayed medical practice after the war in Roulette, Pennsylvania, and retired in 1934. Almost blind, he shuffled around from relative to relative in Philadelphia and Florida, dying on 19 February 1939 at the Philadelphia Naval Hospital. The cause of death was coronary heart disease.

Smith, Claud. Smith was a hunter and a trader in Kenya in the early 1900s. When John Boyes was arrested for "waging war, setting shauri, impersonating government, leading punitive expeditions, and dacoity" in 1901 and imprisoned at Fort Jesus, Smith—an erstwhile comrade of Boyes but not a particularly close friend—traveled four hundred miles from his hunting camp at Naivasha to pay the bail of 10,000 rupees. In his book *King of the Wa-Kikuyu,* Boyes cited Smith's act as an example of the splendid camaraderie that existed among the pioneer hunting community.

Smith, Eric. An English officer, Captain Smith held a commission in the 1st Regiment of Life Guards before being seconded to duties in East Africa. He led an IBEA (see glossary) survey team from Mombasa to Lake Victoria in December 1890. Members of the team included Arthur Neumann and James Martin.

As a major in the early 1890s Smith was commander of the IBEA chartered company outpost at Kampala in Uganda, where he gave assistance to the Portal mission in 1893. Portal relieved him as part of the government takeover from the IBEA and sent him back to Kenya on 1 April 1893 with a letter recommending that Smith be reappointed to a senior Uganda post in the new imperial government. On his safari back to the coast, Smith, a dedicated elephant hunter, carried forty-four loads of ivory.

Smith lost an arm after being gored by a rhino in the 1890s, but apparently the amputation was not total, because John Boyes referred to his losing "a hand" (1911). Smith eventually retired as a colonel. ROWLAND WARD 1928: ELEPHANT (114 AND 108 POUNDS).

Smith, Norman Bayley (1864–xxxx). This British trophy hunter operated in Africa from about 1892, including Somaliland in the early 1890s, British East Africa in 1899, Kilimanjaro in 1900, Barotseland in 1905, Dinka territory in 1909, and BEA again in the 1920s.

Highly respected as a hunter, Smith went for difficult trophies rather than dangerous game. In his long career he shot only five elephant and eight rhino. Smith was a contributor to the 1932 Lonsdale Library volume *Big Game Shooting in Africa.*

In a letter to Denis Lyell in 1916, he said he had owned only a few rifles in his career—a .256 for light game, a 10-bore Paradox for elephant and rhino, and a .577-500 BP Express for lion hunting. He had used a borrowed .400 cordite rifle to kill the last of his elephant. ROWLAND WARD 1928: ELAND, LEOPARD, NILE LECHWE, LESSER KUDU (NO. 1), SOMALI HARTEBEEST.

Smith, Percy (xxxx–1939). A settler living near Eldoret, Smith was the first European to capture a bongo, that most elusive member of the antelope family. He caught the animal in a game pit in the northern Aberdares and sold it to a European zoo for a reported £1,000. The newspapers made so much of his feat that for a time he became known as Bongo Smith. He later bought a giant forest hog from professional hunter Eric Rundgren for £25 and then sold it to the same zoo for £750.

Smith, Tom Murray. A professional hunter employed by the firm of Safariland, Ltd., in the 1920s.

Smith, William Lord. Smith was a Massachusetts doctor who went on a fishing and hunting trip to Norway with A. Donaldson Smith in 1893. William Smith had already planned a subsequent hunting trip to Somaliland. Donaldson

Smith asked to come along, and the pair apparently had a wonderful vacation, shooting six lion (Somaliland was famous for its lion) as well as elephant, rhino, and other game. This adventure prompted Donaldson Smith to make his larger expedition to Lake Rudolf a year later.

Smith, Tom Murray. A professional hunter in Kenya from the 1920s through the 1960s, Smith was a decorated veteran of both World Wars, a close friend of Philip Percival, and the president of the East African Professional Hunter's Association. He was the brother-in-law of district commissioner Geoffrey Rimington and the son-in-law of Kenya pioneer Jackie Lethbridge.

Smith wrote a book called *The Nature of the Beast,* which is more of a series of wildlife anecdotes than a memoir and contains only a minimum of autobiographical material. Nevertheless, we can surmise a few facts about his life and career. As a young man Smith learned his craft under the tutelage of professional hunter George Hurst. Hurst was a reckless man and Smith described hunting with him as a "hair-raising experience." Smith often worked for the game department and mentions doing elephant control work in Tanganyika in the 1920s and also in northern Kenya; he was badly injured by an elephant in Tanganyika in 1929.

In 1934 Smith was commissioned by Kenya to shoot out a number of lions in the Masai territory. Just before World War II he held a government contract shooting rinderpest-infected buffalo around Meru; after the war he was hired by the government of Northern Rhodesia to supply Polish refugees with fish from Lake Tanganyika. This last commission involved setting up a fledgling fishing industry and shooting a large number of the local crocodiles, including a huge eighteen footer. In his younger days Smith occasionally captured animals for sale to European zoos, a practice he discontinued as immoral. His main income was derived from guiding professional hunts, including for the maharajah of Jodhpur in 1932 and 1935. He got along well with the Indian nobility and escorted a number of other princes and maharajas. Smith was one of three white hunters employed by the production crew of the film *Mogambo* in 1953.

Smuts, Hendrik. Smuts was an elephant hunter in the Kunene River area in the middle of the nineteenth century. Little is known about his life, but he left his mark in the form of wagon-wheel ruts along his well-traveled hunting route. According to Lawrence Green in his *Lords of the Last Frontier,* as late as the 1940s the local Africans still referred to these tracks as "the road Smuts made."

Snow, H. A. An American wildlife photographer, he shot some motion-picture film in Africa and displayed it in the United States in 1922. Snow was sharply criticized because much of his footage was obviously staged.

Sommer, Francois. A French hunter and author, Francois Sommer (pronounced Somm-aire) first went big-game hunting in Africa in 1934. In that year he went on safari in Tanganyika, where he stayed at a hunting camp by Lake Manyara that had been built originally by filmmaker Martin Johnson. He later hunted and photographed all through Africa, gaining a firsthand knowledge of big game and big-game hunters. Although his experiences in Africa perhaps were not as comprehensive as those of many of the better British hunters, Sommer was a popular star in his native France.

The German-born professional hunter Ossie Koenig, who knew Sommer only casually, wrote in his 1954 memoir *Pori Tupu* that mere mention of Sommer's name was sufficient to get him waved right through French customs. Sommer's book, *Man and Beast in Africa* (1953), is especially interesting because it is one of the few English sources covering French hunters in any detail. It also boasts an introduction by Ernest Hemingway.

Southey, Sir Richard (1808–1901). Southey, a distant relative of the poet Robert Southey, was born in Devonshire but moved to South Africa in 1820. He tried his hand as a farmer and a clerk but was bored, and in 1829 he went on a long trading and hunting expedition into the Transvaal.

The trip was exciting but not a financial success, and he took to cattle ranching upon his return. Southey had served in the militia as early as 1828, and when the latest Frontier War broke out in 1834 he was commissioned captain of a company of scouts attached to Sir Harry Smith's corps. His combination of basic ability and the bush skills he had learned on his hunting expedition served to make him a valuable asset to the British armed forces. He was rewarded for his service in 1835 by an appointment as Native Agent, but the post was abolished a year later.

Harry Smith returned to South Africa in 1847 and appointed Southey, who had been raising and selling cattle, as secretary to the high commissioner. Southey served in this capacity at the Battle of Boomplaats. Upon the surrender of the Boers and the withdrawal of the main British army, Southey remained in Bloemfontein in charge of the occupation forces. The defeated Boers were required by terms of the capitulation to surrender an indemnity, and

Southey, who generally was a tactful man, managed to collect the fines without causing any undue rancor.

During the remainder of his life Southey held a number of administrative offices, including acting secretary of Cape Colony (1852–1854), treasurer (1861–1864), colonial secretary (1864–1872), and lieutenant governor of Griqualand West (1873–1875). His tenure in the last post was marred by civil disturbances at the mines, and Southey felt it necessary to call in the troops to restore order. He finished his career as a member of the Cape Colony Parliament until 1878.

Southey was made CMG in 1872 and KCMG (see glossary for these titles) in 1891. The interesting thing about his long and successful career in public service was that it all began with a hunting trip—his youthful trek through the Transvaal gave him the experience he needed to excel as a scout in the Frontier War. Southey serves as a splendid example of how bushcraft and the outdoor life were woven into the very fabric of early African colonial life.

John Hanning Speke, at the age of seventeen, on first receiving his commission in the Indian army.

Sparrmann, Anders (1748–1820). Also seen as Sparrman and the year of birth also seen as 1747. The son of a clergyman, Sparrmann was a Swedish doctor and botanist—he collected plant specimens for his teacher Linnaeus—who visited China as a ship's doctor in 1765–1767. He then traveled and hunted in South Africa in 1772–1776. He shot quagga, lion, buffalo, rhino, and elephant, and he wrote extensively about the Khoi-Khoi and Bushmen. Sparrmann spent the rest of his days as a curator and professor in northern Europe, dying at Stockholm in 1820. He was the author of *A Voyage to the Cape of Good Hope* (1785).

Speke, John Hanning (1827–1864). Speke was born to a relatively well-off family in Somerset, England. An obsessive hunter, he went to India at age seventeen and began to collect trophy heads and hides for the sporting museum he one day dreamed of opening. As an officer of the 46th Bombay Native Infantry, he spent his annual vacations hunting in Tibet to vary his sport. At some point he acquired the odd desire to eat the embryos found in female game animals that he had killed, a habit that even his contemporary Victorians, who were nearly as prone to culinary experimentation as the ancient Romans, found distasteful.

Speke first came to Africa in 1854 on a trip to Aden, where he planned to go off by himself on a shooting expedition. The British resident in Aden would not allow him to go hunting alone in the interior, so he wound up signing on to an 1855 expedition that Richard Burton was organizing to the Nile via Somalia. This venture was a disaster: The Burton safari was promptly attacked at night by Somali bandits, and Burton was badly wounded with a spear through his mouth while another officer, Lieutenant Stroyan, was killed. Speke was momentarily captured but managed to escape in the confusion. Needless to say, that was the end of that particular expedition.

Speke and Burton seemed to hit it off, however, and plans were made for a new attempt at the Nile source in 1857. There is no need to go into the details of that journey here, for they are well known. Suffice it to say that Speke and Burton, who began as friends of a sort, wound up despising each other, an emotion that would only get worse in the years to come.

One of the chief sources of animosity between the two British officers was Speke's claim that he had discovered the source of the Nile in Lake Victoria. Burton, who had missed the trip to the lake because he was recuperating from malaria in Tanganyika, felt strongly that Speke had not seen enough of the lake to make that assertion. Burton was undoubtedly correct in principle, given the fact that Speke had scouted only a small portion of the lake and had no clear idea of any of its outlet rivers or even its actual size. The fact that Speke's assertion proved more accurate than that of any other great Nile explorer can only be attributed to intuition, or luck.

Speke returned to the lake in 1860–1863, this time accompanied by the faithful James Augustus Grant. He spent a great deal of time in what is now Uganda, consorting with the Africans and even possibly fathering a child (current historians bitterly dispute whether Speke engaged in sexual shenanigans while in Africa). In 1863 he and Grant finally moved northward, where they expected to find a relief column moving south down the Nile, led by the British Vice Consul in Khartoum, a man named Petherick. Instead they met Samuel Baker and his wife Florence. Baker was a casual acquaintance of Speke (and a famous hunter in his own right). While grateful to Baker, Speke never forgave Petherick and, upon his return to England, did his best to ruin the man by spreading false stories of graft and slave dealing.

Upon his triumphant return in 1863, Speke published a book entitled *Journal of the Discovery of the Source of the Nile.* Burton meanwhile spread his own version of events, and British geographical circles (it was a big thing then) polarized around the two men and their conflicting opinions. At first, public opinion was wildly in Speke's favor, and he was adulated as the explorer who found the legendary source, while Burton was looked down upon as the man who gave up. Speke's pride proved his undoing, however. His treatment of Petherick was soon revealed as insanely petty and spiteful, and the fact that he had prevented his loyal friend Grant from seeing Victoria Nyanza (Speke had left the Scotsman in camp as he completed that leg of their journey) brought back earlier doubts about his similar behavior toward Burton. Plus, he stiffed the Royal Geographical Society with his promised report on his explorations, giving the society only a cursory outline while reaping large profits from a detailed book timed to come out just in time for Christmas.

Burton and Speke were scheduled to debate the matter in August 1864, but on the day before the debate Speke, an expert with a gun, died in an odd shooting accident at his uncle's estate. Under the circumstances, it is natural to suspect that he committed suicide, but the coroner returned a verdict of accidental death, and many modern authorities agree. Historians still dispute the verdict, however, and the full truth will never be known.

John Hanning Speke escapes from a group of angry Somali bandits in 1855.

Stabb, Henry (1835–1888). Maj. Henry Stabb was an officer of the 32nd Duke of Cornwall Light Infantry Regiment. He fought in the Indian Mutiny and its aftermath in 1857–1859. He spent the 1860s serving in India and in the early 1870s was stationed in Mauritius, commanding four detached companies of his regiment. In 1874–1876 he was in South Africa, usually stationed at King William's Town.

In 1875 he went on a hunting trip through Matabeleland with a brother officer named James Jocelyn Glascott, about whom little is known. The safari was detailed in Stabb's journal, which was long believed lost but was finally published in South Africa in 1967 as *To the Victoria Falls via Matabeleland,* with editing and footnotes by E. C. Tabler.

Stabb returned to Britain in 1876 but was back in South Africa for the final days of the Zulu War in 1879. He fought at the Battle of Ulundi and was mentioned in dispatches. He later commanded a commission that investigated claims for settler reparations and was the officer entrusted by Queen Victoria to erect a monument on the spot where the Prince Imperial, the Bonaparte heir to the French throne, had been killed by the Zulus. Stabb married Janetta Mander in 1885; he died young of heart disease in Pietermaritzburg in 1888. His last station was as commander of British forces in Natal shortly before he died.

Stairs, William Grant (1865–1892). Stairs, a Canadian from Halifax, Nova Scotia, was sent to the Merchiston Castle School in Edinburgh at age twelve and then to Royal

Military College at Kingston, Ontario, three years later. Trained as a civil engineer, he worked as a surveyor in New Zealand until June 1885, when he was commissioned as lieutenant in the Royal Engineers. Bored with peacetime army routine, he soon applied for a post in Stanley's 1887 Emin Pasha relief expedition and was accepted.

His service under Stanley was generally considered excellent. Stairs was close friends with Arthur Jephson, and together the two had a rather serious row with Stanley, but Stanley still trusted Stairs enough to leave him in charge at Fort Bodo when Stanley had to backtrack to find the missing Rear Column. Stairs was also the officer chosen to supervise the exploration of Ruwenzori.

Stairs got himself into an uncomfortable situation in August 1888 when he wrote a letter to Maj. Edmund Barttelot severely criticizing Stanley, and entrusted it to a man named Wadi Mambruki for delivery. The messenger drowned en route, and his personal effects, including the letter, were recovered and given to Stanley. Stanley brooded over the contents—which included allegations of brutality, selfishness, and hoarding of supplies on his part—and relations between the men were never afterward the same.

From then on Stanley made sure to assign Stairs to the most onerous tasks that had to be done. For a time Stairs was placed in charge of the expedition's sick camp, a static, depressing, and unhealthy situation for a young officer. When the expedition was stationary near Lake Victoria, waiting for Emin Pasha to gather those of his people who were to flee with them to the coast, Stairs was ordered to conduct the foraging drives needed to collect the requisite food. These unpleasant affairs consisted of burning villages, fighting through ambushes, and stealing cattle on a large scale—on one day alone Stairs and his men brought in over three hundred head of cattle. This type of activity seems to have been against Stairs's nature, but he followed his orders.

Upon his return to England in 1890, Stairs was assigned to Aldershot, then in 1891 promoted to captain and posted to an infantry regiment. Stairs was then commissioned by King Leopold to lead an expedition to Katanga under the auspices of the Thys subsidiary, the Compagnie du Katanga. This mission Stairs carried out with dispatch, starting out in July 1891. Three similar parties, sent out roughly simultaneously, all lagged behind.

His main assignment was to force a treaty upon the Katanga king, Msiri. Stairs demonstrated his fidelity to his new employer, Leopold, at the expense of his loyalty to his country when he intercepted and destroyed a letter to Msiri from Alfred Sharpe, who was attempting to win the area for Britain. When Msiri nevertheless proved reluctant to sign his treaty, Stairs attempted to arrest him. Msiri and Stairs's lieutenant, Omer Bodson, were killed in the resulting fracas. Stairs promptly settled the political status of Katanga by dividing the kingdom and placing puppets on the various thrones. He tore down Msiri's palace to build a fort, where he spent Christmas Eve of 1891 proudly feasting his surviving officers and looking forward to the future.

He was a bit premature. Katanga was beset by famine, and hundreds of the local people and some seventy of Stairs's Swahili troops died of malnutrition. An additional ninety or so deserted. Stairs decided to return to civilization by going eastward, down the Zambezi. He fell ill with either blackwater fever (Harry Johnston, 1897) or simple malaria (*Scottish Geographical Magazine,* January 1893) and died in the summer of 1892 at Chinde, the British port at the Zambezi mouth, while waiting for a steamer to take him to Zanzibar. Stairs's diary was published in 1994 under the title *Victorian Explorer.*

Stanley, Sir Henry Morton (1841–1904). The career of Henry Stanley is one of history's stranger rags-to-riches stories. Born in Denbigh, Wales, as Henry Rowlands and abandoned as a child, Stanley came to the United States at a very young age. He grew up in the Midwest. During the American Civil War he managed to participate as an enlisted man on both sides, fighting as a Confederate infantryman at the Battle of Shiloh and as a Union seaman later in the war. Drifting into newspaper work, Stanley (he had taken the name of a New Orleans merchant who had befriended him) got a journalistic scoop by wiring the news of the British victory at Magdala during the Abyssinian campaign just moments before the telegraph cable snapped, which prevented the news from reaching Britain. Readers in London first heard the news from Stanley's paper, the *New York Herald,* and Stanley was marked as an ambitious, enterprising young reporter.

In 1869 Stanley received his famous commission to locate the Scottish missionary David Livingstone, a task he accomplished in late 1871. Stanley's book, *How I Found Livingstone in Central Africa,* catapulted him into the front rank of African explorers. Stanley was quick to capitalize on his success, returning to Africa in 1874 to organize a massive safari of nearly four hundred men. Through many hardships (not the least of which was his own violent and abrasive leadership style), Stanley led his expedition from the east coast of Africa through the Lakes district and down the Congo to the sea. He reached the Atlantic Ocean in 1877 with 115 survivors.

While it has become popular to denigrate and despise Stanley in recent years, it is nevertheless true that this was only the third time Europeans had crossed the continent of Africa, behind Cameron and David Livingstone. Once back in European-held territory, Stanley received repeated offers to leave his men and return to a hero's reception in Britain. He refused, so that he could see his men safely back to Zanzibar. With all his faults and richly deserved reputation for selfishness and severity, it is important to acknowledge that Stanley possessed some good qualities as well, not least among them his sense of loyalty to the African members of his expeditions. It is also a mistake to think of Stanley as a man who was always brutal. He was more of a pragmatist (albeit an emotional one) than a brute. It's true that whenever he felt he had to move fast and decisively he drove his men hard and didn't hesitate to resort to force, but when he could, as during his days as Congo administrator, he often approached his duties in a thoughtful and deliberate manner. No man is a total stereotype, and Henry Stanley was a more complex character than most. This has been recognized over the years by the large number of biographies written about him.

In 1879 Stanley was hired by King Leopold as director of the International Association of the Congo to investigate and develop the commercial opportunities inherent in the Congo. He spent five years in West Africa supervising the construction of trading and military stations and organizing the infrastructure of what became the Congo Free State. He earned the nickname Bula Matari (also seen as Matadi), the "breaker of rocks," for his dynamic construction methods and determination to overcome any obstacle. The nickname grew a larger significance, and for many years was used by the Congolese as another name for the Belgian-dominated government. Stanley's tenure must be regarded as a disappointment. The Congo never quite produced the vast natural wealth that Leopold had anticipated, and the resulting frustration and greed poisoned the atmosphere of the Free State. Stanley must bear a significant share of the responsibility for the creation of what must be regarded as one of the most distasteful governments of modern times.

His final African adventure began in 1887 as an attempt to rescue Emin Pasha and his rumored hoard of ivory. Like most of Stanley's activities, this expedition was marred by trouble and violence. Stanley was especially criticized for abandoning part of his force, the so-called "Rear Column," in an attempt to streamline his safari and make quicker progress toward Emin and Lake Victoria. By the time Stanley reached his goal, it was questionable who was rescuing who: Emin's men were well fed and clothed in immaculate uniforms while Stanley's bedraggled and starving porters were dropping by the dozens from hunger and disease. The one commodity Emin did need, modern rifle ammunition, Stanley didn't have, and to make it worse, the Pasha didn't even want to be rescued. He was quite happy to stay where he was, but Stanley needed to accomplish the "rescue" if he was to avoid ridicule back home. After much argument and coercion, Stanley convinced Emin to come along to East Africa, a journey of some twelve hundred miles. Emin survived a near-fatal fall from a balcony in Tanganyika, and Stanley returned to Europe and what he believed would be a triumphant reception.

Henry Stanley in the uniform of the Congo Free State, wearing his self-devised "Stanley cap."

At first he was correct. The story of the Emin Pasha Relief Expedition captured British hearts, and Stanley, who had previously earned some resentment in England for his high-handedness, found himself the man of the hour. But inevitably, stories of the Rear Column began to filter in, and Stanley found himself the center of a bitter controversy.

The Rear Column had fallen on disaster. Beset by hostile Africans, starving in the middle of a green jungle, and wracked by strange and lethal diseases, the men who had been left in equatorial Africa by Stanley had fallen against each other like desperate wolves. The atrocity stories created a sensation in the press. One English officer was even accused of purchasing a young slave girl so he could watch the local cannibals eat her. As was his wont, Stanley blamed everybody but himself for the disaster. His subordinates, his men, his feckless Arab allies, everyone was to blame for the tragedy except Henry Morton Stanley.

The controversy dogged Stanley for the rest of his days and blackens his reputation even today. But materially it had no real impact on the former Welsh waif. He won a knighthood and made a fortune from his African adventures. The only real insult was one he never even knew about: The British refused to allow him to be buried next to Livingstone in Westminster Abbey.

Heroes of the Dark Continent, a massive 1889 book by J. W. Buel, is an interesting example of the two schools of thought concerning Stanley, in this case combined in one volume. Its main body, written after Stanley had returned from the Emin Pasha Relief Expedition but before the Rear Column scandal exploded, is adulatory in tone when discussing the Welsh explorer. In an appendix, however, Buel explored the Rear Column and other controversial aspects of Stanley's adventures. Buel made it clear that he had totally reevaluated his earlier high opinion and made much of the fact that the main source of information on Stanley's activities in Africa was always Stanley himself.

Buel even went so far as to repeat an insinuation that, in all fairness, seems to be a blatant libel of Stanley. Many onlookers had noted that while Stanley had survived his numerous expeditions, most of his officers had not. Jameson, William Shaw, William Farquhar, Major Barttelot, the Pocock brothers—a long list of ardent young Europeans had embraced the chance to go to Africa with Stanley and then died there. Stanley was known to be insanely jealous of anyone else gaining recognition for what he viewed as his accomplishments alone, and there were rumors of poisoning, but they were just that—rumors.

This kind of speculation and suspicion thrived in the murky and evil atmosphere surrounding the Congo Free State. James Jameson's passing in 1888 was certainly

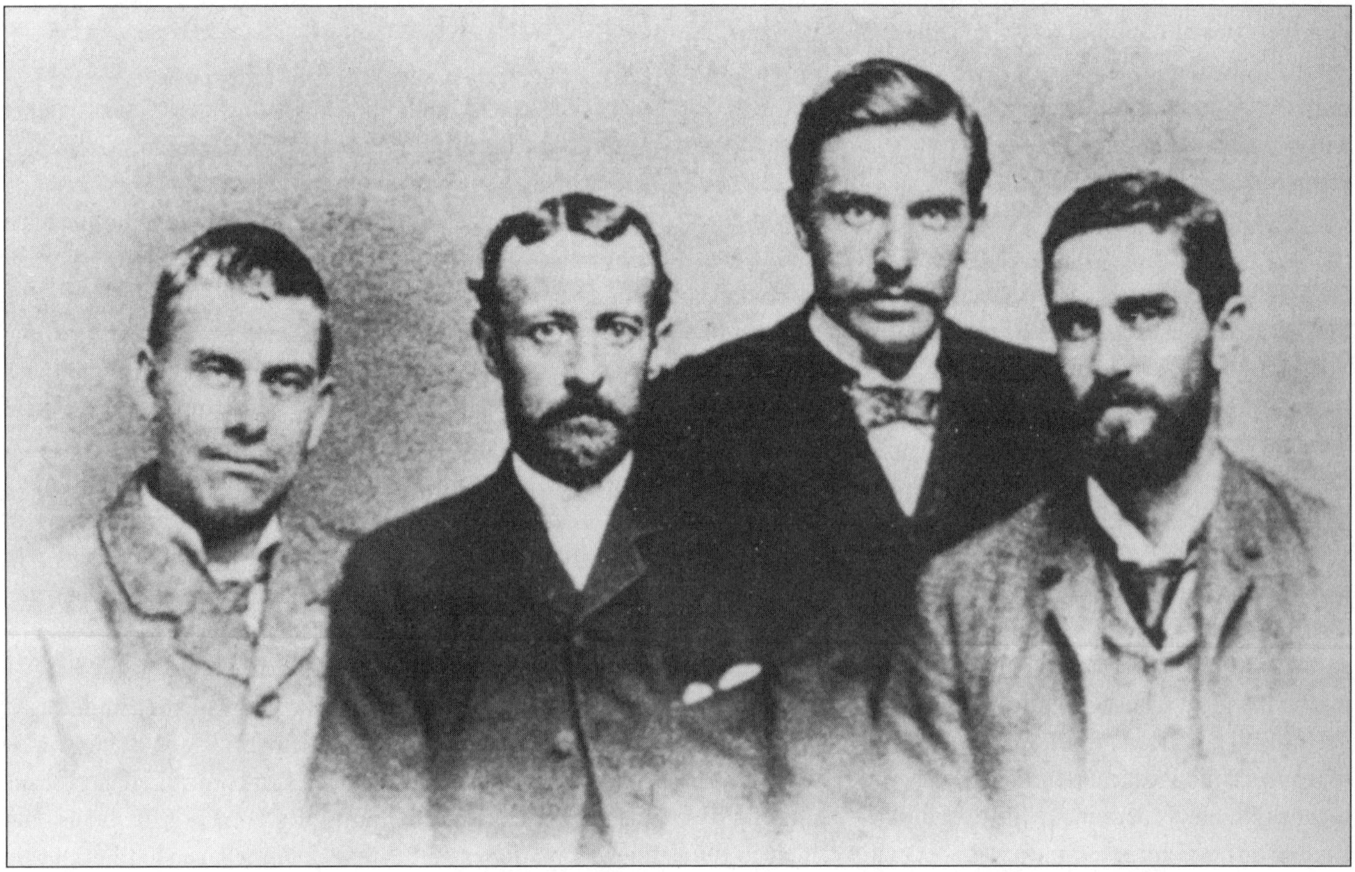

Associates of Henry Stanley. From left to right: E. J. Glave, Alfred Parminter, Herbert Ward, and Roger Casement.

considered suspicious, but the time between the onset of his final illness and his death was not out of the ordinary. African diseases have a way of killing a man very dead very quickly. For that matter, Tippu Tib (a Machiavellian prince if ever there was one) seems to have believed that the Belgians murdered Jameson, not Stanley. More likely the culprit was the abysmal sanitation, the drinking water, or the mosquito. It says much about Stanley's character, however, that he could even be suspected of such crimes. Other African explorers were not so charged. Harry Johnston, for example, could be a ruthless man when he wanted to be, but nobody accused him of throwing Walter Doggett to the crocodiles when that poor man died in Lake Victoria.

Stanley's books and the controversy surrounding his activities and character firmly established in the European mind the fact of cannibalism in Africa. The "Dark Continent" was not unique in this regard. Sailors' stories, missionary letters, and explorers' memoirs had long counted anthropophagy as one of the hazards of life in the world's remote places. Cannibal legends arose about Africa, the Americas, and the Far East, sometimes with a kernel of truth behind them and sometimes not.

There are several types of cannibalism, including eating another human as part of a religious service, being forced to eat human flesh so as to remain alive in a survival situation like a famine or an airplane crash, and what is called gustatory cannibalism, the outright, everyday use of human beings as food. In recent years it has become fashionable to dismiss stories about such "market" cannibalism as being either overtly racist or part of a great historical tradition in which cultures tend to accuse other, "alien" cultures of indulging in the practice. It is very difficult to get to the truth of the matter. A lot of ink has been expended trying to prove or disprove the existence of the practice.

This is not a recent dispute. During the public outcry over the fate of Stanley's Rear Column, a story broke into the news that catapulted cannibalism onto the forefront of European consciousness. One of Stanley's officers, the aforementioned James Sligo Jameson, was said to have placidly watched and even sketched the murder of a young slave girl at the Congo headquarters of Tippu Tib.

When the story broke initially, it was largely overlooked. In 1890, however, the fate of the Rear Column became a hot topic in Europe and America. The dispute centered on who was to blame for the disasters that had befallen the Column, Stanley or his officers. Almost as a side issue, the tale of Jameson and the slave girl was resuscitated. For details of that episode, see the entry on Jameson.

For the next fifty years, nearly every European writer with long experience of the Congo or West Africa discussed cannibalism as an established practice. Harry Johnston published a treatise on the subject in 1888 and covered it extensively in later books such as *British Central Africa* (1897) and *George Grenfell and the Congo* (1908). Johnston was no fool. He was vehemently imperialistic, pragmatic almost to the point of cruelty, tactless, and by today's standards a racist (but not any worse, and indeed more enlightened, than most of his contemporaries). But he wasn't stupid. He wasn't intellectually dishonest either. Originally a defender of King Leopold and the Congo Free State, Johnston publicly turned against the king once a careful assessment of the evidence convinced him that Leopold had encouraged the atrocities in the Congo. On most things Johnston is an excellent source, so his comments on cannibalism should not be reflexively discarded. He claimed to have once inadvertently partaken in a cannibal feast in West Africa, and his books are full of references of cannibalistic activities and photographs of alleged cannibal paraphernalia.

The redoubtable George Grenfell, a missionary in the Congo with immense experience, routinely recorded instances of cannibalism. During an 1885 safari to the Juapa River district, for instance, Grenfell unsuccessfully tried to ransom a man held prisoner by a cannibal tribe—he was slated to be their next meal. On the same trip another group of cannibals offered to purchase a husky crewman from the Grenfell party, making no secret that they wanted him for the cooking pot. Another of Stanley's men, Herbert Ward, wrote extensively of his firsthand knowledge of cannibalism in the Congo and claimed that he had been offered human meat as food—"lumps of human flesh on sticks, together with bunches of bananas, dried monkey, and a few bony fowls" (*Scribner's Magazine,* 1890).

The explorers du Chaillu, William Winwood Reade, and Mary Kingsley all knew the West African Fang people intimately, and all wrote of their cannibalism. Kingsley, for example, wrote of sleeping in a hut in a Fang village and awakening to a noxious odor coming from a sack. It contained "a human hand, three big toes, four eyes, two ears . . . The hand was fresh, the others only so-so, and shriveled." She was fond of the Fang and not one to cast aspersions lightly, and her work is generally highly regarded. In fact, she is often lionized as a progressive reformer and amateur anthropologist.

The stories did not abate in the first part of the twentieth century. The hunter George Rushby claimed to have been fed human flesh in the 1920s. As late as the 1950s, writer Stuart Cloete's book *The African Giant* (1955), essentially a routine travelogue, had five separate index items on cannibalism. Cloete's stories were all secondhand, but they make it clear that the British district officers of the time, at least in West Africa, firmly believed in African cannibalism as an ancient tradition that still existed underground. One local legislature of a famine district had even vetoed a proposal to buy meat from French colonies because they couldn't be certain the meat wasn't human.

However, historians and anthropologists have raised some serious doubts about the existence of the practice. Right off the bat, they say, European explorers and missionaries were misled by their ignorance of African languages. In the idiom of many of these tongues, "to eat" means the same as "to destroy." So when an African warned against, say, the Zulus, crying, "They will eat you!" it is well established that this was meant in a metaphorical and not a physical sense. In fact, the war cry *"Usuthu,"* exclaimed by a Zulu warrior whenever his spear plunged into an enemy, translates literally as "I have eaten." The Fang people, subject of Mary Kingsley's allegations of cannibalism, used the same verb for "to kill" and "to eat."

Second, anthropological research has disclosed that many peoples and cultures tended to accuse their enemies of cannibalism. It seems to have been almost a historical universal. In many cases, burial practices or other rites are misinterpreted by ignorant foreigners. For example, a forest culture that kept the bones of its ancestors on display for the purpose of venerating them would invariably be termed cannibals by the European explorer or hunter who didn't take the time to discover the real reason human bones were visible in a village hut. Sometimes such artifacts were kept for religious reasons or for sentiment, not for soup.

Third, the evidence for cannibalism is often anecdotal, circumstantial, or comes from a questionable source. Especially in South America (excluding ritual religious cannibalism by societies like the Aztecs), the stories often can easily be explained by other scenarios. Early explorers tended to accuse a people of cannibalism on minimal evidence, and everyone else just repeated that initial claim. Eyewitness accounts are notoriously unreliable, particularly when they are an attempt to interpret a foreign culture.

Of course, all the above objections could be applied to many historical controversies—the Belgian atrocities in the Congo Free State, for instance, and the recently resurrected controversy over the conduct of the British during the Kenya "troubles" of the 1950s. History is rarely cut-and-dried. All too often the preconceptions and mores of current society color how it considers conventional history.

The Kingsley case is an interesting example. Mary Kingsley was an adventurous woman who accomplished a lot on her own. Therefore it is often assumed she must have been a feminist, though even a cursory reading of her writings shows her to have been a strongly conventional woman who didn't believe in female suffrage. Her anthropological work is widely applauded, although experts on the field have pointed out that she covered no new ground and made no new discoveries. Her work, while good, frankly received the attention it did (and does) because of her gender. All well and good. It was indeed difficult for a woman of her background to do what she did, but countless men and at least some other women, particularly missionaries and missionary wives, did much more. Regardless of why she has been granted such exalted status, it is inconsistent to applaud her anthropological work in general but deny her evidence on cannibalism because it is now socially unacceptable.

Just as the history of warfare is written by the victors, however, cultural history is written by those who hold the ascendant cultural views. The lenses that are applied today are not much more accurate than the lenses of the past. It is ironic that the evidence supporting the existence of cannibalism is the same type of evidence that supports the European atrocities of the Belgian Congo, yet one is accepted while the other is increasingly denied.

One of this book's goals is to note historical controversies and to point the reader toward additional information if desired. But the entire subject is riddled with bias and preconceptions—it all depends on who you listen to. There is simply no consensus of method used in the study of recent African history. What you get are opinions backed by fairy tales or selected facts. Eyewitness accounts are contradictory and useless; secondhand reports are worse. Oral testimony is accepted in one instance (the British atrocities in Kenya) but rejected in another (cannibalism). Unfortunately, the facts of the past are often determined by whatever is considered acceptable in the university classrooms of today.

Statham, J. L. B. This English sportsman was the author of *Through Angola* (1922). His first trip to Africa was a pilgrimage to the tree where Livingstone's heart was buried. Statham had a distinguished hunting career, including shooting the first several nyala antelope to be found near Beira in Mozambique, the species having been previously unknown in that district. His shoots were interrupted by World War I, in which he was wounded. After recovering, he hunted giant sable in Angola in 1920, and was criticized for killing several of this very rare subspecies. Eventually he met a grisly end, stung to death by bees in India. He also wrote *With My Wife Across Africa by Canoe and Caravan* (1924). ROWLAND WARD 1928: ELAND, PATTERSON ELAND, LORD DERBY ELAND, GIANT SABLE, SITATUNGA.

Steinacker, Ludwig. Steinacker was an eccentric militia officer who claimed he was born of a Prussian military family. During the Boer War he led an irregular unit called "Steinacker's Horse" that was stationed around the part of the Transvaal that later became Kruger National Park. The unit suffered occasional losses to the man-eating lion of the area. A martinet given to wearing a gaudy uniform of his own design, Steinacker was eventually relieved of his command when he went AWOL on a trip back to London. He hung around the district for a while, alternately trying to bully or whine himself back into a job, and then faded into obscurity.

Stephens, F. T. Major Stephens was commissioner of police in Nyasaland in the 1920s and 1930s, and a renowned target-shooter and prolific elephant hunter. As police commissioner he traveled all over British Central Africa and took it upon himself to carry out elephant control work wherever he went. He once shot through thick bush at an elephant that kept poking its head through the undergrowth. Closer investigation revealed that he had shot and killed five elephant, each of them dead with a brain shot.

The Junior Mackinnon Cup was a trophy offered to rifle teams from all over the British Empire who competed at Bisley. Stephens was a member of the 1909 Southern Rhodesia team and the 1929 trophy-winning Nyasaland team, and was captain of the first-place 1932 Nyasaland squad.

Sterk, Hans. The son of a Dutch father and an English mother who were murdered by African warriors when he was still a boy, Sterk was one of the premier Boer elephant hunters of the nineteenth century. He used the typical Boer technique of moving all his worldly goods in an oxwagon to a pristine area, setting up a homestead, and shooting out the area's elephant until it was time to trek on. Once, down to his last thirteen bullets, he used them to take down four bulls carrying a total of five hundred pounds of ivory.

Despite often-serious antipathy between Boer and English residents of Cape Colony, Sterk was popular among the British and was well received in Cape Town society. He was also known for his eagerness to enlist in any and all punitive campaigns, in that way perhaps avenging the deaths of his parents. Sterk was the subject of *The Adventures of Hans Sterk* by A. W. Drayson.

Stevenson, Gilbert. Stevenson served with Harry Johnston in the 1891–1893 antislavery campaigns in Nyasaland. While campaigning against the Arab slaver Liwonde in early 1893 Stevenson was shot near the kidney and almost died. He recovered and worked as a collector in the Mlanje District of British Central Africa. He died in a gun accident while hunting in September 1896.

Stevenson-Hamilton, James (1867–1957). James Stevenson-Hamilton began his career as a British soldier, an officer of the Inniskilling Dragoons. He acquired early substantial experience in Africa, for he was fond of hunting and other outdoor activities, and took every opportunity he could to escape into the bush for a quick hunting holiday. When the Boer War was over, he had attained the rank of major and was asked if he would consider a brief temporary assignment as warden of the Sabi Game Reserve. The reserve had been set aside as a protected area for wildlife some five years previously, in 1897, but the exigencies of war had prevented any development of the wildlife sanctuary. In fact, the local military unit, an irregular cavalry battalion called Steinacker's Horse, had been living off the Sabi's antelope for a few years. The reserve, in the northeastern corner of the Transvaal, had once been a legendary hunting ground teeming with game of all kinds.

By 1902, however, the game there had been largely shot out. The eastern Transvaal had been a favorite hunting spot of men like Henry Glynn, Abel Erasmus, and David Schoeman. Predators predominated, and lion, leopard, cheetah, and African hunting dogs seemed to be everywhere. Non-predatory game had taken a beating from the Boer riflemen. The few remaining elephant were survivors, most having fled to Portuguese East Africa during the Boer War. Wildebeest were extremely rare, and impala and other antelope were relatively few. The situation was so bad that until 1926 the rangers had a policy of shooting predators, particularly lion, on sight.

Stevenson-Hamilton first arrived in the Sabi in the summer of 1902, seconded from his regiment. He considered himself at this point a career soldier (he stayed on as warden until 1946) and looked upon the posting to the reserve as a nice little temporary job that would allow him to indulge in his second love, wildlife and hunting. He was not the first choice for the job. A man named Walker had been appointed warden in 1901 but never actually arrived there, thanks to the chaos of the Boer War, and a well-known South African hunter named Farmer Francis was slated for the job until he was killed in one of the last battles of the war near Mambatine just north of the Sabi River. With the end of hostilities, a new proclamation was issued by the Transvaal government reaffirming the reserve's existence, and Stevenson-Hamilton was selected as warden by Sir Godfrey Langdon, the Transvaal commissioner of native affairs.

After a quick tour, Stevenson-Hamilton set out to hire capable rangers to help him patrol the reserve. The first one hired was Paul Bester, who had a short and undistinguished career. After Bester, Stevenson-Hamilton was more fortunate, or skillful, in his hiring—the rangers of the early Sabi Reserve formed an effective and unique group of colorful outdoorsmen. Men like Wolhuter, Healy, Duke, and De Laporte established an outstanding tradition of excellence for future rangers to follow.

The reserve got off to a shaky start. Stevenson-Hamilton was beset from all sides. Few Transvaal citizens in 1902 could understand why tax dollars should go to protecting animals. Native Africans who had hunted the area for centuries were now "poachers" and required to stop, though many were permitted to reside inside the reserve's boundaries for years to come. Poachers and ranchers from Portuguese East Africa liked to cross the border to hunt and graze their herds. The hunters of European descent were an even greater problem, and Stevenson-Hamilton had to take firm measures to put them in their place. He had to be an outstanding game warden, a policeman, and a politician, constantly traveling to the capital to fend off yet another attack on the reserve's meager budget and even its existence. One recurrent battle was the constant effort to open the reserve to grazing interests. Even many of the reserve's supporters felt that it should be only temporary—ban shooting for a few years so as to replenish the game supply, and then open it up for hunting once again.

Ever so slowly, Stevenson-Hamilton succeeded in changing the public perception of the reserve's role. Gradually the rangers and native policemen of the Sabi earned the respect of their neighbors, and gradually physical improvements were made. Roads were built, tourist accommodations set up, and other parcels of land added, and the game animals began returning. Eventually the predator control policy was abandoned and the lion became a prime tourist attraction. The final step in the reserve's protection was to bring it national park status, which happened in 1926, when it became the core of Kruger National Park.

Stevenson-Hamilton's constant promotion, aided by public-relations campaigns such as that of artist Stratford Caldecott, ensured the park's eventual growth. Tough and single-minded, he was the perfect man for the job in the reserve's doubtful early years. Stevenson-Hamilton made a concerted effort to concentrate as much authority in the person of the Sabi Game Warden as possible, using various political and legal machinations to become, at one time or another, the area's native commissioner, customs agent, railway supervisor, and civil magistrate. By accumulating all of this power he hoped to invest the office of warden with enough authority both to stave off threats to the reserve and to shape it in the way most beneficial to wildlife. He succeeded in his attempt to make the warden virtually all-powerful in the reserve, thereby ensuring both its existence and its growth during the difficult period of the 1910s–1920s, when outside farming, ranching, and hunting interests wanted to throw the place open for their own destructive use.

In 1928 there were 122 miles of road inside the reserve's borders. That increased to 382 miles in 1929, 450 miles in 1930, and over 900 miles by 1936. During the same period the number of cars allowed in rose from three in 1927 to more than 6,000 in 1935. The total number of tourists went from about twelve to 26,000 annually. People who had never thought of wild animals other than as something to shoot, or had never thought of wild animals at all, came out to gawk at lion and zebra and giraffe. There were still problems, of course, including the inevitable continuing debate over the park's purpose (people or wildlife) and the fact that the macho atmosphere surrounding the rangers earned them an international reputation for rudeness. But the validity of the park's concept and its intrinsic value were firmly established under the hand of the first warden.

Few men are lucky enough in their professional lives to garner the kind of job satisfaction that Stevenson-Hamilton must have felt. A 1936 account by Mary L. Jobe Akeley entitled *Restless Jungle* describes his accomplishment in building up the park using terms generally reserved for miracles. During his long career he occasionally took extended leaves to try his hand at other vocations, including service in World War I and a stint as director of the Khartoum Zoo, but it is Kruger National Park for which Stevenson-Hamilton will always be remembered. He was very much the standard ex-military British official, tough but proper, but his actions and writings reveal a man who definitely marched to his own drummer. He was years ahead of his peers, for instance, when it came to realizing the need for wildlife protection, and he seems to have lacked some of the more egregious racial attitudes of the time. In his book *The Low Veld* Stevenson-Hamilton recommended that local folk remedies for snakebite be studied by Western scientists, citing several examples in which the remedies proved effective. "I think we should do well to recollect," he wrote, "that native doctors, in spite of the contempt, often born of ignorance and racial prejudice, with which they are regarded by the white man, are by no means fools, and that it would be an astonishing thing if in thousands of years they had not evolved some efficient remedy against one of the most present and serious dangers to which they and their clients are exposed." Another passage in the same book makes it clear that Stevenson-Hamilton had tried, at least once, the local habit of smoking hemp and found that "smoking of this weed in moderation does not do much harm, and indeed a few whiffs after a long journey act as a pick-me-up."

He retired in 1946, but kept his home in the Transvaal until his death at age ninety. One intriguing feature of his retirement home was a large marula tree that overlooked his bungalow. The marula grows to about thirty feet tall but is known more for its fruit than its shade. All over its range, the acidic, yellow plums are fermented into a refreshing beer that is, shall we say, very popular. As Stevenson-Hamilton put it (1934), when the fruit is in season "the whole country-side is either preparing to get drunk, actually drunk, or getting over being drunk."

In addition to the national park, Stevenson-Hamilton left another very valuable legacy, his books. Not content to write a simple autobiography or hunting memoir (*South African Eden* comes closest, if that's what you're looking for), Stevenson-Hamilton recorded his observations about the land he loved with a meticulous attention to detail that's almost unique. Discounting his 1947 book *Wild Life of South Africa* (virtually a lightly updated rehash of 1912's *Animal Life*), the three remaining volumes form a classic library in themselves.

Animal Life in Africa (1912) presents an engaging and thorough (539 pages) look at the wildlife of the Dark Continent, not just game animals but everything from ratels to fish to birds to snakes. There are sections on observing wildlife, the dangers of fishing, managing porters, and using *machilas*, horses, and bicycles. Many writers of his day wrote chapters on the organization of African safaris, but Stevenson-Hamilton blows the others away with his scrupulous attention to detail. An appendix includes the entire text of the lengthy Transvaal game ordinance.

The Low Veld: Its Wildlife and People (1929) is a somewhat lesser accomplishment. Ostensibly divided into three parts, the sections on geology and wildlife are relatively weak. The strength of the book lies in the third part, covering the indigenous people of the Transvaal and their history and customs. Many of the warden's observations on race relations were decades ahead of their time.

The third book in his African troika, *South African Eden* (1937) must be considered a classic of the genre. Stevenson-Hamilton recorded the entire history of the Sabi Game Reserve/Kruger National Park year by year, with details on the personalities and political events that shaped the formation of the great sanctuary. The latter part of the book, dealing with the national park, is not quite as strong as the half that focuses on the reserve, but nevertheless the work as a whole dwarfs all other African park histories, even the redoubtable *Wankie* by Warden Ted Davison. A century after the events that Stevenson-Hamilton wrote about, a reader can still transport himself to the early days of the Transvaal through the magic of his books. ROWLAND WARD 1928: ELEPHANT, NILE LECHWE, WHITE-EARED KOB, LION.

Stigand, Chauncey Hugh (1877–1919; birth year also given as 1875). A professional soldier, Stigand was stationed with the King's African Rifles at Zomba in Nyasaland in the first years of the twentieth century. There he enjoyed hunting with Brander-Dunbar, Mostyn, and Denis Lyell, with whom he later collaborated on several books. Stigand was a tough, muscular man, much respected for his physical strength and both soldierly and hunting skills. He was a legendary marksman but had his share of bad luck, being at various times roughed up by a lion, a rhino, and an elephant.

The rhino incident happened in early 1905. Stigand was walking through the bush when two black rhino charged him, apparently without provocation. He put a bullet into one rhino's head at point-blank range, but the other smacked him in the chest and laid him flat. After goring him and rolling him along the ground, it suddenly stopped the attack and trotted away. Stigand had numerous scrapes and a bad horn wound to the chest, but no vital organs were damaged and he quickly recovered.

The lion accident followed just two months later. Stigand was hunting at the appropriately named railway station of Simba in Kenya. The big cats of Simba were particularly troublesome and had even been known to attack people right in the station building. Stigand staked out a position near a water tank where the animals frequently went to drink. He killed three and wounded one. When he went to follow up the fourth lion, it sprang out at him from some tall grass, knocked him down, and bit him in the shoulder. Stigand managed to punch the lion in the snout. As luck would have it, his earlier bullet had wounded the animal in the face, and, startled by the pain, it ran off.

Stigand was rushed by train to Nairobi and immediately hospitalized. Blood poisoning set in (the bites of lion and leopard are often septic due to the decayed meat between their teeth), and for a time it seemed he wouldn't survive. As it was, Stigand was left with a stiff arm and nerve damage that bothered him for years.

Stigand rose to high office, becoming governor of Mongalla province in the Sudan. He is one of the few great hunters who predicted the manner of his own death, exactly and in writing. Considering the number of times he was mauled by game animals, you might think he predicted getting chomped by a hippo or thumped by a buffalo, but somehow he imagined and wrote about just how native spearmen would someday do him in.

Chauncey Hugh Stigand, Uganda, 1912.

In his best book, *Hunting the Elephant in Africa* (1913), he wrote about punitive expeditions against native tribesmen, stating that it usually went a certain way, but that "on the hundredth occasion, all starts as it started before, but either the strength or the courage of the enemy has been underrated or a small column becomes detached. Nothing is seen of the assailants except a few flying men. Suddenly, there is a rush in thick grass or bush and the little column gets massacred." That is precisely how Stigand died on 8 December 1919, leading a column of troops on a punitive expedition against the Dinkas. He and another officer, Major White, stepped ahead of their troops to check some compass points on the map. Suddenly there was a rush of tribesmen, a flurry of shots, a flashing of spears, and Stigand and White lay dead along with a dozen or so spearmen. He was buried where he fell, at a speck on the map called Kor Rhaby in the Sudan.

In addition to his own books, Stigand is mentioned frequently by other hunters, especially Denis Lyell. Lyell's *African Adventures* contains not only letters from Stigand to Lyell but also missives from other hunters discussing Stigand, which are very interesting. Abel Chapman writes about why he admired Stigand, Norman Smith discusses the Dinkas and the governor's death, and Millais tells why he didn't like Stigand's books. It's an interesting read.

One odd work by Stigand was published after his death. *Cooking for Settler and Trekker,* by Captain and Mrs. Stigand, came out in 1920. It's a 124-page cookbook with some very unusual recipes.

Stockley, Charles Hugh (1882–1955). Lieutenant Colonel Stockley was the author of *Big Game Shooting in the Indian Empire* (1928) and *African Camera Hunts* (1948). A veteran with a long history of big-game hunting, Stockley went on safari to Kenya's Tana River district in 1952. He was disappointed with the overall wildlife situation in the region and particularly concerned with the low state of morale in the game department, so when his hunt was over he wrote a long letter to Archie Ritchie, the country's chief game warden, expressing some of his concerns. In the letter Stockley quoted an unnamed game department control officer who had griped about the state of affairs, no doubt over a few drinks. Stockley's point was merely to illustrate that there was an overall problem that Ritchie might want to look into.

In the classic response of bureaucrats everywhere, Ritchie missed the point entirely and set out to punish what he regarded as an act of disloyalty. Looking down the list of control officers to see who might have been so low as to betray the hallowed department, his eyes fell upon the name of Eric Rundgren, the hot-headed rogue who had been control officer at Nanyuki since 1944. True, Nanyuki was nowhere near the Tana River, where Stockley had been hunting, but that didn't stop Ritchie from leaping to the conclusion that Rundgren was the man responsible for this blemish on the department.

Ritchie called Rundgren on the carpet at his headquarters in Nairobi. Rundgren denied any knowledge of Stockley or the incident. The thirty-four-year-old Swede's first reaction was to reasonably point out that he had nothing to do with the Tana River area, but Ritchie, in a style that would do any civil servant proud, countered with the fact that Rundgren was known to have hunted there in the past. So had most of Kenya, and probably every single control officer and game warden, but that didn't stop Ritchie. Rundgren, who generally reacted to these situations like Attila the Hun on speed, and who this time had the added encouragement of being entirely in the right, promptly went berserk and a full-fledged row developed in Ritchie's office. It ended with Rundgren stomping out with Stockley's Nyeri address in his hand and vowing to get to the bottom of the matter.

When confronted by an angry Rundgren (an awesome sight), Stockley calmly pointed out that the identity of the control officer who had made the remarks was not the point—he was simply drawing Ritchie's attention to a potential morale problem. Ritchie's behavior obviously led credence to the disgruntled officer's charges. Commendably, Stockley refused to reveal the control officer's name, even though Rundgren not unreasonably pointed out that his own reputation was now at stake. It was an unfortunate situation all around, and the fault was entirely Ritchie's. Weak executives often punish any criticism of their organization rather than investigate it.

Ritchie, one of the last remaining game department heads hired solely because of personal skill with a rifle (he had held the post of Kenya's chief warden since 1924), had simply lost touch with the situation on the ground. The game department at this point was woefully underfunded and understaffed and had no real "mission statement." Department policy was to respond to problems, not to initiate policies or programs, and Ritchie saw nothing wrong with asking individual wardens to cover wild areas the size of an American state. Ritchie encouraged the use of his department's personnel to hassle white hunters over picayune licensing violations while ignoring the major threats to Kenya's wildlife. Considering that the remote areas of East Africa were packed with dangerous game, savage bandits, medieval warriors, and commercial poachers, and that he was charged with protecting his country's most valuable resource, Ritchie should have spent every waking minute fighting for more money and personnel instead of hanging at the Muthaiga Club and nitpicking over regulations. The very real problems of the Kenya Game Department were covered up by skillfully romanticizing the wardens and control officers as knights of civilization holding back the tide of barbarism.

The result of the Stockley affair was a serendipitous one, under the circumstances. Rundgren resigned from his job and was promptly snapped up by a safari company as a professional hunter. His annual salary immediately went from £624 (out of which he had to pay his own transportation expenses) at the game department to £3,000 at Safariland. The safari industry got a legend-in-the-making, and Ritchie was no doubt relieved that he had rid himself of a troublesome, if singularly skilled, troublemaker.

Stokes, Charles (xxxx–1895). Stokes was a Christian Missionary Society missionary in British East Africa who lost his calling and found a career running guns to the Africans. He also did general trade and safari work, arranging for porters and provisions at his clients' behest. In 1882 he was of great assistance in organizing Bishop James Hannington's first trip to East Africa. He accompanied Hannington all the way from Saadani on the coast to Lake Victoria, where he left the party. Along the way he managed the caravan for the benefit of the totally inexperienced missionary, even leading the armed Swahili porters in skirmishes against local bandits. Hannington described Stokes as speaking in a thick Irish brogue. Two years later Stokes was the outfitter of Harry Johnston's prolonged Kilimanjaro safari (Johnston always thought very highly of Stokes).

In 1890 Stokes was carrying a large load of weapons to Uganda when he was intercepted by Lugard and forced to turn back. Lugard confiscated some one hundred fifty Snider rifles and three hundred muskets, and these contraband weapons were a decisive factor in Lugard's upcoming campaign.

Subsequently Stokes went into business trading guns for ivory with the distinctly unfree Africans of the Congo Free State. This was during the period of almost continuous African and Arab revolt against the Belgian authorities. The Belgians and their mercenary officers (drawn from all over Europe and the United States) were drastically outnumbered and trusted their technological and tactical superiority to give them the upper hand in the jungle warfare. Stokes's operation threatened to diminish that superiority. For his part, Stokes relied upon his British citizenship and the ephemeral legal environment of Central Africa to protect him and his activities.

In January 1895 Stokes was invited to a conference by a Belgian officer named Captain Lothaire. He showed up suspecting nothing, apparently believing it was a routine meeting called to discuss permits or bribes. He even left his numerous armed retainers behind so as not to further offend the Europeans: This was a fatal mistake. Without any ceremony, Lothaire had Stokes dragged before a kangaroo court, tried, convicted, and hanged all within a few hours.

The illegality of the proceeding bothered some people, but not very many and not very much. After diplomatic protests from Great Britain, Lothaire was indicted for murder. He was thrice tried, thrice acquitted, and soon thereafter promoted by King Leopold and given a lucrative managerial position in one of the concessionaire companies that was busy exploiting the Congo. Harry Johnston (1908) was one of the few who wrote fondly of Charlie Stokes, describing him as "handsome-looking" and "trustworthy," but even he had to admit that the Belgians were justified in taking offense to Stokes's trading activities. His rifles, after all, were killing their troops. Johnston and a few other English writers with Imperialist agendas tried to make a martyr of the dead gunrunner, but the material just wasn't there. Johnston argued that Stokes should have been imprisoned or deported at most, but what was done was done, and the judicial murder soon faded from public consciousness.

Stone, Charles Pomeroy (1824–1887). Charles Stone was born in Greenfield, Massachusetts, and graduated from the United States Military Academy at West Point in 1845. He served with distinction in the Mexican War and, after retiring from the Army in 1856, led a scientific survey in the Mexican state of Sonora and Baja California from 1857–1861. When the Civil War erupted he was commissioned a brigadier general of volunteers in the Union army, but after a humiliating defeat at Ball's Bluff in October 1861, he was temporarily jailed, disgraced, and finally relegated to minor commands. In 1863 he was demoted to colonel. Resigning in 1864, he ran a mining concern in postwar Virginia until 1870. At that time Stone joined the Egyptian service as lieutenant general and chief-of-staff to the Khedive, becoming the most senior of the many American Civil War officers who went to Egypt. He served the Khedive competently for thirteen years before returning to the United States, where he was chief engineer in charge of erecting the Statue of Liberty. General Stone died three months after the Statue's opening ceremony.

Strombom, Jan Oscar. A British trader, he arrived in Africa about 1862. Four years later he established a store at Lake Ngami and was the main white trader in the area until his death in 1892 or 1893. He was well liked and considered brave, despite being of slight stature.

Strong, Richard Pearson. Dr. Strong was the leader of the 1927 Harvard African Expedition. He had listings in the 1928 Rowland Ward records for buffalo (a bull with 47-inch horns shot south of Lake Edward) and elephant (Ituri forest). A key member of the expedition staff was Dr. Harold Coolidge, who collected mountain gorilla specimens and later wrote the 1929 paper "Revision of the Genus Gorilla," which differentiated between the subspecies of mountain gorilla and the lowland gorilla.

Stroud, E. P. W. Stroud was the senior cultivation protector assigned to the Tanganyika Game Preservation Department in 1930. He supervised Tanganyika Territory's Elephant Control Scheme and supervised temporary officials such as David Blunt and Mickey Norton. Stroud was based in Masai.

Strydom, Hendrick. This Boer hunter owned a small homestead in the Colesburg area of Cape Province in the 1850s. Strydom and his family lived by hunting and by making ash, which other Boers used as an ingredient in making soap. Described as a tall, bearded, wild-looking man, Strydom was an exceptionally skillful hunter. In their short acquaintanceship he taught Gordon Cumming a great deal about stalking and hunting. A nice example of Gordon Cumming's superior prose is his description of Strydom's wife: ". . . rather a nice little woman, with a fresh color, and fine dark eyes and eyebrows; and [she] demonstrated her good taste by taking a fancy to me . . ."

In Gordon Cumming's memoir Strydom is shown to be an absolutely superb huntsman—for instance killing a springbok with a head shot at three hundred yards—and a great stalker and tracker, yet even he made mistakes. The Scotsman reports how he and Strydom pursued a herd of quagga at dusk, finally bringing a couple down. Close examination showed the first dead "quagga" to be a gelding—they had been hunting a neighbor's horses.

Sutherland, James (1872–1932). The elephant hunter's elephant hunter, Jim Sutherland arrived in Cape Colony in 1896 eager for adventure. He had a nest egg of £500 with him, but that was soon gone. At one point he got into some kind of fracas that resulted in his getting a bullet in the leg. Sutherland was no one to fool with, being a fine athlete and a very good boxer, once sparring with champion Kid McCoy.

He started hunting ivory in 1898, mainly in Portuguese and German East Africa. By 1912 he was good enough and famous enough to warrant a book, *The Adventures of an Elephant Hunter.* To Sutherland, elephant hunting was a grand affair involving many porters and their women and virtual tent cities. Some of his safaris had as many as eight hundred members. He later was unfairly depicted as an "ivory king" in the popular press, which claimed he was carried about from elephant to elephant in a *machila.* This story possibly started later in his career when he was recovering from the effects of poison. Another canard circulated about Sutherland was that he supposedly took credit for tuskers that his African retainers had shot.

Yet another story had it that the German East African government gave Sutherland an Iron Cross plus unlimited license to kill elephant in return for services rendered in the 1905 Maji Maji rebellion. It's more likely that Sutherland's hunting operation was so successful that he was able to bribe his way into an unlimited license several years before the revolt. The Iron Cross story is doubtful because the medal is historically authorized only at the start of a major war—e.g., the Franco-Prussian War or World War I. Sutherland did win British, French, and Belgian medals in the 1914 war, however.

During World War I Sutherland worked for British intelligence in East Africa as a member of the Nyasaland Intelligence Field Force. He served with distinction and, as noted above, was decorated for merit. After the war he shifted his hunting operations first to East Africa and then to the Belgian Congo, Chad, and Ubangi-Shari. The French-governed areas such as the last named were the most attractive to Sutherland because they still offered commercial licenses that permitted shooting unlimited numbers of elephant.

He and Charlie Grey once bet £100 on who would die first—each man would put the other down for that amount

James Sutherland in East Africa, 1907.

in his will. When Grey was killed by a buffalo in 1930, Sutherland collected his bet.

Sutherland did not long survive his friend. His death is shrouded in mystery. The generally accepted version is that he was poisoned. Struggling to survive in a drastically depressed ivory market, Sutherland somehow incurred the ire of a powerful native chief or witch doctor of the Azande tribe. Poison was slipped into his food. Whether the dosage was miscalculated or Sutherland was just heartier than most, we'll never know. The lingering effects of the poison, however, crippled him and over the course of months his once-proud body began letting him down. His incapacity during this period is what probably led to those *machila* rumors that haunted his legend. He finally succumbed to the poison on 26 June 1932. Some accounts of Sutherland's death leave out the poison, claiming he died from a simple illness. Foran, for instance, reported in *Kill or Be Killed* (1933) that Sutherland succumbed to dysentery.

Since he wrote only the one book, in 1912, there are many gaps in the record of Sutherland's career. He was much admired and envied as a man who spent his life doing exactly what he wanted to do. It became fashionable to mention his name when writing one's memoirs, and many writers took liberties with the truth when they did so. One such was Marcus Daly, who claimed it was his (Daly's) influence that inspired Sutherland to go elephant hunting in the first place. This claim is at variance with all known facts except those concerning Daly's integrity.

Sutton, Richard L. (1879–1952). Sutton was a Kansas City dermatologist who also lectured at the University of

Missouri campus in Columbia. He made several hunting and collecting trips to Africa and Asia in the 1920s and 1930s; many of the artifacts obtained currently belong to the University of Missouri Museum of Anthropology.

Sutton took his twenty-one-year old son to Africa in the late 1920s as a reward for getting good grades in college. They hunted in South Africa, Kenya, and Tanganyika. In addition to shooting, they took some 1,800 photographs. Sutton wrote about the trip in his *The Long Trek* (1930). Other books by Sutton include *An African Holiday* (1924), *Tiger Trails in Southern Asia* (1926), and *An Arctic Safari* (1932). He was a Fellow of the Royal Geographic Society and the Geographical Society of Paris.

Swann, Alfred J. (1855–1928). Swann was an experienced sailor who was hired by a Scottish missionary society to operate a steamer for it on Lake Tanganyika. He had to supervise the movement of the vessel from Zanzibar to the lake, and its reassembly once there. Swann also led troops for Harry Johnston during the recurring slaver wars in Nyasaland. As a mission employee, he had to keep his martial activities secret from his bosses in Scotland. He worked for the mission from 1882–1894 and then transferred over to Johnston's administration, remaining in the Nyasaland civil service until 1908.

Swann was the author of *Fighting the Slave Hunters in Central Africa* (1910). It's a readable and popular work and Swann gives a lot of interesting detail on the everyday aspects of fighting slavers and hunting leopard, hippo, and waterbuck. His style translates well for a modern reader and it has been reprinted at least once; the introduction is by Harry Johnston. The text can even be found for free on the Internet.

Swartz, Lucas Martinus (xxxx–1877). This Boer hunter from the Transvaal chased elephant in the Zambezi Valley from 1854 until his death.

Swayne, Eric John Eagle (1863–1929). Brigadier General Swayne was commissioner of the Somaliland Protectorate in the first decade of the twentieth century. He is mainly remembered for raising a military unit called the Somali Levy in 1900. This battalion, an elite unit despite the name, consisted of a thousand infantrymen and five hundred cavalry led by twenty British officers and fifty Sikh havildars from the Indian army. The Levy (also called the 6th Battalion of the King's African Rifles) fought against the so-called "Mad Mullah" until 1905, when the Somali troops were replaced by Sikh enlisted men and transferred into a new militia.

Swayne took an active interest in sport and wildlife and was a keen observer of the changes that took place from his arrival in the country in 1891 until 1905. In that year he wrote a pessimistic report on the state of Somali game, sounding a dire warning about overhunting. Not that he was the nineteenth-century equivalent of a tree-hugger—far from it. On one two-day surveying safari he and his brother, H. G. C. Swayne, shot two lion, five rhino, and numerous other creatures. General Swayne also seems to have lost an important "in-country" assignment in 1888 because it was felt he'd spent too much official time hunting elephant.

Swayne's November 1905 rough census of game in the Somaliland Protectorate is interesting not only for its own sake but also for its insights into the mind of an intelligent and attentive sportsman. Swayne estimated that less than a thousand elephant, a thousand greater kudu, two thousand lesser kudu, and no zebra or buffalo survived in the entire country. Among predators, he arrived at a figure of three thousand lion and five thousand leopard. Leopard are traditionally undercounted, being furtive and largely nocturnal, but the figure for lion is shocking considering that Somaliland was famous for that particular animal. Swayne's 1905 report, accurate or not, was clearly a wake-up call for the growing number of concerned Edwardian sportsmen.

Swayne, Harold George Carlos (1860–1940). Captain (later Colonel) Swayne was a British army officer (brother of E. J. E. Swayne) who made numerous trips through Somaliland and the Northern Frontier District in the 1890s. His safari in 1893 was turned back by the same hostile Galla tribesmen who had just harassed the Italian expedition led by Ruspoli and Bottego. Later that year he gave much helpful advice to the American explorer A. Donaldson Smith.

Swayne was a contributor to the 1932 Lonsdale Library volume *Big Game Shooting in Africa* and was the author of *Seventeen Trips Through Somaliland and a Visit to Abyssinia* and *Through the Highlands of Siberia*. Some fifty years after his death, Swayne's lost diaries were found in an old trunk in an attic. These were published in 1996 as *Early Days in Somaliland and Other Stories*. ROWLAND WARD 1928: GEMSBOK, GERENUK, ELAND, LESSER KUDU. ROWLAND WARD 1899: SWAYNE HARTEBEEST (NO. 1, 20¼ INCHES), SOMALI DIK-DIK, KLIPSPRINGER, WATERBUCK, ARABIAN GAZELLE, SPEKE GAZELLE, PELZELN GAZELLE, SOEMMERRING GAZELLE, DIBATAG, GERENUK, BEISA oryx, Abyssinian bushbuck (No. 1, 17 inches), greater kudu, lesser kudu, black rhino, tiger.

Swynnerton, Charles Francis Massy (1877–1938). British hunter and game warden. Swynnerton, a charming, intellectually gifted man, was director of game preservation (chief game warden) of Tanganyika in the 1920s. Sometime around 1930 Swynnerton became head of a newly formed tsetse research department (some books say he took over that office about 1933, but Julian Huxley wrote in his *Africa View,* published in 1931 but written a year or two earlier, that Swynnerton was already leading the "anti-tsetse department").

As game warden, Swynnerton was responsible for curtailing crop damage by hungry elephant. In 1925 he inaugurated the Tanganyika Elephant Control Scheme and hired a number of "temporary" cultivation protectors who worked on salary and took direction from the game department. These men, assisted by Africans armed with magazine rifles but given only small amounts of ammunition (to discourage poaching), went to areas troubled by crop-raiding elephant and shot the worst offenders. The tusks belonged to the government. The system was effective because elephant are very intelligent and soon learned to stay away from human habitations and fields.

One of Swynnerton's employees was temporary cultivation protector David Blunt, a former submarine commander in the Royal Navy. Blunt wrote in *Elephant* (1933) that Swynnerton was "the most energetic man I have ever known, never sparing himself; when sick and wanting to travel he carries on until he is definitely ordered to hospital."

The British writer Julian Huxley saw Swynnerton at the Tanganyika town of Shinyanga about 1930. Huxley wrote that Swynnerton was "suffering from a triple bill of malaria, bilharzia, and relapsing fever—a veritable museum of tropical diseases, caused by three very different kinds of parasites and conveyed by three very different kinds of hosts, one by an insect, one by a mollusk, and one by an arachnid." Huxley went on to say, "He seemed to be congratulating himself on not having sleeping sickness as well." A two-month stint at Mrs. Maynard's sanatorium in Ibadakuli got Swynnerton back on his feet.

Swynnerton, G. H. The son of the chief game warden of Tanganyika, Jerry Swynnerton was a game ranger in the same country. He was coauthor (with R. W. Hayman) of the article "A Checklist of the Land Mammals of the Tanganyika Territory and the Zanzibar Protectorate" (*Journal of the East African Natural History Society,* No. 20, 1951).

Sykes, C. A. Elephant hunter and Brig. Gen. C. A. Sykes wrote *Service and Sport on the Tropical Nile* (1903). One day in the Sudan, as he was running from some elephant, Sykes reportedly swore off foxhunting because he could now identify with the poor fox. Rowland Ward 1928: Eland.

T

Talbot, P. Aumory (1877–1945). A colonial official in the Oban district of Southern Nigeria and the Cameroons, Talbot was a detailed observer of West African culture and traditions. He and his wife accompanied Olive Macleod on her 1910 safari to central Africa to investigate the murder of Macleod's boyfriend, Boyd Alexander. Talbot was the author of *In the Shadow of the Bush* (1912) and *Life in Southern Nigeria* (1923).

Tallian, Emil (xxxx–1912). A Hungarian hunter operating in the Athi River area of Kenya in the 1920s. He is mentioned in Kittenberger (1926).

Tappenbeck, Hans (1861–1889). Lieutenant Tappenbeck was a top German explorer who frequently traveled with Lieutenant Kund. The pair were active in the Congo throughout the mid to late 1880s, exploring the Lukenye River in 1885 and opening up the south Congo basin and the Cameroons interior to German traders.

In October 1887 Tappenbeck and Kund, accompanied by a zoologist named Dr. Weissenborn and a botanist named Braun, landed at Great Batanga in the Cameroons and, after a month of preparation, started up the Kribi River heading east. At a point about 175 miles inland they reached what they took to be the ethnic boundary between the Bantu people and the Nilotic races from the Sudan. The local people, called the Bakoko, lived in strongly fortified villages as a defense against Arab slavers from the north, and were unfriendly.

The Bakoko launched raid after raid against the German expedition. In one major attack, Tappenbeck was wounded near his right ear and knocked unconscious, and then Kund was shot, first in the forehead and then twice in the elbow. The Bakoko were finally driven off, but the Germans had lost ten men killed and twenty-six wounded. The wounds of the two leaders were not life-threatening, but it was decided to retreat immediately to the coast because the constant fighting had used up most of their ammunition. The Bakoko followed all the way, spearing stragglers and occasionally sneaking up close to fire a random musket shot. It took twenty-one days of skirmishing and starvation (they saw little or no game) to reach Great Batanga, where Tappenbeck was laid up under the care of Dr. Weissenborn and Kund returned to Europe for medical treatment.

The August 1888 edition of *Scottish Geographical Magazine* reported that fifteen of the Bakoko men who had fired on the retreating expedition were arrested by the German authorities but does not say what was done with them. Their fate would not have been pleasant. The usual German response would have been hanging or a firing squad.

By August of 1888 Kund was recovered and back in Great Batanga and waiting for Tappenbeck, who had apparently gone back to Germany on leave. In early 1889 the intrepid pair went on an expedition past the Sanaga River, into territory never before seen by Europeans. On 10 June they returned to the German station at Epsumb, which they had founded, between the Upper Njong and Sanaga Rivers. From there Tappenbeck returned to the coast, reaching the Cameroons on 12 July. He was still there on 31 July 1889, when he succumbed to a sudden attack of fever.

Tarlton, Alan. With forty years of professional experience, Alan Tarlton was one of most respected of Kenya's white hunters. He had good DNA for the job, being Leslie Tarlton's nephew and the son of hunter/jockey Henry Tarlton. Alan's early clients included Martin and Osa Johnson—indeed, Tarlton was a pioneer of the early photographic safari. He also had a reputation as a superb stalker and was one of the relatively few professionals who carried a .45 on his hip as a backup. Most preferred to rely on a second rifle. Tarlton felt that the .45 automatic was sufficient as a last-ditch defense against a charging lion. He should have known, for he killed more than 150 of the animals.

Like Ionides, Tarlton was something of a "snake man." He maintained a puff-adder farm where hundreds of the creatures were kept in pits. The venom was used to produce vitamin K. During World War II his serpentarium held more than three thousand snakes. Their venom was shipped to the South Africa Institute of Medical Research. He also provided the seventeen-foot python and the spitting cobra that threatened Stewart Granger in the movie *King Solomon's Mines.* Tarlton's wife Morea had a reputation as quite an elephant hunter herself.

Tarlton, Henry. An early Kenya professional hunter, he was the brother of Leslie and father of Alan. Born in Australia, Henry Tarlton was also a talented jockey during Nairobi's frantic pioneer horse-racing days.

Tarlton, Leslie Jefferis (1877–xxxx). Leslie Tarlton is sometimes called the first white hunter. He was certainly one of the early ones, being considered immensely experienced when he led the Theodore Roosevelt safari in

1909. Leslie arrived in British East Africa from Australia (via the Boer War) in 1904. He promptly teamed up with Victor Newland to form Newland & Tarlton, the first great safari company. Their first client, personally guided by Leslie, was Carl Akeley. The American taxidermist liked to tell the story in later years of his initial visit to the Newland & Tarlton offices. The two hunters were furiously pounding on a typewriter in an effort to convince him how busy and businesslike they were. Later he found out that the typewriter was broken. No matter—soon the Newland & Tarlton stable of PHs included such men as Alan Black, George Outram, R. J. Cunninghame, Fritz Schindelar, Philip Percival, and Bill Judd.

Newland & Tarlton had a run of fifteen years and then dissolved in 1919. The next year Tarlton started Safariland, Ltd., with much the same clientele and many of the same hunters. Unlike many safari-company executives, Leslie Tarlton liked to keep his hand in as a professional. A founding member of EAPHA (see glossary), he was a hunter first and a businessman second. His lifetime total of lion killed (they were considered vermin most of his life) stood at 284. It wasn't all one-sided—Tarlton was once badly chewed up by a lion near Thika. He married a fine young woman named Jessie Wright and was a life member of the New York Zoological Society.

Leslie Tarlton and cheetah shot by Kermit Roosevelt, 1909.

Leslie Tarlton, Theodore Roosevelt, and the big lion shot by President Roosevelt.

Taylor, J. B. (1860–xxxx). Taylor was born and raised in South Africa, a member of a moderately well-to-do family, and early on got used to quickly winning and losing fortunes, mainly through mining and trade. He was one of those characters who find themselves in the center of everything, and his 1939 autobiography, *A Pioneer Looks Back,* is full of stories about Cecil Rhodes and Paul Kruger and many lesser-known political and financial figures of the day like Abe Bailey and Alfred Beit. Taylor was an enthusiastic hunter all his life, and he frequently crossed paths with men like Selous and Bill Finaughty. In 1878 Taylor and Finaughty, who had recently retired from elephant hunting, went on a trading trip north of the Hartz River. The trip ended prematurely when Lobengula refused them entry to Matabeleland.

After the Finaughty venture, Taylor enlisted as a gunner in Maj. Owen Lanyon's volunteer regiment fighting Griqua rebels under Donkin Malgaas and Jantjie. Taylor fought in skirmishes at Gomeperi, Lataku, and in the Langeberg Mountains. The Griquas were essentially starved into submission when the British captured their cattle.

Taylor went on to a successful career as a miner and businessman in South Africa and Rhodesia, rubbing elbows with Cecil Rhodes and Starr Jameson. He was a very close friend of the writer Sir Percy Fitzpatrick and never lost his taste for blood sports. He was the founder of the Rand Rifle Association.

When Taylor was running a brokerage in Barberton in the Transvaal, the nearest telegraph office was 136 miles away at Middelburg. Taylor employed a messenger, a man named Harry Pitt, to regularly carry his coded business telegrams to and from Middelburg. As a cover, Taylor would grab his gun and his dogs and ride out of town, meet Pitt, decode the telegrams, encode the new ones, shoot a bird, and ride back to Barberton. None of his rivals ever guessed that he was getting the equivalent of "inside" information.

His middle-aged years were spent on an estate in Scotland, where he leased the shooting and fishing rights on thirty thousand acres of prime deer and trout territory. In his old age Taylor returned to live in South Africa. During WW1 he was involved in protecting the interests of South Africans serving in the British forces.

His 1939 memoirs are interesting in that they present a fairly detailed look at life in the South African diamond- and gold-mining districts, as well as various hunting tales and anecdotes involving well-known figures. One odd recurring motif, however, is Taylor's ongoing bad (or is it good?) luck with poisonous snakes. While almost all African books emphasize the secretive nature of these reptiles and how few encounters there are between man and snake, Taylor recounts at least a dozen close encounters with venomous reptiles during his life, including several when only his thick boots stopped the fangs from piercing him. What was it with this guy and snakes?

John Taylor wearing a turban.

Taylor, John "Pondoro" (1904–1969). Born in Ireland, Taylor left home as a young man due to fears that his pro-British attitude had marked him for death at the hands of the Irish Republican Army. After a short trip to Canada, Taylor joined the Rhodesian police but was soon fired for purposely letting a prisoner escape. He had felt the prisoner was a victim of injustice and acted in accordance with his conscience, regardless of the consequences, an attitude that would get him into much trouble during his life.

Taylor learned his hunting skills by shooting marauding lion on one of South Africa's biggest cattle ranches. He then gravitated to elephant hunting, operating in Nyasaland and Portuguese East Africa. He was extraordinarily successful, albeit not overly concerned about trifling matters such as licenses and game laws. In the 1930s he began writing letters and articles for various magazines, some of which are reprinted in an appendix to Capstick and Marsh's *A Man Called Lion*.

Often broke, on a scale that would depress even Bror Blixen, Taylor was frequently forced to stop hunting due to high ammunition prices or the inability to buy rifles. He still managed to shoot about fifteen hundred elephant in his career, most of them illegally. The money from the ivory was generally invested unwisely, given away, or spent on guns and booze. In the 1940s he began writing books: *Big Game and Big Game Rifles* and *African Rifles and Cartridges* are both classics of African hunting literature and ballistics.

Taylor, in his classic semibiography *Pondoro* (1955), devoted an entire chapter to what he termed the "Great Tana Raid." In it he claimed that he and several accomplices—called Hamisi, Mir Khan, and Hidayetulla in the story—had conducted a large-scale, military-style poaching sweep of a protected area in the Tana River valley.

According to Taylor, the four men (two of whom were Pathans from the Khyber Pass region) and their staff led authorities on a wild-goose chase, ending up on the Indian Ocean coast after plundering the Tana's wildlife resources and in general making fools of the vaunted Kenya Game Department. Taylor was intentionally vague in his book about the date of this escapade, saying, "It's far too recent." According to Capstick and Marsh, authors of *A Man Called Lion,* he told friends that it took place in 1936.

Ever since, the truth or falsehood of Taylor's story has been the subject of controversy. Kenya Game Department folks understandably denied it—couldn't happen, they said, not on their watch. Capstick and Marsh reached the conclusion that the logistics of the operation were impossible. They left open the possibility that Taylor, a known raconteur, may have embellished the telling of what was actually a smaller, lesser raid.

Taylor's later years were tragic, bringing him to probably the worst end imaginable for an African adventurer. An alcoholic and a homosexual (he frequently lived for years in the bush with just his favorite African male companion), and a self-confessed poacher to boot, he was not exactly the type preferred by the staid British authorities. Acting supposedly on his poaching activities, they deported him from Nyasaland back to London in the late 1950s. He spent the last years of his life drinking heavily, living in a one-room flat, and working as a night watchman at a small zoo and kennel. He frequently talked of returning to Africa, but there was never any money for it. At the time of his deportation, the great elephant hunter didn't even own a rifle, having pawned all his weapons.

Teare, Philip. A professional hunter and game official, Teare made his reputation as a buffalo hunter in Rhodesia. He was assigned to the Tanganyika Game Department in 1930 at Shinyanga, and later became the game warden of Tanganyika.

Teleki von Szek, Count Samuel (1845–1916). Also seen as Teleki. Teleki was a wealthy Hungarian nobleman—fond of wine, dining (he lost ninety-seven pounds on his famous safari), and fine horses—who decided to go hunting in East Africa after reading Joseph Thomson's *Through Masai Land.* The Austro-Hungarian Crown Prince Rudolf encouraged him to broaden his expedition into one of exploration as well. Teleki agreed to take Ludwig von Hoehnel (1856–1942), an Imperial Navy officer attached to Rudolf's personal staff, as second-in-command.

Von Hoehnel was the navigation officer aboard Rudolf's yacht, the *Greif.* He had long wanted to make a trip into the African interior, but the first meeting between the two explorers was not propitious. Teleki disliked the idea of sharing the spotlight with another European, while von Hoehnel (like many others) was a little skeptical that a man as overweight as Teleki could withstand the rigors of exploration. Prince Rudolf, who combined a decadent lifestyle with a fairly scientific mind, finally convinced Teleki that von Hoehnel's navigation and cartography skills would add immensely to the geographic value of the expedition. The initial announcement of the upcoming safari in the March 1888 edition of *Scottish Geographical Magazine* read simply, "It is announced that Count Teleky and Herr von Haehnel (sic) intend to lead a large expedition, consisting of 400 armed bearers, through Masai-land to Mount Kenia, and to push northward to Lake Samburu."

The goal was to explore the area north of the Masai homeland. A lot of planning went into this safari, but it was not necessarily practical. Basically, von Hoehnel purchased a bunch of miscellaneous supplies while Teleki informally sought advice from some English hunting friends. Sir Richard Burton convinced him to increase the expedition's firepower, so when they eventually set out, nearly three hundred armed men were in the caravan. Teleki tried to hire James Martin, late of the Thomson expedition, as a guide, but he was already committed to leading a hunt for Sir Robert Harvey, a wealthy Briton. The original route was changed many times, because Teleki had a practical and pragmatic nature and wasn't committed to any one line of march.

The Teleki expedition formed up in Zanzibar during the winter of 1886–1887. In addition to the count and von Hoehnel, the members included the intrepid interpreter Dualla Idris, a roguish ivory trader named Juma Kimameta, a cook called Mhogo who had served with Speke and Cameron, nine askaris, nine guides, three personal servants, and approximately three hundred porters. One article that was not neglected during the planning stage was weaponry: For his personal use Teleki brought two 8-bore double rifles, two .500 Express rifles, a .577 Express, and a 10-bore. The men carried two hundred muzzleloading rifles, eighty Werndl breechloaders, twelve Colt repeating rifles, and various sidearms. In addition, Teleki had gathered a small group of Somali bodyguards, each of them and the three personal servants armed with a modern magazine rifle.

The first part of the journey took them from the port of Pangani on the Ruvu River to the town of Taveta, about 150 miles inland. The expedition got off to a shaky start. Over sixty porters deserted in the first fortnight, and only seventeen were recaptured by von Hoehnel. Halfway to Taveta some of Teleki's porters mistreated a local girl, and several men on both sides were killed in the ensuing brawl. Nature also threatened—members of the safari were attacked by *siafu* (African driver ants), crocodiles, scorpions, and swarms of bees, the bees panicking the column on three separate occasions.

Things got a bit better at Taveta, a very amenable location. Teleki set up camp there for several weeks, trading with the local villagers, an offshoot of the Masai. Von Hoehnel was temporarily left in charge while the count led sixty-six men westward to Mount Meru. His original intent was to climb the 14,979-foot peak, but torrential

Count Samuel Teleki in Africa.

downpours caused him to change his mind, and he headed back to Taveta. This tangential trip was noteworthy because it was Teleki's first contact with the real Masai—he met large parties of them near Kilimanjaro. He handed over some small presents and was allowed to pass unmolested.

Teleki and von Hoehnel then made another side trip, this time to climb Mount Kilimanjaro. It was now the middle of June 1887. Hiring local guides who had worked for Harry Johnston three years earlier, the two Europeans made it within a few thousand feet of the summit. They then returned to Taveta to organize their main safari to the northward, and traveled through Masailand unmolested by those fearsome warriors.

Von Hoehnel now tried his hand at hunting big game. He easily took down four rhino, but his first attempt at an elephant was a different story. Unused to the recoil of the heavy 8-bore elephant rifle, von Hoehnel was smashed in the face by the gun's hammer, ripping open both his nostrils. The injury, while not serious, was painful and took six weeks to heal. The elephant got away.

On 7 September 1887 the expedition left Ngong and entered the land of the Kikuyu. Teleki had ordered the safari to keep its weapons handy because the Kikuyu were known for their propensity for ambush. The events of the next six weeks proved the wisdom of this order. The Kikuyu, ostensibly friendly, harassed the safari at every opportunity. Every river crossing meant paying tribute, or *hongo*; every stop to trade meant arguing and bullying. A flurry of arrows would come out of nowhere, and then arrogant Kikuyu warriors would saunter up to Teleki or von Hoehnel as if nothing had happened. On at least four separate occasions, members of the expedition were wounded. Finally Teleki and the others had had enough.

It was Dualla, the interpreter, who started things going. A Kikuyu warrior threatened him with a spear and a short sword called a *simi*. The warrior reached forward and pulled the devout Somali's prayer beads off his neck. Dualla fired a shot, and the much-beleaguered askaris and the Somali members of the bodyguard went on the offensive. They burned several villages and confiscated ninety cattle and thirteen hundred sheep and goats. The loss of life is not known. There was no more trouble with the Kikuyu, and by 17 October the Teleki expedition was camped on the banks of a cold, clear stream called Nairobi. They halted there when von Hoehnel took sick.

With von Hoehnel laid low by dysentery, Teleki took a small force to climb Mount Kenya. They reached an altitude of 15,355 feet before turning back. This was the very first penetration of the Mount Kenya area by Europeans.

The safari then quick-marched over the Laikipia Plateau, where they had the gratification of discovering that the Masai had been greatly impressed by their military strike against the Kikuyu. Von Hoehnel took a short side trip to look for the mythical Lake Lorian while Juma Kimameta stopped to trade for ivory, buying over eleven hundred pounds from Wandorobo hunters. Teleki took the largest part of the expedition up to Lake Baringo, with the others to follow. Things seemed to be going well.

Everyone snapped back to reality at Baringo, where they intended to buy food. They had been told that the Lake Baringo area was a lush paradise similar to Taveta. Instead they found starvation, illness, and death caused by a famine devastating the district. The safari was almost out of food. Von Hoehnel, already suffering from dysentery, survived the next few weeks only because a clutch of ostrich eggs was found and used to supplement his meager diet. Teleki was forced to shoot for the pot while Dualla led a trading safari to Miansini to buy some grain. He was gone over five weeks.

It was here that Teleki proved his hunting skills. With over two hundred mouths to feed, plus the need to make dried meat for the march ahead, every shot counted. In one day he shot thirty-eight large animals for the pot. In all during this period the Hungarian nobleman shot ten elephant, sixty-one buffalo, twenty-one rhino, nine zebra, six hartebeest, four eland, and two waterbuck, providing over five thousand pounds of biltong. He was charged no less than eleven times by wounded buffalo. Finally Dualla returned with enough grain for the expedition to attempt its final objective, exploration of the north frontier to look for the existence of rumored great lakes.

It was February 1888 when the safari, down to 220 men, set out over uncharted ground. They discovered an unknown range of hills that Teleki named after Major General Mathews, the commander-in-chief at Zanzibar. For the next month they suffered from half-rations, heat in the daytime and cold at night, and from the very real threat of dying of thirst. Finding a small amount of water in a dry riverbed, Teleki had the safari rest there while he and von Hoehnel once again went hunting for the pot. Then they moved on.

Finally, on 5 March 1888, Lake Rudolf was seen by a European for the first time: "At that moment all our dangers, all our fatigues were forgotten in the joy of finding our exploring expedition crowned with success at last," von Hoehnel wrote in 1894. Teleki named the lake after the Austrian crown prince who had been his benefactor, not knowing that Rudolf had shot himself in the Mayerling scandal. Their joy was dampened only a bit when they found that the waters of their great lake were brackish and unpleasant to the taste, albeit drinkable. For the next several weeks the expedition explored and hunted along the lakeside. Not all was fun and games—eight men had been lost for one reason or another since they'd left Lake Baringo. Teleki shot hippo and rhino along the lakeshore, but the closest call came when he and Dualla were hunting an elephant from two small boats. Wounded, the great bull charged Dualla's boat, causing its occupants to dive overboard into the croc-infested water. The elephant crushed the fragile canoe and flung it contemptuously aside, then disappeared behind a peninsula.

The expedition (by now nicknamed "slow safari" by the Swahili porters) explored along the east shore of Rudolf, meeting the primitive Dassenach people. Rumors abounded about a second lake to the east. The Dassenach refused to provide guides but finally at least gave directions. Teleki found the second lake to be a seasonal and unattractive body of water, brackish and teeming with vultures and crows that fed on the lungfish that flopped in the receding shadows. He named it after Rudolf's wife, the Princess Stephanie, presumably as a compliment.

Frightened by a smallpox epidemic among the Dassenach, the safari quickly packed and began to head homeward on 14 May 1888. Trying to pack along enough food to prevent the hunger troubles of the outward trip, each porter was forced to carry about 125 pounds. It took a march of sixteen days down the eastern shore to reach the southern point of the lake. One man came down with smallpox and voluntarily remained behind to perish in the wilderness. His name deserves to be remembered—Matchako.

Soon the men of the safari were feeling more at ease. Teleki named an active volcano after himself, and the first meetings with the Turkana people took place. The Turkana were aggressive and fairly belligerent, enjoying making threats and mock attacks. They were hard to trade with because their principal need was tobacco and Teleki had none. Nature was uncooperative as well, and in several days of hunting Teleki was unable to provide any meat for the pot, except for a warthog and two crocs. Beyond these animals, the safari was subsisting largely on wild figs and berries, and even as they moved southward little food could be found. To make matters worse, it was the rainy season and the skies opened up daily.

Desperate, Teleki OK'd a plan to raid the local *shambas*. This was sheer, unprovoked aggression, which the Europeans justified as a matter of survival. A force of nineteen men under the command of Dualla raided the friendly Pokot villages, stealing cattle. Dualla and his captive herd hastened after Teleki, chased by two hundred warriors. The Pokot had no experience of firearms, and the pursuit was soon discouraged. The expedition was saved.

Back in Masai country, Teleki and von Hoehnel were again delighted to see that the Masai, already respectful, were even more impressed by their defeat of the Pokot. The stock of the Teleki expedition was very high with the nomadic warriors. Even the Kikuyu were friendly this time around.

The last leg of the trip, a march to Mombasa, was essentially uneventful. At a place called Kikumbulyu, Teleki shot the last rhino of the safari, his eighty-third (von Hoehnel had shot about twenty). The Teleki expedition proudly marched into Mombasa on 24 October 1888.

They had a right to be proud. Von Hoehnel in particular provided detailed notes that enlightened the world to the geography and conditions of the hinterlands of East Africa. Three new species of chameleon, seventy-five insects, and a number of plant species were unveiled to science, and a beautiful mountain flower was named *Lobelia telekii.*

Teleki continued his privileged life, later going on extended hunting trips to India and Indonesia. There is an unconfirmed report that he returned to Kilimanjaro once more in an attempt to climb it but was unsuccessful. He died in Hungary on 10 March 1916. Von Hoehnel went on safari again in 1892 with William Astor Chanler, only to be badly gored by a rhino. He later had a successful government career, becoming both naval aide to the Austrian Emperor Franz Josef and head of a trade mission to the Emperor Menelik of Abyssinia. In 1909 he decided to marry against the wishes of his superiors and was forced to retire with the naval rank of commander. Three years later he was promoted, while still in retirement, to rear admiral so as to augment his pension. He died in Vienna on 23 March 1942, a relic of a bygone age. Unfortunately, von Hoehnel's personal papers were seized at his death by the Nazi government and have disappeared.

Temple-Perkins, E. A. A New Zealander, Temple-Perkins spent over thirty years in the Colonial Administrative Services Department of East Africa and was one of the most famous hunters of his time. At the time of his death he held seven No. 1 hunting records for Uganda, where he had spent most of his career.

He arrived in the country in 1919 and took a post as commissioner for the Teso district in northeastern Uganda just south of Karamoja. He held this position from 1919 to 1923, when he had to return to New Zealand for a short time for health reasons, having contracted blackwater fever.

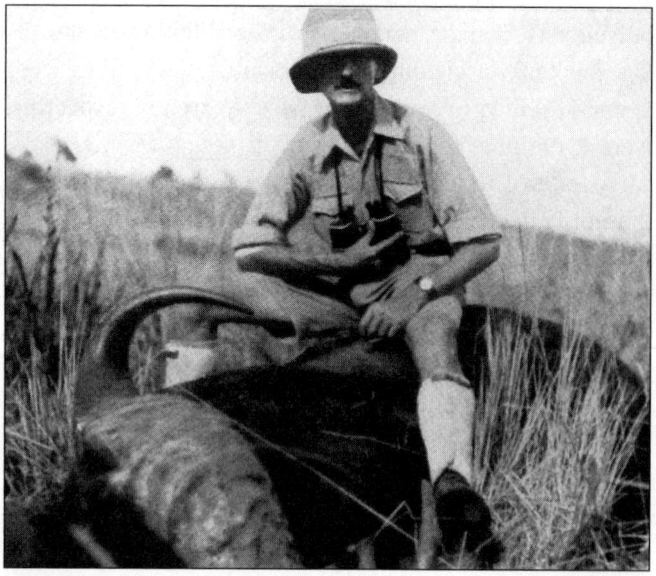

Temple-Perkins with buffalo.

He was district commissioner at Ankole from 1924–1929, then spent short terms in the Eastern province and as DC at Lango. In 1931 he retreated to the Kenya Highlands for another convalescent stretch (blackwater fever again), then from 1931–1944 served as DC of the Masaka district on the western shore of Lake Victoria. In 1944–1945 he was British resident commissioner (effectively the British ambassador) to the Buganda Kingdom, a traditional African monarchy that was a sort of "shadow government" for much of Uganda. Thereafter this tall, bearded eccentric lived in retirement for many years in a modest home in the middle of a game reserve.

One of his duties as district commissioner was to help out the understaffed game department with wildlife control. During a sixteen-week period in 1924, at least 161 people in the Ankole district of Uganda were taken by lion. Temple-Perkins had just taken office when the outbreak began at Sanga, a locality inhabited by Bahima tribesmen only twenty-three miles from his headquarters. Temple-Perkins immediately began an energetic campaign to eliminate the menace. Part of the plan was to have the local inhabitants organize their own hunts. It did not all go smoothly. During one such hunt villagers attacked two lion but gave up after two men were killed and four wounded, one mortally. In another episode five men were wounded (again one mortally), but at least the lion was killed.

Rethinking his approach, Temple-Perkins set out to trap, shoot, and poison the man-killers. This time he was much more successful. He personally shot a few lion, his African rangers took a few more, and others fell to poisoned baits. All in all, seventeen lion were killed, one of which was believed to have killed eighty-four people and another over forty. There was a brief flurry of similar activity in 1930, but it was quickly snuffed out.

Temple-Perkins wasn't a particularly healthy individual, at various times suffering from blackwater fever (twice), malaria (constantly), and typhoid. It's somewhat of a wonder that he had such a long career. He was hardly the office-bound type of district commissioner either, and was always grasping at any excuse to grab a rifle and go out on control duties. He made a point of supplementing his salary every year by taking the two elephant allowed on his license, and he hints in his excellent memoir, *Kingdom of the Elephant* (1955), that he was not above sparing a large tusker during control duties so he could come back and shoot it later on license. That way he could keep the ivory instead of turning it over to the treasury. Temple-Perkins generally used a .404 for dangerous game, a .475 double as backup,

District commissioner E. A. Temple-Perkins (right).

and a .318 for lighter animals. When ammo was relatively cheap in the 1930s he used the .475 more often. He was also a noted sport fisherman.

As he got older Temple-Perkins mellowed quite a bit and took to hunting almost exclusively with a camera. On various photographic safaris he guided such notables as Cherry Kearton, Sir Geoffrey de Havilland, and Jim Corbett of *Maneaters of Kumaon* fame.

Although a government official, Temple-Perkins was not the most avid conservationist. In the early 1920s black rhino were common in Uganda while white rhino were extremely rare. Harrison Gibbs was a Uganda coffee planter who went on a hunt for a white rhino with Temple-Perkins at Christmas holiday in 1922. They were inexperienced—Gibbs was new in the country and Temple-Perkins had been there for just three years and at that time had shot only one elephant and a few buffalo. While waiting for a steamer *(Samuel Baker)* at the Lake Albert port of Butiaba, they filled in the time by tracking a problem elephant north of the town. T-P brought the animal down a few yards outside a game reserve.

The men then took the steamer up to Rhino Camp on the west bank of the Nile. Early on the morning of 31 December they came upon a solitary white rhino bull and Temple-Perkins killed it with one round from his .470 Rigby double-barreled rifle. The bull had an excellent horn that was 36 inches in length, and in fact made the Rowland Ward record list. The next day the two hunters were following a small rhino herd when Gibbs severely sprained his ankle and the hunt had to be called off. As they sailed back to Butiaba aboard the steamer *Lugard,* Temple-Perkins shot a fourteen-foot crocodile called "George," a legendary reptile that had been locally famous for its ability to avoid hunters.

Taken to task by Governor Sir Geoffrey Archer for shooting the endangered white rhino, Temple-Perkins pointed out that the licensing law then in effect said that the licensee was entitled to one rhino but did not differentiate between species. Although Archer countered that the regulation clearly intended to mean just the black rhino, the letter of the law was on Temple-Perkins's side. Archer got the law clarified a few days later, but Temple-Perkins got to keep his trophy and avoided any sanctions. The source for this story, which speaks volumes about the level of commitment of many British game officials, is Temple-Perkins himself, who thought his exploit rather clever.

Thesiger, Sir Wilfred (1910–2003). Born in Addis Ababa, Wilfred Thesiger came from a distinguished family. His grandfather, Frederic Augustus Thesiger (1827–1905) was the Lord Chelmsford who commanded the British armed forces in the 1879 Anglo-Zulu War. His father,

Wilfred Gilbert Thesiger (1871–1920), served as an army captain in the Boer War and in diplomatic posts in Asia Minor, Taranto, Belgrade, Saint Petersburg, the Belgian Congo, and as Minister to Abyssinia from 1909–1919. It was during this latter posting that young Wilfred Patrick Thesiger was born.

His formative years were spent in outstanding company. Arnold Hodson, the remarkable hunter and official who later served as governor of Sierra Leone, was a family friend, as was Kenya pioneer Geoffrey Archer. Thesiger used to borrow Archer's fowling piece to shoot shorebirds on the Indian Ocean beaches. As a boy Thesiger met most of the ruling class of Abyssinia, including Ras Tafari, better known to history as the Emperor Haile Selassie. The Thesigers returned to England in 1919, where in January 1920 the older Wilfred died suddenly while shaving. Wilfred Patrick went on to be schooled at St. Aubyns, at Eton, and at Oxford, where he displayed a real talent for boxing.

During summer vacations from Oxford, Thesiger went on a series of interesting adventures, including a 1930 visit to Abyssinia where he hunted for kudu and buffalo (in the latter case unsuccessfully), and a season on a fishing trawler near Iceland the following year. In 1933 he returned to Abyssinia on a collecting commission from the London Natural History Museum and spent a year exploring the Awash River and the Danakil region. During this trip he was accompanied by a friend, David Haig-Thomas. The two youths adroitly delivered a rare blue-winged goose (only the second collected by a Western museum; the first was in 1868) and an Abyssinian or Simien wolf, as well as a trophy-book mountain nyala and numerous more common specimens.

Before leaving for Africa, Thesiger had applied for entry into the Sudan Political Service, a prestigious government department of only 130 men, with a reputation for quality approaching that of the excellent Indian Civil Service. Upon his return to England in the summer of 1934 he was notified that his application had been approved, and he was sent to a four-month course learning Arabic.

Thesiger arrived in Sudan in January 1935 and was posted as a probationary assistant district commissioner at Kutum in northern Darfur, an isolated station some five hundred miles to the west of Khartoum. The district commissioner at that time was Guy Moore, a hard-tasking but dedicated man who spent most of his time on the trail visiting the remote villages of his bailiwick. Moore took an immediate liking to his assistant and was willing to overlook the younger man's dislike of protocol and his strong sense of independence. Moore taught Thesiger the ropes and provided support when he got himself into trouble—for instance, when Thesiger once went on safari to a neighboring district without notifying his counterpart of his presence. Local nomads spread reports of unknown armed white men visiting an oasis, and, until Thesiger confessed that it was just he, the British authorities in Khartoum were in a state of near panic, believing that the incident might be the spearhead of an Italian invasion. Thesiger was chewed out by Civil Secretary Sir Angus Gillan, the number-two man in the colony and the head of the Political Service, but the incident had no permanent effect on his record.

On another occasion Thesiger forwarded a medical report up the chain of command without carefully reading it over beforehand. There had been twenty-nine cases of chickenpox in the Kutum clinic, a mildly interesting point but hardly cause for general concern. Thesiger's African medical assistant, however, had inadvertently written smallpox instead of chickenpox, an altogether different matter. An outbreak of smallpox was a catastrophic event and cause for a massive mobilization of medical resources. Fortunately, the doctor at the provincial headquarters in Fasher caught the mistake before the document went any further, and checked out the story before notifying Khartoum. Moore merely cautioned Thesiger to be more careful in the future.

Thesiger's stay in Darfur lasted until 1937 and can be considered as the last step in the education that had begun at Eton and Oxford. The young colonial officer learned many critical things, such as how to travel through an arid wilderness and the importance of learning the languages and customs of the people of the district. He honed his hunting skills and became such a lethal lion hunter that, like Jules Gerard in Algeria a century before, shepherds and cattle-men came from miles around to ask for his help with stock raiders.

Northern Darfur had a thriving lion population but plains game was relatively thin on the ground, so naturally the lions (and leopards as well) took readily to domestic goats and cattle as substitutes for their natural prey. Some villages just a few miles from the district headquarters were losing two or three animals each week, a rate that could not be sustained. The herders and shepherds also suffered casualties: One lioness killed three men and maimed four others in a fight over a cow. Thesiger later reckoned that he killed some thirty lions during his three years in Kutum, always hunting in daylight and never from a machan or a blind. He most often pursued *simba* on foot, but occasionally used a horse. One of his hard-earned lessons was that if you dismount from your horse while a bayed lion is facing you, the animal will almost invariably launch an immediate charge.

The regulations of the Sudan Political Service required the officer, after a probationary period, to take advanced examinations in Arabic and Sudanese law. The normal procedure was then to assign him to a post in one of the more civilized districts or to a job in Khartoum so that the officer could learn additional skills that would be helpful in his career. This included providing agricultural advice and dealing with administrative and personnel matters. Thesiger was loath to leave his wild district of Kutum and, besides, was one of those people who don't test well, so in 1937 he approached Gillan with an unusual offer. He would resign the Political Service, forfeiting his pension rights, and immediately be hired back as an independent contractor. In return, Gillan would allow him to deviate from the usual career path and, instead of assigning him to an agricultural or suburban post, would permit him to serve in one of the wild frontier districts. It's an indication of the impression that Thesiger had made in just three years in the Sudan that Gillan not only agreed to the contract arrangement but gave him a slight increase in salary to compensate for the loss of his pension. Such contract district officers were relatively rare but not unheard of; the situation usually developed when an officer wanted to stay in the same district for longer than the usual period of a few years. Civil Service district commissioners were generally rotated to a new district every two years or so as a matter of course. Contract officers often remained at the same post for seven or eight years or even longer.

Thesiger had in mind remaining at Kutum, but the need was greater elsewhere, so Gillan wound up sending him to the Nile district of the western Nuer, an isolated place that had only been administered by the British since 1921. The only Englishmen in western Nuer were Thesiger and District Commissioner H. G. Wedderburn-Maxwell (known simply as Wedderburn). The district consisted of 20,000 square miles of swamp and bush and was notably unhealthy; the previous DC had recently died from blackwater fever. It wasn't just the mosquitoes that could kill you, either, for as recently as 1927 a district commissioner had been speared to death by Nuer warriors. The area was so underdeveloped that the district headquarters was on board a paddle-steamer called the *Kereri*. The *Kereri* had a barge lashed to it, aboard which any of the local populace that had cause to be visiting the district commissioner were allowed to set up camp, along with their associated goats and chickens. The steamer was usually tied up at the town of Malakal on the Nile, where the military and police lines were also situated. Both Thesiger and Wedderburn lived on the *Kereri* when at headquarters and shared a tiny bathroom. Fortunately for the junior officer, Wedderburn was an amiable and easygoing man, and had himself only been posted to the district a few weeks before, succeeding H. A. Romilly, who had transferred to another station.

The nature of Thesiger's service in western Nuer can perhaps best be illustrated by a description of his very first assignment there in 1937. Wedderburn told the younger man to take his rifles and a few guides and strike out into countryside to do some shooting while, at the same time, generally familiarizing himself with the district. He was to keep his eyes and ears open and to be particularly alert for anything that might pertain to a disturbing rumor about the Nuer that they had just recently taken to eating the flesh of dogs. As there was no famine in the area, this change of diet was believed to have religious connotations. But it could also possibly be akin to the *chappatties* (biscuits of unleavened bread) that were passed around India as a conspiratorial sign just before the Sepoy Rebellion of 1857. The colonial government of the Sudan was constantly on the watch for signs of an uprising, and for good reason: The rural population was fierce, independent in nature, and quite capable of resorting to arms for any reason. In 1921, for example, members of a religious sect suddenly attacked the *boma* of the Nyala district in southern Darfur and killed the DC, the station veterinary officer, and all of the district police.

Thesiger was impressed by the Nuer who were tall, athletic, and carried themselves with a stern martial grace that bespoke their prowess as warriors. They had a peculiarly warlike culture, even to the extent of encouraging their children to fight, and that trait as well as the terrain accounted for the fact that they had never been conquered before the arrival of the British. The Nuer were one of the very few people of Central Africa who had not been decimated by the slave raids of the nineteenth century, and they remained proud of their independent nature and their institutions. Capt. Vere Fergusson, the district commissioner who was murdered in 1927, had provoked their ire by insisting upon their adherence to a European code of conduct and by forcing them to return cattle they had stolen from the neighboring Dinkas.

One of Fergusson's ambitions was to get the Nuer to wear pants—like many of the Nilotic peoples, they went around entirely naked—and this sometimes had comic consequences. The Nuer abhorred European clothing, and universally refused to wear it after Fergusson's death, but they retained a vague realization that the British somehow equated clothing with dignity. Accordingly, many Nuer chiefs would don pants or shorts when a British official visited his village, simply as a mark of respect. Thesiger remembered one well-endowed chief, uncomfortable in the foreign garment but big-heartedly trying his best to impress the visiting district officer, who solved his tightness problem without being disrespectful by undoing his fly buttons and innocently allowing the compressed parts to just hang out in the open.

Thesiger's tenure in western Nuer consisted of many safaris like the first, just wandering the district almost aimlessly, hunting and getting to know the people. Every six weeks or so he would return to the *Kereri* to rendezvous with Wedderburn, who was conducting his own expeditions. Both men always brought a large number of porters with them on these treks, many more than necessary. The strategy was to become friendly with the porters so that when they reached the home villages of these men Thesiger or Wedderburn would be welcomed by the families of their porters. The more men they had, the more villages they were accepted into. Thesiger apparently never discovered the truth behind the rumors of dog-eating, or at least didn't mention it in his autobiography if he did.

Thesiger resumed his career as a killer of stock-raiding lions, shooting forty in his two years in the western Nuer district (giving him a total of seventy in the five years he served in the Sudan bush). Spending most of his time in the wilds, he took advantage of the opportunity to hunt leopard, sitatunga, and roan antelope. He bagged his first several buffalo (having stalked them unsuccessfully in Abyssinia years before), and shot a tremendous crocodile that the local Nuer said was the biggest that they had ever seen. The reptile measured out at sixteen and a half feet, causing Thesiger ever after to be skeptical of claims of Nile crocs measuring twenty feet or more.

Thesiger took a lively interest in hunting and considered it a valuable tool in establishing close relations with the local Africans. He even joined with the Nuer in one of their traditional hippo hunts with harpoons, in the course of which one man was badly cut up. The Nuer were formidable elephant hunters, attacking the animals en masse and on foot with razor-sharp throwing spears. In 1936, before Thesiger's arrival in the district, a huge herd of elephant had migrated through western Nuer, and the concentrated warriors had killed some 200–300 of them with their primitive weapons. Thesiger was better equipped, with a personal arsenal consisting of a .275 Rigby Express rifle, a .350 magnum, and a .450 double. The Sudanese game license allowed for two elephants each year, and Thesiger shot his bag of four during his term. The biggest he killed had tusks of 83 and 81 pounds, and the other three were all in the 70s; he gave the meat to the Nuer.

In 1938 Thesiger went on leave to the mountains of Tibesti, in Chad. There he hunted Barbary sheep (the meat was "rank-smelling and very tough") and dorcas gazelle. Upon his return to the *Kereri,* he was delighted to find out that he was scheduled to soon be reassigned back to Kutum. The western Nuer district had been an interesting experience, but he had never lost his love for his first station. He returned to England on a short leave before reporting to Kutum, but the outbreak of the Second World War suddenly overturned his plans. Thesiger received peremptory orders to return immediately to Africa, and on 3 September 1939, the very day Britain declared war on Germany, he sailed for Alexandria on the passenger liner *Montcalm.* If a German U-boat had happened to attack the ship, the results would have been interesting. As Thesiger noted in his memoirs, "promotion in the Sudan Political Service might have been spectacular, for nearly half the officials, including several provincial governors, were on board."

Almost immediately upon his return Thesiger was selected as one of thirty Political Service officers who would receive commissions in the Sudan Defence Force. After a six-week "very well-run and essentially practical" training course, he was sworn in as a *bimbashi*, a commissioned rank of the Anglo-Egyptian army. The peculiarities of military seniority dictated that even though Thesiger was promptly assigned as second-in-command of an infantry company, his *bimbashi* rank was considered as junior even to the most newly commissioned second lieutenant of the regular army.

Thesiger was given command of a platoon and assigned to an ancient fort at Gallabat on the Ethiopian frontier, overlooking positions held by Italian colonial troops. His orders in the event of enemy attack were to live long enough to send warning of the invasion. No wireless was available, so the warning would have to be by lorry.

Italy entered the war on 10 June 1940. Thesiger heard the word on the BBC and immediately directed several long bursts of machine-gun fire on the Italian positions. Moments later, urgent orders came through from Khartoum to take no offensive action. Thesiger was not punished for having prematurely violated this order, and indeed was always proud of the fact that he had fired the first shots of the Abyssinian campaign.

Thesiger's war work is mostly beyond the scope of this book, but a short summary is in order. The Italians attacked his sector in late July 1940, forcing a temporary evacuation, but the British came back three months later and recaptured Gallabat. Thesiger was then assigned to the Ethiopian invasion force led by the abrasively eccentric Orde Wingate. Thesiger served as a staff officer and as a liaison to Abyssinian rebels who had been fighting the Italians since Mussolini's invasion in 1935, very dangerous missions indeed. These irregulars, called the "Patriots" by the British, were fierce and highly motivated but dismally armed; the English supplied what weapons they could, but the modern items were being kept for the defense of the homeland. The Patriots received whatever could be spared, in most cases old antiques including Martini-Henry rifles dating back to the Anglo-Zulu War. Nevertheless, they provided tremendous assistance to Wingate's invasion force, if not always on the battlefield then at least with supplies and intelligence.

With Abyssinia liberated and Haile Selassie returned to the Imperial throne, Thesiger was reassigned for a short time to the Lebanon-Syria theater, and then to the Special Operations Executive, that cloak-and-dagger outfit commissioned by Churchill to "set Europe ablaze." From 1942–1943 he served in the western desert as a member of the elite Special Air Service, undertaking long-range reconnaissance missions in machine-gun Jeeps, hundreds of miles behind enemy lines.

Thesiger served capably, even brilliantly, but he was only human—and one of the few who wasn't afraid to admit it in his autobiography. Thus, we know as much about his failures as his accomplishments: One important mission was aborted because Thesiger, adept as he was at riding camels and horses, didn't know how to change a flat tire on a Jeep. On another occasion he was hotly pursued by a squadron of German armored cars. It was only after the war ended that he discovered that one of those armored cars was occupied by no less than Field Marshall Erwin Rommel.

In 1944 Thesiger was reassigned once again, this time to a diplomatic post in Abyssinia, where he served as an aide to the emperor's son. He idled the days away hunting ducks and snipe on a magnificent Arab stallion given him by the crown prince. When the war ended, Thesiger, who had a lifelong fascination with things Arabic, joined the International Locust Control Organization and explored the forbidding Empty Quarter of Arabia on its behalf. Starting in 1946 he made two trips through the Empty Quarter and visited many places never before seen by a Westerner.

Thesiger spent the remainder of his very long life traveling to exotic places, including Kurdistan, Afghanistan, Pakistan, and several times back to Ethiopia. In 1950 he spent two weeks duck-hunting in the Iraqi marshes at the head of the Persian Gulf, and was so taken with the place that he returned every year until a revolution barred his entry in 1958. In addition to hunting and fishing, he also indulged himself in the strenuous sport of mountain climbing. Thesiger served as an honorary game warden in Kenya and was actively involved in the antipoaching campaign. He finished his days living in northern Kenya, at the village of Maralal close by the Samburu people.

Tough, eccentric, observant, and brutally honest, Thesiger was the author of several books, including *Arabian Sands* (1959), *The Marsh Arabs* (1964), *Visions of a Nomad* (1987), and *The Life of My Choice* (1987). The latter work is an excellent study for anybody interested in Ethiopia, the Sudan, or the life of a British colonial officer during the three decades before these countries achieved independence.

Thewles, J. E. An Englishman living in Mozambique in the 1930s, Thewles worked under contract with the Portuguese colonial authorities as an ad-hoc elephant control officer. His regular position was recruiter for the South African mining companies, but when small herds of elephant ravaged local farms, he would be hired to go out and kill them. Thewles shot at extremely close range, often under ten feet, even though he was considered an above-average marksman. For many years he lived alone with his houseboy in the remote town of Bela Vista, on the Maputo.

Thomas, David. In 1885 Thomas, the son of a South African pioneer missionary, settled on an island in the Zambezi River near its junction with the Lufua River. From there he traded and hunted the area north of the Zambezi. One night Batonga warriors sneaked in and murdered him and stole all of his property, including two modern breechloading elephant rifles that had been borrowed from Fred Selous.

The elephant hunter Bill Buckley recorded a radically different version of Thomas's death in his book *Big Game Hunting in Central Africa* (1930). Buckley got his version from an enemy warrior in the 1893 Matabele War. According to the Matabele soldier, David Thomas was an induna, or subchief, appointed by Lobengula to lead a group of warriors to punish some Barotse who had refused to pay tribute. Thomas had deployed his warriors as small skirmishing parties when the section he was personally leading was surrounded and overcome. In the fight Thomas was speared to death. Buckley claimed that Lobengula ordered the entire group executed for failing to properly guard their commander.

Thompson, Bird. Thompson was assistant administrator of the British Protectorate north of the Tana River in 1893. He accompanied Commander Dundas on his 1891 expedition up the Tana River.

Thompson, Charles. An American from Key West, Florida, Thompson was Ernest Hemingway's hunting companion on his 1933 safari. Thompson drew Hemingway's ire by consistently bagging better trophies than the writer.

Thompson, Francis R. "Matabele" (1857–1927). A British explorer and hunter who occasionally acted as an interpreter between Lobengula and representatives of Cecil Rhodes. As a young boy he had watched Matabele warriors murder his father by pushing a ramrod down his throat. Young Thompson grew up to hunt and trade among these same people. He was instrumental in obtaining various "concessions" (treaties) that led to the downfall of the Matabele. Lobengula grudgingly called him the "white man who lied the least." His autobiography was published in 1936.

Thomson, Joseph (1858–1895). Thomson was a Scotsman who rewrote the map of East Africa. As a twenty-year-old in 1878, Thomson accompanied Keith Johnston, leader of a Royal Geographical Society expedition to Lake Nyasa. Johnston quickly sickened and died, and Thomson, not too healthy himself, took over command of the mission. It was a serendipitous choice.

Thomson was gifted with remarkable patience and a wisdom beyond his years. He led the expedition to the northern end of Lake Nyasa (the first European to visit the northern shore) and then started up the western shoreline of Lake Tanganyika. When the natives began to get hostile, he returned to the eastward, discovering Lake Rukwa.

In 1881 Thomson went on a three-month expedition to investigate the mineral resources south of the Ruvuma River, a mission commissioned on behalf of the Sultan of Zanzibar. The results were reported in the *Scottish Geographical Magazine* as "honest but disappointing." Two years later he and James Martin entered Masai country, leading a Royal Geographical Society expedition to Lake Victoria. The Masai had a ferocious reputation at this time and were inclined to be difficult. Thomson, a masterful amateur psychologist, instinctively knew when to be firm with the Africans. More important, he knew to be passive when the Masai tried to provoke him. By a combination of calm demeanor and schoolboy conjuring tricks, Thomson managed to win the Masai over, at least to the point where they tolerated his expedition's presence in their country. After a temporary return to the coast, prompted by the Masai's warlike attitude in the aftermath of the expedition of Gustav Fischer (a German explorer who had skirmished with both the Masai and the Kikuyu), Thomson and Martin worked their way through, visiting Lakes Naivasha and Victoria and discovering Lake Baringo and Mount Elgon. They returned to the coast in May of 1884.

Three years later Thomson went into what is now Nigeria on a pseudo-diplomatic mission of exploration. He visited Sokoto, Gandu, and other northern Nigerian states and signed trading treaties with their leaders. This was done primarily to forestall German designs on those areas. After this venture, Thomson was considered for the Emin Pasha relief expedition, but that task eventually went to Stanley.

In 1888, for a change of pace, Thomson went to North Africa and explored the Atlas Mountains, accompanied by Lt. Harold Crichton Browne. On this trip Thomson was thrown hard onto the pommel of his saddle by his mule and suffered an internal injury that plagued him for the rest of his days, and presumably hastened his death.

In 1890 Thomson visited Matabeleland and the southern shore of Lake Nyasa accompanied by T. A. Grant, son of the Grant who went with Speke. They were the first to cross the Muchinga Mountains to Lake Bangweulu. This expedition was subject to numerous hardships, not the least of which was an epidemic of smallpox. After reaching Msiri's territory, Thomson collapsed from illness and was forced to turn back.

He returned to Europe in 1891 and spent the rest of his life trying to recover his health. After a bout of pneumonia, he made one trip to South Africa to visit Cecil Rhodes, and another to Italy, and his condition seemed to improve, but upon his last return to Britain he came down with influenza and never recovered. It seems his immune system had been fatally compromised in Africa—he couldn't shake old diseases anymore and kept on developing new ones. His once-robust constitution ruined by injury, tropical fevers, and quite possibly tuberculosis, he died at age thirty-seven on 2 August 1895 at the house of a friend in York Gate. He was buried in his hometown at Thornhill.

Besides being a dedicated naturalist and a fine hunter, Thomson was the author of several books, including *To the Central African Lakes and Back* (1881), *Through Masai Land* (1885), *Travels in the Atlas and Southern Morocco* (1889), and *Mungo Park and the Niger* (1890). Disappointed by the fictionalized picture of Africa drawn by Rider Haggard, Thomson even collaborated with a Miss Harris-Smith on a novel called *Ulu: An African Romance.* The novel was nowhere near as successful as Haggard's stories like *She* and *King Solomon's Mines.*

Many modern historians have belittled Thomson's accomplishments and his political, anthropological, geographical, and biological observations as haphazard and disorganized. It is true that he would often focus with great detail on minor aspects of a situation and miss the big picture, and that he lacked the scientific training of many of his contemporaries. Still, he was clearly in the top rank of explorers in his time. It is estimated that during a total of six trips to Africa, Thomson walked a total of fifteen thousand miles.

Joseph Thomson and Wilhelm Junker.

Thornton, Richard (1837–1863). A young geologist, Thornton accompanied Livingstone on the Zambezi expedition. He was fired in 1859 due to conflicts with Livingstone and his brother Charles Livingstone, and went to accompany the German explorer Baron von der Decken on his explorations in East Africa.

In summer 1862 Thornton rejoined Livingstone on the Shire River. He died of fever and dysentery on 13 April 1863 after a debilitating overland journey to Tete to fetch livestock for the hungry expedition. "He was a fool," the unsympathetic Livingstone wrote in a letter, "and went off to Tete to buy goats for the ladies though he had my written orders to geologize in a healthy quarter."

A gifted geologizer, Thornton made extensive surveys of mineral deposits around Tete and in the Shire Highlands. These areas are known to be rich in gold, copper, iron, asbestos, and graphite. Thornton wrote his notes in his own personal code that, unfortunately, no one has ever been able to decipher.

Thruston, Arthur Blyford (1865–1897). Thruston was a British officer (rank of major) who in the 1890s traveled to the west coast of Lake Albert and led the survivors of Emin Pasha's army out of Emin's Equatoria Province to the eastern section of the Uganda Protectorate and even western Kenya. The Sudanese troops were blamed for bringing with them a devastating sleeping-sickness epidemic that caused nearly a quarter-million deaths in the next decade. Not only that, but the sixteen hundred Sudanese soldiers, reformed into a unit called the Uganda Rifles, soon began to mutiny against the British.

In retrospect it is hard to blame them. Most of them had been serving the British for years, far away from their homes, and even the low wages they were entitled to were paid only sporadically. Worse, many of them had settled down in Equatoria and started to raise families, and the abrupt move tore them away from all that was familiar and thrust them into an unknown country surrounded by alien people. It would have taken far sterner discipline than the Sudanese were capable of to vanquish the feelings of bitterness and outrage that sparked the mutiny.

Thruston, a popular officer who spoke fluent Arabic, believed (like many other Imperial officers at the onset of the Empire's various mutinies, particularly the 1857 Indian Rebellion) that he had nothing to fear personally from his own soldiers. He was wrong—they imprisoned him and went over to the mutineers. As loyal columns led by Frederick Jackson and Maj. J. R. L. MacDonald closed in during October 1897, the Sudanese executed Thruston and two other captive officers at Fort Luburan. The British forces, composed largely of Swahili askaris with white officers, brutally suppressed the mutiny. Thruston was the author of *African Incidents* (1900).

Thys, Albert (1849–1915). A Belgian military officer, Thys was tasked by King Leopold with assisting in the preparation of the 1876 Brussels Geographical Conference. Utterly devoted to the idea of Belgian colonization, Thys in the 1880s founded the Compagnie du Congo pour le Commerce et l'Industrie, with the goal of developing the railway and other commercial interests in the area. Thys became a financial powerhouse and was effective in blocking the ambitions of Cecil Rhodes and others with their eyes on the Congo. Under his direction the Compagnie du Congo branched out into numerous subsidiaries, including companies designed to exploit rubber, ivory, trade, and local agriculture, and geographically based corporate entities like the Compagnie du Katanga.

Till, Jim. Assistant warden to Ted Davison at Wankie in the 1930s. The two men worked together on elephant control outside the reserve.

Timmler, C. H. Timmler was a resident of Fort Jameson and a friend of Owen Letcher. The two men hunted elephant, rhino, and crocodile together in 1909. One day during this trip Timmler used a .400 Mauser to shoot two large bull antelope across the Luangwa River. The animals were either nyala, hitherto unknown in that country, or bushbuck rams on steroids. To his chagrin, his native trackers refused to swim the croc-infested river and retrieve the trophies, despite the offer of a large reward. Notice that Timmler didn't dive into the water himself. By the time a canoe could be found the next morning, the rams were gone, pulled into the water by the ravenous reptiles. Smart trackers, those.

Tinne, Alexandrine Petronella Francisca (1839–1869). Also seen as Alexine, and many accounts show her birth date as 1835. A Dutch (born at The Hague) heiress of English descent, Tinne was already an experienced traveler (Europe and Asia Minor) when she first arrived in Africa in 1862. With her mother and aunt she explored the Nile River to Gondokoro, and the Sobat and Bahr el Ghazal regions until 1864. Between 1865 and 1869 she toured the Mediterranean littoral, dressed in Arab garb.

In 1869 Tinne set out on what was to be a grand safari, aiming to become the first European woman to cross the Sahara. On 28 August she was murdered at a place called Murzuk, either by bandits or by a treacherous escort. She was twenty-nine years old (born 17 October 1839), although some modern sources list her age as thirty-three.

Tippu Tib (c. 1850–1905). Also given as Tippoo Tip, Tippoo Tip, and other variations, as well as his real name, Hamidi bin Muhammed or Hamed bin Muhammed. The Tippu Tib name is supposedly derived from the sound of crashing gunfire. Whatever you call him, he was an Arab-African trader and slaver, powerful from Zanzibar to the Upper Congo during the late nineteenth century. He was also a provincial governor of the Congo Free State, a post that was not as incongruous as it might seem at first blush. The Belgians were simply seeking to take advantage of his power and influence in the region. The title certainly didn't do much to abate Tippu Tib's slave-trading and other illegal activities.

Born on the island of Zanzibar, Tib led his first trading expedition into the African central-lake district starting in 1867, returning with a profitable load of slaves and ivory. During this safari he met David Livingstone. The missionary's influence doesn't seem to have worn off—Tib was perfecting the Arab slaving method of capturing and enslaving an entire village, forcing the slaves to carry loads of ivory to the coast, and there disposing of both slaves and ivory. As a result he grew rich, but he spent this part of his life in almost constant warfare.

For a while Tippu Tib was the ruler of a vast Arab slaving and trading empire, headquartered at Kasonge. On several of his excursions in the 1860s into what would become Northern Rhodesia, Tippu Tib brought along his brother, Kumbakumba, as a lieutenant. He would leave Kumbakumba and an armed force at a captured village to be used as a base and a depot. On one occasion in 1873 Kumbakumba was defeated by Chishinga tribesmen, which prompted an all-out revolt against Tippu Tib, a revolt that was bloodily repressed.

By his own lights Tib was a reasonable man, and indeed he dealt fairly with the Europeans he met. He was of great assistance to Cameron in 1874 and to Henry Stanley in both 1876 and 1887. Stanley arranged for his appointment as the Congo Free State governor of the Stanley Falls district. Tib was also a convenient scapegoat when Stanley needed someone to blame for the disasters that befell his so-called "Rear Column" during the Emin Pasha relief expedition.

Tib retired back to Zanzibar as the days of the slave trade wound down. When the last Arab slavers revolted in the Congo in 1890, they beseeched him to join them but he refused. A clear-sighted, intelligent man, Tib knew that those days were gone forever. He lived comfortably until his death on 13 June 1905.

Tiran, Paul. Paul Tiran was a veteran elephant hunter in the French colonies. In 1930 he was on safari in Chad when he came upon the camp of chief game warden Bruneau de Laborie, who had been badly mauled by a lion. Tiran carried the wounded man to Doba, the nearest town. Tiran wasn't always in strict compliance with the game laws, so this rescue might have paid off big in brownie points—had de Laborie not died of infection within a fortnight.

Tiran had begun his career some years earlier as an ivory poacher. Like his contemporary, Etienne Canonne, he switched to rhino hunting in the middle 1920s when the price of horn skyrocketed temporarily. Also like Canonne, he later shot hippo on the Shari River, selling the dried meat to the railway gangs for about a franc per pound—a good profit, given that each animal produced an average of two hundred pounds of meat.

Tjader, Richard. Journalist, hunter, and author of *The Big Game of Africa* (1911). In 1906 he led the Tjader East Africa Expedition, a collecting safari for the American Museum of Natural History in New York. *Big Game* is a well-written and well-illustrated book (with photographs by the author) that you don't hear much about anymore. It has all the standard chapters on the different types of game animals, which are done well. Tjader is not prone to exaggeration. For instance, he cites the length of "monster" crocodiles as eighteen feet or so, a remarkably conservative estimate for 1911. Other chapters cover the composition of the safari and tips about itineraries and supplies. There is even an excellent forty-nine-page appendix that will have you speaking Swahili in no time. This is not one of those "Tarzan" glossaries that you see in many books but rather a complete dictionary and grammar that tackle the difficult plurals and verb tenses and even include exercises like those in your old high-school Spanish text. The book, however, is rather offensive even for its time, which I suspect is why it has not been reprinted. The racial attitudes are offputting, outdated, and prominent, while Tjader had a penchant for photographing wounded animals in their death throes.

Tjader was a man of some means and also hunted with the American naturalist Herbert Lang.

Trappe, Margarete (1884–1957). Trappe was the wife of a German settler, Ulrich Trappe, who served in the Tanganyika Schutztruppe (defense force) at the outset of World War I. Margarete had considerable hunting and riding skills and so volunteered as a courier for the German general von Lettow. An adventuresome woman, Trappe soon expanded this role into active scouting and spying, frequently slipping through English lines in the dead of night festooned with pistols and rifles and cartridge belts like a Mexican bandit. Her talents in the bush were honed to such a fine degree that she became almost a legend to the

Alexandrine Tinne.

local Africans, who credited her with supernatural talents such as the ability to milk elephant and talk to hippo. Von Lettow was concerned, however, by the British propaganda claiming that the Germans were so hard up for men that they had to enlist women, and he may also have worried that she was liable to be shot as a spy (he was a chivalrous sort at heart). Accordingly he ordered Trappe to surrender to the English, which she did. After the war she became one of the very few female professional hunters and one of the first to tame African wild dogs.

Treatt, Maj. Chaplin Court. Chaplin Court Treatt was commissioned as a lieutenant in the British army on 26 July 1906. In 1913 he resigned his commission and took a job as an assistant at the British Museum of Natural History, but he was back in uniform when war broke out a year later. Promoted to captain, he accepted the temporary rank of flight lieutenant so that he could serve in the Royal Flying Corps. In 1919 he was awarded the Order of King George by the Greek government. Two years later he was demobilized from the RAF and promoted to major.

Court Treatt traveled extensively in East Africa and in the Sudan in the 1920s and 1930s—hunting, filming, and writing of his adventures, which appeared in *Out of the Beaten Track* (1931). The book is dedicated to his wife, Stella. She was an expert photographer in her own right and accompanied him on many of his travels. Unlike Osa Johnson, who she resembled, Stella Court Treatt was no farm girl from the Midwest, nor was she the glamorous type you read about in Ruark; she was true Rhodesian pioneer stock. Her grandfather, one of the pioneering Jennings brothers, once shot ten elephants in one morning on the Gwaai River. There is a portrait of her (dated 1925) in London's National Portrait Gallery. Stella was the author of two books, *Cape to Cairo* (1928) and *Sudan Sand* (1930).

The Court Treatts are best remembered for their wildlife and travel films, several of which have achieved a certain cult status and are available on VHS today. These include *Cape to Cairo* (1922) and *Stampede* (1921). The latter movie was considered a "lost film" for several decades, with only a few reels known to exist, but recently a full print of the American release was discovered and the picture restored as *Africa in Flames.* Chaplin Court Treatt also apparently had some talent as a musician, for he is given "composer" credit for the 1936 movie *White Hunter.*

In 1929 Court Treatt (called "CT" by his friends) traveled to Darfur so that he could film the Habbania Arabs hunting elephants and hippos with spears. He hired local natives to act as extras in the film, but every night they would all run away. A considerable amount of time was lost each day rounding up the reluctant villagers and warriors that were needed to add authenticity to the picture. He finally discovered that, due to a clumsy translator, the local natives were under the misconception that the Court Treatts were actually slavers, and the casting calls were really the prelude to a long march to the slave market.

Treich-Laplene, Marcel. This French explorer of the Congo in the late 1880s worked for the Verdier trading company.

Trollope, Harold. In 1925 Harold Trollope, a veteran of the Boer War, was appointed to a ranger post at the Sabi Game Reserve. It was a demanding post that required a man to act effectively in conditions of hardship and extreme solitude; in fact, Trollope replaced the previous ranger who had collapsed with a nervous breakdown after just a few months on the job. Trollope was experienced and tough, and daring to the point of recklessness.

In its early days, the Sabi Game Reserve, which became Kruger National Park in 1926, had an official "shoot-on-sight" policy when it came to lions and other predators. The policy was set at the insistence of neighboring cattle ranchers and justified by the belief that antelope and buffalo herds would grow healthier if the lions were eliminated. This latter belief is false: Animal population dynamics are complicated, and a healthy predator population is actually a requirement for a balanced ecosystem. But in the 1920s few people had given the matter much thought, and the extermination policy remained on the books through the 1930s.

Trollope's boss, James Stevenson-Hamilton, was one of the few outdoorsmen who had considered the matter, and by the mid-1920s he was starting to have his doubts about all this lion-killing. He also suspected that the presence of big cats would draw tourists to the reserve, and, therefore, he was reluctant to wage all-out war against the lions. Nevertheless he was under strong political pressure to continue the policy, and, accordingly, he ordered Trollope to consider lion-shooting as one of his primary duties.

Prior to Trollope, the shooting of lions for control purposes, contrary to the ethics of sport hunting, was conducted largely over bait and usually at night. The job, after all, was to remove the predators from the food chain quickly and efficiently. Trollope started out this way but soon found the shooting of lion over baits distasteful. He switched to pursuing the animals on foot and on horseback, taking such extreme risks that some of his fellow rangers began to question his sanity. It was said that Trollope, who seems to have enjoyed living dangerously, would deliberately provoke a charge before shooting in order to give the lion an even chance. During his two years in the park, he shot and killed an estimated four hundred lions without ever getting hurt himself.

Trollope's tenure at Kruger was marred by one serious accident. He went hunting for leopard one day just outside of the reserve with his father-in-law, the septuagenarian Glen Leary, and Harry Wolhuter's brother-in-law, a man named Yates. They were hunting with dogs and Leary walked right into a wounded leopard in tall grass. The panicked animal charged and tore the old man up. Trollope shot the leopard off of his father-in-law, but it was too late. Leary died a short time later.

Trollope left Kruger soon afterward and in the early 1930s wound up taking on the job of restoring the Addo elephant herd. This herd, originally numbering nearly two hundred animals, had been almost wiped out by P. J. Pretorius in a government-ordered extermination campaign shortly after World War I. By the time Pretorius was done, there were less than twenty elephants left—frightened, nervous animals hiding in and around the thick Addo bush. That same government that had ordered their destruction now ordered that they not only be spared, but restored, so that future generations could enjoy the sight of South Africa's last remaining wild herd.

This job of building an elephant herd instead of destroying it must have been perceived as an interesting challenge and change of pace. Severely persecuted by Pretorius, a legendarily efficient elephant killer, the few remaining Addo animals had taken to roaming the surrounding countryside where they were a nuisance to farmers. They would have to be lured back into the very jungle from which they had been driven. The problem was compounded because the Addo elephants were remarkably fierce and aggressive, in part because of their persecution. They killed several people during this period, including an African game ranger and a woman caught walking alone down a deserted road at night.

As a first step Trollope dug bore holes throughout the Addo to remedy a longstanding shortage of natural water holes. Then he chased the elephants back into the Addo Bush. This was tough because the scared, nervous, and crafty survivors were scattered, hiding in nooks and crannies all over the district, surviving by raiding farms at night and hiding in the thick vegetation in the daytime. Trollope set out regular feeding stations loaded with oranges, pumpkins, pineapples, and hay in order to keep the elephants eating at home, so to speak. Then he began to harass the elephants back into Addo, which had been declared a sanctuary. That Trollope managed to do this while shooting only one bull is a tribute to his skill and his understanding of elephant behavior.

The park board had established a specific section of the Addo bush as the elephants' new home. In a climactic moment, Trollope and scores of young African assistants drove the last twenty or so survivors about twenty-five miles in the space of a few weeks, moving them with horns and firecrackers toward the designated area. Finally the confused and tired animals were safe in their new refuge.

And so the battered remnants of the Addo herd returned to the bush, where their descendants live to this day. The area was proclaimed Addo Elephant National Park in 1931, and an effective elephant-proof fence was finally constructed around the park in 1954. It now contains a healthy breeding herd of about two hundred individuals and is currently approaching maximum population density for the species, if it hasn't reached it already.

Tuckey, James Kingston (1776–1816). Captain Tuckey of the Royal Navy was commander of an 1816 African Association expedition to the Congo River. Large and well equipped, this safari was to be the definitive exploration of that region. Unfortunately, the expedition had gone only a short distance upriver when the men started coming down with malaria. In short order Captain Tuckey and most of his men died and the mission was aborted.

Twigg, Hamilton (xxxx–1916). Hamilton Twigg was a professional hunter, based in Arusha, who guided Kenyon Painter and his bride Maud on their honeymoon safari in 1910–1911. He died of blackwater fever in 1916 while in the field campaigning against the Germans in East Africa.

U

Udet, Ernst (1896–1941). Udet, a famous German fighter ace in World War I, made a living traveling the world as a stunt pilot after Germany's defeat in 1918. In 1930 he was hired as an aviation advisor by a film company shooting in East Africa. At the conclusion of that job, Udet went on safari with Bror Blixen, who described him in a letter as an "always cheerful little German." The pair went hunting for buffalo at Mount Hanang near Blixen's home at Arusha, Tanganyika. Udet was using a .600 Jeffery rifle borrowed from Dick Cooper. After an exciting stalk, Udet shot and killed a big bull buffalo with a horn spread of over 48 inches. The German ace was so pleased that he presented Blixen with a prized Walther pistol as a gratuity.

While Udet was Blixen's guest, the PH noted that the German's plane had been jury-rigged with a repaired wing. The wing had been broken in a crash (see entry on Friedrich Siedentopf for details) and no replacement could be found, so a makeshift wing was put together at Arusha. When the plane was parked on the ground, the wing went up at a 30-degree angle, but Udet assured his worried host that it was workable and not a safety problem. On his way back to Europe, however, the future field marshal had to make a forced landing in the remote Sudan. After several days with no food and little water, and suffering from exposure to the elements, Udet was rescued by Tom Black, Beryl Markham's partner in the aviation business.

John Hunter in his 1957 *Hunters Tracks* tells how Udet—head of the Luftwaffe at the time, according to Hunter—was knocked out of the sky in the Serengeti by a leaping lioness that he buzzed with his Fokker. This episode must in actuality have been the Siedentopf mishap mentioned above, in which another pilot in Udet's plane clipped an anthill while chasing a rhino. The only known crash by Udet in Africa (and the Luftwaffe didn't even exist at the time) was his 1930 forced landing in Sudan, and that doesn't match the other details in Hunter's story. Just one more example of how an actual event (see the Ryall entry for another) would be altered so many times in its retelling around African campfires and in Nairobi bars that several barely recognizable versions would eventually appear in print.

The remainder of Udet's life consisted of a meteoric rise and a spectacular fall. He became Hermann Goering's right-hand man in the Nazi Luftwaffe and was placed in charge of strategic planning after the death of the able General Wever in a 1936 plane crash. The consensus among historians is that Udet was a gifted flier and a personable and charming man with few of the reprehensible qualities prevalent among leading Nazis, but out of his element in a planning and development job at the Luftwaffe. He committed suicide when the tide of war began to turn against Germany in 1941.

Uechtritz, Baron von. Uechtritz undertook the exploration of South-West Africa in 1892, on behalf of a German development company. He planned to travel from Windhoek over the Okavango, but was turned back by hostile Hereros and instead went north to Ovambo country. Adding a contingent of twelve Bushmen to his safari, Uechtritz surveyed the Kunene River, the border between German territory and Portuguese Angola. He did a lot of hunting along the way, specifically shooting ostrich, gnu, giraffe, crocs, and hippo. At one point he took a long detour on the trail of a rumored elephant herd but never caught up with them.

Shortly after his Kalahari expedition, Uechtritz also explored in the Cameroons and along the Niger. Dr. Siegfried Passarge was a member of both expeditions.

Ulyate, Ray (1884–1948). Ulyate was born in South Africa and moved to the Kijabe district of Kenya in the early 1900s. He was taking clients out on safari as early as 1907 when he guided the American banker Kenyon Painter. In 1910 he worked with the Buffalo Jones expedition. Ulyate was associated with the safari firm of Newland & Tarlton.

Ulyate moved to Arusha in 1923 and purchased a coffee farm called Meru Estate, a property that had been confiscated from its German owners in World War I. He grew coffee for five years, until the market crashed in 1928. Meru Estate was later bought by Kenyon Painter and is now the site of the Tanzania Parks Department headquarters.

Ulyate also leased and managed the New Arusha Hotel, which was apparently built and owned by Painter. Ulyate was constantly referred to in contemporary newspaper articles as the "proprietor." The first guest at the New Arusha was the Prince of Wales, who was honored at a reception held there in December 1927. Ulyate and his family ran the New Arusha until 1947.

Ulyate ran the African Tours and Hotels company and pioneered the concept of photo safaris, taking clients out to the Serengeti and Ngorongoro to film lion. He dragged bait carcasses behind a truck until the cats got used to the free meal and would come running whenever Ulyate and his guests showed up with their cameras. The practice was eventually banned by the game department. Ulyate had six children—four boys (including one named Kenyon) and two girls.

Upsher, Bill. Upsher was a big-game hunter out of Beira in Portuguese East Africa. Upsher's prime was right around the turn of the twentieth century, and he often hunted with a partner named Rever. Spectacularly bald, he wore a toupee to protect his vanity. Once while out prospecting for gold deep in the bush of PEA, he had himself lowered down a test shaft on a rope. The rope was held by a pair of backwoods Africans who had very limited exposure to European ways. As Upsher was being lifted up the shaft, he absentmindedly removed the hairpiece so he could wipe the sweat off of his scalp. The workers, astonished at the sight of this white man so casually removing his hair, dropped the rope and let him fall to the bottom of the shaft. Upsher was badly hurt and had a great deal of difficulty climbing out of the hole. He died in England sometime in the 1920s.

Uzes, Duc d' (1868–1893). The young Duc d'Uzes, a French nobleman named Jacques Marie Geraud, set out on his African safari in 1892. His plan was to travel along the Congo until he reached a point near the equator, then head northeast to the Nile, and finally ascend the Nile to Cairo, where he had already arranged to meet his mother. The column consisted of Senegalese porters guarded by fifty Algerian *zouaves* (elite French light infantry) and several French officers. It was designed to be a comfortable trip, such as many British aristocrats were taking, and no expense was spared in its preparation.

The mission started out at a leisurely pace. At the end of six months d'Uzes was only on the Ubangi, slowly steaming north. The duke spent seven weeks socializing at Brazzaville and then, concerned about reports of marauding Arabs near Stanley Falls, decided to change his itinerary. The new plan was to steam up the Ubangi to Abiras and then proceed on a line considerably to the north of the Free State border. This would serve the additional purpose of expanding French influence in a new territory, something the duke may have decided upon in conversations with French officials at Brazzaville. These officers certainly provided the duke with blank treaty forms for nonaligned African chiefs to sign along the way.

Throughout the expedition the duke sent a stream of letters home to his mother. These were later published as *Le Voyage Mon Fils au Congo*. As they moved north on two steamers, d'Uzes wrote often about the varied wildlife and native people he encountered along the banks.

The caravan left Brazzaville on 24 September 1892 and arrived at Bangui on 3 November. The steamers could go no farther, so they landed and waited for a month for sufficient small boats to be purchased and leased. Eventually they headed north in sixteen boats, reaching Mobaye on 6 January and Abiras on 11 January. There matters took a fatal turn.

Ray Ulyate and eland calf brought in by Masai, 1909.

The garrison at Abiras was incensed because a nearby tribe, the Bubus, had recently murdered a Frenchman named de Poumayrac. They asked for the duke's assistance. He eagerly agreed, and the *zouaves*, along with the men of the garrison and some Nsakkara allies, smashed the Bubus, burning their main villages and inflicting heavy casualties.

It was the end of the expedition, however. Abiras was in an unhealthy spot, and much time was wasted chasing the Bubus, burning down their homes, and then nursing the French wounded. By the time the safari was ready to move on, most of them, including the duke and his chief officers, were sick. So sick that it was decided to speed back down the Ubangi and the Congo and try to get medical attention at Brazzaville before it was too late.

The letters home to his mother stopped at this point—the duke barely had enough strength to scribble in his journal each day. He did reach Brazzaville, just as the *zouaves* and the Senegalese began to drop like flies. From there d'Uzes was sent by *machila* (carried platform) to the coast and then shipped first to Landana and then to Cabinda preparatory to being sent home. He never made it, dying at Cabinda on 20 June 1893, leaving his mother to publish his letters and parts of his journal.

V

Vanden Bergh, Leonard John. An American missionary stationed in Uganda and the Kavirondo district 1896–1905. Dr. Vanden Bergh returned to Africa from September 1919 through August 1920 as a member of the Lowie Ethnological Expedition. He was the author of *On the Trail of the Pigmies* (1921).

Trail of the Pigmies is one of my favorite African books, not because of any innate literary worth or sporting or adventure value but due to its unintentionally comic nature. It often borders on hilarity. First, the book is 264 pages long in its reprinted edition and devotes only one chapter to the Pygmies of the title. Vanden Bergh admitted in the introduction that he knew little about those fascinating people and that it would have been "difficult" for him to discover more. He was not the most relentless of researchers. Second, in addition to being rather fat and lazy, Vanden Bergh was something of a prig and therefore wrote with a far different perspective than we normally would expect from an anthropologist. He was clearly appalled by Masai sexual practices, for instance, and apparently dedicated most of his missionary career trying to get the local warriors to wear trousers.

An idea of his limited approach to anthropology can be derived from this line: "The Kavirondo call themselves Luo and resent being labeled Kavirondo, whatever that name may mean." Given that he was the first missionary among the Kavirondo, couldn't he simply have asked somebody what the word meant? In the book's introduction Vanden Bergh refers to the cultural practices that he purportedly studied as "weird and often disgusting and revolting customs." In another passage he describes the Shilluck people of the Nile as wearing a hairstyle that makes them look "very ridiculous." This is hardly cultural relativism at its best.

Vanden Bergh blamed promiscuity among the Masai for destroying the birth rate, and predicted the tribe's extinction within a generation. He cited Kenya tax records as proving that only 20,000 Masai still existed. It apparently never occurred to him that the overwhelming majority of those martial people had simply moved to Tanganyika. That ugly fact would have ruined his hypothesis that somehow a lot of sexual activity cuts down on the number of babies being born.

I could cite dozens of additional examples. *Trail of the Pigmies* is heartily recommended to any historian who wants to understand how the stereotype of the bumbling, thickheaded missionary developed. Don't expect much adventure—Vanden Bergh admits that during his time in Africa ". . . thrilling events . . . have been very few." Missionary literature, as a whole, is distinctly different from what you see in hunting books. Hunters, almost to a man, walked through Africa and proudly recounted the hardships; missionaries were carried in *machilas* (platforms) or even, when crossing streams and swamps, on the shoulders of strong porters. You'll never see a hunter complaining about the perils of *machila* travel as J. H. Morrison did in his 1919 book *Streams in the Desert* (he wailed that it was hard to read when being bounced around in a litter), or bitching about how they got wet when porters carried them clumsily through vile swamps, as John Roscoe did in *Twenty-Five Years in East Africa.* Compare this to memoirs by elephant hunters like P. J. Pretorius, who crawled for miles through the jungle with broken legs and bayonet wounds to escape the Germans at the start of World War I, or Arthur Neumann, who took one of the nastiest beatings on record from a cow elephant.

One final additional illustration: Vanden Bergh, as noted above, spent 1904–1905 as a missionary in the Kavirondo region, supposedly the first to set up shop there. His big thing was not to fight illiteracy or disease or even to promote religion, but to get the Luo to wear pants. "Well do I remember how I struggled to get them to wear clothes," he wrote years later. "White people were beginning to pour into Uganda and the embarrassing situation which arose when ladies or Sisters arrived was acute." He approached commissioner Sir Charles Eliot to ask for a decree forbidding anyone not wearing proper clothing from entering town limits (in fairness, many localities did adopt such ordinances). Eliot scoffed at the idea and said, probably with malicious enjoyment, "Didn't Adam and Eve go about the same way?" Vanden Bergh was still pouting over the rebuff fifteen years later. He tried one further ploy, giving free clothes to the local girls to wear on Sundays, but the young ladies promptly sold the hats and dresses to Swahili traders ("the girls went straight from my camp to the market"). Additional efforts were curtailed when Vanden Bergh developed a protracted case of malaria, no doubt to the relief of all concerned.

Van der Byl, P. B. Van der Byl was a well-traveled sportsman and a graduate of Oxford University. Starting in the 1880s, he hunted in North America, India, and the Austrian Alps as well as in Africa. Known as "Baccy," he was once hunting on a grassy plain in Rhodesia when he spotted a leopard and wounded it with his Mannlicher rifle. The leopard ran off at high speed and van der Byl ran after it. After about three hundred yards, the leopard disappeared behind a slight rise. When van der Byl reached the rise, he found that the leopard had taken advantage of the cover to turn and wait for him. The leopard charged, and van der Byl got one shot off before the furious cat sent him sprawling. Fortunately for the hunter, his lucky bullet had somehow broken both of the leopard's canine teeth, and so, even though the animal was biting him furiously, no real damage was done. One of van der Byl's trackers then ran up and killed the leopard with an ax. ROWLAND WARD 1899: NILE LECHWE, LECHWE. ROWLAND WARD 1928: MOOSE (MANITOBA), WAPITI, BRINDLED GNU, COMMON REEDBUCK, INDIAN GAZELLE, SPEKE GAZELLE, SOEMMERRING GAZELLE, GERENUK, BEISA ORYX, GREATER KUDU, LESSER KUDU, ELAND, CHAMOIS (AUSTRIA), ROCKY MOUNTAIN GOAT, BLACK RHINO.

Van der Stel, Simon (1639–1712). To van der Stel belongs the credit of establishing the first conservation laws in southern Africa, when in 1652 he extended limited protection to buffalo, eland, rhino, and hippo. This early Dutch governor of Cape Colony was also famous for introducing winemaking to the country.

Vandervelde (xxxx–1888). A Belgian officer, Vandervelde went with Stanley to the Congo in late 1882. In 1883 he led an expedition that founded a station, Rudolfstadt, at the mouth of the Kwilu River. He then went up the river and rescued Captain Grant Elliott, another Free State explorer who was incapacitated by illness in the interior. In 1887 he led a battalion of fifty Hausa and Bangala soldiers to restore the authority of the Congo Free State at Stanley Falls station, which had been abandoned due to Arab raids. Vandervelde died of fever at Leopoldville in early 1888 while organizing an expedition to Stanley Falls.

Van der Westhuizen. This young Boer outdoorsman worked as a scout for the Imperial German Army during the Herero Rebellion in 1904. He once went hunting with Selous and the teenage John Burger. Both Burger and van der Westhuizen were shocked to discover that the legendary Selous was only a middling shot (which he always readily admitted—his prowess and success were earned from his bushcraft and character). Indeed, the young Boer consistently beat the legend at shooting.

Something of a prima donna when it came to shooting, van der Westhuizen made a habit of holding fire until the last possible second, so as to make a perfect shot. If the situation involved a charge by a dangerous animal such as a buffalo, this would produce a very dramatic and artistically satisfying kill. On one occasion, however, his rifle misfired and his artistic flair left no room for error. The buffalo killed him.

Van Dyke, Woodbridge Strong (1889–1943). A Hollywood filmmaker, W. S. van Dyke directed the motion picture *Trader Horn* in 1930. The movie, based on the best-selling but much exaggerated "biography" of Alfred Aloysius Smith, was one of the first Hollywood productions to be filmed in Africa. Van Dyke wrote a book about his extended stay in the Dark Continent, entitled *Horning into Africa* (1931), which contains some stories about hunting elephant, crocodile, and topi.

Trader Horn has been re-mastered and is an amazing document of Old Africa. Filmed on location (but not entirely: some scenes had to be re-shot in Mexico), the movie boasts wonderful footage of wild animals, native life, and scenery. It starred Harry Carey, Edwin Booth (who caught a notorious case of fever during the filming), Aubrey Smith, and Duncan Renaldo. Stock footage left over from the production was spliced into African adventure films for decades. Much of the natural history information given in the film (the lead character gives his protégé a guided tour of the Serengeti) is more accurate than that contained in contemporary scientific books. There are also some authentic hunting sequences, as well as numerous "staged" battles like that between a pair of leopards and some hyenas.

Incidentally, the crew of *Trader Horn* was widely blamed for ruining the local economy, at least as far as visiting photographers and filmmakers were concerned. The story goes that the production unit wanted a snippet of movie film of a particularly impressive East African chief, so they offered him the outrageous sum of £40 for the privilege. That set the going rate; even twenty years later the Masai and Samburu were often demanding as much as £1 for a still photo.

Van Dyke went on to make *Tarzan of the Apes* (1932, with Johnny Weissmuller and the incomparable Maureen O'Sullivan), as well as *The Thin Man* (1934) and *Manhattan Melodrama* (1934). The latter was the Clark Gable–William Powell movie that John Dillinger watched just before he was shot by the FBI. Van Dyke made more than seventy-five films during his career. He was known as a fast worker and often got a bonus for each day he brought a film in under schedule.

Van Gele. Captain van Gele was commissioned by the Congo Free State to lead an 1886 expedition surveying the Ubangi River system. According to *Le Mouvement Geographique* of 8 May 1887, van Gele went most of the way on board the steamer *Henry Reed.* When further navigation proved impossible, he and a Lieutenant Lienart proceeded on foot. "The white travelers were everywhere hospitably received." Van Gele reported discovering a tribe called the Baloi, "a race of pirates, the terror of their neighbors, who carry on their predatory excursions as far as the Congo; they also traffic in ivory." Van Gele also reported that cannibalism was common in the district. In June 1888 van Gele led a small military force that peacefully reoccupied the abandoned Free State station at Stanley Falls.

Van Gele led another expedition from Leopoldville in May 1889, this time taking the steamers *En Evan*t and *A.I.A.* up the Ubangi River. He established a station at Zongo on that waterway and explored two tributaries, the Kwango and the Benghi. At the end of May he visited the capital of one Dayo, chief of the Yakoma, who had hitherto been hostile to the Europeans. Van Gele and Dayo signed a treaty of peace, and van Gele left to continue his survey. His chief navigational officer on this trip was Paul le Marinel.

Van Kerckhoven, Guillaume (1854–1892). Van Kerckhoven, a Belgian captain, was sent out by King Leopold in February 1891 to march on Emin Pasha's old base at Wadelai and seize it for the Congo. Leopold hoped to fill the vacuum left by Emin's departure with Belgian troops before the disorganized British could establish themselves there. Van Kerckhoven had fourteen Europeans and six hundred African soldiers to accomplish this mission. He was also ordered to make the expedition show a profit by grabbing all the ivory possible on his way.

No one can ever say that van Kerckhoven was lax in following his orders. His battalion acted like one giant robber band, stealing ivory and shooting Arab ivory merchants whenever they resisted. In a series of engagements beyond the Uele rain forest in October 1891 he stole over eight hundred elephant tusks and killed some eighteen hundred Arab soldiers. The expedition stirred up not only the Arabs but also the French, who felt the Belgians were encroaching on their territory, and the British, who belatedly realized that Leopold was making a grab for the Nile headwaters.

The first direct results of van Kerckhoven's ivory raiding were the murders of Hodister and Michiels in May of 1891 and the subsequent Arab-Belgian Ivory War. Van Kerckhoven was already past the Congo and closing in on the Nile, but just before he got there he was robbed of his triumph by being accidentally shot and killed by his gunbearer on 10 August 1892.

Vannutelli, Lamberto (1871–1966). An Italian naval officer, Lieutenant Vannutelli was the geographer on the 1895 Bottego expedition. Along with Citerni, he was captured in the attack that killed Bottego (17 March 1897), kept in chains for ninety-eight days, and then brought to Addis Ababa. There the two surprised prisoners were treated graciously by Menelik and released. The men coauthored a book about the expedition, *Seconda Spedizione Bottego: L'Omo-Viaggio D'Esplorazione Nell'Africa Orientale* (1899) that received excellent reviews.

After his repatriation, Vannutelli led Italian Geographic Society expeditions to Turkey in 1904 and 1906 and fought in the Italian-Turkish War of 1911 and in World War I. He died in Rome in 1966, the last living member of the Bottego expedition.

Van Reit, William. Van Reit was a trooper of the Bechuanaland Police (or, less likely, the BSAC [see glossary] police) who got lost while traveling on Mashonaland's "Pioneer" road in 1891. While heading toward Salisbury he went hunting for his supper one day and then couldn't find his way back to his wagon. The countryside adjoining the road was heavily wooded, and it was all too easy to become disoriented. Van Reit had only a handful of rifle cartridges with him and soon expended them all in a futile attempt to signal his friends or anybody else that he was lost. When the bullets were gone he threw his rifle away, thinking it was an encumbrance.

After wandering aimlessly for a few days van Reit found a small pond and decided to settle down alongside it to await rescue. Lacking food or weapons, he took to eating rock-hard native fruit and figs, breaking his teeth and badly cutting his gums. He also cut his hands by digging up roots. The only other foods he managed to find were some small lizards he caught by hand and ate raw. At night he would crawl into an aardvark hole for shelter.

After a month of this brutal existence his reason began to slip and van Reit began to contemplate suicide. The best solution appeared to be drowning, and on several occasions he filled his pockets with rocks and dove into the pond. The attempts failed. Even when he lost consciousness, he invariably woke up on the banks of the little pool. The American hunter "Curio" Brown noted that in later life, whenever van Reit drank too much, he would have an attack of "diving fits" whereby he would holler out boisterously, "Look out, boys, I'm going to make a dive!" and then crash to the ground. On one occasion he nearly broke his shoulder by diving from the bed of a wagon to the ground. On another he smashed a table at a military hospital, destroying plates and food and deeply upsetting the hungry soldiers.

Van Reit was eventually rescued after forty-seven days by two hunters who visited his pond and found him cowering in his aardvark hole. Six Catholic nuns and a priest named Father Prestige nursed him back to health. He seems to have made a nearly complete recovery, and worked for a while as an orderly at the hospital in Salisbury. That was where he met Brown, who was suffering from a spear wound received in the 1896 Mashona Rebellion. Adrian Darter gave van Reit's name as van Dencken in his 1914 *Pioneers of Mashonaland.*

Van Rensburg. Van Rensburg (also seen as Van Rensberg) was an experienced Afrikaner elephant hunter of the 1930s and 1940s. He had a legendary adventure at a camp on Balambala Island in the Tana River district one day, at least two versions of which exist.

According to George Adamson (1987), van Rensburg was suffering from a hangover one morning just before the start of World War II and didn't accompany his partners when they left camp to look for elephant. As he lay sick in his tent, a huge bull elephant blundered into camp. Van Rensburg staggered to his feet and shot it. The tusks proved to weigh over 170 pounds a side.

Dennis Holman and Eric Rundgren (1969) placed the incident somewhat later. The amount of detail in their account lends credence to this version. They stated that Rundgren was on safari with his first wife (who he married in 1945, six years after Adamson's version of events) when they visited the riverside camp of Martinus Nel, another well-known Boer hunter. According to Rundgren, Nel was showing them his recent bag, a dozen tusks each weighing more than 100 pounds. The largest pair checked in at 164 and 163 pounds. Rensburg came over from his island camp and stated that he had just shot an enormous bull. Nel, Rundgren, and the others all went over to the island and found the animal, whose tusks each weighed 174 pounds.

Rundgren wrote that he and his wife remained in the area and shot four elephant with an average tusk weight of 116 pounds (the best pair was 143 and 138). He also got a fleeting glimpse of one huge bull with an immense, record-book-approaching 200 pounds per side, but saw the animal only for a second, in profile and in heavy bush. With no time left on his annual leave and having used up his licenses (one license must have been in his wife's name, a common misdemeanor practiced even by game department officials), Rundgren went back to work, vowing to return and bag the so-called "Island Elephant."

Unfortunately for Rundgren, word of the Island Elephant leaked out (Nel had also been stalking him) and dozens of hunters flocked to Balambala Island. Many of them bagged elephant in the 100-pound class, including Ralph "Slim" Metcalfe, nephew of Karamojo Bell, who took one with tusks of 154 pounds per side. By the time Rundgren returned to the Tana the next year, he had little hope of finding the Island Elephant (one reason for his delayed return was that Archie Ritchie asked him to attend a meeting of the Rumuruti Farmer's Association, further support for Holman and Rundgren's dating of the incident because Rundgren worked for Ritchie from 1944 to 1952). Rundgren made a cursory search of the island but saw nothing and went off to hunt a nearby swamp, eventually killing an elephant with tusks of 117 and 115 pounds.

Rundgren finally caught up with the Island Elephant, almost by accident, toward the end of his leave. He was walking back to camp one afternoon when suddenly the enormous animal slipped out from a wall of vegetation, unaware of the hunter's presence. There was no doubt it was the long-sought quarry. Rundgren shouldered his rifle, readying himself for a heart shot, then stopped. The Island Elephant, seen so fleetingly the year before, had but one tusk. The tradition was to let large one-tusked bulls go as potential breeders, so Rundgren reluctantly lowered his rifle. He didn't mention in his memoirs whether he let the other hunters in on the secret or allowed them to waste their time chasing this chimera.

Van Rooyen, Cornelius (1860–1915). Van Rooyen (also seen as Van Royen) was a famous South African hunter and a dark-horse candidate for greatest African hunter of all time. Known as "Nellis," van Rooyen explored and hunted around most of modern Zimbabwe from the Zambezi River and the Wankie area down to Bulawayo and points south and east. His primary residence was a farm at Mangwe, southwest of Bulawayo.

His claim to the title of Africa's greatest hunter rests upon the judgment of no less than Fred Selous, who expressed that opinion to Adrian Darter, one of the 1890 "Pioneers" of Mashonaland. Darter believed that the affable van Rooyen would have returned the compliment. Darter (1914) described the hunter as "brave, modest and quiet. An inveterate smoker, a dead shot, mild of manner, medium height, massive frame, enormous strength and untiring energy."

In addition to his reputation as a hunter, van Rooyen was adept in many other fields. He is credited with being the only man to develop an internationally recognized breed of dog, the Rhodesian ridgeback, also known as the African lion dog. Van Rooyen possessed a wide variety of frontier skills, including riding, blacksmithing, leatherworking, carpentry, ranching, farming, military scouting, tracking, and shooting. He had a special gift for veterinary medicine. Along with hunting for himself and guiding others, he collected living animals for sale to European zoos.

Van Rooyen commanded a mixed English and Boer force in a besieged *laager* (see glossary) at Mangwe during the 1896 Matabele Rebellion. His son-in-law, Hans Lee, was second in command. The men had lost their oxen at the outbreak of the war and had opted to fortify and ride the thing out. Around the turn of the century he took a young boy named John Burger along on a hunting trip (Burger also hunted with Selous around the same time).

Van Someren, Victor Gurner Logan (1886–1976). A dentist, doctor, surgeon, and naturalist, van Someren arrived in East Africa in 1912 and began studying birds. He was honorary secretary of the East Africa and Uganda Natural History Society and author of *Bird Life in Uganda* and *Notes on Birds of Uganda and East Africa.*

Van Zyl, Hendrik Matthys (1828–1880). A hunter in South-West Africa.

Van Zyl, Jan. Van Zyl was leader of a group of Boer hunters who chased 104 elephant into an Angolan swamp in 1879. The elephants became stuck in the mire, and Van Zyl and company shot down the entire herd. The sporting community expressed much outrage at this horrific slaughter.

Van Zyl, W. Van Zyl was a grizzled Boer who in 1899 transported Denis Lyell and his baggage from Bulawayo to Salisbury for a fee of £5. Van Zyl was a veteran elephant hunter who had shot with Selous in his youth. According to Lyell, Van Zyl was married with five "wild" children and owned a farm in the Transvaal where he bred trek oxen. On the 1899 trip he was loaded with a large shipment of tinned meat and whisky.

Vardon, Frank. Vardon hunted with Livingstone and Oswell in the 1850s and was with the latter when the two men shot eighty-nine rhino in one season, most of them white rhino. The antelope known as the puku *(Cobus vardoni)* is named after him.

Varian, H. F. "Frank" (1876–xxxx). Born in Ceylon, Varian was a British railway official and the author of *Some African Milestones* and of the Angola chapter in H. C. Maydon's *Big Game Shooting in Africa* (1932), part of the Lonsdale Library. His father, a famous hunter, had in 1882 shot the record Ceylon elephant, a legendary creature called the Malanpe Rogue. Varian Jr. arrived in Mozambique in May of 1898 and started a prosperous career working as a railroad surveyor and planner. He worked on Mashonaland Railways and the Victoria Falls Bridge, and in 1902 started a survey of Angola to find the best rail route. He supplied his work gangs by shooting buffalo and antelope with a Martini-Henry.

Varian wrote occasionally for sporting magazines. In a 20 March 1909 article in *The Field* entitled "The West Coast Duiker," he mentioned that a sable antelope with 54½-inch horns had been shot by a Mr. Essington Brown a few years before. At the time nobody realized that this was the first print reference to the Angolan giant sable.

Varian's article started a controversy about the accuracy of his claim (common sable were much smaller). Such controversies were a regular and entertaining part of the sporting press in those days. This led to a veritable crusade by Varian to prove the existence of this animal, which was finally accepted as real in 1916.

In World War I Varian served with a railways unit in France. Afterward he returned to Angola to help complete the Benguela railroad, which was finished in 1929. He finally retired to a long and apparently happy retirement in East Africa. Varian never lost his interest in the giant sable and was instrumental in protecting it by getting the Cabinde District closed to hunting when Boer hunters—known for their rapacity—began operating there. ROWLAND WARD 1928: ORIBI, ANGOLAN SABLE.

Varndell, C. R. Varndell led a shooting party in 1894 in Zululand that killed six extremely rare white rhino at the junction of the Black Umfolozi and White Umfolozi Rivers. The ensuing outrage led to the animal being declared royal game.

Vasconcelos, Joao Teixeira de. Portuguese big-game hunter who worked in northern Angola from 1914 through the 1920s. He is reputed to have shot some two hundred elephant. His memoirs were published in 1924 but have not been translated into English.

Vasse, Guillame (William). Vasse was a French hunter who spent several years in Portuguese East Africa in the early 1900s. Shooting for a museum, he collected buffalo, leopard, elephant, sable, lion, bushpig, and various antelope along the Rhodesian border and on the Zambezi and Pungwe Rivers. He also collected insects, and a species of mantid fly is named after him *(Perlamantispa vassei).* Vasse was the author of *Three Years' Sport in Mozambique* (1909).

Vaudet, A. (xxxx–1859). Vaudet, uncle of the brothers Poncet, was commissioned by the king of Sardinia as pro-consul in Khartoum. Vaudet did a bit of hunting and exploring in the area but was killed by Bari tribesmen near Gondokoro in 1859.

Vaughan-Jones, T. G. C. Vaughan-Jones was a career official of the British Colonial Office assigned to Northern Rhodesia in the 1930s as a district officer. In 1937 he was seconded to work as a sort of ad-hoc national game ranger. Northern Rhodesia didn't establish its game and tsetse control department until 1942, and the quality of Vaughan-Jones's work had been good enough that he was naturally chosen to be the first director. He established buffer zones, known as Controlled Hunting Areas, around the country's game reserves. The reserves acted as breeding grounds for wildlife while the CHA offered opportunities for a fledgling safari industry as well as a transitional zone between the reserves and the local populace. Under his stewardship some 6 percent of Northern Rhodesia was designated as either national park or game reserve.

Vernay, Arthur Stannard. Vernay was a British-born antiques dealer with offices in New York and London. As a sort of sideline he began to undertake collecting expeditions for the American Museum of Natural History, traveling to Africa and shooting animals for display and research purposes. He led fifteen such expeditions between 1923 and 1946.

On one such venture, the 1925 Vernay Angola Expedition, he collected sixty-one large mammals including fourteen rare giant sable. During this trip he stayed with Frank Varian. His last expedition was to Nyasaland in 1946. In the Akeley Hall of African Mammals in 1940 the mounted specimens listed as donated by Vernay consisted of giant sable, gemsbok, springbok, blesbok, and white-tailed gnu. Vernay had listings in the 1928 edition of Rowland Ward's record book for kongoni, Thomson gazelle, and springbok.

Veth, Daniel David (1850–1885). As a young man David Veth, son of a famous Dutch explorer named Prof. P. J. Veth, worked as a manager of the Zurich Railroad. In 1877–1878 young Veth led two Dutch expeditions to Sumatra, exploring the Padang Highlands and Palembang. Upon his return to Europe in 1881 he was appointed the Dutch Geographical Society delegate to the Geographical Congress and exhibition at Venice. In 1882 Veth worked in the administration of Java and was also tasked with organizing the 1883 Colonial Exhibition at Amsterdam.

Veth made his first visit to Africa in 1884 as leader of the Dutch Central Africa Expedition. Its primary goal was to communicate with and show support for those Boers who had settled in Portuguese territory along the Kunene River. Veth and his people made some explorations in Angola and visited the Mondombe people, but hadn't accomplished very much when Veth developed a fever and died in May 1885. His Angola papers were published by his father in 1887.

Viljoen, Jan Willem (1812–1893). A legendary Boer hunter of French Huguenot ancestry, he was hunting elephant on the Matabele border as early as 1857. He spent most of his life roaming the African interior, hunting with his sons and other Boer hunters. In 1859 he hunted the Transvaal with Petrus Jacobs, and together they counted for ninety-three elephant. Six years later the two Boers were the first known white men to hunt Mashonaland, having been granted permission by the Matabele king, Mzilikazi, and brought back the tusks of 210 elephant from this expedition.

In 1875 we catch a glimpse of Viljoen hunting at Mangwe on the Simbookie River, where his family resided while he and his sons and sons-in-law went shooting. By 1878 he was trying his luck at Gwenia on the Gwelo River, where Selous encountered his wagons.

In his long career Viljoen dropped hundreds of elephant, all in fair-chase conditions and most, if not all, with primitive black-powder weapons. There is no record of his ever being injured by his quarry. He left a large progeny, and the family name creeps up many times in the history of the Boer Wars and of South Africa.

Personally affable and very highly respected, he hated the British government and was almost hanged when captured after the Battle of Boomplaats in 1848. He escaped with his life, but his farm near Winburg was impounded. Viljoen established a new farm at Marico called "Faer-genog" (Far Enough).

He held a number of civil and military posts during his life and in 1853 led a Boer column against the BaKwena chieftain Sechele. During the course of the campaign troops under his command ransacked and looted David Livingstone's vacant house at Colobeng. Mrs. Viljoen later asked Livingstone's brother-in-law, John Smith Moffatt, not to blame her husband for the raid because some of his men had simply gone out of control (the incident was widely blamed on the local Africans). Moffatt would later witness this type of behavior firsthand. For many years Viljoen held the rank of field cornet at Marico, a Boer post roughly equivalent to a combination police chief/military commander/district commissioner.

On Christmas Day 1880 Viljoen was commander of a Boer force that occupied the pro-British town of Zeerust in the Transvaal. The first Anglo-Boer war had just broken out, and the Boers were trying to consolidate their position and make sure that the English settlers in the district did not take up arms against them. Viljoen arrested John Moffatt, the local native commissioner, and ordered the former missionary to resign his post and sign a pledge of neutrality. Moffatt refused. Several of the Boers prepared to shoot him down in the middle of the main street while Viljoen looked on, according to Moffatt, "in a maze." The impromptu firing squad hesitated, because some of their own men were in the line of fire behind Moffatt, and then Viljoen "seemed to snap out of a trance and suddenly rushed forward, his horse between me and my assailants" (Moffatt, 1921) and ordered the execution to stop. Moffatt was placed under loose arrest and confined to a friend's ranch for the rest of the war.

Selous (1881) described Viljoen as small for a Boer, "very tough and wiry with a quick, vivacious manner and keen dark eyes." The impression one gets from the various memoirs and letters that mention him is of a quiet man who tried to do his duty when his people called but who infinitely preferred the solitude and peace of the wide-open spaces. He remains one of the most respected South African hunters of the early period. He kept a low profile during the remainder of the 1881 Anglo-Boer War, acting as an ambassador to the African tribes in a largely successful attempt to keep them out of the conflict. Viljoen died quietly in 1893 at the age of eighty-two.

The association between hunting and the Viljoen name did not end with his passing. Jan's son Hendrick is mentioned in Selous's book *A Hunter's Wanderings in Africa,* which relates how he hunted down a man-eating lion that killed a goat herd in 1876. In 1908 the government of a section of Rhodesia called Lomagundi proclaimed open season on elephant to trim the numbers of crop-raiders. Hunters came flocking in, and one group that killed eighty-one elephant was led by a Viljoen, presumably a relative of the old patriarch.

Villiers, C. Villiers was an officer in the Royal Horse Guards who accompanied Sir Gerald Portal on the 1893 mission to Uganda. He had arrived in East Africa on leave with the intention of going on an extended hunting safari. When he heard that Portal was in the area preparing his expedition, he quickly sought permission to join up, obtaining approval at almost the last minute. On 26 February 1893 the progress of the expedition was halted as the officers went out to hunt some hartebeest they had spotted a few hundred yards ahead of the column. During the stalk the men suddenly heard a cry from behind them. A huge rhino had decided to charge the line of porters. Villiers and Raymond Portal (Sir Gerald's brother) were the first to close the range and begin firing. With five officers firing and a hundred porters darting about in panic, the scene struck Portal as so funny that "our laughter and haste seriously interfered with our aim" (Portal, 1894), but finally the rhino fell. Fourteen bullets were found in the carcass, almost all .577 caliber, and two or three had gone straight through the heart. Villiers got the horns, for he had drawn first blood.

Vincent. A hunter named Vincent was one of the codefendants in the notorious Atkinson murder trial of 1902 (see entry on Atkinson for details). Readers interested in divine justice may be pleased to know that a few years later Vincent was savaged by a wounded leopard and lamed for life.

Vincent, John. Col. Jack Vincent was a South African naturalist who accompanied Rear Admiral Lynnes on an ornithological safari in the 1920s. Vincent later collected birds in Mozambique, Angola, Kenya, and Ethiopia, including several species that had been unknown to science. After serving in the Natal Carabiniers in World War II (winning numerous decorations for merit and bravery), Vincent retired to his farm on the Mooi River. In 1949 he accepted a post as secretary of the Natal Parks Board, which he held until he retired in 1963. As secretary he helped oversee the successful white rhino conservation and transplant program at Umfolozi Reserve.

Vogel, Eduard (1829–1856). A German-born explorer, Vogel was working as an astronomer in London in 1853 when he was commissioned by the British government to undertake a mission to the Sudan. He explored the area around Lake Chad for three years, meeting up with fellow traveler Heinrich Barth. In 1856 Vogel was killed by Wadai tribesmen, but his fate remained unknown until 1873, when it was ascertained by Nachtigal.

Vogelsang, Heinrich (1862–1914). Vogelsang was an unscrupulous agent who worked for Lüderitz in the 1880s. In 1883 he negotiated the notorious "miles treaty," which, by using the different English and European definitions of "mile," cheated the local Africans into ceding much more land than they had intended to.

Vojnich, Oscar (1864–xxxx). Hungarian sportsman who hunted Central Africa in the early years of the twentieth century.

W

Wackernie. A French elephant hunter of this name operated in Ubangi-Shari in the late 1920s. He is said to have shot some 150 elephants before opening a trading post. Wackernie joined the Free French in World War II and was killed fighting against the Germans.

Wahlberg, Johan August (1810–1856). Swedish naturalist who explored southwestern Africa beginning in the 1830s. Wahlberg who was associated with the Swedish State Museum sent thousands of specimens back for study, especially butterflies and other insects. He sometimes traveled with the hunter Fred Green, with whom he visited Lake Ngami in 1855. Wahlberg was killed by an elephant in 1856 while hunting in Matabeleland.

Waal, David Christiaan de (1845–1909). An important Dutch politician in Cape Colony and a close friend of Cecil Rhodes, de Waal accompanied Rhodes on trips to Mashonaland in 1890 and 1891. There they met with Lord Randolph Churchill (visiting the area for sport and to make money as a journalist) and also Lobengula. De Waal wrote an account of the trip called *With Rhodes in Mashonaland* (1896). From a sporting perspective, the book is interesting mainly in that de Waal and company shot at virtually every animal they saw. For example: "I could not make out what kind of animal they were. Without dismounting, I fired a shot at them…" In this case, the creatures were wild pigs. De Waal must have been a nuisance to travel with, for in his book he complains about every little thing.

De Waal's political career suffered from his unfaltering loyalty to Rhodes, even after the fiasco of the Jameson Raid. He lost the support of his Boer friends and was out of politics for good by 1903.

Walker Brothers. The Walkers—Harry, Chris, and Mackie—were elephant-hunting brothers in Southern Rhodesia in the 1920s. They assisted the American geologist-turned-animal-collector Wynant Hubbard in his 1923–1924 efforts to capture specimens for the Pretoria Zoo. The Walkers themselves had three tame elephant on their farm, obtained as calves by way of shooting the mother cow.

Walker, Eric Sherbrooke. Trained as an Anglican minister, Eric Walker took a position in 1908 as scout commissioner and private secretary to Lord Baden-Powell, founder of the Boy Scouts. When World War I broke out, Walker joined the Royal Flying Corps. He was shot down and captured, and escaped from several POW camps in Germany. After the war he served in British Military Intelligence and fought in the Russian Revolution on the side of the Whites.

In the 1920s Walker worked as a merchant and trader, and as a bootlegger in Prohibition-era America (he wrote *Confessions of a Rum Runner* under the pseudonym James Barbican). In the early 1930s he settled in Kenya, where he opened first the Outspan Hotel and then the famous Treetops Hotel.

Walker enlisted in the RAF in World War II but was turned down for flying duty because of his age. After transferring to the army, he served in the Abyssinian theater and in the Western Desert campaign. After the war he returned to Treetops, which under his management soon became the fashionable place to observe wildlife.

Built over a water hole frequented by elephant, rhino, leopard, warthog, and other animals, Treetops at that time was a primitive but friendly place with just the right mix of comfort and wilderness. Guests were guided by professional hunters from their cars down a long path to the hotel. Spaced at intervals along the path were broad, easy-to-climb safety ladders, which were often used to escape curious rhino and elephant. The ladders were used fairly frequently, at least once by the governor of Kenya and his wife. Treetops achieved international fame in February 1952, when Princess Elizabeth, who was vacationing there, received word of her father's death and became Queen of England. A semipermanent guest in his old age was the legendary tiger hunter Jim Corbett (1875–1955), author of *Maneaters of Kumaon* and other classics. Lord Baden-Powell, founder of the Boy Scouts and a successful hunter and soldier in his younger years, also frequented Treetops and died at nearby Nyeri in 1941.

When the Mau Mau insurgency erupted, Walker and others were somewhat puzzled that Treetops was not immediately attacked. Its prominence and remote location seemed to make it a logical target, but for some inexplicable reason the terrorists left it alone. In May 1954 an informant among Walker's Kikuyu staff provided the answer. It seems that the driver of the lorry that brought supplies to Treetops every morning—necessities like milk, bread, and eggs—was a Mau Mau sympathizer who was also dropping food off to the terrorists along the roadway. Attacking Treetops would have stopped the flow of their own supplies. The British authorities decided to lay a trap. Walker and his daughter, Honor, in the company of six policemen armed with Greener guns (Mauser-style bolt-action magazine rifles in .318 Nitro Express caliber) arranged an ambush. The attempt to capture or kill the terrorists was unsuccessful. Shots were exchanged, but the guerrillas escaped back into the forest. With their supply operation uncovered, the Mau Mau no longer had any incentive not to attack the hotel. Inevitably, Treetops was burned to the ground a few days later. It was later rebuilt on a much more luxurious scale.

Walker, L. H. "Tommy." The brother of Eric Sherbrooke Walker, Tommy Walker worked as a hunter at Treetops. He was once walking through a reedy area close to a river when a buffalo bull charged him from a distance of a few feet. As Walker fell he was able to fire one desperate shot, and the bull crashed to a stop nearly on top of him, shot dead through the heart. It was such a close call that the buffalo landed on Walker's hat.

Later that same day he was about to cross a stream by walking on a log when something caused him to suddenly stop and take a much closer look. Then he carefully raised his rifle and put a bullet into the log, killing the crocodile with a shot right in the eye.

Wallace, Sir Lawrence A. Wallace was the administrator of North-East Rhodesia in the early years of the twentieth century and the first European to explore the Chambezi River swamp (late 1890s). One day Wallace was charged by an elephant and tripped, and the enraged animal drove his tusk into the ground in an attempt to kill him. The Administrator's companion shot and killed the elephant. Wallace was unhurt. He had a listing in the 1928 Rowland Ward record book for Lichtenstein hartebeest.

Waller, Sydney. Waller was a professional hunter hired as a backup to Alan Black for the 1928 safari of the duke of Gloucester (brother of the Prince of Wales). He worked for both the Newland & Tarlton and Safariland firms.

Walmsley, Leo (1892–1966). Walmsley was a popular nature writer and novelist who found himself in the British army at the start of World War I. Not wanting to stay in the trenches, he transferred to the Royal Flying Corps, the forerunner of the RAF. After his preliminary flight training and evaluation, he wasn't considered skilled enough to be a pilot, so he was trained instead as an observer for the Be2c, an antiquated biplane with a reputation as a "flying coffin"; the famous Baron von Richthofen ran up much of his score shooting these things down. Walmsley served over Kenya and Tanganyika during the East African campaign against the Germans under von Lettow-Vorbeck.

Assigned to Number 26 (South Africa) Squadron, Walmsley survived an amazing fourteen plane crashes and was mentioned in dispatches for bravery. He planned to write a book about his wartime experiences and so kept a journal, but he lost the notebook and had to reconstruct everything from memory. The resulting book, *Flying and Sport in East Africa* (1920), combines military flying with the hunting of lion and elephant. He went on to have a distinguished writing career and is the subject of the 1997 biography *Shells and Bright Stones* by Nona Stead.

Walsh, Mary (xxxx–1922). Mary Walsh left Ireland for Australia as a young bride of seventeen. She and her first husband tried their hands at prospecting for gold in the Outback and at raising sheep, but they were unsuccessful at both endeavors. After Mary's husband and both of their children died (one child from a snake bite, the other child from drowning), she moved to Rhodesia in an attempt to start over. There she met and married John Walsh, a wandering hunter and trader.

In 1896 the couple rambled into East Africa, where they went prospecting for several years around Lake Magadi with a partner, Tom Deacon; they also established the first general store at Naivasha. Around the year 1907 they were living at a farm in Uganda, the only European settlers—as opposed to functionaries like missionaries and military men—in the colony at that time. The Walshes conducted a profitable transport business from Kenya to Uganda; Mary Walsh would often lead the caravan of mules herself all the way from Mombasa to Lake Victoria. Business was hurt by the growth of the Uganda Railway, but they kept at it and also ran a number of small general stores along the road.

The Walsh's were fated to have a lot of money and opportunities pass through their hands over the years—they lived simply and without luxuries and never amassed a fortune. John Boyes, who knew them in western Kenya in the late 1890s, attributed this to their "open-handed hospitality and careless, happy-go-lucky Irish temperament" (1911), but there were some bad business decisions, as well: John Walsh, for instance, sold the mineral rights to Lake Magadi to a man named Commerell Cowper Coles in November 1902 for £15. Coles promptly worked out a lucrative deal with the East Africa Syndicate mining company, which made millions extracting and selling soda from the lake. The place is still producing soda today.

Mary Walsh tried her hand at a variety of jobs, including trading, ranching, and setting up bakeries and trading posts. Her main line of work was the donkey transport business, running from Mombasa to Nairobi and beyond. She was a formidable woman—a wiry, redheaded firecracker who often wore men's clothes and always carried a revolver. She also carried a *kiboko*, a hippo-hide whip, which accounts for her African nickname, Bibi Kiboko. The Europeans called her "Pioneer Mary" because of her toughness and the legend that she had been one of the first European woman to settle in Rhodesia, in Uganda, and in central Kenya. Mary liked to drink to excess and was often in trouble with the law, but her acerbic tongue and readiness to use the *kiboko* made the African constables extremely reluctant to confront her. She died on 20 June 1922 and was buried in an unmarked grave, presumably because her husband lacked the money for a monument.

By nature John Walsh was a quieter sort and was generally content to assist his wife in her trading and transport business. After his wife died, John turned to hunting antelope for the meat market in Nairobi. He also worked as a guide on Martin and Osa Johnson's first African safari later that same year at the fee of $5 per day.

John Walsh died soon afterward in an odd shooting accident. While out shooting one day, his Model T Ford broke down. Walsh walked the two miles back to camp and ordered his staff to hitch up an ox wagon to tow the automobile back. The men had trouble hooking up the wagon and Walsh, in a rage, began hollering and waving his arms madly about. The shotgun was still in his hands and the violent gesturing caused it to fire, hitting him in the knee. Walsh didn't lose consciousness but bled to death while his men tried to carry him to the nearest doctor.

Wambua Ngula. This African poacher from the Voi area was in his prime during the second quarter of the twentieth century. A Waliangulu hunter, he had a prodigious reputation and a memory to match. When finally captured in 1955 he confessed to a poaching record that included more than three hundred elephant, thirty-one buffalo, and sixteen lion, all killed with a bow. Like many others like him, after arrest he became a successful tracker for the anti-poaching forces.

Wantenaar, John. A noted gunsmith in Salisbury, Rhodesia, in the 1920s as well as a successful hunter.

Ward, F. A. In Kenya in 1909, Freddy Ward was one of the owners of the Boma Trading Company, which equipped the Buffalo Jones expedition among others. During the Boer War he had been a captain in the British army. During the famous Roosevelt safari Ward hosted a dinner for the ex-president and his party.

While lion hunting in the Sotik region of Kenya shortly afterward, Ward happened to shoot a leopard. The shot led to the classic wounded-leopard scenario: Ward followed the cat into brush and was severely mauled, surviving only because his Somali gunbearer literally shot the leopard off him. Ward lost an ear, and his jaw was broken. When he was released from the hospital weeks later, his bed was immediately taken by another victim of a leopard mauling. It's a rough sport.

Ward, Herbert (1863–1919). Herbert Ward was the son of naturalist and taxidermist Edwin Ward and the nephew of Rowland Ward. After exploring in Borneo, Ward joined the Congo Free State administration in 1884. He worked in the Congo for three years (first at Isanghila and then in 1886 as commander of the station at Bangala) and was preparing to go home to England (and from there to California, where his father owned a fruit farm) when he learned of the 1887 plans to rescue Emin Pasha. Anxious for a shot at what he thought would be glory, Ward recruited three hundred porters on his own initiative and intercepted Henry Stanley's safari. He then offered to turn the men over to Stanley provided he himself was allowed to join the expedition.

Stanley was in desperate need of additional porters and so agreed to the offer. Besides, he had personally vetted Ward's 1884 application and thus already had a good opinion of the man. He placed Ward in command of a company of Zanzibari troops. When Stanley split the expedition into two parts, Ward was left with the so-called Rear Column under the psychotic Major Barttelot while Stanley pushed on to find Emin.

Stanley's plan was for Barttelot to gather additional men and supplies (with the assistance of the Arab trader/Belgian governor Tippu Tib) and then eventually move forward to succor Stanley and Emin in Equatoria. Unfortunately, Tib had trouble providing the requisite assistance and Barttelot proved a complete incompetent, and so the Rear Column self-destructed amidst murder, sickness, and starvation. Ward did his best to help the situation but was often confined to his tent with fever. He was apparently prone to illness—he had almost died of malaria years earlier during his travels in northern Borneo.

It is difficult to imagine two 1880s African explorers more different than Ward and Barttelot. Ward was an intellectual with a genuine affection for the local Africans while Barttelot was an insecure, sadistic brute who despised them as racial inferiors. Barttelot soon found an excuse to send Ward on a ridiculous errand—a march of some fifteen hundred miles to a Portuguese telegraph station to wire London a stupid question. And he compounded the indignity by later sending Ward an insulting letter warning him not to steal any company property along the way. No coward, Ward sent back a reply that he would seek "satisfaction" from the major upon completion of his mission. Ward did indeed carry out his petty task, but was then ordered by Barttelot not to return to the Rear Column's main depot but to establish himself at Bangala. Ward never got his desired duel—Barttelot was shot dead by one of his disgruntled porters.

Upon his return to Europe, Ward refused to jump on the pro-Stanley bandwagon. At first he kept quiet, acknowledging Stanley's accomplishments and keeping mum about his flaws. After Stanley started pinning the blame on everybody else for the Rear Column disaster, however, Ward began talking. He then played a key part in publicizing the Rear Column scandal, which marred Stanley's reputation in the world press and with posterity.

Ward served in World War I and drew praise for his bravery. He died a year after the Armistice. He was the author of *Five Years with the Congo Cannibals* (1890), *My Life with Stanley's Rearguard* (1891), and *A Voice from the Congo* (1910).

Herbert Ward at Bangala, Central Africa, circa 1890.

Ward, Rowland (1848–1912). Rowland Ward was an expert taxidermist with a shop called "The Jungle" in Piccadilly. He was the son of Henry Ward, an early taxidermist and a companion of John James Audubon during Audubon's travels in America. Rowland's brother Edwin was also a taxidermist and had the patronage of Britain's royal family from 1871 until he moved to California. Rowland's nephew, Edwin's son Herbert, accompanied Stanley on the Emin Pasha Relief Expedition.

Taxidermy in the 1800s was generally a shabby affair, with stuffed mounts looking little more realistic than a sack jammed with potatoes with a pair of glass eyes stuck on. In the 1880s and 1890s Ward and others, such as American Carl Akeley, began to revolutionize the art by using new techniques and, more important, a new philosophy designed to make the animal look as lifelike as possible. The results were often amazing. This visual evidence of one's skill as a hunter helped spark the increased interest in big-game hunting that swept England and much of America around the year 1900.

In 1892 Ward decided to publish a series of books that would become known as *Records of Big Game,* listing the best specimens submitted to his studio. It was a brilliant marketing idea, not only fanning the interest in hunting but also ensuring that Rowland Ward got the lion's share (pun intended) of the trophy business coming in from Asia and Africa. "The Book" was the *Baseball Encyclopedia* of the safari world—every young hunter yearned to see his name under one of the headings. It was updated every few years, new editions being published in 1896, 1899, 1903, 1907, 1910, 1914, 1922 (interrupted by the war), 1928, and so on through the present day. No matter where you were in Africa, no matter how remote a swamp you were in or how far up the Congo you were, if you could find a hunter's camp you found a copy of the record book. So popular was the ubiquitous book that Denis Lyell, in describing the meager possessions of the typical poverty-challenged hunter living in the African bush, mentioned a rifle, a cow or two, a natural-history and shooting notebook, some ratty clothes, and the Rowland Ward record book.

The early editions of the book did not contain a lot of information about the trophies themselves, not even the date they were taken. Each listing simply gave the trophy's dimensions, place of origin, occasionally a photograph, and the name of the current owner. This last would not necessarily be the name of the hunter. The 1928 Rowland Ward book, for instance, listed D. D. Lyell as owner of an Angolan giant sable head with horns measuring more than 58 inches. Lyell, however, wrote in *Memories of an African Hunter* (1923) that the sable had been given to him by H. F. Varian. In the same edition there is a photograph of a bushbuck skull and horns that had belonged to Lyell's friend, Barnshaw, but was sold to the Tring Museum of Lord Rothschild. It is identified in the book only as belonging to Rothschild. Rarely, usually when the trophy was in a museum, the record book would list its location and then, parenthetically, the name of the hunter who had donated it—e.g., "British Museum (13th Earl of Derby)."

Ward went into the publishing business in a big way, coming out with original works by Selous, Powell-Cotton, Arthur Neumann, and other authorities. He also sold secondhand books and reprints but on a smaller scale, and wrote his own books on taxidermy (although he seems to have lifted some passages wholesale from his brother Edwin's earlier works).

"The Book" virtually created an entirely new class of outdoorsman, the trophy hunter. These were men who stalked game selectively, taking only those prime specimens that would get them listed in records. Once listed, they tried to work their way up, always seeking better heads and bigger tusks. The archetype of this breed was Norman B. Smith. The Rowland Ward company continued functioning for many years after its founder's death, but eventually the name was purchased by an American group and moved across the sea. In the 1990s a family in South Africa purchased the company, and the record book is still being published there today.

Ward, Vivian. A professional hunter employed by the firm of Safariland, Ltd., in the 1920s.

Ware, Harry. Despite claims (usually by Kenyans) that the job of professional hunting guide was invented in Kenya around the turn of the century, there is a long record of such folks before then. In the 1880s, for instance, a man named Harry Ware was advertising in European and English papers for clients for his Zambezi River hunting trips. Ware also promised to show the sportsmen Victoria Falls.

Also a trader, Ware was instrumental in the British South African Company's bid to take over Barotseland. In 1889 Ware convinced the Barotse king, Lewanika, to sign a twenty-year concession giving him (Ware) mining rights over an area bigger than Ireland. The price was a parcel of Martini-Henry rifles, ammunition, cloth, and a promise to pay £200 annual rent plus 4 percent of the gross. Ware promptly turned around and resold the concession for a profit to Cecil Rhodes's BSAC, beginning the company's thirty-five-year control of Northern Rhodesia.

Warren, Sir Charles (1840–1927). An officer of the Royal Engineers, Warren was one of those uniquely Victorian individuals who combined two widely disparate talents. In his case he was both a competent military officer and an excellent amateur archaeologist.

In 1882–1883 Warren led what was termed the Palmer Search Expedition in the Sinai and in Egypt. Three Englishmen—Palmer, Charrington, and Gill—had disappeared in the desert without a trace. Rumor had it they had been murdered. Sir Charles Warren led a column into the Sinai to find the men, or at least discover their fate. After much searching and conflict with the Bedouin, Warren found the men's bones and clothing in a shallow grave in the Wadi Sadr. He also found the culprits and brought them back to Cairo to face justice, making this the sort of adventure-drama the Victorian public just loved.

Two years later Warren led an expedition of four thousand men into Bechuanaland that marked the beginning of the British dominion over that country. The invasion (for that's what it was) was remarkably efficient, and Warren effectively annexed the entire territory without losing a single man. He also helped Cecil Rhodes in early negotiations with Lobengula.

Warren went on to serve as commissioner and chief of the London Metropolitan Police, commander of Singapore, and commander of the Thames district, and led the 5th division during the Boer War.

Waterall, L. S. Waterall presents the type of ghostly record often turned up by those investigating Africa's past. Owen Letcher wrote in 1911 of a Mr. L. S. Waterall "of M'Pika," who was the recipient of unprovoked attacks by two rhino and an elephant during his first few months in North-East Rhodesia. In 1933 David Blunt wrote of a settler named Waterall who was a game ranger in Tanganyika. In fact, the 1930 EARB (see glossary) confirms that L. S. Waterall was living at Morogoro in Tanganyika Territory at the approximate time, around 1929. So far, that's all we've found.

Waters, Vinston. In 1899 near Nairobi, Dr. Waters went out to shoot some elephant that were raiding native farms. Spotting a large bull, he tried a heart shot at close range with a .577 double. Two huge bullets had no discernible effect on the tusker, and Waters ran for his life. The elephant was just about to grab him with its trunk when Waters disappeared! He had fallen into a Kikuyu game pit. Fortunately for him, the pit wasn't staked at the bottom. The confused elephant stomped around a bit and wandered off. Waters, a bit bruised but otherwise OK, clambered out and, in true frontier style, finished the hunt.

Watkins. A man named Watkins was manager of the Luangwa Cotton Plantation around 1905. A few years later he took up elephant hunting on a large scale in German East Africa. After initial success, he developed recurrent fever and died.

Watteville, Vivienne de (1899–1957). Also seen as Waterville. Vivienne de Watteville went on a collecting expedition for the Berne Museum in 1923–1924 with her father, the Swiss naturalist Bernard de Watteville (1877–1924). The safari was run on a shoestring, like many non-American museum expeditions. There was no professional hunter and no motor vehicles, just a headman, a gunbearer (named Kongoni), a cook, a few skinners, thirty porters, and six donkeys. Things didn't go too well—Papa was soon killed by a lion in the Congo near the Uganda border. Unflinchingly, Vivienne buried her father and finished up the job, bagging the buffalo, antelope, and white rhino for which the museum had contracted. She later wrote a book about the experience, *Out of the Blue.* A later book, *Speak to the Earth,* was about a safari she made in 1935. Her work suffers from that annoying "wisecracking" style that was so prevalent in the 1930s.

Vivienne married George Goschen (1887–1953) in 1930. As a young girl Vivienne had introduced her cousin, a sparkling beauty named Catherine Bechet de Balan, to a promising nobleman, the younger son of the Earl of Winchilsea. Balan and the young aristocrat hit it off and for a time seemed destined to marry. Ultimately, however, Catherine married an army colonel named Lucas, and the rejected suitor, who always looked back on her as the great lost love of his life, moved to Africa, where he pursued various interests including hunting and Karen Blixen. Catherine Lucas named her second son Denys after her lost suitor, Denys Finch Hatton. Vivienne's own wedding was attended by Finch Hatton, and the best man was Sir Alan "Tommy" Lascelles, assistant private secretary to the Prince of Wales. ROWLAND WARD 1928: (BERNARD DE WATTEVILLE) TSESSEBE, BLACK LECHWE, LICHTENSTEIN HARTEBEEST, KONGONI, HIROLA, LION, SITATUNGA, ROAN, GIANT FOREST HOG, (VIVIENNE) WHITE RHINO.

Wayland, E. J. Government geologist of Uganda from 1919 to the 1940s, Wayland was appointed by Sir Robert Coryndon to lead the Uganda Geological Survey. He began his work by hiking nine hundred miles through the countryside, checking out the land and surveying the various types of terrain. He was very interested in finding prehistoric human artifacts, of which he collected some thirty thousand, storing them in a shed. The entire project took years of grueling fieldwork. After his retirement the government allowed Louis Leakey to look at the collection. He found that all of the labels and other documentation showing where the items had been found had been eaten by termites—what remained was virtually worthless. After Leakey took his pick of the artifacts, the rest were just tossed over a cliff.

Weatherley, Poulett. Weatherley was a British sportsman and hunter who lived in Awemba territory in the 1890s and had a great relationship with chiefs Ponde and Mporokoro. He was also friendly with Sir Harry Johnston, who at the time was commissioner of the British Central Africa Protectorate (later Nyasaland), and would often feed intelligence to Johnston. Weatherley was instrumental in brokering a peace treaty between Johnston and Mporokoro.

Wells, Carveth (1887–1957). Wells was popular newspaperman and writer and a member of the Cudahy-Massee-Milwaukee Museum Expedition in 1928–1929. The expedition originally spent several months in Tanganyika and southern Kenya collecting specimens for taxidermic groups. When the rest of the party moved northward, Wells (as part of a pre-arranged plan) went on to Mount Ruwenzori. In 1929 Doubleday published a book of his African experiences, titled *In Coldest Africa.* The title reflects the author's surprise at spending freezing nights atop the Mountains of the Moon; he had expected a truly tropical experience. Unfortunately, Wells was a devotee of the 1920s-vintage wisecracking style of writing that was peculiar to American journalists of the day and that many modern readers find annoying.

Wells was originally trained as an engineer and spent several years working in Canada before moving to London as a young man. After a two-year teaching stint at the South Kensington Imperial College of Science and Technology, he took a post in the colonial administration and served in Malaya as a surveyor for six years. In addition to his popular writing, he authored *The Field Engineer's Handbook.* He was a success on the lecture circuit.

Werthor, Waldemar. He was a German officer and hunter who brought the first specimens of the aardvark back to Germany in the 1890s.

Wessels, Peter. In 1950 Peter (Piet) Wessels and his wife Minnie, after failing at several occupations, decided to take advantage of the fact that crocodiles were considered vermin in Tanganyika and thus could be hunted without license or limit. Their croc-hunting operation was one of the most profitable and successful in Africa. They would patrol the remote Kilombero and Manyara Rivers in thirty-five-foot outboard canoes, shooting and harpooning the reptiles. Their biggest occupational hazard was the hippo. On numerous occasions the animals attacked the Wessels's canoe, one of their African assistants was bitten in half by a hippo, and Minnie boasted a permanent scar under one eye from one that charged her on land. The Wessels were also concerned about raising their young daughter alongside a river teeming with crocodiles.

In the dry season it was possible to shoot crocs by day, but in the rainy season the hunting had to be done at night. It was a risky business in more ways than one—the price of crocodile skin fluctuated between three and fifty-three shillings per foot during their career (only the belly skin of the crocodile has commercial value). Several times they had to quit temporarily due to market conditions and take up other professions—in Piet's case, mica mining. Eventually crocodiles became too rare in the area to make hunting profitable.

Piet and Minnie Wessels.

In addition to making a living, the Wessels viewed themselves as performing a public service. Piet Wessel was lauded for killing a crocodile in the Kihange River that had killed four hundred people, as well as a Zambezi River animal that allegedly had three hundred victims to its credit.

Westbeech, George Copp (1844–1888). George Westbeech was perhaps the most famous of the Zambezi Valley traders in the nineteenth century. After arriving in Africa in 1862, he built a station in the Pandamatenga Hills and employed native hunters to procure ivory and hides for him. His chief partner was George Phillips. Panda-ma-tenga, as it was frequently written, became a major base for trading and hunting operations in Zambezia, and Westbeech became the most important trader, especially of ivory, on the upper Zambezi.

The Matabele called Westbeech "Georos" and the Barotse called him "Jolosi," both corruptions of his first name. Westbeech had close relationships with Mzilikazi, Lobengula, and the Barotse chief Lewanika. In fact, he held the tribal rank of a Barotse headman. He often hired African hunters to roam the hinterland shooting elephant and other big game for him. In 1874 Selous, for instance, ran into one of Westbeech's hired hunters, a Griqua named Jacob Ourson, at the confluence of the Zambezi and Chobe Rivers.

Policeman Arnold Hodson (later governor of Sierra Leone) reported that the ruins of Westbeech's store still stood in 1910 on a "ragged, sparse-bushed spur" of the hills (*Trekking the Great Thirst,* 1912).

Wet, de. The hundreds of books written by and about African big-game hunters are full of stories of courage and adventure. Most of these rugged men were at least in some respects admirable. Every once in a while, however, a scoundrel slips in, as happens with any group of people anywhere. For every paragon of sport and fair play there is a less-than-noble counterpart.

C. G. Schillings wrote about one of the scoundrels in his 1905 *With Flashlight and Rifle.* This man was a Boer hunter who went by the name of de Wet. In 1903 he presented himself to the German authorities in Tanganyika and received permission to live-trap marabou storks, those bizarre-looking "undertakers" related to the vulture. De Wet claimed he had discovered a technique whereby he could prune a few valuable feathers off each stork and then return the bird to the wild, living and unharmed. He hoped to make a modest income from the sale of the feathers.

This seemed harmless enough, so the Germans granted him permission to set up his operation by certain lakes near Mount Kilimanjaro. Since there was to be no killing involved, the authorities didn't even require a license fee or any tax on the feathers. The ponds in question had been discovered by the German hunter Moritz Merker and were known as the "Merker lakes." Schillings had been by them in 1899 and counted some one hundred fifty hippo making their homes there.

When Schillings returned four years later, he found only a dozen or so hippo left alive. The culprit was de Wet and his feather operation. It seems the Boer hunter had used the hippo as stork bait; he would shoot them and leave the carcasses by the lakeside to attract his birds. And his method of stork capture was far from innocuous. Rather than trap the marabous, he simply shot them and then sold the feathers (as well as the hides and teeth from the hippo) to Greek businessmen. Schillings turned him in and he was arrested. An investigation disclosed that he had been perpetrating similar schemes in various parts of Africa for at least seven years. Schillings and the local German commandant hoped to put him away for a long time. His influential business partners, however, managed to get the punishment commuted to a hefty fine, which they paid. De Wet then disappeared, presumably to set up shop elsewhere.

The African big-game hunter has been both the beneficiary and the victim of the world's publishers. For many years their adventures were glorified, and book after book created an unrealistic portrait of the "great white hunter." In modern days the tide has turned, and the current stereotype—cruel, greedy, unthinking—is just as inaccurate. Few of today's readers would guess that hunters played a key role in the preservation of Africa's wildlife. I'm sure many kids grow up today thinking that the original Africans and the kind missionaries and antihunters were all vegetarians and lived in perfect harmony with kittenish lion in a Garden of Eden setting occasionally bespoiled by the mean and greedy men with the double rifles. Hunters then and now did great things and unspeakable things, kind things and cruel things. Objective history demands the telling of both sides of the story.

Weyand, Karl. A Boer elephant hunter in the 1870s and 1880s, Weyand also hunted in northern Mashonaland with an Englishman named Grant in late 1883. By the mid-1880s the white rhino, which had once roamed southern Africa by the thousands, had been reduced to a few small groups living in scattered pockets. In 1886 Weyand and Jan Engelbrecht discovered one of these pockets in Matabeleland and killed ten rhinos for their hides and their horns.

Weyers, John. Weyers was another of the Boer hunter–traders of Panda-ma-tenga. In 1888 he traveled with Fred Selous from there to Wankie's Town hoping to trade for ivory.

White. A man named White accompanied William Baldwin on his disastrous 1852 hippo-hunting trip to Saint Lucia Bay. Of the thirteen men associated with the venture, at least seven died during or shortly afterward, mainly from fever. White was a veteran elephant hunter, and apparently generated the idea of the entire Saint Lucia expedition. From Baldwin's memoirs it appears that White left the main group once everybody started becoming sick and dying. This didn't cause any hard feelings, apparently, because for a year after the fiasco White and Baldwin shared a shack on a farm where they eked out a living trading cattle.

White, Stewart Edward (1873–1946). White was a prolific and popular novelist (and a major figure in the Spiritualist movement) who jumped on the Theodore Roosevelt safari bandwagon. He wrote such books about his African trip as *Land of Footprints* (1912) and *African Campfires* (1913). They are typical post-Roosevelt fare, replete with details such as the trip to Mombasa, preparations for the hunt, etc.

Despite the opportunistic nature of his African literary work, White was a true sportsman. Professional hunter R. J. Cunninghame told Teddy Roosevelt that White was the best rifle shot he had ever seen. White returned to East Africa in 1925, hunting lion with a bow and arrows with the American archers Art Young and Saxton Pope. Both Pope and White wrote books about this safari. White's was titled *Lions in the Path* (1926). ROWLAND WARD 1928: LION, THOMSON GAZELLE.

Whitehouse, William Fitzhugh (1877–1955). A Yale graduate from Illinois, Whitehouse was only twenty-two years old when he joined Lt. Col. James Harrison in 1899 for what became known as the Harrison-Whitehouse Expedition to Lake Turkana. For details on that expedition see the entry on Harrison. Suffice it to say the young American enjoyed his first real adventure and above all his first elephant hunt. In 1902 he returned to Ethiopia for a ten-month hunting trip with Lord Hindlip, who wrote about this adventure in his 1906 book *Sport and Travel: Abyssinia and East Africa.*

Whitehouse was gassed while fighting with the 77th Infantry Division as a captain in France during World War I. He later moved to the wealthy resort town of Newport, Rhode Island, and served in the state legislature and with the Boy Scouts and other organizations. He never went back to Africa except for one brief trip to the Congo in 1952. ROWLAND WARD 1928: SOMALI HARTEBEEST, LESSER KUDU.

Whittet, R. Captain Whittet became an assistant game warden in Kenya in 1925 and was still listed in that post in 1930. He was stationed at Meru.

Whittingstall. A businessman from Acornhoek in the Transvaal, he for many years had the supply and catering contracts for Sabi Game Reserve and Kruger National Park. On one occasion a bull giraffe attacked him in his car, kicking in the radiator and wrecking it.

Whittingstall's favorite pastime was lion hunting, which he did on foot with one or two local trackers in the bush just outside the reserve's borders. He had great success at this, once killing a charging lion with a brain shot at a distance of three feet. One lioness caught him, however, as he was following her up in thick cover, and only the quick action of his trackers saved him, one spearing the lioness and the other pulling her tail.

Whyte, Alexander (1831–1912). A Fellow of the Royal Zoological Society and the Scottish Geographical Society, Whyte was appointed official botanist and natural history collector of British Central Africa by Harry Johnston in 1891. Previously he had owned and operated a successful plantation on Ceylon. He got the post in Johnston's administration by answering a "help wanted" advertisement in *The London Times.* Zoologist Philip Sclater helped Johnston make the selection.

It was a good choice. In Africa, Whyte founded a botanical garden at Zomba and was the first scientist to describe the African conifer *Widdringtonia whytei,* which has since been widely exported to various other countries including Great Britain. He displayed a natural aptitude for taxidermy and collecting, working in Nyasaland, Kenya, and Uganda. In 1904 he transferred to a similar post in Liberia and then finally retired in 1906.

Whyte was a prodigious writer, authoring numerous articles and several books, including *The Development of Africa* (1890).

Wickenburg, Eduard Ernst Karl Maria (1866–1936). An Austrian count, Wickenburg first visited Africa in 1897 on safari to Somalia. Refused permission to cross Ethiopia by the Emperor Menelik, Wickenburg returned to Vienna, only to come back to Africa in 1899 to climb Mount Kilimanjaro and do some museum collecting. In 1901 he conducted a long safari through the Northern Frontier Province, visiting Marsabit, Lake Rudolf, Lake Stephanie, and the Lorian Swamp.

From 1911–1914 Wickenburg went on an extensive expedition through South America. Unfortunately for posterity, he never wrote a book about his adventures and his diaries were destroyed during World War II. He died at the age of seventy while mountain climbing in Austria. In the 1980s Wickenburg's daughter traveled along the Kenya portion of his original route.

Wikar, Hendrik Jacob. Of Swedish origin, Wikar was an officer employed by the Dutch at Cape Town in the 1770s. Disgraced because of gambling debts, he deserted and lived for four years in the bush along the Orange River, hunting elephant in a forest of kokerboom trees *(Aloe dichotoma).* He kept a detailed diary during his hermitage. Wikar, who had a way with words and was not without charm, eventually wrote a letter to the Dutch governor Van Plettenburg that was so eloquent and moving that the governor pardoned him.

Wilhelm, Prince (1885–1965). Prince Wilhelm of Sweden went on an extensive gorilla-hunting expedition in 1921, centered on the White Fathers' mission at Lulenga in the Congo. He put quite a dent in the local gorilla population, shooting at least fourteen. There was a general consensus among sportsmen and the public alike, even then, that the gorilla was too grand an animal to be wantonly slaughtered, and the Prince (and others like him, such as the American, Burbridge) was much criticized.

Wilkinson, J. F. "Cap." Captain Wilkinson was a South African hunter of the 1860s.

Williams, Francis Wigley Greswolde. Frank Greswolde Williams arrived in Kenya in 1907 and took up cattle ranching. A leading member of the decadent "White Highlands" social set, Williams was that circle's chief source of morphine and cocaine. He had the drugs flown in from Port Said, and the transactions took place in the exclusive Muthaiga Club. He was known to give away generous amounts of coke to, for example, keep a band playing later than usual. In October of 1928 Williams was bodily ejected from the club by game warden Archie Ritchie after offering the Prince of Wales a blast of cocaine.

The faux pas apparently did not affect his social standing too much, given that Williams remained friendly with such as Lord Delamere and Denys Finch Hatton. Despite his unconventional social habits (he was an alcoholic as well as a drug dealer) and his appearance (he was overweight and had lost an eye in a 1917 shooting accident), Williams was a superb tracker and hunter. He was also generous and apparently had a great deal of unpretentious personal charm. Very wealthy, he lived on a ranch he called Knightwick and owned several other houses and estates in both Britain and East Africa. Karen Blixen hunted buffalo on his ranch in 1917 and lion in 1919. A few years later he arranged an illegal abortion for Beryl Markham in London. His only son was killed in action in German East Africa during World War I. ROWLAND WARD 1928: BUFFALO, LION, RED-FRONTED GAZELLE, PATTERSON ELAND.

Williams, Frederick Raban (1874–1944). As a young man of eighteen, Raban Williams prospected for gold in Canada. He found none but learned how to survey land and to hunt for food. In 1897 he came to Africa as a soldier, serving in the Bulawayo Burgher Force during a Zulu uprising. When that skirmish (or massacre, pick your term—it was basically a "Wounded Knee" type of affair) was over, Williams went hunting and prospecting. He teamed up for a while with Fred Selous, and then tried his hand working on a tramp steamer.

After a few years at sea Williams took a job with the Benguela Railway. Like many professional hunters of his day, he made a living shooting buffalo to feed the rail workers. He also did surveying work and exploration for the railroad companies, traveling and hunting his way through the Belgian Congo and British East Africa.

Shortly after the outbreak of the 1914 war, Williams married a rich mining heiress, a beautiful and charming nineteen-year-old. He was commissioned a lieutenant in the British army and was wounded on the Western Front at the Battle of Loos. Like Karamojo Bell, he wound up in the Royal Flying Corps as a pilot. Unlike Bell, he wanted to stay with the RAF in the postwar years, but the effects of his wounds forced him to retire from the military in 1920.

Williams spent his remaining years doing railroad survey work in Canada, Alaska, and Egypt, as well as a 1925–1930 stint with the Uganda Railway. He retired to England in 1930 and died fourteen years later after serving as a member of Britain's Home Guard against the potential Nazi invasion.

Williams, George Washington (1849–1891). Col. George Washington Williams was a black American journalist with no military experience—he had been made an officer of the Minnesota militia as a reward for making a donation to the state treasury. After several failed business ventures and a term as the American minister to Haiti, he applied to Belgium's King Leopold for a post in the Congo but was rejected. Williams went to Africa on his own and was appalled at the brutal methods the Europeans were using to exploit rubber and other resources from the Congo.

In 1890 Williams wrote an open letter to Leopold that caused a minor sensation in the world press. In this letter he tasked the king for his hypocrisy, accusing him of mouthing philanthropic platitudes while permitting the brutal and immoral acts that characterized the Free State. One of the first public denunciations of Leopold and the Free State, Williams's letter was attacked by Leopold's propaganda machine and widely dismissed by the public.

Williams also earned a spot in the books with his innovative research methods. In preparing two noteworthy books, *A History of Negro Troops in the War of the Republic 1861–1865* and *History of the Negro Race,* Williams pioneered the use of oral history, interviewing veterans of the American Civil War and other events. The use of eyewitness accounts from men who were common soldiers, not generals or admirals or Presidents, was not only ahead of its time but also an early divergence from the prevailing "Great Man" theory of history.

Williams died at age forty-one from tuberculosis. He left both a wife and a fiancée.

Williams, J. H. A British Royal Artillery officer, Capt. J. H. Williams led a detachment of reinforcements to Uganda in 1891. The explorer Frederick Lugard was attempting to secure the country for the British East Africa Company but was meeting with stolid resistance. Williams was technically senior to Lugard but wisely allowed the more experienced man to retain command.

Lugard put Williams in charge of whipping the ragtag army of Zanzibaris, Swahilis, and Sudanese into shape, a job at which he proved very adept. When in early 1892 it appeared the IBEA (see glossary) was going to abruptly evacuate the country, leaving it open to annexation by the Germans or French, Williams agreed with Lugard that if necessary they would launch an unauthorized military coup and claim Uganda for Britain. As it turned out, the 1892–1893 expedition led by Sir Gerald Portal took the matter out of Williams's hands in an entirely satisfactory way, by proclaiming a British Protectorate over the region.

Williams was promoted to major and left in charge of the country in Lugard's absence. Portal recorded in his diary entry for 21 March 1893 how Williams had just returned from a hunting trip with *The Times* correspondent Gedge. The two had shot twenty-four Speke antelope.

Williams, Sir Ralph (1848–1927). This British civil servant, a friend of Selous, penetrated Africa's interior as early as 1883, when his wife was quite possibly the first white woman to see Victoria Falls.

In 1904 Williams became resident commissioner of Bechuanaland. Upon leaving that post, he took a farewell safari with Arnold Hodson to Victoria Falls, arriving there twenty-three years to the day after his first visit (16 August 1906). In 1909–1912 he was governor of Newfoundland.

Throughout his career he was an eager hunter and sportsman. On the 1906 safari, Hodson saw him fire four times. The first shot killed a jackal at two hundred yards with a .303, the second shot killed a tsessebe, the third and fourth were left and rights with a double, bringing down two more jackal. Hodson later saw Williams shoot a crocodile through the eye at two hundred yards.

Willis Brothers. Well-known elephant- and buffalo-hunting brothers P. W. Willis and C. Willis were affectionately known as "Pump" and "Clinkers." They hunted tuskers in South Africa in the 1890s. At the start of the Boer War they had just returned from a hunting trip in the interior when, along with Harry Wolhuter, they joined Steinacker's Horse. While on guard duty one night, Clinkers Willis narrowly escaped becoming the victim of a man-eating lion whose claw reached through a barricade behind which Willis was posted. The paw flashed in and out, missing Willis by inches. No more was seen of that lion until days later when future Sabi ranger Major Francis tracked him down and killed him.

Clinkers Willis later became a fireman on the railroad that went through the Sabi Game Reserve, while Pumps ran a general store out of a corrugated iron shack at Acornhoek.

Willoughby, Sir John Christopher (1859–1918). A British officer during the First Matabele War of 1893, Willoughby worked for the British South Africa Company. He was the author of *East Africa and Its Big Game* (1889) and *A Narrative of Further Excavations at Zimbabye* (Mashonaland) (1893).

Wilmot, Edward Cronje (1890–xxxx). Born in Grahamstown, South Africa, Wilmot moved to Bechuanaland when he was fifteen and spent the rest of his life there. He was a successful rancher who gained an immense amount of big-cat hunting experience by shooting leopards and lions in protection of his livestock. When his wife Enid Maud passed away in the early 1940s, Wilmot deeded the ranch to his son Bobby. He then took a position with the Maun veterinary services department as a tsetse fly ranger, in one of those unfortunate programs where thousands of game animals were shot in an attempt to check the spread of the fly. About the best that can be said about such programs is that they were thought necessary at the time. Wilmot was the author of *Okavango Adventure* and *Always Tread Lightly.*

Wilson, Allan (1856–1893). Major Wilson was the General Custer of the 1893 Matabele War. After the initial battles of the campaign, the Matabele had fled from their capital of Bulawayo, led by the despotic king Lobengula. Wilson, an adroit leader of a battalion of scouts (the unit's personnel included both Bill Buckley and Frederick Burnham), was detached with a special flying column of less than forty men in an attempt to capture the fugitive king. Rising floodwaters isolated the squadron from the main army across the Shangani River, and they were surrounded and wiped out by the Matabele in a furious last stand. The fate of the Shangani Patrol stood as an inspirational example of desperate courage for several generations of Rhodesians.

According to Buckley (1930), when peace was made the Matabele told an interesting story. Two British troopers named Wilson and Daniels had been on outpost duty at the time of Lobengula's flight. The defeated king had sent a high-born emissary to find an appropriate authority to sue for peace and given the emissary £1,000 in gold pieces as tribute. The first white men the emissary found were Wilson and Daniels, who took the gold and promised they would pass the message on. They didn't. If they had, many lives might have been saved, including those of Major Wilson and his thirty-five men.

The Matabele could describe the soldiers who had taken the gold but didn't, of course, know their names. The authorities were furious and began to investigate the incident. Wilson and Daniels attracted suspicion by apparently dumping stacks of gold coins on various poker tables, and were arrested and identified by the Matabele as the soldiers involved. The two men were lucky to get off with stiff prison terms of fourteen years apiece. The terms were later commuted when they volunteered to serve in the 1896 Matabele uprising.

Wilson, Benjamin "Matabele" (1861–1959). Born in England, Wilson moved to South Africa at the age of twenty and was a member of Charles Warren's Bechuanaland expedition in 1883. Directly afterward he explored the Kalahari and visited Bulawayo as early as 1888. Wilson fought in both the 1893 Matabele War and the 1896 rebellion; he later settled down as a rancher. He died in Cape Town at an advanced age.

Wilson, James C. (1900–1995). James Wilson rode a motorcycle from Lagos to Khartoum and then to Eritrea in 1927–1928. Wilson was accompanied by a friend named Francis Flood. Both were graduates of the University of Nebraska, Wilson having been out of school for five years and Flood seven at the time of their adventures. They were an unlikely pair for an African odyssey: Wilson was a farmhand and an itinerant musician who played in subways and honkytonks while Flood was a writer for an agricultural news syndicate and had never even been on a motorcycle. This wasn't their first adventure together, for five years before they had "dish-washed ourselves to Alaska" and taken a rowboat down the Yukon River.

The two Americans arranged a passage to Africa on board a freighter belonging to the Shipping Board. While on the ship, they worked out the details of their partnership. Flood agreed to produce travel articles about their ports-of-call for the agricultural syndicate while Wilson (an accomplished saxophone player) would help with the writing and also entertain the colonial officials and natives they met along the way with a banjo.

Their original plan was to travel along the west coast of Africa without venturing into the interior. While visiting Lagos, Nigeria, the men heard people talking about an Englishman named Frank Gray who had driven an automobile laterally across Africa. Flood suggested that they jump ship and attempt the same journey on motorcycles, a feat that had never before been accomplished. He and Wilson managed to procure two British-made light motorcycles with sidecars attached (nicknamed "Rough" and "Tumble"). After loading up with maps and spare parts, they left Lagos on the first leg of their 3,800-mile journey.

The route went from Lagos to Jebba to Bida-Kano-Zinder to Lake Chad to Moussoro to Abeshr-el Obeid to Khartoum and then almost straight eastward to Massawa. They were aided in their meetings with the local tribesmen by Wilson's proficient use of the banjo and had little trouble, at least with people. Nature was another story, for they encountered floods, rains, sand storms, and drought. They went hunting for elephant with a French officer named Captain Le Blanc near Lake Chad but came up empty-handed. By the time they reached decent game country near the town of Mao, they had discarded their rifles on account of the weight. The final leg of their trip was uneventful, and when they reached Massowa they sold their motorcycles and booked first-class passage to India.

Wilson was the author of *Three Wheeling Through Africa* (1936), as well as a long *National Geographic* article of the same name in January 1934. The book is your standard travel account, nothing special and rather on the dull side, with only the sections that concern the drought and the effects of running out of water meriting any real interest.

After his return from Africa in 1928, Wilson got a job as an English professor at Iowa State University. After three years he was forced to resign because of his lack of a Ph.D. He and his wife Alice moved to Chicago (years later Wilson wrote that their total life savings consisted of $212, a broken down Chevy, and a tent) so that he could look for work. Before leaving Iowa State, he composed a song and submitted it as an entry in a contest to pick the new college anthem. After he had arrived in Chicago and just before he had given up hope of finding a job, Wilson was notified that his entry had been chosen as the winner. The song, "The Bells of Iowa State," is still the official anthem of the school. With the money from the contest, Wilson was able to buy a small cottage where he could raise his family.

Winter, W. A. Bill Winter was a hunter at Treetops Hotel in the 1930s and 1940s.

Winton, Sir Francis de (1835–1901). Winton was administrator general of the Congo operations of the International Association of the Congo 1884–1886, and administrator of the IBEA (see glossary) 1890–1891. He was also a director of the IBEA from its inception in 1888.

Wissmann, Herrmann von (1853–1905). Wissmann (the von came later) was born in Frankfurt-am-Oder in 1853. As a young man, Lieutenant Wissmann (Prussian army) was the only member of the 1880 Pogge expedition to successfully cross the African continent from Angola to Zanzibar, completing the trans-Africa trip in 1881–1882. From 1882 to 1887 he was in the employ of Leopold II and the Congo Free State (exploring the Kasai River in 1883, for instance), after which he was named imperial commissioner for German East Africa.

In 1886–1887 Wissmann made his second trip across Africa. He was thus the fifth and the tenth European to cross the continent. He left the mouth of the Congo in October 1886 with eighty-nine followers. The size of the safari was later increased to about a thousand men when various African leaders loaned him porters and guides.

Wissmann started heading on a northeasterly course but, after meeting much difficulty, gave up that plan and instead went southeast, along the lines of the route he had taken five years earlier. He found that the Beneki country, which had been lush and populous before, had in the interim been devastated by a combination of tribal warfare, the slave trade, and smallpox. Wissmann continued on through the Zambezi Valley and the Lake Nyasa district before reaching the eastern shore.

In 1888–1890 Wissmann organized the administration of German East Africa and crushed the Arab Abushiri revolt in Tanganyika. Afterward he concentrated on combating the Arabs in the Lake Nyasa district. Harry Johnston, his British counterpart in East Africa, held Wissmann in great esteem as an honorable man and an extremely capable administrator.

Wissmann was one of the most able and respected of the German colonial administrators, a group generally distinguished by their severity rather than by any particular talent. He has a unique place in the history of conservation. As governor of German East Africa, Wissmann was instrumental in setting up the first International Conference for the Protection of Wild Animals in 1900. Attendees included representatives from the United Kingdom, Germany, France, Spain, Portugal, Italy, and the (Belgian) Congo Free State. More symbolic than effective, this meeting was still a milestone in conservation history. Von Wissmann did take some effective conservation measures, particularly setting aside game reserves and promoting restrictive game laws. He was the first major colonial figure to push for a ban on the sale of immature elephant tusks, prohibiting it in German East Africa and pressuring Zanzibar into accepting the ban in 1904.

Like many of the great colonial figures in the days before antibiotics, Wissmann died young. He was the author of *Im Innern Afrika* (1888) and *Unter Deutscher Flagge Quer Durch Afrika* (1889).

Wolhuter, Harry Christopher (1877–1964). Born 14 February 1877 at Beaufort West, the Karoo, South Africa, Wolhuter took his first job at age fourteen at a trading post in Maraisburg. From there he went to a bar and pool hall in Johannesburg, where he learned to play pool and other urban skills. After a time he longed for the country and returned to his family, who had relocated to Legogote in the eastern Transvaal. While running a trading post and cattle ranch, he was all but wiped out by the rinderpest epidemic of 1896. Shortly thereafter he was drafted to fight in the Magato campaign, where he apparently saw some skirmishing action.

When the campaign ended, Wolhuter started hunting in the area that is now Kruger National Park, only to enlist in Col. Ludwig Steinacker's volunteer cavalry shortly after the start of the Boer War. He eventually rose to the odd rank of "de facto" officer, drawing officer's pay but not holding official rank. His duties centered around scouting and foraging.

When peace settled in, Steinacker's Horse was used to garrison the northeast corner of the Transvaal. At this time the newly appointed Warden of the Sabi Game Reserve, Maj. James Stevenson-Hamilton, was looking for qualified game rangers. Wolhuter was recommended to him as a superb scout and hunter. After some discussion, Wolhuter took the job at the salary of £1 per day, not a lot of money even by 1902 standards. He was the second ranger hired after Paul Bester. Wolhuter took over the northern and western parts of the reserve and started the job of administering the area, hiring native police (at £2 per month), and erecting the first primitive buildings at his base at Pretorius Kop.

On 26 August 1903, after just about a year on the job, an event happened that emblazoned Wolhuter's name forever in the annals of hunting history. Wolhuter was on a mounted patrol with his dog, Bull, trotting faithfully by his side, riding alone at sunset toward a water hole called Metsimetsi Spruit. Suddenly a charging lion knocked him off his horse, full on top of another lion. The second lion bit into his right shoulder and started dragging him away while the first lion chased after the fleeing horse. Bull went running after the horse and lion. Unlike Livingstone, Wolhuter immediately felt excruciating pain in his shoulder, worsening every time the lion shook its head to bump him over weeds and rocks. Wolhuter noted that the lion was purring loudly the whole time. The distance he was dragged was later stepped off as sixty yards.

Carefully, Wolhuter reached with his left hand down to his belt and found that his sheath knife was still there. This in itself was a miracle—twice before he had been thrown from his horse and the knife had fallen out. The wounded ranger carefully calculated the best place to aim to hit the lion's heart and then stabbed the animal twice in quick succession behind the left shoulder.

The lion roared furiously, and Wolhuter stabbed it again, this time in the throat. Miraculously, he severed the lion's jugular vein. The lion backed away, spraying blood all over, and slunk off into the deepening dusk.

Badly hurt, Wolhuter could hear the wounded lion moaning nearby and started shouting at it, hoping to scare it away. Then he remembered that yet another lion was about. He managed to clamber twelve feet up a tree, just in time to hear the one lion die and the other arrive. The tree was leaning over and not impossible for a lion to climb. Wolhuter thought his number was up, but then his dog Bull reappeared out of nowhere and kept the lion distracted by barking and dodging for an hour. Finally some of Wolhuter's African staff appeared and chased the surviving lion away.

After rubbing the wounds with salt in a desperate attempt to avoid infection, Wolhuter had to be carried for five days to reach medical treatment. Even so, the doctors thought he would die. The wounds turned septic, and his arm and shoulder were greatly swollen and stank of infection. It took several weeks for him to recover—indeed, he never again had full use of his right arm. For the next forty years he could barely manage to lift the arm enough to fire a rifle, but manage he did. His courageous dog Bull was later killed by a baboon.

In 1903 Denis Lyell met Wolhuter's brother in Durban. Retelling the tale in his 1923 *Memories of an African Hunter,* Lyell indicates that some folks were initially skeptical of the lion story. The incident was well documented, however, and to this day visitors to Kruger National Park can see the site of the attack and the tree in which Wolhuter sought refuge.

Wolhuter continued his amazing career as a game ranger, retiring in 1946. He had many other experiences, such as gunfights with native poachers (one of whom just barely missed his much abused right shoulder with a black-powder gun), and was charged several other times by lion while on horseback. During the early years the reserve had a policy of shooting lion on sight. The theory was that a reduced lion population would permit the herds of grazing animals to recover. Wolhuter excelled at this task (as did his chief, Stevenson-Hamilton) and shot at least 150 lion during these years.

A tall, wiry man, he had some quirks to his character. For instance, he had stolen the knife that killed the lion from a shop where it was being used to cut cheese. He felt it was inappropriate to use such a fine knife on such a mundane task, so when the shopkeeper wasn't looking, he switched it with a much cheaper blade.

Harry C. Wolhuter.

On another occasion, while he was with Steinacker's Horse, Wolhuter was unhorsed while carrying the unit payroll. The horse started to run off with the money in the saddlebags, so he shot it—his own horse! To avoid ridicule from his fellow troopers, he made up a story about the beast dying from *nagana* (see glossary). Such little slips of character were presumably just remnants of his youthful pool-hall days. His courage and ability were never in doubt and were proven time and again.

In 1948 Wolhuter wrote his memoirs, *Memories of a Game Ranger.* An interesting book, it has a certain additional charm in that he tends to focus more on everyday details such as the lives of his pet dogs and the eccentricities of animals and so-called witch doctors than on more dramatic events.

Wollaston, A. F. R. (1875–1930). Wollaston was a naturalist who made several trips through East Africa, Tanganyika, and the Congo. His book *From Ruwenzori to the Congo* (1908) contains chapters on big-game hunting, botany, and African diseases.

Wolverton, Lord (1864–1932). The author of *Five Months Sport in Somaliland* (1894), Lord Wolverton hunted the area northeast of Jubaland with Col. Arthur Page in the early 1890s. Typical of the exorbitant bags collected by the early explorer–hunters, the pair shot thirty-two lion.

Wood, George. (xxxx–1882). The brother of hunter Swithin Wood and the half-brother of Thomas Wood, George Wood is virtually forgotten today but in his time was recognized as one of the great elephant hunters. Among his contemporaries he was comparable only to Fred Green, Bill Finaughty, Jan Viljoen, Henry Hartley, and Piet Jacobs for experience and total number of kills. By the time Selous first hunted with him in 1872, the future legend could write that Wood had "probably shot more elephants than any Englishman living." Wood, a regular member of the southern African hunting syndicates of the 1860s, continued his activities even though other hunters had given up when the elephants disappeared from all but the tsetse-fly zones.

Wood hunted with Selous for the better part of two years in the early 1870s. During the course of one four-month trip in 1872, Wood shot about fifty elephants while Selous killed forty-two; their Matabele partners accounted for nearly another forty. The following year they were hunting buffalo when Wood's quick reflexes and superior marksmanship prevented a tragic accident. When one of the party wounded a cow buffalo, the buffalo charged, and the hunters scattered. Even though the men were mounted and on open ground, the buffalo caught up to one of Selous's Hottentot servants who was riding a borrowed horse that belonged to Lobengula. The buffalo hit the horse right in the thigh, sending the rider sprawling to the ground. Wood reined in and coolly put a bullet right between the buffalo's shoulders, stopping the charge just before the animal could turn on the fallen servant.

George Wood visited Barotseland in 1882, but his entire party contracted malaria and perished to a man. Wood died at Deka, not far from what is now Hwange National Park.

Wood, Thomas (xxxx–1868). Thomas Wood was a South African elephant hunter of the 1860s, and half-brother of George and Swithin Wood, both hunters themselves. Thomas also worked as a carpenter and a trader. He died of fever in Mashonaland with Christiaan Harmse in 1868. George Wood died of malaria in 1882.

Woodhouse, C. W. An assistant game ranger in Kenya from 1911–1918, Woodhouse carried the first living specimen of lungfish ever to leave Africa to the Reptile House of the Regent's Park Zoo. He ensured its safe journey by packing it in a tin of thick mud. Once safely in London, he washed it off with warm water to revive it, and it suddenly tried to bite his fingers off.

In 1914 Woodhouse was on predator control duty, shooting lion around Naivasha. In the process he killed a lion that measured 11 feet, 1 inch, dressed, from tip of nose to tip of tail, earning him a listing in the 1928 edition of *Rowland Ward's Records of Big Game.*

Woodruff, Louis. A professional hunter employed by the firm of Safariland, Ltd., in the 1920s.

Woosnam, Richard Bowen (1880–1915). R. B. Woosnam is one of the forgotten men of the early Kenya wildlife scene. Born in Builth, Wales, he served in the Boer War and then went on a hunting and collecting trip to the Persian Gulf and the Black Sea. He returned to Africa in 1905 as a member of the British Museum's Ruwenzori Expedition, collecting birds and mammals at Ruwenzori and in the Ituri Forest with a friend named Dent.

In 1910 Woosman was appointed the senior game ranger in Kenya, succeeding John Patterson and serving until 1915. He specialized in lion control and also did quite a bit of collecting work for the British Museum. During the First World War, Woosnam first commanded an intelligence unit at British headquarters in East Africa. After being transferred to the Mediterranean, he was killed at Gallipoli in 1915. His collections of natural history and ethnographic artifacts are housed in the British Museum.

Worthington, Bayley. Cousin of Norman B. Smith, he hunted East Africa circa 1910.

Wright, Sandy. Wright was a Scottish farmer who settled in Kenya in the early 1900s. He obtained his stake by shooting buffalo and selling their hides in the Kavirondo district, where they were used to make warriors' shields. He took payment in cattle and soon bought a ranch near Lake Nakuru. Wright eventually assumed a seat on the Legislative Council.

Y

Yebes, Count Edward De. A Spanish big-game hunter with a preference for the 9.3mm magnum rifle, Yebes was the author of *Twenty Years a Big Game Hunter* (1943).

York, Duke and Duchess of. The duke and duchess of York went on a well-publicized East African safari in 1924. ROWLAND WARD 1928: (DUKE): PATTERSON ELAND, NILE LECHWE, ELEPHANT, WHITE RHINO, KONGONI, BUFFALO, LELWEL HARTEBEEST. ROWLAND WARD 1928: (DUCHESS): KONGONI, NILE LECHWE.

Young, Art (1883–1935). An American archery enthusiast, Young in the 1920s decided to test his theory that modern bowhunting did not require firearms as a backup. He went to Alaska in 1923 and hunted brown bears armed only with a bow. In 1925 he accompanied his friend Saxton Pope and the Spiritualist writer Stewart Edward White on a seven-month bowhunting trip to the Serengeti. Together the three men killed fifty-two male lion.

Young, Edward Daniel (1831–xxxx). A lieutenant in the Royal Navy, Young led a Livingstone rescue expedition in 1867. Hunter Henry Faulkner accompanied him in this unsuccessful quest. Young later (1875–1876) mapped the Lake Nyasa region. He was the author of *Nyassa* (1877).

The duke (far left) and duchess of York, with Osa Johnson (far right) and staff members.

Yule, James B. (xxxx–1914). Yule owned a ranch in Northeastern Rhodesia in the early 1900s and often went elephant hunting to supplement his income. This habit proved his undoing. In May of 1914 he was charged by a wounded elephant that first seized his rifle and threw it into the bush and then drove a tusk right through his abdomen. Yule's African assistants scared the elephant off, but he died the next day from his injuries. ROWLAND WARD 1899: LICHTENSTEIN HARTEBEEST, KLIPSPRINGER, WARTHOG.

Z

Zaphiro, Fotios. Fotios Zaphiro, called Philip, was a Kenyan taxidermist and professional hunter of Greek descent who accompanied William McMillan on his abortive 1903 Blue Nile expedition. From 1905 to 1908 Zaphiro was the boundary inspector for Kenya's northern border and worked with Gwynn's Abyssinian Boundary Commission. It was Zaphiro who convinced Gwynn to adjust the border in order to put the best water holes on the Kenya side. He was also responsible for overseeing the construction of Fort Harrington at Moyale.

For several years Zaphiro was the only official British presence in what became the Northern Frontier Province, assisted by perhaps twenty or thirty African policemen. He was the father of Dennis Zaphiro, a game warden and hunter of the postwar era.

Zarafi. This African chief was on the slavers' side during the 1890s Nyasaland campaign. Zarafi, whose stronghold was a town on a rugged hilltop some twenty miles east of Fort Johnston, was a formidable enemy. When J. G. King led a mixed assault force of Sikhs, Zanzibaris, and Angoni warriors against him in February 1892, Zarafi not only smashed the column (badly wounding King in the process) but also captured a seven-pounder cannon. Losing an artillery piece was a huge symbolic disgrace to a nineteenth-century army, and the loss of the gun probably rankled more than the defeat itself. The gun was recovered when a stronger British force assaulted his mountain in 1895, and Zarafi fled into the wilderness of Portuguese East Africa.

Zimmerman, Paul. A Silesian native, Zimmerman served in the German army during World War I and arrived in Kenya in 1929. He had been in Africa on and off since 1911, making a trip back to the Fatherland in 1914. Zimmerman had studied taxidermy at the Wiesbaden Natural History Museum and set up shop in Nairobi. He quickly became known as a first-class preparer of mounts and trophies and handled many difficult specimens for rich British and American sportsmen, European aristocrats, and prestigious museums. At his firm's peak in the 1950s and 1960s, he employed 130 African assistants, all experts in the art of taxidermy.

Zintgraff, Eugen (1858–1897). Dr. Zintgraff explored the rivers and other waterways of German Cameroon in 1887, attempting to locate a navigable channel to the interior of the country. He explored the Vuri, Dibombe, and Meme Rivers and was the first European to explore the Bakossi Mountains. In 1888 he and thirty porters made an abortive attempt to build an observatory at Lake Elephant in the Cameroons. On an expedition that began 1 January 1889, Zintgraff set out from Lagos with 180 Africans to explore the area around the Benue River. He met immediate resistance from the Banyang tribe, who first tried to stall him with a subterfuge and then repeatedly attacked the column when he proceeded on. Passing into a peaceful district, Zintgraff spent two months collecting ivory and building a trading station, and then marched on to Ibi on the Benue. On the way back the expedition was camped one night on a hill about six hundred feet high when a storm broke. The wind, rain, and hail were so severe and the temperature dropped so much that overnight sixteen of his men died. The survivors returned to the coast in July without further incident.

Zintgraff also was the first European to encounter various African tribes in the area. Sometimes these encounters were not to his benefit: In January 1891, for example, Zintgraff's safari was attacked by the Barfut tribe at Baghirmi (southeast of Lake Chad) and a third of his men were killed.

Zwilling, Ernst A. (1904–1990). Though not well known in the English-speaking world, Ernst Zwilling was a hunter and an extremely popular writer whose books sold by the hundreds of thousands in his native Europe. Born in Austria in 1904, Zwilling earned a college degree in agriculture and moved to Cameroon in 1928, taking a position as assistant manager of a tobacco plantation. As with so many of his contemporaries, Zwilling was hit hard by the Great Depression and lost his job when the plantation went bust in 1930.

He took his life's savings, bought a rifle and hunting outfit, and went into the bush. For the next decade he wandered West Africa from Cameroon to Lake Chad, traveling on horseback in search of big and exotic game. Zwilling made his living by supplying European zoos and museums with rare specimens, and also wrote a series of books about his adventures. These were published largely in Germany and Austria (one English-language edition, *Jungle Fever,* was issued in London in 1956) and proved hugely popular.

Zwilling's career was interrupted by the outbreak of war in 1939, and he didn't return to the bush until 1956, when he went hunting in Angola. The following year he moved his operation to Uganda and began an affiliation as a

PH and game manager with the semigovernmental Uganda Wildlife company, an association that he maintained until the late 1970s.

Ernst Zwilling died in his native Austria in 1990. His autobiography was published posthumously in German in 1991 under the title *Der Wildnis Verfallen.*

Annotated Glossary

Askari. An African soldier in European service, or safari guard.

Assegai. A type of spear popular in southern Africa. A light variation was used for throwing, and the Zulu king Shaka popularized a heavier, shorter version, used for stabbing. In the hands of trained warriors it was as deadly as the short sword used by Roman legionaries.

Baas. A term of respect, like "Master" or "Bwana."

Bilharzia. Also known as bilharziasis and schistosomiasis, bilharzia is a deadly disease named after its discoverer, a German parasitologist named Bilharz (1825–1862). The disease is transmitted by immature snail flukes that can be found in many freshwater sources in tropical Africa. The tiny threadlike flukes enter the bodies of those humans unwise enough to wade in infested water, taking up residence in various organs such as the liver and brain. Scientist R. T. Leiper was the first to realize the role of the snail fluke in the progression of the illness. The disease is painful and debilitating and eventually fatal. For many years the standard treatment was to poison the patient with what was hoped to be a sublethal dosage of antimony tartrate. Precautions have hugely reduced the incidence of bilharzia. The disease was practically an epidemic in the British army in Egypt during World War I, but almost nonexistent in the same army in the same place twenty years later.

Biltong. Uncooked meat, dried in the sun (usually in a cool breeze) and often heavily seasoned with pepper and other spices to make a long-lasting, nutritious form of jerky.

Blackwater fever. A much feared complication of malaria (fatal in up to ninety percent of cases) characterized by darkened urine that looks like port wine (hence the name) and dehydration. Blackwater was the scourge of the tropics as long as quinine was the main anti-malarial drug in use. Various theories were proposed about precisely how malaria turned into blackwater. Many hunters and settlers suspected that it was caused by too much quinine being taken by somebody who wasn't used to it. It is now believed that blackwater was indeed a symptom of quinine overdose, and the disease largely disappeared once quinine was replaced by Atabrine in the 1940s as the number one anti-malarial prophylactic. Professor Robert Koch of Germany was the first to recognize the connection between blackwater and quinine, but his warning went unheeded.

Boma. A fortified place, particularly a government headquarters.

Bonosoora. Kabarega's elite bodyguard, recruited from escaped slaves.

BSAC. British South Africa Company, the charter company that was also the de facto government of Rhodesia until the 1920s. Chartered in 1889.

Buffalo bean. An inoffensive-looking vine with little reddish-brown bean pods covered by tiny hairs. The irritation and itching caused by touching the pod are so bad it is considered one of the major curses of Africa. Consider this 1933 statement from a very tough man, Commander David Blunt: "Scratching does no good, for it only spreads the irritation; rubbing with dry earth or sand has little effect, but the irritation is so intense that one rubs the skin until it is raw." To make matters worse, the hairs of the buffalo bean linger in clothing, causing renewed attacks when the careless victim tries on an old shirt or sweater. The buffalo bean is presumably the same loathsome plant called the *chitasi* bean by Lyell in 1923. Recalcitrant African workers in the Belgian Congo were sometimes punished by being doused with a powder made from the buffalo bean.

Bwana. Master, or Sir—a term of respect used by Africans toward Europeans.

Charter Company. Any of several commercial enterprises specially commissioned by the British Crown to develop or operate in a specific area. Some of the more famous charter companies were the British South Africa Company, the Imperial British East Africa Company, the African Lakes Company, and the Royal Niger Company. In African historical literature, in the absence of any other reference point "charter company" often refers to the BSAC.

Chemosit. A cryptid of East Africa; also called the Nandi Bear.

Chila. A communal hunt in Rhodesia.

Chitemene. A form of slash-and-burn agriculture, common in Rhodesia.

Chui. Leopard.

Collector. An early term for district commissioner.

Cornac. Elephant trainer at the Belgian Congo training schools, analogous to the Indian mahout.

Cryptid. An animal that is suspected to exist but is not accepted by conventional scientists.

Cryptozoology. The study of cryptids or "unknown animals," creatures that conventional scientists consider mythical, extinct, or in some cases foreign to that particular area—for example the Loch Ness Monster, Bigfoot, the thylacine, dinosaurs in the modern Congo, and lion and tiger in southern England.

Dagga. Marijuana. In widespread use in the Zambezi Valley and the Congo during the historical period covered by this book—also in my high school in the 1970s.

Dak bungalow. Dak bungalows were government rest houses set out at intervals along the road, for use by officials traveling on government business. Originally developed in India, the concept was imported to British East Africa in the last days of the nineteenth century. In BEA the dak houses were catered by J. A. Nazareth & Company, a Goanese firm, and tended to resemble inns more than they did the original official houses. Meals were provided at nominal cost, and were served by white-coated waiters along with wine stewards and barmen. Elspeth Huxley late in life recalled that "the food was pretty dreadful and the drinks tepid" (1985). Comments in the guest book frequently remarked on the pervasive stench of garlic. Coming from Mombasa, the first dak bungalow was at Voi, a hundred miles inland, and there were several more before the terminus in Uganda.

DBS. Distressed British Subject—official classification for indigent or vagrant British subjects in foreign territory. A DBS could apply to the British consul for a loan, charity, or a ticket (in steerage) back to England.

Debi. [also spelled Debbi]. Airtight four-gallon tin originally used for gasoline or paraffin but often adapted for other uses.

Dingonek. East African cryptid—a fifteen-foot aquatic horned beast.

District Commissioner. The basic administrative officer of British colonies. The district commissioner was subordinate to the provincial commissioner but superior to the district officer, and was the Crown's representative to the African people in the district. Kenya and Tanganyika usually had about thirty to forty district commissioners each, while Uganda had about fifteen and Nyasaland approximately twenty.

District Officer. Administrative officer subordinate to the district commissioner in a British colony. The typical DC had three to five district officers. The term was occasionally used to mean both DCs and DOs.

Donga. Dry streambed.

DSO. Distinguished Service Order.

Duka. A small general store, often owned by Indians.

EAPHA. East African Professional Hunter's Association. Formed at Nairobi's Norfolk Hotel on 12 April 1934, it was an elite group; in the late 1930s there were only twenty-one members. EAPHA was disbanded when Kenya banned hunting in the late 1970s.

EARB. The *East African Red Book*, an invaluable almanac published sporadically in the 1920s and 1930s. It contained a wealth of information on the histories, game laws, economics, and governments of Kenya, Uganda, Tanganyika and Zanzibar. The EARB also contained resident directories that listed most of the European families of those colonies.

EAUNHS. East Africa and Uganda Natural History Society. Based in Nairobi, the Society was established in 1909 by C. W. Hobley and Sir Frederick Jackson. Blayney Percival was vice president of the society for many years, and Archie Ritchie was a Trustee. It ran a museum that became the Coryndon Museum (now the National Museum of Kenya) when ownership was transferred to a Board of Trustees in 1930.

Elephantiasis. A disease caused by the *Filaria* parasite. It can cause arms and legs to resemble those of an elephant, hence the name, and the testicles to swell to over a foot in diameter. The parasite, *Filaria bancrofti*, grows to three inches in length and lives in the victim's lymphatic system. Its microscopic young are transmitted by the mosquito *Culex fatigans*. According to Elspeth Huxley (1987), for many years it was thought the disease was caused by eating limes.

EPRE. Emin Pasha Relief Expedition.

Fataki. Cheap, muzzleloading percussion-cap muskets, usually manufactured in Birmingham, England, that were used as trade goods in East Africa in the early 1900s.

Ferik. A nomad camp in the Sudan.

Filaria. A gruesome tropical disease in which threadlike worms invade the eyeball, causing blindness. Mary Kingsley came across a typical case in West Africa in 1894: ". . . the entire white of one eye being full of the active little worms and a ridge of surplus population migrating across the bridge of the nose into the other eye, under the skin, looking like the bridge of a pair of spectacles." (Kingsley, *Travels in West Africa*, 1897). The parasite that causes filaria is named *Stephanofilaria dinniki* and it has an unusual association with the black rhino, which see. The same type of parasite causes the disease elephantiasis.

Fisi. Hyena.

Frontiers: Frontier police—paramilitary force in British Sierra Leone, African askaris with European officers and Creole NCOs. The frontiers were formed in 1890.

Funza. Jiggers or sand fleas.

Gamaxene. An insect poison used mixed with bran to kill locusts during their flightless "hopper" stage.

GCMG. British title—Knight Grand Cross of the Order of Saint Michael and Saint George ("God Calls Me God") see KCMG.

Goat bag. The British colonial establishment in Africa was known for efficiency, incorruptibility, and, above all, parsimony. The degree of sheer bureaucratic nonsense that surrounded any attempt to tap Britain's treasury was astronomical. Indeed, a persistent legend has it that a contributory cause of the defeat at Isandhlwana in 1879 was the reluctance by supply officers to give out ammunition without a proper receipt.

One of the recurring problems in the routine administration of the region was that very few bush Africans possessed any hard cash or specie. Accordingly, hut taxes, fines, and other financial obligations, even toward the Crown, had to be met in kind. Maj. Robert Foran suffered a nervous breakdown over the inability of the authorities back in London to understand that if a tax was paid by the remission of, say, fifty sheep at a village, there wouldn't be exactly fifty sheep when the walking, breathing taxation arrived at the *boma*. Some sheep would have died, some wandered off, new ones born, and some eaten by lions in transit. So the books would never precisely balance. Yet the Treasury could never understand this.

It was the district commissioners of the Northern Frontier District who first figured how to use this anomaly to their advantage. Taxes and other official debts in that remote area were invariably paid in the form of goats, for cows were too valuable. The goats would be assessed and then would usually wind up in the stewpots of the nearby King's African Rifles detachment. About 1920, some bright district officer instituted a time lag of one breeding season between arrival of the goats and disbursement of the stew. This allowed the flock to grow, creating extra goats and a sort of slush fund that could be tapped whenever an unusual expenditure had to be made, perhaps an expenditure that the Treasury might be reluctant to approve. These extra animals could be sold "off the books," and the resulting income was invisible as far as the Treasury was concerned. Additionally, the skins of goats legally killed for soldiers' rations were also sold and those monies added to the secret slush fund.

The initiative was astoundingly successful. Soon district officers in every remote area of the Empire began creating a "goat bag" of the uncounted and unofficial lambs of the previous season's tax. Whenever an expense had to be paid that might raise eyebrows or cause consternation at the government level (Elspeth Huxley gives the example of blood money for an unsolved accidental killing of a Masai girl in her 1985 *Out in the Midday Sun*), the goat bag could cover the unexpected expense, in the sure knowledge that the next year's lambing season would recoup the expenditure. Thus the wheels of colonialism were greased, and the machinery of state allowed to run smooth. And DCs everywhere could rest easy, knowing that they had ample resources of their own, safe from the grasping oversight of the Treasury.

Over time, the goat bag was expanded to include revenue from other unofficial sources. District Commissioner Charles Chenevix Trench in his 1993 *Men Who Ruled Kenya* noted that unofficial fines (of a kangaroo-court variety or for small infractions) and the profits from the *boma* vegetable gardens ended up in the goat bag. He observed that goat-bag money was often spent on things like prizes for school sports and to pay for oxen slaughtered at holiday feasts. Most expenditures were relatively small, but at times the goat bag could rise to quite a substantial level. Chenevix Trench knew one DC who built an entire medical clinic from goat-bag funds.

Groundnut Scheme. The Groundnut Scheme was a hopelessly ill-thought effort to make groundnuts (known to Americans as peanuts) a major cash crop in Tanganyika. In the late 1940s more than £36,000,000 was wasted clearing land, building infrastructure, and planting the groundnuts, for no return whatsoever. Thousands of wild animals were killed during the bush clearing, and the reduction of natural food is thought to have caused numerous cases of man-eating lions and leopards in the early 1950s.

Harrisbuck. [after hunter W. C. Harris]. Sable antelope.

Havildar. [Indian]. Indian army rank equivalent to sergeant.

Header, taking a. This really has nothing to do with hunting, and I can't say I ever gave it much thought, but I always assumed that the expression "he took a header," meaning "he fell head-first," was modern slang. Then I came across this passage, in Denis Lyell's 1923 *Memories of An African Hunter*: "It seems that the husband of the woman had been in the hut when the lion got through the wall, and he immediately took a header through the opposite side, leaving his spouse for the invader." The lion got the woman, the man lived, and his cowardly act has provided a bit of lexicographic enlightenment. After I wrote the above, I found an even earlier reference. Mary Kingsley, *Travels in West Africa* (1897), describing falling off a tree-trunk bridge: ". . . whereupon I took a header, and am thereby able to inform the world that there is between fifteen and twenty feet of water each side of that log."

Hongo. Tribute paid to an African chief, particularly as a toll for passage through his district. The practice apparently began as compensation for foodstuffs consumed while large slave-and-ivory caravans were passing through a tribe's land. Often paid in the form of rolls of fabric.

IBEA. Imperial British East Africa Company. Chartered in 1888, the IBEA controlled Uganda until 1893.

IDB. "Illicit Diamond Buying," a serious crime in the South African mining districts. An intensive network of informants and detectives was constructed to monitor the practice, and draconian punishments were used to deter hired laborers from pocketing precious stones at the mines and selling them themselves on the black market. Still, the practice was widespread and it was generally believed that the best diamonds were turned in only if one of the mine owners or a guard fortuitously happened to be standing by when the gem was found.

Impi. A Zulu or Matabele regiment, battalion, or army. An impi was an armed force of any size.

Indaba. A formal tribal meeting.

Indirect rule. Philosophy and system of British colonial government pioneered by Goldie but associated chiefly with Lugard, in which the colonial power used existing social and political structures and personnel to form the primary level of colonial administration. To the extent possible, daily affairs under "indirect rule" were managed by popularly recognized African chiefs and authorities, with minimal European interference. Major decisions and policies were monitored by British district and provincial commissioners, responsible to the European governor. This system had the theoretical advantage of allowing a degree of freedom to the African population, while preparing them for some far-off and hazily foreseen day of independence—as well as the very real advantage of minimizing British financial and personnel requirements.

Induna. An odd and interesting term. An induna (plural *izinduna*) was a rank in Zulu and Matabele society that has no specific equivalent in English. It is often translated as general, but that is only one of the possible functions. An induna was an administrative official appointed directly by (and answerable to) the king himself, for a specific task; it could be to lead an impi, administer a territory, act as an ambassador or counselor, or simply carry a message. Perhaps the best equivalent might be the European concept of minister without portfolio. Whatever the specific function of an individual induna, the office carried great authority as the personal representative of the king.

IPHA. International Professional Hunters' Association.

Jebels. Hills.

Jess. A term for the peculiarly thick Rhodesian bush, composed of thorns entangled in a dense mass twice the height of a man. It was and is a perfect hiding place and refuge for elephant and wounded buffalo. The term derives either from a Bantu term *muchesa* meaning "thick bush," or the falconry term *jesses*, the restraining strap for a falcon, which resembles the thorns of the jess. British falconers favor the latter derivation while the rest of the world recognizes the Bantu one.

Jiggers. Sand fleas, otherwise known as *funza* and, in Rhodesia, *maundu*. These tiny fleas lay their eggs under the toenail, causing stupendous itching and infection if the pea-sized egg sac is broken in a removal attempt. In severe cases the entire toenail is eaten by the fleas.

Kabaka. The traditional King of Buganda.

Kali. [Indian]. Very dangerous, evil, satanic. Used to describe animals that seem to have supernatural help in stalking humans—for example, "a *kali* herd," or "that is a very *kali* elephant."

KANU. Kenya African National Union, a nationalist party.

KAR. King's African Rifles, a military unit composed of British officers and African soldiers.

Karama. A thanksgiving festival in the Sudan.

KCMG. British title—Knight Commander of the Order of St. Michael and St. George ("Kindly Call Me God" runs the old joke).

Kiboko. A *sjambok* or whip made from hippo or rhino hide. The word literally means "hippo" in Swahili.

Kissra. A food made from flour rolled into a flat pancake and dried in the sun.

Knobkerrie. A long club with a thin shaft and a circular head.

Kraal. African word for home, camp, or corral—typically a collection of huts built into the wall of, or in the center of, a brush stockade.

Kungu. Tiny gnat found on Lake Nyasa that is collected by the local people by the billions and pounded into cakes. Livingstone said that they tasted like caviar, or salted locusts.

Laager. To laager is to fortify one's temporary camp by circling the wagons and filling the gaps with thornbushes and other impediments. The resulting fortified camp is also called a laager.

Leopard men. See "Theriomorph."

Lobola. The "bride price" or reverse dowry paid in many African cultures. The groom and his family paid a fee to the bride's family. In many areas the fee was in cattle, in others goods and services were allowed, and later cash payments became common. It was not considered buying a wife but rather sealing a contract.

Machan. [Indian]. A shooting platform built in a tree.

Machila. A hammocklike sling used to carry a person, typically a woman, between two porters. Use of a machila in British Africa was looked upon as somewhat effete unless you were female, sick, or perhaps an Indian maharajah on safari. After his poisoning, Jim Sutherland often used a machila, giving rise to the legend that he had lived a glorious, pampered life as some sort of "Ivory King." Other nationalities, particularly the Portuguese, attached no such stigma to the machila. The secret to machila travel was that a team of up to fourteen bearers was used. They would relieve each other on the fly every few minutes, thereby preventing excessive fatigue. The machila is not quite the same as the teepoy.

Malaria. Malaria means, literally, "bad air." Although not unknown in Europe (it was endemic in parts of Italy, for instance), particularly virulent strains of this disease contributed to the legend of Africa as the "White man's grave." The disease is caused by the protozoa *Plasmodium*, transmitted by the bite of an infected Anopheles mosquito. Symptoms include a fever of up to 106 degrees F, chills, headache, nausea, and sweating. These symptoms show up from twelve to thirty-six hours after being infected. Quinine was the great preventative once the disease was half-understood. It was only in 1898 that the connection between mosquitoes and malaria was positively established. Even then, for some years scientists believed that other factors besides the mosquito could transmit the disease. The 1900 Annual Report of the Smithsonian Institution, for example, discussed a theory that the malarial parasites could be transmitted by so-called "black spores" that could lie dormant on the ground for years.

Before then, in the nineteenth century, it is eerie to see how close some early hunters were to guessing the causal connection between Anopheles and malaria. In *Wild Beasts and their Ways* (1890), for instance, Samuel Baker wrote, "the air, sultry and redolent of malaria, was humming with mosquitoes." How much closer can you get? Richard Burton was actually warned by an Arab, before his visit to the forbidden Ethiopian city of Harar in 1853, to avoid mosquito bites as they caused fever. He dismissed any connection between mosquitoes and fever as a mere coincidence of timing. William Finaughty also made no connection between cause and effect. Finaughty first suffered a malarial attack in 1875, after many years of travel and sport in the interior. It was always a mystery to him why he came down with fever then, after so many years of being disease free. In his old age he speculated that his long immunity stemmed from either his moderation in drinking or just a strong constitution. As he admitted in his 1916 book, "It was certainly not because I took any precautions against mosquitoes, for the mosquito theory had not been thought of in those days and I have slept and hunted in country where the mosquitoes swarmed to such an extent that one's face would be black with them when one slept." As with most things in life, it just seems that some folks get malaria and some don't.

Malawi sausages. A local delicacy, this is another name for mice on a stick. Local children catch mice, boil them whole, then salt them and sell them on bamboo sticks. The mice are eaten whole, fur, innards, everything.

Mandala. Universally used native name for the African Lakes Corporation, Ltd.

Martini-Henry. Single-shot falling-block breechloading rifle used by the British army in the 1870s and 1880s.

Maria Theresa dollar. A silver coin that was in universal use from Nigeria out to Kenya, the Sudan, Somalia, Abyssinia and Arabia. Minted by the Imperial government of Austria-Hungary, the dollar originally appealed to merchants due to its high quality—it was struck in .883 fine silver. The coin bears a portrait of the Austrian Empress Maria Theresa (1717–1780). A company in Trieste seems to have been the first to promote the coin in its trade with the Arabs. The dollar found universal acceptance; indeed, so taken were the primitive peoples to whom it was traded that they would only accept dollars stamped with the date "1780" as genuine. During its periodic re-issues, the Austrian government has continued to use the eighteenth-century date. In 1941 three million pounds worth were minted in England (the Austrian mint being in evil hands) for use in Abyssinia, and a further 500,000 coins in 1949. There

The machila *for carrying white men along bush paths was a Portuguese innovation, readily adopted by the British.*

have also been more recent issues, and the dollar, always dated "1780," is still accepted in much of the Persian Gulf and the Horn of Africa. In Kenya in the 1920s a Maria Theresa dollar was worth about 5 shillings, or one-quarter of a pound sterling.

Marula. A medium-sized tree, *Scelocarya caffra.* The marula tree bears an acidic fruit that looks like a yellow plum, which is used to make a local African beer. It is very popular, and when the marula fruit is ripe certain tribes devote all of their energies to the preparation and use of the beverage; as Stevenson-Hamilton put it (1934): "the whole countryside is either preparing to get drunk, actually drunk, or getting over being drunk."

Masuku. Springs of water found in the mountains of the eastern Congo; occasionally tectonic gases released from inside the mountain along with the water overwhelm and kill anyone who breathes them in.

Maundu. Rhodesian word for jiggers.

MC. Military Cross. British medal awarded for "distinguished service in the field."

Memsahib. [Indian]. A term of respect from an African to a European woman. The female equivalent of Bwana.

Mentioned in dispatches. A form of military recognition unique to Great Britain. Soldiers and sailors were rewarded for valorous or meritorious acts by being "mentioned in dispatches," it was the equivalent of a minor decoration.

Mericani. Coarse, unbleached calico cloth once used as an article of trade throughout Africa. Also called Merican or Americani, the name was a corruption of "American," from the source of the textile, which was made in the mills of Massachusetts and New Hampshire.

Mfecane. "The Crushing," the Mfecane was the period of bloody Zulu victories and civil wars that gave them dominance over southeastern Africa, 1820–1834.

Mngwa. A ferocious cryptid of Tanganyika, resembling a large furry lion.

Moran, el-moran. A warrior, one of a specific age group and caste. (Morani is the plural.)

Mpango. In Northern Rhodesia, the "bride price." See lobola.

Muhlambela. A cryptid of South Africa, a one hundred-foot serpent.

Mumbo jumbo. A term now meaning "gibberish," especially gibberish of an arcane type ("scientific mumbo jumbo"). Better dictionaries will also give the word a meaning of a "fetish: an object believed to have supernatural powers." The term originally came from Mandingo, and it first appears in the works of Mungo Park. The mumbo jumbo was an idol that was used by harried husbands to discipline bitchy wives.

Mzee. An old man.

Nagana. Horse sickness; the invariably fatal affliction carried by the tsetse fly that precluded bringing domestic animals into fly-zones.

NFD. Northern Frontier District, the barren northern half of Kenya, long the scene of constant irregular warfare between the Somalis and the local tribes. In popular parlance the area was still called the NFD long after the official name had been changed to Northern Frontier Province in the 1920s.

Ngalisio. A common game throughout sub-Saharan Africa, *ngalisio* is played by crouching men who move small stones from one small hole to another. The nuances of the game consist in determining what stones to move when and in what combinations. No adequate description of the rules has ever been given by a Westerner; suffice to say that the players understand full well the consequences of each move but have never deigned to explain them. A handful of pebbles will be chosen and moved, and the onlookers will gasp and shake their heads in disbelief that anyone could be so inept, yet a seemingly identical transfer will have the watchers nodding and whistling in admiration.

It is tempting to say that *ngalisio* needs its Hoyle but the folks who play the game seem to understand it just fine.

Ngula mtwe. A special Mozambique drum beat, meaning "a man is eaten." It consists of two short thumps followed by a long one and is played when a lion takes a human victim.

Nimrod. A Victorian euphemism for "hunter," derived from the Biblical story of Nimrod, the son of Cush and grandson of Ham (just check your begats if you don't believe me), a great hunter who went on to found the Assyrian Empire.

Ntarago. A cryptid of Uganda, resembling a leopard-lion cross.

Nullah. A dry waterway.

Nyika. Wilderness.

Panga. A thick bush knife, like a machete.

Permanganate of potash. Chemical compound that was used as a disinfectant and antibiotic by early European travelers in Africa. Permanganate of potash came in packets of crystals. When a leopard or lion bit or clawed someone, quick action had to be taken, as the rotting flesh always found under the claws of a predator could quickly lead to blood poisoning. First, using a sharp knife, a deep gash would be made along the lines of the scratch. Then a few crystals would be ground up in a 10 percent water solution and sprayed into the gash with a glass syringe with a long nozzle. This application was thought to disinfect the wound and avoid septicemia and gangrene. And, yes, it would sting. Permanganate of potash began to be used for all types of medical problems, and was held by many to be a cure-all for everything. Virtually all of the great hunters swore by permanganate, and ascribed to it healing powers far beyond penicillin and the shrine at Lourdes.

The fact that it probably did more harm than good in most circumstance somehow eluded them for years. Denis Lyell, for example, used it on two snakebite victims with good results. In another case, a French elephant hunter named Audet was mauled by a lion while hunting in Ubangi-Shari. The animal bit right through his hand. The canoe trip back to Fort Archambault, the nearest settlement, was nine days long. Audet spent the time with his hand soaking in a gourd filled with permanganate solution, and his recovery was quick and complete. Hunter's faith in permanganate should not be scoffed at; modern studies indicate that the psychological aspect of medicine is extraordinarily important, which explains the popularity of acupuncture, herbalism, chiropractic, and holistic healing. Combined with the placebo effect, belief in the effectiveness of permanganate was much more powerful medicine than the alternative, which in the field was often no treatment at all.

PH. Professional hunter. Generally, a licensed safari guide.

PHASA. Professional Hunter's Association of South Africa.

Pombe. Locally brewed African beer; a thick, powerful brew, with a consistency more like oatmeal than like Budweiser.

Porters. The lack of transport, roads, and the prevalence of the domestic animal-killing tsetse fly dictated that supplies had to be carried on the shoulders of human beings. The weight of the individual load varied, from a maximum of sixty pounds in colonial Kenya to forty pounds in other locales, and frequently became an issue during safaris and exploratory expeditions. District officers often helped to organize the recruitment of porters for hunting safaris; during the First World War hundreds of thousands of Africans were recruited or drafted to carry supplies for the various armies. The automobile gradually replaced human portage in the 1920s and 1930s, but even today expeditions in remote areas often rely on the strength of the human back.

Punda. Donkey.

Punda miliya. Zebra (literally, "donkey stripes").

Rasn. A prize awarded in the Sudan to the hunter who first speared an elephant in a communal hunt.

Reim. An Afrikaner term, a reim is, according to Selous (1881): "the soft though tough rawhide thong used universally in South Africa for tying up bullocks and horses." Pieces of buffalo hide would be cut into long strips that would be hung from a tree with a weight attached. With a stick, the strip would be twisted around as tightly as possible. When the stick was yanked out the strip would quickly unwind. This process would be retreated for a few days, with the strip being well oiled throughout. Finaughty estimated that fifty reims could be made from a bull buffalo and forty from a cow. Along with ivory, rhino horn, and sjamboks, reims were a major source of income for the South African hunter.

RGS. Royal Geographical Society of London, established 1831.

Roer. Traditional Boer hunting rifle. Weighing sixteen-pounds, the typical roer was a long-barreled muzzleloading percussion smoothbore, firing lead bullets that weighed four ounces apiece.

Royal game. Animals protected by law, that is, animals forbidden to hunt. From the medieval concept that all game animals belong to the king.

RW28. [reference]. The ninth edition of Rowland Ward's *Records of Big Game*, published in 1928. Used in the text to indicate some listings by certain hunters.

RW99. [reference]. The third edition of Rowland Ward's *Records of Big Game*, published in 1899. Used in the text to indicate some listings by certain hunters.

Safari. Originally, any journey. The term quickly came to mean a hunting expedition with porters and askaris, and now stands for virtually any excursion into the wild.

Sago. A starchy food made from the trunks of palms and occasionally used as a cheap, transportable staple.

Salted. A domesticated animal (usually a horse) that had been exposed to and recovered from the "horse sickness" caused by the bite of the tsetse fly. Salted horses could be expected to survive in fly zones and generally cost about ten times the price of an unsalted animal. They always came with a guarantee, that if the horse died within a period of months (usually three) the purchase price would be refunded.

Serolomootlooque. Bushbuck.

Setyot. Setyot *(Mimulopsis solmsii)* is a seasonal vine that grows alongside bamboo that forms an important part of the bongo's diet. The flowers of the vine appear only once every seven years, and dies immediately after flowering. The dead vine undergoes a chemical transformation that produces a toxin, and it is reported that the bongo population crashes dramatically from the poison in the second year after the setyot flowering. Giant forest hog are also reported to suffer from this peculiar poisoning. The toxin appears to act as a laxative and death comes quickly from dehydration. Setyot also figures in several important tribal circumcision ceremonies.

SGM. [reference]. *Scottish Geographical Magazine,* the journal of the Scottish Geographical Society.

Shaber. A forked pole about six to eight feet long used to fetter slaves. The forked pole would be lashed to the slave's neck while the straight end would rest on the slave in front of him, who was similarly burdened.

Shenzi. A barbarian, a savage.

Siafu. African driver ants, much feared and voracious insects that travel in armies. They are small, red, and they bite. It is safe to say that no memoir of African hunting or bush life is complete without mention of siafu. Blunt mentions having to strike camp at one A.M. due to an invasion of ants. Owen Letcher likewise was chased from his bed, likening their bite to "so many red hot needles" (1911). Kittenberger described the same bite as "very painful, itches like the sting of a nettle, and by brushing them off only the body is removed, while the head stays in the skin like those of ticks, itching and burning continuously" (1927). Mining surveyor J. M. Moubray had a similar experience in Rhodesia in 1906. Often the ants were more deadly. Pretorius reported on two tethered goats that had been completely devoured by the voracious ants. Beryl Markham, no city girl, confessed (1942) that siafu composed her greatest nightmares: "Give me beetles and bugs, spiders, puff adders, and tarantulas like buttons of cozy wool—but not siafu. They are minions of the Devil."

Woe betide the infant child left unattended in the path of the driver ant. Mary Kingsley (1899) had this last thought in mind one night when she responded to a cry of help from a native village in West Africa. The adults of the family had safely evacuated their hut from an onslaught of siafu, but were still in an incredibly agitated state. Kingsley tried to decipher what the problem was, and through sign language and snippets of pidgin realized that a baby was still inside. The young Englishwoman burst into the hut and spotted the tiny form, "a mere inert black mass, with hundreds of cruel Drivers already swarming upon it." She gathered the form into her arms and completed the rescue. The parents thanked her joyfully, for saving their prized (and joy) ham.

Denis Lyell (1923) mentioned the Hollywood favorite called the "ant death," where the victim is ordered smeared with honey by a village chief and then tied to a tree. The ants did the rest. Sometimes the ant armies could be fought off. Foa's camp in the Zambezi Valley was raided by siafu one night, apparently attracted by meat and blood that had spilled on the ground. The porters and askaris repelled the attack with burning brands, while Foa arranged hot coals around the iron legs of his camp bed and went back to sleep, "as I did not wish to disturb myself."

Simi. Double-edged short sword, about two feet in length.

Sisal. A sharp-leafed plant of the daffodil family that can weigh up to three hundred pounds, used to make sacking and rope. Native to the Americas, sisal was first transplanted to Africa in the 1890s.

Sjambok. A long leather whip made from the hides of wild animals such as rhino, hippo, and buffalo. A short version was used as a horse whip.

Skerm. The South African equivalent of a *boma*, but cozier. Branches and bush placed in a semicircle with a fire at the opening.

Skokiaan. A strong, distilled liquor popular in Rhodesia, also called "Matabele moonshine." Reputed to produce an extremely magnificent hangover.

Snider rifle. Single-shot, breechloading weapon often carried by African askaris. The Snider was a modified Enfield rifled-musket in .577 caliber, altered by the introduction of the breech mechanism and loaded with a brass cartridge.

Strip roads. Unique to Rhodesia, these roads consisted of two narrow strips of tarmac that a vehicle would drive along like a train. Common around the 1930s.

Stuck up. "Stuck up," in the sense of snobbish or arrogant, is another one of those phrases that sound very recent but have a surprisingly long history. In the 1890s the American missionary Sam Lapsley wrote in a letter, explaining why he was fond of the Africans near his mission, "I like the black folks very much. They are not stuck up, though they are ready to stand up for themselves."

Syce. [Indian]. A groom or horse attendant.

Taenia. South African term for the symptoms of tapeworm.

Tapans. According to Hodson, tapans are "horrible crablike insects with a painful bite, which are very common in parts of the Kalahari" (1912). The unattractive vermin live in the sand underneath shade trees near habitation, and upon smelling humans or animals march forth to devour their prey. Hodson found his oxen covered with welts, and a parade of the little monsters marching up his bedpost.

Tej. Strong barley wine made in Ethiopia or the Sudan.

Theriomorph. A theriomorph ("beast-forms") is a term coined to denote Africans who were coerced, forced, trained, or persuaded to adopt the form of a wild beast, usually to no good end. In this group fall the various "lion men" and "leopard men" of indigenous folklore. In the usual scenario, orphans or kidnapped children are kept for years in isolated cages, fed like beasts and sewn into the skins of wild animals. Eventually, with no mind of their own, they are the perfect instrument of assassination, with the added benefit that death at their claws will invariably be attributed to wild animals.

Tanganyika has been a hotbed of such activity. In the 1890s lion-men killed scores of Christian converts around the Badouinville mission on Lake Tanganyika. A few decades later George Rushby killed a slew of real lions before he reached the conclusion that most, if not all, of the depredations in the area had been committed by lion-men. There has even been speculation that the famous "Man-eaters of Tsavo" were actually theriomorphs; this is thought highly unlikely.

Modern writers tend to disparage the old tales and to discount the reality of theriomorphs. P. Jay Fetner, in his excellent 1987 photographic work *African Safari* calls such stories "beyond the pale of the outer reaches attracted by this compendium." Suffice to say that virtually all the old-time hunters and colonial officials, as well as the older generations of Africans, believed these stories to have a solid base in truth; furthermore, trials were held and men were hanged on the basis of theriomorphic activity. It may be that "lion men" and "leopard women" were not as widespread as the old stories would have it, but for contemporary writers to flat-out dismiss such tales as being unlikely is to selectively tamper with the historical record.

Tikoloshe. Tikoloshe is a mischievous, tiny, dwarflike character with attributes like a fairy, pixie, or brownie. He likes to throw stone sand clods of earth into dwellings through windows and doors.

Tembo. Elephant.

Toto. The young of any species, human or animal.

Tsetse. A large biting fly (various *Glossina* species) that has caused great tragedy and, conversely, helped save much of Africa's wildlife. The tsetse carries sleeping sickness *(Trypanosoma gambiense)* and nagana (also known as horse sickness). Its presence in an area (called a fly zone or belt) effectively excludes domestic animals from entry. If they are not salted, that is, immune to the disease from exposure, the huge majority of horses, mules, and cattle die a quick death in a fly zone. In colonial days this meant that no farms or ranches could be built in these areas, and that any safaris had to go on foot. Finaughty, like many of the South African "interior men," stopped elephant hunting when the last herds in his area retreated into fly country, and he could no longer hunt on horseback.

The sleeping sickness affected humans, and sometimes depopulated entire areas. Pretorius wrote of an island in Lake Victoria that went from a population of sixty thousand to zero in less than a year. The first symptoms of sleeping sickness are fever and headache, followed by trademark pains in the back of the neck and delirium. Hunger and lassitude are prominent symptoms as well. Sir David Bruce led the Royal Commission that first established the link between the fly and both sleeping sickness and nagana. He conducted a series of experiments in Zululand in the early 1900s that established the ability of wild game animals to act as a reservoir of the disease without falling sick themselves. Prior to the Royal Commission, it had been known for at least a century by both Africans and Europeans that the presence of tsetse in a district was fatal to domestic animals. It was not known, however, or even widely suspected, that the fly transmitted sleeping sickness and other human diseases. Henry Stanley, even in the second edition of his wildly popular *How I Found Livingstone* (1895), maintained that the bite of the fly was harmless to humans. He quoted Livingstone's 1868 *Missionary Travels*: "On man the bite has no effect, neither has it on wild animals." A few short years were to prove them both wrong. By the turn of the century, the fly was vaguely suspected as being harmful to humans.

Great efforts were made to eliminate the fly, but the programs were misguided and scientifically unfounded. Tsetse control was a very controversial, wasteful, and ultimately futile program. It was believed that the fly needed the game to survive. Selous, for example, had noted that on his first trip to the Chobe River valley there had been many buffalo and many tsetse; however, in 1912 Selous was asked to write the foreword for Hodson's *Trekking the Great Thirst,* and he noted that Hodson had found no buffalo and no fly. The conclusion seemed inescapable: One way to eliminate or at least contain tsetse was to eradicate the game. A few hunters spoke out against this form of tsetse control—Denis Lyell called it a "senseless crime" in 1935, but by and large most European naturalists in Africa reluctantly endorsed the program. (Lyell believed that the flies ate plants as well as blood, and, therefore, couldn't be eradicated at all.) Rangers killed every large mammal in designated zones and belts in order to try to keep the fly away from livestock areas.

The slaughter was horrific. In the early 1950s it was estimated that as many as 100,000 animals a year were being shot for tsetse control purposes. From 1952 to 1962 in Uganda, 60,000 antelope were shot; in 1920s the government of Natal shot over 500,000 animals. It was also estimated that between 1932–1959 over 550,000 creatures in Rhodesia were destroyed. In South Africa between 1942 and 1950 every animal that entered a buffer zone near the Umfolozi River was shot, with the exception of the rare white rhino.

Other, less wasteful, methods of control were also attempted. Areas of brush would be intentionally burned away by the control teams. For some time experiments with different color panels were tried since it was known that the fly was drawn to certain pigments. In the 1930s, South African R. H. R. Harris invented an effective tsetse trap, which in a fly zone would catch 300–400 flies daily. Provincial Commissioner Temple-Perkins tried to persuade the Uganda Game Department to adopt the trap, but the initial test was ineffective due, Temple-Perkins felt, to a lack of flies in the test area. He was unsuccessful. Uganda, like the other governments, went on killing game. By the late 1950s, it was becoming obvious that the large-scale slaughter of game animals was both incredibly wasteful and a very ineffective method of controlling the fly. One of the last colonial governments to actively shoot game animals as a form of fly control was Uganda, where thousands of large mammals were slaughtered every year through the 1960s, despite growing international protests. Progressive administrators like W. Steel of Northern Rhodesia began programs of clearing the brush from known tsetse breeding areas but leaving the game alone. This was more effective, less costly, and obviously less damaging to wildlife interests.

Ironically, however, the tsetse fly has to be credited with saving far more wildlife than was ever destroyed in its name. By denying large areas of Africa to agricultural use, it preserved the habitat that the game needed. Habitat loss being the single greatest threat to African wildlife, the greatest danger to what remains is the development of successful tsetse prophylaxis techniques.

As a side note, the fly also carries other microorganisms, such as the crocodile parasites *Trypanosoma grayii,* and *Hepatozoon petiti.*

UAC. United Africa Company.

Ulendo. A safari or expedition, especially in Rhodesia.

Warburg's Fever Tincture. A patent malaria medicine mentioned by many hunters and explorers, including Selous (1881), Portal (1894), and Darter (1914). Selous, in particular, recommended the medication very highly. Warburg's Tincture could be made with or without aloes. The full formula, with aloes, consisted of about 60 percent alcohol, 2.75 percent socotrine aloes, 2 percent quinine sulphate, 0.91 percent rhubarb root, 0.91 percent angelica fruit, 0.03 percent opium, and small amounts of other ingredients including saffron, cinnamon, black pepper, elecampane root, zedoary root, white agaric, ginger, myrrh, fennel, gentian, camphor, and chalk. It was invented by a Dr. Warburg of London.

White Fathers. French-based Roman Catholic missionary order founded in 1848 by Cardinal Lavigerie to build missions in Algeria. They soon spread to other areas, including Uganda. In 1891 they established a mission at Mambwe on the Stevenson Road between Lake Tanganyika and Lake Nyasa. By 1918 the White Fathers were active throughout Northern Rhodesia, especially among the Awemba.

White hunter. A licensed professional who guides amateur hunters on safari. The term began as a convenient way to distinguish European hunters from local Africans; a white hunter can be any nationality or race.

Zareba. (also spelled zariba). A thorn barricade designed to keep out wild animals.

BIBLIOGRAPHY

This is a list of those books that were most helpful. I also relied heavily on the published reports of the Scottish Geographical Society, the Smithsonian Institution, the *Dictionary of National Biography,* and the archives of Safari Press. In addition, I benefited from various government postings on the Internet, such as the United Kingdom's Gazette archives, the Royal Navy archives, and the U.S. Immigration and Naturalization Service's Ellis Island database.

Adamson, George. *Bwana Game.* London: Collins Harvill, 1968.

Adamson, George. *My Pride and Joy.* New York: Simon and Schuster, 1987.

Aflalo, F. G. *A Book of the Wilderness and Jungle.* New York: Dodge Publishing. Undated.

Ahlefeldt-Laurvig-Bille, Count Gregors. *Tandalla.* London: Routledge and Keegan Paul, 1951.

Akeley, Carl E. *In Brightest Africa.* New York: Garden City Publishing, 1920.

Akeley, Mary L. Jobe. *Carl Akeley's Africa.* New York: Dodd, Mead & Company, 1929.

Akeley, Mary L. Jobe. *Restless Jungle.* New York: National Travel Club, 1936.

Akeley, Mary L. Jobe. *The Wilderness Lives Again.* New York: Dodd, Mead & Company, 1940.

Alderson, E. A. H. *With the Mounted Infantry and the Mashonaland Field Force 1896.* London: Methuen, 1898.

Alexander, Boyd. *From the Niger to the Nile.* London: Edward Arnold, 1907.

Altrincham, Lord. *Kenya's Opportunity.* London: Faber, 1955.

Andersson, Charles John. *Lake Ngami.* London: Hurst and Blackett, 1856.

——. *The Okavango River.* New York: Harper, 1861.

Arbuthnot, Thomas S. *Grand Safari.* London: William Kimber, 1954.

Arnot, F. S. *Bihe and Garenganze.* London: J. E. Hawkins and Son, 1893.

Askins, Charles. *Asian Jungle African Bush.* Harrisburg: Stackpole, 1959.

Austin, Herbert H. *Among Swamps and Giants in Equatorial Africa.* London: Arthur Pearson, 1902.

——. *With MacDonald in Uganda.* London: Edward Arnold, 1903.

——. *Some Rambles of a Sapper.* London: Edward Arnold, 1928.

Baden-Powell, R. S. S. *The Downfall of Prempeh.* London: Methuen, 1896.

Bailey, Henry (as Bula N'Zau). *Travel and Adventure in the Congo Free State and its Big Game Shooting.* London: Chapman and Hall, 1894.

Baker, Samuel W. *The Albert N'Yanza, Great Basin of the Nile, and Explorations of the Nile Sources.* London: Macmillan, 1866.

——. *The Nile Tributaries of Abyssinia and the Hamran Arabs.* London: Macmillan, 1867.

——. *Ismailia.* London: Macmillan, 1874.

——. *Wild Beasts and Their Ways.* London: Macmillan, 1890.

Baldwin, William Charles. *African Hunting and Adventure.* Bulawayo: Books of Zimbabwe, 1981. First published in 1863.

Barclay, Edgar N. *Big Game Shooting Records.* London: Witherby, 1932.

Barker, R. De La Bere. *Rufiji.* London: Robert Hale, 1956.

Barkly, Mrs. *Among Boers and Basutos.* London: Remington, 1893.

Barnes, Alexander T. *The Wonderland of the Western Congo.* London: Putnam, 1920.

——. *Across the Great Craterland to the Congo.* London: Ernest Benn, 1923.

——. *An African Eldorado.* London: Methuen, 1926.

Barrett, S. A. (editor). *The Cudahy-Massee-Milwaukee Museum African Expedition, 1928–1929.* Milwaukee: Milwaukee Public Museum, 1930.

Bates, Marston. *Where Winter Never Comes.* New York: Scribner's, 1952.

Beard, Peter. *The End of the Game.* San Francisco: Chronicle Books, 1988.

———. *Zara's Tales.* New York: Alfred Knopf, 2004.

Beaton, K. de P. *A Warden's Diary.* Nairobi: East African Standard, 1949.

Beck, Henry Houghton. *History of South Africa and the Boer-British War.* Philadelphia: Globe Bible Publishing, 1900.

Becker, Peter. *Dingane: King of the Zulu 1828–1840.* New York: Thomas Crowell, 1965.

———. *The Pathfinders.* New York: Viking, 1985.

Bell, W. D. M. *Wanderings of an Elephant Hunter.* Long Beach: Safari Press, 1989. Originally published in 1923.

———. *Karamojo Safari.* Saffron Walden: Neville Spearman, 1986. Originally published in 1949.

———. *Bell of Africa.* Saffron Walden: Neville Spearman, 1985. Originally published in 1960.

Bernatzik, Hugo Adolf. *Gari-Gari.* New York: Henry Holt, 1936.

Bertram, Brian. *Pride of Lions.* New York: Scribner's, 1978.

Bierman, John. *Dark Safari.* New York: Alfred A. Knopf, 1990.

Binks, Herbert K. *African Rainbow.* London: Sidgwick and Jackson, 1959.

Biss, H. C. J. *The Relief of Kumasi.* London: Methuen, London, 1901.

Bjerre, Jens. *Kalahari.* New York: Hill and Wang, New York, 1960.

Blackwell, Lionel. *African Occasions.* London: Hutchinson & Company, 1938.

Blake, Robert. *A History of Rhodesia.* New York: Alfred Knopf, 1978.

Bland Sutton, J. *Man and Beast in Eastern Ethiopia.* London: Macmillan, 1911.

Blennerhassett, Rose and Lucy Sleeman. *Adventures in Mashonaland.* London: Macmillan, 1893.

Blixen-Finecke, Baron Bror von. *African Hunter.* New York: St. Martin's Press, 1986. Originally published in 1938.

Blixen-Finecke, Baron Bror von. *The Africa Letters.* New York: St. Martin's Press, 1988.

Blunt, David E. *Elephant.* London: East Africa Press, 1933.

Bompiani, Sofia. *Italian Explorers in Africa.* London: Religious Tract Society, 1891.

Booth, Martin. *Rhino Road.* London: Constable, 1992.

Borer, Alain. *Rimbaud in Abyssinia.* New York: William Morrow, 1991.

Boyce, W. B. *Notes on South African Affairs.* Cape Town: C. Struik, 1971. Originally published in 1838.

Boyce, William D. *Illustrated Africa.* Chicago: Rand McNally, 1925.

Boyes, John. *King of the Wa-Kikuyu.* London: Methuen, 1911.

———. *The Company of Adventurers.* Alexander: Alexander Books, 1998. Originally published in 1927.

Bradford, Phillips Verner and Harvey Blume. *Ota Benga.* New York: Delta, 1992.

Bradnum, Frederick. *The Long Walks.* London: Victor Gollancz, 1969.

Brander, Michael. *Hunting and Shooting.* New York: Putnam's, 1971.

———. *The Big Game Hunters.* New York: St. Martin's Press, 1988.

Bright, Michael. *Man-Eaters.* New York: St. Martin's Press, 2002.

Brocklehurst, H. C. *Game Animals of the Sudan.* London: Gurney and Jackson, 1931.

Brodie, Fawn. *The Devil Drives.* New York: W. W. Norton, 1967.

Brook-Shepherd, Gordon. *Between Two Flags.* New York: Putnam, 1972.

Brooke Worth, C. *Mosquito Safari.* New York: Simon and Schuster, 1971.

Brown, Leslie. *Ethiopian Episode.* London: Country Life, 1965.

Brown, William Harvey. *On the South African Frontier.* London: Sampson, Low, Marston & Company, 1899.

Bryce, James. *Impressions of South Africa.* London: Macmillan, 1899.

Bryden, H. Anderson. *Gun and Camera in Southern Africa.* London: Edward Stanford, 1893.

Buchholzer, John. *The Horn of Africa.* London: Angus and Robertson, 1959.

Buckley, William. *Big Game Hunting in Central Africa.* New York: St. Martin's Press, 1988. Originally published in 1930.

Buel, J. W. *Heroes of the Dark Continent.* Philadelphia: Historical Publishing Company, 1889.

——. *Conquering the Dark Continent.* Philadelphia: Historical Publishing Company, 1899.

Bull, Bartle. *Safari: A Chronicle of Adventure.* London: Viking, 1988.

Bulpin, T. V. *Shaka's Country.* Cape Town: Howard Timmons, 1952.

——. *Storm Over the Transvaal.* Cape Town: Howard Timmons, 1955.

——. *To The Shores of Natal.* Cape Town: Howard Timmons, undated.

——. *The Hunter is Death.* Johannesburg: Nelson, 1962.

Burchell, William. *Travels in the Interior of Southern Africa.* London: Longman, Hurst, Rees, Orme & Browne, 1822 and 1824.

Burger, John. *Horned Death.* Long Beach: Safari Press, 1992.

——. *African Adventures.* Long Beach: Safari Press, 1993.

——. *African Jungle Memories.* London: Robert Hale, 1958.

——. *African Camp-Fire Nights.* London: Robert Hale, 1959.

——. *My Forty Years in Africa.* London: Robert Hale, 1960.

Burnham, Frederick Russell. *Scouting on Two Continents.* New York: Doubleday, Doran and Company, 1928.

Burton, Richard F. *First Footsteps in East Africa.* Cologne: Koenemann, 2000. Originally published in 1856.

Burton, Sir Richard Francis and James Macqueen. *The Nile Basin.* New York: De Capo Press, 1967. Originally published in 1864.

Buxton, Edward North. *Two African Trips.* London: Edward Stanford, 1902.

Caillou, Alan. *South from Khartoum.* New York: Hawthorn Books, 1974.

Campbell, R. J. *Livingstone.* New York: Dodd, Mead, & Company, 1930.

Cameron, V. L. *Across Africa.* London: Daldy Isbister, 1877.

Cannadine, David. *The Decline and Fall of the British Aristocracy.* New Haven: Yale University Press, 1990.

Cansdale, G. *Reptiles of West Africa.* London: Penguin Books, 1955.

Capstick, Peter Hathaway. *Safari.* New York: St. Martin's Press, 1984.

——. *The Last Ivory Hunter.* New York: St. Martin's Press, 1988.

——. *Sands of Silence.* St. Martin's Press, New York. 1991.

——. *The African Adventurers.* New York: St. Martin's Press, 1992.

——. *A Man Called Lion.* Long Beach: Safari Press, 1994.

——. *Warrior.* New York: St. Martin's Press, 1998.

Caputo, Philip. *Ghosts of Tsavo.* Washington: National Geographic, 2002.

Caras, Roger. *Dangerous to Man.* Philadelphia: Chilton, 1964.

Carnochan, F. G. and H. C. Adamson. *The Empire of the Snakes.* London: Hutchinson, circa 1935.

——. *Out of Africa.* New York: Dodge Publishing, 1936.

Carpenter, H. D. *A Naturalist on Lake Victoria.* London: Nisbett, 1920.

Carrington, Richard. *Elephants.* New York: Basic Books, 1959.

Carty, Wilfred and Martin Kilson (ed.). *The Africa Reader: Colonial Africa.* New York: Vintage Books, 1970.

Casati, G. *Ten Years in Equatoria.* London: Frederick Warne, 1891.

Chadwick, Douglas H. *The Fate of the Elephant.* San Francisco: Sierra Club, 1992.

Chaillu, Paul B. du. *Explorations and Adventures in Equatorial Africa.* London: John Murray, 1861.

———. *The Country of the Dwarfs.* London: Sampson Low Son and Marston, 1872.

———. *Adventures in the Great Forest of Equatorial Africa and the Country of the Dwarfs.* London: John Murray, 1890.

Chanler, William Astor. *Through Jungle and Desert.* New York: Macmillan, 1896.

Chapman, Abel. *On Safari.* London: Edward Arnold, 1908.

———. *Savage Sudan.* London: Gurney and Jackson, 1921.

———. *Memories of Fourscore Years Less Two, 1851–1929.* London: Gurney and Jackson, 1930.

Chapman, F. Spencer. *Lightest Africa.* London: Chatto & Windus, 1955.

Chase, John Centlivres. *The Cape of Good Hope and the Eastern Province of Algoa Bay.* Cape Town: Struik, 1967. Originally published in 1843.

Chilvers, Hedley A. *The Seven Wonders of Southern Africa.* Johannesburg: South African Railways and Harbors, 1929.

———. *The Seven Lost Trails of Africa.* London: Cassell and Company, 1930.

Christie, Cuthbert. *Big Game and Pygmies.* London: Macmillan, 1924.

Churchill, Winston Spencer. *My African Journey.* London: Holland, 1908.

———. *My Early Life.* London: Scribner's, 1930.

Clarke, James. *Man is the Prey.* New York: Stein and Day, 1969.

Clark, James L. *Trails of the Hunted.* Boston: Little, Brown & Company, 1928.

Cloete, Stuart. *The African Giant.* Boston: Houghton Mifflin, 1955.

Cloudsley-Thompson, J. L. *Animal Twilight.* London: Foulis, 1967.

Cohen, Louis. *Reminiscences of Johannesburg and London.* London: Robert Holden, 1924.

Cole, Sonia. *Leakey's Luck.* New York: Harcourt, Brace, Jovanovich, 1975.

Collins, Robert O. (ed.). *Documents from the African Past.* Princeton: Markus Wiener Productions, 2001.

Collins, W. B. *They Went Into the Bush.* London: MacGibbon & Kee, 1961.

Colvile, Sir Henry. *The Land of the Nile Springs.* London: Edward Arnold, 1895.

Cooper-Chadwick, J. *My Three Years with Lobengula and Experiences in South Africa.* London: Cassell, 1894.

Cotlow, Lewis. *Zanzabuku.* New York: Rinehart, 1956.

Coupland, Reginald. *Kirk on the Zambesi.* Oxford: Clarendon Press, 1928.

———. *East Africa and Its Invaders.* London: Oxford University Press, 1938.

Court Treatt, Maj. C. *Out of the Beaten Track.* New York: Dutton, 1931.

Cowie, Mervyn. *The African Lion.* London: Arthur Barker Ltd., 1966.

———. *Fly, Vulture.* London: George Harrap, 1962.

Crawford, D. *Thinking Black.* New York: Doran, 1913.

Croke, Vicki. *The Modern Ark.* New York: Avon, 1998.

Cronwright-Schreiner, S. G. *The Migratory Springbucks of South Africa.* London: Fisher Unwin, 1925.

Cullen, Anthony and Sydney Downey. *Saving the Game.* London: Jarrolds, 1960.

Cumming, Roualeyn Gordon. *A Hunter's Life in South Africa.* London: John Murray, 1850

———. *Wild Men and Wild Beasts.* Edinburgh: Edmonston and Douglas, 1871.

Curtis, Charles P. and Richard C. Curtis. *Hunting in Africa East and West.* Boston: Houghton Mifflin, 1925.

Daly, Marcus. *Big Game Hunting and Adventure, 1897–1936.* London: Macmillan, 1937.

Dane, R. M. *Sport in Africa and Asia.* London: Andrew Melrose, 1921.

Darley, Henry. *Slaves and Ivory.* London: Witherby, 1926.

Darling, F. Fraser. *Wild Life in an African Territory.* London: Oxford University Press, 1960.

Darter, Adrian. *The Pioneers of Mashonaland.* Bulawayo: Books of Rhodesia, 1977. Originally published in 1914.

Dasman, R. F. *African Game Ranching.* Oxford: Pergamon, 1964.

Davidson, Basil. *The Lost Cities of Africa.* Boston: Little, Brown, and Company, 1970.

——. *Africa History.* New York: Collier Books, 1991.

Davis, Charles Belmont. *Adventures and Letters of Richard Harding Davis.* New York: Scribner's, 1917.

Davison, Ted. *Wankie: the Story of a Great Game Reserve.* Cape Town: Books of Africa, 1967.

Dawnay, Guy. *Campaigns: Zulu 1879, Egypt 1882, Suakin 1885.* London: privately printed, c.1886.

Dawson, E. C. *James Hannington: A History of his Life and Work, 1847–1885.* London: Seeley, 1887.

Denman, E. *Animal Africa.* London: Robert Hale, 1957.

Desowitz, Robert S. *The Malaria Capers.* New York: W. W. Norton, 1991.

Dinesen, Isak. *Letters from Africa, 1914–1931.* Chicago: The University of Chicago Press, 1981.

Ditmars, Raymond L. *Guide to the New York Zoological Park.* New York: New York Zoological Society, 1939.

——. *Thrills of a Naturalist's Quest.* New York: Macmillan, 1932.

Dorst, Jean. *Before Nature Dies.* Boston: Houghton Mifflin, 1970.

Douglas-Hamilton, *Iain and Oria. Battle for the Elephants.* New York: Viking, 1992.

Downey, Fairfax. *Burton: Arabian Nights Adventurer.* New York: Scribner's, 1931.

Dracopoli, I. N. *Through Jubaland to the Swamp.* Philadelphia: Lippincott, 1914.

Drummond, Henry. *Tropical Africa.* New York: Scribner and Welford, 1887.

Duff, Hector Livingston. *Nyasaland under the Foreign Office.* London: George Bell, 1903.

Dugard, Martin. *Into Africa.* New York: Broadway Books, 2003.

Duggan, Alan. *Illustrated Guide to the Game Parks and Nature Reserves of Southern Africa.* Cape Town: Reader's Digest Association of South Africa, 1990.

Dugmore, A. Radclyffe. *The Wonderland of Big Game.* London: Macmillan, 1925.

——. *African Jungle Life.* London: Macmillan, 1928.

Earl, Lawrence. *Crocodile Fever.* London: Collins, 1954.

East African Standard, Ltd. *The East African Red Book for 1930–1931.* Nairobi: East African Standard Limited, 1930.

Edgerton, Robert B. *The Fall of the Asante Empire.* New York: Free Press, 1995.

Edwards, Hugh. *Crocodile Attack.* New York: Harper & Row, 1989.

Eliot, Sir Charles. *The East Africa Protectorate.* New York: Barnes & Noble, 1966. Originally published in 1905.

Elliot, G. F. S. *A Naturalist in Mid-Africa.* London: A. D. Innes, 1896.

Ellis, Richard. *No Turning Back.* New York: Harper Collins, 2004.

Evans, Mrs. Frank. *Some Legendary Landmarks of Africa.* London: Cassell, 1893.

Farson, Negley. *The Way of a Transgressor.* New York: Carroll & Graf, 1984. Originally published in 1936.

——. *Behind God's Back.* New York: Harcourt, Brace and Company, 1941.

——. *Last Chance in Africa.* New York: Harcourt, Brace and Company, 1950.

Farwell, Byron. *Burton.* London: Longmans, Green & Company, 1963.

——. *Prisoners of the Mahdi.* New York: Harper & Row, 1967.

——. *The Great Anglo-Boer War.* New York: Harper & Row, 1976.

———. *The Great War in Africa.* New York: W. W. Norton, 1986.

Felkin, R. W., MD. *On the Geographical Distribution of Tropical Diseases in Africa.* Edinburgh: William Clay, 1895.

Fetner, P. Jay. *African Safari.* New York: St. Martin's, 1987.

Fife, C. W. Domville. *Savage Life in the Black Sudan.* London: Seelee and Service, 1927.

Finaughty, William. *The Recollections of an Elephant Hunter, 1864–1875.* Bulawayo: Books of Zimbabwe, 1980. Originally published in 1916.

Fitzpatrick, Sir Percy. *Through Mashonaland with Pen and Pencil.* Johannesburg: Argus Printing and Publishing, 1892.

———. *Jock of the Bushveld.* London: Longmans Green, 1907.

Fleming, Reverend Francis. *Southern Africa.* London: Arthur Hall, Virtue, & Company, 1856.

Fletcher, Colin. *The Winds of Mara.* New York: Alfred A. Knopf, 1973.

Flint, John. *Cecil Rhodes.* London: Hutchinson, 1976.

Foa, Edouard. *After Big Game in Central Africa.* Long Beach: Safari Press, 1986. Originally published in 1899.

Foran, Maj. W. Robert. *Kill or be Killed.* New York: St. Martin's, 1988. Originally published in 1933.

———. *Fifty-Two Tales of Wildlife and Adventure.* London: Hutchinson, 1935.

———. *A Breath of the Wilds.* London: Robert Hale, 1958.

———. *The Kima Killer.* Nairobi: East African Railways, 1961.

Foreign Office (Great Britain). *British Possessions.* London: His Majesty's Stationary Office, 1920.

Fothergill, E. *Five Years in the Sudan.* London: Hurst and Blackett, 1910.

Fotheringham, Low Monteith. *Adventures in Nyasaland.* London: Sampson and Low, 1891.

Fox, James. *White Mischief.* New York: Random House, 1982.

Frank, Katherine. *A Voyager Out.* New York: Ballantine, 1986.

Fraser, Donald. *Winning a Primitive People.* London: Seeley, Service, & Company, 1914.

Freeman, T. B. *Journal of Two Visits to the Kingdom of Ashanti.* London: John Mason, 1843.

French-Sheldon, M. *From Sultan to Sultan.* London: Saxon, 1892.

Frump, Robert R. *The Man-Eaters of Eden.* Guilford, CT: Lyons Press, 2006.

Furber, Percy Norman. *I Took Chances.* Leicester: Backus, 1954.

Fyfe, Christopher. *A Short History of Sierra Leone.* London: Lowe & Brydone, 1975.

Gardner, Brian. *The African Dream.* New York: Putnam's, 1970.

Gatti, Attilio. *The King of the Gorillas.* Garden City: Doubleday, Doran & Company, 1932.

Geil, William Edgar. *A Yankee in Pigmy Land.* New York: Dodd, Mead and Company, 1905.

Gibbons, A. St. H. *Africa from South to North through Marotseland.* London: John Lane, 1904.

Gide, Andre. *Travels in the Congo.* New York: Alfred Knopf, 1929.

Gillham, Nicholas Wright. *A Life of Sir Francis Galton.* New York: Oxford University Press, 2001.

Gillmore, Parker. *Through Gasa Land and the Scene of Portuguese Aggression.* London: Harrison and Sons, 1890.

Golding, Harry (editor). *The Wonder Book of the Wild.* London: Ward, Lock, and Company, 1925.

Gordon, Charles. *General Gordon's Khartoum Journal.* New York: Vanguard Press, 1961.

Gouldsbury, Cullen and Hubert Sheane. *The Great Plateau of Northern Rhodesia.* London: Edward Arnold, 1911.

Graham, A. and Peter Beard. *Eyelids of Morning.* San Francisco: Chronicle Books, 1973.

Grattan Guinness, Mrs. H. *The New World of Central Africa.* London: Hodder and Stoughton, 1890.

Green, Lawrence G. *Lords of the Last Frontier.* Cape Town: Howard Timmins, 1962.

Greene, Graham. *Journey Without Maps.* London: Pan Books, 1948.

Gregory, J. W. *The Rift Valleys and Geology of East Africa.* London: Steeley & Service, 1921.

Grogan, Ewart and Alfred Sharpe. *From The Cape to Cairo.* London: Hurst and Blackett, 1900.

Grotpeter, John J. *Historical Dictionary of Zambia.* Metuchen New Jersey: Scarecrow Press, 1979.

Grundy, Kenneth. *The Lands and Peoples of Kenya, Uganda and Tanzania.* London: Adam and Charles Black, 1968.

Grzimek, Dr. Bernhard and Michael Grzimek. *Serengeti Shall Not Die.* London: Hamish Hamilton, 1960.

Grzimek, Dr. Bernhard. *Among Animals of Africa.* London: Collins, 1971.

——(ed.) *Animal Life Encyclopedia.* New York: Van Nostrand and Reinhold, 1975.

Guggisberg, Charles Albert Walton. *Simba.* Cape Town: Howard Timmons, 1961.

——. *Crocodiles.* Harrisburg: Stackpole Books, 1972.

——. *Wild Cats of the World.* New York: Taplinger, 1975.

——. *Early Wildlife Photographers.* New York: Taplinger, 1977.

Gunther, John. *Inside Africa.* New York: Harper, 1955.

Haagner, A. K. *South African Mammals.* Cape Town: H. F. & G. Witherby, 1920.

Haardt, Georges-Marie. *The Black Journey.* New York: Cosmopolitan, 1927.

Hale, John. *Settlers.* London: Faber & Faber, 1960.

Hallet, Jean-Pierre, and Alex Pelle. *Animal Kitabu.* New York: Random House, 1967.

Hallet, Robin. *Africa since 1875.* Ann Arbor: University of Michigan Press, 1974.

Hanna, A. J. *The Beginnings of Nyasaland and Northeastern Rhodesia 1859–1895.* Oxford: Clarendon Press, 1956.

——. *The Story of the Rhodesias and Nyasaland.* London: Faber and Faber, 1965.

Hanzak, Dr Jan, with Dr Zdenek Veselovsky and David Stephen. *Encyclopedia of Animals.* New York: St. Martin's Press, 1979.

Hardwick, Alfred Arkell. *An Ivory Trader in North Kenia.* London: Longmans, Green, and Company, 1903.

Hardy, R. *The Iron Snake.* New York: Putnam's, 1965.

Harper, F. *Extinct and Vanishing Animals of the Old World.* New York: New York Zoological Park, 1945.

Harris, William Cornwallis. *Wild Sports of South Africa.* Cape Town: Struik, 1987. Originally published in 1852.

Hawker, George. *The Life of George Grenfell.* New York: Fleming H. Revell Company, 1909.

Hayes, Harold T. P. *The Last Place on Earth.* New York: Stein and Day, 1977.

Heck, Lutz. *Animals.* London: Methuen and Company, 1954.

——. *Animal Safari.* London: Methuen, 1956.

Hediger, H. *Wild Animals in Captivity.* New York: Dover, New York. 1964. Originally published in 1950.

Heminway, John. *No Man's Land.* Harcourt, Brace, Jovanovich, San Diego. 1983.

Herne, Brian. *White Hunters.* New York: Henry Holt, 1999.

Heuvelmans, Bernard. *On The Track of Unknown Animals.* New York: Hill and Wang, 1959.

Hibben, Frank. *Under the African Sun.* Long Beach: Safari Press, 1999.

Hibbert, Christopher. *Africa Explored.* New York: Cooper Square Press, 2002.

Hillaby, John. *Journey to the Jade Sea.* London: Constable, 1964.

Hillegas, Howard C. *Oom Paul's People.* New York: Appleton, 1899.

Hinde, Captain Sydney L. *The Fall of the Congo Arabs.* London: Methuen, 1897.

Hobley, C. W. *Bantu Beliefs and Magic.* London: Frank Cass & Company, 1967. Originally published in 1938.

Hochschild, Adam. *King Leopold's Ghost.* Boston: Houghton Mifflin, 1998.

Hodson, Arnold W. *Trekking the Great Thirst.* Bulawayo: Books of Zimbabwe, 1987. Originally published in 1912.

———. *Where Lion Reign.* London: Skeffington, no date.

Hoehnel, Ludwig von. *Discovery by Count Teleky of Lakes Rudolf and Stephanie.* London: Longmans, Green, 1894.

Holman, Dennis, with Eric Rundgren. *Inside Safari Hunting.* New York: Putnam's, 1970.

Holmes, William D. *Safari, R.S.V.P.* New York: Coward McCann, 1960.

Hornaday, William T. *Our Vanishing Wild Life.* New York: New York Zoological Society, 1913.

———. *Tales from Nature's Wonderlands.* New York: Scribner's, 1924.

Horne, C. Silvester. *The Story of the London Missionary Society.* London: Snow and Company, 1894.

Hotchkiss, Willis R. *Then and Now in Kenya Colony.* New York: Fleming H. Revell Company, 1937.

House, Adrian. *The Great Safari.* London: Harvill, 1993.

Howarth, David. *The Shadow of the Dam.* New York: Macmillan, 1961.

Hubbard, Wynant D. *Wild Animals.* New York: Appleton, 1926.

Hunter, John A. *White Hunter.* Long Beach: Safari Press, 1986.

———. *Hunter.* New York: Harper & Brothers, 1952.

———. *Hunter's Tracks.* New York: Appleton-Century-Crofts, 1957.

Hunter, John A. and Daniel Mannix. *Tales of the African Frontier.* New York: Harper & Brothers, 1954.

Hutchinson, G. H. *From the Cape to the Zambesi.* London: John Murray, 1905.

Huxley, Elspeth. *Out in the Midday Sun.* New York: Viking, 1987.

———. *With Forks and Hope.* New York: Morrow, 1964.

Huxley, Elspeth, and Hugo van Lawick. *Last Days in Eden.* New York: Amaryllis, 1984.

Huxley, Julian. *Africa View.* New York: Harper & Brothers, 1931.

Hyatt, Stanley Portal. *The Old Transport Road.* Bulawayo: Books of Rhodesia, 1969. Originally published in 1914.

Imperato, Pascal James. *Historical Dictionary of Mali.* Metuchen, New Jersey: Scarecrow Press, 1977.

———. *Quest for the Jade Sea.* Boulder, Colorado: Westview Press, 1998.

Imperato, Pascal James and Eleanor M. Imperato. *They Married Adventure.* New Brunswick: Rutgers University Press, 1992.

Ingham, Kenneth. *A History of East Africa.* New York: Frederick Praeger, 1967.

Isemonger, R. M. *Snakes of Africa.* Johannesburg: Thomas Nelson, 1962.

Jack, E. M. *On the Congo Frontier.* London: Fisher Unwin, 1914.

Jackson, Henry Cecil. *Behind the Modern Sudan.* London: Macmillan, 1955.

James, F. L. *The Wild Tribes of the Sudan.* London: John Murray, 1883.

Jameson, James Sligo. *The Story of the Rear Column of the Emin Pasha Relief Expedition.* London: Lovell, 1890.

Jeal, Tim. *Livingstone.* New York: Putnam's, 1973.

Jeary, Bertram F. *Pride of Lions.* London: Longmans, Green and Company, 1936.

Jenkinson, Michael. *Beasts Beyond the Fire.* New York: E. P. Dutton, 1980.

Johnson, Martin. *Camera Trails in Africa.* New York: Grosset & Dunlap, 1924.

———. *Lion.* New York: Putnam's, 1929.

Johnson, Osa. *I Married Adventure.* Philadelphia: Lippincott, 1940.

Johnston, Alex. *The Life and Letters of Sir Harry Johnston.* London: Jonathan Cape, 1929.

Johnston, Sir Harry. *Livingstone, and the Exploration of Central Africa.* London: George Philip and Sons, 1891.

———. *British Central Africa.* London: Methuen, 1897.

———. *The Uganda Protectorate.* London: Hutchinson, 1902.

——. *The Nile Quest.* London: Lawrence and Bullen, 1903.

——. *Britain across the Seas: Africa.* London: National Society's Depository, c. 1911.

——. *George Grenfell and the Congo.* London: Hutchinson and Company, 1908.

——. *Pioneers in West Africa.* London: Blackie and Son, 1912.

——. *The Story of My Life.* Indianapolis: Bobbs Merrill, 1923.

Johnston, James. *Dr. Laws of Livingstonia.* London: S. W. Partridge, c. 1910.

Jones, Charles H. *Africa.* New York: Henry Holt, 1875.

Jonveaux, E. *Two Years in East Africa.* London: T. Nelson and Sons, 1875.

Jordan, John Alfred. *The Elephant Stone.* London: Nicholas Kaye, 1959.

Junker, Wilhelm. *Travels in Africa during the Years 1882–1886.* London: Chapman & Hall, 1892.

Kearton, Cherry. *In the Land of the Lion.* New York: Robert McBride, 1930.

Kennedy, Pagan. *Black Livingstone.* New York: Viking, 2002.

Ker, Donald I. *African Adventure.* Harrisburg: Stackpole Company, 1957.

Kerr, Walter Montagu. *The Far Interior.* London: Sampson Low Marston Searle & Rivington, 1886.

Kingdon, Jonathan. *The Kingdon Field Guide to African Mammals.* San Diego: Academic Press, 1997.

Kingsley, Mary. *Travels in West Africa, Congo Francais, Corsico and Cameroons.* London: Macmillan, 1897.

——. *West African Studies.* London: Macmillan, 1899.

Kittenberger, Kalman. *Big Game Hunting and Collecting in East Africa, 1903–1926.* London: Rowland Ward, 1929.

Klineburger, Bert. *International Hunter.* Long Beach: Safari Press, 1999.

Knight, Ian. *Warrior Chiefs of Southern Africa.* London: Firebird Books, 1994.

Koenig, Oskar. *Pori Tupu.* London: Michael Joseph, 1954.

——. *The Masai Story.* London: Michael Joseph, 1955.

Kollmann, Paul. The Victoria Nyanza. London: Swan Sonnenschein, 1899.

Lacy, G. *Pictures of Travel, Sport, and Adventure.* London: Arthur Pearson, 1899.

Lagus, Charles. *Operation Noah.* New York: Coward-McCann, 1960.

Lake, Alexander. *Killers in Africa.* Garden City: Doubleday, 1953.

Landor, A. H. S. *Across Widest Africa.* London: Hurst and Blackett, 1907.

Lardner, Edgar George Dion. *Soldiering and Sport in Uganda.* London: Walter Scott, 1912.

Leakey, L. S. B. *White African.* New York: Ballantine Books, 1966. Originally published in 1937.

Leakey, Richard E. *One Life: An Autobiography.* London: Michael Joseph, 1983.

Legendre, Sidney J. *Okovango: Desert River.* New York: Julian Messner, 1939.

Leonard, A. G. *How We Made Rhodesia.* Bulawayo: Books of Rhodesia, 1973. Originally published in 1896.

Letcher, Owen. *Big Game Hunting in North-Eastern Rhodesia.* New York: St. Martin's, 1986. Originally published in 1911.

Lewis, Roy and Yvonne Foy. *Painting Africa White.* New York: Universe Books, 1971.

Liebowitz, Daniel. *The Physician and the Slave Trade.* New York: W. H. Freeman, 1998.

Listowel, Judith. *The Other Livingstone.* New York: Scribner's, 1974.

Little, Reverend Henry W. *Henry M. Stanley.* London: Chapman and Hall, 1890.

Livingstone, David. *Missionary Travels and Researches in South Africa.* London: John Murray, 1857.

——. *The Last Journals of David Livingstone.* London: John Murray, 1874.

Livingstone, David and Charles Livingstone. *Narrative of an Expedition to the Zambesi and its Tributaries.* London: John Murray, 1865.

Lloyd, Albert. *Uganda to Khartoum.* London: Fisher Unwin, 1906.

Lockhart, J. G. and C. M. Woodhouse. *Cecil Rhodes.* New York: Macmillan, 1963.

Long, Charles Chaille. *Central Africa.* London: Sampson Low Marston Searle & Rivington, 1876.

Lord, John. *Duty, Honor, Empire.* New York: Random House, 1970.

Lovell, Mary S. *A Rage to Live.* New York: Norton, 1998.

——. *Straight on till Morning.* New York: St. Martin's Press, 1987.

Loveridge, Arthur. *I Drank the Zambesi.* New York: Harper and Brothers, c. 1950.

Luard, Nicholas. *The Last Wilderness.* New York: Simon & Schuster, 1981.

Lucas, T. J. *Camp Life and Sport in South Africa.* London: Chapman and Hall, 1878.

Lugard, F. D. *The Rise of our East African Empire.* London: William Blackwood & Sons, 1893.

——. *The Diaries of Lord Lugard.* Evanston, Illinois: Northwestern University Press, 1959.

Lumley, E. K. *Forgotten Mandate.* London: Archon Books, 1976.

Lydekker, R. *The Game Animals of Africa.* London: Rowland Ward, 1926.

Lyell, Denis D. *Memories of an African Hunter.* New York: St. Martin's, 1986. Originally published in 1923.

——. *African Adventures.* New York: St. Martin's, 1988. Originally published in 1935.

Maberly, C. T. Astley. *Animals of East Africa.* Howard Timmins, Cape Town. 1962.

MacDonald, Reverend James. *Light in Africa.* London: Hodder and Stoughton, 1890.

MacKenzie, John. *Day-Dawn in Dark Places.* London: Cassell, 1883.

MacKenzie, W. Douglas. *South Africa.* Boston: Home Library Company, 1899.

——. *John Mackenzie.* New York: Armstrong & Son, 1902.

MacNair, James. *Livingstone's Travels.* London: Reader's Union, 1956.

Makin, W. J. *Across the Kalahari Desert.* London: Arrowsmith, 1929.

Mallows, Wilfrid. *The Mystery of the Great Zimbabwe.* New York: Norton, 1984.

Manthorpe, Victoria. *Children of the Empire.* London: Victor Gollancz, 1996.

Markham, Beryl. *West with the Night.* San Francisco: North Point Press, 1983. Originally published in 1942.

Marsh, Brian. *Baron in Africa.* Long Beach: Safari Press, 1997.

Martelli, George. *Leopold to Lumumba.* London: Chapman & Hall, 1962.

Martin, Annie. *Home Life on an Ostrich Farm.* London: George Philip and Son, 1890.

Mathers, E. P. *Zambesia.* London: King, Sell and Railton, 1891.

Mattenklodt, Wilhelm. *Fugitive in the Jungle.* Boston: Little, Brown, and Company, 1931.

Matthiessen, Peter and Eliot Porter. *The Tree Where Man Was Born.* New York: Dutton, 1972.

Matthiessen, Peter and Hugo van Lawick. *Sand Rivers.* New York: Viking, 1981.

Maugham, R. C. F. *Africa as I Have Known It.* New York: Negro Universities Press, 1969. Originally published in 1929.

Maxwell, Marius. *Stalking Big Game with a Camera.* New York: Century Company, 1924.

McCord, James B. and John Scott Douglas. *My Patients Were Zulus.* New York: Rinehart, 1951.

McGuire, Harry (editor). *Tales of Rod and Gun.* New York: Macmillan, 1931.

McLynn, Frank. *Hearts of Darkness.* New York: Carroll & Graf, 1983.

McLynn, Frank. *Stanley: Sorcerer's Apprentice.* London: Constable, 1991.

McSpadden, J. Walker. *To the Ends of the World and Back.* New York: Thomas Crowell, 1931.

M'Dermott, P. L. *British East Africa or IBEA.* London: Chapman and Hall, 1893.

Mecklenburg, Duke Adolphus Frederick. *In the Heart of Africa.* London: Cassell, 1910.

Melland, Frank. *In Witch-bound Africa.* London: Seeley Service, 1923.

Melliss, Capt. C. J. *Lion Hunting in Somaliland.* New York: St. Martin's Press, 1991. Originally published in 1895.

Mellon, James. *African Hunter.* Long Beach: Safari Press, 1985. Originally published in 1975.

Meredith, Martin. *Elephant Destiny.* New York: Public Affairs, 2001.

Merfield, Frank G. *Gorilla Hunter.* New York: Farrar, Straus and Cudahy, 1956.

Meyer, Hans. *Across East African Glaciers.* London: George Philip and Son, 1891.

Middleton, Dorothy. *Baker of the Nile.* London: Falcon Press, 1949.

Millais, John G. *A Breath from the Veldt.* London: Sotheran, 1899.

——. *Wanderings and Memories.* London: Longmans, 1919.

——. *The Life of Frederick Courteney Selous DSO.* London: Longmans Green, 1919.

——. *Far Away up the Nile.* London: Longmans Green, 1924.

Miller, Charles. *The Lunatic Express.* New York: Macmillan, 1971.

Mills, Lady Dorothy. *The Golden Land.* London: Duckworth, 1929.

Moffatt, The Reverend Robert. *Missionary Labors and Scenes in Southern Africa.* London: John Snow, 1846.

Moffatt, Robert U. *John Smith Moffatt.* London: John Murray, 1921.

Mohr, Jack. *Hyenas in My Bedroom.* New York: A. S. Barnes, 1969.

Monson, Ronald A. *Across Africa on Foot.* New York: Dodd, Mead, & Company, 1931.

Moorehead, Alan. *The Blue Nile.* New York: Random House, 1986. Originally published in 1962.

——. *No Room in the Ark.* London: Hamish Hamilton, 1959.

Morell, Virginia. *Ancestral Passions.* New York: Simon and Schuster, 1995.

Morkel, Bill. *Hunting in Africa.* Cape Town: Howard Timmins, 1980.

Morris, Donald R. *The Washing of the Spears.* New York: Touchstone, 1965.

Moss, Cynthia. *Portraits in the Wild.* Boston: Houghton Mifflin, 1975.

Mostert, Noël. *Frontiers.* New York: Alfred Knopf, 1992.

Moubray, J. M. *In South Central Africa.* London: Constable, 1912.

Murray, J. *How to Live in Tropical Africa.* London: George Philip, 1895.

Myers, Norman. *The Long African Day.* New York: Macmillan, 1972.

Nalder, L. F. (editor). *A Tribal Survey of Mongalla Province.* London: Oxford University Press, 1937.

Nesbitt, L. M. *Hell-Hole of Creation.* New York: Alfred Knopf, 1935.

Neumann, Arthur H. *Elephant Hunting in East Equatorial Africa.* Bulawayo: Books of Zimbabwe, 1982. Originally published in 1898.

Nicholson, G. *The Cape and Its Colonists.* London: Henry Colburn, 1848.

Oates, Frank. *Matabeleland and the Victoria Falls.* London: Kegan Paul, Trench, 1881.

Oliver, Roland. *Sir Harry Johnston and the Scramble for Africa.* London: Chatto & Windus, 1959.

Oswell, W. Edward. *William Cotton Oswell, Hunter and Explorer.* London: Heinemann, 1900.

Pakenham, Thomas. *The Scramble for Africa.* London: Weidenfeld and Nicolson, 1991.

Pakenham, Valerie. *Out in the Noonday Sun.* New York: Random House, 1985.

Parke, T. H. *My Personal Experiences in Equatorial Africa.* London: Sampson Low Marston, 1891.

——. *Guide to Health in Africa.* London: Hawkins and Son, 1893.

Patterson, Bruce D. *The Lions of Tsavo.* New York: McGraw-Hill, 2004.

Patterson, Frederick B. *African Adventures.* New York: Putnam's, 1928.

Patterson, J. H. *The Man-eaters of Tsavo.* London: Macmillan, 1907.

———. *In the Grip of the Nyika.* London: Macmillan, 1909.

Pavitt, Nigel. *Kenya: The First Explorers.* New York: St. Martin's Press, 1989.

Pease, Sir Alfred. *Travel & Sport in Africa.* London: Arthur Humphreys, 1902.

———. *The Book of the Lion.* London: John Murray, 1913.

———. *Edmund Loder: A Memoir.* London: John Murray, 1923.

Penny, Malcolm. *Alligators & Crocodiles.* New York: Crescent, 1991.

Percival, A. Blayney. *A Game Ranger's Note Book.* London: James Nisbet, 1924.

———. *A Game Ranger on Safari.* London: James Nisbet, 1928.

Peters, Carl. *New Light on Dark Africa.* London: Ward, Lock and Company, 1891.

Petherick, John. *Egypt, the Soudan, and Central Africa.* Edinburgh: William Blackwood, 1861.

Petherick, Mr. and Mrs. *Travels in Central Africa.* London: Tinsley Brothers, 1869.

Pitman, C. R. S. *A Game Warden among His Charges.* London: James Nisbet, 1931.

———. *A Game Warden Takes Stock.* London: James Nisbet, 1942.

Player, Ian. *The White Rhino Saga.* New York: Stein and Day, 1973.

Pollard, John. *Adventure Begins in Kenya.* London: Robert Hale, 1957.

———. *African Zoo Man.* London: Robert Hale, 1963.

Portal, Sir Gerald. *The British Mission to Uganda in 1893.* London: Edward Arnold, London, 1894.

Post, L. van der. *Venture to the Interior.* New York: William Morrow, 1951.

———. *The Lost World of the Kalahari.* London: Hogarth, 1958.

Powell-Cotton, P. H. G. *A Sporting Trip through Abyssinia.* London: Rowland Ward, 1902.

———. *In Unknown Africa.* London: Hurst & Blackett, 1904.

Preston, R. O. *Descending the Great Rift Valley.* Nairobi: Colonial Printing Works, undated.

Pretorius, Maj. P. J. *Jungle Man.* New York: Dutton, 1948.

Prorok, Count Byron de. *In Quest of Lost Worlds.* New York: E. P. Dutton, 1935.

Pruen, S. Tristram. *The Arab and the African.* London: Seeley, 1891.

Quammen, David. *Monster of God.* New York: W. W. Norton, 2003.

Raby, Peter. *Bright Paradise.* Princeton: Princeton University Press, 1996.

Rainier, Peter W. *My Vanished Africa.* New Haven: Yale University Press, 1940.

Ravenstein, E. G. *The Strange Adventures of Andrew Battell.* London: Hakluyt Society, 1901.

Rayne, H. *The Ivory Raiders.* London: Macmillan, 1923.

Reitz, Deneys. *Commando.* New York: Charles Boni, 1930.

Riddell, James. *In the Forests of The Night.* New York: A. S. Barnes, 1946.

———. *African Wonderland.* London: Robert Hale, 1956.

Ritter, E. A. *Shaka Zulu.* London: Longmans, 1955.

Roberts, Brian. *Cecil Rhodes and the Princess.* Philadelphia: Lippincott, 1969.

Robins, Eric. *Africa's Wild Life.* New York: Taplinger Publishing, 1963.

Robinson, Reverend Charles Henry. *Nigeria.* London: Horace Marshall and Son, undated.

Rocco, Fiammetta. *The Miraculous Fever-Tree.* London: Harper Collins, 2003.

Roosevelt, Kermit. *The Happy Hunting Grounds.* New York: Barnes and Noble, 2004. Originally published in 1920.

Roosevelt, Kermit Jr. *Sentimental Safari.* New York: Alfred Knopf, 1963.

Roosevelt, Theodore. *African Game Trails.* New York: St. Martin's, 1988. Originally published in 1910.

Roosevelt, Theodore and George Bird Grinnell. *Hunting in Many Lands.* New York: Boone and Crockett Club, 1895.

Roosevelt, Theodore and Edmund Heller. *Life Histories of African Game Animals.* New York: Scribner's Sons, 1914.

Roscoe, John. *Twenty-five Years in East Africa.* Oxford: Cambridge University Press, 1921.

Rose, W. *The Reptiles and Amphibians of Southern Africa.* Cape Town: Maskew Millar, 1950.

Rosenthal, Eric. *Stars and Stripes in Africa.* London: George Routledge and Sons, 1938.

———.(editor) *Encyclopaedia of Southern Africa.* London: Frederick Warne, 1970.

Rotberg, Robert. *Joseph Thomson and the Exploration of Africa.* London: Chatto & Windus, 1971.

Rotberg, Robert (editor). *Africa and Its Explorers.* Cambridge: Harvard University Press, 1973.

Rushby, George. *No More the Tusker.* London: W. H. Allen, 1965.

St. Barbe Baker, Richard. *Africa Drums.* London: Lindsay Drummond, 1942.

Samkange, Stanlake. *Origins of Rhodesia.* New York: Frederick Praeger, 1969.

Sanchez-Ariño, Tony. *The Last of the Few.* Long Beach: Safari Press, 1995.

———. *Elephant Hunters: Men of Legend.* Long Beach: Safari Press, 2005.

Sanderson, Ivan. *Animal Tales.* New York: Alfred Knopf, 1946.

———. *The Dynasty of Abu.* New York: Alfred Knopf, 1962.

———. *Ivan Sanderson's Book of Great Jungles.* New York: Julian Messner, 1965.

Sauer, Hans. *Ex Africa.* Bulawayo: Books of Rhodesia, 1973. Originally published in 1937.

Schaller, George. *The Year of the Gorilla.* Chicago: University of Chicago Press, 1964.

———. *Golden Shadows, Flying Hooves.* New York: Alfred Knopf, 1973.

Schiffers, Heinrich. *The Quest for Africa.* New York: G. P. Putnam's Sons, 1957.

Schillings, C. G. *With Flash-light and Rifle.* New York: Harper & Brothers, 1905.

Schweinfurth, G. *The Heart of Africa.* London: Low Marston & Searle, 1874.

Scobie, Alastair. *Animal Heaven.* London: Cassell, 1954.

Seabrook, William B. *Jungle Ways.* New York: Blue Ribbon Books, 1931.

Seaver, George. *David Livingstone: His Life and Letters.* New York: Harper & Brothers, 1957.

Selous, Frederick Courteney. *A Hunter's Wanderings in Africa.* Bulawayo: Books of Zimbabwe, 1981. Originally published in 1881.

———. *Travel and Adventure in South-East Africa.* London: Rowland Ward, 1893.

———. *African Nature Notes and Reminiscences.* London: Macmillan, 1908.

Severin, Timothy. *The African Adventure.* New York: E. P. Dutton, 1973.

Seymour, Frederick. *Roosevelt in Africa.* New York: McCurdy, 1909.

Sheldrick, Daphne. *Animal Kingdom: The Story of Tsavo, the Great African Park.* Indianapolis: Bobbs-Merrill, 1973.

———. *The Tsavo Story.* London: Collins and Harvill, 1973.

Shipman, Pat. *To the Heart of the Nile.* New York: HarperCollins, 2004.

Shoshani, Jeheskel. *Elephants.* London: Simon and Schuster, 1992.

Siedentopf, A. R. *The Last Stronghold of Big Game.* New York: National Travel Club, 1946.

Simon, Noel. *Between the Sunlight and the Thunder.* London: Collins, 1963.

Smith, A. Donaldson. *Through Unknown African Countries.* London: Edward Arnold, 1897.

Smith, Tom Murray. *The Nature of the Beast.* London: Jarrolds, 1963.

Smith, W. H. B. and Joseph E. Smith. *The Book of Rifles.* Harrisburg: Stackpole, 1965.

Smithers, R. H. N. *The Mammals of Botswana.* Salisbury: National Museums of Rhodesia, 1971.

———. *The Mammals of the Southern African Subregion.* Pretoria: University of Pretoria, 1983.

Smuts, J. C. *Jan Christian Smuts.* New York: William Morrow, 1952.

Sommer, Francois. *Man and Beast in Africa.* London: Herbert Jenkins, 1953.

Southworth, A. S. *Four Thousand Miles of African Travel.* New York: Baker, Pratt, 1875.

Speke, John Hanning. *Journal of the Discovery of the Source of the Nile.* Edinburgh: William Blackwood, 1863.

———. *What Led to the Discovery of the Source of the Nile.* Edinburgh: William Blackwood, 1864.

Stabb, Henry. *To the Victoria Falls via Matabeleland: The Diary of Major Henry Stabb.* Cape Town: C. Struik, 1967.

Stanley, H. M. *How I Found Livingstone in Central Africa.* London: Sampson Low Marston Low & Searle, 1872.

———. *Through the Dark Continent.* New York: Dover, 1988. Originally published in 1878.

———. *In Darkest Africa.* London: Sampson, Low, Marston, Searle & Rivington, 1890.

Stevenson-Hamilton, J. *Animal Life in Africa.* London: Heinemann, 1912.

———. *The Low Veldt: Its Wild Life and Its People.* London: Cassell and Company, 1934.

———. *South African Eden.* London: Collins, 1974.

———. *Wild Life in South Africa.* Norwich: Jarrold, 1947.

Stigand, C. H. *The Game of British East Africa.* London: Horace Cox, 1909.

———. *To Abyssinia Through an Unknown Land.* London: Cassel, 1910.

———. *Hunting the Elephant in Africa.* London: Macmillan, 1913.

Stonehouse, Bernard. *Saving the Animals.* New York: Macmillan, 1981.

Street, Philip. *Wildlife Preservation.* Chicago: Henry Regnery, 1971.

Streeter, Daniel. *Denatured Africa.* New York: Putnam's, 1926.

Stuart, J. M. *The Ancient Gold Fields of Africa.* London: Effingham Wilson, 1891.

Summers, Gerald. *An African Bestiary.* New York: Simon and Schuster, 1974.

Sutherland, James. *The Adventures of an Elephant Hunter.* Long Beach: Safari Press, 2002. Originally published in 1912.

Swann, Alfred. *Fighting the Slave-Hunters in Central Africa.* Philadelphia: Lippincott, 1910.

Swayne, H. C. G. *Seventeen Trips through Somaliland.* London: Rowland Ward, 1895.

Sykes, Frank W. *With Plumer in Matabeleland.* Westminster: Archibald Constable & Company, 1897.

Tabler, E. G. *The Far Interior.* Cape Town: Balkema, 1955.

Taylor, J B. *A Pioneer Looks Back.* London: Hutchinson, 1939.

Taylor, John. *Big Game and Big Game Rifles.* London: Herbert Jenkins, 1947.

———. *African Rifles and Cartridges.* Georgetown, SC: Samworth, 1948.

———. *Pondoro.* New York: Simon and Schuster, 1955.

Temple-Perkins, E. A. *Kingdom of the Elephant.* London: Andrew Melrose, 1955.

Terres, John K. (editor). *Discovery.* Philadelphia: Lippincott, 1961.

Thesiger, Wilfred. *The Life of My Choice.* New York: Norton, 1987.

Thomas, Lowell. *Rolling Stone.* Garden City: Doubleday, Doran, & Company, 1934.

Thomson, Joseph. *To the Central African Lakes and Back.* London: Sampson, Low, Marston, Searle & Rivington, 1881.

———. *Through Masai Land.* London: Sampson, Low, Marston, Searle & Rivington, 1885.

———. *Travels in the Atlas and Southern Morocco.* London: George Philip and Son, 1889.

———. *Mungo Park and the Niger.* London: George Philip and Son, 1890.

Thomson, Ron. Mahohboh. Long Beach: Safari Press, 1997.

Thornhill, Christopher J. *Taking Tanganyika.* London: Stanley Poul, 1937.

Thruston, Arthur Blyford. *African Incidents.* London: John Murray, 1900.

Thurman, Judith. *Isak Dinesen.* New York: St. Martin's Press, 1982.

Tjader, Richard. *The Big Game of Africa.* London: D. Appleton, 1911.

Toniolo, Elias and Richard Hill (ed.). *The Opening of the Nile Basin.* New York: Barnes & Noble Books, 1975.

Trench, Charles Chenevix. *Men Who Ruled Kenya.* London: Radcliffe Press, 1993.

Trzebinski, Errol. *Silence Will Speak.* Chicago: University of Chicago Press, 1977.

———. *The Kenya Pioneers.* New York: W. W. Norton, 1986.

———. *The Lives of Beryl Markham.* New York: W. W. Norton, 1993.

Turner, Myles and Brian Jackman. *My Serengeti Years.* New York: W. W. Norton, 1988.

Vanden Bergh, Dr. Leonard John. *On the Trail of the Pygmies.* New York: James McCann, 1921.

Van Sinderen, Adrian. *Africa.* Syracuse, NY: Syracuse University Press, 1950.

Vaughan Kirby, F. *In Haunts of Wild Game.* London: Blackwood, 1896.

———. *Great and Small Game of Africa.* London: Rowland Ward, 1899.

Vaughan, Megan. *Curing Their Ills.* Stanford, CT: Stanford University Press, 1991.

Von Wolfe, J. F. *Mammals of Ethiopia and Principal Reptiles.* Salisbury: Rhodesian Litho, 1955.

Waal, D. C. de. *With Rhodes in Mashonaland.* Johannesburg: J. C. Juta, 1896.

Walker, Eric Sherbrooke. *Treetops Hotel.* London: Robert Hale, 1963.

Walker, H. F. B. *A Doctor's Diary in Damaraland.* London: Edward Arnold, 1917.

Walker, John Frederick. *A Certain Curve of Horn.* New York: Atlantic Monthly Press, 2002.

Wallace, H. F. *Big Game Wanderings in Many Lands.* London: Eyre and Spottiswoode, 1934.

Wallis, J. P. R. *The Story of Sir Percy FitzPatrick.* London: Macmillan, 1955.

Ward, Rowland. *Records of Big Game,* Third Edition. London: Rowland Ward, 1899.

———. *Records of Big Game,* Ninth Edition. London: Rowland Ward, 1928.

———. *Records of Big Game,* Eleventh Edition. London: Rowland Ward, 1962.

Wauters, A J. *Stanley's Emin Pasha Expedition.* London: Nimmo, 1890.

Weidensaul, Scott. *The Ghost with the Trembling Wings.* New York: North Point Press, 2002.

Wellby, M. S. *Twixt Sirdar and Menelik.* London: Harper & Brothers, 1901.

Wells, A W. *Southern Africa.* London: J. M. Dent, 1956.

Wells, Carveth. *In Coldest Africa.* New York: Doubleday, Doran and Company, 1929.

Werner, H. *A Visit to Stanley's Rearguard.* London: Longmans, 1897.

Western, D. *In the Dust of Kilimanjaro.* Washington: Island Press, 1997.

White, Jon Manchip. *The Land God Made in Anger.* Chicago: Rand McNally, 1969.

White, Stewart Edward. *Lions in the Path.* Garden City: Doubleday, Page, & Company, 1926.

Whitehouse, P. *To Lake Rudolf and Beyond.* London: Chatto & Windus, 1900.

Whyte, Arthur Silva. *The Development of Africa.* London: George Philip and Son, 1890.